Cisco Software-Defined Wide-Area Networks

Designing, Deploying, and Securing Your Next Generation WAN with Cisco SD-WAN

Jason Gooley CCIE No. 38759

Dana Yanch, CCDE No. 20130071, CCIE No. 25567

Dustin Schuemann, CCIE No. 59235

John Curran

D1592017

Cisco Press

221 River St.

Hoboken, NJ 07030 USA

Cisco Software-Defined Wide-Area Networks

Jason Gooley
Dana Yanch
Dustin Schuemann
John Curran

Published by:
Cisco Press

Library of Congress Control Number: 2020937215

ISBN-13: 978-0-13-653317-7

ISBN-10: 0-13-653317-5

Warning and Disclaimer

1 2020

Trademark Acknowledgments

All terms mentioned in this book that are known to be trademarks or service marks have been appropriately capitalized. Cisco Press or Cisco Systems, Inc., cannot attest to the accuracy of this information. Use of a term in this book should not be regarded as affecting the validity of any trademark or service mark.

Special Sales

For information about buying this title in bulk quantities, or for special sales opportunities (which may include electronic versions; custom cover designs; and content particular to your business, training goals, marketing focus, or branding interests), please contact our corporate sales department at corpsales@pearsoned.com or (800) 382-3419.

For government sales inquiries, please contact governmentsales@pearsoned.com.

For questions about sales outside the U.S., please contact intlcs@pearson.com.

Feedback Information

At Cisco Press, our goal is to create in-depth technical books of the highest quality and value. Each book is crafted with care and precision, undergoing rigorous development that involves the unique expertise of members from the professional technical community.

Readers' feedback is a natural continuation of this process. If you have any comments regarding how we could improve the quality of this book, or otherwise alter it to better suit your needs, you can contact us through email at feedback@ciscopress.com. Please make sure to include the book title and ISBN in your message.

We greatly appreciate your assistance.

Editor-in-Chief: Mark Taub

Alliances Manager, Cisco Press: Makarand Chitale

Director, Product Management: Brett Bartow

Managing Editor: Sandra Schroeder

Development Editor: Christopher Cleveland

Technical Editors: Phil Davis, Aaron Rohyans

Project Editor: Lori Lyons

Copy Editor: Bart Reed

Editorial Assistant: Cindy Teeters

Cover Designer: Chuti Prasertsith

Production Manager: Aswini Kumar / codeMantra

Composition: codeMantra

Indexer: Tim Wright

Proofreader: Donna Mulder

	Americas Headquarters	Asia Pacific Headquarters	Europe Headquarters
	Cisco Systems, Inc.	Cisco Systems (USA) Pte. Ltd.	Cisco Systems International BV
	San Jose, CA	Singapore	Amsterdam, The Netherlands

Cisco has more than 200 offices worldwide. Addresses, phone numbers, and fax numbers are listed on the Cisco Website at **www.cisco.com/go/offices.**

About the Authors

Jason Gooley, CCIE No. 38759 (RS and SP), is a very enthusiastic and spontaneous person who has more than 25 years of experience in the industry. Currently, Jason works as a Technical Evangelist for the Worldwide Enterprise Networking Sales team at Cisco Systems. Jason is very passionate about helping others in the industry succeed. In addition to being a Cisco Press author, Jason is a distinguished speaker at Cisco Live, contributes to the development of the Cisco CCIE and DevNet exams, provides training for Learning@Cisco, is an active CCIE mentor, is a committee member for the Cisco Continuing Education Program (CE), and is a program committee member of the Chicago Network Operators Group (CHI-NOG), www.chinog.org. Jason also hosts a show called MetalDevOps. Jason can be found at www.MetalDevOps.com, @MetalDevOps, and @Jason_Gooley on all social media platforms.

Dana Yanch, CCIE No. 25567 (RS,DC) CCDE No. 20130071, at the time of writing content for this book was a Global Technical Solutions Architect at Cisco focused on designing and deploying SD-WAN solutions for large enterprises around the world. Prior to spending the last six years working with Viptela and other SD-WAN technologies, Dana had a focus on fabric-based data center technologies. Dana has presented at several Cisco Live Events worldwide and has a passion for public speaking and mentorship. Dana can now be found at Aviatrix, the multi-cloud networking platform, designing cloud connectivity architectures every single day. Dana can be found at www.danayanch.com or @DanaYanch on Twitter.

Dustin Schuemann, CCIE No. 59235 (R&S), is a Technical Solutions Architect at Cisco Systems. Within the Demo CoE organization, Dustin is a subject matter expert on all things SD-WAN, including development of SD-WAN demo offerings and CPOC labs for some of Cisco's largest customers. He has been a distinguished speaker at Cisco Live multiple times, where he has presented on multiple topics around Cisco SD-WAN. Dustin has more than 17 years of experience in the network engineering field, and before Cisco he was a network architect for multiple firms within the manufacturing and financial industries. He is very passionate about giving back to the IT community and helping to mentor other network engineers. Dustin currently resides in Raleigh, North Carolina. Dustin can be followed on Twitter as @dschuemann.

John Curran is a Technical Solutions Architect with Cisco's Global Virtual Engineering team, where he assists customers and partners with the design of their next-generation networks. John is a subject matter expert in routing and SD-WAN and is excited to spend time teaching and training on these topics. John presents regularly at Cisco Live events around the world and has been repeatedly recognized as a Distinguished Speaker. In his prior role at Cisco, John worked as a Network Consulting Engineer for Cisco's Advanced Services team, supporting government and education customers. John holds a Bachelor of Science degree in Computer Engineering Technology from the University of Cincinnati.

About the Technical Reviewers

Phil Davis, CCIE No. 2021, is a Senior Systems Engineer with Aviatrix, specializing in cloud networking and security architecture. Phil has more than 25 years of experience in the industry and is a subject matter expert on SD-WAN. His background includes routing, switching, security, data center, and cloud networking, and he holds multiple certifications from Microsoft, VMware, Cisco, and Aviatrix. Phil has been instrumental in helping enterprise customers design and architect their networks while working for Cisco, VMware, and Viptela. Phil's current role at Aviatrix allows him to expand his work with enterprise customers and focus on their cloud and multi-cloud architectures. When Phil is not traveling all over the Midwest, he lives in Cincinnati, Ohio, with his beautiful wife, Karen, and their two wonderful children, Meredith and Max.

Aaron Rohyans, CCIE No. 21945, CCNP, is a Technical Marketing Engineer with Cisco Systems and has technical expertise in Cisco Security, Routing/Switching, as well as Unified Communications solutions. Aaron helps to drive the ~$3B in annual routing revenue through various SD-WAN enablement activities such as competitive comparisons, technical evangelism (Cisco Live, roadshows), pre-sales deal support and sales acceleration (PoC/PoV, Customer Workshops, Training), and as a feedback liaison among field teams and product development.

Dedications

Jason Gooley:

This book is dedicated to my wife, Jamie, and my children, Kaleigh and Jaxon. I love you all more than anything! I also want to dedicate this book to my father and brother for always having my back. In addition, this book is dedicated to all the people who supported me over the years and all the candidates who are studying or trying to improve themselves through education.

Dana Yanch:

This book is dedicated to James Winebrenner and Paul Ho, two of the best colleagues and mentors anyone could ask for. You have both championed me tirelessly and provided so many challenges for me to take on and succeed at over the past years. I look forward to building something new with you every single day. I also want to thank my friends and family for their patience and understanding for my being a complete ghost while working in this industry. It can be a bit addictive.

Dustin Schuemann:

This book is dedicated to my lovely wife, Heather. Thanks for putting up with all my crazy projects such as this book. I promise I won't be taking on any more projects for at least a little while. I love you. I would also like to dedicate this book to my mother and father.

John Curran:

This is dedicated to my wonderful wife, Rebecca, and my daughter, Grace. Thank you for your enduring support and unending encouragement throughout this process. I couldn't have done it without you. I love you both so very much.

Acknowledgments

Jason:

Thank you to Brett and Marianne Bartow as well as Chris Cleveland at Cisco Press! It's always a pleasure to work with such amazing and talented people!

Thank you to my team, Worldwide Enterprise Networking Sales, at Cisco for always supporting me through all the awesome projects I am fortunate enough to be a part of! #TeamGSD

Thank you to all the people who follow me on my journey, whether through social media or in person. You are much appreciated!

Dana:

I would like to thank Ali Shaikh for being so patient with me during my early Viptela days. I am certain I asked hundreds of questions over the years and never once received an incomplete response from you. I would also like to thank Aaron Rohyans for providing such incredibly detailed information around Cloud onRamp for Colocation and both Aaron and Phil Davis for their incredible tech editing work.

Dustin:

First off, I would like to thank my fellow authors, Jason, Dana, and John. We had a lot of laughs and a lot of stress throughout this project, but we got it done. Congratulations.

Secondly, I would also like to thank our tech editors, Aaron and Phil. I appreciate the feedback you provided, even if it was hard to swallow sometimes. Ultimately it made this a better book.

Thanks to the Demo CoE leadership team at Cisco. You've always supported me throughout all my endeavors. A special thank-you goes to my fellow teammates Steve Moore, Fish Fishburne, Paul Patrick, Christine Strom, and Gavin Wright. Now I can get back to work.

There are a few individuals who have helped with this book and various other projects throughout my career. I will always appreciate the support and willingness they've provided. A special thank-you to Brad Edgeworth, Mosaddaq Turabi, Ali Shaikh, Gina Cornett, Joe Astorino, Thomas Mckinnon, Tom Kunath, Fred Damstra, and Seth Lechlitner.

John:

I would like to send a special thanks to Brent Colwell, Phil Davis, Dana Yanch, Ali Shaikh, and Larry Roberts for all of the help and training with Viptela across the years.

This project wouldn't have been possible without the support of the leadership of Cisco's Global Virtual Engineering team. In particular, special thanks to Henry Carmouche for saying "yes" to that first unreasonable request, Jeff Sweeney for helping this vision and many others become a reality, Femi Ajisafe for seeing this project through to completion, and John Ellis for all the support throughout these adventurous years.

A special thanks to Todd Osterberg, Jason Dumars, Shaker Nazer, and Brad Edgeworth. Each of you were always more than willing to take a chance on me, and I owe you each so much. I only hope that I will be able to pay it forward. Thank you.

Contents at a Glance

Reader Services

Register your copy at www.ciscopress.com/title/9780136533177 for convenient access to downloads, updates, and corrections as they become available. To start the registration process, go to www.ciscopress.com/register and log in or create an account.* Enter the product ISBN 9780136533177 and click Submit. When the process is complete, you will find any available bonus content under Registered Products.

*Be sure to check the box that you would like to hear from us to receive exclusive discounts on future editions of this product.

Contents

Command Syntax Conventions

The conventions used to present command syntax in this book are the same conventions used in the IOS Command Reference. The Command Reference describes these conventions as follows:

- **Boldface** indicates commands and keywords that are entered literally as shown. In actual configuration examples and output (not general command syntax), boldface indicates commands that are manually input by the user (such as a **show** command).

- *Italic* indicates arguments for which you supply actual values.

- Vertical bars (|) separate alternative, mutually exclusive elements.

- Square brackets ([ ]) indicate an optional element.

- Braces ({ }) indicate a required choice.

- Braces within brackets ([{ }]) indicate a required choice within an optional element.

Figure Credits

Cover image	Cisco Brand Exchange, Cisco Systems, Inc.
UNFIG11-01	© 2020, Amazon Web Services, Inc.
UNFIG11-02	Microsoft Azure, © 2020 Microsoft
UNFIG11-03	© 2020, Amazon Web Services, Inc.
UNFIG11-04	Microsoft Azure, © 2020 Microsoft
FIG13-10	VMWare Settings Window screenshot, © Microsoft 2020
FIG13-11	Add Hardware Wizard screenshot, © Microsoft 2020
FIG13-12	Create new virtual disk, screenshot, © Microsoft 2020

Foreword

It's a great pleasure for me to write the foreword for the first complete guide to SD-WAN. Being the founder of Viptela (Cisco SD-WAN), I am delighted to read a really comprehensive work on SD-WAN. SD-WAN is one of the major disruptions wide area networks have seen since MPLS was created in the 90s.

Since SD-WAN requires people to understand both technology and implementations of the new age WAN, I feel this book will provide a great reference guide for the reader. The topics covered will benefit both the novice and expert reader. Because this book is structured to walk you through from basic principles to advanced topics, it can be used as a reference guide.

This book is written by a team of individuals who have been instrumental in deploying and testing the largest SD-WAN networks.

I would strongly recommend reading this comprehensive book on the Cisco SD-WAN networking technology.

Khalid Raza, Founder/CTO Viptela

Introduction

The Implementing Cisco SD-WAN Solutions (ENSDWI 300-415) exam is a concentration exam for the CCNP Enterprise certification. If you pass the ENSDWI 300-415 exam, you also obtain the Cisco Certified Specialist – Enterprise SD-WAN Implementation certification. This exam covers core SD-WAN technologies, including SD-WAN architecture, controller deployment, Edge router deployment, policies, security, quality of service, multicast, and management and operations.

Implementing Cisco SD-WAN Solutions (ENSDWI 300-415) is a 90-minute exam.

Tip You can review the exam blueprint from Cisco's website at https://learningnetwork. cisco.com/s/ensdwi-exam-topics.

This book gives you the foundation and covers the topics necessary to start the CCNP Enterprise certification, with a focus on SD-WAN concentration exam or Cisco Certified Specialist – Enterprise SD-WAN Implementation certification.

The CCNP Enterprise Certification

The CCNP Enterprise certification is one of the industry's most respected certifications. In order for you to earn the CCNP Enterprise certification, you must pass two exams: the ENCOR exam and one concentration exam of your choice, so you can customize your certification to your technical area of focus. This book focuses on the Implementing Cisco SD-WAN Solutions (ENSDWI 300-415) concentration exam.

Tip The ENCOR core exam is also the qualifying exam for the CCIE Enterprise Infrastructure and CCIE Enterprise Wireless certifications. Passing this exam is the first step toward earning both of these certifications.

The following are the CCNP Enterprise concentration exams:

- Implementing Cisco Enterprise Advanced Routing and Services (300-410 ENARSI)
- Implementing Cisco SD-WAN Solutions (300-415 ENSDWI)
- Designing Cisco Enterprise Networks (300-420 ENSLD)
- Designing Cisco Enterprise Wireless Networks (300-425 ENWLSD)
- Implementing Cisco Enterprise Wireless Networks (300-430 ENWLSI)
- Implementing Automation for Cisco Enterprise Solutions (300-435 ENAUTO)

Tip   CCNP Enterprise now includes automation and programmability to help you scale your enterprise infrastructure. If you pass the Developing Applications Using Cisco Core Platforms and APIs v1.0 (DEVCOR 350-901) exam, the ENCOR exam, and the Implementing Automation for Cisco Enterprise Solutions (ENAUTO 300-435) exam, you will achieve the CCNP Enterprise and DevNet Professional certifications with only three exams. Every exam earns an individual Specialist certification, allowing you to get recognized for each of your accomplishments, instead of waiting until you pass all the exams.

There are no formal prerequisites for CCNP Enterprise. In other words, you do not have to pass the CCNA or any other certifications in order to take CCNP-level exams. The same goes for the CCIE exams. On the other hand, CCNP candidates often have three to five years of experience in implementation enterprise networking solutions.

The Exam Objectives (Domains)

The Implementing Cisco SD-WAN Solutions (ENSDWI 300-415) exam is broken down into six major domains. The contents of this book cover each of the domains and the subtopics included in them as illustrated in the following descriptions.

The following table lists the breakdown of each of the domains represented in the exam.

Domain	Percentage of Representation in Exam
1: Architecture	20%
2: Controller Deployment	15%
3: Router Deployment	20%
4: Policies	20%
5: Security and Quality of Service	15%
6: Management and Operations	10%
	Total 100%

Here are the details of each domain:

Domain 1: Architecture: This domain is covered in Chapters 1, 2, and 3.

1.1 Describe Cisco SD-WAN Architecture and Components

    1.1.a Orchestration plane (vBond, NAT)

    1.1.b Management plane (vManage)

    1.1.c Control plane (vSmart, OMP)

    1.1.d Data plane (vEdge)

    1.1.d [i] TLOC

    1.1.d (ii) IPsec

1.1.d (iii) vRoute

1.1.d (iv) BFD

1.2 Describe WAN Edge platform types, capabilities (vEdges, cEdges)

Domain 2: Controller Deployment: This domain is covered primarily in Chapter 13.

2.1 Describe controller cloud deployment

2.2 Describe controller on-prem deployment

 2.2.a Hosting platform (KVM/hypervisor)

 2.2.b Installing controllers

 2.2.c Scalability and redundancy

2.3 Configure and verify certificates and whitelisting

2.4 Troubleshoot control plane connectivity between controllers

Domain 3: Router Deployment: This domain is covered primarily in Chapters 3 and 4.

3.1 Describe WAN Edge deployment

 3.1.a Onboarding

 3.1.b Orchestration with Zero Touch Provisioning/Plug and Play

 3.1.c Single/multi data center/regional hub deployments

3.2 Configure and verify SD-WAN data plane

 3.2.a Circuit termination/TLOC-extension

 3.2.b Underlay–overlay connectivity

3.3 Configure and verify OMP

3.4 Configure and verify TLOCs

3.5 Configure and verify CLI and vManage feature configuration templates

 3.5.a VRRP

 3.5.b OSPF

 3.5.c BGP

Domain 4: Policies: This domain is covered primarily in Chapters 5, 6, 7, and 8.

4.1 Configure and verify control policies

4.2 Configure and verify data policies

4.3 Configure and verify end-to-end segmentation

4.3.a VPN segmentation

4.3.b Topologies

4.4 Configure and verify SD-WAN Application-Aware Routing

4.5 Configure and verify Direct Internet Access

Domain 5: Security and Quality of Service: This domain is covered primarily in Chapters 9 and 10.

5.1 Configure and verify service insertion

5.2 Describe application-aware firewall

5.3 Configure and verify QoS treatment on WAN Edge routers

5.3.a Scheduling

5.3.b Queuing

5.3.c Shaping

5.3.d Policing

Domain 6: Management and Operations: This domain is covered primarily in Chapters 4, 6, and 7.

6.1 Describe monitoring and reporting from vManage

6.2 Configure and verify monitoring and reporting

6.3 Describe REST API monitoring

6.4 Describe software upgrade from vManage

Steps to Passing the Implementing Cisco SD-WAN Solutions (ENSDWI 300-415) Exam

There are no prerequisites for the ENSDWI exam; however, students must have an understanding of implementing networking solutions.

Signing Up for the Exam

The steps required to sign up for the ENSDWI exam as follows:

1. Create an account at https://home.pearsonvue.com/cisco.

2. Complete the Examination Agreement, attesting to the truth of your assertions regarding professional experience and legally committing to the adherence of the testing policies.

3. Submit the examination fee.

Facts About the Exam

The exam is a computer-based test. The exam consists of multiple-choice questions only. You must bring a government-issued identification card. No other forms of ID will be accepted.

Tip Refer to the Cisco Certification site at https://cisco.com/go/certifications for more information regarding this and other Cisco certifications.

About *Cisco Software-Defined Wide-Area Networks: Designing, Deploying, and Securing Your Next-Generation WAN with Cisco SD-WAN*

This book maps directly to the topic areas of the ENSDWI exam and uses a number of features to help you understand the topics and prepare for the exam.

Objectives and Methods

This book uses several key methodologies to help you discover the exam topics on which you need more review, to help you fully understand and remember those details, and to help you prove to yourself that you have retained your knowledge of those topics. This book does not try to help you pass the exam only by memorization; it seeks to help you to truly learn and understand the topics. This book is designed to help you pass the Implementing Cisco SD-WAN Solutions (ENSDWI 300-415) exam by using the following methods:

- Helping you discover which exam topics you have not mastered

- Providing explanations and information to fill in your knowledge gaps

- Supplying review questions that enhance your ability to recall and deduce the answers to test questions

- Providing practice exercises on the topics and the testing process via test questions on the companion website

Book Features

To help you customize your study time using this book, the core chapters have several features that help you make the best use of your time:

- **Review All Key Topics:** The Key Topic icon appears next to the most important items in the chapter. The "Review All Key Topics" activity near the end of the chapter lists the key topics from the chapter, along with their page numbers. Although the contents of the entire chapter could be on the exam, you should definitely know the information listed in each key topic, so you should review these.

■ **Define Key Terms:** This section lists the most important terms from the chapter, asking you to write a short definition and compare your answer to the glossary at the end of the book.

■ **Review Questions:** Confirm that you understand the content you just covered by answering these questions and reading the answer explanations.

■ **Web-based Practice Exam:** The companion website includes the Pearson Cert Practice Test engine, which allows you to answer practice exam questions. Use it to prepare with a sample exam and to pinpoint topics where you need more study.

How This Book Is Organized

This book contains 13 core chapters—Chapters 1 through 13. Each core chapter covers a subset of the topics on the Implementing Cisco SD-WAN Solutions (ENSDWI 300-415) exam. The core chapters map to the ENSDWI topic areas and cover the concepts and technologies that you will encounter on the exam.

Here's a brief summary of each chapter:

■ **Chapter 1, "Introduction to Cisco Software-Defined Wide Area Networking (SD-WAN),"** covers an introduction to software-defined networking, controllers, and automation. This chapter also covers the benefits and value of automating management and operations.

■ **Chapter 2, "Cisco SD-WAN Components,"** covers an introduction to the SD-WAN components, including the various controllers. The various types of deployment models are introduced in this chapter as well. The chapter also introduces the control plane, data plane, and cloud integration.

■ **Chapter 3, "Control Plane and Data Plane Operations,"** covers the Overlay Management Protocol (OMP) and how it works to facilitate the orchestration of the control plane and ultimately influences the data plane. This chapter also covers how a secure data plane is constructed with IPsec. As with all routing protocols, there needs to be a loop prevention mechanism. This chapter also discusses the various types of loop prevention within OMP.

■ **Chapter 4, "Onboarding and Provisioning,"** covers how to provision the data plane devices, either manually or via Plug and Play/Zero Touch Provisioning. Templates are also discussed as a means to gain some flexibility and scale with configuration management.

■ **Chapter 5, "Introduction to Cisco SD-WAN Policies,"** covers the basics of Cisco SD-WAN policies. This includes the different types of policies, how policies are constructed, and how they are applied to the Cisco SD-WAN fabric.

■ **Chapter 6, "Centralized Control Policies,"** covers centralized control policies. These policies are used to manipulate or filter the OMP updates in order to manipulate the structure and forwarding patterns in the Cisco SD-WAN fabric. This chapter also covers packet loss recovery techniques, including Forward Error Correction and packet duplication. This chapter discusses a series of use cases that solve for different business requirements.

- **Chapter 7, "Centralized Data Policies,"** covers centralized data policies that are used to manipulate or filter flows in the data plane and override the natural forwarding behavior that is propagated through the OMP. This chapter discusses a series of use cases that solve for different business requirements.

- **Chapter 8, "Application-Aware Routing Policies,"** covers App-Route policies and how these policies can be used to ensure that traffic is forwarded across the SD-WAN fabric using links that meet a required service level agreement (SLA).

- **Chapter 9, "Localized Policies,"** covers localized policies, including local route policies, access control lists (ACLs), and quality of service (QoS).

- **Chapter 10, "Cisco SD-WAN Security,"** covers what SD-WAN security is and why it is relevant to your organization. This chapter also covers how to deploy Application-Aware Enterprise Firewall, intrusion detection and prevention, URL filtering, Advanced Malware Protection (AMP) and Threat Grid, DNS web layer security, cloud security, and vManage authentication and authorization.

- **Chapter 11, "Cisco SD-WAN Cloud onRamp,"** covers what Cisco SD-WAN Cloud onRamp is and how it can optimize your organization's application experience. This chapter also covers how to deploy onRamp for SaaS, onRamp for IaaS, and onRamp for Colocation.

- **Chapter 12, "Cisco SD-WAN Design and Migration,"** covers the methodology behind SD-WAN design across the enterprise. This chapter also covers preparation for SD-WAN migration, data center design, and branch design, as well as overlay and underlay routing integration.

- **Chapter 13, "Provisioning Cisco SD-WAN Controllers in a Private Cloud,"** covers how to deploy the controllers in a private cloud, on premises, or in a lab environment. This chapter also discusses the various methods to handle certificates. Certificates play a critical piece in encrypting and authenticating the control plane.

- **Appendix A, "Answers to Chapter Review Questions,"** provides the answers to the review questions at the end of each chapter.

- **Appendix B, "Example 7-17,"** shows the full and complete policy for all of the configuration that was performed in Chapters 6 and 7.

- The **Glossary of Key Terms** provides definitions for the key terms in each chapter.

The Companion Website for Online Content Review

All the electronic review elements, as well as other electronic components of the book, exist on this book's companion website.

How to Access the Companion Website

To access the companion website, which gives you access to the electronic content with this book, start by establishing a login at www.ciscopress.com and register your book.

To do so, simply go to www.ciscopress.com/register and enter the ISBN of the print book: 9780136533177. After you have registered your book, go to your account page and click the **Registered Products** tab. From there, click the **Access Bonus Content** link to get access to the book's companion website.

Note that if you buy the Premium Edition eBook and Practice Test version of this book from Cisco Press, your book will automatically be registered on your account page. Simply go to your account page, click the **Registered Products** tab, and select **Access Bonus Content** to access the book's companion website.

Please note that many of our companion content files can be very large, especially image and video files.

If you are unable to locate the files for this title, please visit www.pearsonITcertification. com/contact and select the **Site Problems/Comments** option. Our customer service representatives will assist you.

How to Access the Pearson Test Prep (PTP) App

You have two options for installing and using the Pearson Test Prep application: a web app and a desktop app. To use the Pearson Test Prep application, start by finding the registration code that comes with the book. You can find the code in these ways:

- **Print book:** Look in the cardboard sleeve in the back of the book for a piece of paper with your book's unique PTP code.

- **Premium Edition:** If you purchase the Premium Edition eBook and Practice Test directly from the Cisco Press website, the code will be populated on your account page after purchase. Just log in at www.ciscopress.com, click **account** to see details of your account, and click the **digital purchases** tab.

- **Amazon Kindle:** For those who purchase a Kindle edition from Amazon, the access code will be supplied directly from Amazon.

- **Other bookseller eBooks:** Note that if you purchase an eBook version from any other source, the practice test is not included because other vendors to date have chosen not to vend the required unique access code.

Note   Do not lose the activation code because it is the only means with which you can access the QA content with the book.

Once you have the access code, to find instructions about both the PTP web app and the desktop app, follow these steps:

Step 1.   Open this book's companion website, as was shown earlier in this Introduction under the heading "How to Access the Companion Website."

Step 2.   Click the **Practice Exams** button.

Step 3.   Follow the instructions listed there, both for installing the desktop app and for using the web app.

Note that if you want to use the web app only at this point, just navigate to www.pearsontestprep.com, establish a free login if you do not already have one, and register this book's practice tests using the registration code you just found. The process should take only a couple of minutes.

Note   Amazon eBook (Kindle) customers: It is easy to miss Amazon's email that lists your PTP access code. Soon after you purchase the Kindle eBook, Amazon should send an email. However, the email uses very generic text and makes no specific mention of PTP or practice exams. To find your code, read every email from Amazon after you purchase the book. Also do the usual checks for ensuring your email arrives, like checking your spam folder.

Note   Other eBook customers: As of the time of publication, only the publisher and Amazon supply PTP access codes when you purchase their eBook editions of this book.

Customizing Your Exams

Once you are in the exam settings screen, you can choose to take exams in one of three modes:

- **Study mode:** Allows you to fully customize your exams and review answers as you are taking the exam. This is typically the mode you would use first to assess your knowledge and identify information gaps.

- **Practice Exam mode:** Locks certain customization options, as it is presenting a realistic exam experience. Use this mode when you are preparing to test your exam readiness.

- **Flash Card mode:** Strips out the answers and presents you with only the question stem. This mode is great for late-stage preparation when you really want to challenge yourself to provide answers without the benefit of seeing multiple-choice options. This mode does not provide the detailed score reports that the other two modes do, so you should not use it if you are trying to identify knowledge gaps.

In addition to these three modes, you will be able to select the source of your questions. You can choose to take exams that cover all of the chapters, or you can narrow your selection to just a single chapter or the chapters that make up a specific part in the book. All chapters are selected by default. If you want to narrow your focus to individual chapters, simply deselect all the chapters and then select only those on which you wish to focus in the Objectives area.

You can also select the exam banks on which to focus. Each exam bank comes complete with a full exam of questions that cover topics in every chapter. The two online exams that accompany this book are available to you as well as two additional exams of unique questions. You can have the test engine serve up exams from all four banks or just from one individual bank by selecting the desired banks in the exam bank area.

There are several other customizations you can make to your exam from the exam settings screen, such as the time of the exam, the number of questions served up, whether to randomize questions and answers, whether to show the number of correct answers for multiple-answer questions, and whether to serve up only specific types of questions. You can also create custom test banks by selecting only questions that you have marked or questions on which you have added notes.

Updating Your Exams

If you are using the online version of the Pearson Test Prep software, you should always have access to the latest version of the software as well as the exam data. If you are using the Windows desktop version, every time you launch the software while connected to the Internet, it checks if there are any updates to your exam data and automatically downloads any changes that were made since the last time you used the software.

Sometimes, due to many factors, the exam data may not fully download when you activate your exam. If you find that figures or exhibits are missing, you may need to manually update your exams. To update a particular exam you have already activated and downloaded, simply click the **Tools** tab and click the **Update Products** button. Again, this is only an issue with the desktop Windows application.

If you wish to check for updates to the Pearson Test Prep exam engine software, Windows desktop version, simply click the **Tools** tab and click the **Update Application** button. This ensures that you are running the latest version of the software engine.

Chapter 1

Introduction to Cisco Software-Defined Wide Area Networking (SD-WAN)

This chapter covers the following topics:

- **Networks of Today:** This section covers the technologies and challenges of today's networks.

- **Common Business and IT Trends:** This section of the chapter covers the most common trends having a considerable impact on the WAN.

- **Common Desired Benefits:** This section examines the benefits and desired outcomes of what businesses are looking for.

- **High-Level Design Considerations:** This section covers various aspects of WAN design and things that impact the deployment and operations of WANs today.

- **Introduction to Cisco Software-Defined WAN (SD-WAN):** This section examines, from a high level, the benefits and drivers of Cisco SD-WAN.

- **Use Cases Demanding Changes in the WAN:** This section covers a variety of use cases businesses are adopting that are putting pressure on the WAN environment.

- **Building an ROI to Identify Cost Savings:** This section examines the potential cost savings of deploying Cisco SD-WAN and the value of a well-prepared return on investment (ROI).

- **Introduction to Multidomain:** This section examines the purpose of Multidomain and the value associated with having a Multidomain environment.

Networks of Today

The IT industry is constantly changing and evolving. As time goes on, there is an ever-increasing amount of technologies putting a strain on the network. New paradigms are formed as others are being shifted away from. New advances are being developed and adopted within the networking realm. These advances are being created to provide faster innovation and the ability to adopt relevant technologies in a simplified way. This requires the need for more intelligence and the capability to leverage the data from connected and distributed environments such as the campus, branch, data center, and wide area network (WAN). Doing so allows for the use of data in interesting and more powerful ways than ever seen in the past. Some of the advances driving these outcomes are the following:

- Artificial intelligence (AI)

- Machine learning (ML)

- Cloud services

- Virtualization

- Internet of Things (IoT)

The influx of these technologies is putting strain on the IT operations staff. This strain comes in the form of more robust planning, agreed-upon relevant use cases, and having detailed adoption journey materials for easy consumption. All these requirements are becoming critical to success. Another area of importance is the deployment and day-to-day operations of these technologies as well as how they fit within the network environment. Disruption to typical operations is more imminent with regards to some of these technologies and how they will be consumed by the business. Other advances in technology are being adopted to reduce cost of operations as well as reduce complexity. It can be said that every network, to some degree, has inherent complexity. However, having tools that can help manage this burden is becoming a necessity these days.

Automation is something that many in the industry are striving for. This is because the networks of today are becoming more and more complicated. Oftentimes businesses are operating with a lean IT staff, a flat or reduced budget, and are struggling to find ways to increase the output of what the network can do for the business. Another driver for the adoption of these technologies is improving the overall user experience within the environment. This includes users being able to have the flexibility and capability to access any business-critical application from anywhere in the network and have an exceptional experience. In addition to improving user experience, IT operations is searching for ways to simplify the operations of the network.

There are many inherent risks associated with manually configuring networks. There is risk in the form of not being able to move fast enough when deploying new applications or services to the network. Risk could also be seen as misconfigurations that could cause an outage or suboptimal network performance, resulting in impacted business operations and potentially causing financial repercussions. Finally, there is risk that the business itself, relying on the network for some business-critical services, might not be available due to the IT operations staff not being able to keep up with the scalability demand. According to a Cisco Technical Assistance Center (TAC) survey taken in 2016, 95% of Cisco customers are performing configuration and deployment tasks manually in their networks. The survey also stated that 70% of TAC cases created are related to misconfigurations. This means that typos or incorrectly used commands are the culprit for a majority of issues seen in the network environment. This is where automation shines: being able to have the capability to signify the intent of the change that needs to be made, such as deploying quality of service (QoS) across the network, and then having the network configure it properly and automatically. Consistently and correctly configuring services or features with great speed is a tremendous value to the business. Simplifying operations and reducing human error ultimately reduces risk.

A simple analogy for this would be to think of an automobile. As consumers of automobiles, most people use them to meet a specific desired outcome (in this case, it would be to get from point A to point B). An automobile is operated as a holistic system, not a collection of parts that make up that system. For example, there is a dashboard that provides the user all the necessary information of how the vehicle is operating and the current state of the vehicle. When the user wants to use the vehicle, there are certain operational steps required to do so. Drivers simply signify the intent to drive the car by putting it in gear and using the system to get from point A to point B. Figure 1-1 illustrates this analogy.

Figure 1-1   *Automobile as a System*

Why can't networks be thought of in the same way? Thinking of a network as a collection of devices such as routers, switches, and wireless components is how the industry has been doing it for over 30 years. The shift in mindset to look at the network as a holistic system is a more recent concept that stems from the advent of network controllers. The splitting of role and functionality from one another can be described as separating the control plane from the data plane. Having a controller that sits on top of a collection of network devices gives the advantage of taking a step back and operating the network as a whole from a centralized management point—similar to operating an automobile from the driver's seat versus trying to manage the automobile via individual pieces and components. To put this in more familiar terms, think of the command line interface (CLI). The CLI was not designed to make massive scale configuration changes to multiple devices at the same time. Traditional methods of managing and maintaining the network aren't sufficient to keep up with the pace and demands of the networks of today. The IT operations staff needs to be able to move faster and simplify all the operations and configurations that have traditionally gone into networking. Cisco Software-Defined Networking (SDN) and controller capabilities are becoming areas of focus in the industry, and they are evolving to a point where they can address the challenges faced by IT operations teams. Controllers offer the ability to manage the network as a system, which means that policy management can be automated and abstracted. This provides the capability of supporting dynamic, scalable, and consistent policy changes throughout the network.

Common Business and IT Trends

Traditional networking infrastructure was deployed when the security perimeter was well defined. Most applications were low bandwidth, and most content and applications resided in centralized corporate data centers. Today, enterprises have very different requirements. High-bandwidth, real-time, and big-data applications are pushing the capacity limits of the network. In some cases, the majority of traffic is destined for the Internet or public cloud, and the security perimeter, as it existed in the past, is quickly disappearing. This is due to a surge in bring-your-own-device (BYOD), cloud, and dynamic business-to-business (B2B) ecosystems. The downside and risks of staying status quo are significant, and technological innovation has failed to comprehensively address the problem. There has been a huge increase in the use of Software as a Service (SaaS) and Infrastructure as a Service (IaaS) offerings. It seems as if more applications are moving to the cloud each day. The adoption of solutions like Microsoft Office 365, Google Apps, Salesforce.com (SFDC), and other SaaS-based productivity and business applications is not effectively addressed by traditional designs that utilize Internet capabilities out of one or more centralized data centers. The following list contains some of the most common trends being seen in the industry:

- Applications are moving to the cloud (private and public)

- Internet edge is moving to the remote branch sites

- Mobile devices (BYOD and guest access)

- High-bandwidth applications

- IoT devices

The number of mobile devices at the remote sites accessing these applications and accessing the Internet as a result of BYOD and guest services is increasing. The additional load of traffic resulting from all of these devices as well as trends such IoT are putting an additional strain on the network. In addition to everything mentioned, interactive video has finally become the new voice-over IP. Converging voice and data services was an important transition. When it comes to video, however, today's networks not only have to account for optimized QoS handling for video applications, but also need to address the high-bandwidth, latency-sensitive applications that users are demanding. This is going to require rethinking capacity planning to include looking for ways to maximize on current investments. Offloading certain types of traffic and moving to active/active WAN deployment models are some of the ways to accomplish this; however, traditionally these tasks are not easy to implement and require many manual configurations to deploy. Manual intervention when failover or redundancy was required was almost a must. This also led to additional complexity in the network environment.

With everything that was covered from a business and IT trend perspective still in mind, it is important to translate these trends into real challenges that businesses are facing and put them into IT vernacular. As mentioned previously, the WAN is seeing pressure like never before. This is forcing IT teams to look for ways to alleviate that pressure.

Businesses are also looking for ways to improve the user and application experience with what they currently own as well as to drive cost down. Lack of control over visibility, application performance, and keeping up with the ever-growing security attack surface is also contributing to businesses looking for a better way forward. However, organizational silos have also caused many businesses to not be able to achieve the benefits from some of these newer technologies. Breaking down silos to work toward a common goal for the business as a whole is required for businesses to take full advantage of what some of these software-defined advancements have to offer.

Common Desired Benefits

This section of this chapter will cover some of the most common benefits that businesses are looking for from their network and WAN. Designing and deploying the next-generation WAN is about taking advantage of some very useful benefits and the impact they have on the network environment and overall user experience. Here is each of the benefits we will discuss:

- Prioritize and secure traffic with granular control

- Reduce costs and lower operational complexity

- Augment or replace premium WAN bandwidth

- Provide a consistent, high-quality user experience

- Offload guest and public cloud traffic

- Ensure remote site uptime

Oftentimes businesses want to augment or replace premium bandwidth services and move from active/standby WAN transport models to active/active models. This alone will help them to reduce costs. However, the challenge becomes that augmentation of services can increase operational complexity. Complexity is something that must be avoided as businesses look to simplify IT and create a consistent operational model. Ensuring remote site uptime to support business continuity is about more than simply protecting against blackout situations. Critical applications that are impacted by conditions such as latency, jitter, and loss can ultimately render the applications unusable. This is analogous to the applications being completely unavailable. These are called brownouts. Providing a consistent high-quality application experience is top of mind for most businesses today. Because not all applications are created equal, each organization or department might have its own applications that are critical to it and are required to support its business. Voice and video, for example, may be the most critical applications for one business, such as a contact center. However, in the retail vertical, the point of sales (PoS) system or online marketplace may be more critical. It comes down to the level of importance each application plays within a specific organization. Businesses demand the flexibility and power to prioritize applications with granular control. There is a shift to take back control and not have to rely on the service provider for making changes and for ensuring connectivity. This goes beyond typical routing or QoS and extends into application experience and availability. Many businesses are still not comfortable with the Internet edge moving into their remote site edge. This is necessary to more effectively support the rollout of public cloud applications such as Software as a Service (SaaS) and productivity applica tions. This is also needed for more optimized access to Infrastructure as a Service (IaaS). However, many businesses are interested in offloading guest traffic to directly attached Internet connectivity in remote branches. This is because it is better to offload this traf- fic locally rather than consume WAN bandwidth by routing it through a centralized data center for Internet services. This is not efficient and wastes expensive WAN bandwidth.

Networks of today cannot scale at the speed necessary to address the changing needs that the businesses require. Hardware-centric networks are traditionally more expensive and have fixed capacity. They are also more difficult to support due to the box-by-box configurations approach, siloed management tools, and lack of automated provisioning. Conflicting policies between domains and different configurations between services make them inflexible, static, expensive, and cumbersome to maintain. This leads to the network being more prone to misconfigurations and security vulnerabilities. It is impor- tant to shift from a connectivity-centric architecture to an application- or service-centric infrastructure that focuses on user experience and simplicity. Figure 1-2 shows the key factors affecting critical service level agreements (SLAs) that can disrupt business continuity.

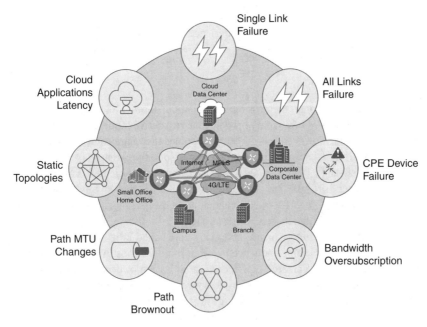

Figure 1-2   *Issues That Impact Critical SLAs*

The solution required to support today's cloud-enabled enterprise needs to be complete and comprehensive. It should be based on the software-defined approach mentioned earlier by leveraging the controller concept. The solution must also include a robust set of capabilities that reduce cost and complexity as well as promote business continuity and rapid innovation. These capabilities should include the separation of the management plane, control plane, and data plane. This will provide more horizontal scaling capabilities and the security of knowing where the data is at all times.

It should provide various consumption models, such as being hosted in the cloud or being managed on-premises, with complete redundancy between the two. The solution must also provide a complete set of network visibility and troubleshooting tools that are all accessible from a single place. Having this type of solution would assist in providing the following business outcomes and use cases:

- Faster branch deployment with no operational interaction
- Complete end-to-end network segmentation for enhanced security and privacy
- Increased WAN performance
- Topology independence
- Better user experience

All of the things mentioned thus far are critical in terms of what businesses are demanding to drive their network into becoming an asset that truly sets them apart from their industry peers. Many organizations rely on the network to function at its best to provide value and competitive differentiation so their businesses can excel. This is what is driving the industry to these types of technologies. This is also why the industry has increased the speed of adoption and deployment of these solutions.

High-Level Design Considerations

Considering the complexity of a majority of the networks out there today, they can be classified in a couple of categories, such as redundant and non-redundant. Typically, redundancy leads to increased complexity. Oftentimes, the simplest of networks do not plan for failures or outages and are commonly single-homed designs with multiple "single points of failure." Networks can contain different aspects of redundancy. There can be redundant links, routers, and service providers when speaking strictly of the WAN portion of the environment. Table 1-1 lists some of the common techniques introduced when dealing with redundancy.

Table 1-1 *Common Redundancy Techniques*

Redundant Links	Redundant Devices
Administrative distance	Redistribution
Traffic engineering	Loop prevention
Preferred path selection	Preferred path selection
Prefix summarization	Advanced filtering
Filtering	

Having a visual of what some of these topologies look like is often helpful. Figure 1-3 showcases some of these various topologies and their associated redundancy types, putting into context how the network will need to be configured and managed to support these types of redundancy options.

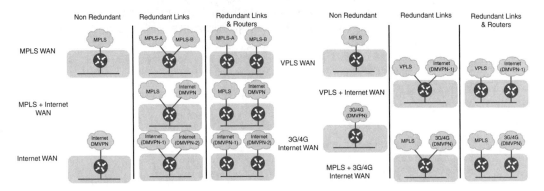

Figure 1-3   *Topology-Based and Link Redundancy Options*

Outside of the complexity associated with redundancy, there are many other aspects of the network that cause complexity within a network environment. Some of these aspects can include things such as securing the network, to shield it from malicious behavior; leveraging network segmentation, to keep traffic types separate for compliance or governance reasons; and even implementing quality of service (QoS), to ensure application performance and increase users' quality of experience. What further complicates the network is having to manually configure these options. The networks of today are too rigid, and things need to evolve. The industry is moving from the era of connectivity-centric network delivery models to an era of digital transformation. A shift is required to transition to a digital trans-formation model. The shift is from hardware and device-centric options to open, extensible, software-driven, programmable and cloud-enabled solutions. Figure 1-4 depicts the transition in a simple summary. Intent-based networking (IBN) is tak-ing the industry by storm. The concept revolves around signifying the intent of the business and automatically translating that intent into the appropriate corre-sponding networking tasks—relying more on automation to handle the day-to-day operational tasks and getting back time to focus on how to make the network pro-vide value to the business. This is delivered through policy-driven, automated, and self-optimizing capabilities. This provides closed-loop, automated service assurance that will empower network operations staff to transition from a reactive nature to a more proactive and predictive approach. Freeing up more of the operations staff's time will hopefully allow them to focus on more strategic initiatives within the business.

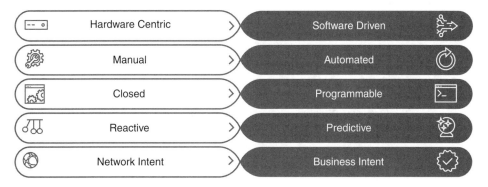

Hardware Centric	>	Software Driven	
Manual	>	Automated	
Closed	>	Programmable	
Reactive	>	Predictive	
Network Intent	>	Business Intent	

Figure 1-4 *Digital Transformation Transition*

Introduction to Cisco Software-Defined WAN (SD-WAN)

Shifting focus from a network-centric model to a business intent-based WAN network is a very powerful change. The WAN architecture can provide simplicity in terms of application deployment and management. However, the mindset must shift from a network topology focus to an application services topology. A common challenge for network operations staff is to support new and existing applications on the WAN. As mentioned previously in this chapter, these applications consume tremendous amounts of bandwidth and are very sensitive to variations in the quality of bandwidth that's available. Things such as jitter, loss, and delay impact most applications, which makes it more important to improve the WAN environment for these applications. Furthermore, cloud-based applications such as Enterprise Resource Planning (ERP) and Customer Relationship Management (CRM) are placing bandwidth demands on the WAN. Non-flexible connectivity options to keep up with the growing amount of cloud applications requiring bandwidth make it costly and difficult to provision new applications and services. Most businesses today have to rely on service providers for MPLS L3VPN to control their WAN routing and network SLAs. This impacts their ability to change and adapt to application delivery methods such as cloud and SaaS. Service providers could take months to implement the necessary changes to their environment in order to support these applications. In addition, some service providers will charge their customers a large amount of money to make these changes, and some may not make the changes at all. Because service providers currently have control of the WAN core, there's no way to instantiate VPNs independent of the underlying transport. Because of this, implementing differentiated service levels for individual applications becomes extremely difficult, if not impossible.

This is why the concept of hybrid WAN was originated. Hybrid WAN is where additional non-MPLS links are acquired by businesses and added to the WAN to provide alternate paths that the applications can take across the WAN environment. These are circuits that businesses have complete control over—from routing control to application performance.

Typically, VPN tunnels are created over the top of these circuits to provide secure transport over any type of link. Examples of these types of links are commodity broadband Internet, L2VPN, wireless, and 4G/LTE. This provides what is called *transport independence*. This allows for the capability to use any type of transport underneath the VPN and get deterministic routing and application performance. This means that some applications can be sent over these commodity links versus the traditional service provider–controlled L3VPN MPLS links. This provides unique granularity of traffic control, redundancy, and resiliency. Figure 1-5 illustrates some common hybrid WAN topologies.

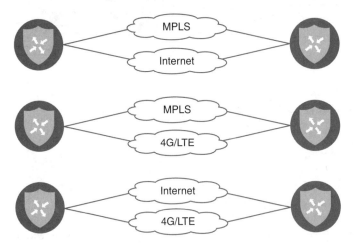

Figure 1-5 *Common Hybrid WAN Topologies*

Hybrid WANs need connectivity that is based on a service topology and can be centrally managed using policies. Currently, WAN connectivity is based on the network topology and managed using a peer-to-peer model. This means routing relationships are established by multiple control planes that operate independently of each other. Routing protocols such as Open Shortest Path First (OSPF) and Border Gateway Protocol (BGP) are used to establish site VPN routes, and IPsec is commonly used to secure the transport. These routing and security control planes run independently of each other and have their own scaling limitations, convergence requirements, and policy enforcement. This means each control plane is required to have its own independent policy and configuration. As a result, when a configuration change is required in the network, it has to be provisioned and propagated across all the control plane peers, for all transports, which creates operational pitfalls. This also creates the potential risk of misconfigurations or missing configuration that might cause applications to suffer.

Transport Independence

Cisco Software-Defined WAN (SD-WAN) leverages a transport-independent fabric technology that is used to connect remote locations together. This is accomplished by using an overlay technology. The overlay works by tunneling traffic over any kind of transport between any destination within the WAN environment. This is the VPN concept that was mentioned earlier in this chapter—for example, being able to connect remote branches that use MPLS to remote branches that use broadband Internet circuits. This gives true flexibility to routing applications across any portion of the network regardless of what type of circuit or transport is in use. This is the definition of transport independence. By having a fabric overlay network, it means that every remote site, regardless of physical or logical separation, is always a single hop away from another. This is of great benefit in terms of application latency and dynamic communication scenarios such as voice or interactive video. This not only provides increased simplicity in terms of network operations, but also provides seamless mobility from a user experience perspective. Transport independence is also one of the primary aspects of Cisco SD-WAN that allows for the use of flexible, lower-cost commodity circuits versus high-cost, inflexible static bandwidth. Although service providers can upgrade the bandwidth of a circuit, cost is usually a barrier. In addition, there are many times that, based on the type of circuit the bandwidth is riding on, an entire physical circuit upgrade or swap may be more likely. An example of this is having a 100Mbps MPLS handoff wherein the physical circuit it is delivered on is also only 100Mbps. In cases like this, another higher-speed port on the provider side is required, such as gigabit or 10-gigabit Ethernet ports. Many times, the circuit may ride over a different type of medium, and the entire circuit and delivery mechanism must be changed—for example, trying to go from a 45Mbps DS3 to a 1-gigabit Ethernet link. All of this takes time, and that is one of the things SD-WAN was created to address. Businesses can typically order a high-speed commodity Internet circuit and have it delivered within weeks. This new Internet circuit can be immediately added to the environment and taken advantage of by using SD-WAN. There are situations where multiple branch locations need to act as a single large branch across the WAN. This means having a virtual fabric over disparate transports such as MPLS and Internet. Given everything that has been covered thus far, it is important to show what an example of a Cisco SD-WAN diagram would look like. Figure 1-6 illustrates the high-level overview of a Cisco SD-WAN environment and how users, devices, and applications fit into the overall design.

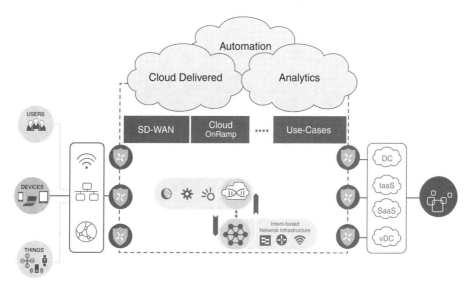

Figure 1-6   *High-Level SD-WAN Overview*

Moving from a network-centric WAN to an application- and services-focused WAN requires a different view of the wide area network. Figure 1-7 illustrates the new view of a business intent–based network, its components, and how they fit within the new model.

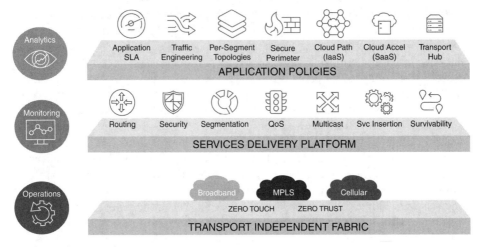

Figure 1-7   *Business Intent–Based Network Components*

Rethinking the WAN

If the current WAN technology and approach were to be redefined, it would have to include some fundamental changes to how WANs are constructed and managed today. These changes would involve the following key areas:

- Secure elastic connectivity

- Cloud-first approach

- Application quality of experience

- Agile operations

From a security perspective, end-to-end segmentation and policy are critical. The control, data, and management planes must be separated across the entire environment. The environment should be able to support native encryption that is robust and scalable, offer lightweight key management, and leverage a zero-trust model, meaning every aspect of the onboarding process must be authenticated and verified.

Rethinking the WAN from a connectivity perspective, these elements would be built on top of security functionality by integrating routing, security, and policy for optimal use of connectivity. The solution must allow for multiple types of transport connectivity options simultaneously and ultimately create a transport-independent operation model. Scale, both horizontally and vertically, is necessary at any layer. Additionally, advanced VPN capabilities and topologies to address any business intent or requirements are critical.

In terms of application support, the solution should support full application awareness across all elements in the system and offer built-in optimization techniques for the networks and applications. The network has evolved to be application aware, and it must be capable of choosing the most optimal path to connect to on-premises or cloud-based applications. The application experience must be optimal in terms of both access and security.

When it comes to the operation of this new application- and services-oriented WAN, network operations staff must be able to define network-wide policies that leverage templates, rather than just a device- or node-level policy. The controller must have the ability to coordinate the paths between the WAN Edge routers, based on centralized policy orchestration. As organizations' network requirements change and evolve over time, the policy should be able to be changed in one single place. This not only reduces the amount of time spent on configuration, but it also lowers the risk associated with misconfiguration errors as well. Programmable, open application programming interfaces (APIs) should be available to provide northbound access for automation and orchestration capabilities. Support of southbound APIs for integration with other solutions should also be included.

Use Cases Demanding Changes in the WAN

In this day and age, there are many reasons to look at enhancing the WAN environment— from load-balancing traffic to ensuring applications have the best performance possible. The following sections cover some of the use cases causing changes to the WAN.

Bandwidth Aggregation and Application Load-Balancing

There are many different use cases that demand changes to the way WANs are handled today. Some are as simple as businesses wanting bandwidth aggregation. This is the ability to use both public and private transports together at the same time. This is what is considered using A + B versus A or B, meaning the secondary transport link (Link B) usually sits idle without any traffic using it until Link A fails. However, in a hybrid WAN approach, being able to leverage multiple links at the same time provides an ability to use bandwidth from both links. This is considered an A + A or an Active/Active scenario. Application load-balancing is achieved using these types of designs as well. This type of hybrid environment allows for greater application performance at a fraction of the cost of two premium transport links. This also increases scale and flexibility without any security compromise. Figure 1-8 illustrates the various options of application load-balancing over multiple links in a hybrid environment. You can see that, by default, per-session Active/Active load-sharing is achieved. Weighted per-session round-robin is also configurable on a device basis. Application pinning, or forcing an application to take a specific transport, is also something that can be enforced via policy. Similarly, Application-Aware Routing or SLA-compliant routing is achieved by enforcing a policy that looks for specific traffic characteristics such as jitter, loss, and delay to determine the path the application should take over the available transports.

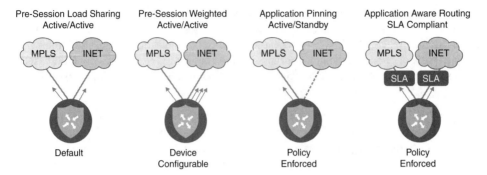

Figure 1-8 *Application Load-Balancing Options*

Protecting Critical Applications with SLAs

Another use case that drives changes in the WAN is the capability to provide an SLA for critical applications. This is accomplished by being able to route traffic based on the application requirements, as mentioned briefly earlier. This also provides statistics on how the applications are performing. Based on the policy that can be created, an SLA determines if the application is adhering to that policy, and performing properly, or if it is experiencing some sort of detriment such as jitter, loss, or delay. If this is the case, the application can be routed to another transport that will ensure the application is within policy and able to perform to the SLA that is expected of it. Figure 1-9 illustrates this particular scenario. A good example of this in a hybrid WAN environment would be an MPLS link and an Internet link. If the MPLS link is experiencing 5% packet loss and the Internet link is not, it might be appropriate to route the application over the Internet link to ensure that the application is functioning properly and users are having the best experience interacting with the application.

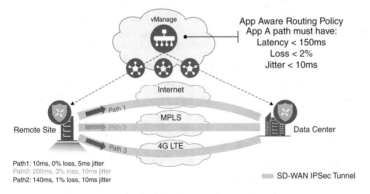

Figure 1-9 *Routing Based on Application Performance*

End-to-End Segmentation

Segmentation is another use case that drives these changes in the WAN. Oftentimes, businesses have different departments that require separation. For example, Research and Development may need to be segmented from the Production environment. There may be extranets that connect to partners, or the business may be merging or acquiring another business in which the networks need to be able to communicate but segmentation may still be required between the two. This may require multiple topologies that can be managed as one. Figure 1-10 depicts an end-to-end segmentation topology, along with how different VPNs are carried over the tunnels. Each of these tunnels terminates at an edge router within the environment.

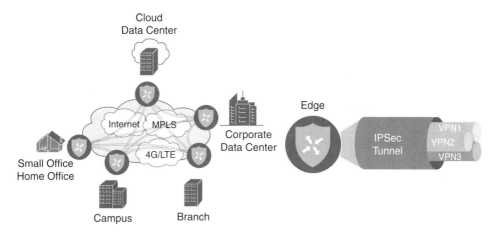

Figure 1-10 *End-to-End Segmentation*

Direct Internet Access

One of the most common use cases is something called Direct Internet Access (DIA). DIA gives branches the capability to send traffic directly out of the local Internet transport instead of carrying it all the way back to a centralized data center to be inspected. This allows for cloud-based applications to go directly to the Internet and cloud service providers without having to use unnecessary WAN bandwidth. This is increasingly becoming the method that is being adopted. Figure 1-11 depicts the traditional way that cloud applications are accessed. This causes suboptimal performance for users trying to access these applications. This also, as mentioned earlier, puts a strain on the WAN infrastructure, as the expensive and limited WAN bandwidth is being consumed by applications that could be sent directly to the Internet from the remote site. This also introduces increased application latency, as the traffic has to cross the entire network to get to the data center to reach the Internet.

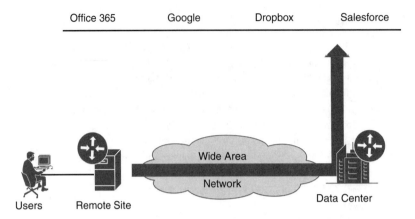

Figure 1-11   *Traditional Cloud Application Access via WAN*

Looking at changing and rethinking the WAN allows for different mechanisms that will allow for better performance and scale. A great example of this is using the Direct Internet Access design to offload the latency-sensitive cloud applications directly to the Internet. This method also gives the flexibility to have a local firewall or inspection device in the branch to ensure the branch is protected from any malicious threats coming into the local branch Internet link.

Figure 1-12 shows an example of what this would look like in a new WAN environment.

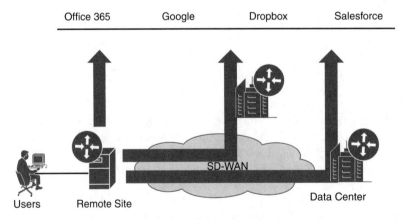

Figure 1-12   *Direct Internet Access and Cloud Access Topologies*

Fully Managed Network Solution

Finally, there is a use case that allows for the business to simply let someone else, such as Cisco or a Cisco Partner, manage the network as a fully managed solution. This provides the flexibility to not only have the network managed as a whole for the business, but also to allow the business to have control over the policy and reporting portion of the managed service. This is becoming a more attractive option for customers who want to move to an OpEx model. This allows them to pay for their network on a subscription basis versus the traditional CapEx model and is analogous to paying an electric or cell phone bill. The consumption models available today are really opening up new options for customers.

Note   All of these use cases and technologies will be covered in detail in the coming chapters of this book.

Building an ROI to Identify Cost Savings

A really important exercise when looking at Cisco SD-WAN is to build a quantifiable return on investment (ROI). Oftentimes businesses investigating Cisco SD-WAN find that removing certain expensive links and leveraging high-speed commodity Internet links for transport not only lowers the overall cost of the WAN but also adds redundancy and resiliency. Typically, these benefits weren't realized in the environment prior to moving to Cisco SD-WAN.

There are many companies that provide these ROI models at no cost to the customer and have proven to be an almost mandatory step in the Cisco SD-WAN journey. Some customers have seen enough cost savings and increases in overall bandwidth that the project was completed without any additional costs to the business. Figure 1-13 shows an example of an ROI calculation. Note the staggering details of a 64% cost savings from moving from a dual MPLS link design to a dual commodity Internet link design. At the very least, this proves the exercise is worthwhile to complete prior to getting started with implementation and deployment.

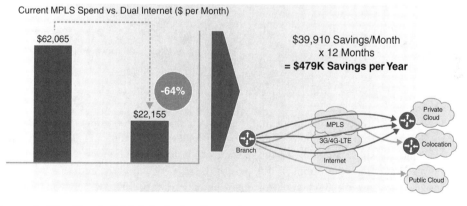

Figure 1-13   *Simple ROI Calculation Example*

> **Note**   These numbers were taken from a real customer example. However, every business will have different ROI calculations based on cost of circuits, type of circuits, and location. These numbers are examples only and will be different for anyone reading this book or having ROI calculations performed on their own environment.

Introduction to Multidomain

A common trend arising in the industry is data being generated and stored in many areas of the network. Traditionally, a majority of the data for a business was stored in a centralized data center. With the influx of guest users, mobile devices, bring your own device (BYOD), and Internet of Things (IoT), data is now being generated remotely in a distributed manner. This means the industry is shifting from data centers to multiple centers of data. That being said, simple, secure, and highly available connectivity is a must to allow for enhanced user and application experience. The other big piece to this is having a seamless policy that can go across these multiple centers of data. An example of this is policy that extends from the campus environment across the WAN and into the data center and back down to the campus. This provides consistency and deterministic behavior across multiple domains. Figure 1-14 illustrates a high-level example of sharing policy between a campus branch location and a data center running Cisco Application Centric Infrastructure (ACI).

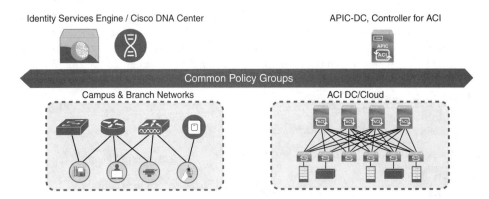

Figure 1-14   *High-Level Multidomain Example*

In future evolutions of Multidomain, the common policy will consequently provide end-to-end policy management across all three domains. This gives the capability of leveraging things like application SLAs from the data center to the WAN and back. This ensures the applications are performing to the best of their ability across the entire network, relieving strain on the WAN and providing a better user experience when using the applications. Figure 1-15 shows a high-level example of what this could look like from a topology perspective.

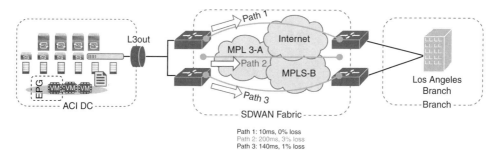

Path 1: 10ms, 0% loss
Path 2: 200ms, 3% loss
Path 3: 140ms, 1% loss

Figure 1-15 *High-Level Multidomain and SD-WAN Example*

Multidomain offers the capability to have the network operate as a holistic system, as mentioned previously in this chapter. This takes intent-based networks to the next level by taking policy across all domains for a seamless application experience. This also implements security everywhere and provides complete granularity in terms of control and operations.

Cloud Trends and Adoption

Cloud adoption has been taking the industry by storm. Over the years the reliance on the cloud has grown significantly, starting with music, movies, and storage and moving into Software as a Service (SaaS) and Infrastructure as a Service (IaaS). Today, there are many aspects of businesses such as application development, quality assurance, and production that are running in the cloud. To make things even more complicated, companies are relying on multiple cloud vendors to operate their business. This requires unique sets of polices, storage capacity requirements, and overall operational skills on a per-vendor basis. Companies are also struggling with things such as shadow IT and backdoor applications in their environment. This means that lines of business are going to cloud providers on their own without any knowledge or guidance from IT departments and spinning up applications on demand in the cloud. This causes major concerns from a security and privacy perspective. In addition, the potential loss of confidential information or intellectual property could damage the brand and reputation of the business. The risks are significant. Furthermore, the applications in the cloud, whether legitimate production or development, still require certain levels of priority and treatment to ensure the applications are being delivered properly to the users who consume them. This is where some of the capabilities of Cisco SD-WAN can help to ensure the applications are being treated appropriately and the experience for the users is adequate. Figure 1-16 illustrates the demand on the WAN and how the Internet is becoming critical to the operations of the business.

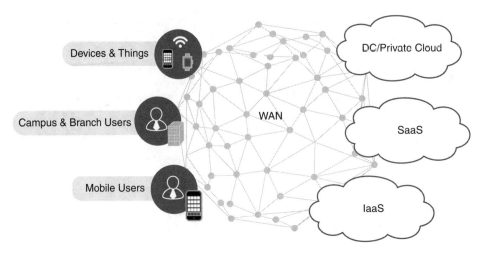

Figure 1-16   *Demand on WAN for Internet-Based Applications*

Having Direct Internet Access can assist with this, as mentioned earlier. By being able to detect application performance through one or more Direct Internet Access circuits, the edge routers are able to choose the best-performing path based on the application-specific parameters. If one of the links to the cloud application fails or has degradation in performance, the application can automatically fail over to another direct Internet link. This process is fully automated and requires no interaction from the network operations staff. Figure 1-17 shows this scenario with multiple Direct Internet Access links.

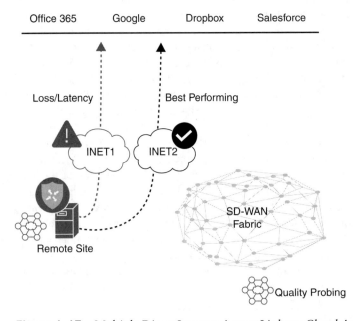

Figure 1-17   *Multiple Direct Internet Access Links to Cloud Applications*

This concept also works in environments that have a remote branch site that has a local direct Internet link as well as an Internet link within a centralized data center. The same process takes place in that the application performance is measured and the path that provides the best performance will be the path chosen for the application. Similarly, blackout or link failures will also be protected against because of redundancy built into the solution by having multiple available paths. Figure 1-18 depicts this scenario of having a local directly attached Internet link and an Internet link available in a centralized data center. Again, this leaves the router to make the decision based on the policy and application parameters that were configured. Not only are these decisions fully automated and made on a per-application and per-VPN basis, but ultimately an amazing amount of flexibility and control over the application performance within the environment is provided.

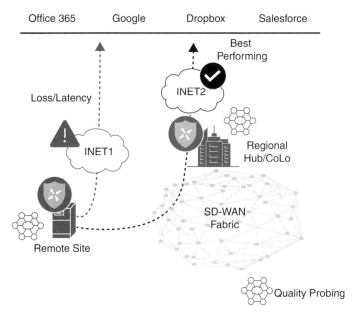

Figure 1-18   *Direct Internet Access and Centralized Internet Link to Cloud Applications*

Summary

This chapter covered a high-level overview of how the networks of today are causing challenges for businesses and their operations staff. The common business and IT trends the industry is seeing and how they impact the networks of today were also covered. The overall benefits desired by organizations and their IT staff lead to the need to rethink the WAN environment. Cloud applications and the influx of the amount of data within the network are causing strain on the WAN. This is causing businesses to look at ways to alleviate the pressure being put on the WAN and the organization as a whole. The use cases covered in this chapter will each be covered in depth in the upcoming chapters in this book. Cost is not the only driver for organizations to look at SD-WAN. Application performance, security, segmentation, improved user experience, redundancy, and resiliency are also key drivers that point to SD-WAN.

Review All Key Topics

Review the most important topics in this chapter, noted with the Key Topic icon in the outer margin of the page. Table 1-2 lists these key topics and the page numbers on which each is found.

Table 1-2   *Key Topics for Chapter 1*

Key Topic Element	Description	Page Number
Section	Transport Independence	10
Section	Protecting Critical Applications with SLAs	14
Paragraph	Direct Internet Access	15
Section	Introduction to Multidomain	18

Key Terms

Define the following key terms from this chapter and check your answers in the glossary:

Multidomain, artificial intelligence (AI), machine learning, cloud, virtualization, Internet of Things (IoT), quality of service (QoS), command line interface (CLI), Software-Defined Networking (SDN), bring your own device (BYOD), Software as a Service (SaaS), Infrastructure as a Service (IaaS), application programming interface (API), Cisco Software-Defined WAN (Cisco SD-WAN), Cisco Application Centric Infrastructure (Cisco ACI), service level agreement (SLA)

Chapter Review Questions

1. What are some of the common IT trends putting pressure on the WAN? (Choose three.)
   a. IoT
   b. Cloud
   c. Fog computing
   d. BYOD
   e. Low-bandwidth applications

2. What are some benefits businesses are looking for from their WAN? (Choose three.)
   a. Lower operational complexity
   b. Increased usable bandwidth
   c. Reduced uptime in branch locations
   d. Topology dependence
   e. Improved overall user experience

3. What are some of the tools or technologies that may be necessary to implement when redundant links are used in branch locations? (Choose three.)

   a. Administrative distance

   b. Traffic engineering

   c. Redistribution

   d. Loop prevention

   e. Preferred path selection

4. Part of having an intent-based network is to move to a hardware-centric approach.

   a. True

   b. False

5. Which of the following are part of the digital transformation journey? (Choose two.)

   a. Automated

   b. Manual

   c. Proactive

   d. Reactive

   e. Predictive

6. Organizations are looking to deploy SD-WAN for what reasons? (Choose two.)

   a. To take all routing control from the service provider

   b. To create end-to-end SLAs for the organization's traffic

   c. To offload all routing control to the service provider

   d. To leverage the service provider's SLA for end-to-end traffic

7. What are some of the benefits of SD-WAN? (Choose four.)

   a. Lower cost

   b. Improved user experience

   c. Transport independence

   d. Increased cloud consumption

   e. IoT devices

   f. Increased bandwidth

8. What are some of the transport options for SD-WAN? (Choose three.)

   a. Dual MPLS

   b. Hybrid WAN

   c. Dual route processor

   d. Hybrid single link

   e. Dual Internet

9. Direct Internet Access is used to offload applications directly to the data center.

   a. True

   b. False

10. What is one of the benefits of Cisco Multidomain?
    a. Single policy across multiple environments
    b. Multiple policies across single domain
    c. Simplified reporting for IoT devices
    d. Enhanced service provider support

Chapter 2

Cisco SD-WAN Components

This chapter covers the following topics:

- **Data Plane:** This section discusses the physical and virtual routers that actually carry data traffic.

- **Management Plane:** This section of the chapter introduces the component that handles most of our day-to-day tasks in managing the Cisco SD-WAN fabric.

- **Control Plane:** This section covers the component that handles all policies and routing.

- **Orchestration Plane:** This section introduces the component that facilitates discovery, authentication, and facilitation of the fabric.

- **Multi-Tenancy Options:** This section introduces the various multi-tenancy options in the Cisco SD-WAN solution.

- **Deployment Options:** This section covers the various deployment options, including Cisco cloud, private cloud, and an on-premises deployment.

This chapter introduces the various components that make up the Cisco SD-WAN architecture as well as the various deployment options. At a high level, these components can be grouped together by what purpose they play in the Cisco SD-WAN solution:

- Data Plane

- Management Plane

- Control Plane

- Orchestration Plane

In traditional networks today, the management plane, data plane, and control plane are all on the same router, and together they facilitate communication within the network. On a traditional router, we have line cards (which handle switching and forwarding of our data packets), a CPU module (which handles calculating our route table and advertising networks to the rest of the network), and the command line interface (CLI) is used to program the router. On the CLI, we type commands, and those commands program the CPU and line cards to act on our intent. Each router in a network has these three components. When you look at a traditional network, you have a number of routers, each of which needs to be programmed independently to achieve the desired operational state of your network. As these networks get larger, the amount of human intervention required to configure this environment dramatically increases, potentially creating complexity. Each router must calculate its own routing table from its perspective of the network. For example, suppose you have a network with 6,000 routes. Whenever there is a change in the network, each router will have to process these routing updates for each of these routes potentially. This requires the router to have the necessary available CPU and memory requirements to process these updates, which in turn creates a lot of overhead. Tuning the routing table on a network with a large number of sites and routes can quickly become very complex to achieve the desired results—be it full mesh, hub and spoke, partial mesh, and so on. Additionally, because each router is programmed individually, when you program the network on a router-by-router basis, you run the risk of undesired results due to an improper design or human error on the CLI.

The Cisco SD-WAN solution is a distributed architecture, meaning Cisco has separated the data plane from the control plane and management plane. Figure 2-1 illustrates how all the components fit into the architecture.

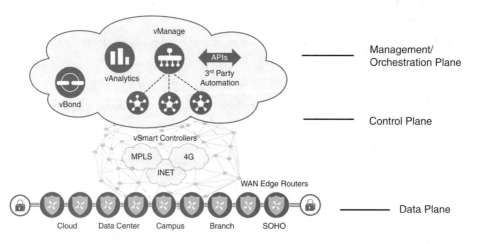

Figure 2-1 *Cisco SD-WAN Distributed Architecture*

This architecture differs from traditional networking in that it allows you to support large-scale networks while reducing operational and computational overhead. This solution separates the data plane, control plane, and management plane from each other. Because the control plane knows about all routes and nodes on the network, you have to calculate the routing table only once and can distribute this to all the necessary nodes as a single routing update rather than have every router send routing updates to the others, with each determining its own Routing Information Base (RIB). This greatly reduces the overhead on the network and enables you to reduce required resources on the routers so that you can bring additional features and capabilities to your edge devices. Because you have a complete view of the network, you can create a common network policy across the entire SD-WAN fabric—with the need for the management plane to program it once. As new devices are added to the network, they receive the same policy as well, ensuring the network is operating as expected. This book will show you how you can create various topologies and policies with ease, while increasing scale and capability.

Data Plane

Traditionally, the data plane is composed of the physical interfaces that our physical layer plugs into (for example, Ethernet, fiber and serial, and so on). As mentioned previously, this is analogous to the line cards on routers and switches. The Cisco SD-WAN solution refers to the data plane as WAN Edges. WAN Edges could be Cisco vEdge routers or Cisco XE SD-WAN routers. Throughout this section, you will learn the differences and features that these two platforms bring and how to select which one meets your business requirements. Data plane devices are deployed at branches, data centers, large campuses, colocation facilities, or in the cloud. At each site you can have a single WAN Edge or multiple WAN Edges, depending on redundancy requirements.

The data plane is where the SD-WAN overlay resides and is the layer that forwards user, server, and other network traffic. Both IPv4 and IPv6 are supported for transport within the data plane. In addition, data policies (such as QoS, Application-Aware Routing, and so on) are enforced within the data plane.

Each router will form data plane connections to other routers within the SD-WAN overlay for the purposes of transporting user traffic. Data plane connections are only established between data plane devices. These tunnels are secured via Internet Protocol Security (IPsec). As described previously, the data plane has native segmentation. The original IPv4/IPv6 payload is encapsulated utilizing RFC 4023. By using RFC 4023, you have segmentation across the SD-WAN overlay. Segmentation allows the network administrator to build separate instances of the data plane, depending on business requirements and regulations. The original data packet is encapsulated with IPsec, providing encryption and authentication. Figure 2-2 depicts the SD-WAN header representation.

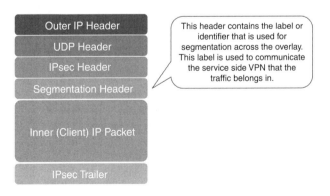

Figure 2-2 *Cisco SD-WAN Packet Format*

The Cisco SD-WAN solution can support diverse topologies unique to each VPN segment or data plane instantiation. Each of these VPN segments is completely isolated from communicating with each other unless policy allows it. These VPNs are carried in a single IPsec tunnel. For example, corporate users could have a full-mesh topology while PCI or HIPAA requirements could dictate that you have a hub-and-spoke topology for other devices. Figure 2-3 provides a graphical representation of this concept. On the LAN, or service side, the data plane supports OSPF, EIGRP, and BGP for routing protocols. For smaller locations that don't utilize a routing protocol, VRRP is supported to provide first-hop gateway redundancy.

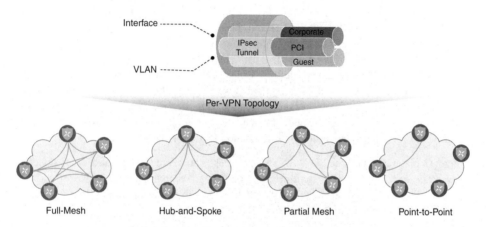

Figure 2-3   *Segmentation and Per VPN Topologies*

Note   In the Cisco SD-WAN solution, Virtual Private Network (VPN) is synonymous with Virtual Routing and Forwarding (VRF) instances from a generic routing perspective. VRFs and VPNs provide a method to separate the control and data plane into different logical parts. Segmentation in the data plane is accomplished by building multiple, isolated routing table instances and binding specific interfaces to those instances.

WAN Edges have built-in security to prevent unauthorized access from the network. The WAN-facing interfaces only allow connections from authenticated sources, such as control plane and management plane elements. These interfaces explicitly allow IPsec connections only from other WAN Edges in the fabric. The WAN Edges learn of these other data plane devices from the control plane elements in the solution. The WAN-facing interface firewall on the WAN Edge, by default, will block everything that isn't allowed explicitly. Inbound services that can be enabled are SSH, NETCONF, NTP, OSPF, BGP, and STUN. Outbound services that are allowed are DHCP, DNS, and ICMP.

Bidirectional Forwarding Detection (BFD) is used inside IPsec tunnels between all WAN Edges. BFD sends *Hello* packets to measure link liveness as well as packet loss, jitter, and delay. Each WAN Edge will make its own determination on how to react to this BFD information. Depending on the policy defined by the management plane, routing across the data plane could be adjusted, such as having applications prefer one transport over the other, depending on performance. BFD operates in echo mode, which means that the neighbor doesn't actually participate in the processing of the BFD packet; instead, it is simply echoed back to the original sender. This greatly reduces the impact on the CPU, as the neighbor doesn't need to process the packets. By comparison, if the neighbor was involved in the processing of the BFD packets, and the remote neighbor's CPU was busy with some other processing, there could be potential delay in responding to the BFD packet. By eliminating this, you can reduce outage detection time and improve user experience. BFD cannot be turned off, but timers can be tuned in the SD-WAN fabric to identify and illicit a response to potential issues more quickly. Another advantage of using echo mode is that the original packet is echoed back to the original sender, and from this information the WAN Edge has a complete round-trip view of the transport.

When the WAN Edge initially gets connected to the network, it first tries to reach out to a Plug and Play (PNP) or Zero Touch Provisioning (ZTP) server. Figure 2-4 illustrates a high-level overview of the PNP/ZTP process. This process will be discussed further in Chapter 4, "Onboarding and Provisioning," but for now know that this is the process in which the router connects to the orchestration plane and learns about all of the various components in the network. Once the control plane is established, the last step is to build data plane connections to all other WAN Edges. By default, a full-mesh topology will be built, though policy can be built to limit data plane connections and influence the routing topology. It should be noted, as well, that if PNP or ZTP isn't available, there are other options available to manually bootstrap the configuration using the CLI or a USB thumb drive.

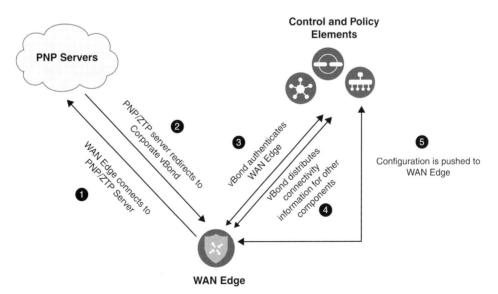

Figure 2-4 *High-level Overview of the Plug and Play/Zero Touch Provisioning Process*

Note There are two methods of auto-provisioning of WAN Edges: PNP and ZTP. PNP uses HTTPS to connect to Cisco PNP servers, and ZTP uses UDP port 12346 to connect. Cisco XE SD-WAN routers use PNP, while Cisco vEdges use ZTP for provisioning.

There are two methods of deployment—physical and virtual. Physical platforms that are supported are the Cisco Integrated Services Router (ISR), Cisco Advanced Services Router (ASR), and Cisco vEdges. Virtual platforms are supported on public or private clouds. Supported virtual platforms are the Cisco Cloud Services Router (CSR1000v) running XE SD-WAN and Cisco vEdge Cloud. At press time, supported public clouds are Amazon Web Services, Google Cloud and Microsoft Azure. Virtual platforms can also be deployed on a private cloud, which can run either on VMware ESXi or KVM hypervisors. If the use case requires it, virtual platforms can be supported at the branch as well via the Cisco Enterprise Network Compute System (ENCS) and Cisco Cloud Services Platform (CSP). These platforms open the door to provide service chaining with VNFs—including firewalls and third-party virtual appliances. Table 2-1 outlines the supported WAN Edge platforms.

Table 2-1 *Current SD-WAN Supported Platforms*

Cisco XE SD-WAN Platforms	Cisco vEdge Platforms	Virtual Platforms
Cisco ISR1000 Series	Viptela 100 Series	Cisco CSR1000v
Cisco ISR4000 Series	Viptela 1000 Series	Viptela vEdge Cloud
Cisco ASR1000 Series	Viptela 2000 Series	Cisco ISRv
Cisco ENCS	Viptela 5000 Series	
Cisco CSP		

Check https://www.cisco.com/c/en/us/solutions/enterprise-networks/sd-wan/index.html for the complete supported list of platforms.

When considering which WAN Edge to go with, you will need to understand your throughput requirements, data plane tunnel requirements (for example, how many other branches the router will be communicating with), and what type of interfaces are needed. Cisco vEdge platforms support Ethernet, LTE, and wireless interfaces, while Cisco XE SD-WAN platforms support additional interface types, including voice and serial interfaces. Both platforms are interoperable on the SD-WAN fabric and can terminate data plane tunnels between XE SD-WAN and vEdge platforms.

Viptela platforms run Viptela OS. Cisco SD-WAN platforms run IOS-XE SD-WAN software. If there is an existing deployment of Cisco ISRs and ASRs, then you can leverage this existing investment and upgrade them from IOS-XE to an IOS-XE SD-WAN image in the same way you would upgrade any other Cisco router.

Note Upgrading Cisco IOS-XE to IOS-XE SD-WAN may require a ROMMON upgrade as well. You can find more information on the procedure to upgrade Cisco IOS-XE routers at https://www.cisco.com/c/en/us/td/docs/routers/sdwan/configuration/sdwan-xe-gs-book/hardware-and-software-installation.html.

Some of the most important features supported on XE SD-WAN routers are advanced security use cases. By overlaying security on top of the Cisco SD-WAN solution, you can introduce new Direct Internet and Direct Cloud Access use cases at the branch, in addition to securing traffic within the overlay. Moving security to the branch facilitates the capability to leverage existing Internet transports at the branch. This is referred to as Direct Internet Access (DIA), or sometimes as Local Internet Access. Figure 2-5 illustrates these concepts.

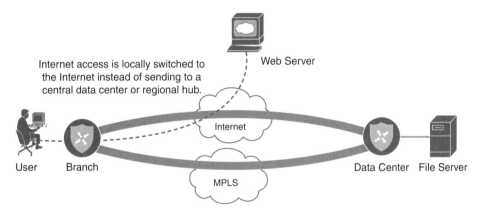

Figure 2-5 *Direct Internet Access Overview*

Security use cases will be discussed in more detail in Chapter 10, "Cisco SD-WAN Security," but here is a list of currently supported security features:

- DNS Security (Cisco Umbrella)

- Endpoint Protection (Cisco AMP for Endpoints)

- Application-Aware Firewall

- Intrusion Detection System/Intrusion Prevention System

- URL Filtering

Traditionally, security requirements dictate that all Internet access is backhauled to a data center, colocation, or regional site. The reason for this was due to the fact that it was more cost-effective to implement security at a central site due to the cost of implementing and managing disparate security components at all sites. With Cisco SD-WAN security, businesses can move security to the branch and can now offload Internet access at remote sites. Here are some other areas where a business might see benefits from DIA:

■ Reduced bandwidth requirements and latency on costly WAN circuits

■ Guest access

■ Improved user experience to Cloud SAAS and IAAS applications

Chapter 7, "Centralized Data Policies," discusses DIA in more detail.

When a WAN Edge attempts to join the fabric, it attempts to build control connections across each transport deployed at that site. By default, if a transport doesn't have control connectivity to any of the Cisco SD-WAN controllers, then it won't build a data plane connection across that transport either. This is very common with cloud deployments where the controllers are in a public or private cloud and your MPLS transport has no connectivity to the Internet.

Note   There are a few options to still achieve data plane with no control connectivity. One option is to disable control connections on that transport via the **max-control-connections** command. Be aware that when control connections aren't established on an interface, there will be no control plane monitoring over that transport. You still have monitoring from a data plane perspective, however.

Management Plane

As mentioned previously, network devices of the past would be managed via the CLI independently. Cisco SD-WAN, however, introduces vManage, which is a network management system (NMS) that provides a single pane of glass to manage the SD-WAN solution. vManage can be utilized for onboarding, provisioning, policy creation, software management, troubleshooting, and monitoring. Though vManage has a rich feature set, if the preference is to interface with vManage via an API, vManage also supports communication via REST and NETCONF. By having a full API, the user can build and utilize scripts and interface with vManage in an automated fashion. This API also allows the user to use existing and future toolkits for integration. As you can see in Figure 2-6, vManage provides an intuitive and easy-to-consume dashboard. When first logging in to vManage, you will be presented with statistics outlining what the current state of the network is.

vManage is also highly scalable, depending on the needs of the environment. When vManage is clustered, redundancy can be provided, with multiple clusters deployed regionally or globally. A single cluster is made up of three or more vManage NMSs but must always be an odd number to avoid a split-brain scenario. A vManage cluster can manage up to 6,000 WAN Edges, with each cluster node handling 2,000 WAN Edges.

vManage can use multiple authentication sources, including RADIUS, TACACS, and SAML 2.0 for external user connectivity. By default, vManage is deployed in a single tenant mode, though, if the requirements call for support of a service provider model, multi-tenancy is supported as well.

Figure 2-6 *Cisco vManage Overview*

All configuration for the SD-WAN fabric should be performed within vManage in order to maintain consistency and scalability. Discussed further in Chapter 4, device configurations are built in vManage via feature or CLI templates. Policies, controlling things such as network topology, routing, QoS, and security, are also configured here. When necessary, vManage is also where troubleshooting and monitoring of the network will occur. Network administrators can simulate traffic flows to show data paths, troubleshoot WAN impairment, and access the configuration and routing tables of all devices. This greatly reduces operations as there is no longer a need to log in to each WAN Edge individually. Instead, troubleshooting can be accomplished via a single dashboard.

Each WAN Edge will form a single management plane connection to vManage. If the device has multiple transports available, only one will be used for management plane connectivity to vManage. If a cluster is in place, then the control connection will get load balanced across cluster nodes. If a transport hosting the management plane connection experiences an outage, then the WAN Edge will briefly lose connectivity to vManage and any changes made will get pushed when the device reconnects.

The last component in the management plane is vAnalytics. vAnalytics gives the network administrator predictive analytics to provide actionable insight into the WAN. With vAnalytics, the business can perform trending, capacity planning of circuits, as well as review how application performance is trending globally. With capacity planning, you can see how new applications may interact on your WAN before actually deploying them, allowing the business to rightsize connectivity. vAnalytics ingests data from the network and uses machine learning to predict trends on capacity. vAnalytics requires additional licensing and isn't on by default. It is important to note that vManage should be used for a real-time, raw data view of the network, while vAnalytics should be used as a tool to review the historical performance of the network—which provides forward-looking insight into network adjustments.

Control Plane

Previously, you learned how the control plane has been separated from the data plane in the traditional sense. The component that provides control plane functionality is vSmart. vSmart is the brain of the SD-WAN fabric. vSmart is highly scalable and can handle up to 5,400 connections per vSmart server with up to 20 vSmarts in a single production deployment. With these numbers, a deployment can support very large WANs. vSmart is responsible for the implementation of control plane policies, centralized data polices, service chaining, and VPN topologies. vSmart also handles the security and encryption of the fabric by providing key management.

Separating the control plane from the data and management planes allows the solution to achieve greater scale while simplifying network operations. If you look at traditional link state routing protocols such as OSPF and IS-IS, each router knows about the state of the whole network and calculates its own routing table based off the link state database information. This can be very CPU intensive and offers only a limited, autonomous view of the network. Distance vector routing protocols operate a little differently in that they only know what their neighbors tell them about the rest of the network. In turn, they may make suboptimal routing decisions because they don't have the whole picture of the network. With the Cisco SD-WAN solution, all routing information is learned by all vSmarts. vSmarts then calculate the routing table and distribute it to the WAN Edges. Because the vSmart has a complete picture of the network state, you are able to simplify the best path calculation and reduce complexity of the entire network while still increasing scale. A WAN Edge can connect to up to three vSmarts at a time but only needs connectivity to one to get policy information.

The protocol the vSmart uses to communicate all this information is called Overlay Management Protocol (OMP). Though OMP handles routing, it would be a disservice to consider it simply a routing protocol. As such, OMP is used to manage and control the over-lay beyond just routing (key management, configuration updates, and so on). As illustrated in Figure 2-7, OMP runs between vSmart and the WAN Edges inside of a secured tunnel. When a policy is built via the management plane, this policy is distributed to vSmart via NETCONF, and the vSmart will distribute this policy via an OMP update to the WAN Edges.

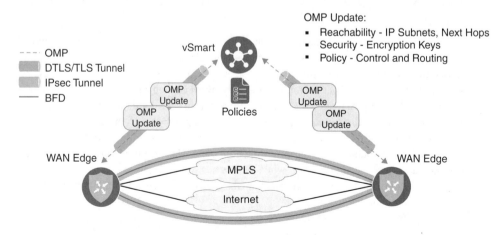

Figure 2-7   *Cisco Control Plane and Data Plane Overview*

The vSmart operates similarly to a BGP route reflector in iBGP. The vSmart receives routing information from each WAN Edge and can apply policies before advertising this information back out to other WAN Edges. vSmart is also where different topologies are defined per VPN. The control policy is defined in the management plane, the management plane then distributes the policy, and vSmart applies the policy to the fabric. In this example, topology modification is achieved by manipulating what routes get distributed and how the data plane is built between WAN Edges.

The control plane is also responsible for encryption of the fabric. In more legacy WAN technologies, securing the network required a considerable amount of processing power, as each device would compute its own encryption keys and distribute these keys to peers using a protocol such as ISAKMP/IKE. This is usually referred to as "IPsec Phase 1" in legacy nomenclature and is covered in more detail in IETF draft *draft-carrel-ipsecme-controller-ike-00*. In Cisco SD-WAN, key exchange and distribution have been moved to the vSmart. Each WAN Edge will compute its own keys per transport and distribute these to the vSmart. The vSmart will then distribute them to each WAN Edge, depending on defined policy. In addition, the vSmart is also responsible for rekeying of the IPsec Security Associations (SA) when they expire. By moving key exchange to a centralized location, we achieve greater scale as each WAN Edge doesn't need to handle key negotiation or distribution. Review Figure 2-7 for an overview of how the control and data planes are built. Chapter 3, "Control Plane and Data Plane Operations," will also cover this in more detail.

If there is a situation where control connectivity was established but, due to an outage, has been lost, then data plane connectivity will continue to flow. By default, WAN Edges will continue forwarding data plane traffic in the absence of control plane connectivity for 12 hours, utilizing the last-known state of the routing table, though this is configurable, depending on your requirements. When control plane connectivity is reestablished, WAN Edges will be updated with any policy changes that were made during the outage. When the control connection is restored, the route table is flushed and the newly received route table is installed. This will cause a brief outage to the data plane when this occurs.

For redundancy, best practice dictates that you have at least two vSmarts geographically dispersed. vSmarts should have an identical policy configuration to ensure network stability. If these configurations aren't identical, you risk having suboptimal routing and potential blackholing of traffic. vSmarts will maintain a full mesh of OMP sessions among themselves and exchange control and routing information, though each vSmart will operate autonomously (that is, there is no database synchronized between the two). Figure 2-8 shows how OMP is established between numerous vSmart controllers. It is with this full mesh that the vSmart controllers stay synchronized. If there are more than two vSmarts in the network, control connections from the WAN Edges will be load balanced. If a vSmart goes down, these control connections will get rebalanced across the remaining vSmarts.

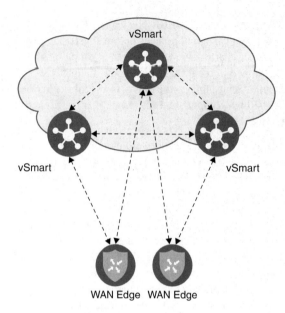

Figure 2-8   *OMP Session Establishment*

 ## Orchestration Plane

The final, and probably the most important, component in the Cisco SD-WAN solution is the vBond. This component is so important because it provides initial authentication for participation on the fabric and acts as the glue that discovers and brings all other components together. Multiple vBond servers can be deployed to achieve high availability. Though a WAN Edge can point to only a single vBond, it is recommended to have the WAN Edge use DNS and have a single A record point to all vBond IPs. When the WAN Edge tries to resolve the DNS record for the vBond, it will receive each IP address and try to connect to each one sequentially until a successful control connection is made.

When a WAN Edge first joins the overlay, the only thing it knows about is the vBond. It receives this information via one of four methods:

- Plug and Play

- Zero Touch Provisioning

- Bootstrap configuration

- Manual configuration

The WAN Edge will attempt to build a temporary connection to the vBond over each transport. Once the control plane connectivity is up to vSmart and vManage, the connection to the vBond will be torn down. At the time that the WAN Edge connects to the vBond, it goes through an authentication process. Each component authenticates each other and, if successful, a Datagram Transport Layer Security (DTLS) tunnel is established. The vBond then distributes the connectivity information for the vSmart and vManage to the WAN Edge. This is why the vBond is essentially referred to as the glue of the network, as it tells all the components about each other. This process will be discussed in more detail in Chapters 3 and 4.

One remaining functionality that the vBond provides is network address translation (NAT) traversal. By default, the vBond operates as a STUN Server (RFC 5389). The WAN Edge operates as a STUN client. What this means is that the vBond can detect when WAN Edges are behind a NAT device such as a firewall. When the WAN Edge goes to establish its DTLS tunnel, the interface IP it knows about will be written into the outer IP header and noted within a payload of the message. When the vBond receives this information, it performs a XOR operation comparing the two values. If the two values are different, it can be inferred that NAT is in the transit path of the WAN Edge (since the outer IP header was changed to a NAT'd IP address and no longer matches the IP address noted in the payload of the packet). The vBond will communicate this back to the WAN Edge, and the WAN Edge can communicate this information to the rest of the overlay components—ultimately allowing data plane connectivity to be established through a NAT device. There are, however, some scenarios where this won't work, such as with symmetric NAT. This will be discussed in more detail in Chapters 3 and 4. Figure 2-9 explains how STUN is utilized to detect when a WAN Edge or other control plane component is behind a NAT.

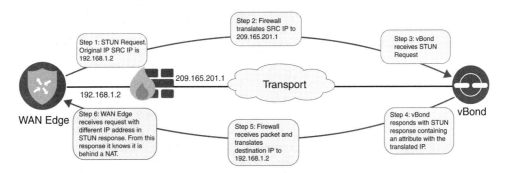

Figure 2-9 *STUN NAT Detection Method*

When you're deploying a vBond, special consideration must be made around IP connectivity. The vBond must be publicly addressable, though this could be via 1:1 static NAT. The vBond is the only component that must be set up this way. Other components like vManage and vSmart can be behind port address translation (PAT) as long as they have connectivity to the vBond. The control plane and management plane use the same NAT discovery method of STUN as the WAN Edge.

Multi-Tenancy Options

The Cisco SD-WAN solution supports multiple modes of segmentation in the control, data, management, and orchestration planes. Referencing Figure 2-10, the first mode is dedicated tenancy. In this mode, each tenant has dedicated components and the data plane is segmented as well. The second option is VPN tenancy. This mode segments only the data plane of the VPN topology and allows you to define read-only users who can view and monitor their VPN within vManage. VPN tenancy still shares the same SD-WAN components, however. The third option is enterprise tenancy. With this mode, the orchestration and management planes are operating in multi-tenancy mode, but the control plane requires dedicated, per-tenant appliances. Because the control plane is dedicated, it can be deployed as a container or nested virtual machine to decrease scalability concerns.

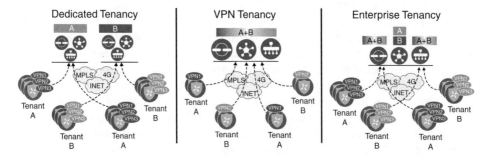

Figure 2-10   *Cisco SD-WAN Multi-Tenancy Options*

Deployment Options

With the Cisco SD-WAN solution, multiple controller deployment options are supported. The most common deployment utilizes the Cisco Cloud. With Cisco Cloud, Cisco builds all the SD-WAN components that you have been introduced to in this chapter. This greatly simplifies the deployment, allowing the network administrator to focus on configuration and policy administration of the Cisco SD-WAN fabric. Cisco will work with the business to collect the requirements needed to support their use cases and deployment—such as if you have requirements to have controller redundancy globally. In such a case, Cisco will work to deploy disparate controllers.

If the business has a requirement (due to regulatory or business compliance) that necessitates the Cisco SD-WAN controllers be deployed in a different cloud besides the Cisco-managed cloud, then private cloud is the deployment method you would most likely select. Currently supported private clouds are Amazon AWS and Microsoft Azure. When deploying in a private cloud, ensure you have the necessary TCP and UDP ports open for control plane connectivity and that vBond, in particular, has a public IP address or is behind a static 1:1 NAT.

The last deployment option is an on-premises deployment. If business requirements dictate that the Cisco SD-WAN controllers are deployed in a more traditional data center, then an on-premises deployment is what you should review. On-premises deployments will have specific requirements around CPU, memory, and storage in addition to the previously mentioned specific network requirements. On-premises may also be the type of deployment selected when deploying for testing and proof of concept. Chapter 13, "Provisioning Cisco SD-WAN Controllers in a Private Cloud," covers deploying on-premises controllers in much more detail.

Summary

This chapter introduced the components that make up the Cisco SD-WAN solution. The data plane was discussed, wherein user traffic will be routed and forwarded across the WAN. The data plane is similar to routers that would be deployed in a traditional WAN, though in Cisco SD-WAN, these are referred to as WAN Edges. vManage was also introduced as the management plane. The management plane is where all Day 0, Day 1, and Day N functions will be performed, including WAN Edge configuration, routing and control policies, troubleshooting, and monitoring. The next component that was introduced was vSmart. vSmart is the brain of the Cisco SD-WAN fabric and is responsible for calculating and deploying all control and data policies as well as handling the distribution of encryption keys for data plane connectivity. The last component introduced was the vBond. vBond makes up the orchestration plane and is responsible for authenticating components on the fabric in addition to distributing control and management plane information to the WAN Edges. The vBond is the component that aids in discovery of the fabric for all other components (such as when devices are behind NAT). The final topic discussed was the deployment options. The most common deployment method is via Cisco Cloud, but there are two other options to consider: private cloud and on-premises. By supporting all three deployment options, the Cisco SD-WAN solution can support all business requirements.

Review All Key Topics

Review the most important topics in the chapter, noted with the Key Topic icon in the outer margin of the page. Table 2-2 lists these key topics and the page numbers on which each is found.

Table 2-2 *Key Topics*

Key Topic Element	Description	Page
Figure 2-1	Cisco SD-WAN Distributed Architecture	26
Section	Data Plane	27
	The data plane is where user traffic traverses. Data plane traffic is influenced by the control plane.	
Table 2-1	Cisco SD-WAN Supported Platforms	30

Key Topic Element	Description	Page
Section	Management Plane	32
	How vManage is utilized to manage the SD-WAN fabric from Day 0, Day 1, and Day N.	
Section	Control Plane	34
	Overview of how the SD-WAN control plane operates.	
Section	Orchestration Plane	36
	How vBond brings the fabric together and authenticates all the components.	

Key Terms

Define the following key terms from this chapter, and check your answers in the glossary:

Data plane (WAN Edge), management plane (vManage), control plane (vSmart), orchestration plane (vBond), Overlay Management Protocol (OMP)

Chapter Review Questions

1. What are the three controllers that make up the Cisco SD-WAN solution?
   a. vSmart
   b. vBond
   c. WAN Edge
   d. vManage
   e. vController

2. How does the Cisco SD-WAN architecture differ from traditional WAN technologies? (Choose three.)
   a. Single pane of glass
   b. Increased scale with centralized control plane
   c. Reduced uptime in branch locations
   d. Topology dependence
   e. Distributed architecture

3. What are the three functions of vManage in the SD-WAN solution?
   a. Troubleshooting
   b. Configuration
   c. Redistribution
   d. Loop prevention
   e. Monitoring

4. WAN Edges provide data plane encryption via IPsec.

   a. True

   b. False

5. What traditional networking concept does vSmart closely relate to?

   a. BGP route reflector

   b. Router

   c. Switch

   d. Hub

6. What functions does the vBond provide in the SD-WAN environment? (Choose two.)

   a. Authentication and whitelisting of the SD-WAN components

   b. NAT detection and traversal

   c. Pushing configuration to WAN Edges

   d. Software upgrades

7. The Cisco SD-WAN solution supports multi-tenancy.

   a. True

   b. False

8. Which routing protocols are supported on the service side of the Cisco SD-WAN solution? (Choose three.)

   a. EIGRP

   b. OSPF

   c. RIP

   d. OMP

   e. BGP

9. What three attributes are measured with BFD?

   a. Delay

   b. Loss

   c. Jitter

   d. Out-of-order packets

10. The Cisco SD-WAN solution is able to provide segmentation and different topologies per VRF.

    a. True

    b. False

References

T. Worster, Y. Rekhter, and E. Rosen, Ed. RFC 4023, "Encapsulating MPLS in IP or Generic Routing Encapsulation (GRE)," Network Working Group, https://tools.ietf.org/html/rfc4023, March 2005

D. Carrel and B. Weis. IETF Draft, "IPsec Key Exchange Using a Controller," IETF, https://tools.ietf.org/html/draft-carrel-ipsecme-controller-ike-00, January 2018

J. Rosenberg, R. Mahy, P. Matthews, and D. Wing. RFC 5389, "Session Traversal Utilities for NAT (STUN)," Network Working Group, https://tools.ietf.org/html/rfc5389, October 2008

Chapter 3

Control Plane and Data Plane Operations

This chapter covers the following topics:

- **Control Plane Operations:** This section covers the Overlay Management Protocol (OMP) and how the three routing updates (TLOC, OMP route, and service routes) build the control plane.

- **Data Plane Operations:** This section covers how the data plane is established and secured, along with how network address translation (NAT) interacts with overlay provisioning.

As discussed in Chapter 2, "Cisco SD-WAN Components," four different planes make up the Cisco SD-WAN solution, as illustrated in Figure 3-1 and described in the list that follows:

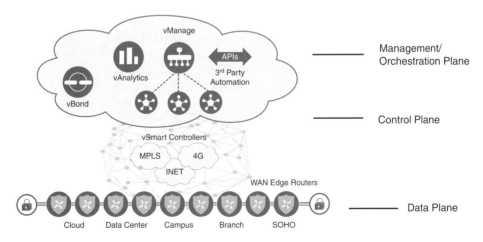

Figure 3-1 *Cisco SD-WAN Distributed Architecture*

- **Data plane:** The data plane is where user traffic flows and utilizes information learned from the control plane to build connections between branches. The data plane can be full mesh, partial mesh, point-to-point, hub-and-spoke, or a combination thereof. The data plane in the Cisco SD-WAN solution is extremely flexible and can be designed to meet the needs of most deployments.

- **Management plane:** The management plane is provided by vManage. vManage is the single pane of glass for onboarding, provisioning, monitoring, and troubleshooting. Once SD-WAN components are deployed, this is where most day-to-day operations will be performed.

- **Orchestration plane:** Orchestration plane functionality is provided by the vBond controller. vBond authenticates and authorizes all other SD-WAN components while providing connectivity information about vSmart and vManage controllers. In addition, vBond facilitates NAT-traversal capabilities.

- **Control plane:** The component responsible for control plane functionality is referred to as vSmart. The vSmart provides all routing and data plane policies to the routers in the environment.

This chapter is broken into two sections. The first section will be on the SD-WAN control plane and how OMP facilitates building the control plane. In this section, three route types will be introduced: TLOC Routes, OMP Routes, and Service Routes. These routing updates are used to influence how WAN Edges build the data plane.

The second section covers data plane operations. Multiple new concepts will be introduced in this section, including colors, VPNs, tunnel groups, Restrict, and IPsec. NAT is integrated seamlessly in the solution and will be covered too.

Control Plane Operations

In the Cisco SD-WAN solution, control plane mechanisms are facilitated by the Overlay Management Protocol (OMP). OMP allows for a secure and scalable fabric across all transport types, whether private (MPLS, Layer 2 VPNs, and point-to-point networks) or public connectivity methods (Internet and LTE). As discussed in Chapter 2, the component responsible for the control plane is the vSmart controller. This controller facilitates a scalable control plane and is responsible for disseminating all policy information to the WAN Edges. The vSmart's functionality is often compared to that of a BGP route reflector. With that thinking in mind, the vSmart will take all routing and topology information received from the clients, calculate best-path information based off of configured policy, and then advertise the results of this to the WAN Edge (route reflector clients).

Note   BGP route reflectors are defined in RFC 4456 (https://tools.ietf.org/html/rfc4456).

In traditional networks, the control plane is only focused on how data flows through the network. This was accomplished by consuming routing updates, performing best-path selection operations, and feeding this information into forwarding tables. Configuring security with these protocols is usually an intensive and often manual process that generally required downtime while the network administrator transitions to these security mechanisms. Security was often an afterthought and usually implemented after the routing domain was established. As such, security should be critical to any routing domain, as you need to validate and trust all routing updates so that no malicious routing information is processed.

With that in mind, security is at the heart of the Cisco SD-WAN solution. Control plane tunnels are encrypted and authenticated via Datagram Transport Layer Security (DTLS) or Transport Layer Security (TLS). In Figure 3-2, DTLS/TLS connections are maintained between all personas in the SD-WAN overlay (vBond, vSmart, WAN Edges, and vManage). These tunnels are negotiated using SSL certificates, wherein each component will authenticate the other end and establish a one-way tunnel. In this negotiation, each device will validate that the received certificate is signed by a trusted root CA and has a valid serial number with a matching organization name. See Figure 3-3 for an example of a tunnel between a WAN Edge and vSmart controller.

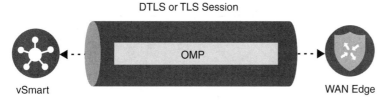

Figure 3-2   *DTLS Tunnel*

Note   DTLS and TLS are defined in RFC 6347 and RFC 5246, respectively. Keep in mind, WAN Edges don't maintain control plane connections among themselves, only IPsec tunnels. This allows the solution to be scalable and on-demand.

By default, DTLS is the protocol of choice. DTLS communication occurs over UDP port 12346. It is recommended that this port remain open to and from the vBond to all WAN Edges. TLS is also supported if requirements call for it (note that TLS operates using the TCP protocol and is therefore stateful). In both cases, the DTLS protocol is able to handle out-of-order or lost packets. Furthermore, vSmart and vManage are deployed as a virtual machine that supports multiple cores (up to eight). Each core has a base port associated with it. Inbound DTLS/TLS connections will initially target port 12346; however, they can be transitioned to one of the other base ports. This is how vManage and vSmart are able to distribute control connection load across the CPU. Table 3-1 provides the core-to-port mappings. Recommended practice dictates allowing all base ports through transit devices so that vManage and vSmart can properly balance inbound control plane connectivity.

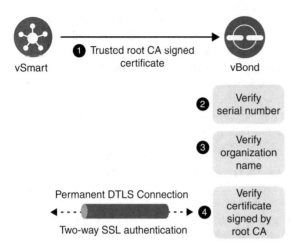

Figure 3-3   *DTLS Tunnel Authentication*

Table 3-1   *Core to UDP Port Mappings*

Core	UDP Port
Core 0	12346
Core 1	12446
Core 2	12546
Core 3	12646
Core 4	12746
Core 5	12846
Core 6	12946
Core 7	13046

After control plane tunnels are up, other protocols can use these sessions as well. For example, besides OMP, Simple Network Management Protocol (SNMP) and Netconf will use these secure channels. By utilizing established DTLS/TLS tunnels, we no longer need to be concerned about the disparate security native to these protocols or the flaws that may be present in them. Figure 3-4 shows an example of what resides inside the DTLS or TLS session between the components. Some common protocols inside the tunnel are OMP, SNMP, and Netconf.

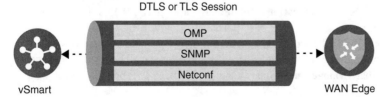

Figure 3-4   *Protocol Communications*

Overlay Management Protocol

Within the Cisco SD-WAN solution, the routing protocol selected is the Overlay Management Protocol (OMP), but it would be a disservice to limit OMP to just routing. OMP is the director of all control plane information and provides the following services:

■ Facilitation of network communication on the SD-WAN fabric, including data plane connectivity among sites, service chaining, and multi-VPN topology information

■ Advertisement of services available to the fabric and their related locations

■ Distribution of data plane security information, including encryption keys

■ Best-path selection and routing policy advertisement.

OMP is enabled by default and doesn't need to be explicitly enabled. As components in the fabric learn about their respective control elements, they will automatically initiate control connections to them. With this information, reachability can be achieved, which ultimately allows for the orchestration of the topology.

As discussed in subsequent chapters of this book, all of this information can be manipulated by user-defined policies via vManage. OMP interacts with all forms of legacy routing including static routes and traditional interior gateway routing protocols, such as Open Shortest Path First (OSPF), Border Gateway Protocol (BGP), and Enhanced Interior Gateway Routing Protocol (EIGRP). OMP differs from traditional IGPs, however, in that the peering is not between all members in the routing domain. Peering only occurs between the WAN Edges and the vSmart controller(s). This operates very similarly to a BGP route reflector in an Internal Border Gateway Protocol (IBGP) domain. From a scaling perspective, this is beneficial as the domain starts to grow. By establishing peering with only the vSmart controller, we reduce CPU cycles on the data plane devices since they don't need to handle and respond to excessive routing updates and best-path recalculations.

OMP also supports graceful restart. Graceful restart allows WAN Edges to cache forwarding information if connectivity to the vSmart controllers becomes unavailable. In such a case, the WAN Edge will continue to use the routing information that was last received. Graceful restart is enabled by default on the vSmart controllers and WAN Edge routers with a default timer of 12 hours. This timer can be modified with a minimum value of 1 second and a maximum value of 7 days. Keep in mind that there should be a valid IPsec encryption key during the duration of the graceful restart period; otherwise we risk having the data plane tunnels being torn down when the graceful timer expires. By doing this we can ensure that there is no IPsec rekey while OMP is down. Best practice is to set your IPsec rekey timer to be twice the value of the graceful restart timer.

Note The graceful restart timer can be configured from vManage via a CLI template or in an OMP feature template. Feature templates will be discussed further in Chapter 4, "Onboarding and Provisioning."

When a peering session with the vSmart controller becomes unavailable, it continues to re-establish a connection. If the WAN Edge is reloaded, however, this cached information is lost. The WAN Edge will need to reestablish an OMP session with the vSmart and receive new forwarding information before it can begin forwarding traffic on the SD-WAN fabric again.

As mentioned previously, OMP runs between the vSmart controllers and WAN Edge routers and advertises the following types of routes:

- **OMP routes (sometimes referred to as vRoutes):** Network prefixes that provide connectivity services to data centers, branch offices, or any other endpoint in the SD-WAN fabric. OMP routes will resolve their next hop to a TLOC route (discussed next).

- **Transport locations (TLOCs):** The TLOC is an identifier that ties an OMP route to a physical location. The TLOC is the only IP address that is known and reachable from the underlying network.

- **Service routes:** Identifies a network service to the SD-WAN overlay. This route identifies the service's physical location. A service could be a firewall, IPS, IDS, or any other device that can process network traffic. Service information is advertised in service routes and OMP routes.

Figure 3-5 shows examples of how these three types of routes interact in the Cisco SD-WAN solution.

OMP Routes

Each WAN Edge at a site will advertise routes to the vSmart controllers. These updates are similar to traditional routing updates in that they include reachability information for prefixes the WAN Edge handles. OMP can advertise connected, static routes and routing updates via redistribution from traditional protocols such as OSPF, EIGRP, and BGP. Along with reachability information, the following attributes are also advertised:

- TLOC
- Origin
- Originator
- Preference
- Service
- Site ID
- Tag
- VPN

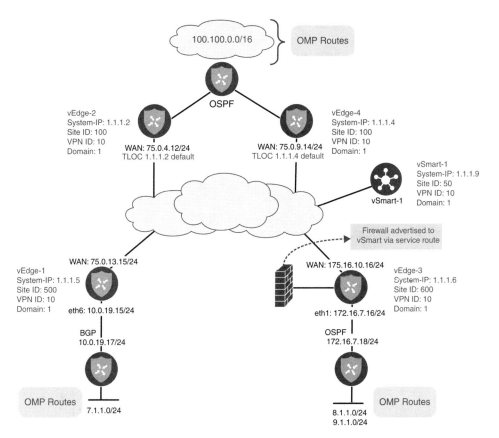

Figure 3-5   *Examples of the Three Types of OMP Routes*

Some of these attributes can be modified by the network administrator to influence routing decisions:

- **TLOC:** The Transport Location (TLOC) identifier is the next hop of the OMP route. This attribute is very similar to the BGP_NEXT_HOP attribute. Within the TLOC, there are three values:

  - **System IP Address:** This can be thought of as a router ID. Though this IP address doesn't need to be routable, it needs to be unique across all WAN Edges. The system IP is a way to identify the WAN Edge that originally advertised the route.

  - **Color:** This will be explored more in the data plane section of this chapter, but color is a way to mark a specific WAN connection that can later be used for influencing policy and how the topology is built.

  - **Encapsulation Type:** This value will advertise what encapsulation type is being used for the data plane tunnel; possible options include IPsec and GRE.

- **Origin:** This is the source of the route. As the route is advertised into the routing domain, the original source of the route is inserted into the update. The source may contain an identifier (BGP, OSPF, EIGRP, Connected, or Static), along with the protocol's original metric. Origin is used in the best-path selection for OMP routes as well and, as with most attributes policy, can be configured to influence how this information is reacted to.

- **Originator:** The Originator attribute identifies where the route was originally learned from. This value will be the system IP of the advertiser. The network administrator can then construct policy that can take into account this attribute.

- **Preference:** This is sometimes referred to as OMP Preference, though it should not be confused with TLOC Preference. The Preference value can be modified to influence the best-path selection criteria for a given route. A higher preference is preferred over a lower one. Preference operates similarly to LOCAL_PREF in BGP terminology.

- **Service:** The Cisco SD-WAN solution also supports service insertion. If a service (a firewall, for example) is associated to this route, then it will be indicated here. Service routes will be discussed in further detail later in this chapter.

- **Site ID:** The Site ID attribute is similar to a BGP autonomous system number (ASN). This value will be used for policy orchestration and influencing routing decisions. All sites should have a unique site ID. If there are multiple devices at a site, they should have the same site ID for loop prevention.

- **Tag:** This is an optional, transitive attribute that an OMP peer can apply to the route, which can be acted upon via policy. Redistributing to or from OMP does not carry the tag, however. This attribute functions like a route tag in traditional routing protocols.

- **VPN:** When discussing segmentation within the solution, this value communicates what VPN/VRF this route was advertised from. VPN tags allow the use of overlapping subnets, provided they are in different VPNs/VRFs (for example, 10.0.0.0/24 in VRF RED and 10.0.0.0/24 in VRF BLUE). Segmentation will be discussed in more detail in the data plane section.

Note In the Cisco SD-WAN solution, VPNs and VRFs are used interchangeably. VPNs/VRFs are used in the network to be logically segmented into multiple data paths and have separate routing instances per VPN or VRF.

Example 3-1 shows an example of an OMP route for the network prefix of 10.1.0.0/24. This example is generated with the command **show omp routes 10.1.0.0/24**.

Example 3-1   *OMP Routing Update*

```
--------------------------------------------------
omp route entries for vpn 10 route 10.1.0.0/24
--------------------------------------------------
            RECEIVED FROM:
peer            12.12.12.12
path-id         8
label           1004
status          C,I,R
loss-reason     not set
lost-to-peer    not set
lost-to-path-id not set
    Attributes:
    originator       10.1.0.2
    type             installed
    tloc             10.1.0.2, mpls, ipsec
    ultimate-tloc    not set
    domain-id        not set
    overlay-id       1
    site-id          100
    preference       not set
    tag              not set
    origin-proto     connected
    origin-metric    0
    as-path          not set
    unknown-attr-len not set
```

Note   In Example 3-1, **peer** is where the routing update was received from. On the SD-WAN overlay, all routing updates will be received from the vSmart controller.

C,I,R stands for "chosen, installed, resolved." This designation means that the route was selected and installed into the routing information base (RIB). For a route to be selected, the next hop (TLOC) must be resolvable.

Note   OMP uses an administrative distance of 250 on Viptela OS routes and 251 on XE SD-WAN routers. XE SD-WAN routers use 251 because the Next Hop Resolution Protocol (NHRP) already uses an administrative distance of 250.

TLOC Routes

TLOC (Transport Location Identifier) routes identify the physical location of this device on that transport. The TLOC is the only addressing that is routable to the underlay and represents the endpoint of the data plane tunnels (similar to a GRE tunnel with **tunnel source** and **tunnel destination** commands). A TLOC is made up of three attributes: the system IP address of the WAN Edge, the transport color, and the encapsulation type. If a WAN Edge has multiple transports, a TLOC route will be advertised for each interface. System IPs are used in the TLOC due to the fact that IP addresses can and will change (such as when DHCP is being utilized). By using the system IP address, the TLOC remains easily identifiable. Figure 3-6 shows an example.

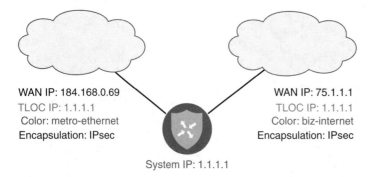

WAN IP: 184.168.0.69
TLOC IP: 1.1.1.1
 Color: metro-ethernet
Encapsulation: IPsec

WAN IP: 75.1.1.1
TLOC IP: 1.1.1.1
 Color: biz-internet
Encapsulation: IPsec

System IP: 1.1.1.1

Figure 3-6   *TLOC Route Example*

A critical attribute of the TLOC route is Color, which is a mechanism to identify the transport. Ideally, each of your transports will have a different color. Policy can then be constructed to use Color to influence how the data plane is built. At this time, there are 22 predefined colors to choose from. Colors also define whether the underlying transport is private or public in nature and, hence, what IP address should be used when forming a data plane tunnel to the remote site. By default, WAN Edges will attempt to build data plane tunnels to every other site using every color available. This may not be desirable, as it could lead to inefficient routing—such as if MPLS sites attempt to build tunnels to public Internet sites. Though the connectivity may exist, the tunnels may have formed over a path that was unintended. This behavior can be controlled with the **restrict** command and/ or tunnel groups, however. More about this will be discussed in the data plane section.

A TLOC route advertisement will contain the following pieces of information:

- **TLOC private address:** This attribute will contain the private IP address derived from the physical interface of the WAN Edge.

- **TLOC public address:** As the WAN Edge builds its control plane connections, it is notified via STUN (RFC 5389) that it may be behind a NAT device. This attribute contains the publicly routable or outside IP address assigned to the WAN Edge. This is critical in supporting data plane connectivity across a NAT boundary. If both the public and private addresses match in a TLOC route, the device is considered to not be behind a NAT.

- **Color:** As discussed earlier, this is the defined color of the transport. Possible options are **3g**, **biz-internet**, **blue**, **bronze**, **custom1**, **custom2**, **custom3**, **default**, **gold**, **green**, **lte**, **metro-ethernet**, **mpls**, **private1**, **private2**, **private3**, **private4**, **private5**, **private6**, **public-internet**, **red**, and **silver** The color **default** will be used if no color is administratively defined.

- **Encapsulation type:** This attribute refers to the tunnel encapsulation type. Options available are IPsec and GRE. Both sides of the tunnel must match for data plane connectivity.

- **Preference:** Similar to OMP Preference, this attribute allows the network administrator to prefer one TLOC over another when comparing the same OMP route. A higher Preference value is preferred.

- **Site ID:** Value that identifies the originator of this TLOC route and is used to control how data plane tunnels are built.

- **Tag:** Similar to route tags and OMP tags. A value can be defined that can control how prefixes are exchanged and, ultimately, how traffic will flow.

- **Weight:** Another path selection method. This is utilized just like BGP Weight and is locally significant. A higher Weight value is preferred over a lower one.

Example 3-2 provides an example of a TLOC from the peer of 12.12.12.12 for the MPLS color. The command to retrieve this output is **show omp tlocs detail**.

Example 3-2 *Example of a TLOC Route*

```
-------------------------------------------------
tloc entries for 10.1.0.1
                mpls
                ipsec
-------------------------------------------------
            RECEIVED FROM:
peer              12.12.12.12
status            C,I,R
loss-reason     not set
lost-to-peer    not set
lost-to-path-id not set
    Attributes:
      attribute-type      installed
      encap-key           not set
      encap-proto         0
      encap-spi           256
      encap-auth          sha1-hmac,ah-sha1-hmac
      encap-encrypt       aes256
      public-ip           172.16.10.2
      public-port         12366
```

```
            private-ip        172.16.10.2
            private-port      12366
            public-ip         ::
            public-port       0
            private-ip        ::
            private-port      0
            bfd-status        up
            domain-id         not set
            site-id           100
            overlay-id        not set
            preference        0
            tag               not set
            stale             not set
            weight            1
            version           3
          gen-id              0x80000006
            carrier           default
            restrict          1
            groups            [ 0 ]
            border               not set
          unknown-attr-len    not set
```

Service Routes

Service routes advertise a specific service to the rest of the overlay. This advertisement can then be used for service chaining policies. Service chaining allows data traffic to be routed to a remote site through one or more services (such as firewalls, intrusion detection/prevention systems, load balancers, or an IDP) before being routed to the traffic's original destination. These services can be utilized on a per-VPN basis. A common example of service chaining might be when thinking about compliance and regulations. In such a use case, a need exists for data to flow through firewalls that might be at a data center or regional hub—such as with Payment Card Industry Data Security Standard (PCI DSS). Devices that provide services for the overlay must be Layer 2 adjacent for traffic to be redirected through them (that is, there cannot be any intermediate hops between the WAN Edge device and the device performing the service). Keep in mind that Layer 2 adjacency can be achieved with IPsec or GRE tunnels as well. To enable service chaining in the overlay, the following workflow should be used:

1. The network administrator defines the service via a feature template.

2. WAN Edge routers advertise the services available to the vSmart controllers. Note that multiple WAN Edges can advertise the same service, if needed, for redundancy.

3. WAN Edge routers also advertise their OMP and TLOC routes.

4. The network administrator applies a policy defining traffic that must flow through these advertised service(s). Traffic is processed by the service before being forwarded to the final destination.

The example in Figure 3-7 describes how service chaining functions in the Cisco SD-WAN solution. The network has a central hub and two remote sites. Business requirements state that all traffic between "Local Site 1" and "Local Site 2" must flow through a firewall at the central hub. The network administrator will define a service chaining policy to enable this traffic flow.

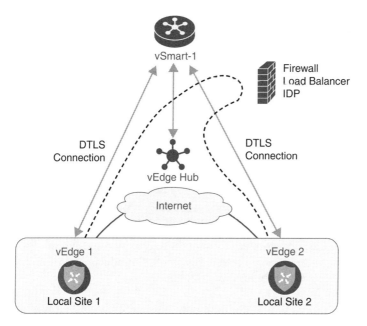

Figure 3-7   *Service Chaining Example*

The site offering the service (in this case, the hub) will advertise a service route via a Subsequent Address Family Identifier (SAFI) in the OMP Network Layer Reachability Information (NLRI). This information is advertised to the vSmart controller, where it is propagated to the WAN Edges. The service route update will contain the following information:

- **VPN ID:** Attribute defines what VPN this service applies to.

- **Service ID:** Defines the service type that is being advertised. Seven predefined services are available:

    - **FW:** Service type of firewall (maps to a value of **svc-id 1**).

- **IDS:** Service type of intrusion detection system (maps to a value of **svc-id 2**).

- **IDP:** Service type of Identity Provider (maps to a value of **svc-id 3**).

- **netsvc1, netsvc2, netsvc3, and netsvc4:** These are reserved for custom services and map to the service values of **svc-id 4**, **svc-id 5**, **svc-id 6**, and **svc-id 7**, respectively.

- **Label:** OMP routes that have traffic that must flow through this service will have the Label field in their advertisement replaced with this label.

- **Originator ID:** System IP address of the node advertising the service.

- **TLOC:** Transport location address where the service is located.

- **Path ID:** An identifier for the OMP path.

Example 3-3 shows the output of **show omp services** from the vSmart controller. This output shows that WAN Edge 10.3.0.1 advertised an FW service. Similar to the OMP route, the Status field shows that the route is installed.

Example 3-3 *Example of a Service Route*

```
ADDRESS                                                    PATH
FAMILY   VPN    SERVICE   ORIGINATOR    FROM PEER     ID    LABEL    STATUS
-----------------------------------------------------------------------------
---------------------
ipv4     10     FW        10.3.0.1      10.3.0.1      66    1006     C,I,R
                                        10.3.0.1      68    1006     C,I,R
```

This is just an introduction to service chaining. The process to construct and apply service chaining policies is covered in more depth in Chapter 5, "Introduction to Cisco SD-WAN Policies," and Chapter 6, "Centralized Control Policies."

Path Selection

As with traditional routing protocols, OMP has best-path selection criteria to choose the best route available and avoid routing loops. The best-path selection process draws some similarities to BGP. A WAN Edge will install an OMP route into its routing table only if the TLOC (next hop) is valid. A TLOC is valid if there is a BFD session that is associated to that TLOC.

As WAN Edges advertise OMP routes to the vSmart controller, the vSmart controller will perform best-path selection and advertise the result to the WAN Edges. Best-path selection can be influenced by policy either inbound (before best-path selection) or outbound (after best-path selection).

The best-path selection occurs in the following order:

1. **Valid OMP route:** For an OMP route to be considered valid, the TLOC needs to be valid. For a TLOC to be valid, there must be an active BFD adjacency for that TLOC. This is similar to BGP, where the NEXT HOP must be valid.

2. **Locally sourced OMP route:** On the WAN Edge, prefer a locally originated route versus a route learned from the vSmart controller.

3. **Lower administrative distance:** If multiple routes for the same prefix are received, select the one with the lower administrative distance.

4. **Higher OMP Preference:** Prefer the route with a higher OMP Preference.

5. **Higher TLOC Preference:** Prefer the route with a higher TLOC Preference.

6. **Prefer Origin:** Compare the origin type in the following order (first match wins):

   ■ Connected

   ■ Static

   ■ EBGP

   ■ EIGRP Internal

   ■ OSPF intra-area

   ■ OSPF inter-area

   ■ OSPF external

   ■ EIGRP external

   ■ IBGP

   ■ Unknown

7. **Lowest Origin metric:** If origins match, prefer the route with the lowest origin metric.

8. **Highest System IP:** Prefer the route with highest System IP.

9. **Highest TLOC private address:** Prefer the route with the highest TLOC private address.

vSmart can advertise up to 16 equal-cost routes, if configured. By default, the advertisement is 4 equal-cost routes.

The following is an example of best-path selection when choosing routes that will be advertised to an OMP peer:

A vSmart controller receives four paths for the prefix of 10.0.0.0/24.

■ First path doesn't have a valid TLOC.

■ Second path has a TLOC Preference of 500.

■ Third path has an OMP Preference of 300.

■ Fourth path has an Administrative Distance of 249.

Walking through the process described previously, let's review these paths. The first path is ignored because the TLOC isn't valid. This leaves three valid paths. If we compare the remaining routes, the second has a TLOC Preference of 500 and the third has a higher OMP Preference. If we stop there, the third route wins, as it has a higher OMP Preference, which beats TLOC Preference. However, in the example, the fourth path received wins because it has a modified Administrative Distance of 249.

OMP Route Redistribution and Loop Prevention

Just like other routing protocols, OMP supports redistribution. OMP supports mutual redistribution between OSPF, BGP, EIGRP, connected routes, and static routes. By default, OMP will automatically redistribute **Connected, Static, OSPF intra-area,** and **OSPF inter-area** routes into OMP. To avoid routing loops and less-than-ideal routing, redistribution of BGP, EIGRP, and OSPF external routes must be explicitly configured. In these cases, the network administrator would create an OMP and OSPF template (see Figure 3-8 and Figure 3-9, respectively) or a CLI template (see Example 3-4 and Example 3-5).

Figure 3-8   *OMP Template Configuration (Redistribute into OMP)*

Figure 3-9   *OSPF Template Configuration (Redistribute into IGP)*

Example 3-4 *Redistribution into OMP*

```
show run omp
omp
 no shutdown
 ecmp-limit       8
 graceful-restart
 advertise ospf external
 advertise connected
 advertise static
!
```

Example 3-5 *Redistribution into IGP*

```
show run vpn 10
vpn 10
 router
  ospf
   default-information originate
   timers spf 200 1000 10000
   redistribute omp
   area 0
    interface ge0/1
    exit
   exit
  !
 !
```

When redistributing into OMP, the origin and sub-origin are also set. This information is used in the best-path selection criteria mentioned earlier (specifically step 6). Table 3-2 describes the various OMP origin types and their subtypes.

Table 3-2 *OMP Origin Types*

OMP Route Origin Type	OMP Route Origin Subtype
BGP	External
	Internal
Connected	N/A
OSPF	Intra-area
	Inter-area
	External
Static	N/A
EIGRP	External
	Internal

Additionally, OMP also carries the metric from the redistributed protocol. A metric of 0 indicates a connected route. This is used in step 7 of the best-path selection criteria described previously.

For reference, Table 3-3 lists the default administrative distances for WAN Edges.

Table 3-3   *WAN Edge Default Administrative Distances*

Protocol	Administrative Distance
Connected	0
Static	1
Learned via DHCP	1
EBGP	20
EIGRP Internal	90
OSPF	110
EIGRP External	170
IBGP	200
OMP	250 (251 on Cisco XE SD-WAN devices)

Networks that have multiple exit points to the WAN are susceptible to routing loops. This can commonly occur when two or more routers have mutual redistribution from the WAN routing protocol and the LAN routing protocol. Consider Figure 3-10, where we have two WAN Edges and OMP and OSPF are doing mutual redistribution.

OMP has native loop prevention mechanisms built into it when interfacing with EIGRP, OSPF, and BGP. In migration scenarios, where the network is being migrated from a legacy site, the network administrator will need to take this into consideration and eliminate any potential loops by either filtering routes or using the traditional method of route tagging. At this time, OMP does not support filtering via a route tag, so this type of filtering will need to be handled outside of the WAN Edges, such as at the core of the network.

Walking through the process below, you can see how the OSPF Down bit can be utilized to prevent a routing loop.

1. WAN Edge 1 and WAN Edge 2 learn 10.0.0.0/24 via OMP from the data center and install this route in their routing table.

2. WAN Edge 1 and WAN Edge 2 advertise 10.0.0.0/24 into OSPF.

3. The core router(s) advertises the route to WAN Edge 1 and WAN Edge 2 via OSPF.

4. Here is where the loop can be formed. Both WAN routers are learning the route via OSPF and OMP. Remember that OMP has an administrative distance of 250 and OSPF has a route of 110. In this case, the route via OSPF will be installed in the routing table due to a lower administrative distance. This will create a loop since the OSPF route will remove the route from OMP, which, in turn, will eventually remove the route via OSPF and blackhole traffic.

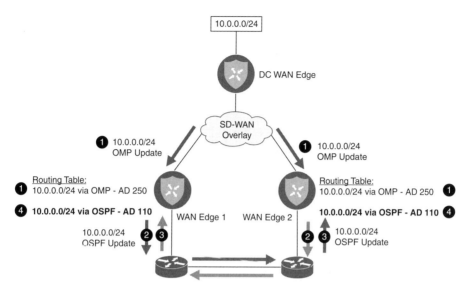

Figure 3-10   *Routing Loop*

RFC 4577 has been implemented to solve the loop prevention problem with OSPF. RFC 4577 implements a concept called a "down bit." When a route is being redistributed from OMP to OSPF, the WAN Edge sets this bit. As this Link State Advertisement (LSA) moves throughout the rest of the network, and ultimately gets to the other WAN Edge, it is dropped due to the down bit being set. Example 3-6 shows the LSA in the database for 10.0.0.0/24. Figure 3-11 represents this graphically.

Example 3-6   *OSPF Database Entry*

```
            OSPF Router with ID (10.3.10.2) (Process ID 10)


            Type-5 AS External Link States


LS age: 30
Options: (No TOS-capability, DC, Downward)
LS Type: AS External Link
Link State ID: 10.0.0.0 (External Network Number )
Advertising Router: 10.3.10.2
LS Seq Number: 80000001
Checksum: 0xCB3B
Length: 36
Network Mask: /24
      Metric Type: 2 (Larger than any link state path)
      MTID: 0
      Metric: 16777214
      Forward Address: 0.0.0.0
      External Route Tag: 0
```

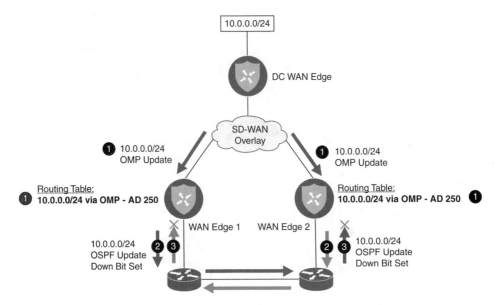

Figure 3-11 *OSPF Loop Prevention with Down Bit*

Walking through the process below we can see how the OSPF Down bit can be utilized to prevent a routing loop.

1. WAN Edge 1 and WAN Edge 2 learn 10.0.0.0/24 via OMP from the data center and install this route in their routing table.

2. WAN Edge 1 and WAN Edge 2 advertise 10.0.0.0/24 into OSPF and set the down bit.

3. The core router(s) advertises the route with the down bit set to the WAN Edges via OSPF. The LSA is rejected.

Conversely, BGP loop prevention is handled with site of origin (SoO), which is a BGP extended community where the value is set to the OMP site ID. When the other WAN Edge receives the BGP update from the core network, it will see that the site of origin community matches its own site ID, and the BGP update will be dropped. For this loop prevention mechanism to function properly, all BGP peers in the network must send BGP extended communities and have the same site ID. Figure 3-12 represents this graphically.

In this example BGP site of origin is utilized to prevent a routing loop.

1. WAN Edge 1 and WAN Edge 2 learn 10.0.0.0/24 via OMP from the data center and install this route in their routing table.

2. WAN Edge 1 and WAN Edge 2 advertise 10.0.0.0/24 via BGP and set the site of origin extended community to 100.

3. Core router(s) advertises the route with the extended community set. The WAN routers drop the BGP update.

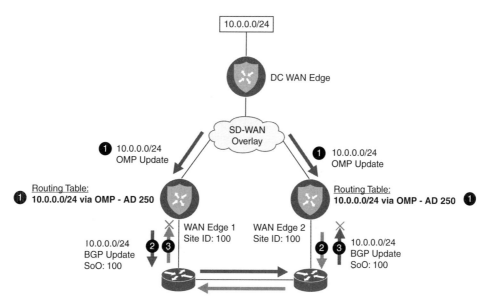

Figure 3-12 *BGP Loop Prevention with Site of Origin*

Example 3-7 shows a BGP routing update with an SoO extended community set. You can see that this matches the site's ID of 100.

Example 3-7 *BGP Update with Site of Origin Set*

```
BGP routing table entry for 10:10.0.0.0/24, version 2
Paths: (1 available, best #1, table 10)
  Advertised to update-groups:
     1
  Refresh Epoch 1
  100
    10.3.10.3 (via vrf 10) from 10.3.10.3 (192.0.2.1)
      Origin incomplete, metric 1000, localpref 100, valid, external
      Extended Community: SoO:0:100
      rx pathid: 0, tx pathid: 0
```

Because EIGRP is supported on XE SD-WAN routers, we need a method to support loop prevention there as well. New features have been added to the Cisco SD-WAN solution to support this. When redistributing from OMP into EIGRP, the External Protocol field is set to a value of OMP-Agent. When the other WAN Edge receives the update and installs the route into the EIGRP topology table, it sets the "SD-WAN-Down" bit and sets its Administrative Distance to 252. This, in turn, makes OMP the preferred route because it has an Administrative Distance of 251. Figure 3-13 represents this graphically.

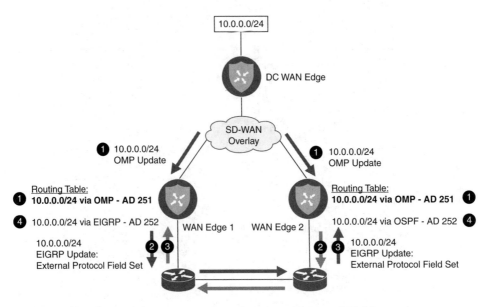

Figure 3-13   *EIGRP Loop Prevention with External Protocol Field*

Here we walk through how EIGRP with the external protocol field can be used to prevent routing loops.

1. WAN Edge 1 and WAN Edge 2 learn 10.0.0.0/24 via OMP from the data center and install this route in their routing table.

2. WAN Edge 1 and WAN Edge 2 advertise 10.0.0.0/24 via EIGRP and set the **External Protocol** field to **OMP-Agent.**

3. Core router(s) advertises the route with the **External Protocol** field set. When the WAN routers receive this route, they place the route into their EIGRP topology table with SD-WAN Down bit set and an Administrative Distance of 252.

Example 3-8 provides an example of an EIGRP routing update with the external protocol field set.

Example 3-8   *EIGRP Topology Table with External Protocol Set*

```
EIGRP-IPv4(100): Topology base(0) entry for 10.1.10.0/24
  State is Passive, Query origin flag is 1, 1 Successor(s), FD is 1
  Descriptor Blocks:
  10.1.0.2, from Redistributed, Send flag is 0x0
      Composite metric is (1/0), route is External
      Vector metric:
        Minimum bandwidth is 0 Kbit
```

```
       Total delay is 0 picoseconds
       Reliability is 0/255
       Load is 0/255
       Minimum MTU is 0
       Hop count is 0
       Originating router is 10.3.10.3
    External data:
       AS number of route is 0
       External protocol is OMP-Agent, external metric is 4294967294
       Administrator tag is 0 (0x00000000)
```

Data Plane Operations

The data plane in any traditional network is responsible for moving packets from one location to another. This is commonly referred to as the forwarding plane. From a WAN perspective, common transports utilized to transmit data packets consist of the public Internet or private WANs (such as DMVPN, MPLS, or point-to-point connections). All of these technologies build on some type of overlay for encapsulating and securing the data packets. As wide area networks grow, the legacy transports start to have trouble scaling—particularly when securing the control and data planes enters the discussion. These functions consume a large amount of CPU cycles to process key exchanges and routing updates. Figure 3-14 shows a common deployment scenario for a WAN.

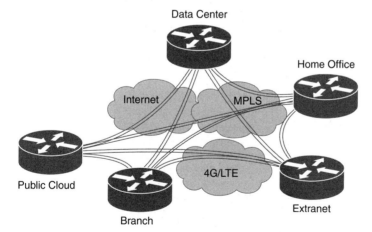

Figure 3-14   *Traditional Wide Area Network*

Security in the data plane is usually achieved by encrypting the data with IPsec and its suite of tools. In networks that traditionally use IPsec to secure the data plane, scale becomes a concern, as the processing power to handle key exchanges is exponentially larger than the number of nodes in the WAN. For example, a full mesh network that has 100 nodes would require 10,000 key exchanges (n^2). Each device would have to maintain 999 keys ($n-1$). The Cisco SD-WAN solution is no different in that IPsec is used to secure the data plane. However, modifications have been made to support larger-scale deployments. To support larger numbers, a centralized controller is utilized to distribute keys and routing information (vSmart). By having vSmart handle key distribution, the ability to scale out to larger networks is greatly increased by not requiring each WAN Edge to negotiate its keys with the other nodes in the network.

Additionally, networks also face scalability challenges when network requirements call for supporting segmentation or different topologies per network segment. Traditional methods to provide segmentation across a WAN utilizing technologies such as MPLS L3VPN and 2547oDMVPN (MPLS over DMVPN) can be very complex and generally require more seasoned network engineers to implement, operate, and troubleshoot. In the Cisco SD-WAN solution, segmentation is natively implemented and doesn't require advanced experience to implement and support. Network segmentation also allows for different topologies per network segment. For example, corporate users could have a full mesh topology and PCI/HIPAA devices could be hub and spoke. Later on in this chapter, segmentation and multi-topology will be discussed. In Figure 3-15, you can see an example of how network segmentation is achieved between Gidget and Mowgli.

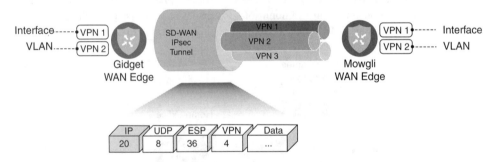

Figure 3-15 *Cisco SD-WAN Segmentation*

The remainder of this chapter will dive deep into these technologies and discuss how the Cisco SD-WAN solution implements data plane routing, encryption, authentication, and segmentation.

TLOC Colors

As discussed earlier, TLOC is an OMP route type that provides reachability information to the WAN Edges on how to build the data plane to the rest of the WAN Edges in the network. TLOCs are what identify the WAN Edge to the physical underlay. A key attribute to TLOCs is their color. Colors are utilized to mark or categorize a specific transport. The network administrator will assign transports their respective colors when provisioning the routers. For example, all sites that have the same type of Internet circuit might use the same color. Policies can then be defined that control how data traffic flows across the overlay between these colors. Currently, there are 22 pre-built colors broken into two categories (public and private). The color selected signifies when NAT is in play. Private colors are only to be used when there is no NAT between devices on the overlay. If there is a NAT device between WAN Edge devices, then use a public color. Refer to Table 3-4 to see how colors break down.

Table 3-4 *TLOC Colors by Category*

Public Color(s)	Private Color(s)
3g	metro-ethernet
biz-internet	mpls
public-internet	private1
lte	private2
blue	private3
bronze	private4
custom1	private5
custom2	private6
custom3	
gold	
green	
red	
silver	

Note If there is no color defined, then **default** is the color that will be advertised with the TLOC route.

When establishing the IPsec data plane, routers will attempt to establish full mesh connectivity between all routers in the fabric by default. If two colors have IP reachability, they will establish the data plane no matter what the color is. For example, assume router 1 has a color of **biz-internet** and another router has a color of **public-internet**. Since they have IP connectivity, they will build an IPsec tunnel. This may be desired, or it may not be. A common design where this decision comes into play is if your private WAN (MPLS) does not have IP connectivity to the Internet. In such a case, you don't want MPLS-connected routers attempting to build connections to Internet-connected routers. Another design may be with global deployments. Here, depending on country or region, you may want full mesh tunnels. However, across countries or regions (such as between the US and Europe), you want to use a point-to-point tunnel between hub sites.

Looking at Figure 3-16 you can see a graphical representation of this.

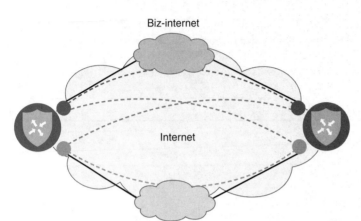

Figure 3-16 *TLOC colors with No Restrict*

Both routers have two transports: mpls and public-internet. When these devices establish their control plane connections, they will advertise two TLOCs each: one for the public-internet color and another for the biz-internet color. Both of these routers will learn these TLOC routes and begin to establish data plane connectivity. Since both of these colors have Internet connectivity and reachability between them, the routers will build data plane connections across all colors. This means that each router will have four IPsec tunnels to the other WAN Edge:

■ WAN Edge 1: biz-internet ⟷ WAN Edge 2: biz-internet

■ WAN Edge 1: public-internet ⟷ WAN Edge 2: public-internet

■ WAN Edge 1: biz-internet ⟷ WAN Edge 2: public-internet

■ WAN Edge 1: public-internet ⟷ WAN Edge 2: biz-internet

Let's say that either of the colors don't have IP connectivity between the TLOCs or the design calls for them not to build data connectivity across colors. In this case, there are two options. You can advertise the **restrict** attribute with the TLOC, or you can configure tunnel groups. These attributes tell the other devices in the fabric not to attempt to build connectivity to the restricted color. Let's examine this concept using the **restrict** keyword first. Restrict is an OMP attribute inside the TLOC route. This value needs to be defined per site as either on or off. An example of a TLOC route with **restrict** is shown in Example 3-9. Notice that this TLOC uses the color of **biz-internet**. Toward the bottom of the advertisement, notice the **restrict** attribute that is set to 1. A **restrict** attribute of 1 means that this device will only form tunnels with other TLOCs advertising the **biz-internet** color. If this was 0, then the color would be unrestricted to form tunnels with other colors. Taking the previous example in Figure 3-16, if **restrict** is not set, you will end up with four data plane tunnels per device, as we'll build IPsec tunnels across all colors.

Example 3-9   *TLOC Route with Restrict Set*

```
--------------------------------------------------
tloc entries for 10.1.0.1
                 biz-internet
                 ipsec
--------------------------------------------------
             RECEIVED FROM:
peer            12.12.12.12
status          C,I,R
loss-reason     not set
lost-to-peer    not set
lost-to-path-id not set
   Attributes:
     attribute-type    installed
     encap-key         not set
     encap-proto       0
     encap-spi         256
     encap-auth        sha1-hmac,ah-sha1-hmac
     encap-encrypt     aes256
     public-ip         172.16.10.2
     public-port       12366
     private-ip        172.16.10.2
     private-port      12366
     public-ip         ::
     public-port       0
     private-ip        ::
     private-port      0
     bfd-status        up
     domain-id         not set
     site-id           100
     overlay-id        not set
     preference        0
     tag               not set
     stale             not set
     weight            1
     version           3
    gen-id             0x80000006
     carrier           default
     restrict          1
     groups            [ 0 ]
     border             not set
     unknown-attr-len  not set
```

Figure 3-17 shows how data plane would be established if **restrict** was set. Each WAN Edge would have two IPsec tunnels, one per color.

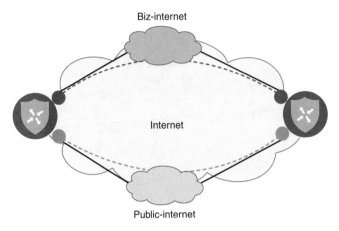

Figure 3-17   *TLOC Colors with Restrict*

Tunnel Groups

Just as with the previous example, both routers have two transports: biz-internet and public-internet. In this case, **restrict** is configured on the two transports. When these devices establish their control plane connections, they will advertise two TLOCs each: one for the public-internet color and another for the biz-internet color. Both of these routers will learn these TLOC routes and begin to establish data plane connectivity. Since restrict is configured, these routers will only build connections across their like colors. This means that each router will have two IPsec tunnels to the other WAN Edge:

- WAN Edge 1: Biz-internet ⟵⟶ WAN Edge 2: Biz-internet

- WAN Edge 1: Public-internet ⟵⟶ WAN Edge 2: Public-internet

Another option to restrict data plane connectivity is using tunnel groups. Only tunnels with matching tunnel groups, or no tunnel group defined, will form data plane connectivity (independent of the color). It is recommended that, if using tunnel groups, all sites have tunnel groups defined. A common deployment for this is when a data center has two physical connections to the same MPLS provider but the branch sites only have one physical connection, though the design calls for building connectivity across both physical interfaces in the data center. The tunnel group is advertised as an attribute in the TLOC route, as demonstrated in Example 3-10. The possible values for tunnel groups are between 0 and 4294967295.

Example 3-10 *TLOC Route with Tunnel Groups*

```
-----------------------------------------------
tloc entries for 10.1.0.1
                  mpls
                  ipsec
-----------------------------------------------
            RECEIVED FROM:
peer              12.12.12.12
status            C,I,R
loss-reason       not set
lost-to-peer      not set
lost-to-path-id not set
    Attributes:
     attribute type     installed
     encap-key           not set
     encap-proto         0
     encap-spi           256
     encap-auth          sha1-hmac,ah-sha1-hmac
     encap-encrypt       aes256
     public-ip           172.16.10.2
     public-port         12366
     private-ip          172.16.10.2
     private-port        12366
     public-ip           ::
     public-port         0
     private-ip          ::
     private-port        0
     bfd-status          up
     domain-id           not set
     site-id             100
     overlay-id          not set
     preference          0
     tag                 not set
     stale               not set
     weight              1
     version             3
    gen-id               0x80000006
     carrier             default
     restrict            0
     groups              [ 500 ]
```

Looking at Figure 3-18, we see three sites: a data center and two remote sites. The data center has three physical transports: two to the MPLS provider and one to the Internet provider. All of the MPLS transports will have a tunnel group ID of 10 and the Internet transports will have a group ID of 20.

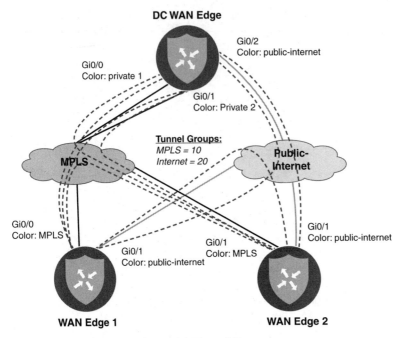

Figure 3-18   *TLOC Colors with Tunnel Groups*

Because the design calls for data connectivity to be built from the single MPLS connection at the remote sites to both MPLS physical interfaces at the data center, we are using two colors: **private 1** and **private 2**. A single color of **mpls** is used at the remote branches on the MPLS transport. Each remote site will build five tunnels—three over the MPLS provider and two over the Internet provider:

- WAN Edge 1 and 2: Public Internet ←→ DC WAN Edge: Public-internet

- WAN Edge 1 and 2: Mpls ←→ DC WAN Edge: Private 1

- WAN Edge 1 and 2: Mpls ←→ DC WAN Edge: Private 2

- WAN Edge 1: Mpls ←→ WAN Edge 2: Mpls

- WAN Edge 1: Public-internet ←→ WAN Edge 2: Public-internet

Because the tunnel groups aren't the same between the MPLS and Internet transports, data connectivity will not be attempted. Example 3-11 shows the CLI output from these devices.

> **Note**   An important note regarding color is that you can only have one interface per WAN Edge using that color. You can't have multiple interfaces on the same WAN Edge using the same color. This won't work, as it breaks the uniqueness of the TLOC route at that point.

Example 3-11   *CLI Output from Each Device Showing Data Plane BFD Sessions*

```
DC-WAN-Edge# show bfd sessions
                                SOURCE TLOC      REMOTE TLOC              DST PUBLIC
SYSTEM IP   SITE ID   STATE     COLOR            66  COLOR   SOURCE IP    IP
-----------------------------------------------------------------------------------
2.2.2.2     2         up        public-internet  public-internet  192.168.1.2  192.168.10.2
2.2.2.2     2         up        private1         mpls             100.64.0.2   100.64.10.2
2.2.2.2     2         up        private2         mpls             100.64.1.2   100.64.10.2
3.3.3.3     3         up        public-internet  public-internet  192.168.1.2  100.64.20.2
3.3.3.3     3         up        private1         mpls             100.64.0.2   100.64.30.2
3.3.3.3     3         up        private2         mpls             100.64.1.2   100.64.30.2


WAN-Edge-1# show bfd sessions
                                SOURCE TLOC      REMOTE TLOC              DST PUBLIC
SYSTEM IP   SITE ID   STATE     COLOR            COLOR        SOURCE IP   IP
-----------------------------------------------------------------------------------
1.1.1.1     1         up        public-internet  public-internet  192.168.10.2  192.168.1.2
1.1.1.1     1         up        mpls             private1         100.64.10.2   100.64.0.2
1.1.1.1     1         up        mpls             private2         100.64.10.2   100.64.1.2
3.3.3.3     3         up        public-internet  public-internet  192.168.10.2  100.64.20.2
3.3.3.3     3         up        mpls             mpls             100.64.10.2   100.64.30.2


WAN-Edge-2# show bfd sessions
                                SOURCE TLOC      REMOTE TLOC              DST PUBLIC
SYSTEM IP   SITE ID   STATE     COLOR            COLOR        SOURCE IP   IP
-----------------------------------------------------------------------------------
1.1.1.1     1         up        public-internet  public-internet  100.64.20.2  192.168.1.2
1.1.1.1     1         up        mpls             private1         100.64.30.2  100.64.0.2
1.1.1.1     1         up        mpls             private2         100.64.30.2  100.64.1.2
2.2.2.2     2         up        public-internet  public-internet  100.64.20.2  192.168.10.2
2.2.2.2     2         up        mpls             mpls             100.64.30.2  100.64.10.2
```

Note   Tunnel groups can be utilized with the **restrict** attribute as well. The rules of the two still follow, with **restrict** and **color** taking precedence. This means that if **restrict** is set on a color, and a tunnel group set, the router will only build IPsec tunnels between routers with not only the same color, but also the same tunnel group ID (or no tunnel group ID).

Network Address Translation

When discussing the data plane of any tunneling mechanism, network address translation (NAT) must be examined. As the IPv4 pool is exhausted more and more,

WAN termination points are relying on NAT to conserve address space. As with
most traditional tunneling technologies, there are some NAT designs that work and
some that don't. Cisco SD-WAN is no different. It goes without saying that the best
possible solution is to assign your WAN Edge a public IP address to avoid having to
worry about NAT, but that is not always possible. In this section, we'll discuss which
designs work and which don't. Before we begin, let's review the various types of
NAT deployments.

Full Cone NAT

The first type of NAT construct is *full cone NAT* (sometimes referred to as either
one to one NAT or static NAT). Full cone NAT is the only type of NAT where the
address and port are always open. All external hosts initiating connections to this
port are allowed and translated to the internal host. You can have multiple full cone
NATs configured using the same public IP, but the ports that are being translated
internally must be different per internal host. Additionally, the internal and external
ports don't need to match. Review Figure 3-19 for an example of how full cone NAT
works.

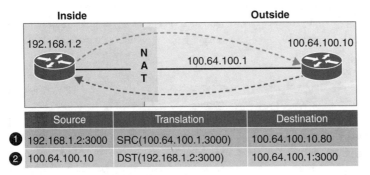

Figure 3-19 *Full Cone NAT*

In this example, we have two hosts with a NAT device in the middle configured
with NAT. The internal host, 192.168.1.2, has a service running on port 3000. We
also have an external host at 100.64.100.10.

Starting with step 1, we can see how the traffic flow occurs with full cone NAT.

1. Traffic initiated from the inside host to the outside host with a source port
   of 3000 will have its source IP in the IP header translated to the outside
   zone with a source IP of 100.64.100.1. **SRC IP:** *192.168.1.2* translated to
   100.64.100.1.

2. When the outside initiates a connection to 100.64.100.1:3000, the destination IP in the IP header will be translated to the inside zone with a destination IP of 192.168.1.2 by the NAT device. **DST IP:** *100.64.100.1* translated to
   192.168.1.2.

Symmetric NAT

The second type of NAT construct, and probably the most common, is *symmetric NAT* (also referred to as dynamic PAT). Symmetric NAT has the advantage of allowing a large number of hosts behind a single IP address. Symmetric NAT is common in deployments where a number of users need access to the Internet, but the administrator does not want to consume a unique IP per user. With symmetric NAT, the original source IP will be translated to the outside IP address, and the source port will be translated to another port. This allows a theoretical limit of up to 63,335 hosts behind a single public IP. With symmetric NAT, each internally initiated conversation to an outside host will be mapped to a NAT translation table. This is a key difference with full cone NAT. Because the mapping is created only when traffic is initiated from an internal host, external hosts cannot initiate connections to the internal host. This mapping is dynamic and will expire eventually, if there is no traffic matching that mapping entry.

Figure 3-20 illustrates how symmetric NAT works.

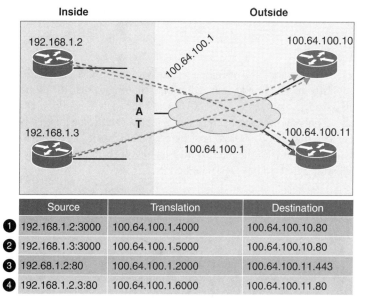

Source	Translation	Destination
① 192.168.1.2:3000	100.64.100.1.4000	100.64.100.10.80
② 192.168.1.3:3000	100.64.100.1.5000	100.64.100.10.80
③ 192.68.1.2:80	100.64.100.1.2000	100.64.100.11.443
④ 192.168.1.2.3:80	100.64.100.1.6000	100.64.100.11.80

Figure 3-20 *Symmetric NAT*

In Figure 3-20, there are four hosts. Two are behind a NAT device configured with symmetric NAT. The two hosts are initiating various connections to the external hosts of 100.64.100.10 and 100.64.100.11. Let's review these conversations:

1. Traffic is being initiated from 192.168.1.2 connecting to the external host 100.64.100.10 with a service running on port 80. As with all TCP/UDP conversations, there is a source and destination port in the header. In this case, the source IP of 192.168.1.2 and the source port of 3000 will be translated to 100.64.100.1:4000. In most TCP/UDP conversations, the source port is selected randomly by the sending host.

2. Similar to conversation 1, traffic is being initiated from 192.168.1.3 connecting to the external host 100.64.100.10 with a service running on port 80. In this case, the source IP of 192.168.1.3 and the source port of 3000 will be translated to 100.64.100.1:5000. Since the NAT device is translating the source port and source IP, you can see that we're able to achieve great scale with symmetric NAT.

3. In this conversation, host 192.168.1.2 is connecting to an external host with the IP of 100.64.100.11 running a service on port 80. The source IP and source port will both be translated to 100.64.100.1:2000.

4. In this conversation, host 192.168.1.3 is connecting to an external host with the IP of 100.64.100.11 running a service on port 443. The source IP and source port will both be translated to 100.64.100.1:6000.

Note   Since the mapping entry is only created when traffic is initiated from the inside hosts, external hosts are unable to initiate connections unless there has been a prior conversation initiated from the internal host.

Address Restricted Cone NAT

The remaining types of NAT are variations of full cone and symmetric NAT. They build off the concepts already introduced but add some additional filtering to the IPs and ports in use. The first option is *address restricted cone NAT*. This type of NAT works similarly to full cone NAT, except it only allows external hosts to communicate to the internal host if that host has communicated with the external host before on any port. The external host can then initiate a connection with the internal host on any ports that have been NAT'ed. Figure 3-21 illustrates how address restricted cone NAT works.

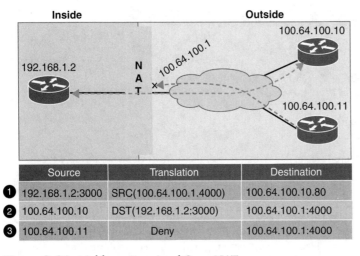

Figure 3-21   *Address Restricted Cone NAT*

In Figure 3-21, there are three hosts. One host is behind a NAT device, where the NAT configured is address restricted full cone NAT. The internal host is initiating connections to the external host of 100.64.100.10. Let's review the conversations:

1. The host behind the NAT device has initiated a connection to the destination IP of 100.64.100.10. The source IP is translated to 100.64.100.1 and the source port is translated from 3000 to 4000.

2. Since the internal host initially connected to 100.64.100.10, 100.64.100.10 can now connect to 100.64.100.1 port 4000, and this traffic will be allowed. The destination IP and port will both be translated to 192.168.1.2:3000.

3. When 100.64.100.11 tries to connect to 100.64.100.1 on port 4000, the traffic will be denied because the internal host has never initiated a connection to 100.64.100.11 previously.

Port Restricted Cone NAT

The final type of NAT construct is *port restricted cone NAT*. This type of NAT is similar to address restricted cone NAT, except it uses the port number as a filter. When an internal host connects to a remote system, it connects to a destination port. This port is then added to the NAT filter, and if any external host wants to communicate with the internal host, it must have the same source port that the internal host used as its destination port. If any external host uses a different source port, the traffic will be denied. If another external host uses the same source port, it will be allowed. Figure 3-22 illustrates how port restricted cone NAT works.

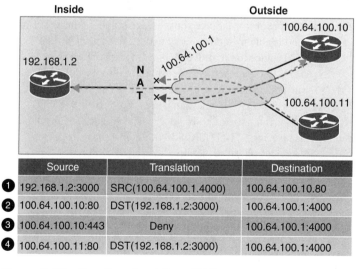

	Source	Translation	Destination
❶	192.168.1.2:3000	SRC(100.64.100.1.4000)	100.64.100.10:80
❷	100.64.100.10:80	DST(192.168.1.2:3000)	100.64.100.1:4000
❸	100.64.100.10:443	Deny	100.64.100.1:4000
❹	100.64.100.11:80	DST(192.168.1.2:3000)	100.64.100.1:4000

Figure 3-22 *Port Restricted Cone NAT*

In Figure 3-22, there are three hosts. One host is behind a NAT device. The NAT configured is *port restricted full cone NAT*. The internal host is initiating connections to the external host of 100.64.100.10. Let's review the conversation:

1. The internal host of 192.168.1.2:3000 initiates a connection to 100.64.100.10 with a destination port of 80.

2. Because the internal host had previously connected to 100.64.100.10 on port 80, the external host is *only* allowed to initiate a connection to the internal host if it uses a source port of 80.

3. In this example, the same external host that was allowed with a source port of 80 is trying to use a source port of 443. This is denied because the internal host has never connected to 100.64.100.10 on port 443.

4. Here, another external host of 100.64.100.11 is trying to connect to the internal host. Since the internal host initially communicated to a destination on port 80, the second external host is allowed to communicate with the internal host as long as its source port is 80.

With the Cisco SD-WAN solution, there are certain types of NAT that work and some that have restrictions. Before discussing those restrictions, let's talk about how the solution handles NAT. As introduced in Chapter 2, the vBond controller operates on the orchestration plane and is the glue of the fabric in regard to how NAT is handled. WAN Edge routers always reach out to the vBond controller first to learn about the rest of the components in the fabric. During this process, they also learn if they are behind a NAT device or not. When the WAN Edge initially connects to the vBond, it inserts its real IP address into the exchange. When this packet passes through the NAT device, the source IP and possibly the source port are translated. Since the message still contains the WAN Edge's real IP and port, the vBond is able to send a message back to the WAN Edge notifying it that it is behind a NAT (since the real IP differs from the NAT'ed IP received in the exchange). The WAN Edge will then insert this information into its OMP TLOC route and send this to the vSmart controller. If these values are different, then the WAN Edge is behind a NAT device. This information will then be reflected to all WAN Edges in the overlay, and they will use this information to build their data plane. The mechanism to achieve this NAT detection is utilizing STUN (RFC 5389). Review the output from Example 3-12 and Figure 3-23 for a graphical depiction.

Example 3-12 *TLOC Route*

```
- - - - - - - - - - - - - - - - - - - - - - - - - - - - - - - - - - - - -
tloc entries for 10.1.0.1
                mpls
                ipsec
- - - - - - - - - - - - - - - - - - - - - - - - - - - - - - - - - - - - -
          RECEIVED FROM:
peer            12.12.12.12
status          C,I,R
loss-reason     not set
```

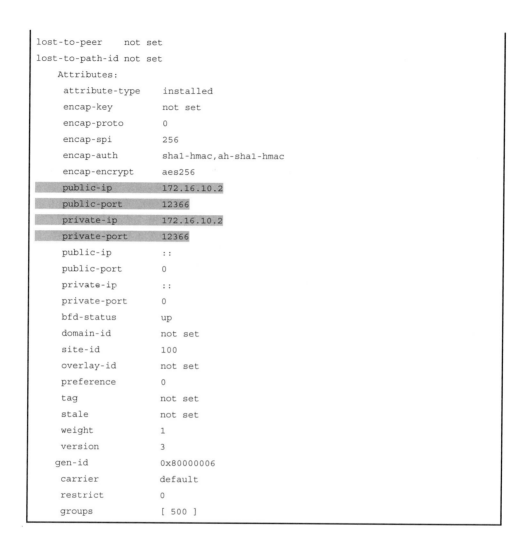

```
lost-to-peer    not set
lost-to-path-id not set
    Attributes:
    attribute-type      installed
    encap-key           not set
    encap-proto         0
    encap-spi           256
    encap-auth          sha1-hmac,ah-sha1-hmac
    encap-encrypt       aes256
    public-ip           172.16.10.2
    public-port         12366
    private-ip          172.16.10.2
    private-port        12366
    public-ip           ::
    public-port         0
    private-ip          ::
    private-port        0
    bfd-status          up
    domain-id           not set
    site-id             100
    overlay-id          not set
    preference          0
    tag                 not set
    stale               not set
    weight              1
    version             3
    gen-id              0x80000006
    carrier             default
    restrict            0
    groups              [ 500 ]
```

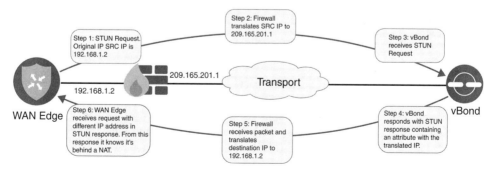

Figure 3-23 *NAT Traversal with STUN*

Note   If the colors being used are private colors, then the private IPs and ports will always be used for data plane connectivity, even if the control connection is behind a NAT device. WAN Edges will only use the NAT address advertised when connecting via a public color.

Symmetric NAT can cause issues for data plane connectivity. Symmetric NAT creates a new mapping for every outbound communication and only allows return traffic from the original destination IP. For example, let's assume we have one WAN Edge that is behind a NAT device using symmetric NAT. When the WAN Edge connects to the vBond, the NAT device will create a NAT mapping with a source IP of the WAN Edge, allowing only the vBond controller's return traffic. Now imagine that a second WAN Edge will receive this TLOC with the public IP and port that was used to communicate with the vBond. When this WAN Edge tries to build an IPsec tunnel to the first WAN Edge using the public IP and port from the advertised TLOC, it is unable to because the initial NAT mapping using that information is unique to the connection with vBond, as illustrated in Figure 3-24.

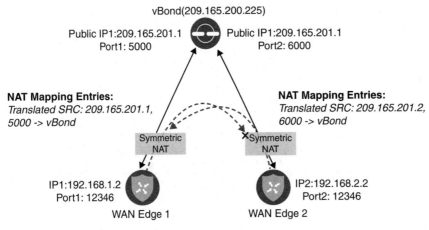

Figure 3-24   *Symmetric NAT Restrictions*

The solution that resolves this requires that at least one of the WAN Edges not use symmetric NAT. When the second WAN Edge (that isn't behind symmetric NAT) attempts to use the TLOC information to establish data plane connectivity, it will be dropped for the same reason as before. However, WAN Edge 1 will also try to establish a tunnel using WAN Edge 2's TLOC information. This should create a new mapping and will be successful, as illustrated in Figure 3-25.

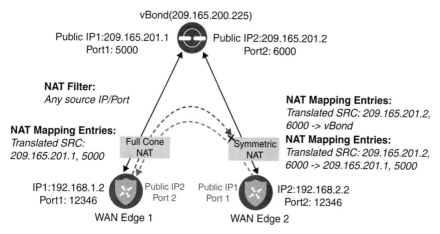

Figure 3-25 *Symmetric and Full Cone NAT*

Table 3-5 contains a breakdown of how the various types of NAT interact with each other.

Table 3-5 *NAT Types and Data Plane Status*

Side A	Side B	Data Plane Status
Public	Public	Successful
Full Cone	Full Cone	Successful
Full Cone	Port/Address Restricted	Successful
Post/Address Restricted	Port/Address Restricted	Successful
Public	Symmetric	Successful
Full Cone	Symmetric	Successful
Symmetric	Port/Address Restricted	Unsuccessful
Symmetric	Symmetric	Unsuccessful

Network Segmentation

As security continues to be a growing concern for most network deployments, more and more network administrators are looking at implementing network segmentation. Network segmentation is nothing new, as networks have been achieving network segmentation for years with solutions such as VLANs and VRFs. Network segmentation allows the network to isolate different lines of business or users from each other, unless specific policy allows communication between them. Here are a few common network segmentation use cases:

- To segment regular users from guest users

- To allow extranet partners to access selective parts of the network

- To separate PCI and/or HIPAA networks due to regulatory requirements

By segmenting the control and data planes, the capability to build disparate topologies per network segment presents itself as well. With the Cisco SD-WAN solution, network segmentation is accomplished via VPNs. Fundamentally, this is the same thing as a VRF, using legacy terminology. There are three different types of VPNs in the Cisco SD-WAN solution, as described in the list that follows and illustrated in Figure 3-26:

■ **Service VPN**: These VPNs are where user traffic lives. These VPNs are defined across the overlay and terminate the LAN side of the routers (service side). You can have multiple service VPNs in the fabric and have multiple topologies for different VPNs. These VPNs have a value from 1 to 511.

■ **Transport VPN**: The transport VPN is where the physical (WAN) underlay transport will terminate. This VPN is usually referred to as VPN 0. VPN 0 is statically assigned as the WAN VPN and cannot be changed.

■ **Management VPN**: This is the out-of-band management interface. It uses a VPN value of 512 that cannot be changed.

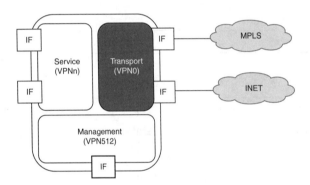

Figure 3-26 *VPN Types*

With the Cisco SD-WAN solution, segmentation is achieved by using VPN identifiers, as shown in Figure 3-27. Each data packet will carry a VPN ID that identifies the VPN it belongs to on the overlay. Once the VPN is configured on WAN Edges, it will have a label tied to it. As the WAN Edge builds its control plane, it will send this label along with the VPN ID to the vSmart controller. The vSmart will then distribute this VPN-ID mapping information to other WAN Edges in the network. The remote WAN Edges in the network will then uses these labels to send traffic for the appropriate VPNs. This solution follows the standard defined in RFC 4023 and operates similarly to MPLS.

Because the control plane and data plane have been separated, the solution allows us to build different topologies per VPN. Common topology types are hub-and-spoke, point-to-point, full mesh, and partial mesh. With no topology defined, all VPNs will be full mesh. Since the TLOC route influences how the data plane is built, we achieve these various topologies by filtering routes and TLOCs. Topologies are defined in a centralized control policy, discussed later in this book.

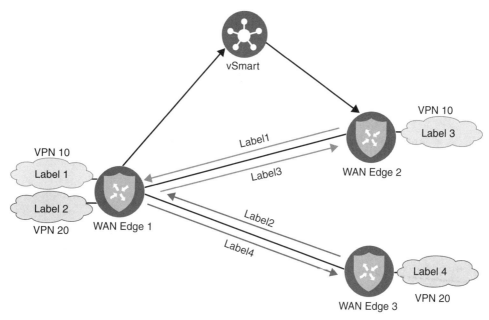

Figure 3-27 *Overlay Label Switching*

Data Plane Encryption

All of the concepts discussed leading up to this point have been related to the control plane's role in building out the data plane. As with most overlay technologies, encryption and authentication are achieved with IPsec, and Cisco SD-WAN is no different. As discussed previously, the biggest difference is how scale is achieved—particularly in how key exchange is handled.

The Internet Key Exchange (IKE) protocol traditionally handles key exchange. In the first phase of the IKE process, two peers will negotiate what type of encryption, authentication, hashing, and other techniques they want to use. This phase is only used to establish a secure channel to negotiate the second phase of the IPsec tunnel. The second phase of IKE establishes a tunnel in which user data is transmitted. For this tunnel to be established, a few things are negotiated. First, phase 2 of IKE will negotiate the use of an encapsulation protocol (either Authentication Header or Encapsulation Security Protocol). Next, the encryption algorithm to use, the type of authentication, and the tunnel lifetime will be agreed upon. The various methods supported in the Cisco SD-WAN solution are listed here:

- **Authentication:** Authentication is the mechanism that ensures the two endpoints communicating with each other are valid and authentic.

  - 2048-bit keys with RSA encryption.

  - Cisco SD-WAN supports Encapsulation Security Payload (ESP) and Authentication Header (AH). These are used to authenticate the origin of the sender.

- **Encryption:** The Cisco SD-WAN solution utilizes the AES protocol with a 256-bit key length to encrypt data.

- **Integrity:** In this step, the data traffic is inspected to ensure that the traffic traversed the network without being tampered with.

  - The Galois Counter Mode (GCM) variant of AES-256 has a built-in hashing mechanism that is used to verify data integrity.

  - Anti-Replay Protection is also enabled to protect against duplication attacks.

Considering this, it's easy to see how this process can become a scalability issue when a network grows larger and larger. Even after the preceding negotiation takes place, the tunnel state must be tracked between devices, which, in turn, continues to burn CPU cycles.

To remedy this, the Cisco SD-WAN solution implements these negotiations within the control plane. Since the WAN Edge already has a tunnel established to the control plane (and these control tunnels have their own encryption, authentication, and integrity), we can leverage this for data plane negotiations. Each WAN Edge will generate an AES-256 bit key (per transport) that is used for encryption and integrity. This key is then advertised in an OMP update to vSmart, along with the WAN Edge's corresponding TLOCs. These route advertisements are then reflected to the rest of the network. Remote WAN Edges will then use this information to build IPsec tunnels between themselves. In essence, this model of key distribution removes the burden of individual negotiations brought forth with IKE. Additionally, to provide enhanced encryption and authentication, WAN Edges will regenerate their keys every 24 hours. This rekey timer can be tuned, if requirements dictate. Renegotiation of keys will not drop existing traffic, as this negotiation happens in parallel with the existing tunnels.

Figure 3-28 illustrates the Cisco SD-WAN key exchange.

The Cisco SD-WAN key exchange process consists of the following.

1. WAN Edge 1 generates an encryption key.

2. WAN Edge 1 advertises the key via an OMP route update. This key is received and reflected by the vSmart controller. (The same process happens on WAN Edge 2 and WAN Edge 3.)

3. Now that the WAN Edges have their respective peer keys, IPsec tunnels can be built.

By default, the key exchange between WAN Edges and vSmart uses symmetric keys in an asymmetric fashion. This means that, not only is the same key used for encryption and decryption, but the shared nature of that key allows WAN Edges to utilize their peer's key rather than their own when sending data. For example, consider that WAN Edge 1 generates key 1. When WAN Edge 1 sends data to WAN Edge 2, it will encrypt the data using WAN Edge 2's key. As WAN Edge 2 receives the data, it will use its key for decryption of that data. WAN Edge 2 will do the same mechanism in reverse with WAN Edge 1's key.

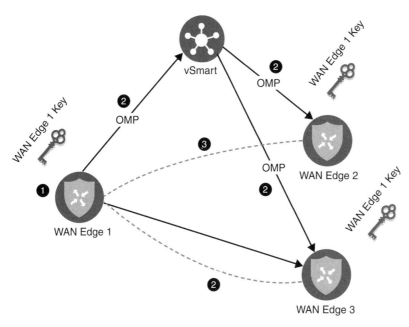

Figure 3-28 *SD-WAN Key Exchange*

Figure 3-29 illustrates how encryption and decryption occur with symmetric key exchange.

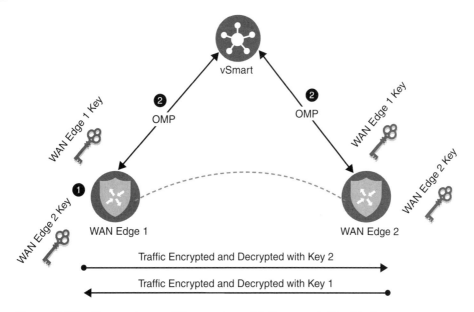

Figure 3-29 *Encryption and Decryption with Symmetric Key Exchange*

Now that both WAN Edges have the peers' respective keys, encryption and decryption occurs using the following process:

1. WAN Edge 1 and WAN Edge 2 generate encryption keys (WAN Edge 1 key and WAN Edge 2 key).

2. Both routers advertise these via OMP.

3. If WAN Edge 1 sends traffic to WAN Edge 2, it will use its WAN Edge 2's key. WAN Edge 2 will use this same key for decryption of that data. For traffic that WAN Edge 2 sends to WAN Edge 1, Key 1 will be used in the same fashion but in reverse.

Data Plane Encryption with Pairwise

A recent introduction to the solution's key exchange model described previously is the use of pairwise encryption keys. Pairwise keys provide some additional security measures in that the same key isn't used across all devices in the fabric for encryption and decryption. Pairwise functions by generating specific key pairs between two WAN Edges. For example, consider a fabric with three routers: WAN Edge 1, WAN Edge 2, and WAN Edge 3. Encryption and decryption between WAN Edge 1 and WAN Edge 2 will use a key that is unique to that pair. Traffic between WAN Edge 1 and WAN Edge 3 will use a different pair. The public key is the only thing exchanged over OMP. The biggest benefit of this is that security-concerned customers don't have to worry about the private key being exchanged as well. Key exchange still occurs via the vSmart, and unique pairs are generated per transport. Figure 3-30 illustrates this process.

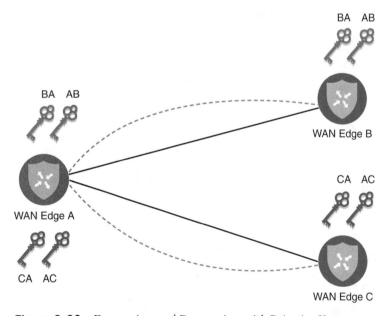

Figure 3-30 *Encryption and Decryption with Pairwise Keys*

With Pairwise keys, the process for encryption and decryption is as follows:

1. Each WAN Edge will generate a key for each transport and each peer. This key will be advertised via OMP to the vSmart.

2. If Edge A needs to send data to Edge B, Session Key AB will be used. In reverse, Edge B will use Session Key BA.

3. If Edge A sends data to Edge C, Key AC will be used. Edge C will use the key of CA when sending traffic in the reverse direction.

It should be noted that pairwise keys are also backward compatible with devices that don't support pairwise keys. Pairwise is disabled by default and can be configured via templates.

Lastly, as with all IPsec tunnels, consider the fact that these technologies add overhead to data plane traffic. This overhead reduces the amount of data that hosts can send into the fabric. To compound this issue, some transports (such as those utilizing PPPoE or LTE) have even further restrictions on payload size per packet (that is, Maximum Transmission Unit). To address this, the Cisco SD-WAN solution utilizes a Path MTU discovery mechanism via the BFD protocol. As discussed throughout this book, BFD is the protocol used within IPsec tunnels to measure loss, latency, and jitter for features such as Application-Aware Routing. The concept of PMTU is to periodically probe the tunnel to determine the maximum packet size. Traditional PMTU packets operate using ICMP. These packets are sent with the Do Not Fragment bit set. If the packet gets dropped, then the sending router can assume that the transport does not support that packet size just sent. The PMTU process will then send another packet with a smaller packet size. This process will repeat until a packet is successful. In the Cisco SD-WAN solution, the PMTU discovery process is integrated within the BFD session. Specifically, the BFD header is padded to include PMTU information. Because BFD traffic (hellos, keepalives, and so on) are continuously sent, the solution is able to continually poll the MTU and adjust as needed. By default, the tunnel is checked every minute. Additionally, since there are IPsec sessions per TLOC, MTU is calculated periodically per TLOC (or IPsec session). However, since this process sends varying packet sizes, issues could arise on low-bandwidth links. Large packets would consume all available bandwidth while the learning process occurs. For this reason, it's recommended to turn PMTU discovery off on low-bandwidth links such as the following:

- VSAT

- LTE

- Metered or low-bandwidth link

Summary

This chapter discussed the control plane process, how OMP is used as the overlay routing protocol, and how the data plane functions. NAT was discussed along with the specific constraints of symmetric NAT and its associated requirements. IPsec was then discussed and the concepts of controller-based key management. Lastly, BFD was also introduced and how it is utilized for Application-Aware Routing and Path MTU discovery.

Bringing this all together, the control plane and data plane build-up process is the following.

1. WAN Edges build DTLS tunnels to the controllers. WAN Edges are authenticated and allowed on the fabric by the vBond. vBond then facilities NAT traversal.

2. OMP routing information and encryption keys are distributed to the vSmart controller.

3. IPsec tunnels are built between WAN Edges utilizing symmetric keys or pairwise keys.

4. BFD sessions are then established inside the IPsec tunnel. BFD is utilized to calculate MTU and monitor WAN metrics for Application-Aware Routing.

Review All Key Topics

Review the most important topics in this chapter, noted with the Key Topic icon in the outer margin of the page. Table 3-6 lists these key topics and the page numbers on which each is found.

Table 3-6   *Key Topics*

Key Topic Element	Description	Page
Section	OMP Routes	48
Section	TLOC Routes	52
Section	Service Routes	54
Section	Network Address Translation	73
Paragraph	NAT is handled within the vBond controllers. The controller operates as a STUN server.	78
Section	Data Plane Encryption	83
Figure 3-29	Encryption and Decryption with Symmetric Key Exchange	85
Section	Data Plane Encryption with Pairwise	86

Key Terms

Define the following key terms from this chapter and check your answers in the glossary:

OMP route, TLOC, service route, vSmart, color

Chapter Review Questions

1. Which controller operates as a BGP route reflector but also is responsible for distributing encryption keys?

    a. vSmart

    b. vBond

    c. WAN Edge

    d. vManage

    e. vController

2. What are the three different types of OMP route advertisements?

    a. OMP vRoute

    b. TLOC route

    c. LSA Type 5

    d. EIGRP Update

    e. Service route

3. Data plane connectivity can be built between two devices behind symmetric NAT.

    a. True

    b. False

4. If using a NAT and a public color, which IPs and port attributes will be used for data plane connectivity?

    a. Post-NAT

    b. Pre-NAT

5. How does the Cisco SD-WAN solution achieve scale with IPsec?

    a. Eliminating need for IKE

    b. Decentralizing control plane from data plane

    c. NAT traversal

6. What port is used for WAN Edges to communicate with the vBond controller?

    a. UDP 12346

    b. TCP 443

    c. TCP 1000

References

E. Rosen, P. Psenak, P. Pillay-Esnault. RFC 4577: OSPF as the Provider/Customer Edge Protocol for BGP/MPLS IP Virtual Private Networks (VPNs), Network Working Group, https://tools.ietf.org/html/rfc4577, June 2006

Cisco SD-WAN Command Line Reference, https://www.cisco.com/c/en/us/td/docs/routers/sdwan/command/sdwan-cr-book.html

F. Audet, Ed., C. Jennings. RFC 4587: Network Address Translation (NAT) Behavioral Requirements for Unicast UDP, Network Working Group, https://tools.ietf.org/html/rfc4587, January 2007

J. Rosenberg, R. Mahy, P. Matthews. RFC 5389: Session Traversal Utilities for NAT (STUN), Network Working Group, https://tools.ietf.org/html/rfc5389, October 2008

Chapter 4

Onboarding and Provisioning

This chapter covers the following topics:

■ **Configuration Templates:** In this section, we discuss various template types, including CLI, device, and feature templates. Design and scaling techniques with templates are discussed in this section as well.

■ **Developing and Deploying Templates:** This section provides step-by-step instructions on how to build and deploy device and feature templates.

■ **Onboarding Devices:** Onboarding of devices with manual bootstrapping as well as automatic provisioning with techniques such as Plug and Play (PNP) and Zero Touch Provisioning (ZTP) are discussed in this section.

Current methods for managing configurations on network devices pose a lot of challenges. These challenges include version control, human error, and scaling considerations when deploying to a large number of devices. Traditionally, network engineers will make individual changes to various network devices via the command line interface (CLI). As networks grow, these configurations are often shared or piecemealed with other network devices (such as QoS or Routing Protocol configurations). Using QoS as an example, many questions must be answered before deployment and, depending on the device, different options exist on how to modify the configuration. Is it MLS queuing or MQC queueing? What hardware platform is it? How many queues has the service provider provided? What DSCP values are you using? This creates a lot of complexity when managing configuration options. In a perfect world, all of our devices and configurations would be standardized across locations. But this isn't realistic due to a multitude of reasons (such as different providers, hardware upgrade cycles, business needs, and so on). As the network grows, the disparity among network devices and network functions makes operations and troubleshooting even more difficult. To compound this issue, network configurations tend to persist as devices are upgraded and replaced. As such, the original intent of the network configuration gets lost as the IT staff turns over or other factors change. In most cases, network device configurations are rarely revisited for cleanup. One last issue to confront is version control. Network administrators tend to make configuration changes on the fly wherein the previous config gets lost. Version control is important, especially when there are outages. Having a working configuration to roll back to can save a lot of headache. Oftentimes, outages don't always get noticed immediately after the change. With no version control or change management in place, rolling back to the last-known configuration becomes difficult, as the previous configuration was not tracked.

With the Cisco SD-WAN solution, configuration management is maintained via a robust templating engine that supports automatic rollback. Templates are all built around your intent wherein the network administrator doesn't need to be concerned with what type of device this configuration is being applied to or the specific configuration options available in that version of the operating system. Templates are built in a modular fashion where they can be reused across differing device types. This allows the network administrator to quickly roll out configurations or changes at a wide scale while also ensuring the syntax is correct and is supported on any platform. Another feature of the Cisco SD-WAN solution is automatic rollback. If a configuration option gets applied to a device and it cuts off the device's ability to be managed by vManage, then the device will automatically roll back and allow the network engineer to correct the issue.

With today's networks getting larger and larger, the need to reduce provisioning and onboarding of devices needs to decrease. For example, to onboard a network device at a branch, the following approach is usually taken:

1. The device ships from manufacturing to IT staff.

2. The network administrator applies configuration to the device.

3. The IT staff drives or ships the device to the location and physically installs it.

This process is expensive for the organization, especially when looking at performing these actions across thousands of devices. If there are issues, and the device won't connect to the network, this adds further delay and operational expense as IT teams work to troubleshoot. In some cases, these installs are performed remotely. While this reduces the cost of traveling, it can create a lot of frustration if and when an issue arises. With a lack of local IT support at the site, network administrators often end up having to rely on non-IT staff to perform operations on the device. This puts a lot of faith in the remote staff and potentially takes them away from their day job. The Cisco SD-WAN solution simplifies onboarding and provisioning of a device. WAN Edge devices support mechanisms such as PNP and ZTP to automatically bring the device online and into the fabric. These onboarding solutions work by allowing the network administrator to pre-configure the device within the vManage controller. Once the vManage controller sees the device, it will automatically apply the specified configuration. WAN Edges can be shipped directly to the remote location and don't require initial configuration from IT staff. Once physically installed at the remote site, the device will automatically locate the vManage controller and begin the provisioning process. By reducing the time to bring up remote sites, the IT staff can bring more devices online more quickly and with fewer errors. This time-savings reduces operational cost, which allows IT staff to focus on bringing additional capabilities to the business.

Configuration Templates

Configurations can be applied one of two ways in the Cisco SD-WAN solution. The network administrator can either apply configuration manually via the CLI (that is, by using SSH to connect to the device or by connecting via the console port) or by using the vManage GUI. Using the vManage GUI is the preferred mechanism, as it is less error-prone and has support for automatic recovery. Configurations provisioned on vManage can be applied to both WAN Edges and vSmart controllers. When vManage is responsible for applying the configuration, it is the single source of truth, and changes can only be applied via vManage.

Note   To apply centralized policy to the vSmart controller, vSmart needs to be under the control of the vManage controller. When a component is managed by vManage, the administrator will be unable to make changes locally to the device.

When applying configuration to WAN Edge devices or controllers using the vManage GUI, a network administrator will apply a device template to a single device or multiple devices. These **device templates** (see Figure 4-1) can either be CLI based or feature template based. When a CLI template is being built, the whole configuration must be in the template (not just specific configuration snippets) as opposed to feature templates. Feature templates can be thought of as building blocks wherein each block is a specific technology feature. Feature templates define what specific feature or technology you want enabled or configured, such as routing protocols, interface parameters, and Overlay Management Protocol (OMP). Feature templates can be reused between multiple device templates, and it is this flexibility that brings greater scale to the solution (and why feature templates are the recommended way of configuring devices). Feature templates can be device type agnostic as well. The network administrator needs only to be concerned with the intent of the configuration. When vManage applies the configuration to a specific device, be it a Cisco IOS-based device or a Viptela OS device, vManage will apply the correct device syntax.

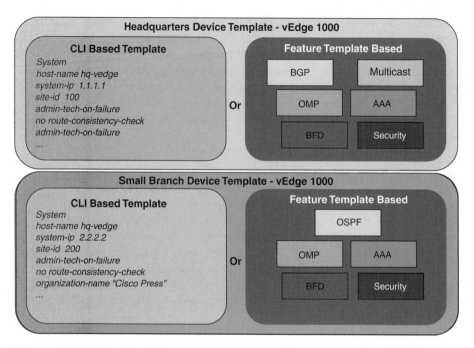

Figure 4-1 *Device Templates*

Device templates are a collection of feature templates and can only be applied to specific device types. For this reason, you may have multiple device templates for the same model of hardware, depending on the device's location, connectivity options, or what role it is playing in the network. A device template can't be shared across different device types, but feature templates can be used across multiple different device types. As illustrated in Figure 4-2, there are four main parts or groups of a device template:

- **Basic Information:** This section includes items such as System, Logging, AAA, BFD, and OMP feature templates.

- **Transport and Management VPN:** This section has templates for configuration of VPN 0 and VPN 512 (such as underlay routing protocol configuration and interface configuration).

- **Service VPN:** This section is where service VPNs or LAN-facing template configurations will exist. This is where BGP, OSPF, and interface parameters are configured.

- **Additional Templates:** This section is for local policies, security policies, SNMP configuration templates, and so on.

Feature templates make configuration options extremely flexible. For example, feature templates provide the option to define variables for configuration parameters. This allows you to reduce the number of templates required in your deployment, yet make it much more modular. To further this example, suppose you have MPLS transports that use different physical interface numbers: Gi0/0, Gi0/1, Gi0/2, and so on. Initially, the thought may be to build a feature template for each physical interface with a different IP address. This would result in three different templates. By using variables for the physical interface and IP address options, the administrator can condense this down to one feature template that can be used across all device templates.

Device Template (Model Type)

Feature Template (Model Type)	Basic Information
Feature Template (Model Type)	(System, Logging, AAA, OMP, BFD,
Feature Template (Model Type)	Security, Archive, NTP)

Feature Template (Model Type)	
Feature Template (Model Type)	Transport and Management
Feature Template (Model Type)	VPN (VPN 0 and 512)

| Feature Template (Model Type) | Service VPNs |
| Feature Template (Model Type) | |

Feature Template (Model Type)	Additional Templates
Localized Policy	(Banner, Policy, SNMP,
Feature Template (Model Type)	Bridge, Cellular)

Figure 4-2   *Device Template Structure*

Figure 4-3 shows how variables can be utilized to control template sprawl. In this example, we have nine different interface templates, depending on if the IP address is assigned via DHCP and what interface is used. By using variables, the network administrator can reduce this down to three different feature templates.

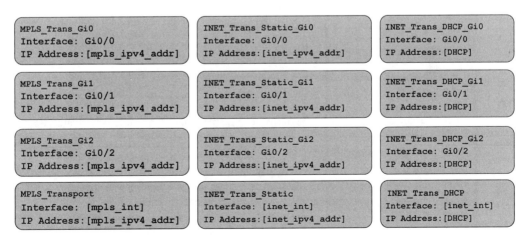

```
MPLS_Trans_Gi0
Interface: Gi0/0
IP Address:[mpls_ipv4_addr]

MPLS_Trans_Gi1
Interface: Gi0/1
IP Address:[mpls_ipv4_addr]

MPLS_Trans_Gi2
Interface: Gi0/2
IP Address:[mpls_ipv4_addr]

MPLS_Transport
Interface: [mpls_int]
IP Address:[mpls_ipv4_addr]
```

```
INET_Trans_Static_Gi0
Interface: Gi0/0
IP Address:[inet_ipv4_addr]

INET_Trans_Static_Gi1
Interface: Gi0/1
IP Address:[inet_ipv4_addr]

INET_Trans_Static_Gi2
Interface: Gi0/2
IP Address:[inet_ipv4_addr]

INET_Trans_Static
Interface: [inet_int]
IP Address:[inet_ipv4_addr]
```

```
INET_Trans_DHCP_Gi0
Interface: Gi0/0
IP Address:[DHCP]

INET_Trans_DHCP_Gi1
Interface: Gi0/1
IP Address:[DHCP]

INET_Trans_DHCP_Gi2
Interface: Gi0/2
IP Address:[DHCP]

INET_Trans_DHCP
Interface: [inet_int]
IP Address:[DHCP]
```

Figure 4-3   *Controlling Template Sprawl*

Three types of values can be defined in a template:

- **Default:** Factory default value. Default values cannot be changed. An example might be using the default BFD timers.

- **Global:** Values set here will be the same wherever this configuration option is used. An example could be SNMP community strings that you want globally applied to all devices utilizing this template. The beauty of this is that, later on (if there needs to be a change to these values), you just update the feature template global option and it updates every device template that is using this feature template.

- **Device Specific:** The value is set via a user-defined variable. This is the preceding referenced example with interface names. The values to these variables are set when the device template is attached to a specific device.

Looking at Figure 4-4, the network administrator can see how these referenced values can be utilized. Some template options might not have all three of these options, depending what is being configured. For example, a BGP AS number won't have a default value.

A large number of feature template options can be configured. Here are some common feature templates:

- **System:** Configure basic system information such as System IP, Site ID, and Hostname.

- **BFD:** Adjust BFD timers and app-route multipliers for each transport or color. BFD timers are used for App-Aware Routing.

- **OMP:** Change graceful restart timers or control redistribution from other routing protocols into OMP.

- **Security:** Change IPsec security settings such as anti-replay, authentication, and encryption.

- **VPN:** Define a service VPN, routing protocol redistribution, or static routing.

- **BGP:** Configuration of BGP in a VPN or VRF.

- **OSPF:** Configuration of OSPF in a VPN or VRF.

- **VPN Interface:** Define an interface that is part of a service VPN or VRF. Common configuration options here include IP Address, QoS, ACLs, and NAT.

As the feature templates are defined, they can be referenced via a device template. After the device template is created, it can be applied to a specific device or a group of devices. Remember, device templates can only be built for a specific device type. If there are any variables defined in the feature template, at the time the device template is attached, these values will need to be populated. Once these values are defined, a configuration syntax check is done in vManage. If successful, the configuration is then pushed to the device. Feature template variable values can be populated either within the vManage template attachment workflow or by using a CSV file. Populating feature template variables via CSV allows an administrator to quickly provision many devices all at once. If, at the time the configuration is pushed to the device, the WAN Edge loses control plane connectivity to the vManage controller, the WAN Edge will start a rollback timer of 5 minutes. If it doesn't re-establish connectivity within that 5 minutes, it will roll back its configuration and reconnect to vManage using the last known-good configuration. At this time, the network administrator will see that the device is out of sync and can correct the issue.

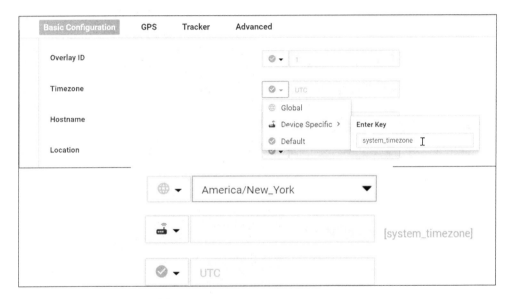

Figure 4-4 *Setting Variables*

If the need arises to change these values after the device template has been applied, an option exists to change these values on a device-by-device basis. If any changes are made to a feature template or device template, vManage will immediately push the updated configuration to all devices utilizing that template. An example of this could be changing the IP address or the username and password of the device.

Developing and Deploying Templates

Template configuration and creation is performed in the vManage GUI. After initial installation of vManage, some default templates are created. These templates can be used as a starting point, or new ones can be created. To create templates, the network administrator will navigate to **Configuration > Templates**.

Step 1.   Go to the configuration section for templates, as illustrated in Figure 4-5.

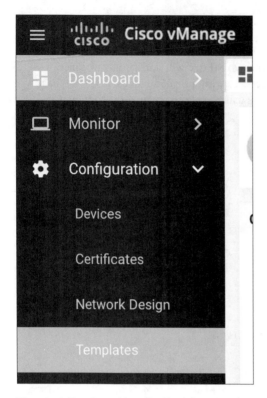

Figure 4-5   *Accessing the Template Configuration Interface*

Step 2.   Once at the template configuration window, you're presented with the option
to configure device templates or feature templates, as illustrated in Figure 4-6.

Figure 4-6   *Configuration Templates Window*

Step 3.   The next step is to begin creating feature templates. Select **Feature (tab) >
Add Template**. Select the devices that this template will apply to and select
the type of template, as illustrated in Figure 4-7.

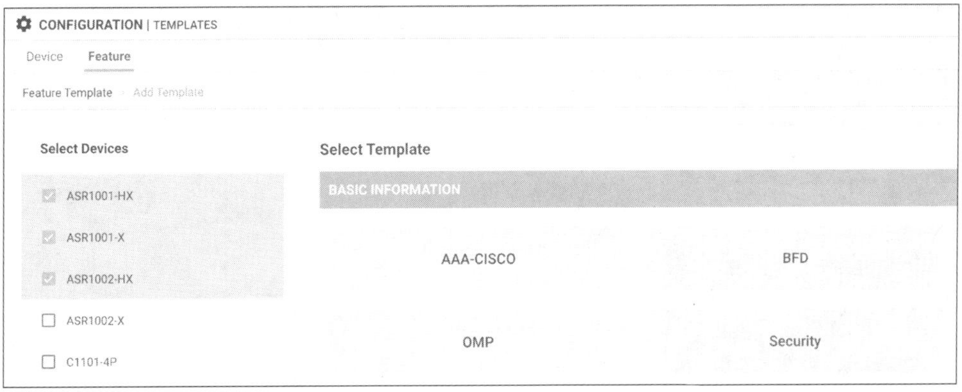

Figure 4-7   *Template Configuration: Device Selection Window*

Step 4.   After selecting the type of feature template you wish to configure, you now have the ability to start setting values, as illustrated in Figure 4-8. These values can be either variables, global parameters, or the default parameter. After the configuration options have been set and the template has been named, click **Save**.

Step 5.   Now that the feature templates have been created, they need to be attached to their respective device templates. Click **Device** (tab) followed by **Create Template**. After you click **Create Template**, the option to create a CLI-based template or a feature-based template is provided. Select **From Feature Template**, as illustrated in Figure 4-9.

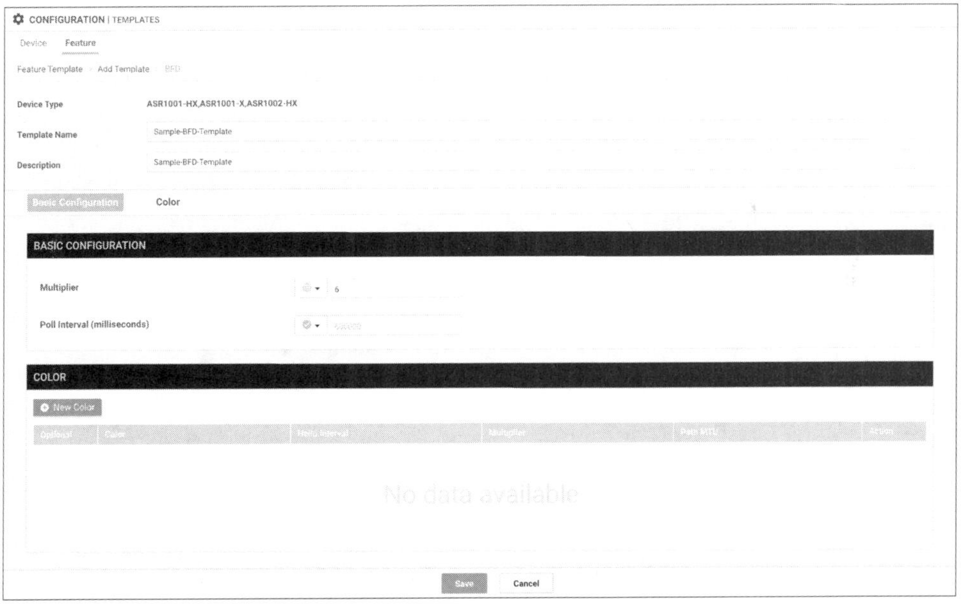

Figure 4-8   *Template Configuration: Setting Configuration Values*

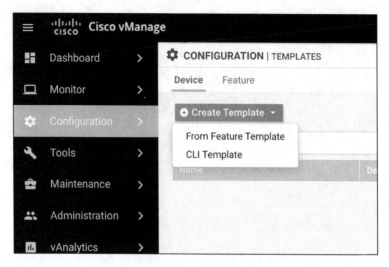

Figure 4-9   *Template Configuration: Device Template Selection*

Step 6.   After selecting a feature-based template, you need to select the device model this template will apply to as well as provide a name for the template, as illustrated in Figure 4-10. Once this is done, you have the ability to start selecting what feature templates to use. In this example, we'll select the BFD template we created in the previous example. Once done, select **Save**.

Figure 4-10   *Template Configuration: Device Template Feature Selection*

Step 7.   Now that the device template is created, you can attach it to devices. From the Device Templates page, click the ellipses next to the template you wish to attach. Select the option to **Attach Devices**, as illustrated in Figure 4-11.

Figure 4-11   *Attaching a Template to a Device*

Step 8.   From here, you can select the devices to apply the configurations to, as illustrated in Figure 4-12. Once you select the device, you have the option to populate any variables.

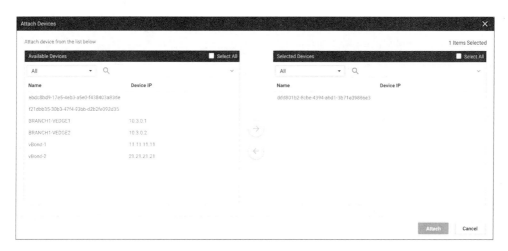

Figure 4-12   *Device Selection Window*

Onboarding Devices

For a WAN Edge to join the SD-WAN fabric, the WAN Edge first needs to establish connectivity to the vBond controller. The vBond controller facilitates discovery of the vManage and vSmart controllers. As the WAN Edge establishes connectivity to each of these controllers, mutual authentication will occur. After the WAN Edge has authenticated to the controller components in the overlay, the device will receive its full configuration from vManage. There are two methods to bootstrap a device with initial configuration so that it can reach vBond. The less preferred, and more obvious, method is to manually apply minimal configuration to the device. The second method is automatically discovering the network using Zero Touch Provisioning (ZTP) or Plug and Play (PNP). If the device is running Viptela OS, it will use ZTP. If the device is an IOS XE-based device, then Plug and Play is utilized. The general process of ZTP and PNP is similar. The following sections elaborate on each process.

Manual Bootstrapping of a WAN Edge

To manually bootstrap a WAN Edge device, the network administrator will begin by applying a minimal configuration to the device. This includes IP addressing, vBond addressing (either DNS hostname or IP), and system identification information. This information is used to establish initial connectivity and authentication. The process to manually bootstrap a device is as follows:

Step 1.   Configure an IP address and default gateway. If DHCP is available, this can be used to assign the IP and gateway automatically.

Step 2.   Configure the vBond IP or hostname. If you are using a hostname, then a DNS server address must be provided, and the device must have reachability from VPN 0.

Step 3.   Configure device identification information, including the system IP, site ID, and organization name.

Examples 4-1 and 4-2 show the minimal configuration for Viptela OS and SD-WAN IOS-XE devices.

Example 4-1   *Minimal Configuration for a Viptela OS–based Device*

```
vEdge# config
vEdge(config)#
vEdge(config)# system host-name hostname
vEdge(config-system)#system-ip ip-address
vEdge(config-system)# site-id site-id
vEdge(config-system)# organization-name organization-name
vEdge(config-system)# vbond (dns-name | ip-address)
vEdge(config)# vpn 0
vEdge(config-vpn-0)# interface interface-name
vEdge(config-interface)# (ip dhcp-client | ip address prefix/length)
vEdge(config-interface)# no shutdown
vEdge(config-interface)# tunnel-interface
vEdge(config-tunnel-interface)# color color
vEdge(config-vpn-0)# ip route 0.0.0.0/0 next-hop
vEdge(config)# commit and-quit
```

Example 4-2 *Minimal Configuration for an IOS-XE based Device*

```
Device# config-transaction
Device(config)#
Device(config)# system host-name  hostname
Device(config-system)# system-ip  ip-address
Device(config-system)# site-id site-id
Device(config-system)# vbond  (dns-name | ip-address)
Device(config-system)# organization-name name
Device(config)# interface Tunnel #
Device(config-if)# ip unnumbered wan-physical-interface
Device(config-if)# tunnel source wan-physical-interface
Device(config-if)# tunnel mode sdwan
Device(config)# interface GigabitEthernet  #
Device(config)# ip address  ip-address mask
Device(config)# no shut
Device(config)# exit
Device(config)# sdwan
Device(config-sdwan)# interface  WAN-interface-name
Device(config-interface-interface-name)# tunnel-interface
Device(config-tunnel-interface)# color color
Device(config-tunnel-interface)# encapsulation  ipsec
Device(config)# ip route 0.0.0.0 0.0.0.0 next-hop-ip-address
Device(config)# ip domain lookup
Device(config)# ip name-server dns-server-ip-address
Device(config)# commit
Device# exit
```

Automatic Provisioning with PNP or ZTP

The second method of provisioning devices allows the network administrator to automatically bring the devices online with minimal effort and involvement. Once powered on, the default configuration on the device tries to receive an IP address via DHCP. Once the device has an IP address, it will reach out to the automatic provisioning server (hosted by Cisco) and learn about the organization's vBond. At this point, the process is exactly the same as the manual bootstrapping process. The device will connect and authenticate to the vBond, learn of vManage and vSmart, and then receive its configuration.

Note   The automatic provisioning servers are managed via the Plug and Play portal at http://software.cisco.com. As devices are purchased from Cisco, their serial numbers will be populated here. vManage can also be configured to synchronize with this portal to automatically populate the organization's devices into vManage.

Before the automatic provisioning process can be initiated, the network administrator needs to attach a device template in vManage for the respective device. The device template must have the system IP and site ID for the device populated as well. If none of this is completed, the process will not succeed. Once vManage sees the device for the first time, it will push the template that is assigned to the matching serial number of the device performing ZTP or PNP.

As briefly described previously, depending on the type of device, the process is slightly different. If the device is a Viptela OS–based device, ZTP will be used. Once the device boots up, it will start the process to receive an IP address and DNS server via DHCP. After this succeeds, it will try to resolve ztp.viptela.com. If successful, the device will connect to the ZTP server and (after the ZTP server verifies what organization the device belongs to) it will redirect the device to the correct vBond for the organization. The ZTP server is able to verify which organization the device belongs to by checking the serial number of the device against its ZTP entries database. Once it's connected to the vBond, the normal process continues. For ZTP to function, two things must happen: DHCP must be available on the WAN (VPN 0) facing interface and the device must be able to resolve **ztp.viptela.com**. Each Viptela OS–based device has specific interfaces that are to be used for ZTP. Refer to the latest product documentation to determine which interface should be used. Figure 4-13 outlines the process, described in further detail in the list that follows.

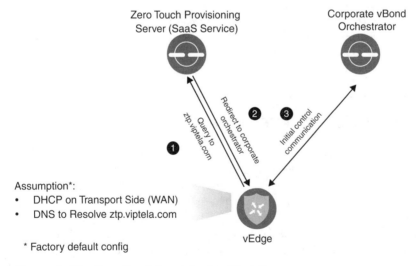

Figure 4-13 *Zero Touch Provisioning Workflow*

1. The vEdge device queries **ztp.viptela.com**. The ZTP server verifies that the device's serial number and organization exist in the ZTP database.

2. If the vEdge performing the ZTP process exists in the ZTP database, the ZTP server responds telling the vEdge what the connectivity information is for the organization's vBond controller.

3. The vEdge then connects to the corporate vBond and goes through the authentication process. If successful, the vBond will tell the vEdge about the vSmart and vManage controllers in the overlay. At this point, vManage will push the necessary configuration to the device.

For Cisco IOS-XE based devices, a slightly different method is used instead of ZTP. PNP operates almost identically to ZTP, except instead of building a DTLS tunnel to the PNP server (**devicehelper.cisco.com**), the device will communicate to the server via HTTPS. After the PNP server validates the device, it will redirect the IOS-XE based WAN Edge to the relevant vBond for the organization. IOS-XE based devices have the same requirements as ZTP devices in that they must get an IP address and DNS server via DHCP and be able to resolve **devicehelper.cisco.com**. Figure 4-14 outlines the process of onboarding a device with PNP.

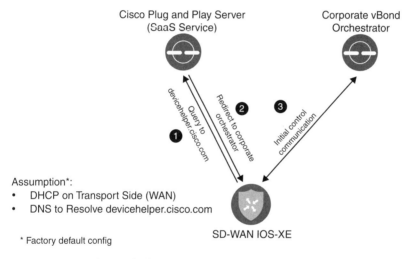

Figure 4-14 *Plug and Play Workflow*

Summary

With the Cisco SD-WAN solution, network configurations are handled with ease via a powerful template engine. Feature templates can be utilized to achieve modularity of configuration that can be reused across various platforms. All of these feature templates are used to form a device template. By using variables within these templates, the network administrator can support a large range of configuration requirements.

Provisioning of devices can occur with one of two methods: either manual or with an automatic process such as Plug and Play or Zero Touch Provisioning. With the manual method, the amount of configuration is very small. The device must have system IP, site ID, organization name, and IP address information. Once the device authenticates to the organization's vBond, it will discover the rest of the controller elements, and vManage can push configuration down to the device. The second option involves using an automatic onboarding process. This process uses either ZTP or PNP, depending on if it's a Viptela OS–based product or a Cisco IOS-based product. Once the device has gone through the automatic method and determined the vBond to use, the process works just the same as with the manual method. This allows the network administrator to deploy a large number devices quickly, even if they have different configuration options.

Review All Key Topics

Review the most important topics in the chapter, noted with the Key Topic icon in the outer margin of the page. Table 4-1 lists these key topics and the page numbers on which each is found.

Table 4-1   *Key Topics*

Key Topic Element	Description	Page
Paragraphs	Device templates are a collection of feature templates or a CLI template. These templates are what are applied to the device.	93
Paragraph	Feature templates make up the building blocks or configuration options for various features. These templates are selected from within the device template. Variables can be utilized to make these templates even more modular.	94
Section	Onboarding Devices Zero Touch Provisioning, or ZTP, is the automatic onboarding process used by Viptela OS–based devices. Connectivity to the ZTP server is established via DTLS tunnel.	101
Section	Automatic Provisioning with PNP or ZTP Just like ZTP, Plug and Play, or PNP, is an automatic process for onboarding Cisco IOS-XE based devices. PNP uses HTTPS to connect to the PNP server.	103

Chapter Review Que   ns

1. What two methods can be used to construct device templates?
    a. CLI
    b. Feature templates
    c. Directly on the device
    d. Multiple CLI Templates

2. What are the three device value types that can be used with feature templates?

    a. Global

    b. Default

    c. Automatic

    d. Imported

    e. Variables

3. Device templates support multiple different device types.

    a. True

    b. False

4. CLI templates can be used in a modular format and achieve the same flexibility of feature templates.

    a. False

    b. True

5. Which automatic provisioning method uses HTTPS for communication?

    a. Plug and Play

    b. Zero Touch Provisioning

    c. NAT traversal

6. Which three things must a device have for automatic provisioning to be successful?

    a. IP address and DNS server via DHCP

    b. Be able to resolve ZTP/PNP domain name

    c. Connectivity to ZTP or PNP server

    d. IPsec tunnel

    e. Connectivity to data center

References

Cisco SD-WAN Command Line Reference, https://www.cisco.com/c/en/us/td/docs/routers/sdwan/command/sdwan-cr-book.html

Cisco SD-WAN CVD – Certificate Deployment, https://www.cisco.com/c/dam/en/us/td/docs/solutions/CVD/SDWAN/CVD-SD-WAN-Design-2018OCT.pdf, October 2018

Chapter 5

Introduction to Cisco SD-WAN Policies

This chapter covers the following topics:

■ **Purpose of Cisco SD-WAN Policies:** This section covers the reasons why customers would choose to use Cisco SD-WAN policies.

■ **Types of Cisco SD-WAN Policies:** This section introduces different types of Cisco SD-WAN policies, including control policies, centralized data policies, and localized policies.

■ **Cisco SD-WAN Policy Construction:** This section covers the building blocks of Cisco SD-WAN policies and how their different components fit together.

■ **Cisco SD-WAN Policy Administration, Activation, and Enforcement:** This section covers how Cisco SD-WAN policies are activated and enforced throughout the Cisco SD-WAN fabric.

■ **Packet Forwarding Order of Operations:** This section examines how different Cisco SD-WAN policies interact with each other when multiple policy types are applied at the same time.

Network administrators use policies in order to configure the Cisco SD-WAN fabric to achieve specific business outcomes. This chapter introduces the different types of Cisco SD-WAN policies. Additionally, this chapter focuses on the necessary components and the process of building policies as well as how the policies are applied and where they are enforced within the network. Chapters 6 through 10 will continue this topic with more detailed discussions about specific types of policies and how to use them to achieve specific business outcomes.

Purpose of Cisco SD-WAN Policies

The ongoing transformation to digital business means that organizations are relying on their IT infrastructure more than ever before. There is more data flowing across the network, and that data is increasingly critical to ongoing business operations. Cisco SD-WAN policies are the mechanism through which administrators can encode their intent into the network fabric and organizations can start to realize new kinds of value. IT administrators today are being tasked to meet new demands from business leaders that have direct implications on the structure and operation of the network. One such objective is to reduce the costs of the WAN transport infrastructure. Realizing this objective often involves moving from an Active/Standby design to a forwarding architecture where all links can be used in parallel. Additionally, administrators are moving away from expensive, leased-line transports and relying more and more on commodity Internet circuits to meet their transport needs. At the same time, business stakeholders require the same application experience that they have traditionally had with MPLS transports. Policies are the way that network administrators configure the Cisco SD-WAN fabric in order to meet their business intentions. Through the next several chapters we will discuss different types of policies and how they can be used with different use cases to solve business problems.

Types of Cisco SD-WAN Policies

Network administrators use several different types of policies in order to meet their business objectives. Policies can be classified as either centralized policies or localized policies.

Broadly speaking, centralized policies control routing information and data that is forwarded across the Cisco SD-WAN fabric. Localized policies control routing and traffic forwarding at the perimeter of the Cisco SD-WAN fabric where WAN Edge routers interface with traditional routers. Figure 5-1 illustrates the relationships between these types of policies.

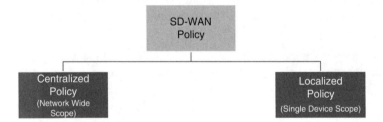

Figure 5-1   *Types of Cisco SD-WAN Policies*

Centralized Policy

Figure 5-2 shows that centralized policies can be further classified as either control policies (called topology policies in the vManage GUI) or data policies (called traffic policies in the vManage GUI). Control policies are used to manipulate the structure of the Cisco SD-WAN fabric by altering the control plane information exchanged by the Overlay

Management Protocol (OMP). Data policies are used to manipulate the data plane directly by altering the forwarding of traffic through the Cisco SD-WAN fabric.

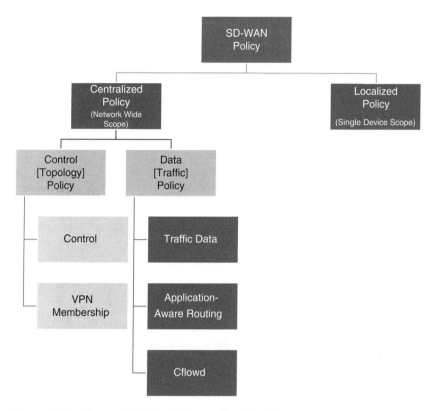

Figure 5-2 *Types of SD-WAN Centralized Policies*

Centralized Policies That Affect the Control Plane

Control policies and VPN membership policies are used to manipulate the propagation of routing information in the control plane, including manipulating or filtering OMP routes and Transport Locator (TLOC) routes. Chapter 6, "Centralized Control Policies," discusses control policies and VPN membership policies in more detail.

- **Control Policies:** Control policies are used for applications such as preferring one site over another for a specific destination (or default routing) and limiting which sites can build tunnels directly across the fabric.

- **VPN Membership Policies:** VPN membership policies are used to limit the distribution of routing information about particular VPNs to specific sites. One common use case for VPN membership policies is for guest segments where Internet access is permitted but site-to-site communication is denied.

Centralized Policies That Affect the Data Plane

While control policies and VPN membership policies are used to manipulate the control plane, centralized data policies and Application-Aware Routing policies directly affect the forwarding of traffic in the data plane.

- **Centralized Data Policies:** Centralized data policies are a flexible and powerful form of policy-based routing and are commonly used to accomplish Direct Internet Access (DIA) for specific applications, network service insertion, and data plane manipulations such as packet duplication and Forward Error Correction (FEC). Chapter 7, "Centralized Data Policies," covers centralized data policies in more detail.

- **Application-Aware Routing Policies:** Application-Aware Routing policies are used to ensure that a particular class of traffic is always transported across a WAN link that meets a minimum service level agreement (SLA). Chapter 8, "Application-Aware Routing Policies," covers these policies in more detail.

- **Cflowd Policies:** Cflowd policies are a special type of centralized data policy that specifies the destination where flow records should be exported so that flow information is available on external systems for analysis.

Localized Policy

Similar to centralized policies, localized policies can be used to manipulate both the control plane and the data plane. Figure 5-3 illustrates the two main types of localized policy: traditional localized policy and security policy. Traditional localized policies include route policy, quality of service, and access control lists (ACLs). The security policy feature set supports use cases such as compliance, guest access, Direct Cloud Access (DCA), and Direct Internet Access (DIA).

Localized policies that affect the control plane, called route policies, can be used to filter or manipulate routes exchanged or learned outside of the SD-WAN fabric via protocols such as BGP, OSPF, and EIGRP. Route policies can also be used to filter routes as they are redistributed from one protocol to another—including into and out of OMP. Route policies are the only way to impact the control plane with localized policy.

Localized policies that affect the data plane include the following:

- **Quality of Service:** Quality of Service (QoS) can be configured on the WAN Edge routers to perform queueing, shaping, policing, congestion avoidance, and congestion management.

- **Access Control Lists:** Access control lists (ACLs) can be created with the localized policy to filter traffic at the interface level. ACLs can also be used to mark or remark traffic for QoS purposes.

■ **Security Policy:** Security policies were first introduced in version 18.2 with the Zone-Based Firewall (ZBFW) feature set and have continued to expand in functionality in subsequent releases. As of version 19.2, the Security Policy feature set currently supports Application-Aware ZBFW, Intrusion Prevention, URL Filtering, Advanced Malware Protection (AMP), and DNS Security. These features are used to affect traffic in the data plane.

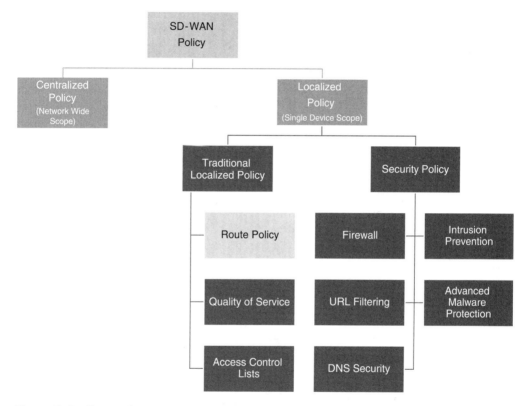

Figure 5-3 *Types of Cisco SD-WAN Localized Policies*

Policy Domains

Figures 5-2 and 5-3 illustrate that both the control plane and the data plane can be manipulated with both centralized policies and localized policies. By comparison, Figure 5-4 illustrates the relationship between centralized control policies and localized control policies. Centralized policies are activated on the vSmart controllers and affect the control plane of the Cisco SD-WAN fabric. Localized route policies are applied to the individual WAN Edge routers and affect the routing domain in the local site that is attached to the Cisco SD-WAN fabric.

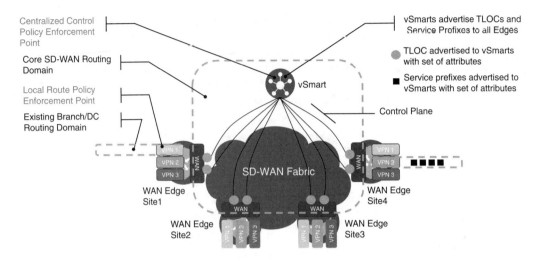

Figure 5-4 *Manipulating the Control Plane with Centralized and Localized Control Policies*

A similar distinction can be made about centralized data policies and localized data policies. Centralized data policies can affect the forwarding of data across the entire Cisco SD-WAN fabric, whereas localized data policies can be applied as narrowly as a single interface on a single router. Figure 5-5 illustrates these relationships.

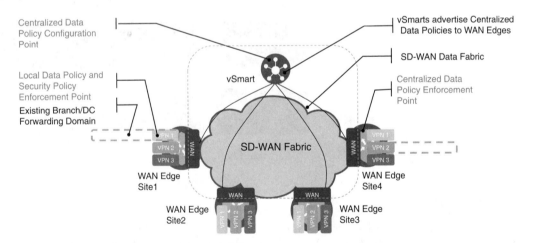

Figure 5-5 *Manipulating the Data Plane with Centralized and Localized Data Policies*

The remaining discussion in this chapter focuses primarily on centralized policies. While most of the concepts are applicable to both centralized and localized policies, there are some key differences in the way that localized policies are constructed and applied. These differences will be discussed in further detail in Chapter 9, "Localized Policies," and Chapter 10, "Cisco SD-WAN Security."

Cisco SD-WAN Policy Construction

Cisco SD-WAN policies may be intimidating or confusing at first look, but they are remarkably similar in construction and operation to routing policies created on traditional IOS routers. Creating a routing policy on a traditional IOS router is a three-step process:

Step 1.   **Define lists to identify the groups of interest.** Lists such as an access control list, an IP prefix list, and an Autonomous System (AS) path list are commonly used for this purpose.

Step 2.   **Define a route map.** A route map is a structured sequence of match and set statements, where traffic of interest from the list defined in the first step is matched and then the specific set of actions to be taken is listed.

Step 3.   **Apply the route map.** In order for the policy to have any effect at all, the route map must be applied. A single route map can be applied in a number of different ways, such as on an interface to configure policy routing in the data plane, or on a routing neighbor to manipulate routing updates in the control plane. Configuring the list and route maps without applying them has no effect on the control plane or data plane of an IOS router.

Example 5-1 illustrates this process by showing a router at a remote site that has a BGP peering with a data center router (BGP neighbor 192.168.1.100). The network administrator creates and applies the following policy in classic Cisco IOS syntax to only accept the default route advertisement from the data center router and to set a specific MED value to that default route.

Example 5-1   *Configuring a Routing Policy in Traditional Cisco IOS with a BGP Route Map*

```
REMOTE_R1#
REMOTE_R1#conf t
Enter configuration commands, one per line. End with CNTL/Z.
! Step 1:  Define the list to identify the traffic of interest
! In this example, an ip prefix-list is defined to match only a default route
REMOTE_R1(config)#ip prefix-list DEFAULT_ONLY permit 0.0.0.0/0
REMOTE_R1(config)#
! Step 2:  Define a route-map to execute the necessary policy actions
! In this example, sequence 10 permits the routes from our prefix-list,
! and sets the MED value to 1000; sequence 20 denies all other routes.
REMOTE_R1(config)#route-map PERMIT_ONLY_DEFAULT permit 10
REMOTE_R1(config-route-map)#match ip address prefix-list DEFAULT_ONLY
REMOTE_R1(config-route-map)#set metric 1000
REMOTE_R1(config-route-map)#route-map PERMIT_ONLY_DEFAULT deny 20
REMOTE_R1(config-route-map)#exit
REMOTE_R1(config)#
! Step 3:  Apply the Route-Map
! In this example, the route-map is applied to one of the configured BGP neighbors
REMOTE_R1(config)#router bgp 100
REMOTE_R1(config-router)#neighbor 192.168.1.100 remote-as 200
```

```
REMOTE_R1(config-router)#neighbor 192.168.1.100 route-map PERMIT_ONLY_DEFAULT in
REMOTE_R1(config-router)#end
REMOTE_R1#
```

While Cisco SD-WAN policies can appear intimidating to new engineers because they are much more flexible than traditional IOS-based policies, the same three-step process is used for configuring policies with Cisco SD-WAN:

Step 1.   **Define lists to identify the groups of interest.** There are many more and different types of lists that can be used with Cisco SD-WAN than with traditional IOS. This, in part, accounts for the greater flexibility with Cisco SD-WAN than with traditional routing policy. In addition to using lists to identify traffic of interest, certain lists can also be used when defining actions and when applying policies. Lists will be discussed in greater detail in the next section.

Step 2.   **Define a policy.** Cisco SD-WAN policies are defined in a structured sequence of match and action statements, where traffic of interest from the list defined in the first step is matched and then the specific set of actions to be taken is listed. There are many different types of policies that can be used with Cisco SD-WAN to accomplish different objectives, but the structure of those policies is similar. The specific criteria that can be matched on and the different actions that can be taken differ between the types of policies.

Step 3.   **Apply the policy.** As with traditional Cisco IOS route maps, in order for the Cisco SD-WAN policy to have any effect at all, the policy must be applied; a route map that has been configured but not applied does not affect the operation of the router. With Cisco SD-WAN, centralized policies are always applied to a site list that matches one or more site IDs. If there are multiple WAN Edge routers at a single site, each of the routers configured with the same site ID will be subjected to the same centralized policy. Depending on the type of policy, the policy can also be applied to a specific VPN and to a specific direction of traffic flow.

Figure 5-6 illustrates this three-step process.

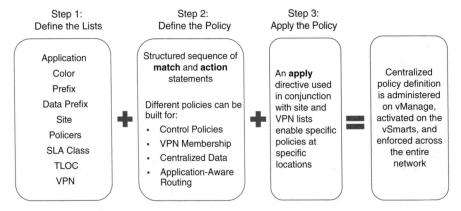

Figure 5-6   *SD-WAN Policy Building Blocks*

In Example 5-2, the three-step process for creating SD-WAN policies is implemented to create a similar routing policy as shown in Example 5-1.

Note   Centralized policies are always rendered in vManage and vSmart such that the policy definitions (Step 2) are displayed first, the lists (Step 1) are displayed second, and the policy applications (Step 3) are displayed third, at the bottom. For this reason, some experienced engineers find it helpful to read policies from the bottom to the top, particularly when troubleshooting.

Example 5-2   *Configuring a Centralized Policy with Cisco SD-WAN*

```
! Step 2:  Define a control-policy to execute the necessary policy actions
! In this example, sequence 1 permits the routes from our prefix-list,
! and sequence 11 permits the TLOC Routes.
! The default action denies all other routes and TLOCs.
policy
 control-policy PERMIT_ONLY_DEFAULT
    sequence 1
     match route
      prefix-list DEFAULT_ONLY
      site-list DC_1
     !
     action accept
     !
    !
    sequence 11
     match tloc
      site-list DC_1
     !
     action accept
     !
    !
  default-action reject
 !
! Step 1:  Define the list to identify the groups of interest
! In this example, a similar prefix-list is defined to match only a default
! route, as was done in Example 5-1.
 lists
  prefix-list DEFAULT_ONLY
   ip-prefix 0.0.0.0/0
  !
! Step 1 (continued): Two site-lists were defined to specify where
! the route is sourced from, and where the policy is applied.
```

```
   site-list REMOTE_1
    site-id 300
    !
   site-list DC_1
    site-id 100
    !
   !
  !
 ! Step 3:  Apply the Policy
 ! In this example, the policy is applied to the remote site specified in the
   site-list REMOTE_1.
apply-policy
 site-list REMOTE_1
  control-policy PERMIT_ONLY_DEFAULT out
  !
 !
```

Later chapters of this book will review the construction of policies in much greater detail; do not be concerned if the meaning of specific commands is not yet clear. The purpose of Examples 5-1 and 5-2 is to review the commonality of the structure of Cisco SD-WAN policies with traditional control and data plane policies in Cisco IOS.

Types of Lists

Lists are the foundational building block of Cisco SD-WAN policies. Lists allow for flexibility and extendibility in both how items are matched and how actions are taken in a Cisco SD-WAN policy. Cisco SD-WAN has many different types of lists that can be used to match different groups of interest in the control plane and the data plane. With centralized policies, the following types of lists can be used:

- **Application List:** An application list can match on a specific application or an application family. These lists are used to assist administrators in creating business-relevant rules using Layer 7 application definitions rather than needing to specify Layers 3 and 4 (IP address and port) values. Common examples would include a "VOICE_AND_VIDEO" application list that would match applications such as RTP (VoIP), WebEx, and TelePresence and a "SCAVENGER" application list that matches non-business-critical applications such as YouTube, Facebook, and Netflix. Application lists are only used as matching criteria.

- **Color List:** As discussed in Chapter 3, "Control Plane and Data Plane Operations," a "color" is an attribute of a TLOC. Color lists can specify a single color or a group of colors. These lists can be used in both control plane and data plane policies and can be used as matching criteria as well as when specifying an action.

- **Prefix List:** A prefix list is used to specify a range of routes in Classless Inter-Domain Routing (CIDR) notation. This list is used for matching routing information in the control plane exclusively and can only be used in control policies. Unlike in traditional IOS, where a single access list or prefix list can be used to match either control plane routes or data plane traffic (depending on how it is used in the policy), Cisco SD-WAN defines two separate lists for these functions: a prefix list and a data prefix list.

■ **Data Prefix List:** A data prefix list is very similar to a prefix list; however, a data prefix list in Cisco SD-WAN can only be used to match traffic in the data plane and is only used in data policies.

■ **Site List:** Every site in the Cisco SD-WAN fabric is assigned a site identifier called a *Site-ID*. A site list can be a single, multiple, or range of site IDs. Site lists are often used as matching criteria in policy statements and to specify which site or sites a particular policy gets applied to. This is discussed further in the following section.

■ **Policers:** Similar to traditional Cisco IOS, a policer is used for limiting the rate of traffic that ingresses or egresses. A policer list can only be used as part of an action statement in a policy and not part of a match statement.

■ **SLA (Service Level Agreement) Class List:** An SLA class list is used with an Application-Aware Routing policy to define an SLA in terms of the maximum loss, latency, jitter, or a combination of the three, that a particular class of traffic should experience.

■ **TLOC Lists:** As discussed in Chapter 3, a TLOC is a Transport Locator and serves as the next-hop address in routing lookups that happen across the SD-WAN fabric. A TLOC list is a set of next-hop addresses and can be used with both control and data policies to manipulate the next-hop address of traffic that is forwarded over the SD-WAN fabric.

■ **VPN List:** A VPN list is a list of service-side VPNs (or VRFs) and is used to specify matching criteria in a control policy for which VPN segment a particular data policy should be applied to.

Policy Definition

While there are many different types of Cisco SD-WAN policies, all of the policies are defined with a similar structure. Each policy is a numbered sequence of **match** and **action** clauses that are evaluated ordinally. Inside of a particular sequence number, you may configure multiple matching conditions and multiple actions. If multiple conditions are specified, then a logical *AND* between the conditions is evaluated, and *all* of the criteria must be met in order to be matched by that sequence. This case can be seen in Example 5-3, where the matching criteria of sequence 1 specifies that routes must match *both* (logical AND) the prefix list **DEFAULT_ONLY** and the site list **DC_1_OR_2**. Any default routes that are not from either Site 100 or Site 200 would not satisfy both of the criteria and therefore would not be matched by sequence 1 and would continue to be evaluated by additional sequences in the policy. Likewise, any routes from Site 100 or Site 200 that are not default routes would also not satisfy both of the criteria and would not be matched by sequence 1.

Example 5-3 *Centralized Policy with Multiple Matching Criteria*

```
control-policy PERMIT_ONLY_DEFAULT
! Sequence 1 accepts routes that are matched by the prefix list DEFAULT_ONLY
! and the Site list DC_1_OR_2.
  sequence 1
   match route
    prefix-list DEFAULT_ONLY
    site-list DC_1_OR_2
   !
   action accept
   !
  !
  sequence 11
   match tloc
    site-list DC_1_OR_2
   !
   action accept
   !
  !
 default-action reject
 !
!
```

Sequence 1 in Example 5-3 shows that multiple lists can be specified as the matching criteria for a single sequence, and in that case, *all* of the matching criteria (both the prefix list and the site list in this example) must be met in order matched by sequence 1. At the same time, each of those lists can contain one or more values, as illustrated by the site list **DC_1_OR_2** in Example 5-4.

Example 5-4 *Lists That Match Multiple Values*

```
lists
 prefix-list DEFAULT_ONLY
  ip-prefix 0.0.0.0/0
 !
 site-list REMOTE_1
  site-id 300
 !
 ! This list, when used as matching criteria, will match multiple values.  Site 100
 OR Site 200
 ! will be matched by this list.
 site-list DC_1_OR_2
  site-id 100,200
 !
 !
 !
```

In the event that the list being used as matching criteria contains multiple values, matching any one value will be sufficient for that criterion: in Example 5-3, sequence 1 will match routes sourced from the Site-ID list **DC_1_OR_2**, which is defined in Example 5-4 to be either site-id 100 or site-id 200. In this way, you can see that the multiple values within a single list, when used as a match condition, are treated as a logical *OR*. As each router is configured with a single site-id, there is no way that a single route could fulfill the matching criteria to be from site-id 100 *AND* site-id 200 at the same time.

Similar to traditional Cisco route maps and ACLs, the matching logic applied in Cisco SD-WAN policies is on a first-match basis. As soon as any given sequence in the policy is matched, those specific actions are taken and no further match statements are evaluated. As such, it is a common practice to put the most specific matching criteria at the beginning of the policy and the broader, more general matches at the end of the policy.

Once a particular sequence number is matched, the first action that an administrator configures is to either "Accept or Reject" in a centralized control policy or "Accept or Deny" in a centralized data policy. Additional, optional actions can be configured in addition to accepting or denying/rejecting the entry, but this choice is mandatory. If the entry in a control policy is rejected, no further actions can be taken. In data policies, if the traffic is rejected, then you have the option to log or count the traffic. If the matching entry is accepted, there are many more possible options that can be taken in both cases. Additional examples of this will be covered in much greater detail in subsequent chapters. Example 5-5 highlights an example of these **action** statements.

Example 5-5   *Policy Actions and Default Action*

```
control-policy PERMIT_ONLY_DEFAULT
   sequence 1
    match route
     prefix-list DEFAULT_ONLY
     site-list DC_1_OR_2
     !
! Every policy sequence either accepts or denies 122(for control policies) /
! rejects (for data policies) entries
    action accept
    !
   !
   sequence 11
    match tloc
     site-list DC_1_OR_2
    !
    action accept
    !
   !
```

```
! Every policy has a default action that applies when no other sequences
! have been matched
 default-action reject
 !
!
```

Each policy also has a default action as the very last sequence. This default action is similar to the implicit denial that is found in traditional Cisco ACLs and route maps, but unlike traditional Cisco route maps, the default action is always configured explicitly. When configuring centralized policies, it is important to keep in mind that the default action exists and is set to Reject or Deny for control and data policies accordingly. Example 5-5 highlights the default action configuration.

Cisco SD-WAN Policy Administration, Activation, and Enforcement

Each of the several different kinds of centralized policies, including control, VPN membership, centralized data, and Application-Aware Routing, is configured as an individual component policy. This process was described in "Step 2: Define the Policy" in the previous section. Each of these component policies has its own specific sequence of **match** and **action** statements and is processed completely independently from the others. These individual policies are then combined into a single centralized policy.

Building a Centralized Policy

Example 5-6 demonstrates the process of combining multiple component policies together. This example continues to build on the policy that was created in Examples 5-4 and 5-5 and adds a centralized data policy to filter the traffic from a specific application on the network. This centralized data policy has a single sequence, sequence 1, that matches on an application list called **BLOCKED_APPS**. In addition to the new centralized data policy, Example 5-6 also includes several new lists, including the application-list **BLOCKED_APPS**, as well as the VPN list **CORP_VPN** and the site list **ALL_BRANCHES**.

Lastly, the apply-policy stanza at the end of the policy has been updated. This stanza now indicates that the new data policy has been applied to the sites indicated by the **ALL_BRANCHES** site list.

Example 5-6 *Centralized Policy with Multiple Component Sub-Policies*

```
policy
 control-policy PERMIT_ONLY_DEFAULT
    sequence 1
     match route
      prefix-list DEFAULT_ONLY
      site-list DC_1_OR_2
     !
     action accept
     !
    !
    sequence 11
     match tloc
      site-list DC_1_OR_2
     !
     action accept
     !
    !
  default-action reject
 !
! The new data policy "_CORP_VPN_BLOCK_BAD_APPS" has been added
 data-policy _CORP_VPN_BLOCK_BAD_APPS
! This policy only applies to traffic in the specified VPN list
  vpn-list CORP_VPN
    sequence 1
     match
      app-list BLOCKED_APPS
     !
     action drop
     !
    !
  default-action accept

 lists
  app-list BLOCKED_APPS
   app youtube
  !
  prefix-list DEFAULT_ONLY
   ip-prefix 0.0.0.0/0
  !
  site-list ALL_BRANCHES
   site-id 300-599
  !
```

```
    site-list REMOTE_1
     site-id 300
     !
    site-list DC_1_OR_2
     site-id 100,200
     !
    vpn-list CORP_VPN
     vpn 10
    !
  !
! The new data policy has been applied to all of the sites referenced
! by the site-list "ALL_BRANCHES".
!
apply-policy
 site-list ALL_BRANCHES
  data-policy _CORP_VPN_BLOCK_BAD_APPS all
 !
 site-list REMOTE_1
  control-policy PERMIT_ONLY_DEFAULT out
  !
 !
```

As Example 5-6 shows, a single centralized policy can consist of many different component policies that can be applied to different subsets of sites in the **apply-policy** stanza to implement the intent of the administrator. The control policy **PERMIT_ONLY_DEFAULT** is only applied to site-id 300, and at the same time, the data policy **_CORP_VPN_ BLOCK_BAD_APPS** is applied to site-ids 300–599. In this way, a single site with the site-id 300 would have both the control and data policy applied, while at the same time sites with site-ids 301–599 would only have the data policy applied.

Centralized data policies will always be applied with a site list, a VPN list, and a direction. The direction is either configured as **from-tunnel**, **from-service**, or **all** (**from-tunnel** means WAN to LAN, and **from-service** means LAN to WAN). These policies can manipulate traffic that is both being received from the fabric and transmitted across the fabric. In Example 5-6, the data policy is configured with the **all** option, indicating that this policy is applied to traffic flowing in both directions. Chapter 7 discusses these options in further detail.

Application-Aware Routing policies will always be configured with a VPN list and a site list, but not with an explicitly configured directionality. As the purpose of an Application-Aware Routing policy is to select the specific tunnel in which the SD-WAN traffic should be forwarded (based on the real-time performance of the site-to-site tunnels), Application-Aware Routing policies can only be used when the traffic is destined across the fabric. The directionality of this policy is always fixed; it is not logical to configure an Application-Aware Routing policy for traffic that is already received across the Cisco SD-WAN fabric and being forwarded out to a local service-side VPN interface. Chapter 8 discusses this in further detail.

Each Cisco SD-WAN fabric can have only a single centralized policy that is active at any point in time. That single policy can have as many different component policies as necessary, and those component policies can apply to different sets of sites or VPNs in order to accomplish the desired business outcomes. In the case of Example 5-6, this complete centralized policy is the combined entirety of the named control and data policies, the lists that are referenced in those policies and the apply-policy stanza that specifies where the policies will be enforced. All of these elements *together* make up a single centralized policy and are indented under the "policy" statement in the very first line.

Activating a Centralized Policy

vManage is the single point of administration for the entire Cisco SD-WAN fabric. This is the place where all management, monitoring, configuration, and troubleshooting is done for the entirety of the solution. This includes the configuration of all policies. While this chapter has primarily dealt with the building blocks of policies with the CLI as an introduction, the following chapters will walk through many different examples of policy configuration and activation using the vManage NMS, which is how most enterprises choose to manage their environments.

Once a centralized policy is built in vManage, it is then activated. When a centralized policy is activated on vManage, vManage writes that policy in its entirety into the configuration of the vSmart controller. This configuration transaction is accomplished through NETCONF—the same mechanism that is used to configure the WAN Edge router configurations from vManage. As NETCONF is being used to modify the configuration of the vSmart controllers, it is typical for the application process to take several seconds. As this process modifies the configuration of the vSmarts, this also means that the policy changes are persistent. Should a vSmart controller reboot for any reason, when it re-initializes, it will have a copy of the last policy that was configured from vManage.

Typical production deployments will have two or more vSmarts, depending on redundancy and scale needs, and it is the responsibility of vManage to ensure that the policy configuration on all of the vSmart controllers remains synchronized. If, for whatever reason, the policy change is not applied successfully to all of the vSmart controllers, vManage will automatically roll back the policy change from all vSmart controllers.

Note   As activating a policy on vManage is actually manipulating the configuration of the vSmart itself, the vSmart controllers must be in "vManaged mode" and have a template applied from vManage. This allows vManage to have authoritative control of the vSmart's configuration. It does not matter whether the vSmarts are running CLI templates or feature templates, but a template must be applied. It is very common for production deployments to use CLI templates for this use case, as they are quick, simple, and do not require administration beyond the initial deployment. Note: This is different from how most production deployments configure both the vBond orchestrators and vManage; it is very common that there are no templates at all applied to vBond and vManage.

While all of the policies in the Cisco SD-WAN fabric are administered on vManage, different types of policies are enforced at different locations in the network. As Application-Aware Routing policies and data policies are manipulating the forwarding of traffic in the data plane (and these policies are enforced on the WAN Edge routers themselves), these policies need to be propagated all the way to the WAN Edge routers. In the Cisco SD-WAN solution, this is accomplished by configuring the policies on the vManage and activating the policies to the vSmart controllers. The vSmart controller then encodes the necessary parts of the policies into an OMP update and advertises these policies to the WAN Edge routers. The left column in Figure 5-7 illustrates this process.

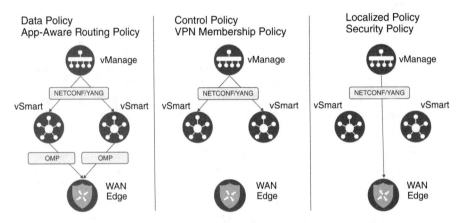

Figure 5-7 *Policy Administration, Activation, and Enforcement*

The architectural decision to encode centralized data policy updates in OMP, rather than to encode them into the configuration of the WAN Edge with NETCONF, has several important implications. Transmitting the centralized data policy as an OMP routing update allows for large-scale changes to be rolled out to the entire SD-WAN fabric very quickly rather than needing to make individual NETCONF configuration transactions on potentially hundreds or thousands of devices (which could take on the order of minutes to tens of minutes). Centralized data policy changes can be rolled out to the entirety of the fabric as quickly as any other routing update can be propagated and processed— typically, in a matter of seconds after the configuration is applied to the vSmarts. Additionally, as the policies are not stored in the configuration of the router, should the router reload for any reason, the policy configuration will be lost and upon re-initialization the router will have no effective policy. This is not considered a problem, as the WAN Edge router will need to establish control connections with the vSmart controllers in order to build fabric tunnels and forward traffic, and therefore will relearn the necessary policy information through OMP updates at that time.

As centralized control policies and VPN membership policies manipulate control plane updates, these policies are enforced on the vSmarts themselves. Fundamentally, these control policies are manipulating or restricting the advertisement of control plane information. As all control plane information flows through the vSmart controllers, enforcing control policies on the vSmart provides an elegant, simple, and scalable solution. There is no need for these policies to be advertised to the individual WAN Edge routers. Instead, the effects of these policies are seen in the routing updates that are propagated from the vSmarts to the WAN Edge routers. The center column of Figure 5-7 shows this relationship.

All localized policies, including traditional localized policies and security policies, are administered on the vManage and configured directly to the WAN Edge routers via device template configuration. In this way, localized policies have much more in common with feature templates than centralized policies. Localized policies and security policies do not directly interact with the vSmart controllers. The rightmost column of Figure 5-7 illustrates this relationship.

> **Note**   It is possible to manually configure policies directly onto the vSmart controllers rather than administer and activate them through vManage. While this is technically feasible, the vast majority of networks are not administered this way, and this model of administration is outside the scope of this book.

Packet Forwarding Order of Operations

As multiple types of policies can be applied to a given site and affect the forwarding of a single flow, it is important to understand the order in which these policies are applied and evaluated, and how they work together. First, as control policies do not directly affect the data plane, they are processed independently of data plane policies. Control policies instead impact the routing information that the data plane is built upon and, in this manner, they are able to impact the forwarding of traffic. As control policies filter, manipulate, summarize, or restrict the advertisement of a specific routing prefix or TLOC, a WAN Edge will have altered control plane information and will build its forwarding plane from this altered control plane information. Figure 5-8 shows the packet forwarding order of operations.

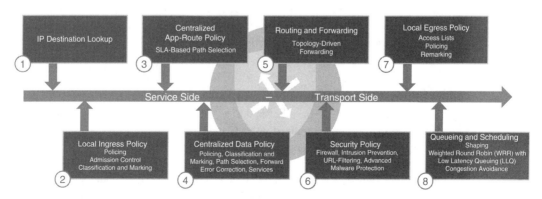

Figure 5-8 *Packet Forwarding Order of Operations*

The following steps are evaluated sequentially when forwarding a packet through a WAN Edge router:

1. **IP Destination Lookup:** The first step in the packet-forwarding process is to perform a routing lookup on the destination IP of the packet in the routing table. This information is then used to inform the rest of the forwarding decisions that are made as the packet is processed through the WAN Edge router.

2. **Ingress Interface ACL:** Localized policy can be used to create ACLs and tie them to interface templates. Interface ACLs can be used for packet filtering, policing, and QoS marking or remarking. If a packet is denied by the ingress ACL, it is dropped at this point and is not processed any further.

3. **Application-Aware Routing:** The Application-Aware Routing policy is evaluated after the forwarding decision has been made based on the routing table. It is important to note that an Application-Aware Routing policy can only make distinctions between equal paths in the routing table. If the routes for a destination's multiple next-hop addresses are not equal-cost paths in the routing table, then the Application-Aware Routing policy will have no effect, and the flow will follow the most preferred path based on the routing table. This will be explored further in Chapter 8.

4. **Centralized Data Policy:** The centralized data policy is evaluated after the Application-Aware Routing policy and is able to override the Application-Aware Routing forwarding decision.

5. **Routing and Forwarding:** Routing lookups are now performed to determine the correct output interfaces so that processing can be continued there.

6. **Security Policy:** If security policies are configured, they are processed in the following order: Firewall, Intrusion Prevention, URL-Filtering, and finally Advanced Malware Protection.

7. **Encapsulation and Encryption:** As packets are prepared to be forwarded across the fabric, the necessary VPN labels and tunnel encapsulations are performed.

8. **Egress Interface ACL:** As with ingress ACLs, local policy is able to create ACLs that are applied on egress as well. If traffic is denied or manipulated by the egress ACL, those changes will take effect before the packet is forwarded.

Summary

This chapter has discussed the basics of building Cisco SD-WAN policies. There are two main types of policies: centralized policies and localized policies. Policies are constructed from lists, which are used to identify groups of interest in both the control plane (such as prefix lists and site lists) as well as in the data plane (such as application lists and data prefix lists). Individual policies are structured sequences of **match** and **action** statements. These component policies are then assembled into a single centralized policy that is activated on the vSmart controller. The vSmart enforces the control policies and then encodes the necessary components of the data policies into OMP updates, which are advertised to the WAN Edge routers where they are enforced in the data plane.

Review All Key Topics

Review the most important topics in the chapter, noted with the Key Topic icon in the outer margin of the page. Table 5-1 lists these key topics and the page numbers on which each is found.

Table 5-1   *Key Topics*

Key Topic Element	Description	Page
Paragraph	Discussion of policies using first-match logic.	121
Paragraph	Discussion of the structure of centralized policies and that there can only be a single centralized policy that is active at one time.	125
Paragraph / Figure 5-7	Centralized data policies are administered on vManage, activated on vSmart, encoded into OMP, and enforced on WAN Edges.	126
Paragraph / Figure 5-7	Centralized control policies are administered on vManage, activated on vSmart, and enforced on vSmart.	126
Paragraph / Figure 5-7	Localized policies are administered on vManage and become part of the configuration on WAN Edges.	127

Define Key Terms

Define the following key terms from this chapter, and check your answers in the glossary:

Centralized policy, localized policy, control policy, data policy

Chapter Review Questions

1. Which of the following are types of Cisco SD-WAN policies? (Choose all that apply.)
    a. Traffic engineering policy
    b. URL-Filtering policy
    c. Application-Aware Routing policy
    d. Centralized data policy

2. Cisco SD-WAN policies use a "best match" (or most specific match) matching logic.

    a. True

    b. False

3. Which of the following are types of lists used in Cisco SD-WAN policy? (Choose all that apply.)

    a. Prefix-List

    b. SLA-Class

    c. Application List

    d. VPN-List

    e. TLOC-List

    f. Site List

4. A single list object can be used to match routes in the control plane and packets in the data plane.

    a. True

    b. False

5. Which of the following can only be configured as part of a local policy?

    a. Forwarding a specific type of traffic over a specific transport link

    b. Filtering specific routes from a BGP peer

    c. Dropping all YouTube traffic

    d. Forwarding voice calls over a link that has less than 150ms of latency

6. Which types of policies are applied to and enforced on the vSmart controller? (Choose all that apply.)

    a. VPN membership policies

    b. Topology (control) policies

    c. Zone-Based Firewall (ZBFW) policies

    d. Cflowd policies

7. Which types of policies are applied to and enforced on the WAN Edge router? (Choose all that apply.)

    a. Application-Aware Routing policies

    b. VPN membership policies

    c. Security policies

    d. Localized data policies

    e. Topology policies

8. Which types of policies are applied to the vSmarts and enforced on the WAN Edges?

    a. Application-Aware Routing policies

    b. VPN membership policies

    c. Security policies

    d. Localized data policies

    e. Topology policies

9. In a typical Cisco SD-WAN deployment, all policies are administered on which device?

   a. WAN Edge

   b. vSmart

   c. vBond

   d. vManage

   e. vPolicy

10. If a single flow matches sequences in both an Application-Aware Routing policy and a centralized data policy, the flow will be forwarded according to which policy?

    a. Application-Aware Routing policy

    b. Centralized data policy

Chapter 6

Centralized Control Policies

This chapter covers the following topics:

- **Centralized Control Policy Overview:** This section discusses the basics of centralized control policies and the directionality of policies when applied to a vSmart.

- **Use Case 1: Isolating Remote Branches from Each Other:** This section covers the process of building and applying a centralized control policy as well as how to limit the data plane tunnels that are built in the SD-WAN fabric.

- **Use Case 2: Enabling Branch-to-Branch Communication Through Data Centers:** This section covers the use of summarization and TLOC lists to enable sites that do not have direct data plane connectivity to still communicate.

- **Use Case 3: Traffic Engineering at Sites with Multiple Routers:** This section covers the use of the TLOC Preference attribute to manipulate how traffic flows into sites with more than one WAN Edge.

- **Use Case 4: Preferring Regional Data Centers for Internet Access:** This section covers the use of the OMP Route Preference attribute to perform traffic engineering on a per-prefix basis.

- **Use Case 5: Regional Mesh Networks:** This section discusses how to create subsets of the fabric that have a full mesh of data plane connectivity, even while the whole fabric does not.

- **Use Case 6: Enforcing Security Perimeters with Service Insertion:** This section covers the use of service insertion to be able to direct a flow from anywhere in the fabric to a local or remote service.

- **Use Case 7: Isolating Guest Users from the Corporate WAN:** This section covers the use VPN Membership policies to be able to restrict which VPNs can join the overlay fabric.

■ **Use Case 8: Creating Different Network Topologies per Segment:** This section covers the use of control policies to create multiple, arbitrary topologies that can be applied on a per-VPN basis.

■ **Use Case 9: Creating Extranets and Access to Shared Services:** This section covers the construction of extranets to enable connectivity with business partners, while still maximizing security posture.

Network administrators can use centralized control policies to manipulate the way traffic flows throughout the Cisco SD-WAN fabric. Fundamentally, centralized control policies are the mechanism through which the control plane information that is advertised by the Overlay Management Protocol (OMP) between the vSmart controllers and WAN Edge routers is manipulated and/or filtered. By manipulating or filtering this information in the control plane, network administrators can influence the way that end-user traffic is forwarded in the data plane in order to accomplish their business objectives. This chapter explores several common business-relevant use cases, the network designs necessary to achieve them, and the centralized control policies used to implement them.

Centralized Control Policy Overview

Throughout the next several chapters, where we examine policies in Cisco SD-WAN, we will be using the topology illustrated in Figure 6-1.

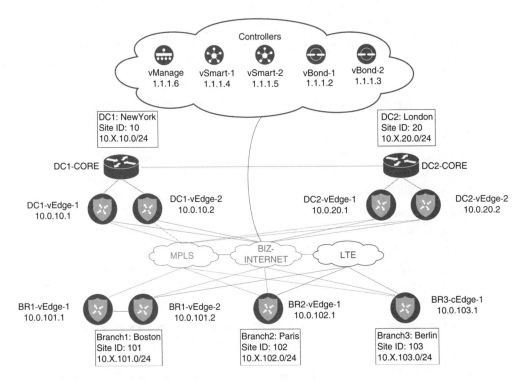

Figure 6-1 *Network Topology Overview*

This simple network topology features two different data centers (DCs) and three branch sites. Each data center has both an MPLS transport and an Internet transport. The branches, in addition to having an MPLS and Internet transport, also have an LTE transport. The hostnames, Site IDs, Router IDs, and network prefixes are also seen in the diagram. The service-side addressing in this network follows the 10.X.Y.0/24 structure, where X signifies the service-side VPN, and Y signifies the Site ID. For the first few use cases in this chapter, we will be focusing on VPN 1. Therefore, all of the service-side addressing will be in the 10.1.Y.0/24 addressing blocks. The SD-WAN controllers and their System IPs are also indicated in this diagram. This topology will allow us to explore different types of policies, how they interact with the SD-WAN fabric, and how network administrators can apply these policies to solve business problems.

As discussed in Chapter 5, "Introduction to Cisco SD-WAN Policies," each type of policy has a specific directionality to it. In the case of centralized control policies, policies can be applied in either the inbound or the outbound direction. This directionality is always from the perspective of the vSmart, as shown in Figure 6-2.

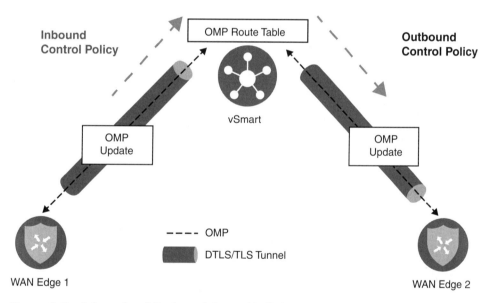

Figure 6-2 *Inbound and Outbound Control Policies*

Inbound policies are applied before the routes are processed through the best-path selection algorithm and before the routes are inserted into the OMP table on the vSmart. As such, any manipulation by inbound control policies will be evident in the vSmart best-path selection process and in turn evident in the OMP advertisements made to all of the other WAN Edge routers. Conversely, policies that are applied outbound are applied after the vSmart best-path selection process has been completed and are limited in scope to only those site IDs listed in the control policy application configuration. In this way, centralized control policies that are applied inbound tend to be much more global in nature, whereas outbound control policies can be much more limited and targeted in their scope and application.

In the following sections, we examine several different sets of business requirements and how network administrators can use centralized control policies to solve for these use cases. These use cases are meant to address common applications of centralized control policies as well as to provide an illustrative review of many of the building blocks of centralized control policies from which network administrators can build their own policies to accomplish their own objectives.

Use Case 1: Isolating Remote Branches from Each Other

The first use case we will be exploring is to turn the topology of the fabric from a full mesh into a hub-and-spoke design, with the data centers as hubs and the branch offices as spokes. Network designs like this are often used for several reasons: In many types of networks, particularly in retail and finance where security is a concern, there is little need to be able to communicate from one branch directly to another branch. As such, the structure of the network can be changed to reflect the desired traffic flow, and the business intent can be encoded directly into the SD-WAN fabric. Furthermore, if this is a large network consisting of hundreds or thousands of spokes, the devices deployed at the branch sites may not have the capacity to build tunnels to all of the other branch offices. In this way, the devices at the branch offices do not need to be sized to handle hundreds or thousands of IPsec tunnels.

As discussed in Chapter 3, "Control Plane and Data Plane Operations," the default state of the Cisco SD-WAN fabric with no policies applied is a full mesh. That is, every WAN Edge router builds an IPsec tunnel to every other router that it has reachability to. In our sample network, since we have the "restrict" attribute set on the tunnel interfaces with the MPLS color, tunnels from the MPLS interfaces will only be built to the other MPLS interfaces. By contrast, tunnels from Biz-Internet will be built to both Biz-Internet and LTE interfaces on other routers. Tunnels from the LTE color will be built to both the Biz-Internet and LTE interfaces on the other routers in the fabric. The result of this behavior (in this relatively simple network of only five sites and only eight routers) is the WAN Edge router at Branch 2 will build 27 different tunnels, as shown in the real-time output in Figure 6-3.

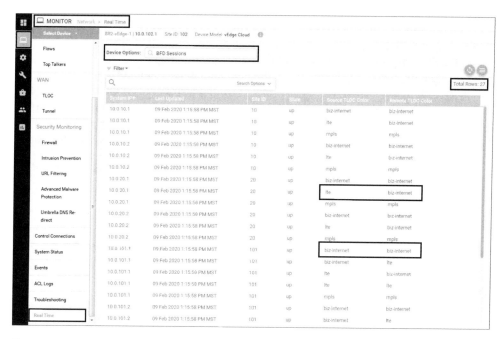

Figure 6-3 *BR2-vEdge1 Tunnels with No Control Policy Applied*

> **Note** The real-time output, as shown in Figure 6-3, is available in the vManage GUI by
> selecting **Monitor > Network > [***Device***]**. The **Monitor > Network** display can be used to
> track lots of information that administrators will find useful throughout the provisioning
> and operation of the SD-WAN fabric. The Real Time option can be found at the very bot-
> tom of the list of elements. Once the Real Time element is selected, the **Device Options**
> field at the top of the page can be used to query the device and display the output of
> practically any **show** command that would be used from the CLI interface. This feature is
> referred to as "Real Time" because it queries the device *in real time* and does not rely on
> cached data like many of the other elements in the Monitor section of vManage. For this
> reason, you might occasionally notice a slight delay, as vManage queries the device for the
> requested real-time output.

As discussed in Chapter 3, the process of building data plane tunnels is controlled by the
advertisement of Transport Locators (TLOCs). If a WAN Edge receives a TLOC from the
vSmart controller, it will attempt to build a data plane tunnel to that TLOC and establish
a Bidirectional Forwarding Detection (BFD) session across the tunnel. As such, monitoring BFD sessions, as shown in Figure 6-3, is a good way to understand if tunnels are trying to be formed and whether they were formed successfully. To change this behavior in

the data plane, you must filter which TLOCs are advertised from the vSmart to the WAN Edge routers.

If the BFD session is working as expected, and there is bidirectional data plane connectivity, the BFD session will be listed in the "Up" state. If the TLOC advertisement was received from the vSmart, but the data plane tunnel is unable to form correctly, the BFD session will be listed in the "Down" state. If the data plane tunnel does not appear in the list of BFD sessions, the WAN Edge is not attempting to build the data plane tunnel. This behavior is generally caused for one of two reasons: either the WAN Edge has not received the TLOC advertisement from the vSmart or the data plane tunnel is prohibited from being built by either the "restrict" or "tunnel-group" settings. Chapter 3 provides a deeper discussion of these settings.

The current state of the network can also be examined from the ways that traffic flows through the network. In Example 6-1, you can see that from Branch 2, the destination address 10.1.103.1 (which resides at Branch 3) is one hop away; that is, it is directly connected.

Example 6-1   *Tracing from BR2-vEdge1 to BR3-cEdge1*

```
Traceroute from BR2-vEdge1 to BR3-cEdge1:
! The traceroute is successful, and shows that the path is direct (1 hop)
BR2-vEdge-1# traceroute vpn 1 10.1.103.1
Traceroute  10.1.103.1 in VPN 1
traceroute to 10.1.103.1 (10.1.103.1), 30 hops max, 60 byte packets
 1  10.1.103.1 (10.1.103.1)  8.227 ms * *
!
! Traceroute from BR2-vEdge1 to DC1-vEdge1:
! The traceroute is successful; resources in the DC are also one hop away
BR2-vEdge-1# traceroute vpn 1 10.1.10.1
Traceroute  10.1.10.1 in VPN 1
traceroute to 10.1.10.1 (10.1.10.1), 30 hops max, 60 byte packets
 1  10.1.10.1 (10.1.10.1)  3.912 ms  5.534 ms  5.596 ms
BR2-vEdge-1#
```

In addition to the prefixes at Branch 3, Example 6-1 also shows that the prefixes in the data center are reachable in one hop. This is also reflected in the routing table, as shown with the real-time output, where the prefix 10.1.103.0/24 is reachable with a TLOC IP of 10.0.103.1 (the system IP of BR3-cEdge1, as shown in Figure 6-1) and prefix 10.1.10.0/30 is reachable with a TLOC IP of 10.0.10.1 (the system IP of DC1-vEdge1), as shown in Figure 6-4.

In order to implement the business intent to eliminate branch-to-branch communication and to reduce the number of tunnels that are established, a centralized policy can be created and applied so that the branches will only build tunnels with the data center WAN Edges. As each WAN Edge router will attempt to build tunnels to all of the TLOCs that it receives from the vSmart controller, such a policy is architected to restrict the TLOCs that are advertised to the branches to be only the TLOCs from the DCs (where the branches should still build their control connections). Figure 6-5 illustrates this process.

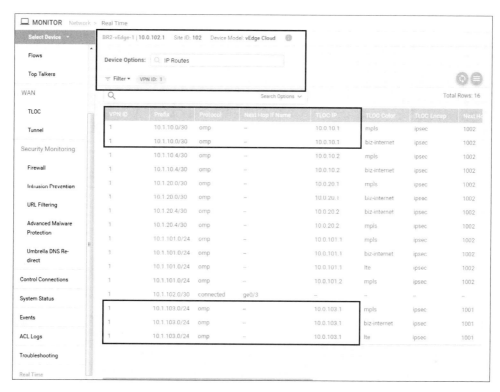

Figure 6-4 *Routing Table for VPN 1 on BR2-vEdge1 with No Centralized Policy Applied*

In Step 1 of Figure 6-5, all of the WAN Edge routers advertise their local TLOCs to the vSmart controllers. In Step 2, the vSmarts advertise all of the received TLOCs back to all of the WAN Edges. For the DC WAN Edge, this means that the router receives all of the TLOCs in the vSmart table, including a copy of its own TLOCs. For Branch 1 and Branch 2, an outbound control policy is applied that restricts the advertisement of the TLOCs to only T1 and T2, which were learned from the data center. Note that the advertisements the data center WAN Edge receives in Step 2 contains all of the TLOCs in the network {T1, T2, T3, T4, T5, T6}, which is different from the TLOCs received by the branches. The outbound control policy has limited the TLOCs that are advertised to the branches to only {T1, T2}, the TLOCs from the data center. The effect of this policy can be seen in Step 3, when the data plane tunnels are built: All of the WAN Edge routers will build data plane tunnels to all of the TLOCs that they have received from the vSmarts. For the data center WAN Edge, this means that tunnels will be built to T3, T4, T5, and T6, the TLOCs of the branch routers. For the branches, tunnels will only be built to T1 and T2, the data center. Note that there is no tunnel built from T3 to T5, or from T4 to T6 in Figure 6-5. Since the WAN Edge router at Branch 1 never received an advertisement for T5 and T6, it is unaware of those TLOCs and will not attempt to build those tunnels. Manipulating and restricting the advertised TLOCs, as shown in Figure 6-5, is the fundamental way to control which data plane tunnels are built in the SD-WAN fabric, and as such, the primary way that network administrators control the structure of the fabric.

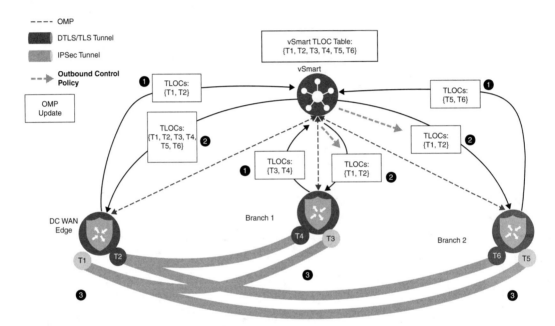

Figure 6-5 *Illustration of Control Policies Filter TLOCs*

Note For the first two policy examples in this chapter, screenshots of the process to build and modify the necessary policies will be provided. For brevity, the remaining policies in this chapter will be provided only with the CLI output. There is no difference in the effect of the policy if it is built with the GUI or with the CLI.

The first step in constructing such a policy would be to open the new Policy Wizard by clicking **Add Policy** from the **Configuration > Policies** screen in vManage, as shown in Figure 6-6.

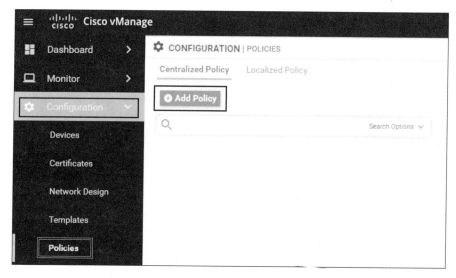

Figure 6-6   *Opening the New Policy Wizard*

From inside of the New Policy Wizard, the first option is to configure all of the criteria (Lists) that will be used within this policy. For this first use case, we will need to create two site lists: one that encompasses the site IDs of the data centers and a second that encompasses the site IDs of the branch offices. You can see these two lists in Figure 6-7. The ranges of site IDs configured in these lists reflect the ranges of site IDs identified in the network topology, as shown in Figure 6-1.

Figure 6-7   *Configuring Site Lists for Use in Centralized Policies*

After we click the **Next** button at the bottom of the Lists page, the wizard moves to the Configure Topology and VPN Membership page. From this page, click the **Add Topology** drop-down and select **Custom Control (Route & TLOC)** from the combo box, as shown in Figure 6-8.

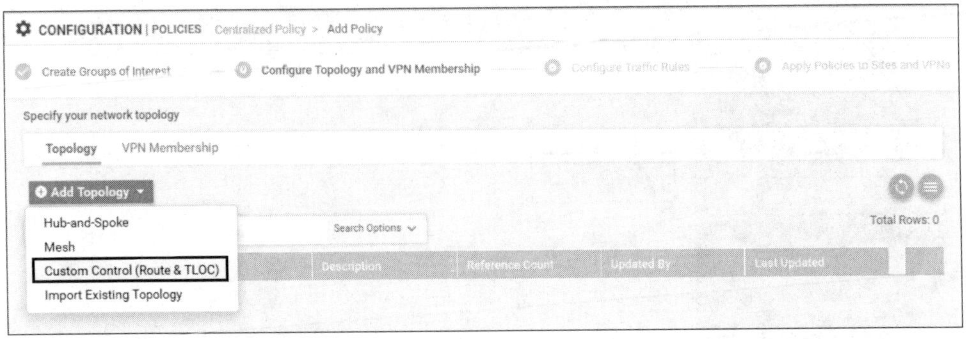

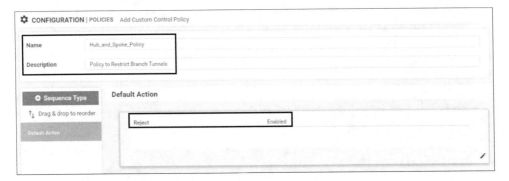

Figure 6-8 *Creating a Custom Control Policy*

> **Note** The vManage GUI includes wizards to build hub-and-spoke and mesh topologies, as can be seen in Figure 6-8. While some network administrators find these assisted workflows easier to use, this chapter will focus on custom control policies to better illustrate the construction of the policies and the principles behind their use.

The first pieces of configuration necessary for every control policy are the policy name and description, as shown in Figure 6-9.

Figure 6-9 *Setting the Default Action in the Control Policy*

It is also important to notice in Figure 6-9 the default action in custom route and TLOC policies: Reject. If an OMP route or a TLOC is not matched by any other sequence in the policy and explicitly permitted, it will not be advertised from the vSmart to the WAN Edge router.

Next, click the **Sequence Type** button and choose a TLOC sequence, as shown in Figure 6-10.

Next, create a new rule in the policy by selecting the **+ Sequence Rule** option. In this sequence, specify a match criteria of a site list and match on the list called "DCs," created previously. Lastly, specify the action **Accept** with no further actions and then **Save Match and Actions**, as shown in Figure 6-11.

Figure 6-10   *Adding a TLOC Sequence to a Centralized Control Policy*

Figure 6-11   *Creating a TLOC Sequence Rule to Accept the DC TLOCs*

This TLOC sequence rule, in combination with the default rule that rejects anything not explicitly permitted, will result in only the DC TLOCs (that is, only the TLOCs from sites specified in the site list "DCs") being advertised to the sites where this policy is applied. Now that the TLOCs from the branch sites have been implicitly filtered, the network will have a topology analogous to what was displayed in Figure 6-5, and data plane tunnels will not form between the branch sites. However, as shown in Figure 6-4, the OMP routes for all of the prefixes that exist at all of the branch sites will still be reflected to all of the other branch sites. Without having received the necessary TLOC advertisements, these

OMP routes will be unresolvable and unused, but bandwidth and compute resources will be wasted in transmitting these network updates.

Rather than continue to transmit routes that cannot be used, a better practice would be to filter out the routes from the branch sites in addition to the TLOCs. In order to accomplish this, select the **+ Sequence Type** button and choose **Route**, as shown in Figure 6-12.

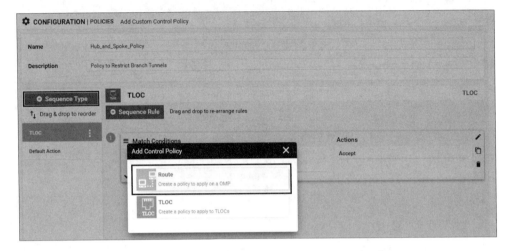

Figure 6-12 *Adding a Route Sequence to a Centralized Control Policy*

In a similar manner as was done for the TLOCs, the route sequence needs to be configured to match on the routes from the site list "DCs" and to accept them. No other sequences need to be configured at this time. You can see this configuration in Figure 6-13.

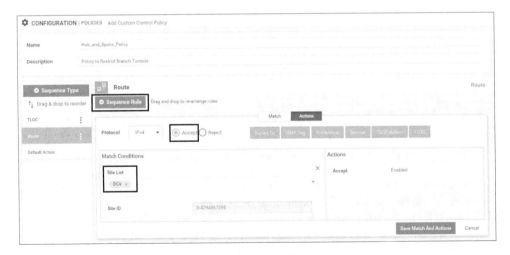

Figure 6-13 *Creating a Route Sequence Rule to Accept the DC Routes*

After the route sequence rule is saved by selecting the **Save Match and Actions** button, the entire policy can be saved by selecting the **Save Control Policy** button at the bottom. Once the control policy is saved, you can progress through the SD-WAN Policy Wizard by clicking **Next** through the Configure Topology and VPN Membership and Configure Traffic Rules screens, until arriving at the Apply Policies to Sites and VPNs screen, as shown in Figure 6-14. On this page, a name and description will need to be configured for the policy. Additionally, under the Topology tab, you must specify where and in what direction the recently created Hub_And_Spoke_Policy should be applied. In this example, the policy will be applied outbound to the branch offices.

Figure 6-14 *Adding Policies to Sites and VPNs*

> **Note** It is the author's recommendation to simply name the centralized policies with version numbers. In this case, the name "Centralized_Policy_v1" was used as the policy name. As discussed in Chapter 5, there will only ever be a single centralized policy that is active at any point in time. From an operational view, it is easy to copy the existing centralized policy, increment the policy number, and then use the Policy Description field to list the changes from the previous version of the policy. This allows for an archive of the policies to be created on vManage. This way, should there ever be a need to roll back a change in the network, the process is as simple as activating a previous version of the policy.

Once the site list the policy is to be applied to is saved by clicking the **Add** button, you can see the CLI of the entire policy by clicking the **Preview** button. Example 6-2 shows the full output of this policy.

Example 6-2   *Use Case 1: Complete Centralized Policy to Create Hub-and-Spoke Topology*

```
policy
 control-policy Hub_and_Spoke_Policy
   sequence 1
    match tloc
     site-list DCs
    !
    action accept
    !
   !
! The reference to the prefix list below was not configured,
! but instead was added automatically by vManage. The matching
! logic remains the same: Match all Routes.
   sequence 11
    match route
     site-list DCs
     prefix-list _AnyIpv4PrefixList
    !
    action accept
    !
   !
  default-action reject
 !
 lists
  site-list BranchOffices
   site-id 100-199
  !
! Only Routes and TLOCs that match this site list will be advertised
! by the policy above.
  site-list DCs
   site-id 10-50
  !
  prefix-list _AnyIpv4PrefixList
   ip-prefix 0.0.0.0/0 le 32
  !
 !
!
! The policy is applied in the outbound direction to the sites that
! match the site list "BranchOffices".
apply-policy
 site-list BranchOffices
  control-policy Hub_and_Spoke_Policy out
 !
!
```

The policy can then be saved by clicking the **Save Policy** button at the bottom of the page with the configuration preview. Once the policy is saved, it can be applied to the SD-WAN fabric by selecting the **Activate** option from the policy menu, as shown in Figure 6-15. As discussed in Chapter 5, the process of activating a policy is where vManage writes the policy into the configuration of the vSmarts.

Figure 6-15   *Activating a Centralized Policy*

Note   As configuring policy on a vSmart from vManage is actually manipulating the configuration of the vSmart itself, the vSmart controllers must be in "vManaged mode" and have a template applied from vManage. This allows vManage to have authoritative control of the vSmart configuration.

Once the policy has been applied, the effects of the policy can be seen using the same monitoring techniques observed before the policies were applied. From **Monitor > Network > BR2-vEdge1 > Real Time**, we can see the current list of BFD sessions, as shown in Figure 6-16. When Figure 6-16 is compared to the output observed before the policy was applied in Figure 6-3, we can see that the policy resulted in the number of BFD sessions (and IPsec tunnels) decreasing from 27 to 12. Furthermore, careful observation of Figure 6-16 shows that all of the remaining BFD sessions come from routers with System IPs of 10.0.10.1, 10.0.10.2, 10.0.20.1, or 10.0.20.2 (routers in Data Center 1 or Data Center 2). All of these tunnels are also established to sites with either Site ID 10 or 20.

Before the policy was applied, we saw in Example 6-1 that we were able to run a **traceroute** from Branch 2 to Branch 3 in one hop. Now, when the same **traceroute** is run from BR2-vEdge1, we can see that the network is unreachable, as signified by the "!N" response from the local host in output of the **traceroute** command in Example 6-3.

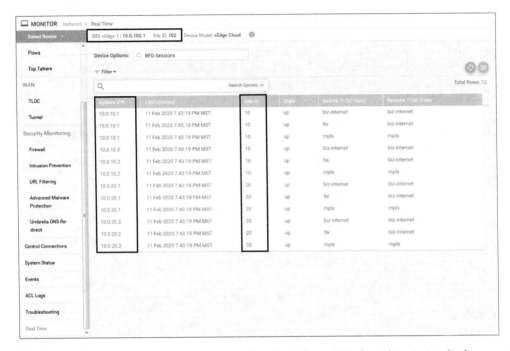

Figure 6-16   *BR2-vEdge1 BFD Sessions after the Hub-and-Spoke Policy Is Applied*

Example 6-3   *Network Unreachable When Tracing from BR2-vEdge1 to BR3-cEdge1*

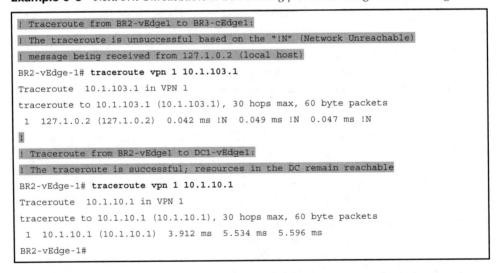

The second **traceroute** to the data center remains successful after the policy has been applied. This behavior can be further explained by examining the IP Routes table in the Real Time output of BR2-vEdge1. As shown in Figure 6-17, after filtering for routes only in VPN 1, we can see that the branch office no longer has a route for the 10.1.103.0/24 prefix, and therefore the network is listed as unreachable. The only routes that remain in the VPN 1 routing table on BR2-vEdge1 are the routes with prefixes 10.1.10.X and 10.1.20.X that originate in the data centers (Site ID 10 and Site ID 20), other than the locally connected route 10.1.102.0/30.

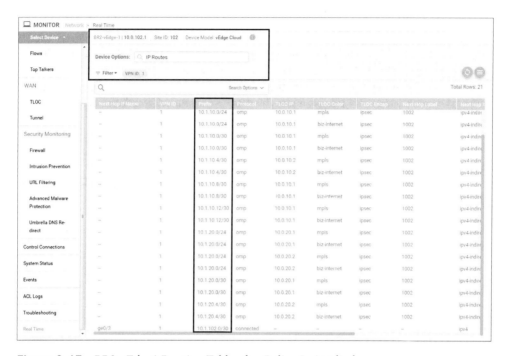

Figure 6-17 *BR2-vEdge1 Routing Table after Policy Is Applied*

Use Case 1 Review

In this use case, we used centralized control policies to prohibit site-to-site communication between branch locations. By encoding the business intent in this fashion into the structure of the SD-WAN fabric, we are able to harden the security posture of the network by preventing unintended east-west traffic flows between branch sites.

Use Case 2: Enabling Branch-to-Branch Communication Through Data Centers

In the previous use case, we saw how centralized control policies can be used to completely isolate branch sites from each other. While this may be appropriate for some use cases where no communication is preferred, there are also use cases where organizations may want to enable site-to-site communications indirectly by proxying traffic through a data center or some other regional hub. This can have the benefits of reducing complexity and scale of the control and data planes at the network edge, while still maintaining full connectivity for the occasional traffic flows that may need to exist between branch locations. There are two different potential solutions we will explore for this use case: summarization and TLOC lists.

Enabling Branch-to-Branch Communication with Summarization

Using summarization, in addition to the centralized control policy discussed in the previous use case, builds on the principle of longest-match routing and is not specific to any technology in Cisco SD-WAN. If a network summary, such as 10.0.0.0/8, or the default route (0.0.0.0/0) was advertised from the DC routers, then traffic would follow the path to the data center WAN Edge routers. The data center routers would then examine their routing tables and follow the route to the more specific match that was advertised from the branch sites. This is a common design mechanism that is used in hub-and-spoke WAN deployments such as with DMVPN Phase 1. Figure 6-18 illustrates this process.

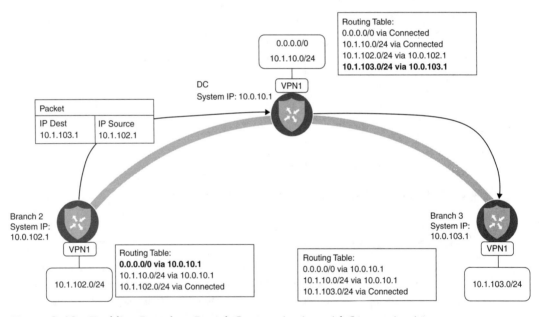

Figure 6-18   *Enabling Branch-to-Branch Communication with Summarization*

As shown in Figure 6-18, when the WAN Edge in Branch 2 does a routing lookup in order to forward a packet to the destination 10.1.103.1, the most specific match in the routing table is the default route. The default route is being advertised from the WAN Edge router in the data center with a System IP of 10.0.10.1, so the packet is forwarded to that router. When the packet arrives at the DC router, it performs a lookup on the destination 10.1.103.1 in its own routing table. As the DC router has not had any routes or TLOCs filtered, it has a more specific route to 10.1.103.1 via 10.0.103.1 and forwards the packet along to Branch 3. In this way, communication is able to be established through the data centers by injecting a default or summary route, without needing to change the SD-WAN fabric or any policies.

For this use case, we have injected a default route in Data Center 1 that is being adver-tised by DC1-vEdge1 and DC1-vEdge2. The specific method used to inject the default route is unimportant. If you have a default route in the routing protocol running in the data center, it can be advertised directly into OMP. Alternatively, you can configure a static default route and advertise that into OMP. Regardless of the method used, once the default route is advertised into OMP, it is then propagated to the branch offices, as seen in Figure 6-19.

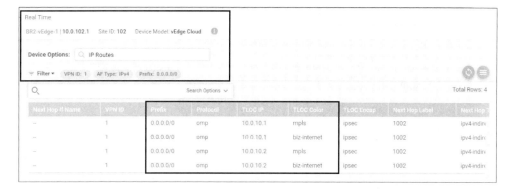

Figure 6-19 *BR2-vEdge1 Routing Table with Default Route*

With the default routes in place, traffic can now be forwarded to the data center and then to a different branch site, as shown in Example 6-4.

Example 6-4 *Tracing from BR2-vEdge1 to BR3-cEdge1 Is Successful with Two Hops*

```
! Traceroute from BR2-vEdge1 to BR3-cEdge1:
! The traceroute is successful, but requires two hops.  The intermediary hop,
! identified by the system ip of 10.1.10.1, is the DC1-vEdge1 router.
BR2-vEdge-1# traceroute vpn 1 10.1.103.1
Traceroute  10.1.103.1 in VPN 1
traceroute to 10.1.103.1 (10.1.103.1), 30 hops max, 60 byte packets
 1  10.1.10.1 (10.1.10.1)  104.163 ms  104.833 ms  105.491 ms
 2  10.1.103.1 (10.1.103.1)  125.817 ms * *
!
! Note that no changes have been made to the centralized control policy that was
! deployed for Use Case 1, and the number of data plane tunnels has not changed.
BR2-vEdge-1# show bfd summary
sessions-total      12
sessions-up         12
sessions-max        27
sessions-flap       15
poll-interval       10000
```

It is important to remember that no changes have been made to the centralized control policy applied for Use Case 1. The **show bfd summary** output in Example 6-4 indicates that there are still 12 BFD sessions (and 12 tunnels) established. This confirms that there are the same number of tunnels as displayed in Figure 6-16, and no new tunnels are established directly between the branches.

Enabling Branch-to-Branch Communication with TLOC Lists

Rather than injecting routes into the Cisco SD-WAN overlay to solve for the desired branch-to-branch communication pattern, it is possible to manipulate the routes that already exist in the overlay to accomplish the same objective.

As discussed in Chapter 3, a Transport Locator (TLOC) serves to uniquely identify the SD-WAN tunnel interfaces in the SD-WAN fabric and also serves as the next-hop attribute that all OMP and Network Service routes use within the overlay. When routes are advertised by the WAN Edge routers to the vSmart (and propagated by the vSmart to the other WAN Edge routers), each OMP route is advertised with the local TLOCs as the next-hop values, as illustrated in Figure 6-20. In Step 1, all of the WAN Edge routers advertise all of their locally reachable prefixes to the vSmart controller with OMP updates. In Step 2, the vSmart controller reflects all of these prefixes to all of the other WAN Edge routers, using TLOC values as the next-hop addresses.

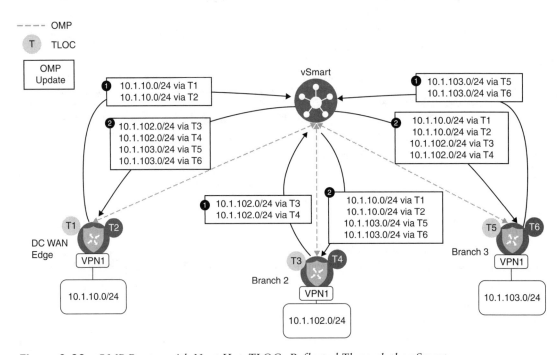

Figure 6-20   *OMP Routes with Next-Hop TLOCs Reflected Through the vSmart*

A centralized control policy can be used to manipulate the TLOC attributes that are advertised as part of the OMP routes and, in effect, change the "next-hop address" that the OMP routes recurse to. Through this process, centralized control policies can be a very powerful tool to perform traffic engineering across the SD-WAN fabric. At the same time, this process maintains simplicity by only having to apply the policy from a single location: the vSmart.

In order to permit the branch-to-branch communication via the data centers without the need for injecting a default route, the policy from Use Case 1 (as shown in Example 6-2) will be modified slightly so that instead of dropping the routes from the other branches, the routes are instead advertised with new TLOCs: the TLOCs of the DC1 WAN Edge routers. Figure 6-21 illustrates the effect of this policy for the routes advertised from Branch 3.

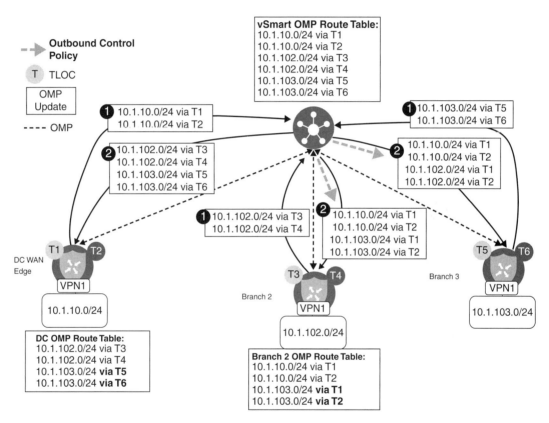

Figure 6-21 *Enabling Branch-to-Branch Communication with TLOC Manipulation*

Figure 6-21 builds on the route exchange process that was discussed in Figure 6-20. In the first step, all of the WAN Edge routers advertise their locally connected prefixes to the vSmart controllers. In the case of Branch 3, this means that the prefix 10.1.103.0/24 in VPN 1 is advertised via OMP as being reachable via TLOCs T5 and T6. The result of this advertisement can be seen in the vSmart OMP table. In Step 2, this advertisement is reflected to the data center routers as is; no manipulation is performed on the advertisement. However, when the route is reflected to the Branch 2 WAN Edge router, an outbound centralized control policy is applied and the TLOCs (next-hop addresses) are overwritten from the original values of T5 and T6 (the TLOCs of the WAN Edge at Branch 3) to TLOCs T1 and T2 (the TLOCs of the data center WAN Edge).

Note   Throughout the next several pages, the detailed process of modifying an existing centralized policy will be reviewed. This section will show the necessary steps in order to create a copy of the policies created in the previous use case and then modify them to meet the requirements of this use case. This same process can be used to construct the policies used throughout the other use cases in this book, but configuration steps in the vManage GUI will not be covered to the same degree of detail as was done in Use Case 1 and Use Case 2.

To begin to construct this policy in the vManage GUI, the first step is to create the new list element that will be needed: a TLOC list. To start this configuration, select the **Lists** item from the **Custom Options** menu on the **Configuration > Policies** window, as shown in Figure 6-22.

Figure 6-22   *Accessing the Lists Configuration for Centralized Policies*

To add a new TLOC list, select **TLOC** from the column of list types on the left and then click the **+New TLOC List** button, as shown in Figure 6-23.

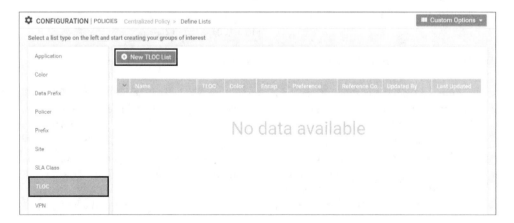

Figure 6-23   *Creating a New TLOC List*

In Figure 6-24, a TLOC list is configured with the name DC_TLOCs. There are a total of four TLOCs specified in the TLOC list: the mpls and biz-internet TLOCs on both DC1-vEdge1 and DC1-vEdge2. Recall from Chapter 3 that each TLOC is a unique combination of the System IP, the color, and the encapsulation. In addition to specifying these three required values, an optional argument of preference can be used to specify different TLOC preference values. This optional attribute was not used in this example and will be discussed in later use cases. Once the list is configured, it can be saved and closed by clicking the **Save** button.

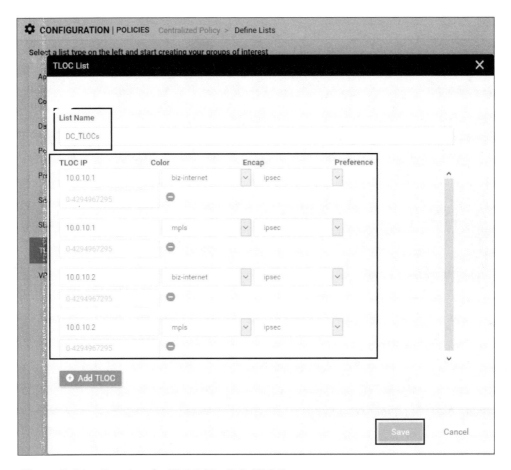

Figure 6-24   *Creating the TLOC List DC_TLOCs*

The next step in the configuration process is to create the necessary centralized control policy to use the TLOC list. In order to do this, select the **Topology** option from the **Custom Options** menu in the upper-left corner, as shown in Figure 6-25.

Figure 6-25   *Selecting Topology from the Custom Options Menu*

In order to copy the existing policy that was created in Use Case 1 so that it can be modified, select the … menu next to the policy and click **Copy**, as shown in Figure 6-26.

Figure 6-26   *Creating a Copy of an Existing Centralized Control Policy*

Every policy is required to be configured with a name and a description. The name and the description for the newly copied policy are shown in Figure 6-27. In this case, the new centralized control policy is named Hub_and_Spoke_TLOC_Lists.

Now that the new copy of centralized control policy has been created from the original policy in Use Case 1, the policy can be edited by selecting the **Edit** option from the … menu, as shown in Figure 6-28.

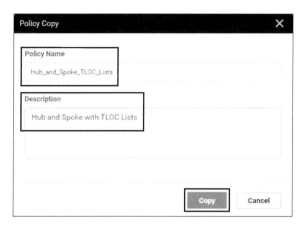

Figure 6-27   *Providing a Name and a Description for the Newly Copied Policy*

Figure 6-28   *Editing the Newly Copied Centralized Control Policy*

This policy needs to be altered such that the routes that are originating from the branch sites are rewritten to resolve to the new DC_TLOCs list that was previously created, as shown in Figure 6-29. In order to accomplish this, select the existing **Route** sequence type on the far left that is highlighted in green in the GUI. Then, click the **+ Sequence Rule** to add a new sequence rule. In this sequence rule, the matching criteria is configured as the BranchOffices site list that was created in the previous use case by clicking the **Match** sub-tab, selecting the **Site** criterion, and then adding the necessary site list (not pictured). Once the matching criteria are specified, select the **Actions** tab at the top of the sequence rule and select the **Accept** radio button. Once the routes are accepted, the **TLOC** action can now be selected and the previously created TLOC list **DC_TLOCs** can be specified. Once all of the configuration is completed, select the blue **Save Match and Actions** button at the bottom of the sequence rule.

Figure 6-29 *Creating a New Sequence to Manipulate Routes Advertised from Branch Sites*

The completed policy with both the existing route sequence rule from the previous use case and the newly created route sequence rule can be seen in Figure 6-30. In summary, the first sequence rule of this policy will match all of the routes being advertised from the DCs and forward them on without any modifications. The second sequence will match all of the routes being advertised from other branches and change their TLOCs (or next-hop attributes) to be the TLOCs of the data centers. The completed policy is saved by selecting the blue **Save Control Policy** button at the bottom.

Now that the centralized control policy has been created, it needs to be imported into a centralized policy. To do this, return back to the main Centralized Policy Configuration screen by clicking on **Centralized Policy** in the breadcrumb trail across the top of the screen, as shown in Figure 6-31.

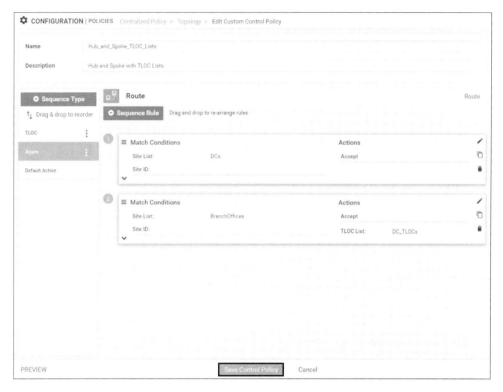

Figure 6-30 *Saving the Centralized Control Policy with Two Route Sequences*

Figure 6-31 *Navigating Back to the Centralized Policy Configuration Screen Using the Breadcrumb Trail*

The next step in the configuration process is to create a copy of the centralized policy that was created in Use Case 1, which will then be modified. As shown in Figure 6-32, this is done by selecting the ... menu and selecting the **Copy** option.

Figure 6-32   *Creating a Copy of a Centralized Policy Before Starting Modifications*

In order to copy the policy, a name and description must be supplied, as shown in Figure 6-33. Once these values are supplied, click the **Copy** button to complete the process.

Figure 6-33   *Configuring a Name and Description for the Copied Centralized Policy*

Figures 6-32 and 6-33 complete the process of copying the centralized policy. This process for copying the centralized policy is the analogue of the steps taken in Figures 6-26 and 6-27 for copying the centralized control policy. In both cases, it would have been possible to modify the existing policies rather than copy them and modify the copies. This process, as illustrated, is considered a best practice, helps to avoid inadvertently applying configuration to the network, and aids in quickly rolling back any configuration changes should the need arise.

Now that Centralized_Policy_v2 has been created, it can be modified to use the new control policy with the TLOC list by clicking the **Edit** option from the ... menu, as shown in Figure 6-34.

Figure 6-34   *Editing a Centralized Policy*

In order to modify this centralized policy for Use Case 2, several changes will need to be made. The centralized control policy created in Use Case 1 will need to be detached from this policy, and the new centralized control policy that was created in Figures 6-26 through 6-30 will need to be imported into this centralized policy. Finally, that new policy will have to be applied to the branch sites. In order to begin with detaching the old centralized control policy, click on the **Topology** tab at the top of the window, as shown in Figure 6-35. On the Topology tab, the Topology sub-tab is already selected and the centralized control policies that are referenced by this centralized policy are listed. Note that there is also a VPN Membership sub-tab that will be used in later use cases. Select the **Detach** option from the ... menu on the **Hub_and_Spoke_Policy** in order to detach this control policy from Use Case 1.

Next, the newly created centralized control policy will need to be attached to this policy by clicking the **+ Add Topology** button and then selecting the **Import Existing Topology** option, as shown in Figure 6-36.

Figure 6-35   *Detaching an Unnecessary Centralized Control Policy from a Centralized Policy*

Figure 6-36   *Importing an Existing Control Policy into a Centralized Policy*

With the Import Existing Topology dialog box, select the radio button for **Custom Control (Route and TLOC)** under **Policy Type** and then select the name of the new centralized control policy **Hub_and_Spoke_TLOC_Lists** from the **Policy** drop-down. Complete the process by clicking the blue **Import** button, as shown in Figure 6-37.

Figure 6-37   *Selecting the Existing Control Policy to Import into a Centralized Policy*

Now that the new centralized control policy has been imported into the centralized policy, the last part of the configuration process is to specify where this policy should be applied. To start this process, move back to the **Policy Application** page by clicking that tab at the top of the window. The Topology sub-tab is selected by default and lists all of the control policies in this centralized policy. The other sub-tabs will be used in later chapters with Application-Aware Routing and centralized data policies.

Under the Hub_and_Spoke_TLOC_Lists policy, select the blue **+ New Site List** button in order to specify the site lists that this policy should be applied to. Add the **BranchOffices** site list to the **Outbound Site List** field. The final step in saving the policy application configuration is to click the **Add** button on the right side and then click the **Save Policy Changes** button at the bottom, as shown in Figure 6-38.

The new centralized control policy has now been saved and can be activated by selecting the **Activate** option from the ... menu, as shown in Figure 6-39. There is no need to deactivate Centralized_Policy_v1 before the new policy is activated. As there can only be a single centralized policy that is active at any point in time, activating the new policy automatically deactivates any other policy.

Figure 6-38 *Configuring the Policy Application for the Imported Control Policy in a Centralized Policy*

Figure 6-39 *Activating a Centralized Policy*

The full CLI configuration of the policy is also visible by selecting the **Preview** option from the ... menu in Figure 6-39. The output of the policy preview displayed in Example 6-5 shows the complete centralized policy used to implement the objectives of this use case.

Example 6-5   *Use Case 2: Hub-and-Spoke Policy with TLOC Lists*

```
! Much of the centralized policy is unchanged from Example 6-2.
! The relevant changes in sequence 21 and the lists are highlighted below.
policy
 control-policy Hub_and_Spoke_TLOC_Lists
    sequence 1
     match tloc
      site-list DCs
     !
     action accept
     !
    !
    sequence 11
     match route
      site-list DCs
      prefix-list _AnyIpv4PrefixList
     !
     action accept
     !
    !
! The new sequence 21 has been added to permit the routes that are
! advertised from the branches, and advertise them with new TLOCs that are
! specified by the "DC_TLOCs" argument to the tloc-list command.
    sequence 21
     match route
      site-list BranchOffices
      prefix-list _AnyIpv4PrefixList
     !
     action accept
      set
       tloc-list DC_TLOCs
      !
     !
    !
 default-action reject
 !
 lists
```

```
   site-list BranchOffices
    site-id 100-199
    !
   site-list DCs
    site-id 10-50
    !
! A new list called "DC_TLOCs" is used to specify which TLOCs should be
! advertised as the next hop addresses of the routes.
   tloc-list DC_TLOCs
    tloc 10.0.10.1 color mpls encap ipsec
    tloc 10.0.10.1 color biz-internet encap ipsec
    tloc 10.0.10.2 color mpls encap ipsec
    tloc 10.0.10.2 color biz-internet encap ipsec
    !
   prefix-list _AnyIpv4PrefixList
    ip-prefix 0.0.0.0/0 le 32
    !
   !
  !
apply-policy
 site-list BranchOffices
  control-policy Hub_and_Spoke_TLOC_Lists out
  !
 !
```

Example 6-5 shows the command line configuration for the TLOC list that was configured in Figure 6-24. The TLOC list is established with the command **tloc-list** {*list-name*}. Once the list is created, each TLOC much be specified individually with the following syntax:

tloc {*system-ip*} **color** {*color*} **encap** {**ipsec**|**gre**} [**preference** *preference*] [**weight** *weight*]

These configuration commands reflect the configuration that was performed in vManage in Figure 6-24. The TLOC list is then referenced in Sequence 21 of the control policy to overwrite the existing TLOC attributes that would have been advertised with the OMP routes from the branch sites. Lastly, the final stanza in Example 6-5 shows that the policy is applied to the site list BranchOffices in the outbound (**out**) direction.

With this new centralized policy applied, we can see the effect by looking at the routing table, as shown in Figure 6-40. In the IP routing table, we can see that we now have four different paths to the prefix 10.1.103.0/24. Careful inspection of those advertisements reveals that the TLOC IP address is not 10.0.103.1 as it was in Figure 6-4 when there was no control policy applied. Instead, it is now listed as 10.0.10.1 and 10.0.10.2, the TLOC IPs of the WAN Edge routers in DC1, as specified in the TLOC list.

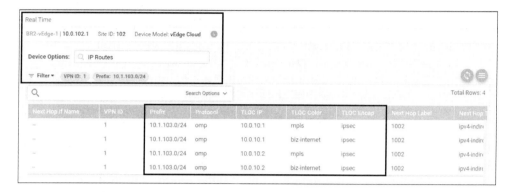

Figure 6-40 *Routing Table on BR2-vEdge1*

It is also important to consider what effect the policy had on the routes that have been advertised to the data center. We can examine the IP routes output from the Real Time view, as shown in Figure 6-41, and see that the routes are received by the DC1-vEdge1 router with all of the original TLOC advertisements.

Real Time

DC1-vEdge-1 | **10.0.10.1**   Site ID: 10   Device Model: **vEdge Cloud**

Device Options: IP Routes

Filter ▼   VPN ID: 1

Total Rows: 22

Next Hop If Name	VPN ID	Prefix	Protocol	TLOC IP	TLOC Color	TLOC Encap	Next Hop Label	Next Hop
ge0/4	1	10.1.10.8/30	connected	--	--	--	--	ipv4
ge0/5	1	10.1.10.12/30	connected	--	--	--	--	ipv4
--	1	10.1.20.0/24	omp	10.0.20.1	mpls	ipsec	1002	ipv4-indire
--	1	10.1.20.0/24	omp	10.0.20.1	biz-internet	ipsec	1002	ipv4-indire
--	1	10.1.20.0/24	omp	10.0.20.2	mpls	ipsec	1002	ipv4-indire
--	1	10.1.20.0/24	omp	10.0.20.2	biz-internet	ipsec	1002	ipv4-indire
--	1	10.1.20.0/30	omp	10.0.20.1	mpls	ipsec	1002	ipv4-indire
--	1	10.1.20.0/30	omp	10.0.20.1	biz-internet	ipsec	1002	ipv4-indire
--	1	10.1.20.4/30	omp	10.0.20.2	mpls	ipsec	1002	ipv4-indire
--	1	10.1.20.4/30	omp	10.0.20.2	biz-internet	ipsec	1002	ipv4-indire
--	1	10.1.101.0/24	omp	10.0.101.1	mpls	ipsec	1002	ipv4-indire
--	1	10.1.101.0/24	omp	10.0.101.1	biz-internet	ipsec	1002	ipv4-indire
--	1	10.1.101.0/24	omp	10.0.101.1	lte	ipsec	1002	ipv4-indire
--	1	10.1.102.0/30	omp	10.0.102.1	mpls	ipsec	1002	ipv4-indire
--	1	10.1.102.0/30	omp	10.0.102.1	biz-internet	ipsec	1002	ipv4-indire
--	1	10.1.102.0/30	omp	10.0.102.1	lte	ipsec	1002	ipv4-indire
--	1	10.1.103.0/24	omp	10.0.103.1	mpls	ipsec	1001	ipv4-indire
--	1	10.1.103.0/24	omp	10.0.103.1	biz-internet	ipsec	1001	ipv4-indire
--	1	10.1.103.0/24	omp	10.0.103.1	lte	ipsec	1001	ipv4-indire

Figure 6-41 *Routing Table on DC1-vEdge1*

As shown in Figure 6-41, the data center routing table entries for the prefixes from the branches are specified with the original TLOC IPs as the next-hop values. When Figure 6-41 is compared to Figure 6-40, it is clear that there are different TLOC IPs, or next-hop attributes, that are advertised to the branch WAN Edge than are advertised to the data center WAN Edge. This is expected because the route manipulation is happening *outbound* to the WAN Edges covered under the BranchOffices site list. There is no manipulation happening on the OMP advertisements being sent to the data center WAN Edge routers.

Furthermore, a **traceroute** from the Branch 2 WAN Edge router is able to confirm that the data plane is working as expected, as seen in Example 6-6.

Example 6-6 *BR2-vEdge1 Is Able to Access the Prefixes in Another Branch by Transiting the Data Center*

```
! BR2-vEdge1 is able to reach the destination 10.1.103.1, but the path requires
! two hops, and must transit through the DC WAN Edge Routers (10.1.10.1).
BR2-vEdge-1# traceroute vpn 1 10.1.103.1
Traceroute  10.1.103.1 in VPN 1
traceroute to 10.1.103.1 (10.1.103.1), 30 hops max, 60 byte packets
 1  10.1.10.1 (10.1.10.1)  3.780 ms  5.017 ms  5.265 ms
 2  10.1.103.1 (10.1.103.1)  15.704 ms * *
BR2-vEdge-1#
```

Use Case 2 Review

In this use case, we explored two different mechanisms to permit branch-to-branch communication in an SD-WAN fabric where TLOCs had been filtered to prohibit the establishment of direct branch-to-branch data plane tunnels. In the first instance, summary prefixes were advertised from the data center in order to draw branch-to-branch traffic, for which the branch routers did not have more specific routes, to the data centers. The data centers, in turn, could then use their more specific routing information to forward the traffic on to its final destination.

In the second example, the construct of a TLOC list was introduced. Using the **set tloc-list** action in the centralized control policy, the OMP routes were manipulated so that the prefixes from remote branches were advertised with the TLOCs of the data centers. Since the WAN Edge routers had already received the DC TLOC advertisements and had built tunnels to the DC WAN Edge routers, the OMP routes with these modified next-hop addresses could be used to forward traffic.

Note TLOC lists are an incredibly powerful tool to create flexible policies in order to implement traffic engineering and meet the objectives of the network administrator. At the same time, "with great power comes great responsibility." Improper application of TLOC lists can cause forwarding behaviors that were unintended and unexpected. Lastly, TLOC lists require a static definition in the centralized control policy and are not updated automatically in the same manner as traditional OMP routing updates. For example, if (years after implementing this policy) an additional transport link is added to the data center and an additional tunnel interface is added to DC1-vEdge1 and DC1-vEdge2, the TLOC list used for this traffic engineering policy would not change automatically. The network administrator would need to remember to update the TLOC list if using all three transport networks is the desired behavior. In a more extreme example, if the WAN Edge routers at DC1 were to be assigned new System IP addresses, the addresses in the TLOC list would not automatically be updated. Traffic flows from branch to branch would then fail, even when the traffic flows from branch to DC would succeed.

Therefore, it is the authors' guidance to use TLOC lists only when they are the only tool able to accomplish the desired outcome. When considering the objective in this use case— that is, enabling branch-to-branch communication without building branch-to-branch tunnels—we would strongly recommend the use of network summarization rather than the TLOC list method.

Use Case 3: Traffic Engineering at Sites with Multiple Routers

Currently in the sample network, three different sites are deployed with redundant routers: Data Center 1, Data Center 2, and Branch 1. The default behavior when forwarding traffic across the fabric is to load-share across all equal paths, and in the case of these three sites, that could mean load-sharing across all of the paths from both routers, as shown in Figure 6-42.

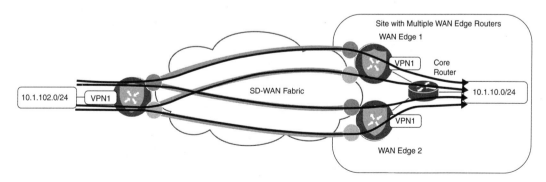

Figure 6-42 *Four Paths to 10.1.10.0/24*

In Figure 6-42, traffic that is destined to the prefix 10.1.10.0/24 may take any of the four established tunnels across the SD-WAN fabric. However, certain issues can arise if a device outside of the SD-WAN fabric, such as the core router in Figure 6-43, forwards the return flow across a different WAN Edge node other than the router on which the original flow was received. As the SD-WAN fabric itself is stateless, there is no inherent problem with using multiple routers for flows to and from a specific destination. However, some advanced data plane services, such as Deep Packet Inspection or the embedded SD-WAN Security feature set, require the ability to see both sides of a traffic flow in order to provide optimal application layer services.

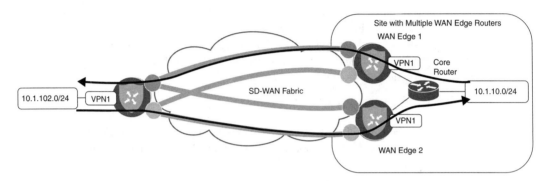

Figure 6-43   *Multipathing on the Fabric May Use Multiple WAN Edge Routers for a Single Flow*

In order to ensure that both halves of a flow are transiting the same WAN Edge router at a given site, it is common to configure the fabric such that all of the traffic traverses one of the routers in steady state, and the other router is not actively passing traffic until a failure occurs.

Note   There are two different pieces in order to complete this configuration: how traffic is forwarded across the SD-WAN fabric to the WAN Edges, and how traffic is forwarded back from the LAN switches to the WAN Edges. Chapter 5 discussed these separate and distinct policy domains.

This use case is going to focus on manipulating the SD-WAN fabric to prefer a single WAN Edge router when traffic is coming in from the fabric. The corresponding configuration for preferring a single WAN Edge router from the LAN side is discussed in detail in Chapter 9, "Localized Policies."

As discussed in Chapter 3, the Preference attribute of both TLOCs and OMP routes is evaluated in the OMP best-path selection process. Preference can therefore be altered to manipulate the OMP path selection. Like many things in networking, there is more than one way to accomplish any given objective. To that end, this use case will explore two different methods for manipulating the TLOC Preference values in order to complete this traffic engineering use case. In the following sections, the manipulations at the data

centers will be completed with a centralized control policy, and changes at Branch 1 will
be made in the WAN Edge configurations locally.

Setting TLOC Preference with Centralized Policy

With the existing policy from Use Case 2, as shown in Example 6-5, both DC1-vEdge1
and DC1-vEdge2 are advertising equal-cost paths to the 10.1.10.0/24 prefix in DC1, as
shown in Figure 6-44.

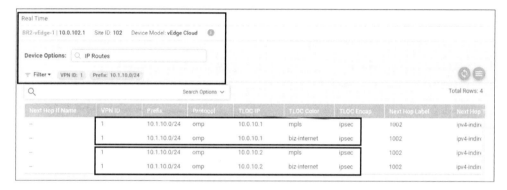

Figure 6-44   *Four Paths to 10.1.10.0/24 Transiting Two Different WAN Edge Routers*

There are a total of four equal-cost paths for the prefix 10.1.10.0/24: two from DC1-
vEdge1 and two from DC1-vEdge2. Each WAN Edge is advertising a path with a color of
MPLS and a color of Biz-Internet.

In the previous use cases, we have explored using centralized control policies applied in
the outbound direction in order to filter and manipulate routes advertised from vSmart.
As the outbound manipulation does not affect the OMP routes and TLOCs in the
vSmart's own tables, they can be more limited in scope, making it easy to apply different
changes in the advertisements to different sites. This was seen in the previous use case
when the TLOC values for certain OMP routes from the branches were overwritten when
advertised to some sites (branches) but not other sites (data centers). Conversely, when
the intent is to make a global change to OMP routes or TLOCs, it is often more appropriate to use an inbound centralized control policy. Inbound centralized control policies
make manipulations before the vSmart best-path selection algorithm is applied and before
the routes are inserted into the vSmart table. The manipulations made by inbound control
policies are apparent in the advertisements to all other OMP peers unless overwritten by
an additional outbound control policy.

As the intention with this use case is to have all of the routers prefer to send their traffic
to vEdge1 over vEdge2 in the data centers, we will use an inbound centralized policy to
achieve this global change. The necessary changes to the centralized control policy to
achieve this objective are shown in Example 6-7.

Note　Parts of the policy in Example 6-7 that are either irrelevant to this use case or are unchanged from the previous use case are omitted for clarity and brevity. The full text of the centralized policy that implements all of the use cases discussed in this chapter can be found in Example 6-24.

Example 6-7　*Use Case 3: Centralized Policy Setting TLOC Preference*

```
policy
 control-policy Hub_and_Spoke_TLOC_Lists
 ! <<<No changes made to this policy from Example 6-5, omitted for brevity>>>
 !
 ! A new control policy is created to set the TLOC preference values
 control-policy Set_DC_TLOC_Preference
    sequence 1
     match tloc
      originator 10.0.10.1
     !
     action accept
      set
       preference 500
      !
     !
    !
    sequence 11
     match tloc
      originator 10.0.10.2
     !
     action accept
      set
       preference 400
      !
     !
    !
    sequence 21
     match tloc
      originator 10.0.20.1
     !
     action accept
      set
       preference 500
      !
     !
```

```
    !
    sequence 31
     match tloc
      originator 10.0.20.2
      !
     action accept
      set
       preference 400
       !
      !
     !
  default-action accept
  !
 lists
 ! <<<No changes made to the lists from Example 6-5, omitted for brevity>>>
  !
 !
 ! The apply-policy statement has been modified to reflect that the new policy
 ! should be applied inbound on advertisements received from the datacenters
apply-policy
 site-list DCs
  control-policy Set_DC_TLOC_Preference in
  !
 ! The existing policy for the branches remains unchanged
 site-list BranchOffices
  control-policy Hub_and_Spoke_TLOC_Lists out
  !
 !
```

The new policy in Example 6-7 introduces a new control policy to add preference values
to the TLOCs that are being advertised from WAN Edge routers in the data centers. In
Sequence 1, a new matching criterion is configured: originator. The originator syntax is
originator {*originator-ip*}, where *originator-ip* is the System IP of the WAN Edge you
are looking to match against. In this particular policy example, as the objective is to set
different values for WAN Edges at the same site ID, matching with site lists would be
ineffective. Once the TLOCs have been matched, the desired preference value is specified in the action statement with the syntax **preference** {*value*}. The acceptable range for
Preference values is 0 through 4294967295 ($2^{32} - 1$). In Example 6-7, the Preference values of 500 and 400 are used.

You can see the effect of this policy in Figure 6-45. The output in this figure is an
updated display of the same output from Figure 6-44 that was taken after the policy in
Example 6-7 has been applied to the SD-WAN network. In this output, only two paths

have been installed in the routing table on BR2-vEdge1: the MPLS path and the Biz-Internet path from 10.0.10.1, DC1-vEdge1.

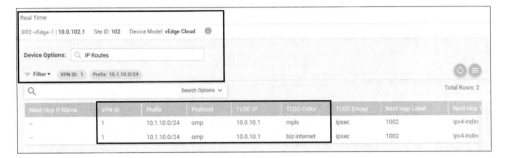

Figure 6-45   *Two Paths to 10.1.10.0/24, Both from 10.0.10.1*

The output in Figure 6-45 represents the routes that have been installed into the routing table for VPN1 on BR2-vEdge1, but this output is not the complete record of all of the routes that OMP has sent to the WAN Edge. In order to see all of the routes that have been sent from the vSmart, we will use the output of OMP Received Routes from the Real Time tab, as shown in Figure 6-46. This figure shows all of the routes that have been received from OMP peers in a similar fashion to how the outputs of the Cisco IOS command **show ip bgp** would display all of the routes received from BGP neighbors (even if they are not the best BGP routes or actually installed in the routing table).

> **Note**   In Figure 6-46, in the Search Options field, there is a search for "1.1.1.4," which is the System IP of vSmart-1. This search has the functional effect of removing all of the duplicate advertisements that would have been received from vSmart-2 (System-IP 1.1.1.5), making it easier for network administrators to understand the table. As the same policy should always be applied to all of the vSmarts, the same route advertisements should come from both vSmarts, and it is safe to filter one set of them from this view.

Last Updated	VPN ID	Prefix	From Peer	Status	Attribute Type	Tloc IP	Tloc Color	Tloc E
13 Feb 2020 ...	1	10.1.10.0/24	1.1.1.4	C I R	installed	10.0.10.1	mpls	ipsec
13 Feb 2020 ...	–	–	1.1.1.4	C I R	installed	10.0.10.1	biz-internet	ipsec
13 Feb 2020 ...	–	–	1.1.1.4	R	installed	10.0.10.2	mpls	ipsec
13 Feb 2020 ...	–	–	1.1.1.4	R	installed	10.0.10.2	biz-internet	ipsec

Figure 6-46   *OMP Route Table on BR2-vEdge1 Showing Four Paths to 10.1.10.0/24*

It is clear from the OMP table that the WAN Edge is still receiving the OMP route advertisements from DC1-vEdge2. These advertisements are the third and fourth entries in the table, with a TLOC IP of 10.0.10.2. The Status column for these routes displays "R," while the Status column for OMP routes from 10.0.10.1 (the first and second rows) is displayed with a status of "CIR." Unfortunately, the key for these status codes does not display in the vManage GUI in this version of software, but the key can be found in the output of **show omp routes** from the CLI, as shown in Example 6-8.

Example 6-8 *OMP Status Code Key*

```
BR1-vEdge-1# show omp routes | table
Code:
C   -> chosen
I   -> installed
Red -> redistributed
Rej -> rejected
L   -> looped
R   -> resolved
S   -> stale
Ext -> extranet
Inv -> invalid
Stg -> staged
U   -> TLOC unresolved
<<<omitted for brevity>>>
```

While the full explanation of these values can be found in the Cisco documentation, a few values are reviewed in Table 6-1.

Table 6-1 *OMP Status Codes*

Status Code	Status Meaning	Explanation
C	Chosen	"Chosen" means that this route is the successor of the OMP best-path selection process.
I	Installed	"Installed" means that the OMP route has been installed into the IP routing table.
R	Resolved	"Resolved" means that the TLOC referenced in the OMP route is present and operational.

As such, the status code of C I R means that the OMP route has been successfully installed in the routing table and is being used for forwarding. The third and fourth OMP routes from 10.0.10.2 have a status code of R. These routes are resolved, but they have not been chosen as the best OMP routes, and they will not be used for forwarding. The reason that these routes have not been chosen can be seen in the output of the OMP TLOCs table, as shown in Figure 6-47.

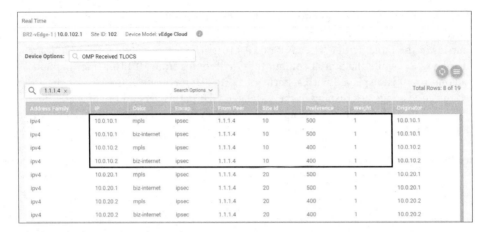

Figure 6-47 *OMP TLOC Table on BR2-vEdge2 Showing TLOCs with Different Preference Values*

Since the TLOCs from 10.0.10.1 have a higher preference value than the TLOCs from 10.0.10.2, the OMP routes that resolved to the TLOCs from 10.0.10.1 have won the best-path selection process, are "chosen," and will subsequently be "installed" in the routing table.

The result of this effect is illustrated in Figure 6-48, which shows that the TLOCs from WAN Edge 1 and 2 are received on WAN Edge 3 with two different TLOC Preference values. As the higher Preference value is received for the TLOCs that are advertised from WAN Edge 1, only the tunnels to WAN Edge 1 will be used for forwarding traffic. Should WAN Edge 1 fail, or both TLOCs be removed from WAN Edge 3, WAN Edge 3 would subsequently use the paths being advertised from WAN Edge 2 and the traffic would fail over to the bottom set of tunnels.

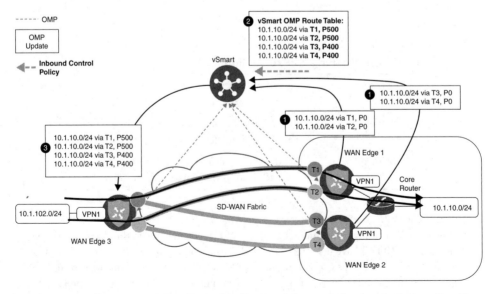

Figure 6-48 *Illustration of the Effects of Different Preference Values on the Forwarding Plane*

Setting TLOC Preference with Device Templates

The previous example reviewed the purpose of setting the TLOC Preference value and how to set that value using centralized control policies. In addition to using centralized control policies to set the TLOC Preference value, you can also configure it directly on the tunnel interface. Typically, WAN Edge configurations are centrally managed using a combination of feature templates and device templates, as discussed in Chapter 4, "Onboarding and Provisioning." While Weight and Preference are configurable on the tunnel interfaces with feature templates, they can also be configured with the CLI on the tunnel interface directly with the command **encapsulation** {**ipsec**|**gre**} [**preference** *preference*] [**weight** *weight*]. Example 6-9 reviews the CLI configuration used to accomplish the same objectives.

Example 6-9   *Tunnel Interface Configuration with Weight and Preference*

```
! The following configuration excerpts from BR1-vEdge1 and BR1-vEdge2 that
! indicate the preference and weight settings that have been configured
! on the tunnel interfaces
!
BR1-vEdge-1# BR1-vEdge-1# sho run vpn 0 | include "interface|color|encap"
 interface ge0/0
  tunnel-interface
   encapsulation ipsec preference 50 weight 20
   color biz-internet
 interface ge0/1
  tunnel-interface
   encapsulation ipsec preference 50 weight 5
   color mpls restrict
 interface ge0/2
  tunnel-interface
   encapsulation ipsec preference 5
   color lte
 interface ge0/3
BR1-vEdge-1#

BR1-vEdge-2# sho run vpn 0 | include "interface|color|encap"
 interface ge0/0
  tunnel-interface
   encapsulation ipsec preference 40 weight 20
   color biz-internet
 interface ge0/1
  tunnel-interface
   encapsulation ipsec preference 40 weight 5
   color mpls restrict
```

```
interface ge0/2
 tunnel-interface
  encapsulation ipsec preference 4
  color lte
 interface ge0/4
 interface ge0/5
BR1-vEdge-2#
```

While the Preference values and their purposes were discussed in depth in the previous section, Example 6-9 also includes the use of the new **weight** attribute. Weight is used to determine the proportional load-sharing among TLOCs with equal preferences. Weight is not part of the best-path selection algorithm, but instead is used after the best paths are determined to forward proportionally among the paths selected through the best-path process. The **weight** attribute can range from a value of 1 (default) to 255. Weight is generally configured in proportion to the bandwidths of the links at a single site. In this example, the **weight** settings of 20 and 5 could represent links with speeds of 20 and 5 Mbps, respectively. Remember, there is no absolute reference value for **weight**; it is only proportional among the transports at the local site.

In Example 6-9, the preferences on the Biz-Internet, MPLS, and LTE links of BR1-vEdge1 are configured as 50, 50, and 5, respectively. The preferences on BR1-vEdge2 for the Biz-Internet, MPLS, and LTE links are configured as 40, 40, and 4, respectively. The result of this configuration is that, in steady-state operation, where all routers and all links are operational, inbound traffic to Branch 1 will be sent over the Biz-Internet and MPLS links of BR1-vEdge1. These links are configured with the highest **preference** values and have won the best-path selection process. Furthermore, traffic will be load-shared on a per-flow basis of 20:5, or 4:1, based on the configured weight values. Should the MPLS and Biz-Internet links on BR1-vEdge1 become inoperable, and the TLOCs are no longer resolvable by other routers in the fabric, then the TLOC advertisements from BR1-vEdge2's MPLS and Biz-Internet links, configured with a TLOC preference of 40, will win the best-path selection process and be used by other routers to send traffic to Branch 1. Only if all MPLS and Biz-Internet TLOCs are unresolvable will the LTE TLOC on BR1-vEdge1 win the best-path selection process with a preference of 5. Lastly, if the LTE TLOC on BR1-vEdge1 is unresolvable, then the last TLOC from Branch 1, the LTE TLOC on BR1-vEdge2 with a preference of 4, will be selected.

You can see the results of these configurations in the TLOCs that have been advertised to DC1-vEdge1, as shown in Figure 6-49.

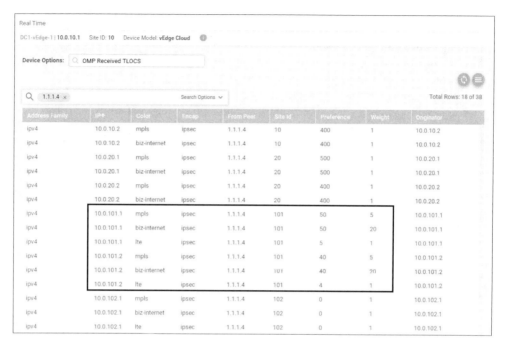

Figure 6-49 *Branch 1 TLOCs Are Received in the DC with the Configured Preference and Weight Values*

Use Case 3 Review

In this use case, we explored two different mechanisms to configure TLOC Preference values and learned how those Preference values can be used to manipulate how traffic flows across the network. We also used the **weight** command to be able to perform unequal-cost load-sharing, which is commonly used when network administrators want to use multiple links of different speeds.

Note Use Case 3 shows two different ways to set the TLOC Preference values. While the ability to write a centralized control policy to override the preferences that are configured on an interface is useful, its primarily utility is for *overriding* the values that were configured on the tunnel interface, not for configuring the values in the first place. It would be the author's recommendation to configure the TLOC Preference values on the WAN Edge tunnel interfaces directly, and only manipulate them with centralized control policies when necessary.

Note   Astute readers will have observed that the choices for Preference values for the data center routers were 500 and 400, while the values used for the Branch 1 location were 50, 40, 5, and 4. While the Preference values have no absolute significance, the decision to use values that were an order of magnitude greater for the DCs than the branches was by intention. By configuring the DCs with values of 500 and 400 and the branch with lower values, should a prefix (or a default route) that belongs to a data center ever be inadvertently advertised or redistributed from the branch office, the rest of the WAN Edges in the fabric will still prefer the advertisements from the data centers because of their higher TLOC preference values. This design choice helps to protect the fabric from mistaken or malicious network updates.

Use Case 4: Preferring Regional Data Centers for Internet Access

A common business objective that network administrators need to account for is the desire to have geographically dispersed users access an instance of a shared resource that is closest to the users. For example, if a service is accessible from the data centers in New York and London, the users in Boston should generally use the service in New York, whereas the users in Paris and Berlin should generally use the service in London. The definition of a service can be anything—an enterprise ERP application, a video conferencing server, or (as we will use in this use case) a default route to provide Internet access. Figure 6-50 shows the topology with the configuration objective.

Before we proceed through this use case, it is once more necessary to inject default routes into the VPN1 routing table from the data centers. As with Use Case 2, the specific method used to inject the default routes is inconsequential. With the default routes advertised from the DCs, we can observe that there are four default routes installed in the VPN1 routing table on BR2-vEdge1, as illustrated in Figure 6-51.

The first two of these four routes have TLOC IPs of 10.0.10.1: the System IP of DC1-vEdge1. The third and fourth routes have TLOC IPs of 10.0.20.1, which are advertised from DC2-vEdge1. This implies that, in our example, half of the traffic from our Paris branch will egress at the London data center, and half of the traffic will be inflicted with the additional latency caused by being routed out of the New York data center.

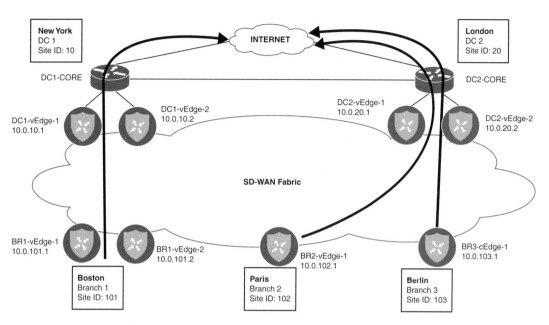

Figure 6-50 *Regionalizing Access to a Service, such as Internet Egress*

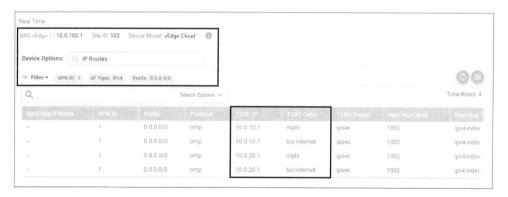

Figure 6-51 *BR2-vEdge1 (Paris Branch) Has Installed Four Default Routes in the Routing Table*

The same is true for our users in our Boston (Branch 1) and Berlin (Branch 3) branches: half of the traffic will egress locally from the geographically local DC, and half of the traffic will be sent all the way across the Atlantic Ocean. This is confirmed by the Simulate Flows output from the Boston branch, as shown in Figure 6-52.

Figure 6-52   *Simulate Flows Output for Destination 0.0.0.0 Confirms That Branch 1 (Boston) Has Four Paths*

Note   The Simulate Flows tool can be found in the **Troubleshooting** section of **Monitor > Network > {***WAN Edge***}**. The Simulate Flows tool is able to provide the expected forwarding path of a flow given the current state of the WAN Edge. This output considers the routes in the routing table, the centralized and localized policies that have been applied, and the current performance of the transport links. This can be a very useful tool to see if the policies that have been applied will have the intended effect. The Simulate Flows tool does not actually generate and forward any traffic in the data plane; instead, it indicates the path that would be taken if a flow had existed to be forwarded.

In order to ensure that users always use the Internet egress closest to their geographic location, the centralized control policy in Example 6-10 can be configured on the network. This policy will build on the policies that were configured for the previous use cases and create separate outbound control policies such that the European branches will prefer the default routes from the European data centers. Likewise, the American branches will prefer the default routes from the American data centers.

Example 6-10 *Use Case 4: Policy for Regionalizing Internet Access*

```
! The control-policy "Hub_and_Spoke_TLOC_Lists" that was configured in
! Example 6-5 has been changed into two separate centralized
! control policies: Europe_Hub_and_Spoke_TLOC and North_America_Hub_and_Spoke_TLOC.
policy
 control-policy Europe_Hub_and_Spoke_TLOC
    sequence 1
     match tloc
      site-list DCs
     !
     action accept
     !
    !
! A new sequence was added to this policy to match the default route from
! the London DC (combination of prefix-list and site-list as matching criteria),
! and set a preference of 100.
!
    sequence 11
     match route
       prefix-list Default_Route
       site-list Europe_DC
     !
     action accept
      set
        preference 100
      !
     !
    !
    sequence 21
     match route
      site-list DCs
      prefix-list _AnyIpv4PrefixList
     !
     action accept
     !
    !
    sequence 31
     match route
      site-list BranchOffices
      prefix-list _AnyIpv4PrefixList
     !
```

```
     action accept
      set
       tloc-list DC_TLOCs
      !
     !
   !
  default-action reject
 !
! Similar to the previous control policy, the following policy matches
! the default route specifically from the New York datacenter and
! sets a preference.  The rest of the policy is unchanged.
!
control-policy North_America_Hub_and_Spoke_TLOC
    sequence 1
     match tloc
      site-list DCs
     !
     action accept
     !
    !
    sequence 11
     match route
       prefix-list Default_Route
       site-list North_America_DC
     !
     action accept
      set
       preference 100
      !
     !
    !
    sequence 21
     match route
      site-list DCs
      prefix-list _AnyIpv4PrefixList
     !
     action accept
     !
    !
    sequence 31
     match route
      site-list BranchOffices
      prefix-list _AnyIpv4PrefixList
```

```
     !
     action accept
      set
       tloc-list DC_TLOCs
      !
     !
    !
 default-action reject
 !
control-policy Set_DC_TLOC_Preference
 ! <<<No changes made to this policy from Example 6-7, omitted for brevity>>>
 !
lists
 ! <<<Some lists without changes from Example 6-5 are omitted for brevity>>>
 !
 ! A new prefix-list is created to match the default route
 !
 prefix-list Default_Route
  ip-prefix 0.0.0.0/0
 !
 site-list BranchOffices
  site-id 100-199
 !
 site-list DCs
  site-id 10-50
 !
 ! New site lists are created to allow for more specific matching criteria
 ! (Europe_DC and North_America_DC) and more targeted policy application scopes
 ! (Europe_Branches and North_America_Branches) .
 !
 site-list Europe_Branches
  site-id 102-103
 !
 site-list Europe_DC
  site-id 20
 !
 site-list North_America_Branches
  site-id 101
 !
 site-list North_America_DC
  site-id 10
 !
!
```

```
!
! Lastly, the policy that prefers the London DC is applied to the European
! branches, and the policy that prefers the American DC is applied to the
! American Branches.
!
!
apply-policy
 site-list Europe_Branches
  control-policy Europe_Hub_and_Spoke_TLOC out
 !
 site-list North_America_Branches
  control-policy North_America_Hub_and_Spoke_TLOC out
 !
 site-list DCs
  control-policy Set_DC_TLOC_Preference in
 !
!
```

With this new centralized policy applied to the SD-WAN fabric, the same outputs from the Paris and Boston offices can be evaluated to further understand the policy's effect. In Figure 6-53, we can see that there are now only two routes installed in the routing table on BR2-vEdge1 (this is in contrast to the four routes present before the policy was applied in Figure 6-51).

Figure 6-53   *BR2-vEdge1 (Paris Branch) Has Two Default Routes Installed in the Routing Table*

The default routes installed on BR2-vEdge1 (Paris branch) have a TLOC IP address of 10.0.20.1, and they originate from the DC2-vEdge1 router (London data center). Further inspection of the OMP Routes table on BR2-vEdge1 in Figure 6-54 shows that all eight default routes have been received by the WAN Edge, but only these two with a Route Preference of 100 have been selected as the best path and have been inserted into the VPN 1 routing table with a status of C I R.

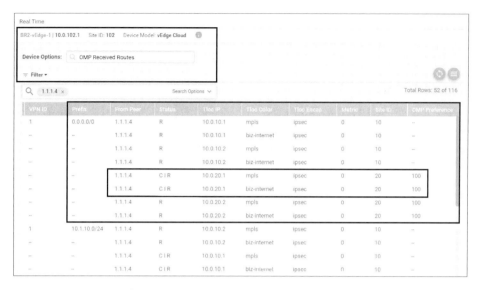

Figure 6-54 *BR2-vEdge1 (Paris Branch) Has Installed Eight Default Routes in the OMP Table*

Figure 6-54 shows that BR2-vEdge1 has received all eight default routes (four data center WAN Edge routers, each with MPLS and Biz-Internet TLOCs). Of these eight routes, the four that are being advertised from the London data center (Site ID: 20) have an OMP Route Preference of 100. Of those four, the two that resolve to the 10.0.20.1 TLOC IPs will have a TLOC preference of 500 and will be preferred over the TLOC Preference of 400 for the TLOCs from 10.0.20.2 (from the policy created in Use Case 3). These two preferred routes are being installed into the routing table with a state of "C I R."

Conversely, the Boston branch has selected two different paths that it will use to forward its traffic toward the Internet, as shown in Figure 6-55.

Figure 6-55 *Simulate Flows Output Confirms That Branch 1 (Boston) Will Egress via the New York Data Center (System IP: 10.0.10.1)*

The Boston branch (BR1-vEdge1) will use the two paths from DC1-vEdge1 (System-IP: 10.0.10.1) that have both a Route Preference of 100 and a TLOC Preference of 500.

Use Case 4 Review

In this use case, we explored how to solve a common traffic engineering problem, such as choosing the closest instance of a shared resource, that often plagues network administrators. While the configurations reviewed in this section may seem overwhelming for a simple network of just five sites, network administrators should consider that the only configuration that would be necessary to expand this design to a network of 500 or 5,000 sites would be to update the definitions of the Europe_Branches and North_America_Branches site lists. This ability to have a single, centralized place to manage the WAN fabric is a fundamental part of the power of Cisco SD-WAN.

While the examples in the previous use case focused on TLOC Preference, this use case highlighted the OMP Route Preference field, and it demonstrated how these two values can be used together. In the best-path selection algorithm, Route Preference is evaluated before TLOC Preference and, as such, can be used to override the selection that would have been made based on TLOC Preference values for a specific prefix or group of prefixes. This type of flexibility allows network administrators the extremely fine control necessary to solve the business's traffic engineering objectives.

Use Case 5: Regional Mesh Networks

In Use Case 1, we explored turning the network from the default state of a full mesh topology into a hub-and-spoke network. While a hub-and-spoke design may meet the needs of some organizations, it is often too rigid for many enterprises. Many times, there are legitimate business purposes for some branch office sites to be in communication with other branch office sites. This communication should be permitted without needing to traverse a corporate data center. Sometimes there are sites that share a geographic proximity; other times, organizations may choose to implement these types of policies based on the business function of a site (such as R&D, Manufacturing, Sales, and so on). Figure 6-56 shows altering the existing topology to form a regional mesh of the European offices.

Building on the policies that were created in the previous use cases, we now need to build regional mesh networks in order to permit the sites in Europe to communicate directly with other sites in Europe without needing to transit a data center to do so. The new data plane tunnel that will need to be created is highlighted in Figure 6-56. Transiting the data centers will still be required in order for a branch office in North America to communicate with a branch office in Europe. A corresponding policy for North America will also be built, but as there is currently only a single branch site in North America, the policy will not have an effect on the network.

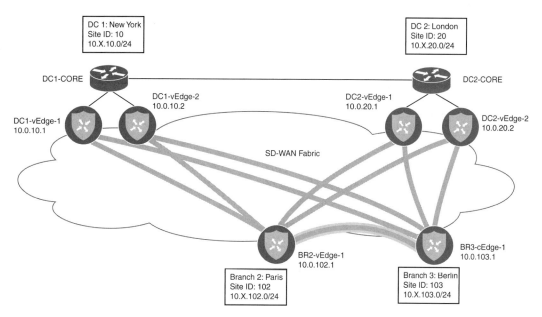

Figure 6-56 *Network Topology with Regional Meshes*

Before the new policy is applied, we can see that there is no direct data plane connection between BR2-vEdge1 and BR3-cEdge1 by looking at the real-time BFD Sessions output, as shown in Figure 6-57. All of the BFD sessions terminate at data center WAN Edges, as indicated by the System IPs of 10.0.10.X and 10.0.20.X.

Real Time

BR2-vEdge-1 | 10.0.102.1   Site ID: 102   Device Model: vEdge Cloud

Device Options: BFD Sessions

Filter ▾

Total Rows: 12

System IP	Site ID	State	Source TLOC Color	Remote TLOC Color	Source IP	Destination Public IP
10.0.10.1	10	up	biz-internet	biz-internet	100.64.102.2	100.64.11.2
10.0.10.1	10	up	lte	biz-internet	100.127.102.2	100.64.11.2
10.0.10.1	10	up	mpls	mpls	172.16.102.2	172.16.11.2
10.0.10.2	10	up	biz-internet	biz-internet	100.64.102.2	100.64.12.2
10.0.10.2	10	up	lte	biz-internet	100.127.102.2	100.64.12.2
10.0.10.2	10	up	mpls	mpls	172.16.102.2	172.16.12.2
10.0.20.1	20	up	biz-internet	biz-internet	100.64.102.2	100.64.21.2
10.0.20.1	20	up	lte	biz-internet	100.127.102.2	100.64.21.2
10.0.20.1	20	up	mpls	mpls	172.16.102.2	172.16.21.2
10.0.20.2	20	up	biz-internet	biz-internet	100.64.102.2	100.64.22.2
10.0.20.2	20	up	lte	biz-internet	100.127.102.2	100.64.22.2
10.0.20.2	20	up	mpls	mpls	172.16.102.2	172.16.22.2

Figure 6-57 *BR2-vEdge1 Does Not Currently Have Any Data Plane Tunnels to 10.0.103.1 / Site 103*

The **traceroute** output in Example 6-11 confirms that while Branch 2 has connectivity to Branch 1 and Branch 3, the data plane must currently transit the data center (10.1.10.1), taking a total of two hops to reach both branch offices.

Example 6-11 *Tracing the Path from 10.1.102.1 to Other Branches via the Data Center*

```
! Tracing a path from BR2 to BR3 is successful, but the data path is indirect
! and transits a datacenter
!
BR2-vEdge-1# traceroute vpn 1 10.1.103.1
Traceroute  10.1.103.1 in VPN 1
traceroute to 10.1.103.1 (10.1.103.1), 30 hops max, 60 byte packets
 1  10.1.10.1 (10.1.10.1)  5.495 ms  6.579 ms  6.593 ms
 2  10.1.103.1 (10.1.103.1)  13.031 ms * *
BR2-vEdge-1#
!
! Tracing a path from BR2 to BR1 is successful, but the data path is indirect
! and transits a datacenter
!
BR2-vEdge-1# traceroute vpn 1 10.1.101.2
Traceroute  10.1.101.2 in VPN 1
traceroute to 10.1.101.2 (10.1.101.2), 30 hops max, 60 byte packets
 1  10.1.10.1 (10.1.10.1)  53.191 ms  55.226 ms  55.268 ms
 2  10.1.101.2 (10.1.101.2)  76.770 ms  77.283 ms  77.456 ms
BR2-vEdge-1#
```

In order to enable a regional mesh for the European locations, the policy in Example 6-12 is applied. In order to form regional meshes, the vSmarts will need to advertise the TLOCs and the routes for the other sites within the mesh that connectivity should be established with. For sites that are outside of the regional mesh, the TLOCs will not be advertised, and the OMP routes will be advertised with the data center TLOCs.

Example 6-12 *Use Case 5: Policy for Establishing Regional Mesh Data Planes*

```
! In the "Europe_Regional_Mesh" control policy, sequence 11 and sequence 41 were
! added to permit the advertisements of the TLOCs and Routes (respectively) from
! other sites in the Site List "Europe_Branches". Additionally, sequence 51 has
! been updated so that only the sites in the "North_America_Branches" site list
! now have their TLOCs updated with the TLOC list.
!
policy
 control-policy Europe_Regional_Mesh
    sequence 1
      match tloc
        site-list DCs
```

```
       !
      action accept
       !
     !
  sequence 11
    match tloc
      site-list Europe_Branches
     !
    action accept
     !
   !
   sequence 21
    match route
     prefix-list Default_Route
     site-list Europe_DC
     !
    action accept
     set
      preference 100
      !
     !
    !
   sequence 31
    match route
     site-list DCs
     prefix-list _AnyIpv4PrefixList
     !
    action accept
     !
    !
  sequence 41
    match route
      site-list Europe_Branches
      prefix-list _AnyIpv4PrefixList
     !
    action accept
     !
     !
  sequence 51
    match route
      site-list North_America_Branches
      prefix-list _AnyIpv4PrefixList
     !
    action accept
```

```
          set
            tloc-list DC_TLOCs
          !
          !
     !
  default-action reject
 !
! Similar to the previous control policy, the following policy permits the TLOCs
! and Routes from the "North_America_Branches" site list to be advertised.
! Additionally, sequence 51 has been updated to only apply to the European
! Branches.
!
control-policy North_America_Regional_Mesh
    sequence 1
     match tloc
      site-list DCs
      !
     action accept
      !
     !
    sequence 11
     match tloc
       site-list North_America_Branches
       !
     action accept
       !
     !
    sequence 21
     match route
      prefix-list Default_Route
      site-list North_America_DC
      !
     action accept
      set
       preference 100
       !
      !
     !
    sequence 31
     match route
      site-list DCs
      prefix-list _AnyIpv4PrefixList
      !
```

```
      action accept
       !
     !
   sequence 41
    match route
     site-list North_America_Branches
     prefix-list _AnyIpv4PrefixList
     !
    action accept
     !
   !
   sequence 51
    match route
     site-list Europe_Branches
     prefix-list _AnyIpv4PrefixList
     !
    action accept
     set
      tloc-list DC_TLOCs
      !
     !
    !
  default-action reject
 !
 control-policy Set_DC_TLOC_Preference
 ! <<<No changes made to this policy from Example 6-7, omitted for brevity>>>
 !
 lists
 ! <<<No changes made to the lists from Example 6-10, omitted for brevity>>>
 !
!
! Lastly, the new policies are applied to the site lists.
!
apply-policy
 site-list Europe_Branches
  control-policy Europe_Regional_Mesh out
 !
 site-list North_America_Branches
  control-policy North_America_Regional_Mesh out
 !
 site-list DCs
  control-policy Set_DC_TLOC_Preference in
!
```

After the policy in Example 6-12 is applied to the network, the necessary TLOCs are exchanged between BR2-vEdge1 (Paris) and BR3-cEdge1 (Berlin) in order to form data plane tunnels. These five additional tunnels between the two sites can be seen in the BFD Sessions output from BR2-vEdge1, as shown in Figure 6-58.

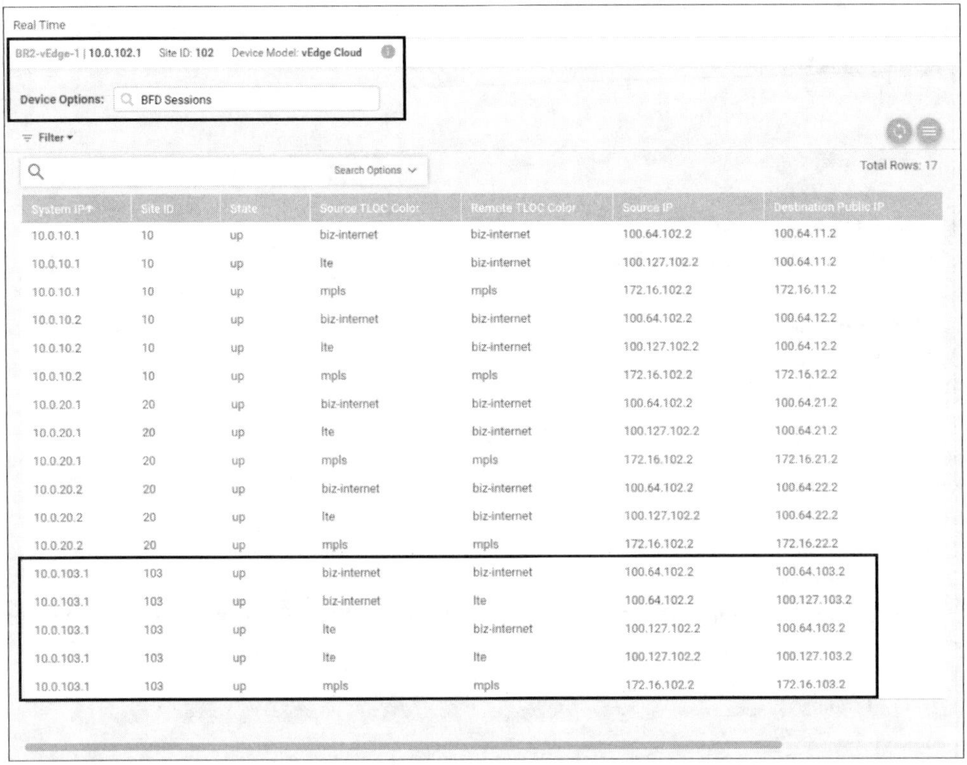

System IP	Site ID	State	Source TLOC Color	Remote TLOC Color	Source IP	Destination Public IP
10.0.10.1	10	up	biz-internet	biz-internet	100.64.102.2	100.64.11.2
10.0.10.1	10	up	lte	biz-internet	100.127.102.2	100.64.11.2
10.0.10.1	10	up	mpls	mpls	172.16.102.2	172.16.11.2
10.0.10.2	10	up	biz-internet	biz-internet	100.64.102.2	100.64.12.2
10.0.10.2	10	up	lte	biz-internet	100.127.102.2	100.64.12.2
10.0.10.2	10	up	mpls	mpls	172.16.102.2	172.16.12.2
10.0.20.1	20	up	biz-internet	biz-internet	100.64.102.2	100.64.21.2
10.0.20.1	20	up	lte	biz-internet	100.127.102.2	100.64.21.2
10.0.20.1	20	up	mpls	mpls	172.16.102.2	172.16.21.2
10.0.20.2	20	up	biz-internet	biz-internet	100.64.102.2	100.64.22.2
10.0.20.2	20	up	lte	biz-internet	100.127.102.2	100.64.22.2
10.0.20.2	20	up	mpls	mpls	172.16.102.2	172.16.22.2
10.0.103.1	103	up	biz-internet	biz-internet	100.64.102.2	100.64.103.2
10.0.103.1	103	up	biz-internet	lte	100.64.102.2	100.127.103.2
10.0.103.1	103	up	lte	biz-internet	100.127.102.2	100.64.103.2
10.0.103.1	103	up	lte	lte	100.127.102.2	100.127.103.2
10.0.103.1	103	up	mpls	mpls	172.16.102.2	172.16.103.2

Figure 6-58 *BR2-vEdge Has New Data Plane Tunnels to 10.0.103.1 / Site 103*

The data plane connectivity can be validated by testing with **traceroute**, as shown in Example 6-13. The first trace shows there is now a direct path established between Paris and Berlin as part of the European regional mesh. There is no longer a need to transit a data center router to facilitate that connectivity, and the path is now only a single hop. However, as the second **traceroute** output indicates, there is no direct data plane path from Paris to Boston. Traffic that is going from Branch 2 (Paris) or Branch 3 (Berlin) to Branch 1 (Boston) must still transit the data center.

Example 6-13   *Tracing the Path from 10.1.102.1 to Other Branches after the Regional Mesh Is Established*

```
! Tracing a path from BR2 to BR3 is successful and the path is now direct (1 hop)
!
BR2-vEdge-1# traceroute vpn 1 10.1.103.1
Traceroute  10.1.103.1 in VPN 1
traceroute to 10.1.103.1 (10.1.103.1), 30 hops max, 60 byte packets
 1  10.1.103.1 (10.1.103.1)  5.783 ms * *
BR2-vEdge-1#
!
! Tracing a path from BR2 to BR1 is successful, but the data path is still ! indi-
  rect and transits a datacenter (2 hops)
!
BR2-vEdge-1# traceroute vpn 1 10.1.101.2
Traceroute  10.1.101.2 in VPN 1
traceroute to 10.1.101.2 (10.1.101.2), 30 hops max, 60 byte packets
 1  10.1.10.1 (10.1.10.1)  5.307 ms  6.238 ms  18.233 ms
 2  10.1.101.2 (10.1.101.2)  30.879 ms  31.555 ms  31.607 ms
BR2-vEdge-1#
```

Use Case 5 Review

In this use case, we explored how to alter the structure of the SD-WAN fabric so that it is not purely a hub-and-spoke network, but now consists of multiple, distinct regional mesh networks. Regional meshes can be deployed by network administrators to permit offices that are in close proximity to each other, or offices that serve the same business function, to communicate without the need for a data center to proxy the communication.

This use case also continued to highlight how trivial it is to create increasingly complex topologies through a single, centrally administered control policy. The only thing necessary to turn the hub-and-spoke network into a regional mesh network was to advertise the TLOCs and OMP routes to the sites that we wanted to communicate with each other.

Use Case 6: Enforcing Security Perimeters with Service Insertion

Enterprises often have a need to inject services into the traffic path of the WAN environment. One of the most frequently used services would be a security device such as a firewall. Other potential services would include IPS/IDS, network sniffers, web proxies, caching engines, WAN optimization appliances, and so on. Regardless of the specific type of service, Cisco SD-WAN can natively advertise the availability of the service across the WAN environment and direct traffic flows to that service. For more information on network services, see Chapter 3.

In this use case, there is a need to ensure that users at branch sites in Europe cannot communicate directly with branch sites in North America without first having their traffic inspected by a firewall, and vice versa. We are going to continue to build on the policies created for the previous use cases and modify them to meet this objective.

The first step in service insertion is the configuration of the service itself. For this use case, we are going to provision a firewall attached to DC1-vEdge1 as a network service, as shown in Figure 6-59. Traffic flows that originate at a European branch site, such as the example in the diagram, must be inspected by this firewall before being forwarded to a branch location in North America.

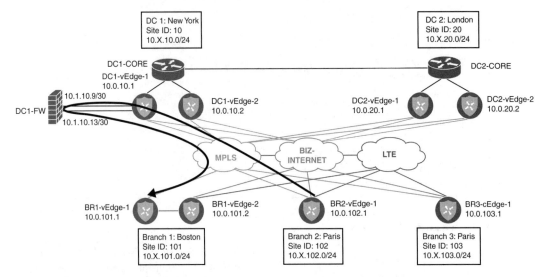

Figure 6-59   *Using a Firewall at the Data Center to Inspect Flows Transiting Between Two Branch Sites*

Example 6-14 shows the necessary configuration to create the service in DC1-vEdge1 and the advertisements on the vSmart controller as soon as the service is provisioned on the WAN Edge. Once the service has been provisioned, a new label is assigned to indicate which traffic received by this WAN Edge should be forwarded to the service. As Example 6-14 shows, the label in this case is 1005.

Example 6-14   *Firewall Service Configuration on DC1-vEdge1*

```
! The minimum configuration necessary for a service is a single line that
! specifies where the service is reachable.
!
DC1-vEdge-1# sho run vpn 1
vpn 1
 service FW address 10.1.10.9
!
!
! As soon as the service is configured, it is advertised to the vSmart and
! ready to be reflected to the entire fabric. Other WAN Edges that want to
```

```
! send traffic to this service should use label 1005.
!
DC1-vEdge-1# show omp services family ipv4 service FW | ex >


                                      PATH
VPN    SERVICE  ORIGINATOR  FROM PEER   ID   LABEL   STATUS
-------------------------------------------------------------------
1      FW       10.0.10.1   0.0.0.0     66   1005    C,Red,R
                            0.0.0.0     68   1005    C,Red,R
```

A service can either be locally attached or reachable across a GRE tunnel. A locally attached service, such as the firewall in this example, is configured with the syntax **service** {*service-name*} **address** {*ip address*}, whereas a remotely accessible service would be configured as **service** {*service-name*} **interface** {*gre_interface_number1*} [*gre_interface_number2*].

Before the policy is applied to the SD-WAN fabric, Branch 2 is able to reach Branch 1 in two hops, as indicated in Example 6-15. Furthermore, this traffic is being forwarded with a label of 1002, which represents VPN 1.

Example 6-15   *Tracing the Path from 10.1.102.1 to Branch 1 Before Service Insertion Is Activated*

```
! Tracing a path from BR2 to BR1 is successful, but the data path transits
! a datacenter.
!
BR2-vEdge-1# traceroute vpn 1 10.1.101.2
Traceroute  10.1.101.2 in VPN 1
traceroute to 10.1.101.2 (10.1.101.2), 30 hops max, 60 byte packets
 1  10.1.10.1 (10.1.10.1)  5.307 ms  6.238 ms  18.233 ms
 2  10.1.101.2 (10.1.101.2)  30.879 ms  31.555 ms  31.607 ms
BR2-vEdge-1#
!
! The OMP Route table indicates that the label that is used to reach
! 10.1.101.0/24 without the service insertion policy is 1002.
!
BR2-vEdge-1# show omp routes 10.1.101.0/24 vpn 1 | nomore


--------------------------------------------------
omp route entries for vpn 1 route 10.1.101.0/24
--------------------------------------------------
            RECEIVED FROM:
peer            1.1.1.4
path-id         232
label           1002
status          C,I,R
```

```
loss-reason      not set
lost-to-peer     not set
lost-to-path-id not set
    Attributes:
      originator        10.0.101.1
      type              installed
      tloc              10.0.10.1, mpls, ipsec
<<omitted for brevity>>>
          RECEIVED FROM:
peer             1.1.1.4
path-id          256
label            1002
status           C,I,R
loss-reason      not set
lost-to-peer     not set
lost-to-path-id not set
    Attributes:
      originator        10.0.101.1
      type              installed
      tloc              10.0.10.1, biz-internet, ipsec
<<omitted for brevity>>>
```

Once the firewall service is configured on the WAN Edge router, only a single line of the centralized control policy needs to be changed in order to direct the branch sites to use the service, as seen in Example 6-16.

Example 6-16 *Use Case 6: Service Insertion for Firewalling Branch-to-Branch Transatlantic Traffic*

```
! The only change that has been made is to change the action in sequence
! 51 from referencing the TLOC Lists to now reference the FW service.
!
policy
 control-policy Europe_Regional_Mesh_with_FW
    sequence 1
     match tloc
      site-list DCs
     !
     action accept
     !
    !
    sequence 11
```

```
   match tloc
    site-list Europe_Branches
    !
   action accept
    !
   !
  sequence 21
   match route
    prefix-list Default_Route
    site-list Europe_DC
    !
   action accept
    set
     preference 100
     !
    !
   !
  sequence 31
   match route
    site-list DCs
    prefix-list _AnyIpv4PrefixList
    !
   action accept
   !
   !
  sequence 41
   match route
    site-list Europe_Branches
    prefix-list _AnyIpv4PrefixList
    !
   action accept
    !
   !
  sequence 51
   match route
    site-list North_America_Branches
    prefix-list _AnyIpv4PrefixList
    !
   action accept
    set
```

```
          service  FW
         !
         !
        !
 default-action reject
 !
control-policy North_America_Reg_Mesh_with_FW
 ! <<<The change in this policy mirrors the change made in the
 ! Europe_Regional_Mesh_with_FW policy, and was omitted for brevity >>>
 !
control-policy Set_DC_TLOC_Preference
 ! <<<No changes made to this policy from Example 6-7, omitted for brevity>>>
 !
lists
 ! <<<No changes made to the lists from Example 6-10, omitted for brevity>>>
 !
 !
!
apply-policy
 site-list Europe_Branches
  control-policy Europe_Regional_Mesh_with_FW out
 !
 site-list North_America_Branches
  control-policy North_America_Reg_Mesh_with_FW out
 !
 site-list DCs
  control-policy Set_DC_TLOC_Preference in
 !
!
```

Once the service insertion policy has been activated, the OMP Route table is updated to reflect the new label that will be used to forward traffic from BR2-vEdge1 to 10.1.101.0/24. Note that the new label in Example 6-17 is 1005, the same label associated with the firewall service in Example 6-14.

The additional hops in the path from Branch 2 to Branch 1 are caused by the firewall that the policy requires these transatlantic flows to transit. At the same time, flows between Branch 2 and Branch 3, both part of the European mesh, go directly between the WAN Edges and are not required to be filtered through the firewall.

Example 6-17   *Tracing the Path from 10.1.102.1 to Branch 1 after Service Insertion Is Activated*

```
! The OMP Route table indicates that the label that is used to reach
! 10.1.101.0/24 without the service insertion policy is 1002.
!
BR2-vEdge-1# show omp routes 10.1.101.0/24 vpn 1 | nomore
---------------------------------------------------
omp route entries for vpn 1 route 10.1.101.0/24
---------------------------------------------------
            RECEIVED FROM:
peer            1.1.1.4
path-id         232
label           1005
status          C,I,R
loss-reason     not set
lost-to-peer    not set
lost-to-path-id not set
    Attributes:
     originator      10.0.101.1
     type            installed
     tloc            10.0.10.1, mpls, ipsec
<<omitted for brevity>>>
            RECEIVED FROM:
peer            1.1.1.4
path-id         256
label           1005
status          C,I,R
loss-reason     not set
lost-to-peer    not set
lost-to-path-id not set
    Attributes:
     originator      10.0.101.1
     type            installed
     tloc            10.0.10.1, biz-internet, ipsec
<<omitted for brevity>>>
!
! Tracing a path from BR2 to BR1 is successful, but the data path now
! has additional hops for the Firewall Service in the datacenter.
!
BR2-vEdge-1# traceroute vpn 1 10.1.101.2
Traceroute  10.1.101.2 in VPN 1
traceroute to 10.1.101.2 (10.1.101.2), 30 hops max, 60 byte packets
 1  10.1.10.1 (10.1.10.1)  6.990 ms  8.770 ms  8.819 ms
```

```
 2  10.1.10.9 (10.1.10.9)  8.787 ms  8.824 ms  8.859 ms
 3  10.1.10.14 (10.1.10.14)  8.830 ms  12.380 ms  14.301 ms
 4  10.1.101.2 (10.1.101.2)  23.016 ms  23.874 ms  26.072 ms
BR2-vEdge-1#
!
!
BR2-vEdge-1# traceroute vpn 1 10.1.103.1
Traceroute  10.1.103.1 in VPN 1
traceroute to 10.1.103.1 (10.1.103.1), 30 hops max, 60 byte packets
 1  10.1.103.1 (10.1.103.1)  7.703 ms * *
BR2-vEdge-1#
```

Use Case 6 Review

In this use case, we reviewed how to provision a network service and manipulate the control policy so that traffic flows were directed to that service. Throughout this example, we used a single firewall that was advertised throughout the fabric. In the real world, it is much more likely that there are redundant sets of network services distributed throughout the WAN fabric. In those cases, the lessons from the previous use cases can be combined with Network Service insertion to ensure that users have reliable, fast access to the services that they need and that the services fail over in a predictable manner.

The traffic engineering that was completed in Use Case 6 was all based on the control plane; the policy was keyed off a specific set of source and destination sites and prefixes. In Chapter 7, "Centralized Data Policies," we will explore how to continue to enhance this policy so that specific applications can be directed through network services, not just an entire site or subnet.

Use Case 7: Isolating Guest Users from the Corporate WAN

Many organizations have sites where guests are permitted onto the network. Basic security can be provided by confining guest users to their own VPN. However, the default behavior of the SD-WAN fabric is such that connectivity within a single VPN is automatically established between different sites through the exchange of TLOCs and OMP routes. While this automatic behavior is desired for the corporate network segments, most organizations do not want to permit guest users to communicate with other guest users across the WAN fabric. In this use case, we will explore the use of VPN Membership policies in order to prohibit the exchange of control plane information from VPN 3 (the guest user VPN) to the vSmarts.

Before any policy is applied to the network, users in the Guest VPN (VPN 3) are able to reach other guest users at different sites, as shown in Example 6-18.

Example 6-18   *Guest VPN Connectivity Between Different Sites*

```
! BR2-vEdge1 is able to reach BR3-cEdge1 in the Guest VPN
!
BR2-vEdge-1# ping vpn 3 10.3.103.1 count 5
Ping in VPN 3
PING 10.3.103.1 (10.3.103.1) 56(84) bytes of data.
64 bytes from 10.3.103.1: icmp_seq=1 ttl=255 time=6.26 ms
64 bytes from 10.3.103.1: icmp_seq=2 ttl=255 time=3.37 ms
64 bytes from 10.3.103.1: icmp_seq=3 ttl=255 time=7.65 ms
64 bytes from 10.3.103.1: icmp_seq=4 ttl=255 time=3.93 ms
64 bytes from 10.3.103.1: icmp_seq=5 ttl=255 time=3.73 ms
```

In order to prohibit this type of site-to-site connectivity in the Guest VPN, a VPN Membership policy will be added to the centralized control policy. Example 6-19 shows the centralized control policy to implement this change.

Example 6-19   *Use Case 7: VPN Membership Policy to Prohibit Guest VPN Connectivity Between Different Sites*

```
! The new piece of this policy is the VPN Membership policy. This VPN membership
! policy permits the VPNs for Corporate (VPN 1), and PCI (VPN 2). All other
! VPNs will be subject to the default action (reject).
policy
 vpn-membership vpnMembership_-950781881
    sequence 10
     match
     vpn-list CorporateVPN
     !
     action accept
     !
    !
    sequence 20
     match
     vpn-list PCI_VPN
     !
     action accept
     !
    !
 default-action reject
 !
```

```
control-policy Set_DC_TLOC_Preference
 ! <<<No changes made to this policy from Example 6-7, omitted for brevity>>>
 !
control-policy Europe_Regional_Mesh_with_FW
 ! <<<No changes made to this policy from Example 6-16, omitted for brevity>>>
 !
control-policy North_America_Reg_Mesh_with_FW
 ! <<<No changes made to this policy from Example 6-16, omitted for brevity>>>
 !
lists
 ! <<<Some lists without changes from Example 6-5 are omitted for brevity>>>
  !
 ! Two new VPN lists were created to work with the VPN membership policy.
  !
 vpn-list CorporateVPN
  vpn 1
  !
 vpn-list PCI_VPN
  vpn 2
  !
 !
!
! Lastly, the VPN Membership policy is applied to the Branch Offices
!
apply-policy
 site-list Europe_Branches
  control-policy Europe_Regional_Mesh_with_FW out
 !
 site-list North_America_Branches
  control-policy North_America_Reg_Mesh_with_FW out
 !
 site-list DCs
  control-policy Set_DC_TLOC_Preference in
 !
 site-list BranchOffices
  vpn-membership vpnMembership_-950781881
  !
 !
```

As Example 6-19 shows, VPN Membership policies follow a similar structure and syntax to the other centralized control policies that we have been working with throughout this chapter. In the most basic sense, the VPN Membership policy specifies which VPNs will be permitted to join the fabric from a specific site. The remaining VPNs are rejected by the default action.

The effect of the VPN Membership policy can clearly be seen by looking at the OMP Services output on the vSmart, as shown in Example 6-20. The command **show omp**

services for VPN 3 lists the service as rejected. In this state, vSmart will not propagate any incoming updates from VPN 3 to other OMP peers, and vSmart will not forward updates about VPN 3 from other WAN Edge routers to these locations that have been rejected. Functionally, this isolates VPN 3 from a control plane perspective. This is proven out in Example 6-20 when users in the guest segment at Branch 2 are no longer able to reach the guest segments at other locations.

Example 6-20   *Use Case 7: Effects of VPN Membership Policy*

```
vSmart-1# show omp services family ipv4 vpn 3
C    -> chosen
I    -> installed
Red -> redistributed
Rej -> rejected
L    -> looped
R    -> resolved
S    -> stale
Ext -> extranet
Inv -> invalid
Stg -> staged
U    -> TLOC unresolved

                                           PATH
VPN    SERVICE  ORIGINATOR  FROM PEER       ID    LABEL   STATUS
----------------------------------------------------------------------
3      VPN      10.0.101.1  10.0.101.1      66    1004    Rej,R,Inv
                            10.0.101.1      68    1004    Rej,R,Inv
                            10.0.101.1      70    1004    Rej,R,Inv
3      VPN      10.0.101.2  10.0.101.2      66    1004    Rej,R,Inv
                            10.0.101.2      68    1004    Rej,R,Inv
                            10.0.101.2      70    1004    Rej,R,Inv
3      VPN      10.0.102.1  10.0.102.1      66    1004    Rej,R,Inv
                            10.0.102.1      68    1004    Rej,R,Inv
                            10.0.102.1      70    1004    Rej,R,Inv
3      VPN      10.0.103.1  10.0.103.1      66    1003    Rej,R,Inv
                            10.0.103.1      68    1003    Rej,R,Inv
                            10.0.103.1      70    1003    Rej,R,Inv
!
!
! BR2-vEdge1 is unable to reach BR3-cEdge1 in the Guest VPN
!
BR2-vEdge-1# ping vpn 3 10.3.103.1 count 5
Ping in VPN 3
```

```
PING 10.3.103.1 (10.3.103.1) 56(84) bytes of data.
--- 10.3.103.1 ping statistics ---
5 packets transmitted, 0 received, 100% packet loss, time 3999ms
BR2-vEdge-1#
!
! Guest Users at BR2-vEdge1 are still able to access the public internet via
! local internet egress even though they can no longer reach other branch sites.
!
BR2-vEdge-1# ping vpn 3 8.8.8.8 count 5
Ping in VPN 3
PING 8.8.8.8 (8.8.8.8) 56(84) bytes of data.
64 bytes from 8.8.8.8: icmp_seq=1 ttl=53 time=17.9 ms
64 bytes from 8.8.8.8: icmp_seq=2 ttl=53 time=15.5 ms
64 bytes from 8.8.8.8: icmp_seq=3 ttl=53 time=16.4 ms
64 bytes from 8.8.8.8: icmp_seq=4 ttl=53 time=17.2 ms
64 bytes from 8.8.8.8: icmp_seq=5 ttl=53 time=16.2 ms
--- 8.8.8.8 ping statistics ---
5 packets transmitted, 5 received, 0% packet loss, time 4003ms
rtt min/avg/max/mdev = 15.559/16.704/17.936/0.830 ms
BR2-vEdge-1#
```

Use Case 7 Review

In this use case, we used a VPN Membership policy to prohibit the Guest VPN from exchanging control plane information with the vSmarts and in turn prohibit the Guest VPN from forwarding traffic across the SD-WAN fabric. While VPN Membership policies can be used to prohibit a VPN from being used at all over the SD-WAN fabric, it can also be used to protect and secure VPNs by prohibiting a WAN Edge that is provisioned either mistakenly or maliciously with a sensitive VPN from being able to exchange control plane information and access the data plane.

Use Case 8: Creating Different Network Topologies per Segment

In this use case, we will continue to revise and combine some of the earlier policies that we have discussed and apply them to different network segments at the same time. Currently, there is a European regional mesh that connects Branch 2 and Branch 3. In this use case, we will keep that forwarding path available for the corporate users in VPN 1, but we will revert the PCI VPN (VPN 2) back to a hub-and-spoke topology.

Before the policy is activated, the output in Example 6-21 confirms that currently both VPN 1 and VPN 2 have direct data plane connections from Branch 2 to Branch 3.

Example 6-21   *All VPNs Are Directly Connected Between Branch 2 and Branch 3*

```
!
! BR2-vEdge1 is one hop away from Branch 3 in VPN 1
!
BR2-vEdge-1# traceroute vpn 1 10.1.103.1
Traceroute  10.1.103.1 in VPN 1
traceroute to 10.1.103.1 (10.1.103.1), 30 hops max, 60 byte packets
 1  10.1.103.1 (10.1.103.1)  5.325 ms * *
BR2-vEdge-1#
!
! BR2-vEdge1 is one hop away from Branch 3 in VPN 2
!
BR2-vEdge-1# traceroute vpn 2 10.2.103.1
Traceroute  10.2.103.1 in VPN 2
traceroute to 10.2.103.1 (10.2.103.1), 30 hops max, 60 byte packets
 1  10.2.103.1 (10.2.103.1)  10.646 ms * *
BR2-vEdge-1#
```

Example 6-22 highlights the necessary changes to the centralized control policy. In order
to enact this policy, a new criterion was added to sequence 41 so that it only applies to
routes from the corporate VPN. Now sequence 41 will match all routes from European
branches in VPN 1 and accept them without any modifications. Additionally, sequence
51 is added to match the routes from European branches in the PCI VPN. These routes
have their TLOCs (next-hop attributes) altered so that the prefixes are advertised as being
reachable from the European DCs.

Example 6-22   *Use Case 8: Multi-Topology Policy*

```
!
! In order to create different logical topologies on a per-VPN basis, the
! routes need to be manipulated on a per-VPN basis.  In this policy, this is
! done in sequence 41, which matches and accepts the routes in the corporate
! VPN, and in sequence 51, which matches routes in the PCI VPN and sets a
! TLOC list with the TLOCs of DC2.
!
policy
 control-policy Euro_Reg_Mesh_with_FW_MultiTopo
    sequence 1
     match tloc
      site-list DCs
     !
     action accept
     !
   !
```

```
      sequence 11
       match tloc
        site-list Europe_Branches
        !
       action accept
        !
       !
      sequence 21
       match route
        prefix-list Default_Route
        site-list Europe_DC
        !
       action accept
        set
         preference 100
         !
        !
       !
      sequence 31
        match route
         site-list DCs
         prefix-list _AnyIpv4PrefixList
         !
        action accept
         !
        !
      sequence 41
        match route
          site-list Europe_Branches
          vpn-list CorporateVPN
          prefix-list _AnyIpv4PrefixList
          !
        action accept
         !
         !
      sequence 51
        match route
          site-list Europe_Branches
          vpn-list PCI_VPN
          prefix-list _AnyIpv4PrefixList
          !
        action accept
```

```
      set
       tloc-list Europe_DC_TLOCs
      !
     !
    !
    sequence 61
     match route
      site-list North_America_Branches
      prefix-list _AnyIpv4PrefixList
      !
     action accept
      set
       service  FW
      !
     !
    !
  default-action reject
  !
  control-policy North_America_Reg_Mesh_with_FW
   ! <<<No changes made to this policy from Example 6-16, omitted for brevity>>>
   !
  vpn-membership vpnMembership_-950781881
   ! <<<No changes made to this policy from Example 6-19, omitted for brevity>>>
   !
  control-policy Set_DC_TLOC_Preference
   ! <<<No changes made to this policy from Example 6-7, omitted for brevity>>>
   !
  lists
   ! <<<Some lists without changes from Example 6-5 are omitted for brevity>>>
   !
   ! A new TLOC List is created for the TLOCs in DC2
   !
   tloc-list Europe_DC_TLOCs
    tloc 10.0.20.1 color mpls encap ipsec
    tloc 10.0.20.1 color biz-internet encap ipsec
    tloc 10.0.20.2 color mpls encap ipsec
    tloc 10.0.20.2 color biz-internet encap ipsec
   !
  !
 !
apply-policy
 site-list Europe_Branches
```

```
   control-policy Euro_Reg_Mesh_with_FW_MultiTopo out
 !
site-list DCs
 control-policy Set_DC_TLOC_Preference in
 !
site-list North_America_Branches
 control-policy North_America_Reg_Mesh_with_FW out
 !
site-list BranchOffices
 vpn-membership vpnMembership_-950781881
 !
!
```

As the multi-topology policy in Example 6-22 shows, creating different logical topologies on a per-VPN basis is a function of manipulating the routes on a per-VPN basis. The centralized policy in this use case created a new TLOC list with the TLOCs from the London data center and applied the TLOC list as the next hop for the routes in VPN 2, the PCI segment. The effect of this policy is that, while the connectivity in VPN 1 will continue to be direct, the communication in VPN 2 will be proxied through the data centers. You can see the effects of this policy in Example 6-23.

Example 6-23   *VPN 1 Has a Direct Data Plane; VPN 2 Must Transit the Data Center When Passing Traffic from Branch 2 to Branch 3*

```
!
! BR2-vEdge1 is one hop away from Branch 3 in VPN 1
BR2-vEdge-1# traceroute vpn 1 10.1.103.1
Traceroute  10.1.103.1 in VPN 1
traceroute to 10.1.103.1 (10.1.103.1), 30 hops max, 60 byte packets
 1  10.1.103.1 (10.1.103.1)  13.625 ms * *
BR2-vEdge-1#
!
! BR2-vEdge1 is two hops away from Branch 3 in VPN 2
!
BR2-vEdge-1# traceroute vpn 2 10.2.103.1
Traceroute  10.2.103.1 in VPN 2
traceroute to 10.2.103.1 (10.2.103.1), 30 hops max, 60 byte packets
 1  10.2.20.2 (10.2.20.2)  4.708 ms  6.235 ms  6.263 ms
 2  10.2.103.1 (10.2.103.1)  20.969 ms * *
BR2-vEdge-1#
```

Use Case 8 Review

In this use case, we created a multi-topology policy by combining the elements that were previously used in prior use cases. This use case demonstrates how network administrators can create different data plane topologies on a per-segment basis to meet their business needs by using the VPN criterion in addition to other criteria to select, filter, and manipulate the control plane updates.

Use Case 9: Creating Extranets and Access to Shared Services

In the final centralized control policy use case, we will explore building an extranet. Extranets are commonly used by enterprises to provide multiple business partners with access to a shared resource, such as an ERP solution, while at the same time ensuring that the partners cannot directly access each other. In our lab, we are going to use VPNs 101 and 102, at Sites 101 and 102, respectively, to represent the business partners. The shared resource that these partners need to access will be in VPN 100 at DC1. Figure 6-60 depicts the extranet that will be built on top of the existing policies from the previous examples.

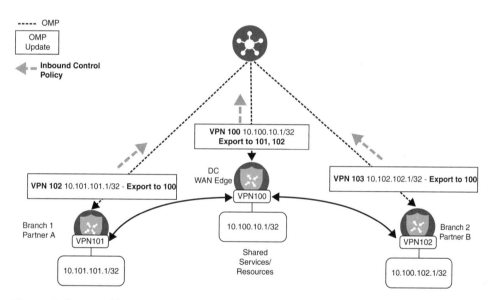

Figure 6-60 *Building an Extranet to Enable Partner Connectivity*

In order to build the necessary connectivity to accomplish this design, there are several key parts of the centralized policy that will need to be either adjusted or created from scratch. The VPN Membership policy created in Use Case 7 will need to be adjusted to account for the new VPNs being used for the extranet. Next, the inbound route policies will need to be either edited (in the case of the data centers) or created (in the case of the branches) so that the route leaking via the **export-to** command can take effect. The Set_DC_TLOC_Preference policy has to be rewritten to include the statements for route leaking. As there can only be a single control policy for a specific site ID applied in a single direction, the functions of setting the TLOC preferences and leaking the routes from VPN 100 to VPN 101 and 102 need to be combined into a single policy. This new policy has been renamed "DC_Inbound_Control_Policy" to reflect a broader purpose than just manipulating the DC TLOCs.

The policy in Example 6-24 implements the necessary changes to completely deploy this extranet. As this is the last set of examples for Chapter 6, the policy is presented in its entirety so that it can be used as a reference.

Example 6-24   *Use Case 9: Extranet*

```
policy
!
! The VPN membership policy is extended to account for the additional VPNs
! that need to be advertised to form the extranet connectivity.  Specifically,
! these are grouped into the CLIENT_VPNS (VPNs 101 and 102), and the
! SERVICE_VPN (VPN 100).
!
 vpn-membership vpnMembership_-1376283532
  sequence 10
   match
    vpn-list CLIENT_VPNS
   !
   action accept
   !
  !
  sequence 20
   match
    vpn-list CorporateVPN
   !
   action accept
   !
  !
  sequence 30
   match
    vpn-list SERVICE_VPN
   !
   action accept
   !
  !
  sequence 40
```

```
     match
      vpn-list PCI_VPN
      !
     action accept
      !
     !
  default-action reject
  !
 !
 ! The former "Set_DC_TLOC_Preference" policy has been renamed to
 ! "DC_Inbound_Control_Policy" and has had sequence 41 inserted in order to perform
 ! the route leaking from VPN 100 to VPN 101 and 102.
 !
 control-policy DC_Inbound_Control_Policy
    sequence 1
     match tloc
      originator 10.0.10.1
      !
     action accept
      set
       preference 500
       !
      !
     !
    sequence 11
     match tloc
      originator 10.0.10.2
      !
     action accept
      set
       preference 400
       !
      !
     !
    sequence 21
     match tloc
      originator 10.0.20.1
      !
     action accept
      set
       preference 500
       !
      !
     !
```

```
   sequence 31
    match tloc
     originator 10.0.20.2
     !
    action accept
     set
      preference 400
     !
    !
   !
   sequence 41
    match route
     vpn-list SERVICE_VPN
     prefix-list _AnyIpv4PrefixList
     !
    action accept
     export-to vpn-list CLIENT_VPNS
     set
     !
     ! An OMP TAG is similar to a route tag that can be found in other
     ! routing protocols.  While it is not strictly necessary to set an OMP TAG
     ! during redistribution, it may become useful in the future to assist with
     ! tracking how routes are propagating as well as creating additional
     ! criteria to filter on.
     !
      omp-tag 100
     !
    !
   !
  default-action accept
  !
 !
! The "North_America_Reg_Mesh_with_FW" policy remains unchanged from previous
! versions.
!
 control-policy North_America_Reg_Mesh_with_FW
    sequence 1
     match tloc
      site-list DCs
     !
     action accept
     !
     !
```

```
   sequence 11
    match tloc
     site-list North_America_Branches
     !
    action accept
     !
    !
   sequence 21
    match route
     prefix-list Default_Route
     site-list North_America_DC
     !
    action accept
     set
      preference 100
      !
     !
    !
   sequence 31
    match route
     site-list DCs
     prefix-list _AnyIpv4PrefixList
     !
    action accept
     !
    !
   sequence 41
    match route
     site-list North_America_Branches
     prefix-list _AnyIpv4PrefixList
     !
    action accept
     !
    !
   sequence 51
    match route
     site-list Europe_Branches
     prefix-list _AnyIpv4PrefixList
     !
    action accept
     set
      service  FW
      !
```

```
    !
    !
  default-action reject
  !
  !
  ! The "Euro_Reg_Mesh_with_FW_MultiTopo" policy remains unchanged from previous
  ! versions.
  !
control-policy Euro_Reg_Mesh_with_FW_MultiTopo
    sequence 1
     match tloc
      site-list DCs
     !
     action accept
     !
    !
    sequence 11
     match tloc
      site-list Europe_Branches
     !
     action accept
     !
    !
    sequence 21
     match route
      prefix-list Default_Route
      site-list Europe_DC
     !
     action accept
      set
       preference 100
      !
     !
    !
    sequence 31
     match route
      site-list DCs
      prefix-list _AnyIpv4PrefixList
     !
     action accept
     !
    !
    sequence 41
```

```
      match route
       site-list Europe_Branches
       vpn-list CorporateVPN
       prefix-list _AnyIpv4PrefixList
       !
      action accept
       !
      !
     sequence 51
      match route
       site-list Europe_Branches
       vpn-list PCI_VPN
       prefix-list _AnyIpv4PrefixList
       !
      action accept
       set
        tloc-list Europe_DC_TLOCs
        !
       !
      !
     sequence 61
      match route
       site-list North_America_Branches
       prefix-list _AnyIpv4PrefixList
       !
      action accept
       set
        service  FW
        !
       !
      !
  default-action reject
 !
 !
 ! A new control policy is created in order to be applied inbound from the
 ! branch sites and export the routes from VPN 101 and VPN 102 to VPN 100.
 ! An OMP tag is again added during the route leaking, and while not strictly
 ! required, it is highly recommended to do so.
 !
 control-policy Branch_Extranet_Route_Leaking
    sequence 1
      match route
       vpn 101
      prefix-list _AnyIpv4PrefixList
```

```
      !
      action accept
        export-to vpn-list SERVICE_VPN
        set
          omp-tag 101
        !
        !
      !
      sequence 11
        match route
          vpn 102
          prefix-list _AnyIpv4PrefixList
        !
      action accept
        export-to vpn-list SERVICE_VPN
        set
          omp-tag 102
        !
      !
    !
  default-action accept
!
lists
 prefix-list Default_Route
  ip-prefix 0.0.0.0/0
 !
 site-list BranchOffices
  site-id 100-199
 !
 site-list DCs
  site-id 10-50
 !
 site-list Europe_Branches
  site-id 102-103
 !
 site-list Europe_DC
  site-id 20
 !
 site-list North_America_Branches
  site-id 101
 !
 site-list North_America_DC
  site-id 10
 !
```

```
  tloc-list Europe_DC_TLOCs
   tloc 10.0.20.1 color mpls encap ipsec
   tloc 10.0.20.1 color biz-internet encap ipsec
   tloc 10.0.20.2 color mpls encap ipsec
   tloc 10.0.20.2 color biz-internet encap ipsec
   !
  vpn-list CLIENT_VPNS
   vpn 101
   vpn 102
   !
  vpn-list CorporateVPN
   vpn 1
   !
  vpn-list PCI_VPN
   vpn 2
   !
  vpn-list SERVICE_VPN
   vpn 100
   !
  prefix-list _AnyIpv4PrefixList
   ip-prefix 0.0.0.0/0 le 32
   !
  !
 !
!
!
! Lastly, all of the policies are applied.  Note, the policies that perform
! route leaking must be applied inbound.
!
apply-policy
 site-list Europe_Branches
  control-policy Euro_Reg_Mesh_with_FW_MultiTopo out
 !
 site-list DCs
  control-policy DC_Inbound_Control_Policy in
 !
 site-list BranchOffices
  control-policy Branch_Extranet_Route_Leaking in
  vpn-membership vpnMembership_-1376283532
 !
 site-list North_America_Branches
  control-policy North_America_Reg_Mesh_with_FW out
 !
!
```

In Example 6-24, route leaking is configured in both the Branch_Extranct_ Route_Leaking and the DC_Inbound_Control_Policy policies with the **export-to** action. The **export-to** action allows the matching routes to be copied from the existing VPN and injected into a different VPN or VPN list using the syntax **export-to** {**vpn** *vpn-id* | **vpn-list** *vpn-list*}.

Route leaking is a powerful and flexible tool that network administrators have at their disposal. However, there are some limitations with how the **export-to** command must be used as of software version 19.2. First, the **export-to** action must be applied on an inbound control policy. If the **export-to** action is applied in the outbound direction, the action will have no effect. Second, the **export-to** command only works to leak routes from a service-side VPN into a different service-side VPN. The **export-to** command cannot be used to leak routes into or out of VPN 0 or VPN 512. The isolation of these VPNs is intentional and, specifically with VPN 0, has significant security implications. As such, there is no native mechanism using policies to leak routes into or out of these special VPNs. There is some discussion in Chapter 12, "Cisco SD-WAN Design and Migration," about different design concepts that look to solve these challenges.

When the policy in Example 6-24 is applied, the results of the route leaking can be seen in the routing tables on BR1-vEdge1 and BR2-vEdge1, as shown in Figure 6-61 and Figure 6-62, respectively. The BR1-vEdge1 and BR2-vEdge1 routing tables have installed the two routes for the Services VPN. These routes are also displayed with a Tag of 100 as a reminder that they originated in VPN 100.

Figure 6-61   *Service Routes from VPN 100 Have Been Imported into VPN 101*

Lastly, the data plane of the extranet can be validated by ensuring that VPN 101 and VPN 102 both have access to the shared services hosted in VPN 100, but that VPN 101 cannot communicate directly with VPN 102. Example 6-25 shows the results from the pings to test the data plane of the extranet.

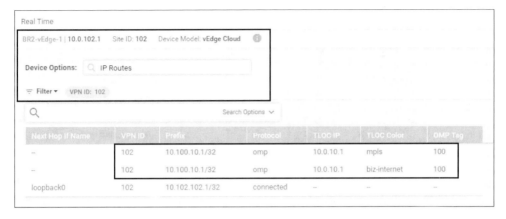

Figure 6-62 *Service Routes from VPN 100 Have Been Imported into VPN 102*

Example 6-25 *Validating the Data Plane Connectivity of the Extranet Connections*

```
!
! BR2-vEdge1 is able to reach the shared services in VPN 100
!
BR2-vEdge-1#
BR2-vEdge-1# ping 10.100.10.1 vpn 102 count 5
Ping in VPN 102
PING 10.100.10.1 (10.100.10.1) 56(84) bytes of data.
64 bytes from 10.100.10.1: icmp_seq=1 ttl=64 time=3.98 ms
64 bytes from 10.100.10.1: icmp_seq=2 ttl=64 time=2.49 ms
64 bytes from 10.100.10.1: icmp_seq=3 ttl=64 time=3.34 ms
64 bytes from 10.100.10.1: icmp_seq=4 ttl=64 time=2.02 ms
64 bytes from 10.100.10.1: icmp_seq=5 ttl=64 time=2.09 ms
--- 10.100.10.1 ping statistics ---
5 packets transmitted, 5 received, 0% packet loss, time 4003ms
rtt min/avg/max/mdev = 2.024/2.787/3.981/0.760 ms
!
! BR2-vEdge1 is not able to directly reach hosts in VPN 101
!
BR2-vEdge-1# ping 10.101.101.1 vpn 102 count 5
Ping in VPN 102
PING 10.101.101.1 (10.101.101.1) 56(84) bytes of data.
From 127.1.0.2 icmp_seq=1 Destination Net Unreachable
```

```
From 127.1.0.2 icmp_seq=2 Destination Net Unreachable
From 127.1.0.2 icmp_seq=3 Destination Net Unreachable
From 127.1.0.2 icmp_seq=4 Destination Net Unreachable
From 127.1.0.2 icmp_seq=5 Destination Net Unreachable
--- 10.101.101.1 ping statistics ---
5 packets transmitted, 0 received, +5 errors, 100% packet loss, time 3999ms
!
!
! BR1-vEdge1 is able to reach the shared services in VPN 100
!
BR1-vEdge-1# ping 10.100.10.1 vpn 101 count 5
Ping in VPN 101
PING 10.100.10.1 (10.100.10.1) 56(84) bytes of data.
64 bytes from 10.100.10.1: icmp_seq=1 ttl=64 time=3.45 ms
64 bytes from 10.100.10.1: icmp_seq=2 ttl=64 time=2.81 ms
64 bytes from 10.100.10.1: icmp_seq=3 ttl=64 time=2.78 ms
64 bytes from 10.100.10.1: icmp_seq=4 ttl=64 time=2.70 ms
64 bytes from 10.100.10.1: icmp_seq=5 ttl=64 time=2.90 ms
--- 10.100.10.1 ping statistics ---
5 packets transmitted, 5 received, 0% packet loss, time 4005ms
rtt min/avg/max/mdev = 2.705/2.931/3.450/0.275 ms
!
! BR1-vEdge1 is not able to directly reach hosts in VPN 102
!
BR1-vEdge-1# ping 10.102.102.1 vpn 101 count 5
Ping in VPN 101
PING 10.102.102.1 (10.102.102.1) 56(84) bytes of data.
From 127.1.0.2 icmp_seq=1 Destination Net Unreachable
From 127.1.0.2 icmp_seq=2 Destination Net Unreachable
From 127.1.0.2 icmp_seq=3 Destination Net Unreachable
From 127.1.0.2 icmp_seq=4 Destination Net Unreachable
From 127.1.0.2 icmp_seq=5 Destination Net Unreachable
--- 10.102.102.1 ping statistics ---
5 packets transmitted, 0 received, +5 errors, 100% packet loss, time 3999ms
BR2-vEdge-1#
```

The output in Example 6-25 confirms that the extranet is working as expected. VPNs 101 and 102 have access to the shared resource that exists in VPN 100, but VPN 101 and 102 are not able to communicate between themselves.

Use Case 9 Review

In this use case, an extranet was created to allow business partners to communicate while still maintaining security and isolation across the SD-WAN fabric. This extranet was configured by establishing a unique VPN for each of the different entities, then leaking routes from the client VPNs (101 and 102) into the Service VPN (100), and vice versa. Route leaking with centralized control policies is a technique that can be used for many different purposes. In addition to creating extranets for shared services access, as was done in this use case, another common use case that requires VPN leaking is using the SD-WAN Security feature set, particularly the Zone-Based Firewall. Cisco SD-WAN Security will be discussed further in Chapter 10, "Cisco SD-WAN Security."

Summary

This chapter discussed one of the key types of SD-WAN policies: centralized control policies. Several different use cases using centralized control policies were reviewed, including how policies can be used to manipulate the structure of the SD-WAN data plane fabric, turning an SD-WAN fabric from a full-mesh deployment to a strict hub-and-spoke deployment or a regional mesh. In addition, many different types of traffic engineering use cases were also reviewed, including using TLOC lists to manipulate the next-hop information of an OMP route, as well as network service insertion. Finally, using centralized control policies to harden the security posture of the network was discussed, including using VPN Membership policies and building extranets with route leaking. This chapter illustrated how these different kinds of policies can be combined and used together to create the architecture necessary to meet any business objective.

Review All Key Topics

Review the most important topics in the chapter, noted with the Key Topic icon in the outer margin of the page. Table 6-2 lists these key topics and the page numbers on which each is found.

Table 6-2   *Key Topics*

Key Topic Element	Description	Page
Paragraph	Data plane tunnels are built from the TLOCs advertisements that a WAN Edge receives from the vSmarts.	137
Paragraph	The status of the BFD session is indicative of the status of the data plane tunnel.	138
Paragraph	The TLOC attribute in OMP routes functions as the next-hop address, and by changing the TLOC attribute, it is possible to redirect traffic flows.	152
Paragraph, Example 6-8	OMP Route Status codes display the current status of the route, and only routes with a status of C I R are going to be used to forward traffic.	175
Table 6-1	OMP Status Codes	175

Key Topic Element	Description	Page
Paragraph, Figure 6-48	When multiple routes to the same prefix via different TLOCs exist, if all of the other route attributes are equivalent, only the routes with the greatest TLOC Preference value will be used.	176
Paragraph	The Weight attribute is used to configure unequal-cost load-sharing.	178
Figure 6-54, Paragraph	When multiple routes with different OMP preferences exist, only the routes with the greatest Preference values will be used.	187
Paragraph	VPN Membership policies can prohibit the acceptance of OMP updates about a specific VPN by the vSmarts, and they stop the vSmarts from forwarding updates about the prohibited VPNs to the WAN Edges.	204
Paragraph	Route leaking can only be performed in control policies applied in the inbound direction.	220

Define Key Terms

Define the following key terms from this chapter and check your answers in the glossary:

Inbound control policy, outbound control policy, TLOC list, originator, service insertion, multi-topology, extranet

Chapter Review Questions

1. What is the default setting of the default action in a centralized control policy?

   a. Accept

   b. Permit

   c. Reject

   d. Deny

   e. There is no default action; one must be configured manually.

2. Which of the following are configuration options for a TLOC list?

   a. Site ID

   b. System IP

   c. Color

   d. Encapsulation

   e. Preference

   f. Weight

   g. VPN

   h. Prefix

3. The TLOC attribute "Weight" is used for which of the following?

   a. The first and most important criterion in the OMP best-path selection process

   b. The final tie-breaker in the OMP best-path selection process

   c. Determining the ratio of flows for load-sharing on the TLOCs that have been selected as the best paths

   d. Turning off the anti-gravity machine

4. OMP Route Preference values can be configured via feature templates and device templates.

   a. True

   b. False

5. What is the status of an OMP process that has been inserted into the IP Routing table?

   a. C I R

   b. C R

   c. R

   d. Rej, R, Inv

6. "Preference" is an OMP attribute associated with which of the following?

   a. TLOCs

   b. OMP routes

   c. Both TLOCs and OMP routes

   d. Neither TLOCs nor OMP routes

7. What are VPN Membership policies used to do?

   a. Determine which users belong to which VPNs.

   b. Determine which routes belong to which VPNs.

   c. Determine which WAN Edges belong to which SD-WAN fabrics.

   d. Determine which VPNs will be permitted to join the overlay fabric on a WAN Edge router.

   e. Determine the ratio of flows for load-sharing on the TLOCs that have been selected as the best paths.

8. Centralized control policies that leak routes must always be applied in the outbound direction.

   a. True

   b. False

9. A centralized control policy can be used to leak routes between service-side VPNs and VPN 0.

   a. True

   b. False

10. Which type of policy is used to export OMP routes from one VPN to another VPN?

    a. Route Import/Export policies

    b. VPN Membership policies

    c. Centralized control policies

    d. Localized control policies

    e. No policy; it is not possible to have the same route in more than one VPN.

Reference

Cisco SD-WAN Command Line Reference, https://www.cisco.com/c/en/us/td/docs/routers/sdwan/command/sdwan-cr-book.html

Chapter 7

Centralized Data Policies

This chapter covers the following topics:

- **Centralized Data Policy Overview**: This section reviews the basics of centralized data policies and the directionality of policies when applied to a WAN Edge router.

- **Centralized Data Policy Use Cases:** This section explores several different sets of common business requirements and explores how network administrators can use centralized data policies to solve for these use cases.

- **Use Case 10: Direct Internet Access for Guest Users:** This section covers a simple data policy to ensure that only publicly routable packets are forwarded to the Internet. This section also reviews how to build a centralized data policy with the vManage GUI.

- **Use Case 11: Direct Cloud Access for Trusted Applications:** This section covers the use of a centralized data policy to change the forwarding path for a specific application and provide direct Internet egress.

- **Use Case 12: Application-Based Traffic Engineering:** This section reviews different methods for performing traffic engineering of flows that traverse the SD-WAN fabric.

- **Use Case 13: Protecting Corporate Users with a Cloud-Delivered Firewall:** This section reviews the use of service insertion to redirect traffic to Cisco Umbrella Secure Internet Gateway.

- **Use Case 14: Protecting Applications from Packet Loss:** This section covers two different methodologies to reconstruct data flows that have been affected by lossy transport networks.

Building on the examples in Chapter 6, "Centralized Control Policies," this chapter will focus on centralized data policies. Unlike centralized control policies that manipulate the routing information in the data plane, centralized data policies are used to override the normal forwarding decisions that would be made by the router and instead follow a specific set of forwarding instructions. These policies can be implemented for a specific flow or application or for all of the traffic at a site. This incredible control provided to network administrators is why centralized data policies are often referred to as "policy-based routing on steroids." However, unlike traditional policy-based routing, centralized data policies are much easier to administer because they are all configured and applied centrally.

Centralized Data Policy Overview

Centralized data policies are a powerful tool that allows administrators to override the normal forwarding actions that would occur in the data plane and specify a different set of actions that should be taken instead. As the use cases in this chapter will show, those new actions could be as simple as dropping a packet, redirecting a flow down a specific path or to a specific service, providing additional data plane services to accelerate data transfers and protect from packet loss, or any combination of these actions.

As discussed in Chapter 5, "Introduction to Cisco SD-WAN Policies," each type of policy has a specific directionality to it. In the case of centralized data policies, policies can either be applied to traffic that is originating "from-tunnel," traffic that is originating "from-service," or traffic that is traversing the WAN Edge router in both directions. Figure 7-1 illustrates these directions.

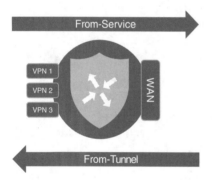

Figure 7-1   *Data Policy Directionality*

Centralized Data Policy Use Cases

In the following sections, we examine several different sets of common business requirements and explore how network administrators can use centralized data policies to solve for these use cases. These use cases are meant to address common applications of centralized data policies as well as to provide an illustrative review of many of the building blocks of centralized data policies, from which network administrators can build their own policies to accomplish their own objectives. The examples in this chapter will continue to build on the network and the examples discussed in Chapter 6. To that end,

Figure 7-2 illustrates the topology we will be discussing throughout this chapter, and you can find the centralized policy that will be used as the starting point in Example 6-24 at the end of the previous chapter.

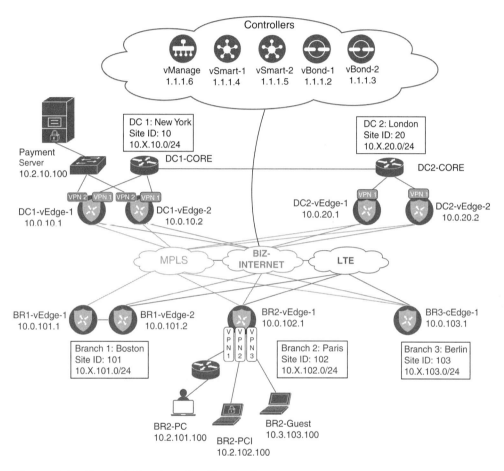

Figure 7-2   *Network Topology for Chapter 7*

Although the network featured in Figure 7-2 is identical to the network used in Chapter 6, there are several changes present in this diagram to highlight some elements that will be used throughout this chapter. Specifically, Branch 2 is drawn in greater detail to illustrate the end hosts that reside in each of the Corporate, PCI, and Guest Service VPNs. Also note that the Payment Processing Server is located in Data Center 1, in the PCI VPN. As noted in Chapter 6, the service-side addressing in this network follows the 10.X.Y.0/24 structure, where X signifies the service-side VPN and Y signifies the site ID. For the first few use cases in this chapter, we will be focusing on VPN 1, and that service-side addressing will be in the 10.1.Y.0/24 address blocks. This topology will allow us to explore different types of policies, how they interact with the SD-WAN fabric, and how network administrators can apply these policies to solve business problems.

Use Case 10: Direct Internet Access for Guest Users

The first use case we will be discussing builds on the VPN membership policy we explored in Chapter 6 to provide Internet access to guest users. In Chapter 6, Example 6-20 showed that users in the Guest VPN on BR2-vEdge1 are able to reach the Internet but not able to reach the other branches. Although true, this is not the complete story, as all of the traffic in the VPN is following the default route. Even traffic that is destined to addresses that are not reachable across the public Internet, such as private (RFC 1918) addresses, is being forwarded out onto the public Internet, where it is eventually dropped, as shown in Example 7-1.

Example 7-1   *Connectivity from the Guest VPN on BR2-vEdge1*

```
!
! BR2-vEdge1 is able to reach the public internet from the Guest VPN
!
BR2-vEdge-1# ping vpn 3 8.8.8.8 count 3
Ping in VPN 3
PING 8.8.8.8 (8.8.8.8) 56(84) bytes of data.
64 bytes from 8.8.8.8: icmp_seq=1 ttl=53 time=18.2 ms
64 bytes from 8.8.8.8: icmp_seq=2 ttl=53 time=16.0 ms
64 bytes from 8.8.8.8: icmp_seq=3 ttl=53 time=17.4 ms

--- 8.8.8.8 ping statistics ---
3 packets transmitted, 3 received, 0% packet loss, time 2001ms
rtt min/avg/max/mdev = 16.018/17.259/18.289/0.951 ms
!
! BR2-vEdge1 is unable to reach BR3-cEdge1 in the Guest VPN as expected
!
BR2-vEdge-1# ping vpn 3 10.3.103.1 count 3
Ping in VPN 3
PING 10.3.103.1 (10.3.103.1) 56(84) bytes of data.

--- 10.3.103.1 ping statistics ---
3 packets transmitted, 0 received, 100% packet loss, time 1999ms
!
! Looking at the traceroute to 10.3.103.1 and the routing table, it is clear
! that BR2-vEdge1 is using the default route to the internet to forward this
! packet, rather than dropping the traffic.
!
BR2-vEdge-1# traceroute vpn 3 10.3.103.1
Traceroute  10.3.103.1 in VPN 3
traceroute to 10.3.103.1 (10.3.103.1), 30 hops max, 60 byte packets
 1  * * *
 2  100.64.102.1 (100.64.102.1)  1.243 ms  1.260 ms  1.320 ms
```

```
 3  192.168.255.1 (192.168.255.1)  3.809 ms  4.031 ms  4.070 ms
 4  192.168.1.1 (192.168.1.1)  4.320 ms  4.359 ms  4.469 ms
 5  * * *
 6  * * *
<<<Omitted for Brevity>>>
29  * * *
30  * * *
!
! The protocol of 'nat' and a nexthop-vpn of 0 indicate that this route is
! being used to nat traffic out to the transit interfaces in VPN 0 for access
! to the internet.
!
BR2-vEdge-1# sho ip route vpn 3 10.3.103.1 detail
Codes Proto-sub-type:
  IA -> ospf-intra-area, IE -> ospf-inter-area,
  E1 -> ospf-external1, E2 -> ospf-external2,
  N1 -> ospf-nssa-external1, N2 -> ospf-nssa-external2,
  e -> bgp-external, i -> bgp-internal
Codes Status flags:
  F -> fib, S -> selected, I -> inactive,
  B -> blackhole, R -> recursive


""------------------------------------------
 VPN 3      PREFIX 0.0.0.0/0
-------------------------------------------
 proto          nat
 distance       1
 metric         0
 uptime         3:23:26:52
 nexthop-ifname ge0/0
 nexthop-vpn    0
 status         F,S
```

As Example 7-1 shows, bandwidth is being wasted by allowing packets to be forwarded out of the Internet interfaces that are destined to private, internal addresses, and therefore cannot possibly reach their destinations across the Internet. Rather than uselessly forwarding these packets out to the Internet, a centralized data policy could be constructed to drop them instead.

The first step in the process of creating a centralized data policy is to create the data-prefix-lists that will be necessary. The menu for creating lists can be found in the upper-right corner of the Configuration > Policies screen under the blue Custom Options menu, as shown in Figure 7-3.

Figure 7-3 *Creating Lists for Use in a Centralized Policy*

The first list that will be needed for this centralized data policy is a Data Prefix list of Bogon addresses. The following is per RFC 3871:

> A "Bogon" (plural: "bogons") is a packet with an IP source address in an address block not yet allocated by IANA or the Regional Internet Registries (ARIN, RIPE, APNIC…) as well as all addresses reserved for private or special use by RFCs. See [RFC3330] and [RFC1918].

Filtering out packets that are destined to networks that cannot exist on the public Internet will help to save resources by not forwarding unnecessary packets. A data-prefix-list to accomplish this filtering can be created by selecting the **Data Prefix** list type, then clicking the blue **+ New Data Prefix List** button. In the **Data Prefix List** configuration window, a list name and the necessary data prefixes are configured, as seen in Figure 7-4.

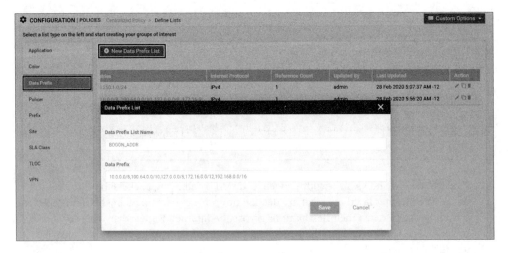

Figure 7-4 *Configuring Data Prefix Lists*

As Figure 7-4 indicates, this data prefix list includes RFC 1918 ranges, the 127.0.0.0/8 home range, and the 100.64.0.0/10 carrier-grade NAT range. None of these ranges are publicly routable, and therefore traffic that is destined to any of these destinations should not be forwarded to the Internet. In order to build a centralized policy to accomplish this filtering, the next step would be to build the data policy itself. Start by selecting

Traffic Policy from the Custom Options drop-down menu shown in Figure 7-3. From the Traffic Policy screen, you see three tabs across the top: Application Aware Routing, Traffic Data, and Cflowd. To create a new traffic data policy, select the **Traffic Data** tab and then select the **Create New** option under the **Add Policy** menu, as shown in Figure 7-5.

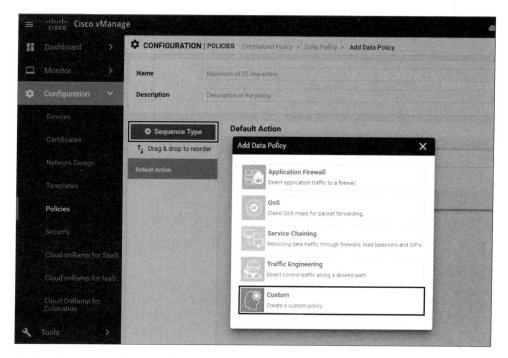

Figure 7-5   *Creating a New Centralized Data Policy*

The first step in creating the new policy is to add a sequence type by clicking the **+ Sequence Type** button, as shown in Figure 7-6. There are many different sequence types available in a centralized data policy, including Application Firewall, QoS, Service Chaining, and Traffic Engineering. These different sequence types expose a limited subset of the available actions to the administrator and attempt to highlight the different actions that may be used to address some of these use cases. The Custom sequence type provides access to all of the action options in the GUI, and many administrators prefer to use this sequence type for all use cases. For this example, select the **Custom** sequence type, as indicated in Figure 7-6.

Figure 7-6   *Add a New Sequence Type to the Data Policy*

This new policy will need to consist of two different sequences, as shown in Figure 7-7. The first sequence will match the packets destined to the addresses in the Bogon data-prefix-list and drop them. There is an additional Counter action that is applied to this sequence as well. A counter named GUEST_DROPPED_PKTS is then specified to track the number of packets that match this sequence. While counters in and of themselves don't provide any impact to how traffic is forwarded, they do provide a useful tool when evaluating and troubleshooting policies.

The second sequence will send all other packets out of the VPN 0 interfaces to the underlay. Matching all other packets is accomplished by not specifying any matching criteria at all in this sequence rule. There are two actions specified in the second sequence rule: NAT VPN and Counter. The NAT VPN action allows us to specify traffic that should be leaked to VPN 0 and forwarded out of a NAT-enabled interface. The VPN argument for this action is always VPN 0. You cannot use the NAT VPN action to leak between service-side VPNs; the NAT VPN action can only be used to leak between a Service VPN and VPN 0 for the purpose of Direct Internet Access (DIA). There is also an optional argument of Fallback, which is not selected in this case. Fallback will be discussed in greater detail in Use Case 11.

For ease of visibility, a counter called GUEST_DIA_PKTS is added to the action statements in this sequence that will count the number of packets forwarded by the second sequence.

Figure 7-7   *Guest Internet Access   Policy*

Once the necessary sequences have been added and a name and description have been added, the centralized data policy can be saved. The next step in the configuration process is to add this data policy to our existing centralized policy from Chapter 6. The easiest way to do that is to select the centralized policy and create a copy of it by selecting that option from the drop-down menu on the right side of the screen, as shown in Figure 7-8.

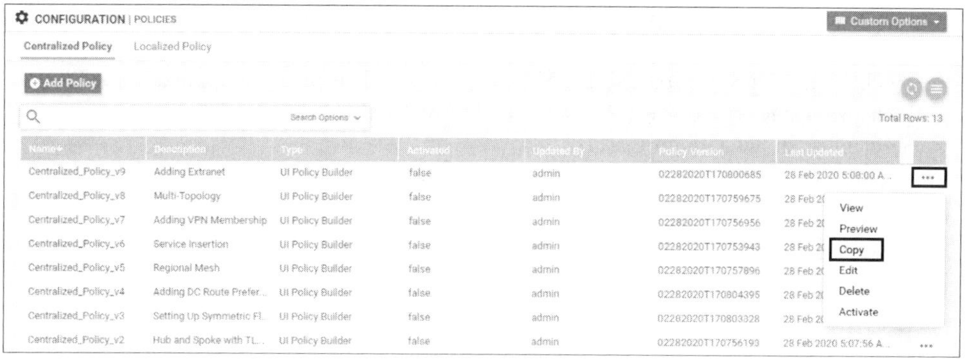

Figure 7-8 *Creating a Copy of a Centralized Policy*

Once the new policy is created, it can be edited by selecting the **Edit** option from the same drop-down menu on the newly copied policy. As shown in Figure 7-9, the Edit Policy page has three main tabs at the very top: Policy Application, Topology, and Traffic Rules. Selecting the **Traffic Rules** tab reveals three more sub-tabs—Application Aware Routing, Traffic Data, and Cflowd—just as there were when the data policy was initially created. After selecting the **Traffic Data** sub-tab, select the **Add Policy** menu in order to import the existing policy as indicated in Figure 7-9.

Figure 7-9 *Edit Policy Window*

When prompted, select the previously created Guest_DIA_Policy, as shown in Figure 7-10, and click the **Import** button.

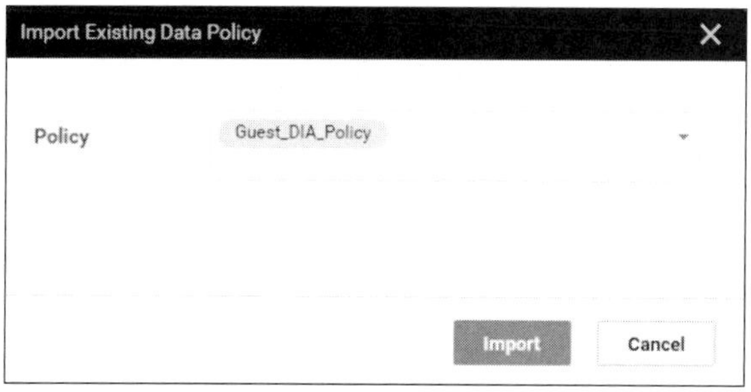

Figure 7-10 *Importing the Guest_DIA_Policy into the Centralized Policy*

Now that the Guest DIA policy is referenced in the centralized policy, the last step in the creation of the centralized policy is to specify where the data policy should be applied by clicking the **+New Site List and VPN List** button. This policy is applied to the Site ID list (BranchOffices), the VPN List (GUEST_ACCESS_VPN), and the direction (From Service), as shown in Figure 7-11.

Figure 7-11   *Applying the New Data Policy*

These configurations are saved by selecting the **Add** button. Once this step is completed, the policy should be saved and activated on the SD-WAN fabric. Example 7-2 shows the relevant changes to the configuration from the full policy that was displayed in Example 6-24.

Example 7-2   *Guest Internet Access Policy*

```
policy
 ! <<<No changes were made to the control policies or VPN membership policies,
 ! and they are omitted for brevity. The full configuration of those policies
 ! can be found in Example 6-24. >>>
 !
 ! The newly created data policy is specified below. Note that the vpn-list
 ! the policy is applied to is specified in the policy definition, not in the
 ! apply-policy section at the end.
 !
```

```
data-policy _GUEST_ACCESS_VPN_Gu_-1821888509
 vpn-list GUEST_ACCESS_VPN
    sequence 1
     match
      destination-data-prefix-list BOGON_ADDR
     !
     action drop
     !
     ! The count action and counter are specified here, and are used for
        ! monitoring and troubleshooting.
      count GUEST_DROPPED_PKTS_-837951389
     !
    !
     ! In the second sequence, all other packets are forwarded using the
        ! "nat use-vpn 0" syntax and also counted. Note that the matching criteria
        ! of any source address were automatically inserted by vManage.

    sequence 11
     match
      source-ip 0.0.0.0/0
     !
     action accept
      nat use-vpn 0

      count GUEST_DIA_PKTS_-837951389
     !
    !
 default-action drop
 !
lists
 ! <<<Some lists without changes from Example 6-24 are omitted for brevity>>>
 !
 data-prefix-list BOGON_ADDR
  ip-prefix 10.0.0.0/8
  ip-prefix 100.64.0.0/10
  ip-prefix 127.0.0.0/8
  ip-prefix 172.16.0.0/12
  ip-prefix 192.168.0.0/16
 !
 site-list BranchOffices
  site-id 100-199
 !
 vpn-list GUEST_ACCESS_VPN
```

```
   vpn 3
  !
!
apply-policy
 site-list Europe_Branches
  control-policy Euro_Reg_Mesh_with_FW_MultiTopo out
 !
 ! The newly created policy is applied to the Site List "BranchOffices"
 ! with the direction "from-service".
 !
 site-list BranchOffices
  data-policy _GUEST_ACCESS_VPN_Gu_-1821888509 from-service
  control-policy Branch_Extranet_Route_Leaking in
  vpn-membership vpnMembership_1710051916
 !
 site-list DCs
  control-policy DC_Inbound_Control_Policy in
 !
 site-list North_America_Branches
  control-policy North_America_Reg_Mesh_with_FW out
 !
!
```

The structure of the data policy, as seen in Example 7-2, is very similar to the structure of the control policies discussed in Chapter 6. Each policy is a structured sequence of match statements that specify the criteria and a list of actions to take. In this policy, the first sequence is matching packets destined to the addresses in the **BOGON_ADDR** list. These packets are dropped and counted with the counter **GUEST_DROPPED_PKTS**. The second sequence matches all other traffic and forwards it out of the VPN 0 interfaces to the Internet using the **nat use-vpn 0** command. This traffic is also being tracked with the counter **GUEST_DIA_PKTS**. In this particular policy, the setting of the default action is irrelevant, because all traffic that wasn't matched by sequence 1 will be matched by sequence 11.

Note   The name of the data policy that was configured in Figure 7-7 was Guest_DIA_Policy, whereas the name of the policy that is rendered in the CLI is _GUEST_ACCESS_VPN_Gu_-1821888509. This name is a concatenation of the VPN list that the policy is applied to, the name of the policy, and a string from vManage to ensure uniqueness. While these additional strings of numbers may make it harder at first glance to follow the naming of the policies, they ensure that the user naming structure and the concatenated names don't overlap.

Users may also note that that counter names are concatenated with strings as well, again ensuring that if the same counter name is used in multiple policies, it will remain unique.

The effects of this policy can be seen in Example 7-3, where users can still access the same resources on the public Internet, but traffic that should not be forwarded to the Internet is dropped instead of consuming that bandwidth.

Example 7-3   *Effects of Data Policy on Users in the Guest VPN*

```
!
! As the centralized data policy is enforced on the WAN-Edge router, the policy
! is encoded as an OMP update by the vSmart controller and advertised to the
! WAN-Edge. The policy is viewable with the "show policy from-vsmart" command.
!
BR2-vEdge-1# show policy from-vsmart
from-vsmart data-policy _GUEST_ACCESS_VPN_Gu_-1821888509
 direction from-service
 vpn-list GUEST_ACCESS_VPN
  sequence 1
   match
    destination-data-prefix-list BOGON_ADDR
   action drop
    count GUEST_DROPPED_PKTS_-837951389
  sequence 11
   match
    source-ip 0.0.0.0/0
   action accept
    count GUEST_DIA_PKTS_-837951389
    nat use-vpn 0
    no nat fallback
  default-action drop
from-vsmart lists vpn-list GUEST_ACCESS_VPN
 vpn 3
from-vsmart lists data-prefix-list BOGON_ADDR
 ip-prefix 10.0.0.0/8
 ip-prefix 100.64.0.0/10
 ip-prefix 127.0.0.0/8
 ip-prefix 172.16.0.0/12
 ip-prefix 192.168.0.0/16
BR2-vEdge-1#
BR2-vEdge-1#
!
! The counters that are configured in the policy can be seen with the "show policy
! data-policy-filter" command. Before any traffic is sent, both counters are 0.
!
BR2-vEdge-1# show policy data-policy-filter
```

```
data-policy-filter _GUEST_ACCESS_VPN_Gu_-1821888509
 data-policy-vpnlist GUEST_ACCESS_VPN
 vpn 3
  data-policy-counter GUEST_DIA_PKTS_-837951389
   packets 0
   bytes    0
  data-policy-counter GUEST_DROPPED_PKTS_-837951389
   packets 0
   bytes    0
!
! After sending four packets to 8.8.8.8, the GUEST_DIA_PKTS counter has
! incremented to 4.
!
BR2-vEdge-1# ping vpn 3 8.8.8.8 count 4
Ping in VPN 3
PING 8.8.8.8 (8.8.8.8) 56(84) bytes of data.
64 bytes from 8.8.8.8: icmp_seq=1 ttl=53 time=22.2 ms
64 bytes from 8.8.8.8: icmp_seq=2 ttl=53 time=26.2 ms
64 bytes from 8.8.8.8: icmp_seq=3 ttl=53 time=21.4 ms
64 bytes from 8.8.8.8: icmp_seq=4 ttl=53 time=22.3 ms
--- 8.8.8.8 ping statistics ---
4 packets transmitted, 4 received, 0% packet loss, time 3003ms
rtt min/avg/max/mdev = 21.414/23.062/26.235/1.874 ms
BR2-vEdge-1#
BR2-vEdge-1# show policy data-policy-filter
data-policy-filter _GUEST_ACCESS_VPN_Gu_-1821888509
 data-policy-vpnlist GUEST_ACCESS_VPN
  data-policy-counter GUEST_DIA_PKTS_-837951389
   packets 4
   bytes    408
  data-policy-counter GUEST_DROPPED_PKTS_-837951389
   packets 0
   bytes    0
!
! After sending five packets to 10.3.103.1, the GUEST_DROPPED_PKTS counter has
! incremented to 5.
!
BR2-vEdge-1# ping vpn 3 10.3.103.1 count 5
Ping in VPN 3
PING 10.3.103.1 (10.3.103.1) 56(84) bytes of data.
```

```
--- 10.3.103.1 ping statistics ---
5 packets transmitted, 0 received, 100% packet loss, time 3999ms
BR2-vEdge-1# show policy data-policy-filter
data-policy-filter _GUEST_ACCESS_VPN_Gu_-1821888509
 data-policy-vpnlist GUEST_ACCESS_VPN
  data-policy-counter GUEST_DIA_PKTS_-837951389
   packets 4
   bytes   408
  data-policy-counter GUEST_DROPPED_PKTS_-837951389
   packets 5
   bytes   510
BR2-vEdge-1#
```

As shown in Example 7-3, the relevant portion of the data policy has been sent to the WAN Edge from the vSmart controllers. Note that this is different than the behavior for centralized control policies. Example 7-2 shows that there is a centralized control policy and a VPN membership policy that has also been applied to the site list BranchOffices; however, only the data policy is visible in the output of **show policy from-vsmart**. This is because the control policies are enforced on the vSmarts directly and therefore have no reason to be advertised to the WAN Edges. The data policies, however, are enforced on the WAN Edges and therefore need to be advertised to the WAN Edges.

The **show policy data-policy-filter** command, as seen in Example 7-3, shows how network administrators can use counters to monitor how flows are being forwarded across the network. The first time the command is run, all of the counters display zeros, as there have been no packets matched by the policy yet. After pinging a destination on the Internet with four packets, the **GUEST_DIA_PKTS** counter reflects that four packets were forwarded. Lastly, the five pings sent to a Bogon address are reflected in the **GUEST_DROPPED_PKTS** counter.

These effects can also be seen using the Simulate Flows tool that can be found under the Troubleshooting menu in the Monitor > Network > [Device] page that was discussed in Chapter 6. When simulating flows that are destined to 8.8.8.8, as shown in Figure 7-12, there is only a next-hop address and an interface specified for the flow. When this output is contrasted against similar output in Figure 6-37, it is clear that this output is lacking the remote system IP, encapsulation, and color that was displayed in that output. This output indicates that the flow is not going to be forwarded across the SD-WAN fabric, but instead is going to egress from the ge0/0 interface, with the next-hop address of 100.64.102.1, which is the upstream ISP router connected to BR2-vEdge1.

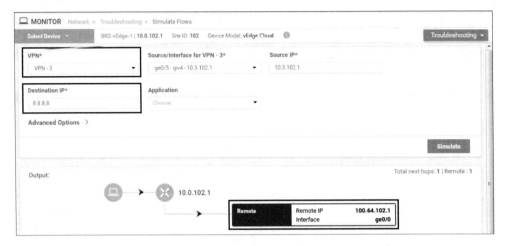

Figure 7-12   *Simulate Flows Output to 8.8.8.8 from VPN 3 Shows That Traffic Is Forwarded to the Internet*

On the other hand, when Simulate Flows is performed for traffic going to 10.3.103.1, the unambiguous results are displayed in Figure 7-13.

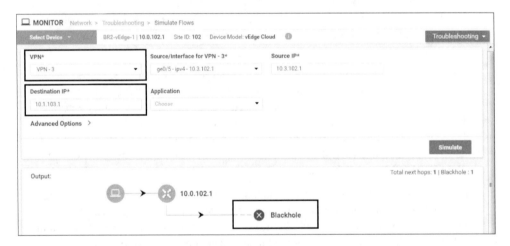

Figure 7-13   *Simulate Flows Output to 10.3.103.1 from VPN 3 Shows That Traffic Is Blackholed*

Use Case 10 Review

In this use case, a simple data policy was created and applied to VPN 3. Through this example, we have seen how data policies can be used to manipulate the forwarding path of traffic. The simple data policy for the guest user VPN illustrates that the structure of data policies is very similar to the structure of control policies, consisting of match and action sequences. While the actual purpose of this policy—dropping packets destined to a specific destination—is relatively straightforward, it is easy to conceive how other policies can be used for much more intricate tasks. For example, it would be trivial to drop traffic destined to a specific port while permitting traffic to other ports with a data policy and impossible to do so with a control policy.

Use Case 11: Direct Cloud Access for Trusted Applications

In addition to providing Internet access for guest users, many organizations are starting to leverage local Internet breakout for employees as well. However, there are significant security implications that come with permitting Direct Internet Access from every branch office to the entirety of the Internet. Detailed discussions on the security features that are built in to the WAN Edge routers can be found in Chapter 10, "Cisco SD-WAN Security." However, one of the ways that organizations can choose to limit the security implications of these choices is to restrict direct access to the Internet from the branch to certain applications or destinations that are deemed to be trusted or lower risk. Such applications may include enterprise services such as Office 365, Google Apps, and Salesforce.com. These types of policies are commonly referred to as *Direct Cloud Access*, in contrast to *Direct Internet Access* policies, which permit unbridled access to all outside destinations.

In this use case, we will build a data policy that allows users to access a specific trusted application, Cisco WebEx, directly from the local branch, while still requiring all other Internet traffic to traverse the main security perimeter through the data centers. Figure 7-14 outlines this traffic pattern for corporate users.

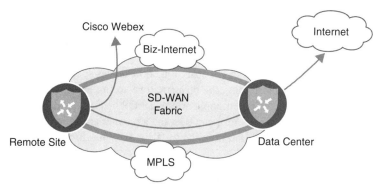

Figure 7-14 *Desired Forwarding Paths Are Different per Application*

Before the policy is applied, all of the traffic from the corporate users behind BR2-vEdge1 traverse through DC2 to reach the public Internet. This can be seen using the Simulate Flows tool in Figure 7-15. The Remote System IP of the device, where the traffic is going to be forwarded, is listed as 10.0.20.1. In this output, the application webex-meeting is specified in the flow criteria.

Figure 7-15   *WebEx Traffic from Users in VPN 1 Would Be Forwarded to DC2 WAN Edge Routers*

Note that with Figure 7-15 and Figure 7-16, different applications are specified, and the destination address of 0.0.0.0 is used. By not specifying a specific address, the tool can leverage the forwarding decisions that would be made for any traffic following the default route in the routing table. However, if a destination address was specified, that would be taken into account when determining the ultimate forwarding path of the flow. By specifying a combination of different applications, DSCP markings, addresses, ports, and/or protocols, the Simulate Flows tool can become a particularly powerful tool for network administrators to understand how the traffic is flowing through the network.

In Figure 7-15 and Figure 7-16, both WebEx traffic and YouTube traffic would be forwarded across the SD-WAN fabric to DC2-vEdge1, indicated in the figures by the remote system IP address of 10.0.20.1. These application flows would be load-shared across both the mpls and biz-internet paths, as indicated by the multiple paths in the output. These outputs, taken before the updated policy is applied, show that the forwarding path for both applications is the same.

Figure 7-16 *YouTube Traffic from Users in VPN 1 Would Be Forwarded to the DC2 WAN Edge Routers*

In order to meet the requirements of this use case and forward the WebEx traffic directly out to the Internet, while continuing to backhaul all other traffic, including YouTube, across to the data centers, the centralized policy from Example 7-2 is modified to include a new data policy that matches the WebEx application and forwards it out the local interface, as shown in Example 7-4.

Example 7-4 *Corporate Direct Cloud Access Policy*

```
policy
 ! <<<No changes were made to the control policies or VPN membership policies,
 ! and they are omitted for brevity. The full configuration of those policies
 ! can be found in Example 6-24. >>>
 !
 ! The data policy below specifies two different VPNs, and each VPN has an
 ! individual set of sequences with different rules. However, the entire policy
 ! is applied to the site list.
 !
 data-policy _CorporateVPN_Branch__1962746902
  vpn-list CorporateVPN
```

```
  sequence 1
    ! In the new sequence for the CorporateVPN, we are matching a specific app-list
    ! for the TRUSTED_APPS. The action (nat use-vpn 0) is the same action that was
    ! used for guest internet access. A new counter was also created and applied
    ! for monitoring.
   match
    app-list TRUSTED_APPS
    source-ip 0.0.0.0/0
    !
    ! The nat fallback configuration specifies the forwarding behavior in the event
    ! that there are no local interfaces that are operational and configured for NAT
   action accept
    nat use-vpn 0
   nat fallback
    count CORP_DCA_-209017211
    !
   !
  ! All non-webex traffic will be matched by the default action and forwarded as
  ! normal across the fabric.
  !
 default-action accept
 !
 ! The Guest_DIA_Policy that was configured as part of Use Case 10 is unchanged.
 !
 vpn-list GUEST_ACCESS_VPN
   sequence 1
    match
     destination-data-prefix-list BOGON_ADDR
     !
     action drop
      count GUEST_DROPPED_PKTS_-1348283274
     !
    !
   sequence 11
    match
     source-ip 0.0.0.0/0
     !
     action accept
      nat use-vpn 0

      count GUEST_DIA_PKTS_-1348283274
```

```
        !
      !
  default-action drop
 !
 lists
 ! <<<Some lists without changes are omitted for brevity>>>
  !
  app-list TRUSTED_APPS
   app webex-meeting
   app webex_weboffice
   app webex
   !
  vpn-list CorporateVPN
   vpn 1
   !
  vpn-list GUEST_ACCESS_VPN
   vpn 3
   !
  !
 !
apply-policy
 site-list Europe_Branches
  control-policy Euro_Reg_Mesh_with_FW_MultiTopo out
  !
 site-list BranchOffices
  data-policy _CorporateVPN_Branch__1962746902 from-service
  control-policy Branch_Extranet_Route_Leaking in
  vpn-membership vpnMembership_373293275
  !
 site-list DCs
  control-policy DC_Inbound_Control_Policy in
  !
 site-list North_America_Branches
  control-policy North_America_Reg_Mesh_with_FW out
  !
 !
```

Example 7-4 shows the modifications to the data policy that were made in order to implement the Direct Cloud Access functionality for corporate users. This builds on the policy that was created in Use Case 10 and adds support for corporate users in a second VPN (VPN 1) with an entirely different set of rules. It is important to understand that these two sets of sequences for the two different VPNs have been concatenated into a single data policy when activated on the vSmart controller, even though they are administered in vManage as two separate data policies (as shown in Figure 7-17). In this case, the _CorporateVPN_Branch__1962746902 policy affects the VPNs specified by both the CorporateVPN and GUEST_ACCESS_VPN lists, albeit with different policies specified in their respective sequence sets. Furthermore, there is no reference to the VPNs that the data policy is applied to in the **apply-policy** stanza at the end of the centralized policy; this is configured by the VPN lists referenced in the data policies.

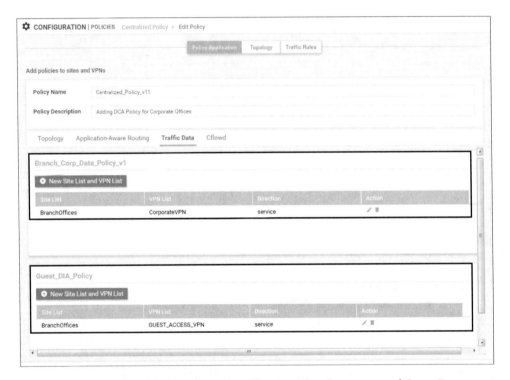

Figure 7-17 *Apply Policy Configuration Showing That Corporate and Guest Data Policies Are Separate Policies*

Once the policy is activated, the results can be validated using the Simulate Flows tool. As shown in Figure 7-18, WebEx traffic now egresses directly to the Internet. This flow pattern is different from what was observed for WebEx traffic before the policy was applied in Figure 7-15, and it's similar to what was seen for traffic in the Guest VPN in Figure 7-12.

Conversely, the forwarding pattern for YouTube traffic, as shown in Figure 7-19 after the policy is activated, is the same as in Figure 7-16 before the policy was activated. All of the YouTube traffic is going to be forwarded across the fabric to the data center and be inspected by the traditional security perimeter there.

Figure 7-18   *WebEx Traffic from Users in VPN 1 Would Egress Directly to the Internet*

Figure 7-19   *YouTube Traffic from Users in VPN 1 Would Continue to Be Forwarded to the DC2 WAN Edge Routers*

As highlighted in Figure 7-7 and Example 7-4, the **nat use-vpn 0** action has an optional configuration argument called **nat fallback**. This argument allows the administrator to specify the desired behavior in the event of a failure. With **nat fallback** enabled, in the event that all of the NAT-enabled VPN 0 interfaces on the local vEdge were to be in a non-operational state, the traffic would follow the forwarding path determined by the routing table. This would typically mean that the traffic traverses across the fabric and egress at a different site (such as a data center). Figure 7-20 illustrates this traffic pattern.

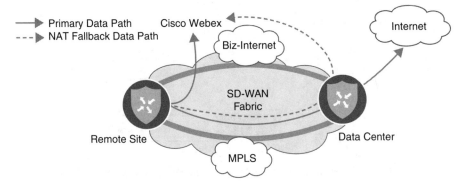

Figure 7-20 *Illustrated NAT Fallback Data Path*

In Use Case 10, the **nat-vpn 0** action is configured for guest Internet access traffic without **nat fallback** enabled. Should all of the local interfaces with NAT configured go down, then guest traffic will not fall back and be forwarded across the SD-WAN fabric and will instead be blackholed. In this use case, the data policy for Corporate VPN does have the **nat fallback** option configured, and this allows for the WebEx traffic to be back-hauled through the data center in the event of a failure of the local Internet connection. Example 7-5 shows both traffic patterns.

Example 7-5 also introduces a new set of tools for monitoring the forwarding decision of flows from the CLI: **show policy service-path** and **show policy tunnel-path**. These two **show** commands are the CLI corollaries to the Simulate Flows tool that has been shown inside of the vManage GUI.

Example 7-5 *WebEx Traffic with Failure of Local Internet Connection*

```
! When all of the transport interfaces are up / up:
!
BR2-vEdge-1# show interface description | until lte


                                       IF      IF      IF
                        AF             ADMIN   OPER    TRACKER
VPN   INTERFACE   TYPE  IP ADDRESS     STATUS  STATUS  STATUS   DESC
-------------------------------------------------------------------------
0     ge0/0       ipv4  100.64.102.2/30  Up      Up      NA       biz-internet
```

```
0    ge0/1    ipv4  172.16.102.2/30   Up      Up      NA      mpls
0    ge0/2    ipv4  100.127.102.2/30  Up      Up      NA      lte
BR2-vEdge-1#
!
! With all of the transports up / up, Webex traffic from VPN 1 will egress
! locally. This output matches Figure 7-17.
!
BR2-vEdge-1# show policy service-path vpn 1 interface ge0/3 source-ip 10.1.102.1
 dest-ip 0.0.0.0 protocol 1 app webex all
Number of possible next hops: 1
Next Hop: Remote
  Remote IP: 100.64.102.1, Interface ge0/0 Index: 4
BR2-vEdge-1#
!
! VPN 3 has connectivity to resources on the internet.
!
BR2-vEdge-1# ping vpn 3 8.8.8.8 count 4
Ping in VPN 3
PING 8.8.8.8 (8.8.8.8) 56(84) bytes of data.
64 bytes from 8.8.8.8: icmp_seq=1 ttl=53 time=26.2 ms
64 bytes from 8.8.8.8: icmp_seq=2 ttl=53 time=25.1 ms
64 bytes from 8.8.8.8: icmp_seq=3 ttl=53 time=33.7 ms
64 bytes from 8.8.8.8: icmp_seq=4 ttl=53 time=26.0 ms
--- 8.8.8.8 ping statistics ---
4 packets transmitted, 4 received, 0% packet loss, time 3004ms
rtt min/avg/max/mdev = 25.141/27.798/33.733/3.457 ms
BR2-vEdge-1#
!
! Turning ge0/0 to a down state, simulating the failure of the local internet link:
!
BR2-vEdge-1# show interface description | until lte


                                     IF      IF      IF
                    AF               ADMIN   OPER    TRACKER
VPN  INTERFACE  TYPE  IP ADDRESS     STATUS  STATUS  STATUS  DESC
----------------------------------------------------------------------------
0    ge0/0    ipv4  100.64.102.2/30   Down    Down    NA      biz-internet
0    ge0/1    ipv4  172.16.102.2/30   Up      Up      NA      mpls
0    ge0/2    ipv4  100.127.102.2/30  Up      Up      NA      lte
BR2-vEdge-1#
!
! With the local internet connection down, Webex traffic will be forwarded across
```

```
! the fabric to destinations 172.16.21.2 and 100.64.21.2. From the OMP TLOCs table,
! we can see that this is DC2-vEdge1 (System IP 10.0.20.1).
BR2-vEdge-1# show policy service-path vpn 1 interface ge0/3 source-ip 10.1.102.1
 dest-ip 0.0.0.0 protocol 1 app webex all
Number of possible next hops: 2
Next Hop: IPsec
  Source: 172.16.102.2 12346 Destination: 172.16.21.2 12366 Color: mpls
Next Hop: IPsec
  Source: 100.127.102.2 12346 Destination: 100.64.21.2 12386 Color: lte

BR2-vEdge-1#
!
! The filters on this command are used to enhance its clarity and brevity
!
BR2-vEdge-1# show omp tlocs ip 10.0.20.1 received | i mpls\|biz\|public\|C,I,R |
  exclude ::\|port | nomore
                  mpls
status          C,I,R
    public-ip            172.16.21.2
    public-ip            172.16.21.2
tloc entries for 10.0.20.1
                  biz-internet
status          C,I,R
    public-ip            100.64.21.2
    public-ip            100.64.21.2
BR2-vEdge-1#
!
! On the other hand, guest traffic originating in VPN 3 does not fallback across
! the fabric and now blackholed:
!
BR2-vEdge-1# ping vpn 3 8.8.8.8 count 4
Ping in VPN 3
PING 8.8.8.8 (8.8.8.8) 56(84) bytes of data.
From 127.1.0.2 icmp_seq=1 Destination Net Unreachable
From 127.1.0.2 icmp_seq=2 Destination Net Unreachable
From 127.1.0.2 icmp_seq=3 Destination Net Unreachable
From 127.1.0.2 icmp_seq=4 Destination Net Unreachable
--- 8.8.8.8 ping statistics ---
4 packets transmitted, 0 received, +4 errors, 100% packet loss, time 2999ms
BR2-vEdge-1# show policy service-path vpn 3 interface ge0/5 source-ip 10.1.103.1
  dest-ip 8.8.8.8 protocol 1 app icmp all
Number of possible next hops: 1
Next Hop: Blackhole
```

Use Case 11 Review

Use Case 11 starts to allude to the true power of centralized data policies: the ability to specify different forwarding behaviors on an app-by-app basis. While the forwarding decisions in this policy were made on the basis of a Layer 7 application definition, centralized data policies can match on a number of different Layer 3, Layer 4, and/or Layer 7 criteria. For example, this policy could be extended to match on a combination of the WebEx application and a source data prefix, such that the rule would only apply to users residing in certain subnets. Users outside of those specific source ranges would follow the traditional forwarding pattern.

Use Case 11 also continues to build on the **nat use-vpn 0** action with the **nat fallback** action. With these combinations of actions, network administrators can create dynamic policies to meet business needs, while at the same time being able to create predictable behavior in the event of a failure. If the network administrators are concerned about conserving limited site-to-site bandwidth, the configurations in this policy can easily be extended to provide access for many different applications using local Internet egress points. The same administrators could then be very selective about which applications would be permitted to "fall back" to the limited site-to-site tunnels. For example, a cloud-hosted payroll application may be considered business critical and permitted to fall back to the site-to-site path. At the same time, Internet radio may be permitted to use the local Internet egress path, but in the event of a failure, it would not be considered business critical and would not be permitted to fall back to the site-to-site path.

Use Case 12: Application-Based Traffic Engineering

Enterprise WANs are becoming increasingly important to the business and are constantly being tasked to provide faster and more reliable connectivity, all while using less expensive transport networks and cutting overall costs. Traditionally, organizations used expensive, leased-line transports with minimal bandwidth and guaranteed service level agreements (SLAs) in order to connect their diffuse sites. As organizations transition to hybrid transport environments (where they may still have expensive, small links that are being augmented with substantially larger circuits without guaranteed SLAs), there is an ever-greater need for new and powerful tools to be able to dictate which paths applications take as they flow across the WAN.

As Figure 7-19 from Use Case 11 shows, the currently configured policy would have non-critical business traffic, such as YouTube, load-shared across the MPLS and Biz-Internet paths. Wasting the limited and expensive MPLS bandwidth is not desired, so in this use case the centralized data policy will continue to be refined so that certain classes of traffic are forwarded across the Biz-Internet path only. This policy will consider two different classes of traffic, YouTube and Facebook, and set different forwarding rules for each. The YouTube application will be preferred across the Biz-Internet SD-WAN tunnels. In the event that the Biz-Internet tunnels are not available, the YouTube traffic will move to any of the other transports available. The second application, Facebook, will be required to use the Biz-Internet tunnels to reach the data centers. In the event that the Biz-Internet tunnels are not available, this application will be unavailable. These traffic patterns are illustrated in Figure 7-21.

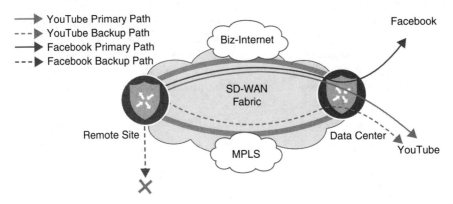

Figure 7-21   *Desired Forwarding Behavior for YouTube and Facebook Applications*

Before the policy from Example 7-4 has been modified, the forwarding behavior as shown in Example 7-6 can be observed.

Example 7-6   *Application Forwarding Behavior Without Policy Changes*

```
!
! Before modifications are made to the policy, both YouTube and Facebook traffic is
! forwarded across both links.
!
BR2-vEdge-1# show policy service-path vpn 1 interface ge0/3 source-ip 10.1.102.1
 dest-ip 0.0.0.0 protocol 1 app youtube all
Number of possible next hops: 2
Next Hop: IPsec
  Source: 172.16.102.2 12346 Destination: 172.16.21.2 12366 Color: mpls
Next Hop: IPsec
  Source: 100.64.102.2 12346 Destination: 100.64.21.2 12386 Color: biz-internet

BR2-vEdge-1# show policy service-path vpn 1 interface ge0/3 source-ip 10.1.102.1
 dest-ip 0.0.0.0 protocol 1 app facebook all
Number of possible next hops: 2
Next Hop: IPsec
  Source: 172.16.102.2 12346 Destination: 172.16.21.2 12366 Color: mpls
Next Hop: IPsec
  Source: 100.64.102.2 12346 Destination: 100.64.21.2 12386 Color: biz-internet

BR2-vEdge-1#
```

Example 7-6 again uses the **show policy service-path** command to be able to determine the path or paths that particular flows would take through a WAN Edge router. This example shows the outputs for the application "youtube" and the application "facebook," indicating that flows from both applications would be load-shared across both the MPLS and Biz-Internet tunnels to DC2-vEdge1. In order to change this behavior, the policy configured in Example 7-7 will use the **local-tloc** action and the **tloc-list** action.

The **local-tloc** action is configured with the syntax

```
set local-tloc color {color} [encap {ipsec|gre}]
```

where *color* is any one of the supported TLOC colors. This action directs packets to be forwarded out of the TLOC that is specified in the **color** argument. If this TLOC is not available (because it is not configured, the tunnel is down, or so on), then the traffic is forwarded out any valid TLOC, as indicated by the routing table. There is also a configuration command called **set local-tloc-list** that allows for the selection of one or more colors. vManage defaults to using this syntax when policies are configured through the vManage GUI.

The **tloc-list** action in a centralized data policy is similar in structure and function to the centralized control policy **tloc-list** action that was explored in Use Case 2. By using the TLOC-List action, a network administrator is statically specifying the fabric tunnel endpoints toward which the flow will be forwarded. This functionality is roughly equivalent to the **set next-hop-address** functionality in a traditional policy-based-routing route-map. With the TLOC-List action, if the TLOCs specified in the list are not available, then the traffic is blackholed, even though there may be a different path available.

In short, the **local-tloc** action selects the *preferred* egress TLOC on the *local* WAN Edge router, while the TLOC-List action *mandates* the TLOCs on the *receiving* WAN Edge that the traffic will be forwarded to. The modified policy in Example 7-7 shows these two different configurations.

Example 7-7 *Application-Based Traffic Engineering Policy*

```
policy
 ! <<<No changes were made to the control policies, VPN membership policies, or
 ! the Guest VPN data policies, and they are omitted for brevity.>>>
 !
data-policy _CorporateVPN_Branch_-1763799758
  vpn-list CorporateVPN
    sequence 1
     match
      app-list TRUSTED_APPS
      source-ip 0.0.0.0/0
     !
     action accept
      nat use-vpn 0
```

```
     nat fallback
     count CORP_DCA_359403425
   !
  !
 !
 ! Sequence 11 uses the local-tloc-list command to indicate the color or colors
 ! on the local WAN Edge that are PREFERRED to be used for forwarding this flow.
 !
 sequence 11
  match
   app-list YouTube
   source-ip 0.0.0.0/0
  !
  action accept
   count CORP_YOUTUBE_359403425
   set
    local-tloc-list
     color biz-internet
     encap ipsec
   !
  !
 !
 !
 ! Sequence 21 uses the tloc-list command to specify the TLOCs that this traffic
 ! MUST be forwarded to. If the TLOCs are unavailable, the traffic will be
 ! dropped.
 !
 sequence 21
  match
   app-list Facebook
   source-ip 0.0.0.0/0
  !
  action accept
   count CORP_FACEBOOK_359403425
   set
    vpn 1
    tloc-list Europe_DC_INET_TLOCS
   !
  !
 !
 default-action accept
!
```

```
  vpn-list GUEST_ACCESS_VPN
   ! <<<Omitted for brevity>>>
  !
 lists
 ! <<<Some lists without changes are omitted for brevity>>>
  !
  app-list Facebook
   app facebook
   app facebook_messenger
   app fbcdn
   app facebook_mail
   app facebook_live
   !
  app-list YouTube
   app youtube
   app youtube_hd
   !
  site-list BranchOffices
   site-id 100-199
   !
  tloc-list Europe_DC_INET_TLOCS
   tloc 10.0.20.1 color biz-internet encap ipsec preference 500
   tloc 10.0.20.2 color biz-internet encap ipsec preference 400
   !
  !
 !
apply-policy
 site-list Europe_Branches
  control-policy Euro_Reg_Mesh_with_FW_MultiTopo out
  !
 site-list BranchOffices
  data-policy _CorporateVPN_Branch_-1763799758 from-service
  control-policy Branch_Extranet_Route_Leaking in
  vpn-membership vpnMembership_373293275
  !
 site-list DCs
  control-policy DC_Inbound_Control_Policy in
  !
 site-list North_America_Branches
  control-policy North_America_Reg_Mesh_with_FW out
  !
 !
```

In sequence 11 in Example 7-7, YouTube application traffic is being matched and then the **local-tloc-list** action is configured to forward this traffic out of the Biz-Internet TLOC, if the TLOC is available. In sequence 21, Facebook traffic is being matched and is being forwarded to Biz-Internet TLOCs on DC2-vEdge1 and DC2-vEdge2, as specified with the **tloc-list** action. The effects of these two different configuration options can be seen in Example 7-8, where the results are shown in both a steady state and a state where an Internet connection of DC2 has failed.

 Example 7-8 *Application Traffic Engineering Behavior with Policy in Steady State and Failed State*

```
!
! When all of the Biz-Internet BFD Sessions to Site 20 are operational:
!
BR2-vEdge-1# show bfd sessions remote-color biz-internet site-id 20
                                        SOURCE TLOC        REMOTE TLOC
                         DST PUBLIC                        DST PUBLIC          DETEC
T      TX
SYSTEM IP         SITE ID  STATE        COLOR              COLOR                SOURCE I
P                          IP                              PORT       ENCAP    MULTI
PLIER  INTERVAL(msec) UPTIME           TRANSITIONS
---------------------------------------------------------------------------
---------------------------------------------------------------------------
-------------------------------------------
10.0.20.1         20       up           biz-internet       biz-internet      100.64.1
02.2                       100.64.21.2                     12386      ipsec   7
       1000                0:00:24:25   6
10.0.20.2         20       up           biz-internet       biz-internet      100.64.1
02.2                       100.64.22.2                     12386      ipsec   7
       1000                0:00:24:25   5
10.0.20.1         20       up           lte                biz-internet      100.127.
102.2                      100.64.21.2                     12386      ipsec   7
       1000                0:03:07:26   1
10.0.20.2         20       up           lte                biz-internet      100.127.
102.2                      100.64.22.2                     12386      ipsec   7
       1000                0:00:47:23   1
!
! In steady state, when all of the links are operational, the two configurations
! have the same effect:  Traffic matching the YouTube app-list and traffic matching
! the Facebook app-list are both forwarded across biz-internet tunnel to
! 100.64.21.2 (DC2-vEdge1).
BR2-vEdge-1# show policy service-path vpn 1 interface ge0/3 source-ip 10.1.102.1
  dest-ip 0.0.0.0 protocol 1 app youtube all
!
```

```
Number of possible next hops: 1
Next Hop: IPsec
  Source: 100.64.102.2 12346 Destination: 100.64.21.2 12386 Color: biz-internet


BR2-vEdge-1# show policy service-path vpn 1 interface ge0/3 source-ip 10.1.102.1
dest-ip 0.0.0.0 protocol 1 app facebook all
Number of possible next hops: 1
Next Hop: IPsec
  Source: 100.64.102.2 12346 Destination: 100.64.21.2 12386 Color: biz-internet


!
! After an internet failure at DC2, all of the Biz-Internet BFD Sessions to
! Site 20 are down:
!
BR2-vEdge-1# show bfd sessions remote-color biz-internet site-id 20
                                   SOURCE TLOC      REMOTE TLOC
            DST PUBLIC             DST PUBLIC         DETECT    TX

SYSTEM IP        SITE ID  STATE    COLOR            COLOR          SOURCE IP
     IP                            PORT       ENCAP  MULTIPLIER  INTERVAL(msec)
  UPTIME
      TRANSITIONS
-----------------------------------------------------------------------------------
-----------------------------------------------------------------------------------
-------------
10.0.20.1      20      down     biz-internet   biz-internet   100.64.102.2
       100.64.21.2                12386      ipsec  7          1000          NA
    11
10.0.20.2      20      down     biz-internet   biz-internet   100.64.102.2
       100.64.22.2                12386      ipsec  7          1000          NA
    10
10.0.20.1      20      down     lte            biz-internet   100.127.102.2
       100.64.21.2                12386      ipsec  7          1000          NA
    4
10.0.20.2      20      down     lte            biz-internet   100.127.102.2
       100.64.22.2                12386      ipsec  7          1000          NA
    4
!
! In a failed state, where there is no longer a path to DC2 via the Biz-Internet color,
! the YouTube traffic will be forwarded across the MPLS path.
!
```

```
BR2-vEdge-1# show policy service-path vpn 1 interface ge0/3 source-ip 10.1.102.1
dest-ip 0.0.0.0 protocol 1 app youtube all
Number of possible next hops: 1
Next Hop: IPsec
  Source: 172.16.102.2 12346 Destination: 172.16.21.2 12366 Color: mpls
!
! The Facebook application, will not failover to the MPLS path. The tloc-list
! action statically specifies the next-hop tunnel endpoints.  If those
! endpoints are not available, the traffic is blackholed.
!
BR2-vEdge-1# show policy service-path vpn 1 interface ge0/3 source-ip 10.1.102.1
dest-ip 0.0.0.0 protocol 1 app facebook all
Number of possible next hops: 1
Next Hop: Blackhole
BR2-vEdge-1#
```

When the network is in a state where all of the Biz-Internet tunnels are operating as expected, Example 7-8 shows that the forwarding behavior for these two configurations is the same: both the YouTube and Facebook flows are forwarded across the Biz-Internet tunnel to 100.64.21.2, the interface IP address of DC2-vEdge1. The difference between these two configurations comes when the network is in a failed state, such as would occur if the Biz-Internet transport to Datacenter 2 was severed by a fiber-seeking backhoe. Example 7-8 shows that the YouTube application, configured with the **local-tloc-list** action, fails over to the MPLS TLOC and continues to operate. The Facebook application, on the other hand, which was configured with the **tloc-list** action where the next hops were statically specified, does not failover, and the traffic is instead blackholed.

Use Case 12 Review

This use case again illustrates that there are often several different design and configuration choices that can be used to accomplish any specific task. It is important for administrators to consider not only the forwarding behavior that is desired, but also to think through the possible outcomes and effects of different failure scenarios, and the effects of design choices on the eventual outcomes. As Example 7-8 shows, TLOC lists are a powerful but unforgiving tool; use them with caution.

This example used Facebook and YouTube as two sample applications for illustration purposes, but these placeholders can easily be replaced with applications that are important to the business: thin clients, enterprise resource planning (ERP) systems, file servers, email, collaboration software, and so on. Network administrators can apply the lessons here to solve the challenges facing their organizations.

Use Case 13: Protecting Corporate Users with a Cloud-Delivered Firewall

Throughout the course of this chapter, we have explored use cases where users were accessing the Internet by egressing directly from the WAN Edge, such as the WebEx application in Use Case 11. In Use Case 12, there were examples of traffic engineering policies that allowed users to access Internet-based applications by backhauling the traffic through a data center. Use Case 13 will explore a third option: integrating a cloud-delivered firewall (CDFW), such as Cisco Umbrella Secure Internet Gateway (SIG), into the SD-WAN fabric, and redirecting traffic flows to Umbrella SIG with service insertion policies. This use case is going to focus on the integration of Umbrella SIG with the SD-WAN fabric and the centralized data policies that are necessary in order to redirect traffic to Umbrella SIG. More information about Cisco Umbrella SIG, and the specific configurations for integrating Umbrella with Cisco SD-WAN, can be found at the end of this chapter and at http://cisco.com/go/umbrella.

In Chapter 6, a firewall inside one of the sites was configured and advertised as a service in the SD-WAN fabric. All of the traffic that was passing between sites was forwarded through the service based on manipulating the routing table with a centralized control policy. In this use case, rather than manipulating the routing table to send all traffic through the CDFW, a centralized data policy will be created to only send a specific set of applications through the firewall—specifically, a variety of Google apps. Figure 7-22 illustrates this traffic flow.

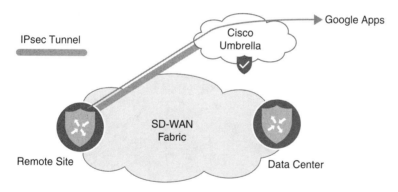

Figure 7-22 *Redirecting Google Apps Traffic to the Cisco Umbrella Secure Internet Gateway*

The first step in this use case will be configuring the connectivity to the CDFW. Next, we'll configure the CDFW as a service in the SD-WAN fabric, as shown in Example 7-9. While this example uses Cisco Umbrella, this integration would also work with most any other CDFW provider that can use IPsec or GRE tunnels to establish connectivity.

Example 7-9 *Local Configuration with CDFW Tunnel*

```
!
! An IPSec tunnel to Cisco Umbrella is configured in VPN0.
!
BR2-vEdge-1# show running-config vpn 0 interface ipsec1
vpn 0
 interface ipsec1
  ip address 10.255.255.253/30
  tunnel-source-interface ge0/0
  tunnel-destination      146.112.82.8
  ike
   version      2
   rekey        28800
   cipher-suite aes256-cbc-sha1
   group        14
   authentication-type
    pre-shared-key
     pre-shared-secret abcdegfhijklmnopqrstuvwxyz
     local-id          SDWAN_BOOK@XXXXXXX-XXXXXXXXX-umbrella.com
     remote-id         146.112.82.8
    !
   !
  !
  ipsec
   rekey                   3600
   replay-window           512
   cipher-suite            aes256-gcm
   perfect-forward-secrecy none
  !
  no shutdown
 !
!
! The IPSec tunnel is in the Up / Up state
!
BR2-vEdge-1# show interface ipsec1
                                      IF      IF      IF
                         AF           ADMIN   OPER    TRACKER
VPN  INTERFACE  TYPE  IP ADDRESS      STATUS  STATUS  STATUS  DESC
--------------------------------------------------------------------
0    ipsec1     ipv4  10.255.255.253/30 Up    Up      NA      -

!
! A service is defined in VPN1 that references the new ipsec tunnel in VPN 0
!
```

```
BR2-vEdge-1# show running-config vpn 1
vpn 1
 service IDP interface ipsec1
 interface ge0/3
  ip address 10.1.102.1/30
  no shutdown
 !
 ip route 10.1.102.64/26 10.1.102.2
BR2-vEdge-1#
```

The first step in the process is to establish the tunnel for connectivity to the CDFW solution, as shown in Example 7-9. The details for establishing these tunnels are typically provided by the CDFW vendor. The documentation for configuring a tunnel with Cisco Umbrella SIG can be found here: https://docs.umbrella.com/umbrella-user-guide/docs/ add-a-tunnel-viptela. After the tunnel interface is configured, the next step is to configure a network service with the **service** command under the service-side VPN. This configuration is very similar to the service that was configured in Chapter 6. In this case, a service type of **IDP** (for Intrusion Detection and Prevention) was selected. After the service is configured, a centralized data policy needs to be created to redirect the traffic of interest to the network service.

Centralized control policies are enforced centrally on the vSmarts and are only evaluated when sending or receiving control plane updates with the Overlay Management Protocol. As such, there is limited impact from the control policies on the vSmarts and no performance impact on the WAN Edge routers. Centralized data policies, however, are forwarded to the WAN Edges from the vSmarts, where each flow is then evaluated against the policy. Hence, there can be significant performance implications to the structure of the policy. It is beneficial to structure the policies in a way that as few of the sequences as necessary are evaluated for each flow. For example, if you have a data policy that is only concerned with external applications, then create the first sequence of the data policy to match all of the internal traffic and eliminate it from consideration of the rest of the sequences in the policy (rather than relying on the default action at the end of the data policy).

While not strictly necessary for this policy in a lab environment, this best practice has been implemented in the policy in Example 7-10 by the first sequence in the policy.

Example 7-10 *SIG Policy*

```
policy
 ! <<<No changes were made to the control policies, VPN membership policies, or
 ! the Guest VPN data policies, and they are omitted for brevity.>>>
 !
 data-policy _CorporateVPN_Branch__1930818813
```

```
vpn-list CorporateVPN
 !
 ! Sequence 1 stops any traffic that is being routed across the fabric from
 ! needing to be processed by any of the rules that are for internet bound
 ! applications.
 !
 sequence 1
  match
   destination-data-prefix-list INTERNAL_ADDRESSES
   !
  action accept
   count INTERNAL_PCKTS_1041684049
   !
   !
 sequence 11
  match
   app-list TRUSTED_APPS
   source-ip 0.0.0.0/0
   !
  action accept
   nat use-vpn 0
   nat fallback
   count CORP_DCA_1041684049
   !
  !
 sequence 21
  match
   app-list YouTube
   source-ip 0.0.0.0/0
   !
  action accept
   count CORP_YOUTUBE_1041684049
   set
    local-tloc-list
     color biz-internet
     encap ipsec
    !
   !
  !
 sequence 31
  match
   app-list Facebook
   source-ip 0.0.0.0/0
```

```
       !
      action accept
       count CORP_FACEBOOK_1041684049
       set
        vpn 1
        tloc-list Europe_DC_INET_TLOCS
        !
       !
      !
     !
     ! Sequence 41 redirects applications matching the "Google_Apps" list to the
     ! local instance of the IDP service. The "IDP" name matches the configured
     ! service in VPN 1.
     !
     sequence 41
      match
       app-list Google_Apps
       source-ip 0.0.0.0/0
       !
      action accept
       count UMBRELLA_PCKTS_1041684049
       set
        service  IDP local
       !
      !
     !
   default-action accept
   !
  vpn-list GUEST_ACCESS_VPN
   ! <<<Omitted for brevity>>>
   !
  lists
  ! <<<Some lists without changes are omitted for brevity>>>
   !
  !
  ! vManage includes, by default, two app-lists: one for Google_Apps, and a second for
  ! Microsoft_Apps. These two lists contain a myriad of different applications that are
  ! produced by the two organizations. Custom app-lists can be created to match
  ! only a subset of apps, but the default app-list is used in this example. The
  ! entire list is not displayed for brevity.
  !
   app-list Google_Apps
```

```
      app gmail
      app google
      app google_translate
      app gmail_drive
      app gtalk
      app youtube
      app youtube_hd
! <<< Output omitted>>>
    !
   app-list TRUSTED_APPS
    app webex-meeting
    app webex_weboffice
    app webex
    !
   app-list YouTube
    app youtube
    app youtube hd
    !
   data-prefix-list INTERNAL_ADDRESSES
    ip-prefix 10.0.0.0/8
    !
   !
 !
apply-policy
 site-list Europe_Branches
  control-policy Euro_Reg_Mesh_with_FW_MultiTopo out
  !
 site-list BranchOffices
  data-policy _CorporateVPN_Branch__1930818813 from-service
  control-policy Branch_Extranet_Route_Leaking in
  vpn-membership vpnMembership_373293275
  !
 site-list DCs
  control-policy DC_Inbound_Control_Policy in
  !
 site-list North_America_Branches
  control-policy North_America_Reg_Mesh_with_FW out
  !
 !
```

Example 7-10 shows the changes that were made to the policy in order to accomplish the objectives of this use case. In sequence 41, packets that match the "Google_Apps" app-list are forwarded to the CDFW with the action **service local** command. The **service**

local action is configured with the following syntax: **set service** *{service}* **local** [**restrict**]. This command is used to forward the traffic to one of the network services that is locally present on the WAN Edge, such as what was configured in VPN 1 in Example 7-9. The *service* value can be any one of the seven supported network services: FW, IPS, IDP, netsvc1, netsvc2, netsvc3, or netsvc4. The optional [**restrict**] value specifies that if the local service is unavailable, the traffic should be dropped.

With the policy changes in Example 7-10 applied to the network, you will see the results in Example 7-11.

Example 7-11 *Validating Service Insertion Policy with CDFW*

```
BR2-vEdge-1# show policy data-policy-filter data-policy-vpnlist CorporateVPN
data-policy-filter _CorporateVPN_Branch__1930818813
 data-policy-vpnlist CorporateVPN
  data-policy-counter CORP_DCA_-240945300
   packets 1
   bytes   96
  data-policy-counter CORP_YOUTUBE_-240945300
   packets 1
   bytes   96
  data-policy-counter CORP_FACEBOOK_-240945300
   packets 141
   bytes   13737
  data-policy-counter INTERNAL_PCKTS_-240945300
   packets 47
   bytes   11748
!
! The counters indicate that traffic is being forwarded to the Cisco Umbrella SIG.
!
  data-policy-counter UMBRELLA_PCKTS_-240945300
   packets 272
   bytes   43518
BR2-vEdge-1#
!
! The "show policy service-path" output for "google" and "gmail", two different!
! services that are covered by the app-list "Google_Apps", are being forwarded
! out of the IPSec tunnel that connects to the Umbrella SIG.
!
BR2-vEdge-1# show policy service-path vpn 1 interface ge0/3 source-ip 10.1.102.1
dest-ip 0.0.0.0 protocol 1 app google
Next Hop: RFC-IPsec

BR2-vEdge-1# show policy service-path vpn 1 interface ge0/3 source-ip 10.1.102.1
dest-ip 0.0.0.0 protocol 1 app gmail
```

```
Next Hop: RFC-IPsec
!
! However, the "show policy service-path" output for "youtube," which is also
! covered by the app-list "Google_Apps", is being forwarded to DC2-vEdge1
! instead of Umbrella SIG.
!
BR2-vEdge-1# show policy service-path vpn 1 interface ge0/3 source-ip 10.1.102.1
dest-ip 0.0.0.0 protocol 1 app youtube
Next Hop: IPsec
  Source: 100.64.102.2 12346 Destination: 100.64.21.2 12386 Color: biz-internet
!
! The "show policy from-vsmart lists app-list" output confirms that the app
! "youtube" is part of two different app-lists: "Google_Apps" and "YouTube".
!
BR2-vEdge-1# show policy from-vsmart lists app-list | i Google\|You\|you
from-vsmart lists app-list Google_Apps
 app youtube
 app youtube_hd
from-vsmart lists app-list YouTube
 app youtube
 app youtube_hd
BR2-vEdge-1#
!
! The "show policy from-vsmart" output indicates why "youtube" is being routed
! differently than "google" and "gmail". The app-list "YouTube" is being matched
! in sequence 11, and has the action "local-tloc-list" applied to it. The
! rest of the sequences are therefore not evaluated for "youtube" traffic. Since
! Cisco SD-WAN policies use a first-match logic, the actions in sequence 41 are
! never applied to "youtube" traffic.
!
BR2-vEdge-1# show policy from-vsmart data-policy vpn-list CorporateVPN seq 11,41

from-vsmart data-policy _CorporateVPN_Branch__1930818813
 vpn-list CorporateVPN
  sequence 11
   match
    source-ip 0.0.0.0/0
    app-list  YouTube
   action accept
    count CORP_YOUTUBE_-240945300
    set
```

```
      local-tloc-list
       color biz-internet
       encap ipsec
 sequence 41
   match
    source-ip 0.0.0.0/0
    app-list  Google_Apps
   action accept
    count UMBRELLA_PCKTS_-240945300
    set
     service IDP
     service local
BR2-vEdge-1#
```

Example 7-11 shows that both the **show policy data-policy-filter** counters and **show policy service-path** can be used to validate that the service insertion policy is successfully redirecting traffic to the Cisco Umbrella SIG service. This example also highlights potential challenges that network administrators may encounter when configuring centralized data policies. In this policy, the application "youtube" was matched by the criteria in both sequence 11 and in sequence 41. Since the sequences are evaluated ordinally, when the application flows were matched by sequence 11, the actions for sequence 11 were performed and no further sequences were evaluated. This resulted in the "youtube" traffic being forwarded across the Biz-Internet tunnel, rather than being redirected with the service insertion action to the CDFW.

Use Case 13 Review

In this use case, service insertion was used to redirect specific traffic flows to Cisco Umbrella Secure Internet Gateway (SIG). Service insertion can be used for many other things than redirecting traffic to CDFWs. As Use Case 6 showed, service insertion can also be used for firewalling traffic traveling between two sites on the fabric. The uses of service insertion aren't limited to inserting security services; other potential uses of service insertion would be redirecting traffic to WAN optimization appliances, load balancers, proxies, network sniffers, and so on.

Use Case 14: Protecting Applications from Packet Loss

In the final use case of this chapter, we will cover several tools that can be used to protect applications from the effects of lossy transport links. IP-based networks, by definition, operate at a best-effort level of packet delivery. There is no mechanism at the IP layer to ensure successful delivery of the packet, regardless of whether the underlying transport is a directly connected cable, a service such as MPLS with a contractually guaranteed SLA, or the public Internet. It is typical for all networks to experience some degree of packet loss, and most applications designed to operate on IP networks are engineered to tolerate some degree of packet loss.

One of the most effective ways to counter the effects of packet loss on the underlying transport networks is simply to move sensitive applications off of transports that are currently experiencing packet loss. In the Cisco SD-WAN fabric, this function is achieved through Application-Aware Routing policies and will be discussed in greater detail in Chapter 8. However, there are often circumstances (such as when there is only a single transport link available, or when all transport links are currently experiencing some degree of packet loss), when simply moving an application off of a lossy transport link is not a viable option. In this use case, two different tools to mitigate the effects of loss in these circumstances will be discussed: Forward Error Correction (FEC) and packet duplication.

Forward Error Correction for Audio and Video

The first technology we are going to examine is Forward Error Correction (FEC). FEC is not a new or novel technology, as different methods have been used with different implementations for decades. The principle behind FEC is that additional information (parity) is transmitted along with the original message such that if a portion of the original message is compromised, the entirety of the original message can be reconstructed. There are many protocols in common use that implement some form of FEC at different layers of the networking stack: 40GBASE-T and 100GE Ethernet standards use FEC at Layer 2, and most Voice over IP (VoIP) protocols implement some form of FEC at Layer 7. With Cisco SD-WAN, we now also have the ability to add FEC to the network layer.

Figure 7-23 shows the current state of the MPLS transport network on BR2-vEdge1. The **Monitor > Network > WAN Tunnel** output indicates that the MPLS network is currently experiencing 4–6% packet loss. In this use case, we will implement FEC in order to mitigate the impact of this lossy transport network on the audio and video applications that the employees are using to collaborate with.

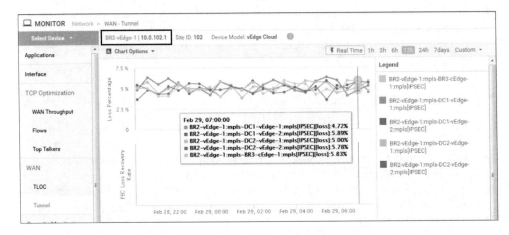

Figure 7-23   *Monitor > Network > WAN Tunnel Shows the Current Packet Loss Rates*

With Cisco SD-WAN, FEC operates on sets of four packets called an FEC block, as illustrated in Figure 7-24. In the first step, the four packets in an FEC block are processed with a mathematical operation called XOR. The result of this operation is transmitted in the fifth packet, called a parity packet. Each of the packets is encoded with a new FEC header and transmitted to the receiver. If any one of the original four packets is lost in transit to the receiver, as indicated in Step 2, but the parity packet is received with the three remaining original packets, the XOR operation is reversed such that the lost packet can be reconstructed from the three that were received and the parity information that is stored in the fifth packet, as indicated in Step 3. If two or more of the five transmitted packets (four data and one parity) are corrupted or lost, the lost packets cannot be reconstructed, and only the correctly received packets will be forwarded on to the end host. In this circumstance, the end hosts will notice that packet loss has occurred.

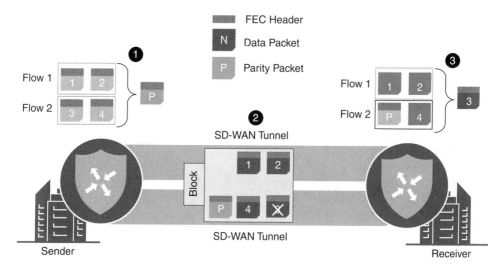

Figure 7-24 *FEC Illustration*

The process of sending five packets (four data packets and one parity packet) for every four packets worth of data being transmitted across the WAN would result in an increase of bandwidth consumption of at least 25% (the parity packet is as large as the largest data packet out of the set of four in the FEC block). While this increase in bandwidth consumption can be beneficial during times of packet loss on the transport links, it may also be unnecessary during a large portion of the time. In order to optimize this, there are two different FEC configuration modes: FEC-always and FEC-adaptive. FEC-always operates exactly as it sounds: the FEC process takes place unconditionally. FEC-adaptive, on the other hand, only operates when the loss percentage on the transport link is detected to be more than 2%. As of 19.2 code, this 2% value is static and is not configurable.

In order to implement this packet loss minimization policy, we will need a new sequence to match on the audio/video application family. Then, we need to enable FEC-adaptive in order to provide FEC when the transport packet losses are above 2%. In addition to configuring this on the data policy that is applied to the branch routers, a corresponding policy will need to be configured on the data center routers so that the traffic that is being forwarded from the data center to the branch sites is also protected by FEC. This policy also configures the **local-tloc** action in order to pin the traffic to the MPLS transport to better illustrate what is happening with the FEC policy. Example 7-12 shows these configurations.

Example 7-12   *FEC Policy*

```
policy
 ! <<<No changes were made to the control policies, VPN membership policies, or
 ! the Guest VPN data policies, and they are omitted for brevity.>>>
 !
 ! Branch Data Policy
 !
data-policy _CorporateVPN_Branch__1623113498
 vpn-list CorporateVPN
  ! Sequence 1 matches all of the applications in the Audio / Video App family
  ! and turns on fec-adaptive.
  !
   sequence 1
    match
     app-list AUDIO_VIDEO_APPS
     source-ip 0.0.0.0/0
    !
    action accept
     count CORP_AUDIO_VIDEO_-548650615
     loss-protect fec-adaptive
     loss-protection forward-error-correction adaptive
     set
      local-tloc-list
       color mpls
     !
    !
   !
   sequence 11
    match
     destination-data-prefix-list INTERNAL_ADDRESSES
     !
    action accept
     count INTERNAL_PCKTS_-548650615
     !
    !
   !<<<<remaining sequences are unchanged and omitted for brevity>>>>
   !
  default-action accept
 !
  vpn-list GUEST_ACCESS_VPN
   ! <<<Omitted for brevity>>>
```

```
 !
 ! A corresponding policy is also configured on the datacenter routers in order
 ! to apply the FEC policy to traffic that is being sent from the DC to the Branch
 !
 data-policy _CorporateVPN_DC_Corp__443359352
  vpn-list CorporateVPN
   sequence 1
    match
      app-list AUDIO_VIDEO_APPS
      source-ip 0.0.0.0/0
     !
    action accept
      count CORP_AUDIO_VIDEO_-1728404761
      loss-protect fec-adaptive
      loss-protection forward-error-correction adaptive
      set
       local-tloc-list
        color mpls
     !
    !
   !
  default-action accept
 !
 lists
 ! <<<Some lists without changes are omitted for brevity>>>
 !
  app-list AUDIO_VIDEO_APPS
   app-family audio-video
   app-family audio_video
   !
   !
  !
 !
apply-policy
 site-list Europe_Branches
  control-policy Euro_Reg_Mesh_with_FW_MultiTopo out
 !
 site-list BranchOffices
  data-policy _CorporateVPN_Branch__1623113498 from-service
  control-policy Branch_Extranet_Route_Leaking in
 vpn-membership vpnMembership_373293275
 !
 site-list DCs
  data-policy _CorporateVPN_DC_Corp__443359352 from-service
```

```
  control-policy DC_Inbound_Control_Policy in
 !
site-list North_America_Branches
 control-policy North_America_Reg_Mesh_with_FW out
 !
!
```

Example 7-12 includes the new sequence that was added into the data policy for the branch sites as well as the new policy that was created and applied to the data center sites. The effects of this policy can be seen with the **show tunnel statistics fec** command, as shown in Example 7-13.

Example 7-13   *Validating FEC Policy from the Command Line*

```
DC2-vEdge-1# show tunnel statistics fec dest-ip 172.16.102.2
tunnel stats ipsec 172.16.21.2 172.16.102.2 12366 12346
 fec-rx-data-pkts       60308
 fec-rx-parity-pkts     15095
 fec-tx-data-pkts       759660
 fec-tx-parity-pkts     189915
 fec-reconstruct-pkts  1100
 fec-capable            true
 fec-dynamic            true
DC2-vEdge-1#
```

Example 7-13 shows the output from DC2-vEdge-1, the recipient of the flows from BR2-vEdge1. The **fec-rx-data-pkts** and **fec-rx-parity-pkts** values are the number of data packets and parity packets, respectively, that have been received by this router. Allowing for slight discrepancies, due to the packets that may have been lost in transit, it is notable that the approximately 60,000 received data packets are approximately four times the 15,000 received parity packets. This is as would be expected since there are four data packets and a single parity packet in each FEC block. The **fec-reconstruct-pkts** value specifies how many packets were able to be recovered based on the received parity packets. This indicates that there were 1,100 times where at least three, but not four, of the data packets in the FEC block were received by DC2-vEdge-1. Using the received parity packet, the router was able to reconstruct the missing packets for these blocks, and the end hosts were unaware that any packet loss occurred during the transmission. The ratio of FEC blocks that were able to be reconstructed versus the total number of missing packets is graphed as the FEC Loss Recovery Rate in Figure 7-25. The **fec-tx-data-pkts** and **fec-tx-parity-pkts** values specify how many data packets and parity packets, respectively, have been sent to BR2-vEdge1.

Packet Duplication for Credit Card Transactions

As Figure 7-25 indicates, while FEC can be effective at dramatically reducing the number of packets that are lost by the end applications, even in the preceding example, there are many times when the Loss Recovery Rate is not 100%. For those circumstances where the utmost effort needs to be made to have zero packet loss, packet duplication may be the appropriate solution.

Figure 7-26 illustrates WAN Edges forwarding traffic flows with a packet duplication policy enabled. For each packet that is forwarded across a tunnel, a duplicate packet is forwarded across a different tunnel between the same pair of WAN Edge routers. The tunnel that is selected to forward the duplicate packet is the tunnel that currently has the lowest rate of packet loss of any of the tunnels between the pair of WAN Edges (excluding the tunnel that was used to forward the original packet).

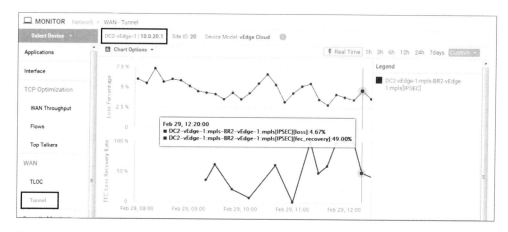

Figure 7-25   *The Current Packet Loss Rates and FEC Recovery Rates*

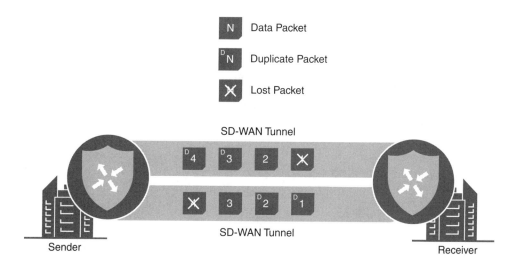

Figure 7-26   *Packet Duplication Illustration*

This type of policy is commonly used in retail environments and applied to credit card transactions. Credit card transactions are typically very small flows, but if a packet is lost in transit and is required to be retransmitted, the end-user experience can be slowed down dramatically. For this reason, network administrators find that it may be worth the "price" of transmitting every packet twice in order to ensure that the latency penalty caused by a packet needing to be retransmitted can be avoided.

Example 7-14 demonstrates the forwarding conditions between the credit card reader in branch 2 and the payment server in the data center through the use of Internet Control Message Protocol (ICMP). The current path between these two sites is experiencing more than 3% packet loss.

Example 7-14 *Packet Loss on PCI Segment Resulting in Slow Credit Card Processing*

```
test@BR2-PCI:~$ sudo ping 10.2.10.100 -i .001 -c 10000 -q
PING 10.2.10.100 (10.2.10.100) 56(84) bytes of data.

--- 10.2.10.100 ping statistics ---
10000 packets transmitted, 9612 received, 3% packet loss, time 50580ms
rtt min/avg/max/mdev = 2.398/4.804/104.705/2.810 ms, pipe 9
test@BR2-PCI:~$
```

Example 7-15 shows the data policies that are configured on the PCI VPNs in order to perform packet duplication and protect this loss-sensitive traffic. Note that two sequences are configured in both the policy applied to the data center and the policy applied to the branches. One sequence matches traffic with a source address of the payment servers; the other sequence matches the return traffic (traffic with a destination address of the payment servers). Structuring the policy this way enables the policy to be used for both the data center and branch locations simultaneously.

Example 7-15 *Packet Duplication Policy*

```
policy
 ! <<<No changes were made to the control policies, VPN membership policies,
 ! the Guest VPN or the Corporate VPN data policies, and they are omitted for
 ! brevity.>>>
 !
 data-policy _CorporateVPN_Branch_-1923459860
  vpn-list CorporateVPN
  ! <<<Omitted for brevity>>>
  !
  vpn-list PCI_VPN
    sequence 1
     match
       source-data-prefix-list PAYMENT_SERVERS
      !
     action accept
```

```
       count PCI_PCKTS_-1949123913
       set
        local-tloc-list
         color mpls
        !
        loss-protect pkt-dup
        loss-protection packet-duplication
     !
    !
   sequence 11
    match
        destination-data-prefix-list PAYMENT_SERVERS
     !
    action accept
     count PCI_PCKTS_-1949123913
     set
      local-tloc-list
       color mpls
      !
        loss-protect pkt-dup
        loss-protection packet-duplication
     !
    !
 default-action accept
 !
 vpn-list GUEST_ACCESS_VPN
 !  <<<Omitted for brevity>>>
 !
data-policy _CorporateVPN_DC_Corp_1741652260
 vpn-list CorporateVPN
 !  <<<Omitted for brevity>>>
 !
 vpn-list PCI_VPN
   sequence 1
    match
        source-data-prefix-list PAYMENT_SERVERS
     !
    action accept
     count PCI_PCKTS_1715988207
     set
      local-tloc-list
       color mpls
      !
        loss-protect pkt-dup
        loss-protection packet-duplication
     !
```

```
      !
      sequence 11
       match
         destination-data-prefix-list PAYMENT_SERVERS
        !
       action accept
         count PCI_PCKTS_1715988207
         set
          local-tloc-list
           color mpls
          !
         loss-protect pkt-dup
         loss-protection packet-duplication
        !
      !
 default-action accept
 !
 lists
 ! <<<Some lists without changes are omitted for brevity>>>
 !
  data-prefix-list PAYMENT_SERVERS
   ip-prefix 10.2.10.0/24
   !
  vpn-list PCI_VPN
   vpn 2
   !
  !
 !
apply-policy
 site-list Europe_Branches
  control-policy Euro_Reg_Mesh_with_FW_MultiTopo out
  !
 site-list BranchOffices
  data-policy _CorporateVPN_Branch_-1923459860 from-service
  control-policy Branch_Extranet_Route_Leaking in
  vpn-membership vpnMembership_373293275
  !
 site-list DCs
  data-policy _CorporateVPN_DC_Corp_1741652260 from-service
  control-policy DC_Inbound_Control_Policy in
  !
 site-list North_America_Branches
  control-policy North_America_Reg_Mesh_with_FW out
  !
 !
```

After the policy in Example 7-15 is applied, the same test is performed again on the credit card reader as was performed in Example 7-14. As Example 7-16 shows, the packet loss has been completely eliminated from the perspective of the end hosts.

Example 7-16   *Results after Packet Duplication Applied to the Network*

```
test@BR2-PCI:~$ sudo ping 10.2.10.100 -i .001 -c 10000 -q
PING 10.2.10.100 (10.2.10.100) 56(84) bytes of data.


--- 10.2.10.100 ping statistics ---
10000 packets transmitted, 10000 received, 0% packet loss, time 45476ms
rtt min/avg/max/mdev = 2.385/4.512/53.553/1.963 ms, pipe 11
test@BR2-PCI:~$
```

Using the Tunnel Packet Duplication Statistics output from the Real Time display on DC1-vEdge1, Figure 7-27 shows in the PKTDUP RX column that only 9,800 of the original 10,000 packets were received on the MPLS tunnel. However, because all 10,000 duplicated packets were received on the Internet tunnel, as indicated by the 10,000 output in the PKTDUP RX OTHER column, the value in the PKTDUP RX THIS column is 10,000. The PKTDUP RX THIS column reflects the total number of original packets that the WAN Edge was able to receive from a combination of the primary tunnel and the tunnel forwarding the duplicate packets.

Figure 7-27   *Real-Time Output Indicating the Packet Duplication Statistics on DC1-vEdge1*

Output in PKTDUP TX and PKTDUP TX OTHER of Figure 7-27 indicate that the 10,000 reply packets were also transmitted down the MPLS tunnel and duplicated down the Biz-Internet tunnel. It is a good thing that the packets were duplicated, because according to the output in Figure 7-28, only 9,812 of the original 10,000 packets were received on the MPLS path. Just as with the DC1-vEdge1 router, the 10,000 value in PKTDUP RX THIS, which represents the number of original packets received across any transport tunnel and ready to be forwarded to the local end hosts, indicates that no packets were lost in transit for which a duplicate did not successfully arrive.

Figure 7-28 *Real-Time Output Indicating the Packet Duplication Statistics on BR2-vEdge1*

Use Case 14 makes extensive use of two different data plane features that are designed to protect against packet loss: packet duplication and Forward Error Correction. There is a third feature, TCP optimization (TCP-Opt), that also fundamentally alters data packets as they are forwarded through the router. All three of these features make fundamental changes to the typical forwarding operations and go well beyond the earlier use cases where a packet was being redirected or remarked.

Unfortunately, the implementations of these three features—Forward Error Correction, packet duplication, and TCP optimization—are different between the Viptela OS–based platforms and the XE-SDWAN-based platforms. While all three features are supported on both platforms, it is not possible in current software (Viptela 19.2 / XE 16.12) to interoperate between the two platform families when using these three features. Network administrators will need to keep this in mind when planning and designing their deployments, and always check the release notes for the latest information about which features are supported on which platforms.

Use Case 14 Review

In this use case, we explored two different methods for reducing the impact of lossy underlying transport networks on business applications: Forward Error Correction and packet duplication. In Chapter 8, another method, Application-Aware Routing, will be discussed in great detail. Application-Aware Routing can also be used to solve similar challenges by moving affected traffic classes off of transports that are currently exhibiting packet loss.

The full and complete policy for all of the configuration that has been performed in Chapters 6 and 7 can be found in Appendix B.

Summary

This chapter discussed one of the key types of SD-WAN policies: centralized data policies. Several different use cases using centralized data policies were reviewed, including how centralized data policies can be used to make per-application forwarding decisions as well as for Direct Cloud Access, injecting services on a per-application basis, and mitigating the effects of using lossy transport networks with Forward Error Correction and packet duplication.

The use cases reviewed in this chapter represent a large cross section of what centralized data policies can accomplish. There are a plethora of actions not included in the use cases in this chapter, however. Some additional topics that network engineers may be interested in learning more about include quality of service (specifically DSCP marking and remarking), setting the forwarding class on a flow to be matched in a Localized policy (for queuing and scheduling purposes, as covered in Chapter 9, "Local Policies"), and using traffic policers. Centralized data policies can also be used to generate Cflowd and NetFlow records that can be exported to an external flow collector for monitoring and reporting purposes. More information and configuration examples for all of these topics can be found in the Cisco documentation.

While these use cases represent some of the most common challenges that network engineers need to solve in order to meet business objectives, the tools and techniques that have been discussed throughout this chapter can also be applied and extended in novel ways to solve practically any set of requirements.

Review All Key Topics

Review the most important topics in the chapter, noted with the Key Topic icon in the outer margin of the page. Table 7-1 provides a reference for these key topics and the page numbers on which each is found.

Table 7-1 *Key Topics*

Key Topic Element	Description	Page
Paragraph, Figure 7-1	Data policy directionality	228
Paragraph	Control policies vs. data policies enforced on WAN Edges via vSmarts	241
Paragraph	Concatenating data policies	247
Example 7-8	Application Traffic Engineering Behavior with Policy in Steady State and Failed State	258
Paragraph	Centralized control policy enforcement behaviors	263
Paragraph	Behavior of the **service local** command	266
Paragraph	FEC block operations	271
Paragraph	WAN Edge forwarding traffic flows with a packet duplication policy enabled	275
Paragraph	Deployment concerns for the data plane features Forward Error Correction, packet duplication, and TCP optimization	280

Define Key Terms

Define the following key terms from this chapter and check your answers in the glossary:

Forward Error Correction, packet duplication, NAT fallback

Chapter Review Questions

1. In a centralized data policy, how do you match all flows?

   a. Using the **match-all** criteria

   b. By not specifying any matching criteria and only configuring the action statements

   c. Only by using the default action

2. When the **nat use-vpn** configuration command is used, which VPN is the traffic going to be NATed into?

   a. VPN 0

   b. VPN 1

   c. VPN 65535

   d. The VPN specified in configuration

3. What is the purpose of the **nat fallback** configuration command?

   a. Provides a backup forwarding path in the event that all of the WAN tunnels go down

   b. Provides a backup forwarding path in the event that all of the local interfaces configured with NAT go down

   c. Provides a backup forwarding path in the event that the destination is not reachable via NAT

4. In a vSmart configuration, how many data policies can applied per site?

   a. Zero: Data policies are not applied in a vSmart configuration.

   b. One: Each site gets one and only one data policy.

   c. Two: Each site gets a data policy that is applied to traffic that is originating from the LAN and a second policy that is applied to the traffic that originates from the WAN.

   d. As many as necessary, but never more than two per VPN per site.

5. When the TLOC specified in the LOCAL-TLOC action is not available, then the traffic that was matched in the data policy sequence is blackholed.

   a. True

   b. False

6. How many packets are in a single FEC block?

   a. One data packet, one parity packet

   b. One data packet, four parity packets

   c. Two data packets, one parity packet

   d. Four data packets, one parity packet

   e. The value is configurable in the policy.

7. When FEC-adaptive data policies are used, what is the loss threshold at which FEC begins to operate?

   a. 0%

   b. 1%

   c. 2%

   d. 5%

   e. The value is configurable in the policy.

8. When packet duplication is configured, which tunnel is used to send the duplicated packets?

   a. The tunnel that is configured in the policy

   b. The least utilized tunnel to the same destination

   c. The same tunnel that the original packets were sent down

   d. The tunnel that is currently experiencing the least amount of packet loss

9. When packet duplication is used, which field indicates the total number of unique packets that have been received?

   a. PKTDUP RX

   b. PKTDUP RX OTHER

   c. PKTDUP RX THIS

   d. PKTDUP TX

   e. PKTDUP TX OTHER

10. Which of the following features are able to interoperate between Viptela OS platforms and XE-SDWAN platforms?

    a. Forward Error Correction

    b. Packet duplication

    c. TCP optimization

    d. All of these are correct.

    e. Forward Error Correction and packet duplication

    f. None of these answers is correct.

References

G. Jones, Ed., RFC 3871: Operational Security Requirements for Large Internet Service Provider (ISP) IP Network Infrastructure, Network Working Group, https://tools.ietf.org/html/rfc3871, September 2004

Cisco SD-WAN Command Line Reference, https://www.cisco.com/c/en/us/td/docs/routers/sdwan/command/sdwan-cr-book.html

Configuring Centralized Data Policy, https://sdwan-docs.cisco.com/Product_Documentation/Software_Features/Release_18.4/06Policy_Basics/04Centralized_Data_Policy/01Configuring_Centralized_Data_Policy

Cisco Umbrella: Add a Tunnel: Viptela, https://docs.umbrella.com/umbrella-user-guide/docs/add-a-tunnel-viptela

Chapter 8

Application-Aware Routing Policies

This chapter covers the following topics:

- **The Business Imperative for Application-Aware Routing:** This section covers the reasons why customers chose to use Application-Aware Routing policies.

- **The Mechanics of an App-Route Policy:** This section covers the necessary steps that must be completed in order to use App-Route policies.

- **Constructing an App-Route Policy:** This section covers the building blocks of an App-Route policy and the process of constructing a simple App-Route policy through the vManage GUI.

- **Monitoring Tunnel Performance:** This section covers the process of using BFD to monitor tunnel performance and how tunnel statistics are calculated.

- **Mapping Traffic Flows to a Transport Tunnel:** This section covers the configuration options inside of an App-Route policy and how those options interact with different transport conditions.

Building on the discussion of centralized data policies in Chapter 7, "Centralized Data Policies," this chapter focuses on a special type of data policy, the App-Route policy. Application-Aware Routing enables organizations to move away from high-cost, guaranteed performance transport links such as MPLS and move to commodity Internet circuits while not sacrificing application performance. This is accomplished by monitoring the characteristics of the transport links in real time and then incorporating that information into the routing process. This enables network administrators to ensure that their applications are always being forwarded down a path that meets or exceeds the requirements of the application.

The Business Imperative for Application-Aware Routing

One of the key business drivers for many organizations to move to SD-WAN is the ability to replace their existing, expensive legacy transport networks with higher-capacity, less-expensive broadband circuits. This transition is enabled in part by Cisco SD-WAN's capability to continue to provide an assured application experience over transports without an underlying SLA commitment.

By moving away from existing legacy transport networks and moving to using the Internet as a transport, many organizations are finding that they can dramatically increase their available bandwidth while at the same time reducing their transport costs. However, there is no guaranteed service level, or service level agreements (SLAs), on the Internet. Many organizations have relied upon their leased-line and MPLS transport providers for an assured level of service. While no solution can guarantee an assured level of service over the Internet, Cisco SD-WAN can leverage the benefits of low-cost Internet transports while at the same time utilizing Application-Aware Routing and packet-loss mitigation technologies to bring leased line benefits to organizations.

Using Application-Aware Routing, network administrators are able to identify business-critical traffic and specify the required service level agreement for that traffic class.

When replacing or augmenting existing MPLS transport circuits with Internet-as-a-Transport, organizations are able to establish multiple connectivity paths between their locations. The ability to move to the Internet as a transport, while still being able to provide for the required end-user experience, enables enterprises to realize cost savings by utilizing all of their bandwidth in an Active/Active fashion, rather than needing to continue to invest in upgrading circuits.

The Mechanics of an App-Route Policy

There are three key parts to the Application-Aware Routing process:

1. **Constructing an App-Route policy:** The first step in Application-Aware Routing is to build an App-Route policy. An App-Route policy is a specific type of centralized data policy that has many similarities with the data policies explored in Chapter 7. Constructing the policy includes defining the necessary lists, building the policy from a sequence of match and action statements, and activating the policy.

2. **Measuring and monitoring the performance of the transport links:** Once the App-Route policy has been created and activated, the next step in the process is to monitor the performance of the SD-WAN tunnels (in real time) to determine which tunnels are in compliance with the required SLA. This performance information is gathered from Bidirectional Forwarding Detection (BFD) packets, which are sent automatically across each of the different tunnels created as part of the SD-WAN fabric.

3. **Mapping application traffic to a specific transport link**: After the tunnel performance has been determined by BFD packets, these metrics are then evaluated against the configured SLA classes to determine which tunnels are in compliance. Forwarding decisions are then made with respect to these SLA compliance states.

The sections that follow explain each of the steps in more detail.

Constructing an App-Route Policy

The first step in building an App-Route policy, just as with the control policies and data policies from Chapters 6 and 7, is to define all of the lists. As we saw with data policies in Chapter 7, a number of criteria can be used to identify traffic of interest. These include traditional Layer 3 and Layer 4 headers, such as IP addresses, protocols, port numbers, and DSCP markings. Administrators can also match traffic based on the Layer 7 application definitions defined as an application-list. Lists are configured from the **Lists** menu under the **Custom Options** menu, as shown in Figure 8-1.

Figure 8-1 *Creating Lists for Use in Policies*

There is a new type of list used specifically for App-Route policies, called an *SLA Class list*. Network administrators use an SLA Class list to define the maximum permitted latency, loss, and jitter (or a combination of the three values) that an application class can tolerate while still maintaining the desired end-user experience. If any one of the Loss, Latency, or Jitter values were to exceed the configured threshold in the SLA Class list, the transport would be deemed noncompliant and the application flow would be moved to a different, compliant transport tunnel. In order to be in a compliant state, all three values must be below the configured thresholds. As some types of traffic, such as real-time voice and video, have much stricter network requirements than other types of traffic, it is common for network administrators to configure multiple SLA Class lists. Figure 8-2 shows an example of an SLA Class list that has been configured for Unified Communications traffic called REALTIME_SLA with a maximum packet loss of 2%, a maximum latency of 100ms, and a maximum jitter of 30ms. The CLI configuration for this and subsequent configuration steps is reviewed later in Example 8-1.

Once the lists have been defined, the next step in building an App-Route policy is to construct the policy from a sequence of match and action statements. As App-Route policies are a type of data policy, the configuration page for App-Route policies is found in the "Traffic Policy" submenu under Centralized Policy, as shown in Figure 8-3.

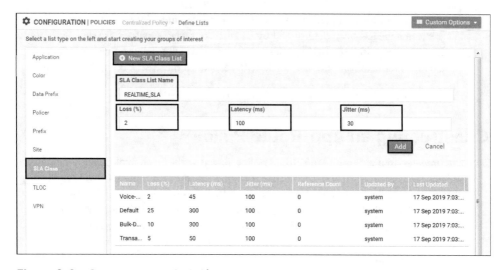

Figure 8-2   *Creating a New SLA Class List*

Figure 8-3   *Opening the Traffic Policy Configuration Menu*

Once you're on the Traffic Policy configuration tab where the Application-Aware Routing subtab is selected by default, a new App-Route policy can be created by clicking the **Add Policy** button and selecting **Create New**, as shown in Figure 8-4.

Figure 8-4   *Creating a New Application-Aware Routing Policy*

The process of building an App-Route policy is identical to the data policies that were built in Chapter 7. The only notable difference is that different actions are used in an App-Route policy. Figure 8-5 shows a simple App-Route policy with a single sequence that matches on traffic marked with DSCP 46 (Expedited Forwarding).

Figure 8-5   *Sample Application-Aware Routing Policy*

As shown in Figure 8-5, all App-Route policies need to be configured with a name and a description. App-Route policies use the same structures of Sequence Type and Sequence Rule that were seen in centralized control and centralized data policies. In the sample policy displayed in Figure 8-5, the matching criterion of a DSCP value of 46 is speci-fied. The primary action taken in an App-Route policy sequence is called SLA Class List in vManage. Two fields have been configured in this action: SLA Class and the Preferred Color. The SLA Class field references an SLA Class list that was previously configured, specifying the maximum permitted loss, latency, and jitter. The Preferred Color field con-tains the color or colors that the network administrator desires to forward this application class across, as long as those colors are in compliance with the SLA class. In this example, the network is configured such that DSCP 46 traffic should be forwarded through the tunnel with the color value of **mpls**, as long as that tunnel is in compliance with the REALTIME_SLA class. A further discussion of logic can be found in the following sec-tion, "Mapping Traffic Flows to a Transport Tunnel." Once the configuration is complet-ed, the sequence rule is saved by clicking the **Save Match and Actions** button, and the policy is saved by clicking the **Save Application-Aware Routing Policy** button.

Finally, all App-Route policies need to be applied through a centralized policy. A new centralized policy can be created by selecting the **Add Policy** button on the Centralized Policy page, as shown in Figure 8-6. The App-Route policy could also be imported into an existing policy by copying and then editing the policy as described in Chapters 6 and 7. That process will not be reviewed in this chapter.

Figure 8-6   *Creating a New Policy with the Centralized Policy Wizard*

As no additional lists or control policies need to be created for this example, click the **Next** button twice to skip the **Create Groups of Interest** and **Configure Topology and VPN Membership** tabs and move to the **Configure Traffic Rules** tab, as shown in Figure 8-7.

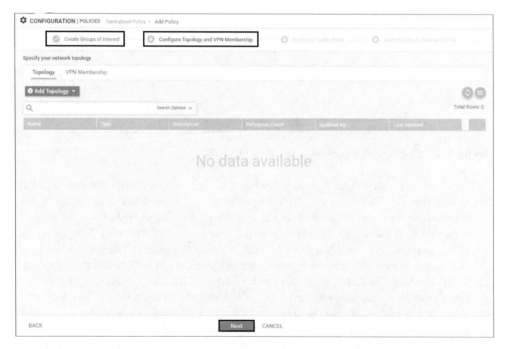

Figure 8-7   *Advancing the Centralized Policy Wizard Through Lists and Control Policies*

On the **Configure Traffic Rules** tab, under the **Application-Aware Routing** subtab, click on the **Add Policy** button and select the **Import Existing** option, as shown in Figure 8-8.

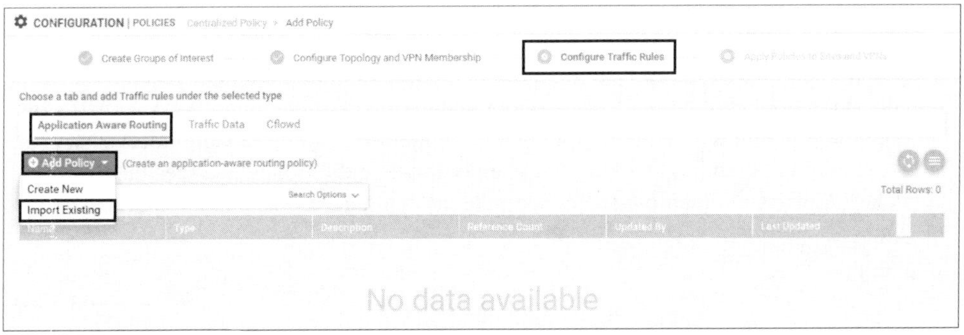

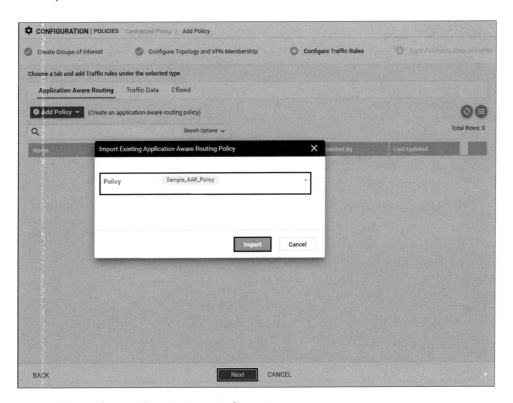

Figure 8-8 *Importing an Application-Aware Routing Policy into a Centralized Policy*

Select the App-Route policy that was created previously and click **Import** in the window. Click the **Next** button at the bottom of the page to proceed. Figure 8-9 shows these steps.

Figure 8-9 *Selecting the App-Route Policy to Import*

The final step in the creation of the centralized policy is to apply the component policies. First, a name and description must be provided for this policy, as shown in Figure 8-10.

In order to apply the App-Route policy, select the **Application-Aware Routing** tab and click the blue **New Site List and VPN List** button under the Sample_AAR_Policy policy. This particular policy is applied to all of the DCs and all of the branch offices by referencing the site lists created in the previous chapters. Next, specify the VPN or VPNs that the policy is to be applied to. In the case of Figure 8-10, this is the CorporateVPN, VPN 10. Finally, click **Add** to save the policy application for this policy and then click **Save Policy**, as shown in Figure 8-10, to complete the centralized policy configuration.

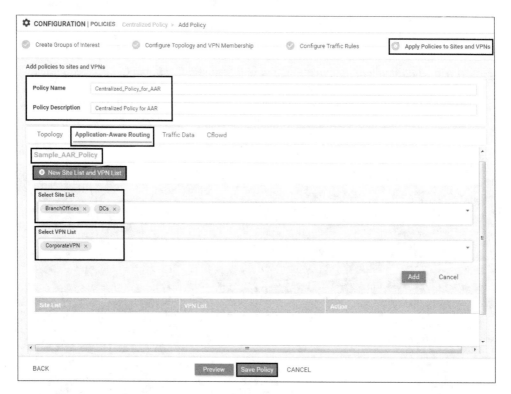

Figure 8-10   *Applying an Application-Aware Routing Policy in a Centralized Policy*

Note   As an App-Route policy is a type of centralized data policy, it is applied on the vSmart controllers, encoded into an Overlay Management Protocol (OMP) update, and advertised down to the WAN Edge routers where the policies are enforced. Chapter 5, "Introduction to Cisco SD-WAN Policies," provides additional details on this process.

Chapter 7 discussed that data policies can be applied in a specific direction—either "from-service" or "from-tunnel." App-Route policies do not have a direction specified when they are applied. App-Route policies are always applied to traffic "from-service" destined to the fabric, as an App-Route policy determines which site-to-site tunnel traffic is forwarded across when it is sent out across the WAN.

Example 8-1 provides the annotated configuration of the entire sample App-Route policy. Just as with the policy examples in Chapter 6, "Centralized Control Policies," and Chapter 7, "Centralized Data Policies," the full CLI for a policy created from vManage is available by selecting **Preview** in the Centralized Policy page. For the remainder of this chapter, AAR policy examples will be presented as configuration snippets for brevity and for illustration. As with all Cisco SD-WAN policies, the configuration can be performed either via the vManage GUI or from the command line.

Example 8-1   *Sample App-Route Policy*

```
policy
! The SLA Class that specifies the required tunnel performance
  sla-class REALTIME_SLA
   latency 100
   loss 2
   jitter 30
   !
! The AAR policy that is composed of 'match' and 'action' sequences
 app-route-policy _CorporateVPN_Sample_AAR_Policy
  vpn-list CorporateVPN
    sequence 1
     match
      dscp 46
      source-ip 0.0.0.0/0
     !
! The sla-class action specifies the SLA Class and the preferred colors
     action
      sla-class REALTIME_SLA  preferred-color mpls
      !
     !
   !
! Additional lists used within the policy. In this case, these lists are used
! when the policy is applied.
 lists
  site-list BranchOffices
   site-id 100-199
   !
  site-list DCs
   site-id 10-50
   !
  vpn-list CorporateVPN
   vpn 1
   !
  !
 !
```

```
! The AAR policy is applied to selected Site Lists and VPN Lists.
! Note: There is no directionality to this policy.
apply-policy
 site-list DCs
  app-route-policy _CorporateVPN_Sample_AAR_Policy
 !
 site-list BranchOffices
  app-route-policy _CorporateVPN_Sample_AAR_Policy
 !
!
```

Monitoring Tunnel Performance

The Bidirectional Forwarding Detection (BFD) protocol is used to monitor the real-time
condition of the underlying transport network. BFD packets are initiated by each router
across every tunnel that is brought up as part of the SD-WAN fabric and serve two different purposes: liveliness detection and path quality monitoring. BFD packets are echoed
bidirectionally across each tunnel and, as such, active BFD neighbors are not formed
across the SD-WAN fabric. Figure 8-11 illustrates this process.

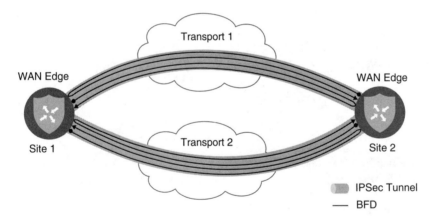

Figure 8-11   *BFD Packets in the SD-WAN Fabric*

As shown in Figure 8-11, each router initiates a BFD packet on each tunnel. When the
packet is received by the router at the far end of the tunnel, it is echoed back to the
originating router. The configuration parameters for BFD probes are set in the BFD
feature template and are referenced in the individual device templates. In this way,
different routers can have different BFD settings.

Liveliness Detection

There are several configurable options inside the BFD template, as seen in Figure 8-12.

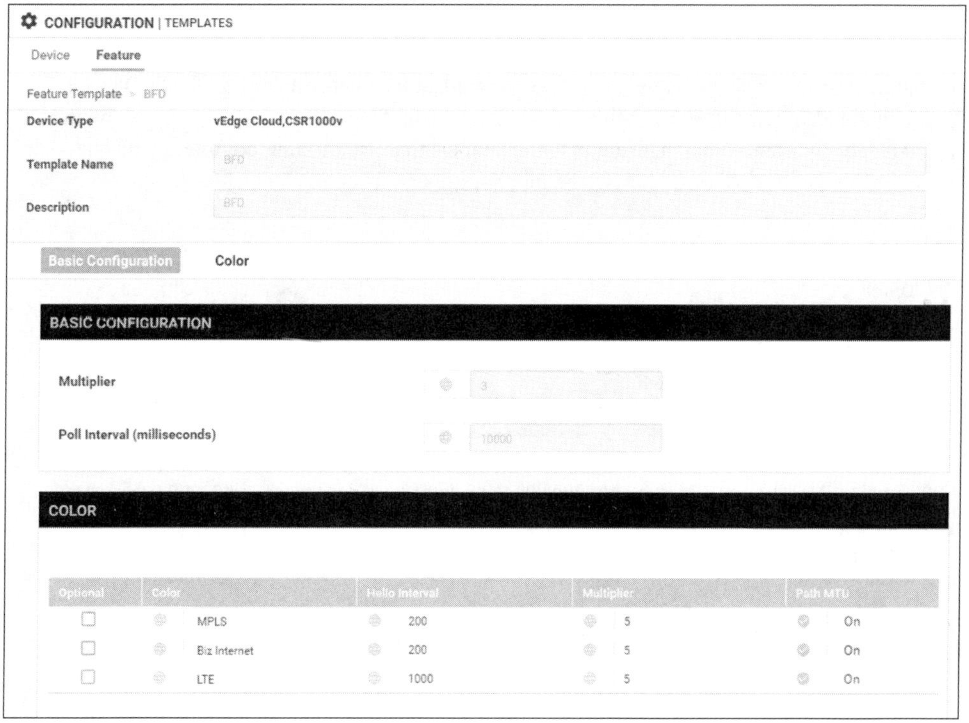

Figure 8-12 *BFD Feature Template*

The two sections to the BFD template are the Basic Configuration section and the Color section. The Basic Configuration section has the configuration elements related to Application-Aware Routing and will be discussed later. The Color section contains two foundational settings: per-color Hello Interval and Multiplier. As shown in Figure 8-12, these two settings allow you to have different values for different colors, providing network administrators the ability to configure different settings for different transport links. A common design choice is to have more aggressive BFD timers on wired connections and more conservative timers on cellular connections where customers are often charged per gigabyte.

Hello Interval

The Hello Interval specifies how frequently a BFD probe will be sent across a given tunnel. The default value for this timer is once per second, and the value is specified in milliseconds. In Figure 8-12, the Hello Interval for the MPLS and Biz-Internet colors is set to 200 milliseconds. The Hello Interval for the LTE color is set to 1000 milliseconds (ms).

However, when different devices have different BFD timers configured for the same tunnel, BFD will negotiate to use the greater of the two values. Figure 8-13 illustrates one example where this negotiation behavior is beneficial. Many times, WAN Edge routers are using different colors at each end of an SD-WAN tunnel. This commonly occurs when transports such as LTE are used to connect to the Biz-Internet TLOCs at other branches or the Biz-Internet TLOCs at the data center, where the LTE TLOC may not be configured at all. In these circumstances, having the tunnels that utilize the LTE TLOCs (at either end of the tunnel) use the slower timers would help to conserve LTE bandwidth, while at the same time ensuring that the tunnels that are running completely on the wireline TLOCs continue to use the more aggressive timers.

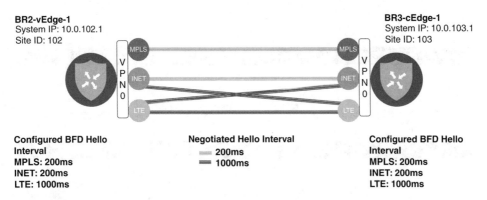

Figure 8-13   *BFD Hello Interval Negotiation*

Figure 8-13 illustrates a scenario where the WAN Edges will negotiate to use the greater of the two configured BFD Hello Intervals for an SD-WAN tunnel. After the configuration shown in the BFD feature template in Figure 8-12 is applied, this effect can be seen by using the Real Time output of BR2-vEdge-1, as shown in Figure 8-14.

System IP	Site ID	State	Source TLOC Color	Remote TLOC Color	Detect Multiplier	Tx Interval
10.0.103.1	103	up	biz-internet	biz-internet	5	200
10.0.103.1	103	up	biz-internet	lte	5	1000
10.0.103.1	103	up	lte	biz-internet	5	1000
10.0.103.1	103	up	lte	lte	5	1000
10.0.103.1	103	up	mpls	mpls	5	200

Figure 8-14   *Effects of BFD Hello Interval Negotiation*

Figure 8-14 shows that the BFD sessions between these two WAN Edges are being negotiated to the greater of the two configured values. In the first row in the table, the tunnel that originates on the Biz-Internet TLOC (configured with a Hello Interval of 200ms), destined to the remote router's Biz-Internet TLOC, is operating with a Tx interval (the negotiated Hello Interval) of 200ms. In the second row in the table, the tunnel that originates from the same TLOC but is destined for the LTE TLOC at the far end of the tunnel has a Tx interval of 1000ms.

Multiplier

The Multiplier value specifies how many consecutive BFD probes can be lost before declaring the tunnel to be down. This feature forms the basis of liveliness detection and is useful for detecting things such as indirect fiber cuts, where the physical interface remains in an "Up" state but no traffic can be sent across a link. In circumstances where the transport interface state changes from Up to Down, there is no need to wait for the multiplier to expire, as the tunnel is immediately set to Down and the corresponding routes are withdrawn. The default Multiplier value is 7, and in Figure 8-12, the value has been changed to 5.

Figure 8-15 illustrates the relationships between the Hello Interval, the Hello Multiplier, and the amount of time it takes to detect a circuit failure for the values configured for the MPLS Color in Figure 8-12.

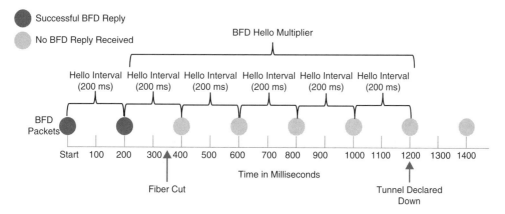

Figure 8-15   *BFD Path Liveliness Detection*

As Figure 8-15 illustrates, with a configured Hello Interval of 200 milliseconds and a con-figured Hello Multiplier of 5, it would take approximately 1,000 milliseconds to detect an indirect circuit failure. With the default Hello Interval of 1 second (1,000 msec) and the default Multiplier of 7, it is possible it would take the SD-WAN solution 7 seconds (1 packet per second × 7 packets) to detect an indirect circuit failure. Further information and recommendations for setting these timers can be found later in this section.

Path Quality Monitoring

In addition to liveliness detection, these same BFD packets are also used to monitor the performance and quality of each of the transport paths. These settings are shown in the Basic Configuration section of Figure 8-12 and include the App-Route Multiplier and the App-Route Poll Interval. As indicated by Figure 8-12, the Poll Interval and the Multiplier are per-device settings; there is only one App-Route polling interval and only one App-Route multiplier setting for each WAN Edge router.

App-Route Poll Interval

The App-Route Poll Interval is defined as a period of time for which the WAN Edge router will calculate the loss, latency, and jitter for each tunnel using the BFD packets sent during that interval. App-Route Poll Intervals are occasionally referred to as "buckets" as they represent the statistics from a collection of individual BFD packets. The WAN Edge routers will then proceed to calculate or recalculate each tunnel's SLA compliance and proceed to forward packets in accordance with the configured App-Route policies until the end of the next App-Route Poll Interval, when the cycle repeats.

Figure 8-16 illustrates a sample poll interval with a duration of 10 seconds where BFD packets were sent every 1 second.

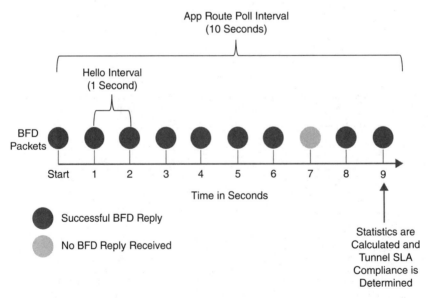

Figure 8-16   *App-Route Poll Interval Illustration*

As illustrated in Figure 8-16, the App-Route Poll Interval is the period of time for which statistics are calculated from the BFD packets sent during that window. The number of

BFD packets and, thus, the sample size for that statistical calculation are not explicitly configured but instead are derived from the combination of the length of the Hello Interval and the length of the App-Route Poll Interval.

Expanding the example illustrated in Figure 8-16 further, we can use the data in Table 8-1 to calculate the loss, latency, and jitter during the App-Route Poll Interval.

Table 8-1   *Individual BFD Packets During an App-Route Poll Interval*

BFD Packet	Received/Lost	Round-trip Time
1	Received	10ms
2	Received	11ms
3	Received	13ms
4	Received	11ms
5	Received	10ms
6	Received	11ms
7	Received	10ms
8	Lost	N/A
9	Received	12ms
10	Received	11ms

At the end of each App-Route Poll Interval, the App-Route statistics are calculated from the BFD packets sent during that interval. Using the data in Table 8-2, the packet loss percentage is calculated from the percentage of BFD packets successfully echoed back to the originating router. The latency is calculated to be 11 milliseconds by the arithmetic mean of the round-trip time for all of the samples where a reply was received ((10+11+13 +11+10+11+10+12+11)/9). The jitter is calculated to be 1 millisecond by taking the mean of the absolute value of the difference in the round-trip time ((1+2+2+1+1+1+2+1)/8).

Table 8-2   *BFD Statistics Calculated after an App-Route Poll Interval*

App-Route Poll Interval	Loss Percentage	Latency	Jitter
0	10%	11 msec	1 msec

Figure 8-16 and Table 8-2 illustrate a key concept about App-Route Poll Interval and BFD Hello Intervals: It is important to ensure that there are enough BFD probes in a particular poll interval in order to generate statistically significant results. In this particular example, there might have been only .05% packet loss, but because a single BFD probe was lost, and that probe represented 10% of all of the probes, the packet loss is recorded as 10%.

When the values in Table 8-2 are compared against the REALTIME_SLA Class list that was configured in Figure 8-2 and Example 8-1, it is clear that the current loss percentage, 10%, exceeds the configured threshold of 2%. As such, the determination would be made at the end of the App-Route Poll Interval that this path would be out of compliance with the REALTIME_SLA Class list at this point in time. This is shown in Figure 8-17 at Time "A" in the next section.

App-Route Multiplier

The App-Route Multiplier specifies how many polling intervals of previously collected BFD probes to consider when calculating tunnel SLA compliance. This can be thought of as how many different "buckets" are evaluated when looking at circuit performance. The maximum configuration value and the default value of the App-Route Multiplier are 6. The configuration shown in Figure 8-10 uses an App-Route Multiplier of 3. In other words, the statistics from a maximum of three different "buckets" will be considered when calculating tunnel performance. Continuing on with the previous example, Table 8-3 illustrates the App-Route Statistics after the completion of a second App-Route Poll Interval.

Table 8-3 *BFD Statistics from Multiple App-Route Poll Interval*

App-Route Poll Interval	Loss Percentage	Latency	Jitter
0	0%	10 msec	1 msec
1	10%	11 msec	1 msec

The original statistics from the first App-Route Poll Interval, Interval 0, are moved down the table to the second row (Interval 1). The new values for tunnel performance are calculated by averaging the values from each of the App-Route Poll Intervals in Table 8-3:

■ Packet Loss = 5%

■ Latency = 10 msec

■ Jitter = 1 msec

Figure 8-17 illustrates these App-Route Poll Intervals and the subsequent calculations to determine compliance with the SLA class that occurs at the end of each App-Route Poll Interval. As discussed previously, at time "A," the circuit would be out of compliance with the SLA class because it experienced 10% packet loss. As there was only a single App-Route Poll Interval that had elapsed, the statistics gathered during this interval are the only statistics available.

At time "B," two different App-Route Poll Intervals have elapsed. While there was no packet loss in the second interval, the 10% loss from the first interval causes the average packet loss to be 5% and, thus, the circuit still exceeds the SLA class requirement of 2%.

After two more App-Route Poll Interval periods have elapsed, the data in Table 8-4 has been gathered to calculate the SLA statistics.

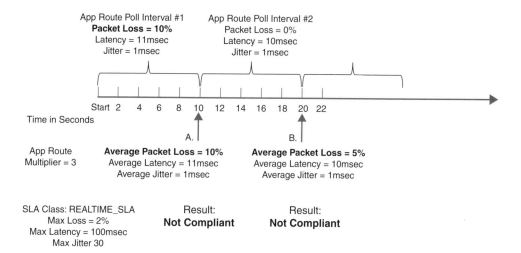

Figure 8-17   *SLA Calculations with Two App-Route Poll Intervals*

Table 8-4   *BFD Statistics from Four App-Route Poll Intervals*

App-Route Poll Interval	Loss Percentage	Latency	Jitter
0	0%	200 msec	25 msec
1	0%	11 msec	0 msec
2	0%	10 msec	1 msec
~	10%	11 msec	1 msec

First, note in Figure 8-17 that the original statistics from the first example gathered in Table 8-2 are now grayed out. As the configured App-Route Multiplier value is 3, only statistics from the three most recent buckets will be considered for the tunnel performance calculation, and these initial values would have aged out of the table and are no longer considered. From the remaining three values, the following averages are calculated:

- Packet Loss = 0%

- Latency = 73 msec

- Jitter = 8 msec

Building on Figure 8-17, Figure 8-18 illustrates what happens after the conclusion of the next two App-Route Poll Intervals, at times "C" and "D."

At time "C," three intervals have elapsed. Even though there has been no additional packet loss, the average packet loss across all three App-Route Poll intervals is 3% and remains out of compliance.

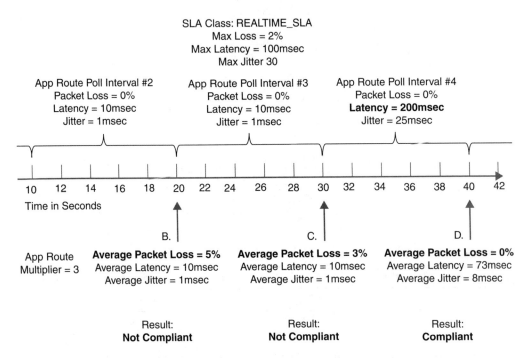

Figure 8-18   *SLA Calculations with Multiple App-Route Poll Intervals*

At time "D," the first App-Route Poll Interval is no longer taken into account, as the App-Route Multiplier is configured as 3. As such, the first interval where the packet loss was experienced is not included in the average, and the packet loss average is now calculated as 0%.

If the App-Route Multiplier had been configured to 1 instead of the current value of 3, then only the statistics from Poll Interval #2 would have been taken into account at time "B," and the transport would have been compliant with the SLA class because the packet loss during Poll Interval #2 was 0%. The same is true at time "C": If the only Poll Interval considered was #3, then the transport would have been considered compliant. In this way, the App-Route Multiplier functions as a hold-down timer and prevents excessive flapping of application flows between SD-WAN paths that would otherwise be caused by transient events in the underlying transport network. Greater App-Route Multipliers allow for more poll intervals and, therefore, longer periods of time to be considered when calculating compliance with SLA classes. At the same time, the opposite effect can also happen: The latency in Poll Interval #4 has now spiked to 200 milliseconds. While this value is above the stated threshold of 100 milliseconds in the SLA class, the value is averaged with the values from the two previous App-Route Poll Intervals. The average value of these three intervals (73 milliseconds) is below the 100 millisecond threshold; therefore, this circuit will be treated as compliant for the time being. Network administrators can configure both the length of the App-Route Poll Interval as well as the App-Route Multiplier to tune the amount of historical performance to consider when evaluating SLA compliance.

SLA compliance is only reevaluated at the end of the App-Route Poll Interval. Other than moving a tunnel to the Down state because of an interface state change or a failure to receive a Hello packet within the Hello Multiplier, changes to the condition of a circuit will only be evaluated at the end of the App-Route Poll Interval. Hello Intervals, App-Route Poll Intervals, and App-Route Multipliers need to be configured to ensure that the network is responsive enough to changes in network conditions, while also having enough BFD data to gather statistically meaningful metrics. While faster BFD hellos and more aggressive timers may make the network react faster to brownouts, they can increase the susceptibility to false positives. This results in traffic moving from tunnel to tunnel unnecessarily and, thus, a potentially higher administrative burden for the team operating the network.

> **Note**   While the specific design objectives and topologies for an SD-WAN deployment will be unique to each individual enterprise, the following settings are a reasonable starting place for many organizations:
>
> - **App-Route Polling Interval:** 120,000 ms (two minutes)
>
> - **App-Route Multiplier:** 6
>
> - **Hello Interval:** 1000 ms (one second)
>
> - **Hello Multiplier:** 7

When these values are considered together, this means that the WAN Edge routers will be able to detect and respond to indirect transport interruptions after 7 seconds (1000ms per BFD hello interval × 7 packets). Individual tunnels will be evaluated for compliance with the SLA classes once every 2 minutes and that compliance will be based on the last 12 minutes of data (2 minutes per polling interval × 6 intervals). Each polling interval will have data from 120 BFD packets (120,000 msec polling interval / 1,000 msec Hello Interval). The higher the number of BFD packets in each polling interval, the better the loss, latency, and jitter statistics will be at truly representing the performance of the underlying transport.

Cisco Validated Design Guides are available at http://cisco.com/go/cvd and can provide additional guidance about tuning these timers for specific network designs.

Mapping Traffic Flows to a Transport Tunnel

After calculating the packet loss, latency, and jitter on a per-tunnel basis, the final step in the Application-Aware Routing process is to map a network data flow to a specific transport tunnel. The process of determining which tunnel should forward a specific flow is first determined by performing the necessary lookup in the traditional routing table. If and only if there are multiple equal-cost matches in the routing table, the App-Route Policy is evaluated to make a forwarding decision.

Packet Forwarding with Application-Aware Routing Policies

This section will continue to use the sample network that has been used throughout Chapters 6 and 7. Specifically, in this chapter, we will be looking at flows that are originating in Branch 2 (10.1.102.0/30) and are destined to Branch 3 (10.1.103.0/24). As such, the validation work and **show** commands that will be undertaken will occur on BR2-vEdge1. Figure 8-19 shows the relevant excerpt of this topology.

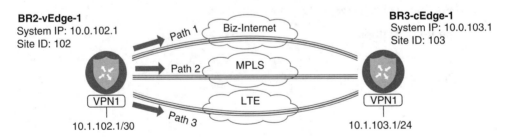

Figure 8-19 *Application-Aware Routing Network Topology*

Traditional Lookup in the Routing Table

Using the topology in Figure 8-19, we can now consider how App-Route policies affect how flows are mapped to transport tunnels. The first step in the process is to perform a normal routing lookup in the routing table.

The routing table is always considered prior to the evaluation of any App-Route policies. If there is more than one equal-cost route for the destination in the routing table, the App-Route policy will be evaluated in order to potentially select one or more paths from the paths in the table. If there is only one OMP best path installed in the table, and there are vsmartnot multiple, equal-cost routes, then the traffic will be forwarded according to the only route in the routing table and the App-Route policy will not be considered. Application-Aware Routing policies are only used to choose between multiple, equal best paths in the routing table.

As seen in Example 8-2, the WAN Edge router has three different paths to the 10.1.103.0/24 segment at Branch 3 installed in the routing table. Note that each of the routes has the status flags of "F,S" set, indicating that these routes have been selected and installed into the Forwarding Information Base (FIB). Additionally, this output displays the **tloc-color** for each of the routes. This indicates that we have one route across the MPLS connection, one across the Biz-Internet connection, and one across the LTE connection, as depicted in Figure 8-19.

Example 8-2   *Equal-Cost Paths Installed in the Routing Table*

```
BR2-vEdge-1# show ip routes vpn 1 10.1.103.0/24 detail

<<<Omitted>>>

Codes Status flags:
  F -> fib, S -> selected, I -> inactive,
  B -> blackhole, R -> recursive


""-------------------------------------------
 VPN 1        PREFIX 10.1.103.0/24
-------------------------------------------
 proto          omp
 distance       250
 metric         0
 uptime         0:00:36:13
 tloc-ip        10.0.103.1
 tloc-color     mpls
 tloc-encap     ipsec
 nexthop-label  1001
 status         F,S
```

```
-----------------------------------------  ---
VPN 1        PREFIX 10.1.103.0/24
-----------------------------------------

proto           omp
distance        250
metric          0
uptime          0:00:36:13
tloc-ip         10.0.103.1
tloc-color      biz-internet
tloc-encap      ipsec
nexthop-label   1001
status          F,S


-----------------------------------------
VPN 1        PREFIX 10.1.103.0/24
-----------------------------------------

proto           omp
distance        250
metric          0
uptime          0:00:36:13
tloc-ip         10.0.103.1
tloc-color      lte
tloc-encap      ipsec
nexthop-label   1001
status          F,S

BR2-vEdge-1#
```

SLA Class Action

If a prefix has multiple equal-cost matches in the routing table and an Application-Aware Routing policy has been created that matches the specific traffic class, then the SLA Class action is evaluated. In this example, we are using an extended version of the policy that was reviewed in Example 8-1. The full policy can be displayed on the vSmart controller using the **show running-config policy** command, as shown in Example 8-3.

Example 8-3 *Expanded Application-Aware Routing Policy*

```
vSmart-1# show running-config policy
policy
 sla-class BULK_DATA_SLA
  loss    10
  latency 300
 !
```

```
sla-class CRITICAL_DATA_SLA
 loss    5
 latency 150
!
sla-class REALTIME_SLA
 loss    2
 latency 100
 jitter  30
!
app-route-policy _CorporateVPN_Expande_-170838785
 vpn-list CorporateVPN
  sequence 1
   match
    source-ip 0.0.0.0/0
    dscp      46
   !
   action
    sla-class REALTIME_SLA preferred-color mpls
    backup-sla-preferred-color mpls
   !
  !
  sequence 11
   match
    source-ip 0.0.0.0/0
    app-list  REALTIME_DATA_TRANSFER
   !
   action
    sla-class CRITICAL_DATA_SLA strict preferred-color mpls
   !
  !
  sequence 21
   match
    source-ip 0.0.0.0/0
    app-list  CRITICAL_DATA
   !
   action
    sla-class CRITICAL_DATA_SLA preferred-color mpls biz-internet
   !
  !
  sequence 31
   match
    source-ip 0.0.0.0/0
    dscp      8
   !
```

```
     action
      sla-class BULK_DATA_SLA preferred-color biz-internet
     !
    !
   !
  !
lists
 vpn-list CorporateVPN
  vpn 1
 !
 app-list CRITICAL_DATA
  app-family audio_video
  app-family erp
  app-family microsoft-office
  app-family microsoft_office
  app-family network-management
  app-family network_management
  app-family terminal
  app-family thin-client
  app-family thin_client
  app-family web
 !
 app-list REALTIME_DATA_TRANSFER
  app tftp
 !
 site-list BranchOffices
  site-id 100-199
 !
 site-list DCs
  site-id 10-50
 !
 !
!
vSmart-1#
```

There have been two new SLA Class lists added to the configuration of this policy: the CRITICAL_DATA_SLA and BULK_DATA_SLA Class lists. Notice that these new SLA classes do not have jitter values configured. In these cases, jitter will not be evaluated as part of the SLA Class criteria.

Reevaluating every tunnel on the WAN Edge router after every poll interval is a CPU- and memory-intensive task. As such, each WAN Edge router is limited to a total of four different SLA Class lists as of software version 19.2. A vSmart policy can contain up to eight different SLA Class lists, but only four of them may be used by the App-Route policies that are configured for a specific WAN Edge. This flexibility is often used by network administrators to configure one set of SLA Classes for their domestic sites and a different set of SLA Classes for their overseas locations.

There have also been several additional sequences added to this App-Route policy. Each one of these sequences is a structured sequence of match and action statements. These sequences are configured with the **sla-class** action. Each **sla-class** action references one of the configured **sla-class** lists (in this example, REALTIME_SLA, CRITICAL_DATA_SLA, or BULK_DATA_SLA), and it lists the preferred TLOC color or colors. The tunnels matching the preferred color or colors, as specified in the SLA Class action, are evaluated against the requirements of the SLA class. If one or more of the preferred colors are in compliance with the SLA class, then that is the color or colors that will be used to forward traffic.

In sequence 1 of the aforementioned policies, the traffic marked with a DSCP value of 46 is configured with the action **sla-class REALTIME_SLA preferred-color mpls**. This configuration should be interpreted to mean that the traffic class, DSCP 46, needs a transport that meets the requirements of the REALTIME_SLA list. If a tunnel with the color of **mpls** can meet that requirement, it will be used to forward the traffic. This process can be seen on the CLI using the commands in Example 8-4.

Example 8-4 *Observing Tunnel Compliance with Configured SLA Classes*

```
BR2-vEdge-1# show app-route sla-class

INDEX   NAME                   LOSS  LATENCY  JITTER
-------------------------------------------------------
0         __all_tunnels__       0     0        0
1         BULK_DATA_SLA         10    300      0
2         CRITICAL_DATA_SLA     5     150      0
3         REALTIME_SLA          2     100      30


BR2-vEdge-1# show app-route stats local-color mpls remote-system-ip 10.0.103.1
app-route statistics 172.16.102.2 172.16.103.2 ipsec 12346 12346
 remote-system-ip 10.0.103.1
 local-color      mpls
 remote-color     mpls
 mean-loss        0
 mean-latency     7
 mean-jitter      1
 sla-class-index  0,1,2,3

        TOTAL            AVERAGE  AVERAGE  TX DATA  RX DATA
INDEX   PACKETS  LOSS  LATENCY  JITTER   PKTS     PKTS
-------------------------------------------------------------
0         10       0     7        1        0        0
1         10       0     7        1        0        0
2         10       0     8        1        0        0
BR2-vEdge-1#
```

As seen in Example 8-4, the **sla-class-index** for the REALTIME_SLA class is **3**. The **show app-route stats** command can then be used to see which SLA classes a particular tunnel is compliant with. Because the MPLS tunnel is compliant with the SLA class, and the MPLS color is configured in the App-Route policy as the preferred color, traffic marked with DSCP 46 will be forwarded across this tunnel.

This can also be validated with the "Simulate Flows" troubleshooting tool in vManage, as shown in Figure 8-20.

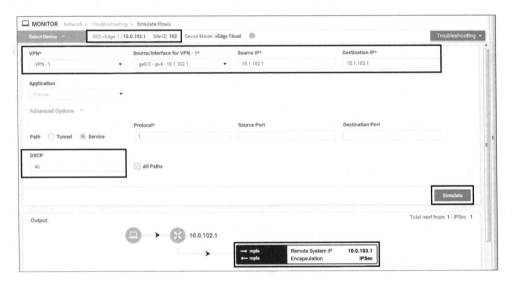

Figure 8-20 *Validating App-Aware Routing with the Simulate Flows Tool*

Continuing on with the **sla-class REALTIME_SLA preferred-color mpls** command and sequence 1 from the preceding policy in Example 8-3, if the MPLS color is out of compliance and other colors are in compliance, the traffic will be forwarded over those tunnels. This can be seen on the CLI using the **show app-route stats** command, as shown in Example 8-5.

Example 8-5 *Observing Tunnel Compliance with Preferred Color Out of Compliance*

```
BR2-vEdge-1# show app-route stats remote-system-ip 10.0.103.1
app-route statistics 100.64.102.2 100.64.103.2 ipsec 12346 12346
 remote-system-ip 10.0.103.1

 local-color      biz-internet
 remote-color     biz-internet
 mean-loss        0
 mean-latency     25
 mean-jitter      18
```

```
 sla-class-index  0,1,2,3

        TOTAL            AVERAGE  AVERAGE  TX DATA  RX DATA
 INDEX  PACKETS  LOSS    LATENCY  JITTER   PKTS     PKTS
 -----------------------------------------------------------
 0      10       0       62       34       0        0
 1      10       0       11       17       0        0
 2      10       0       3        2        0        0


<<<Omitted for Brevity>>>

app-route statistics 100.127.102.2 100.127.103.2 ipsec 12346 12346
 remote-system-ip 10.0.103.1
 local-color       lte
 remote-color      lte
 mean-loss         0
 mean-latency      10
 mean-jitter       13
 sla-class-index  0,1,2,3

        TOTAL            AVERAGE  AVERAGE  TX DATA  RX DATA
 INDEX  PACKETS  LOSS    LATENCY  JITTER   PKTS     PKTS
 -----------------------------------------------------------
 0      10       0       9        11       0        0
 1      10       0       4        1        0        0
 2      10       0       17       27       0        0


app-route statistics 172.16.102.2 172.16.103.2 ipsec 12346 12346
 remote-system-ip 10.0.103.1
 local-color       mpls
 remote-color      mpls
 mean-loss         6
 mean-latency      3
 mean-jitter       3
 sla-class-index  0,1

        TOTAL            AVERAGE  AVERAGE  TX DATA  RX DATA
 INDEX  PACKETS  LOSS    LATENCY  JITTER   PKTS     PKTS
 -----------------------------------------------------------
 0      10       2       2        2        0        0
 1      10       0       4        6        0        0
 2      10       0       2        1        0        0

BR2-vEdge-1#
```

As Example 8-5 shows, the Biz-Internet and LTE tunnels are still listed as in compliance with SLA Class Index 3 (REALTIME_SLA), but the MPLS tunnel at the end of the example is only compliant with SLA Class Index 0 (__all_tunnels__) and 1 (BULK_DATA_SLA). This is caused by the 6% mean packet loss on the MPLS tunnel. In this situation, DSCP 46 traffic will be forwarded across the Biz-Internet and LTE tunnels, as shown in Figure 8-21.

Figure 8-21   *Validating App-Aware Routing with the Simulate Flows tool*

Figure 8-21, which was created using the same criteria as Figure 8-20, illustrates that when the preferred color is not in compliance with the configured SLA class, then all of the available equal-cost tunnels that are in compliance with the SLA class will be used. In this case, there is a total of four different tunnels (the LTE TLOC is also building a tunnel to the receiving router's Biz-Internet TLOC, and vice versa).

In the examples up to this point, the **preferred-color [color]** command has only specified a single color as the preferred color. However, administrators are able to configure multiple colors as arguments to this command. This functionality is demonstrated in sequence 21 of the App-Route policy shown in Example 8-3: **sla-class CRITICAL_DATA_SLA preferred-color mpls biz-internet**. In the case of multiple preferred colors, where multiple colors are in compliance, the traffic will be load-shared on a per-flow basis. In the case that multiple preferred colors are specified but only a single color is compliant, the traffic class will be forwarded across that color. As with Example 8-5, when none of the preferred colors is compliant with the SLA requirements, the traffic is forwarded across any of the nonpreferred colors that are compliant with the SLA class. Another variation of this configuration is where the SLA Class action is specified but no preferred color is specified. In this case, the traffic is load-shared per flow among all of the colors that meet the required SLA.

The last permutation to consider is the behavior of the **sla-class** command when *none* of the TLOCs meet the required SLA, as demonstrated in Example 8-6.

Example 8-6   *Observing Tunnel Compliance with All Colors Out of Compliance*

```
BR2-vEdge-1# show app-route stats remote-system-ip 10.0.103.1 | i app\|sla\|col
app-route statistics 100.64.102.2 100.64.103.2 ipsec 12366 12366
 local-color       biz-internet
 remote-color      biz-internet
 sla-class-index   0
app-route statistics 100.64.102.2 100.127.103.2 ipsec 12366 12366
 local-color       biz-internet
 remote-color      lte
 sla-class-index   0
app-route statistics 100.127.102.2 100.64.103.2 ipsec 12366 12366
 local-color       lte
 remote-color      biz-internet
 sla-class-index   0
app-route statistics 100.127.102.2 100.127.103.2 ipsec 12366 12366
 local-color       lte
 remote-color      lte
 sla-class-index   0
app-route statistics 172.16.102.2 172.16.103.2 ipsec 12366 12346
 local-color       mpls
 remote-color      mpls
 sla-class-index   0
BR2-vEdge-1#
```

When all of the tunnels are out of compliance with the configured SLA class, as indicated in Example 8-6, there are several different configuration options that will dictate the forwarding behavior. In the simplest use case, as seen in sequence 31 of Example 8-7, when there are no further configured actions beyond the **sla-class** action, the traffic is load-shared across all available transports.

Example 8-7   *Configuration Options When SLA Class Cannot Be Honored*

```
vSmart-1# show running-config policy

<<< Omitted>>>

app-route-policy _CorporateVPN_Expande_-170838785
  vpn-list CorporateVPN
   sequence 1
    match
```

```
     source-ip 0.0.0.0/0
     dscp      46
    !
    action
! When the backup-sla-preferred-color command is supplied, traffic is forwarded
! across that color or colors if no colors can meet the required SLA
     sla-class REALTIME_SLA preferred-color mpls
     backup-sla-preferred-color mpls
    !
   !
   sequence 11
    match
     source-ip 0.0.0.0/0
     app-list  REALTIME_DATA_TRANSFER
    !
    action
! When the strict command is supplied, traffic is forwarded across the
! preferred color if the preferred color is able to meet the SLA.  If the
! preferred color does not meet the SLA, but any other color does, the
! traffic will be forwarded on that tunnel.  If there are no colors that
! meet the required SLA, the traffic is dropped.
     sla-class CRITICAL_DATA_SLA strict preferred-color mpls
    !
<<< Omitted>>>
   !
   sequence 31
    match
     source-ip 0.0.0.0/0
     dscp      8
    !
    action
! When no other arguments are configured, and no colors meet the SLA, then the
! traffic is load shared per flow across all available paths.  This functionality
! is equivalent to not having an app-route policy configured.
     sla-class BULK_DATA_SLA preferred-color biz-internet
    !
```

Two alternative configurations could be used in the event that none of the tunnels is able to meet the configured SLA: **backup-sla-preferred-color** and **strict**.

The **backup-sla-preferred-color** action specifies the color that the traffic should be forwarded across in the event that none of the colors is able to support the required SLA class. Sequence 1 in Example 8-7 illustrates the use of the **backup-sla-preferred-color** configuration option. While it might look strange at first glance to have the **mpls** color specified as both the **preferred-color** and the **backup-sla-preferred-color**, this is a rational and often used configuration choice. This configuration should be understood as follows:

1. If the MPLS tunnel meets the required SLA, then forward the traffic on the MPLS tunnel.

2. If the MPLS tunnel does not meet the required SLA but some other tunnel(s) do, then forward the traffic on the tunnels that meet the SLA.

3. If no tunnels meet the required SLA, then forward the traffic on the MPLS tunnel.

Sequence 1 in Example 8-7 would allow for the transmission of sensitive, real-time communications flows over the MPLS path, where we have an SLA agreement with the carrier, as long as that transport was performing to the required SLA. If the MPLS path was failing to meet the SLA but some other transport was able to meet the SLA, this sensitive traffic class would be forwarded over that path. In the event that no transports were able to meet the required SLAs (and the network administrators were having a *really bad day*), then the sensitive traffic classes would be transported over the MPLS path where there is a contractual SLA with the carrier, and hopefully service will be restored soon.

The last option with the SLA Class action is the **strict** command, as seen in sequence 11 of Example 8-7. The **strict** option specifies that if no colors are available that meet the required SLA class, the traffic should be dropped instead of forwarded. **backup-sla-preferred-color** and **strict** are logical opposites of each other. The **backup-sla-preferred-color** option specifies where to forward the traffic if no paths meet the required SLA. The **strict** option indicates that the traffic should be dropped if there is *no path available that meets the required SLA*. As such, these two options are mutually exclusive and cannot be configured at the same time.

Note   Though the **strict** command may have uses for very specific applications (such as SCADA networks, where timely delivery of monitoring traffic is critical), it is not an option that is commonly used by customers. Unfortunately, it tends to provide more confusion than value for most network administrators, and most customers are well served to steer clear of it.

Summary

This chapter has discussed the basics of building App-Route policies with Cisco SD-WAN. Every SD-WAN tunnel that is established in the data plane automatically starts to send BFD probes. These BFD probes serve two purposes: They are able to detect if the forwarding path between two WAN Edge routers is still valid, and they determine the loss latency and jitter conditions of that forwarding path. The information about the real-time condition of the transport paths can then be used to inform the forwarding process and ensure that business-critical applications are sent over paths that are able to meet the required service level agreements. Ultimately, this capability enables organizations to move away from their expensive, legacy transport providers and adopt commodity Internet circuits for transport while not having to compromise on application performance.

Review All Key Topics

Review the most important topics in the chapter, noted with the Key Topic icon in the outer margin of the page. Table 8-5 lists these key topics and the page numbers on which each is found.

Table 8-5 *Key Topics*

Key Topic Element	Description	Page
Paragraph	Ensure that there are enough BFD probes in a particular Poll Interval in order to generate statistically significant results.	299
Paragraph	Path condition will only be evaluated at the end of the App-Route Poll Interval.	303
Paragraph	An App-Route policy can only make forwarding decisions between equal-cost paths that are already installed in the routing table.	305
Paragraph	A vSmart policy can contain up to eight different SLA Class lists, but only four can be used on a single WAN Edge at any time.	308

Define Key Terms

Define the following key terms from this chapter and check your answers in the glossary:

App-Route Poll Interval, App-Route Multiplier, BFD Hello Interval, BFD Multiplier, SLA Class list, preferred color, backup-sla-preferred-color, strict

Chapter Review Questions

1. What is the scope of an Application-Aware Routing policy?

   a. Per site

   b. Per VPN

   c. Per direction

   d. Per site, per VPN

   e. Per site, per direction

   f. Per site, per VPN, per direction

2. Where are App-Route policies applied and enforced?

   a. Applied on the vSmart; enforced on the vSmart

   b. Applied on the vSmart; enforced on the WAN Edge

c. Applied on the WAN Edge; enforced on the vSmart

d. Applied on the WAN Edge; enforced on the WAN Edge

3. Which administratively configured options affect the calculation of the loss, latency, and jitter statistics used for Application-Aware Routing? (Select all that apply.)

a. BFD Hello Interval

b. BFD Hello Multiplier

c. Number of SLA Classes

d. App-Route Poll Interval

e. Number of Tunnels

f. Number of Colors

g. App Route Multiplier

4. What is the maximum number of App-Route Poll Intervals that can be used for tunnel performance calculations?

a. 2

b. 4

c. 6

d. 8

e. 16

5. When are the tunnels (re)evaluated for compliance with the SLA classes?

a. After every BFD packet is received by the WAN Edge router

b. After every Hello Interval

c. After every Hello Multiplier

d. After every App-Route Poll Interval

6. How many different SLA classes can be applied to a single WAN Edge router?

a. 2

b. 4

c. 8

d. 256

e. Unlimited

7. How many different SLA classes can be configured in a vSmart policy?

a. 2

b. 4

c. 8

d. 256

e. Unlimited

8. When is traffic forwarded across the backup SLA preferred color?

a. No tunnels are configured or active with the preferred SLA color(s).

b. None of the preferred SLA color(s) are currently meeting the required SLA class.

c. No colors are currently meeting the required SLA class.

9. When configured, the "Strict" option in an AAR policy will drop the traffic if the preferred color(s) fails to meet the SLA Class requirements.

   a. True

   b. False

10. In order for an Application-Aware Routing policy to have any effect, there must be multiple equal-cost routes in the routing table.

    a. True

    b. False

Chapter 9

Localized Policies

This chapter covers the following topics:

- **Introduction to Localized Policies:** This section covers the different types of localized policies and how these policies relate to other types of policies used by the Cisco SD-WAN solution.

- **Localized Control Policies:** This section covers localized control policies and how they can be used to manipulate routing advertisements to routers outside of the SD-WAN fabric.

- **Localized Data Policies:** This section covers the construction and use of localized data policies and particularly access control lists.

- **Quality of Service Policies:** This section covers the construction and application of quality of service with localized policies, including traffic classification, queuing and scheduling, and congestion management.

As discussed in Chapter 5, "Introduction to Cisco SD-WAN Policies," two main types of policies are used in the Cisco SD-WAN solution: centralized policies and localized policies. Chapters 6–8 focused on the different types of centralized policies; this chapter will discuss localized policies. Just as there are two main classifications of centralized policies (centralized control policies and centralized data policies), there are also localized control policies and localized data policies. This chapter reviews these different types of localized policies, how they are configured and applied, and common use cases for different types of localized policies.

Introduction to Localized Policies

The two main types of localized policies are localized control policies and localized data policies. Just as centralized control policies are used to manipulate the control plane and routing advertisements inside of the Cisco SD-WAN fabric, localized control policies are used to manipulate routing advertisements that happen at the perimeter of the SD-WAN fabric, when the WAN Edge router is communicating with other routers via BGP, OSPF, or EIGRP. Localized control policies can be used to filter routes or manipulate routing attributes such as OSPF cost, BGP local-preference, and EIGRP delay. Localized data policies are used to manipulate individual packets or flows transiting the data plane of the WAN Edge router. There are two main types of localized data policies: access control lists (ACLs) and quality of service (QoS). ACLs can be used to filter, rewrite, or apply additional services to a packet or flow as it transits the router. QoS is used for marking, queuing, and scheduling in order to allow network administrators to prioritize certain classes of traffic. While centralized policies and localized policies share many similarities in their structure, since centralized policies are activated on the vSmart and localized policies are applied as part of the WAN Edge configuration templates, there are no common configuration elements or lists that can be shared between the two different types of policies. Figure 9-1 illustrates the relationships between these different types of policies.

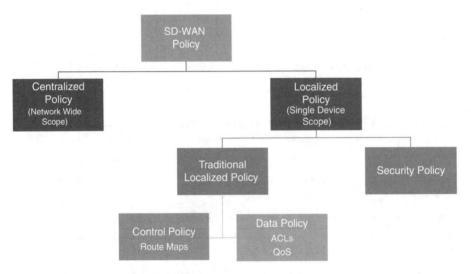

Figure 9-1 *Localized Policy Overview*

In addition to localized control policies and localized data policies, there is a special type of localized policy called a security policy. Security policies will be discussed in detail in Chapter 10, "Cisco SD-WAN Security."

Localized Control Policies

The purpose of localized control policies is to manipulate route attributes or filter out routes completely as they are advertised from the WAN Edge routers into the rest of the routing domain via traditional routing protocols. One of the reasons to do this is to be able to differentially prefer one WAN Edge router over another at a site that is configured with dual routers for high availability. While the Cisco SD-WAN solution deploys an active/active high-availability design, and there is no concept of a "standby" router (each router is always capable of forwarding any received traffic at all times during operation), there are some advantages to deploying a network in such a way that ensures that particular flows always transit particular routers.

This design construct was discussed in great detail in Use Case 3 in Chapter 6, "Centralized Control Policies." While Chapter 6 covered the necessary traffic engineering steps to accomplish this on the WAN side of the router using TLOC preferences, the following example shows how to complete this design using different routing policies on the LAN side of the WAN Edge routers.

Figure 9-2 shows a detailed topology of Data Center 1. We can see, in this example, that there are two WAN Edge routers that connect to a traditional core switch. With default configuration, the core switch will load-share traffic across both WAN Edge routers.

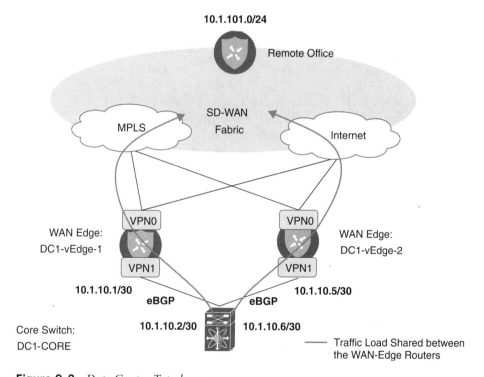

Figure 9-2 *Data Center Topology*

In order to prefer one WAN Edge router and create the desired symmetric flow patterns, we will be adjusting the routing advertisements from DC1-vEdge-1 and DC1-vEdge-2 so that the routes being advertised from the DC1-vEdge-1 are more preferred. Therefore, traffic flowing from the data center across the WAN will prefer DC1-vEdge-1 in steady-state operation. In this case, as the network is using eBGP as the routing protocol between the WAN Edge routers and the data center core, we will be manipulating route preferences with BGP attributes. While different attributes could be used, such as AS

Path Prepending, in this example we will use MED, or the Multi-Exit Discriminator (also called Metric). Since lower MED values are always preferred, we will set the MED value on the routes advertised from DC1-vEdge-1 to 100 and on the DC1-vEdge-2 to 1000.

Before any policy is applied, we can see that DC1-Core has equal-cost paths from each of the WAN Edge routers, indicated by the two next hops for each route (10.1.10.1 and 10.1.10.5). With this default state, the DC1-Core would use ECMP to load-share flows between the two routers, as shown in Example 9-1.

Example 9-1 *DC1-Core Routing Table*

```
DC1-CORE#sho ip route bgp
Codes: L - local, C - connected, S - static, R - RIP, M - mobile, B - BGP
       D - EIGRP, EX - EIGRP external, O - OSPF, IA - OSPF inter area
       N1 - OSPF NSSA external type 1, N2 - OSPF NSSA external type 2
       E1 - OSPF external type 1, E2 - OSPF external type 2
       i - IS-IS, su - IS-IS summary, L1 - IS-IS level-1, L2 - IS-IS level-2
       ia - IS-IS inter area, * - candidate default, U - per-user static route
       o - ODR, P - periodic downloaded static route, H - NHRP, l - LISP
       a - application route
       + - replicated route, % - next hop override, p - overrides from PfR
Gateway of last resort is 192.168.255.1 to network 0.0.0.0

      10.0.0.0/8 is variably subnetted, 11 subnets, 3 masks
B        10.1.20.0/30 [20/1000] via 10.1.10.5, 00:01:49
                      [20/1000] via 10.1.10.1, 00:01:49
B        10.1.20.4/30 [20/1000] via 10.1.10.5, 00:01:49
                      [20/1000] via 10.1.10.1, 00:01:49
B        10.1.101.0/24 [20/1000] via 10.1.10.5, 00:01:49
                      [20/1000] via 10.1.10.1, 00:01:49
B        10.1.102.0/30 [20/1000] via 10.1.10.5, 00:01:49
                      [20/1000] via 10.1.10.1, 00:01:49
B        10.1.103.0/24 [20/1000] via 10.1.10.5, 00:01:49
                      [20/1000] via 10.1.10.1, 00:01:49
DC1-CORE#
```

The process of building a localized control policy is similar to the process of building centralized policies covered in the previous chapters. However, the process of applying that policy is slightly different. In this first example, we will work through the process of configuring the policy in the vManage GUI; for all other examples in this chapter, we will simply review the CLI configuration.

The first step in the configuration process is to create the route policies themselves. The route policies that are used for configuring localized control policies are similar in structure to the centralized control policies reviewed in Chapter 6. For this particular example, we will be creating two different route policies: one that sets a MED value of 100, and the second that sets a MED value of 1000. These route policies can be configured in vManage from the **Configuration > Policies** menu, followed by selecting **Route Policy** from the Custom Options menu in the upper corner, as shown in Figure 9-3.

Figure 9-3   *Accessing the Route Policy Configurations*

Select the **Create New** option under the **Add Route Policy** menu, as shown in Figure 9-4.

Figure 9-4   *Creating a New Route Policy*

The route policy will need to be configured with a name and description. The next step is to add a new sequence type by clicking the **+ Sequence Type** button on the left, as shown in Figure 9-5. In a localized control policy, the only applicable sequence type is a route sequence, so this button will automatically add a new route sequence, as highlighted on the left. In the new route sequence, add a new sequence rule by clicking **+ New Sequence Rule**. As this MED value will apply to all of the routes being advertised by the WAN Edge, there will be no matching criteria specified. In order to have all of the routes permitted by this first sequence rule, click the **Actions** tab and click the **Accept** radio button. From the list of available actions, select the **Metric** action and then specify the MED value of **100**. Finally, select **Save Match and Actions** under the individual sequence and then select **Save Route Policy** at the very bottom of the page to complete the configuration of the route policy.

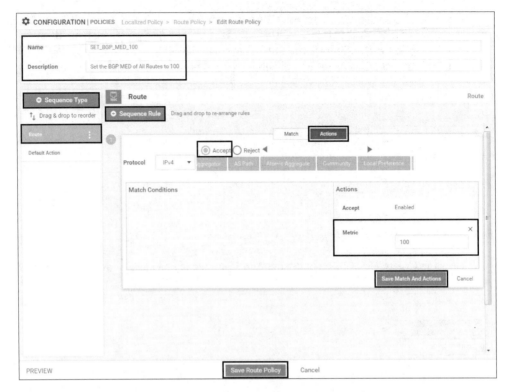

Figure 9-5 *Configuring a Route Policy to Set the BGP MED Value to 100*

The CLI rendering of the policy can also be seen by clicking the **Preview** button in the lower-left corner. Example 9-2 shows the CLI display for this policy.

Example 9-2 *Route Policy to Set the BGP MED Value*

```
route-policy SET_BGP_MED_100
  sequence 1
   action accept
    set
     metric 100
    !
   !
  !
 default-action reject
!
```

> **Note**   The **default-action** step in this policy has no effect, as all of the routes are matched in sequence 1. Ordinarily, network administrators will need to pay special care to the **default-action** statements in **route-policy** configurations.

A second route policy is then created for the second WAN Edge router in order to set the MED to 1000 by repeating all of the steps to create the first policy. Figure 9-6 illustrates that policy.

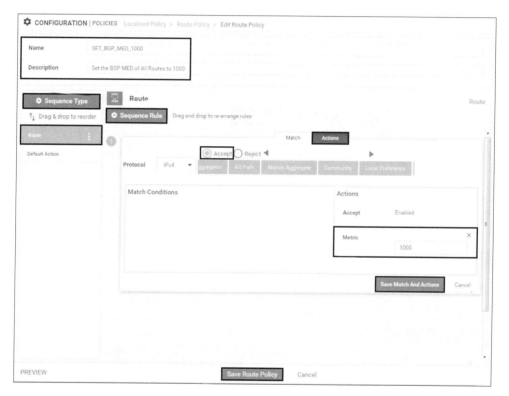

Figure 9-6   *Configuring a Route Policy to Set the BGP MED Value*

Once the route policies have been created, a localized policy will need to be created. As with centralized policies, where a single centralized policy could contain many different component parts, a similar structure is true of localized policies. There is a single localized policy that is applied to any router, but that localized policy can include multiple localized control policies and multiple localized data policies that are applied to different parts of the local router's configuration. In order to create the local policy, select the **Add Policy** option from the local policy screen to start the Local Policy Wizard, as shown in Figure 9-7.

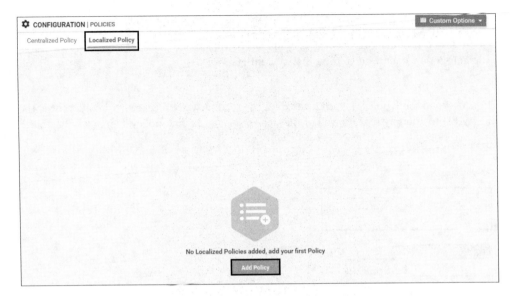

Figure 9-7   *Creating a New Localized Policy with the New Policy Wizard*

Click **Next** in the first several steps of the Local Policy Wizard until you arrive at the **Configure Route Policy** option. On this screen, import the two route policies that were previously created and attach them to this localized policy by clicking on the **+Add Route Policy** button and then selecting the policies, as shown in Figure 9-8 and Figure 9-9.

Figure 9-8   *Import Existing Route Policies into the Local Policy Wizard*

Finally, the local policy will need to have a name and description configured, as shown in Figure 9-10, and then it can be saved by clicking the **Save Policy** button at the bottom of the screen.

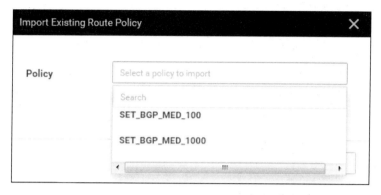

Figure 9-9 *Select the Route Policies to Be Imported into the Localized Policy*

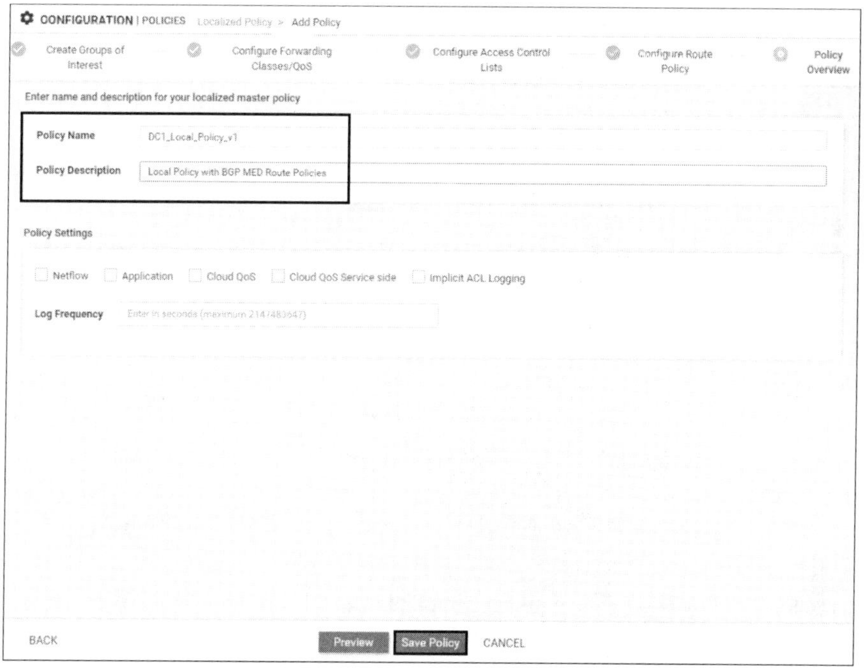

Figure 9-10 *Saving the Localized Policy*

The first step in utilizing the localized policy that was created is to attach it to the device template. This is accomplished by editing the specific device template and then selecting the local policy to be applied from the drop-down in the **Additional Templates** section, as shown in Figure 9-11.

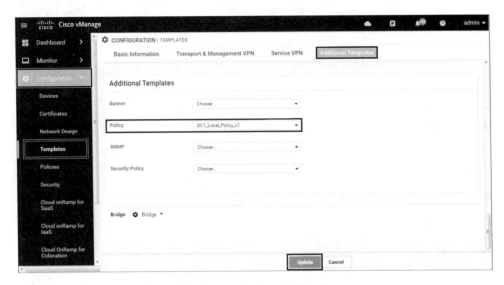

Figure 9-11   *Adding the Local Policy to the Device Template*

Once the local policy has been added to the device template, selecting the **Update** option will immediately push a configuration change to all of the devices that are attached to this device template. If more than one device is attached to the device template, users will receive a warning that they are changing multiple devices.

One of the greatest differences between centralized policies and localized policies is where the policies are applied. Centralized policies are applied to the vSmart's configurations; localized policies are applied as part of each individual WAN Edge router's configuration.

Once the local policy has been created and applied to the device template, it then needs to be applied to the feature template where it will ultimately be used. Similar to a Cisco IOS router, the process of creating a route map does not in and of itself configure the router to utilize the created route map. The route policy will still have to be referenced in the configuration in order to have any effect. This can be seen by examining the configuration of the WAN Edge router from the CLI, as shown in Example 9-3, where the route policies are in the running configuration but are not referenced by the BGP configuration. They, therefore, will not have any effect.

Example 9-3 *Viewing the Route Policies in the Device Configuration*

```
! Route-Policies are visible in the configuration of the WAN Edge router.
!
DC1-vEdge-1# show running-config policy
policy
 route-policy SET_BGP_MED_100
  sequence 1
   action accept
    set
     metric 100
    !
   !
  !
  default-action reject
 !
 route-policy SET_BGP_MED_1000
  sequence 1
   action accept
    set
     metric 1000
    !
   !
  !
  default-action reject
 !
!


! The route polices are not yet applied to any routing protocol.
DC1-vEdge-1# sho run vpn 1
vpn 1
 router
  bgp 65500
   propagate-aspath
   address-family ipv4-unicast
    redistribute omp
   !
   neighbor 10.1.10.2
    no shutdown
    remote-as 10
    address-family ipv4-unicast
     ! <<<No Route Policy Applied Here>>>
    !
   !
  !
 !
```

```
  interface ge0/2
   ip address 10.1.10.1/30
   no shutdown
  !
 !
DC1-vEdge-1#
 !
! The only reference to the name of the policy is in the policy definition.
! The policy is not currently applied anywhere in the configuration.
DC1-vEdge-1# show run | include _BGP_
 route-policy SET_BGP_MED_100
 route-policy SET_BGP_MED_1000
DC1-vEdge-1#
```

Note From an order of operations perspective, the localized policy must be tied to the device template before the individual component policies can be referenced anywhere else in the device configuration. This may be a counterintuitive process for engineers who are unfamiliar with it. If the opposite were done—that is, if the route maps were referenced by the BGP configuration before the localized policy was attached to the device template—then vManage would display a syntax error indicating that a route map was referenced but was not found in the localized policy configuration. Therefore, it is important to always update the localized policy tied to the device template prior to referencing any component parts of that localized policy.

Once the localized policy has been successfully attached to the device template, we can then go back and update the BGP feature template so that the configured BGP neighbors will utilize the new route map. In order to configure this, the **Address Family** radio button will need to be set to **On** and then the **Address Family** combo box will need to be set to **ipv4-unicast**. Under the address family, the **Route Policy Out** radio button will need to be checked and then a variable created for the name of the policy, as shown in Figure 9-12.

By creating a variable for the name of the route policies, we can use the same configuration across both routers and reference the two different route maps that we have created and configured with the local policy. This structure allows for maximum template reuse. Once this configuration is saved, we will be prompted to provide the names of the route policies. We will be using **SET_BGP_MED_100** for DC1-vEdge-1 and **SET_BGP_MED_1000** for DC1-vEdge-2.

Once the changes are applied, this configuration can be seen by looking at the CLI configuration for the BGP protocol in VPN 1 on both of the DC WAN Edge routers, as shown in Example 9-4.

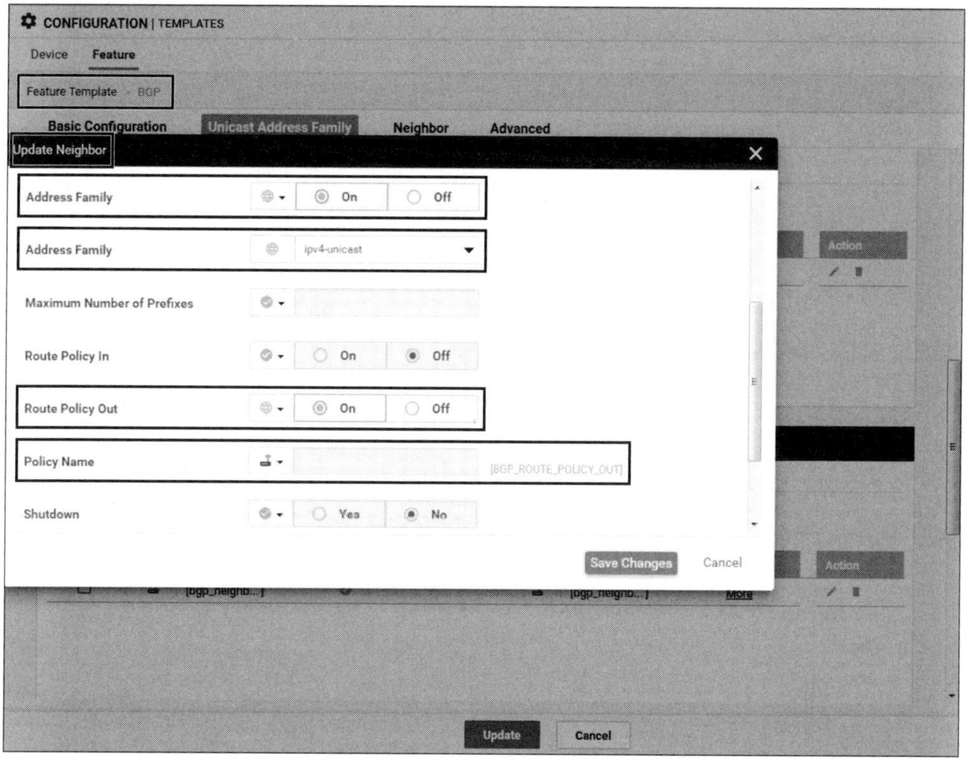

Figure 9-12 *Adding the Local Policy to the Device Template*

Example 9-4 *Viewing the Route Policies Applied in the Device Configuration*

```
! Each WAN Edge router is applying a different route-policy.
!
DC1-vEdge-1# sho run vpn 1
vpn 1
 router
  bgp 65500
   propagate-aspath
   address-family ipv4-unicast
    redistribute omp
   !
   neighbor 10.1.10.2
    no shutdown
    remote-as 10
    address-family ipv4-unicast
     route-policy SET_BGP_MED_100 out
    !
```

```
    !
   !
  !
 interface ge0/2
  ip address 10.1.10.1/30
  no shutdown
  !
 !
DC1-vEdge-1#

DC1-vEdge-2# sho run vpn 1
vpn 1
 router
  bgp 65500
   propagate-aspath
   address-family ipv4-unicast
    redistribute omp
   !
   neighbor 10.1.10.6
    no shutdown
    remote-as 10
    address-family ipv4-unicast
     route-policy SET_BGP_MED_1000 out
    !
    !
   !
  !
 interface ge0/2
  ip address 10.1.10.5/30
  no shutdown
  !
 !
DC1-vEdge-2#
```

After applying the configuration in Example 9-4, we can now return to the DC core router in Example 9-5 and see that the router still receives both sets of BGP advertisements: one from DC1-vEdge-1 and one from DC1-vEdge-2. However, only the routing advertisements from DC1-vEdge-1 are selected as best paths, and only the routes from DC1-vEdge-1 are inserted into the routing table. In this way, we can be assured that the core switch will send all traffic to the DC1-vEdge-1 router in steady state.

Example 9-5   *Viewing the Effects of the Route Policies on Neighboring Routers*

```
!
! Routes from both WAN Edge routers are present in the BGP table, but the different
! MED (metric) values influence the BGP path selection algorithm to select only the
! routes from DC1-vEdge-1.
!
DC1-CORE#sho ip bgp
BGP table version is 16, local router ID is 192.168.255.8
Status codes: s suppressed, d damped, h history, * valid, > best, i - internal,
              r RIB-failure, S Stale, m multipath, b backup-path, f RT-Filter,
              x best-external, a additional-path, c RIB-compressed,
              t secondary path, L long-lived-stale,
Origin codes: i - IGP, e - EGP, ? - incomplete
RPKI validation codes: V valid, I invalid, N Not found

     Network          Next Hop            Metric LocPrf Weight Path
 *   10.1.20.0/30     10.1.10.5             1000           0 65500 ?
 *>                   10.1.10.1              100           0 65500 ?
 *   10.1.20.4/30     10.1.10.5             1000           0 65500 ?
 *>                   10.1.10.1              100           0 65500 ?
 *   10.1.101.0/24    10.1.10.5             1000           0 65500 ?
 *>                   10.1.10.1              100           0 65500 ?
 *   10.1.102.0/30    10.1.10.5             1000           0 65500 ?
 *>                   10.1.10.1              100           0 65500 ?
 *   10.1.103.0/24    10.1.10.5             1000           0 65500 ?
 *>                   10.1.10.1              100           0 65500 ?
!
! The routing table on the DC1-Core router now only lists routes from DC1-vEdge-1.
! This is indicated by the next hop address of 10.1.10.1.
!
DC1-CORE#sho ip route bgp
Codes: L - local, C - connected, S - static, R - RIP, M - mobile, B - BGP
       D - EIGRP, EX - EIGRP external, O - OSPF, IA - OSPF inter area
       N1 - OSPF NSSA external type 1, N2 - OSPF NSSA external type 2
       E1 - OSPF external type 1, E2 - OSPF external type 2
       i - IS-IS, su - IS-IS summary, L1 - IS-IS level-1, L2 - IS-IS level-2
       ia - IS-IS inter area, * - candidate default, U - per-user static route
       o - ODR, P - periodic downloaded static route, H - NHRP, l - LISP
       a - application route
       + - replicated route, % - next hop override, p - overrides from PfR
Gateway of last resort is 192.168.255.1 to network 0.0.0.0

      10.0.0.0/8 is variably subnetted, 11 subnets, 3 masks
B        10.1.20.0/30 [20/100] via 10.1.10.1, 00:03:08
BGP table version is 16, local router ID is 192.168.255.8
B        10.1.20.4/30 [20/100] via 10.1.10.1, 00:03:08
```

```
B        10.1.101.0/24 [20/100] via 10.1.10.1, 00:03:08
B        10.1.102.0/30 [20/100] via 10.1.10.1, 00:03:08
B        10.1.103.0/24 [20/100] via 10.1.10.1, 00:03:08
DC1-CORE#
```

As Example 9-5 shows, localized control policies can be used to manipulate the routing advertisements into or out of the WAN Edges in order to perform traffic engineering at the local site. Administrators should recall that the configuration explained in this section is only half of the configuration necessary to get all of the traffic at a site to flow through a particular WAN Edge. This configuration handles how routers attached to the service VPNs will forward traffic to the WAN Edge. In order to manipulate how other SD-WAN routers will forward traffic to this site across the SD-WAN fabric, see Use Case 3 in Chapter 6.

Localized Data Policies

The second main use of localized policies is to configure data policies (specifically access control lists) used for filtering or remarking traffic at the interface level. In this section, we will continue to expand on the previously configured local policy and add an interface ACL to prohibit SSH sessions through the service-side interface. Before any policy is configured, we can observe that it is possible to connect into the DC1-vEdge-1 router from DC1-Core with the SSH protocol, as shown in Example 9-6.

Example 9-6 *Establishing an SSH Session from DC1-Core to DC1-vEdge-1*

```
! DC1-Core is able to successfully establish an SSH session to DC1-vEdge-1.
!
DC1-CORE#ssh -l admin 10.1.10.1
viptela 19.2.0
Password:
Last login: Mon Nov 11 10:42:08 2019 from 1.1.1.6
Welcome to Viptela CLI
admin connected from 10.1.10.2 using ssh on DC1-vEdge-1
DC1-vEdge-1#
```

In order to filter this data plane traffic with a local policy, a new access control list (ACL) will need to be configured from the **Custom Options** menu, as shown in Figure 9-13.

Figure 9-13 *Creating a New Access Control List*

The objective of dropping SSH traffic can be achieved by matching on a source port of 22 or a destination port of 22 and dropping the traffic, as shown in Figure 9-14. In order to test that the policy is working, we are also configuring a counter on the ACL sequence. Finally, remember when configuring a policy to drop selected traffic like this, it is necessary to change the default action to **accept** in order to permit any other traffic to be forwarded.

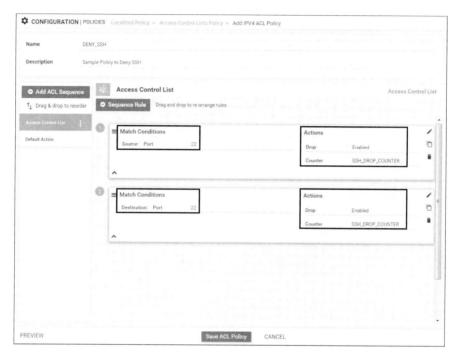

Figure 9-14   *Configuring an ACL to Drop Traffic on Port 22*

This new ACL can then be added into the previously configured local policy by editing the localized policy we created previously and importing this ACL into it, as has been done with other policy examples throughout the book. Example 9-7 shows the full localized policy.

Example 9-7   *Previewing the Localized Policy with Route Policies and ACLs*

```
policy
! New ACL "DENY_SSH" added
 access-list DENY_SSH
    sequence 1
    match
     source-port 22
    !
    action drop
```

```
         count SSH_DROP_COUNTER
        !
      !
     sequence 11
      match
       destination-port 22
       !
      action drop
       count SSH_DROP_COUNTER
       !
      !
  default-action accept
 !
 ! Existing route-policies are still contained in the localized policy
 route-policy SET_BGP_MED_1000
     sequence 1
      action accept
       set
        metric 1000
       !
      !
     !
  default-action reject
 !
 route-policy SET_BGP_MED_100
     sequence 1
      action accept
       set
       metric 100
       !
      !
     !
  default-action reject
 !
 !
!
```

Just as there can only be a single centralized vSmart policy that is activated at any point
in time (although that policy can have many different component parts), the same is true
of localized policies. Each router can only have a single localized policy attached to it
at any given point in time and that single localized policy can have as many component
route policies and/or ACLs as necessary.

Note Because this policy is currently in use by one or more routers, saving changes to the localized policy will result in configuration changes to all of the routers that currently reference this policy. If you would prefer to configure a change to the local policy but to apply that change at a later point in time, this can be achieved by copying the current localized policy and then editing the copy of that policy. When you are ready to apply the necessary changes at some point in the future, this can be achieved by changing which localized policy (LocalizedPolicy_v1 to LocalizedPolicy_v2) is applied in the device template.

Now that the ACL has been configured as part of the localized policy, the last step is to reference the ACL as part of the interface configuration template. This can be achieved by setting the **Ingress ACL – IPv4** option on the interface template to **On** and then specifying the name of the ACL in the **IPv4 Ingress Access List** field, as shown in Figure 9-15.

Figure 9-15 *Configuring the Interface Template to Reference the ACL in the Localized Policy*

The effect of this policy can be seen by attempting to establish an SSH session again from the DC Core to the WAN Edge router, as shown in Example 9-8. It is clear from the example that the SSH session no longer opens correctly. Additionally, the ACL counter is incrementing on DC1-vEdge-1 to reflect that the packets are being matched and dropped by the ACL.

Example 9-8 *Effects of Applying an Access Control List*

```
! The DC1-CORE router is no longer able to SSH into DC1-vEdge-1.
DC1-CORE#ssh -l admin 10.1.10.1
% Destination unreachable; gateway or host down
DC1-CORE#


! DC1-vEdge-1 shows the blocked packets in the ACL counter
DC1-vEdge-1# show policy access-list-counters
NAME        COUNTER NAME      PACKETS  BYTES
-------------------------------------------------
DENY_SSH  SSH_DROP_COUNTER  1        58
```

As this example shows, interface ACLs are useful for filtering traffic flows transiting the router. ACLs can also be used for a number of other actions, including mirroring traffic to an additional destination, manipulating the forwarding path by setting an alternative next-hop address, policing the data rate of a type of traffic, and remarking the traffic by setting a different DSCP value. While these use cases are beyond the scope covered in this book, additional information on these topics can be found in the Cisco documentation.

Note   Tunnel interfaces have implicit ACLs applied to them that automatically restrict the types of traffic permitted to enter these interfaces. Applying an explicit ACL can override this default behavior. Further information about the behavior when explicit ACLs are configured on tunnel interfaces can be found in the Cisco SD-WAN documentation.

Quality of Service Policies

Quality of service (QoS) is also configured with localized policies. As discussed in Chapters 7 and 8, centralized data and App-Route policies can be used to make forwarding decisions in the Cisco SD-WAN fabric. While those two technologies are used to determine which path a specific packet or flow should take, the QoS configuration in the localized data policy is used to perform scheduling and queuing functions. QoS is often used by network administrators to minimize delay and jitter for business-critical applications such as VoIP and video conferencing, and it's used to prioritize the queuing and forwarding of specific traffic classes. It can also be used to manage buffer allocation across different types of traffic, as well as to determine the congestion management behavior when the buffers are full. A detailed discussion of the generic quality of service theory and each of these features is beyond the scope of this book, but there are additional resources available in the Cisco documentation and through Cisco Press. This chapter focuses on the command structure necessary to implement QoS with Cisco SD-WAN.

> **Note** Quality of service configurations are highly dependent on the functionalities supported by the underlying hardware platforms. The following section will deal with features that are common across all hardware platforms. These configuration examples are derived from the vEdge-Cloud virtual routing platform. Additional features may be available depending on the specific code version and hardware platform.
>
> When utilizing QoS functionalities on the vEdge-Cloud—or related platforms such as the vEdge-5000, ISR-1100-4G, ISR-1100-4GLTE, and the ISR-1100-6G—the commands **cloud-qos** and **cloud-qos-service-side** must be configured in the local policy. These commands can be seen in Example 9-14 at the end of this section.

Although it may be overwhelming at first glance, configuring a QoS policy on a WAN Edge router is a simple process that consists of the following steps:

Step 1.   Assign traffic to forwarding classes

Step 2.   Map forwarding classes to hardware queues

Step 3.   Configure the scheduling parameters for each queue

Step 4.   Map all of the schedulers together into a single QoS map

Step 5.   Configure the interface with the QoS map

In the following sections, we will configure each of these steps in turn to observe the entire process of building a QoS policy. The sample policy we will build will have different classes of traffic: a class for voice and video traffic that is placed in the priority queue, a class for business-critical traffic, and a class for everything else.

Step 1: Assign Traffic to Forwarding Classes

The first step in the QoS process is to assign traffic flows to different forwarding classes. This step can be performed with either a centralized data policy or with an ACL from a localized data policy by specifying the **class** action. In this section, we will continue to expand on the existing localized policy we created in Example 9-7. Additional sequences will be added in order to classify traffic into the appropriate forwarding classes, as shown in Example 9-9.

Example 9-9 *Expanding ACL to Perform QoS Classification*

```
policy
<<< omitted for brevity>>>
 access-list DENY_SSH
  !
  ! Sequences 1 and 11 are the existing Sequences to Block SSH traffic
  !
    sequence 1
     match
      source-port 22
     !
```

```
   action drop
    count SSH_DROP_COUNTER
    !
   !
  sequence 11
   match
    destination-port 22
    !
   action drop
    count SSH_DROP_COUNTER
    !
   !
!
! Sequences 21, 31, and 41 match permitted traffic and set the 'class' action
! to specify the forwarding class.
  sequence 21
   match
    dscp 40 46
    !
   action accept
    class VOICE_AND_VIDEO
    !
   !
  sequence 31
   match
    source-data-prefix-list CRITICAL_SERVERS
    !
   action accept
    class CRITICAL_DATA
    !
   !
  sequence 41
   action accept
    class BEST_EFFORT
    !
   !
 default-action accept
 !
lists
 data-prefix-list CRITICAL_SERVERS
  ip-prefix 10.250.1.0/24
  !
 !
!
```

As shown in Example 9-9, three user-defined forwarding classes have been created:

- VOICE_AND_VIDEO
- CRITICAL_DATA
- BEST_EFFORT

Traffic is matched into the VOICE_AND_VIDEO class based on the DSCP markings of the traffic. In Cisco SD-WAN policies, DSCP is always specified in decimal values. Traffic is matched into the **CRITICAL_DATA** class by matching the data prefix list CRITICAL_SERVERS. Any traffic that is not matched into either the **VOICE_AND_VIDEO** or **CRITICAL_DATA** class will be placed into the **BEST_EFFORT** class. While this example matches on DSCP values and IP addresses, any criteria that can be matched in an ACL or a centralized data policy can be used to match traffic and set the **class** action.

Step 2: Map Forwarding Classes to Hardware Queues

The next step in the forwarding process is to assign the forwarding classes to their hardware queues. This configuration is accomplished in the GUI by creating a new type of localized policy list, the *class map*. The class map configuration references the name of the classes that were configured in Step 1 and the specific hardware queue that this traffic will be forwarded through. Example 9-10 shows the class map configuration for the forwarding classes created in Step 1.

Example 9-10 *Class Map Configuration*

```
class-map
 class BEST_EFFORT queue 7
 class CRITICAL_DATA queue 1
 class VOICE_AND_VIDEO queue 0
 !
```

In this example, the **VOICE_AND_VIDEO** class is mapped to queue 0, the **CRITICAL_DATA** traffic is mapped to queue 1, and the **BEST_EFFORT** traffic is mapped to queue 7.

Step 3: Configure the Scheduling Parameters for Each Queue

The next step in the process is to configure the scheduling parameters for each individual queue. Each scheduler will contain a reference to the traffic class, the maximum bandwidth to be used during congestion, the percentage of the buffer that is allocated, the scheduling mechanism (Low Latency Queuing or Weighted Round Robin), and the congestion management technique (tail drop or random early detection). Example 9-11 provides a sample configuration of these features. Note that as of software version 19.2, Cisco SD-WAN only supports the configuration of a single scheduler per queue. When QoS configurations are generated in the vManage GUI, additional classes called **Queue0**,

Queue1, Queue2, and so on are created and the schedulers are tied to these classes. The examples in this section were manually configured to avoid this extra complexity.

Example 9-11   *QoS Scheduler Configuration*

```
!
qos-scheduler VOICE_AND_VIDEO_SCHED
 class VOICE_AND_VIDEO
 bandwidth-percent 20
 buffer-percent 20
 scheduling llq
 drops tail-drop
!
qos-scheduler CRITICAL_DATA_SCHED
 class CRITICAL_DATA
 bandwidth-percent 30
 buffer-percent 40
 scheduling wrr
 drops red-drop
!
qos-scheduler BEST_EFFORT_SCHED
 class BEST_EFFORT
 bandwidth-percent 50
 buffer-percent 40
 scheduling wrr
 drops red-drop
!
```

Currently (as of version 19.2), the Cisco WAN Edge routers support a total of eight queues, numbered 0 through 7. Queue 0 is always configured as a low-latency queue and is the only queue that supports Low Latency Queuing. Additionally, all control traffic that is originated by the WAN Edge router, including DTLS/TLS, BFD probes, and routing protocol traffic, is automatically mapped to queue 0. Any user-defined traffic classes that are mapped to queue 0, such as the **VOICE_AND_VIDEO** class from Example 9-10, must also be configured for Low Latency Queuing. Queues 1 through 7 support Weighted Round Robin forwarding, where the weighting is proportional to the configured bandwidth percent.

Step 4: Map All of the Schedulers Together into a Single QoS Map

The final configuration step in the localized policy for a QoS configuration is to tie all of the schedulers together with a single QoS map that can be referenced under the interface configuration. Example 9-12 demonstrates a sample QoS map configuration.

Example 9-12   *QoS Map Configuration*

```
!
  qos-map MY_QOS_MAP
   qos-scheduler VOICE_AND_VIDEO_SCHED
   qos-scheduler CRITICAL_DATA_SCHED
   qos-scheduler BEST_EFFORT_SCHED
!
```

Step 5: Configure the Interface with the QoS Map

The last part of the process is to configure the interface to use the QoS map that was created in the previous step. This step is analogous to configuring a "service-policy" in traditional Cisco IOS configuration. QoS maps can be applied to any interface to affect the scheduling and queuing of outbound traffic. However, since the available WAN bandwidth is typically lower than LAN bandwidth and, therefore, congestion is most likely to occur on the WAN, QoS maps are most commonly configured on the transport (WAN) interfaces. Example 9-13 demonstrates how to add the QoS map to the transport interfaces.

Example 9-13   *Applying QoS Maps to Transport Interfaces*

```
!
! QoS Maps applied to transport interfaces in VPN 0.
!
DC1-vEdge-1# sho run vpn 0
vpn 0
 interface ge0/0
  ip address 100.64.11.2/30
  tunnel-interface
   <<<omitted for brevity>>>
  !
  no shutdown
 qos-map  MY_QOS_MAP
  !
 interface ge0/1
  ip address 172.16.11.2/30
  tunnel-interface
   <<<omitted for brevity>>>
  !
  no shutdown
 qos-map  MY_QOS_MAP
 !
 !
!
! Sample show commands to validate that the QOS Map is applied
```

```
! to the correct interfaces.
!
DC1-vEdge-1# show policy qos-map-info


QOS MAP      INTERFACE
NAME         NAME
----------------------
MY_QOS_MAP  ge0/0
            ge0/1
 !
 !
! Sample show commands to validate that the QOS Map is configured
! with the correct QoS Schedulers.
 !
DC1-vEdge-1# show policy qos-scheduler-info


                       BANDWIDTH  BUFFER           QOS MAP
QOS SCHEDULER NAME     PERCENT    PERCENT  QUEUE   NAME
-------------------------------------------------------------
BEST_EFFORT_SCHED      50         40       7       MY_QOS_MAP
CRITICAL_DATA_SCHED    30         40       1       MY_QOS_MAP
VOICE_AND_VIDEO_SCHED  20         20       0       MY_QOS_MAP
```

The entirety of the localized policy containing QoS configuration is provided as a reference in Example 9-14. In this example, we can see the ACL used to assign the traffic to forwarding classes (Step 1) and that the forwarding classes are mapped to hardware queues (Step 2), the scheduling parameters are configured in the QoS schedulers (Step 3), and the schedulers are mapped together into a single QoS map that can be referenced under an interface (Step 4).

Example 9-14 *Complete QoS Configuration*

```
DC1-vEdge-1# show running-config policy
policy
 !
 ! 'cloud-qos' and 'cloud-qos-service-side' commands are necessary on
 ! vEdge-Cloud based platforms
 !
 cloud-qos
 cloud-qos-service-side
 lists
  data-prefix-list CRITICAL_SERVERS
  ip-prefix 10.250.1.0/24
  !
 !
```

```
 route-policy SET_BGP_MED_100
  <<<omitted for brevity>>>
 !
 route-policy SET_BGP_MED_1000
  <<<omitted for brevity>>>
!
! Step 2: Class maps are used to map the forwarding classes to hardware queues
!
 class-map
  class VOICE_AND_VIDEO queue 0
  class CRITICAL_DATA queue 1
  class BEST_EFFORT queue 7
 !
 !
 ! Step 1:  Access Lists are used to assign the traffic to forwarding classes
 !
 access-list DENY_SSH
   <<<omitted for brevity>>>
  !
  sequence 21
   match
    dscp 40 46
   !
  action accept
    class VOICE_AND_VIDEO
   !
  !
  sequence 31
   match
    source-data-prefix-list CRITICAL_SERVERS
   !
  action accept
    class CRITICAL_DATA
   !
  !
  sequence 41
  action accept
    class BEST_EFFORT
   !
  !
  default-action accept
 ! !
Step 3: QoS Schedulers are used to configure the forwarding
! parameters of each traffic class.
!
```

```
 !
qos-scheduler BEST_EFFORT_SCHED
 class              BEST_EFFORT
 bandwidth-percent 50
 buffer-percent     40
 drops              red-drop
 !
qos-scheduler CRITICAL_DATA_SCHED
 class              CRITICAL_DATA
 bandwidth-percent 30
 buffer-percent     40
 drops              red-drop
 !
qos-scheduler VOICE_AND_VIDEO_SCHED
 class              VOICE_AND_VIDEO
 bandwidth-percent 20
 buffer-percent     20
 scheduling         llq
 !
 ! Step 4: Map all of the QoS Schedulers together with a QoS Map
 !
qos-map MY_QOS_MAP
 qos-scheduler BEST_EFFORT_SCHED
 qos-scheduler CRITICAL_DATA_SCHED
 qos-scheduler VOICE_AND_VIDEO_SCHED
 !
 !
```

Summary

This chapter reviewed localized policies and how they are used with the Cisco SD-WAN solution. There are two main types of localized policies: localized control policies and localized data policies. Both of these types of localized policies are configured in a single policy section of the WAN Edge router configuration and are device specific in scope. This chapter reviewed examples of how localized control policies are used to manipulate routing advertisements outside of the SD-WAN fabric and how this functionality can be used to achieve certain traffic engineering and outcomes. Localized data policies can be used to create access control lists and manipulate traffic flowing in the data plane through the router. Localized data policies can also be used to configure quality of service on the WAN Edge routers, including queuing and congestion management, in order to prioritize certain classes of traffic over others.

Review All Key Topics

Review the most important topics in the chapter, noted with the Key Topic icon in the outer margin of the page. Table 9-1 lists these key topics and the page numbers on which each is found.

Table 9-1 *Key Topics*

Key Topic Element	Description	Page
Paragraph	Description of where centralized policies and localized policies are applied	328
Paragraph	Description of how each router can only have a single localized policy attached to it at any given point in time	336
Paragraph	Description of the queues supported by Cisco WAN Edge routers	342

Chapter Review Questions

1. Localized policies are configured on which element of the SD-WAN fabric?

   a. vBond

   b. vSmart

   c. WAN Edge routers

   d. vPolicy

2. A single list object can be used in both a centralized policy and a localized policy.

   a. True

   b. False

3. What is the scope of localized policy?

   a. Device-specific

   b. Site-specific

   c. VPN-specific

   d. The entire network

4. Which of the following actions can be taken in a localized control policy? (Select all that apply.)

   a. Accept

   b. Reject

   c. Drop

   d. Inspect

   e. Pass

5. Ensuring symmetric flows through a single WAN Edge router is preferable to equal-cost multi-pathing because it ensures that flows will not be blocked by firewall or NAT state mismatches.

   a. True

   b. False

6. Which of the following actions can be taken in a localized data policy? (Select all that apply.)

   a. Accept

   b. Reject

   c. Drop

   d. Inspect

   e. Pass

7. How many queues are supported on a WAN Edge router interface with 19.2 code?

   a. Zero queues

   b. Two queues

   c. Four queues

   d. Eight queues

   e. 256 queues

8. Which queues support the low-latency queuing and priority queueing functionalities on the vEdge router platforms?

   a. Queue 0

   b. Queue 1

   c. Queue 7

   d. Queue 8

   e. Queues 0 and 1

   f. All queues

9. Which queue is control plane traffic automatically mapped to?

   a. Queue 0

   b. Queue 1

   c. Queue 7

   d. Queue 8

10. Which of the following are part of the localized policy QoS configuration on a WAN Edge router? (Select all that apply.)

    a. class-map

    b. qos-map

    c. shaper

    d. qos-scheduler

Chapter 10

Cisco SD-WAN Security

This chapter covers the following topics:

- **Cisco SD-WAN Security: Why and What:** This section covers what SD-WAN security is and why it is relevant to an organization.

- **Application-Aware Enterprise Firewall:** This section of the chapter covers the concepts and configuration of the Application-Aware Enterprise Firewall.

- **Intrusion Detection and Prevention:** This section of the chapter covers the concepts and configuration of the intrusion prevention and detection engine.

- **URL Filtering:** This section of the chapter covers the concepts and configuration of the URL Filtering engine.

- **Advanced Malware Protection and Threat Grid:** This section of the chapter covers the concepts and configuration of the Advanced Malware Protection engine and Threat Grid cloud.

- **DNS Web Layer Security:** This section of the chapter covers the concepts and configuration of DNS Web Layer security.

- **Cloud Security:** This section of the chapter covers the concepts and configuration of third-party cloud security.

- **vManage Authentication and Authorization:** This section of the chapter covers the concepts and configuration of vManage authentication and authorization.

Cisco SD-WAN Security: Why and What

With the advent of many business-critical applications migrating to the cloud and the rapid adoption of Internet circuits as a business-grade transport, a new and more optimal way to consume applications is being leveraged. Direct Internet Access (DIA) allows end users to reach cloud applications and resources in a more optimal fashion by connecting to the closest and highest-performing point of presence. Most cloud application providers highly recommend not backhauling this traffic through a remote data center or hub but instead going directly from the branch through DIA to the application—leveraging DNS and geo-location services for the best possible performance. In addition, organizations are realizing that they can leverage these same Internet circuits as a means to offload guest traffic to the Internet directly instead of using up WAN and data center resources that would be better used for business-critical applications. Coupled with Cisco SD-WAN Application-Aware Routing and visibility, you have a solution that makes sense for the majority of organizations across most verticals.

Realistically, however, we cannot ignore the security implications of moving the Internet edge to the branch. The DIA model—where Internet access is distributed across many branches, unsecured guest users are allowed Internet access directly, and payment card infrastructure is exposed to these new access models—increases the attack surface of the network. The proliferation of highly publicized massive data breaches has made security compliance, particularly PCI compliance, a critical task for almost every organization. The threat landscape is wide and includes cyber warfare, ransomware, and targeted attacks. These threats can be manifested in many ways (such as security bugs and vulnerabilities, malware, denial of service attacks, botnets, and so on). It is important to note that security threats can come from both inside the network and from outside the network, so all attack vectors must be considered. Figure 10-1 depicts the ever-growing threat surface.

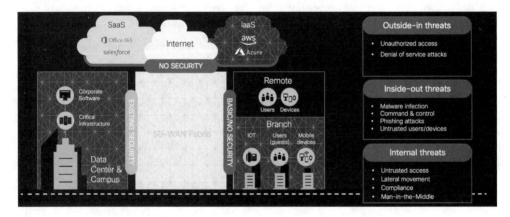

Figure 10-1   *Threat Surface*

It is critical that the appropriate security mechanisms, such as firewalling, intrusion prevention, URL filtering, and malware protection, are leveraged by the branch in order to prevent, detect, and protect the network from all types of threats. The question facing network architects now is how should security services be consumed by the branches? One way to consume Cisco SD-WAN security is by leveraging Cisco's integrated security applications within a rich portfolio of powerful WAN Edge routers, such as the ISR4000 series. On top of the native application-aware stateful firewall, these WAN Edge routers have the capability of dedicating compute resources to application service containers running within IOS-XE to enable in-line IDS/IPS, URL filtering, and Advanced Malware Protection (AMP). The enablement, visibility, and reporting of these integrated security applications are accomplished through a unified management console, Cisco vManage. While this chapter focuses mainly on integrated security at the branch, Cisco SD-WAN security can also be consumed through cloud services or through regional hubs where VNF-based security chains may be leveraged or robust security stacks may already exist. In the end, the appropriate security architecture depends on the organization's technical and business requirements. Figure 10-2 illustrates some of the security deployment models that organizations can choose to deploy.

Figure 10-2 *Security Deployment Models*

Here are some benefits of the Cisco SD-WAN Security suite:

- **Simple and automated security solution:** The intent-based workflow is designed for ease of configuration and deployment of the SD-WAN security solution. The workflow allows you to leverage templates in order to include all of the relevant security capabilities and deploy the policy to multiple devices at the same time.

- **Comprehensive SD-WAN security:** With security capabilities such as Application-Aware Enterprise Firewall and IPS enabled on your WAN Edge device, you can do the following:

  - Restrict access to certain Internet destinations for remote employees and guests, with improved application experience.

  - Protect the internal network from malware and/or malicious content in real time.

  - Incur no additional cost, as deploying the Cisco SD-WAN security solution eliminates the need to deploy any additional equipment within your SD-WAN network to enable security features.

■ **Centralized management:** Deploy, troubleshoot, and monitor the SD-WAN overlay solution with security capabilities across the WAN Edge devices centrally via the Cisco vManage GUI.

As briefly mentioned previously, Cisco SD-WAN security features are centrally configured via vManage in the security section through simple guided workflows. The guided workflow can assist the network operator in building security policy based on well-known use cases such as Compliance, Guest Access, Direct Cloud Access, and Direct Internet Access or based on a custom use case. Figure 10-3 shows the workflow and some of the options that can be configured. The security policy is then assigned to the desired branch through the attached branch template.

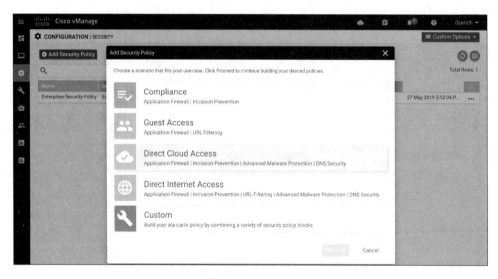

Figure 10-3   *Security Policy Workflow*

Application-Aware Enterprise Firewall

One of the most basic yet crucial forms of security at the branch is firewalling. A proper firewall provides protection of stateful TCP sessions, enables logging, and ensures that a zero-trust domain is implemented between segments in the network. Traditional branch firewall design involves deploying the appliance in either in-line Layer 3 mode or transparent Layer 2 mode behind (or ahead) of the WAN Edge router. This adds additional complexity to the enterprise branch and creates needless additional administrative overhead in managing the added firewalls. Cisco SD-WAN takes an integrated approach and has implemented a robust Application-Aware Enterprise Firewall directly into the SD-WAN code. The Cisco SD-WAN firewall provides stateful inspection, zone-based policies, and segment awareness. Also, through network-based application recognition, it can classify over 1,400 Layer 7 applications for granular policy control. These applications can be secured based on category or on an individual basis, depending on how the feature is lev-eraged in the security policy. Because these policies are VPN aware, they can be applied within a zone, between zones on the same WAN Edge router, or between zones across the Cisco SD-WAN fabric. A *zone* is a grouping of one or more VPNs. Grouping VPNs into zones allows you to establish security boundaries in your overlay network so that you can control the flow of all data traffic that passes between these zones.

Zone configuration consists of the following components:

- **Source zone** is a grouping of VPNs where the data traffic flows originate.

- **Destination zone** is a grouping of VPNs where the data traffic flows terminate.

- **Firewall policy** is a localized security policy that defines the conditions that the originating data traffic flow must match to allow the flow to continue to the destina-tion zone.

- **Zone pair** is a container that associates a source zone with a destination zone and that applies a firewall policy to the traffic that flows between the two zones.

In addition, a self-zone policy exists in order to inspect traffic destined to the WAN Edge router itself, so as to protect from inbound threats, DDoS attacks, and unauthor-ized access to the WAN Edge router. When combined with other Cisco SD-WAN secu-rity features, Application-Aware Enterprise Firewall is an important component of the solution for organizations looking to meet PCI compliance across the enterprise branch footprint. Figure 10-4 provides an overview on the typical zones and traffic flows for an application-aware firewall.

Firewall events and logs can be exported to security information and event management systems through traditional syslog or, for more advanced implementations, via NetFlow v9 to support high-speed logging requirements.

Note   Support for application recognition through firewall policy is currently only available on Cisco IOS-XE SD-WAN software and not Viptela OS. Cisco vEdge and ISR appliances running Viptela OS can still enjoy the benefits of a firewall but must use Layer 3 and Layer 4 criteria to identify traffic.

Through the help of Cisco vManage, implementing a firewall policy at the branch is relatively straightforward. Like all other security features available in Cisco SD-WAN, the first place to start is by navigating to the security section and either building a new security policy (and following the simple workflow to build a firewall policy) or directly navigating to the firewall policy subsection under Custom Options. Figure 10-5 shows the security policy page in vManage. No matter how the firewall policy is configured, it must eventually be tied to an overall security policy, which is then attached to the branch WAN Edge router template.

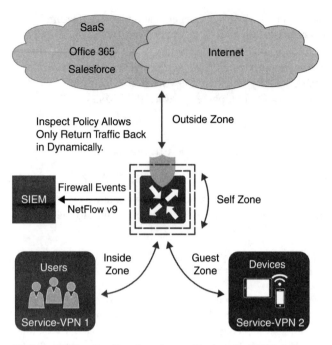

Figure 10-4 *Application-Aware Enterprise Firewall*

Figure 10-5 *Building a Firewall Policy*

Enterprise Application-Aware Firewall is a localized security policy that allows stateful inspection of data traffic flows that are matched based on six different criteria available within the vManage security policy dashboard. The match criteria include source data prefix, destination data prefix, source port, destination port, protocol, and application/ application family. Traffic flows that originate in a given zone are allowed to proceed to another zone based on the policy match and action criteria set between the two zones.

Within a given firewall policy, accepted matching flows can be subjected to the following three actions:

- **Inspect:** When the action is set to Inspect, the Enterprise Application-Aware Firewall tracks the state of the flows and creates sessions. Since it maintains the state of the flows, the return traffic is allowed and there is no need to configure a separate policy to allow the response traffic.

- **Pass:** This action allows the router to forward the traffic from one zone to another zone. The Pass action does not track the state of the flows. In other words, the firewall does not create sessions when the action is set to Pass. The Pass action allows the traffic to flow in only one direction. You must have a corresponding policy to allow the response traffic.

- **Drop:** When the action is set to Drop and packets match against the set match parameters, that packet will be dropped.

> **Note**   When leveraging application recognition for match criteria, the Inspect action will be equivalent to a Drop action.

Based on the flow of traffic between zones, the Enterprise Application-Aware Firewall is further divided into *intra-zone-based security* and *inter-zone-based security*.

The diagram in Figure 10-6 depicts an intra-zone security use case where hosts within the same zone on the same WAN Edge router can be secured with a firewall policy, while the same policy can also secure hosts across the fabric on the same zone. For the firewall policy rule to be impactful, traffic must ingress and egress the WAN Edge router and should not be bypassed via a downstream Layer 3 device.

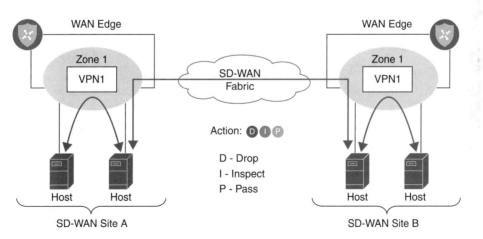

Figure 10-6 *Intra-Zone Firewall Application*

The diagram in Figure 10-7 depicts an inter-zone security use case where hosts on different zones within the same WAN Edge router can be secured with a firewall policy, while the same policy can also secure hosts across the fabric on different zones. For inter-zone connectivity to occur, a vSmart policy that leaks routes between VPNs must first be configured and applied. This is called an *extranet policy* and leverages the "Export to" route-based control policy sequence.

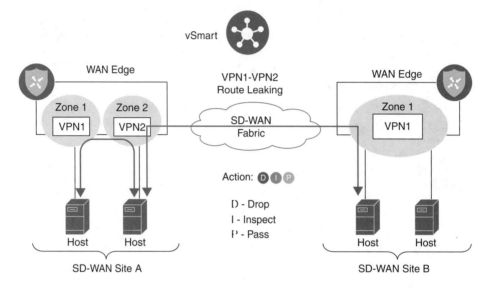

Figure 10-7 *Inter-Zone Firewall Application*

The following is a summary of steps required to configure a firewall policy in Cisco SD-WAN:

Step 1. **Create a new firewall policy.** Name and describe the policy.

Step 2. **Configure zones.** Create your source and destination zones. Today, zones are equivalent to SD-WAN VPNs.

Step 3. **Apply zone pairs.** Group the source and destination zones into a zone pair to define traffic direction. The policy sequences will be applied to this zone pair.

Step 4. **Configure a default action.** This is the action that will take place if a sequence match is not found. Drop, Inspect, and Pass are valid options.

Step 5. **Configure sequence rules.** Match traffic using Layer 3–4 information (such as source data prefix lists, source ports, destination data prefix lists, and so on) or by matching on application category or name.

Once a firewall policy is created, the zones and zone pairs are then created and applied. Figure 10-8 shows the zone and zone-pair configuration in vManage.

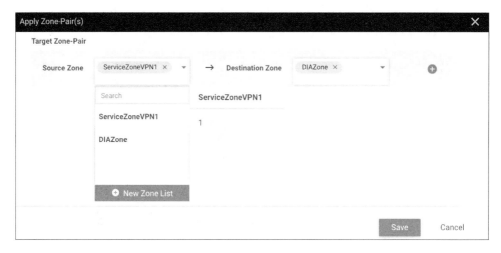

Figure 10-8   *Zone and Zone-Pair Configuration*

After the zones and zone pairs are configured, you will need to build the sequence rules next. You can also specify a default action in the sequence rule configuration shown in Figure 10-9.

Figure 10-9   *Sequence Rule Configuration*

Once all the desired sequence rules are configured, the firewall policy can be saved and other security functions such as IPS/IDS can be enabled through additional workflow tasks. Advanced firewall features such as high-speed logging, policy bypass for direct Internet access, TCP SYN flood limiting, and audit trails for inspection logging can be enabled at the end of the workflow in the Additional Policy Settings section, as shown in Figure 10-10.

Figure 10-10 *Advanced Firewall Features*

The security policy that has the newly built firewall policy can then be referenced in a template that is attached to a branch WAN Edge router under the Additional Templates section. Figure 10-11 shows a summary of how a firewall policy is built, attached to a security policy, and applied to a device template for activation.

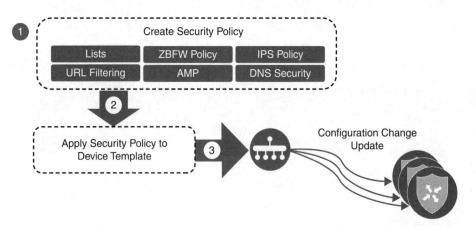

Figure 10-11 *Security Policy Application*

Figure 10-12 demonstrates how to attach a security policy to a device template under the Additional Templates section.

Note   The factory default Security App Hosting template referenced under the container profile section can be selected if no SD-WAN Security feature using application service containers is referenced in the security policy. Cisco Application-Aware Enterprise Firewall does not utilize application service containers.

Additional Templates

AppQoE	Choose...
Banner	All-Banner-dCloud
Policy	BaselinePolicy
SNMP	All-SNMP-Basic
Security Policy	Branch-DIA-Security
Container Profile *	Factory_Default_UTD_Template

Figure 10-12   *Security Policy in Template*

Monitoring of the Application-Aware Enterprise Firewall statistics can be done through the main security dashboard or, for more complete details, through the firewall section of the device dashboard. Both screens are able to show a historical view of inspected/ dropped sessions, though the dashboard view can display the actual firewall policy being hit for more granular reporting, as shown in Figure 10-13.

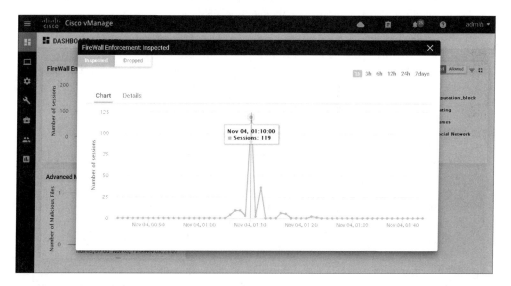

Figure 10-13   *Security Dashboard*

The firewall device dashboard is where traffic statistics can be monitored, along with viewing what policies are applied (and their associated zones). Figure 10-14 shows the Firewall Policy Monitor page in vManage.

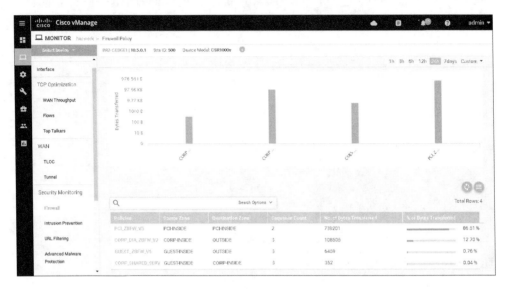

Figure 10-14 *Firewall Device Dashboard*

All ISR, ASR, and CSR platforms that support IOS-XE SD-WAN code are capable of running the Application-Aware Enterprise Firewall functionality.

Please refer to the Cisco SD-WAN Security Configuration guide published on the Cisco documentation site for additional deployment details.

Note   You can gather more detailed firewall statistics through the Real Time section of the device dashboard or via CLI **show** command sets.

Intrusion Detection and Prevention

Intrusion detection and prevention (IDS/IPS) is another important key to branch security and a component of the Cisco SD-WAN security suite. An IDS/IPS can inspect traffic in real time in order to detect and prevent cyberattacks by comparing the application behavior against a known database of threat signatures. Once detected, an IDS/IPS can notify the network operator through syslog events and dashboard alerts as well as stop the attack by blocking the threatening traffic flow. IDS/IPS is enabled through the use of IOS-XE application service container technology. Application service containers allow the network operator to leverage CPU cores and memory on an ISR to host virtual machines directly in IOS-XE and redirect application flows through the container for processing.

The two VM types used by service containers are called Kernel Virtual Machines (KVM) and Linux Virtual Containers (LxC). These two container types differ mainly in how tightly they are coupled to the Linux kernel used in most network operating systems, such as IOS XE. LxC containers use many of the kernel resources of the host, while KVM containers have their own independent kernel. This means that a KVM can be slightly more portable than an LxC container, while an LxC might have a slight performance edge over a KVM. To the end user, however, the container type is completely invisible since all of this is determined by the service container developer. Cisco SD-WAN security leverages LxC containers.

Figure 10-15 shows an example of the application service container architecture in IOS-XE.

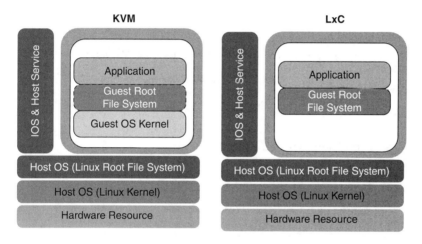

Figure 10-15   *Application Service Container Architecture*

Cisco SD-WAN IDS/IPS runs Snort, the most widely deployed intrusion prevention engine in the world, and leverages dynamic signature updates published by Cisco Talos. The Cisco Talos Intelligence Group is one of the largest commercial threat intelligence teams in the world and is composed of world-class researchers, analysts, and engineers. These teams are supported by unrivaled telemetry and sophisticated systems to create accurate, rapid, and actionable threat intelligence for Cisco customers, products, and services. With Talos, the IDS/IPS system can provide real-time traffic analysis to reliably protect the branch from thousands of threats on a daily basis. Cisco vManage connects to the Talos signature database and downloads the signatures on a configurable periodic or on-demand basis and pushes them down into the branch WAN Edge routers without user intervention. Signatures are a set of rules that an IDS and an IPS use to detect typical intrusive activity.

The two methods for signature update include automatic IPS signature update via vManage and manual IPS signature update using CLI commands available on the WAN Edge device. When a new signature package is updated, the Snort engine will restart and traffic may be interrupted or bypass inspection for a short period (depending on the data plane fail-open/fail-close configuration).

Note   Currently, Cisco does not support manual IPS signature set upload within the vManage virtual-image repository. If you encounter issues performing an automatic signature update from vManage, update the signature manually from the WAN Edge device.

Like all other security features available in Cisco SD-WAN, the first place to start is to navigate to the security section and either build a new security policy (and follow the simple workflow to build an IDS/IPS policy) or directly navigate to the IDS/IPS policy subsection under Custom Options. No matter how the IDS/IPS policy is configured, it must eventually be tied to an overall security policy (which is then attached to the branch WAN Edge router template).

Note   To support IDS/IPS functionality, an ISR must be configured with a minimum of 8GB of DRAM and 8GB of system flash.

The following is a summary of steps required to configure an IDS/IPS policy in Cisco SD-WAN:

Step 1.   **Create a new IDS/IPS policy.** Name the policy.

Step 2.   **Configure signature set.** Specify the desired signature set: Balanced, Connectivity, or Security.

Step 3.   **Configure the signature whitelist (optional).** Specify a list of signature IDs.

Step 4.   **Configure alerts log level (optional):** Specify the alerts log level, from Debug to Emergency.

Step 5.   **Configure target VPNs.** Specify the VPNs to be inspected.

These steps can be accomplished by using the IDS/IPS Policy Workflow in vManage, as shown in Figure 10-16.

Figure 10-16   *IDS/IPS Policy Workflow*

The IDS/IPS engine allows for the network operator to configure three different signature sets: Balanced, Connectivity, and Security. Each of the signature levels contains a list of security vulnerabilities categorized based on the score assigned using the Common Vulnerability Scoring System (CVSS).

Note that CVSS is a free and open industry standard for assessing the severity of security vulnerabilities.

Here are the three signature levels available within vManage IPS:

- **Balanced:** This is the default signature set, which contains rules that are from the current year and the previous two years. The Balanced signature set is designed to provide protection without a significant effect on system performance.

  This signature set is for vulnerabilities with a CVSS score of 9 or greater, and its categories include those listed in Table 10-1.

Table 10-1 *Balanced Signature Set*

Category	Definition
Blacklist	Rules for URIs, user agents, DNS hostnames, and IP addresses that have been determined to be indicators of malicious activity.
Exploit-kit	Rules that are designed to detect exploit kit activity.
Malware-CNC	Rules for known malicious command and control activity for identified botnet traffic. These include call home, downloading of dropped files, and exfiltration of data.
SQL Injection	Rules that are designed to detect SQL injection attempts.

- **Connectivity:** This signature set contains rules from the current year and the previous two years for vulnerabilities with a CVSS score of 10. The Connectivity signature set is less restrictive, with better performance, as there are fewer rules attached to this signature level.

- **Security:** This signature set contains rules that are from the current year and the previous three years. With more added rules, this signature level offers more protection, but overall performance of your WAN Edge device may be lower.

  This signature set is for vulnerabilities with a CVSS score of 8 or greater, and its categories include those listed in Table 10-2.

Table 10-2 *Security Signature Set*

Category	Definition
App-detect	Rules that look for and control the traffic of certain applications that generate network activity.

Category	Definition
Blacklist	Rules for URIs, user agents, DNS hostnames, and IP addresses that have been determined to be indicators of malicious activity.
Exploit-kit	Rules that are designed to detect exploit kit activity.
Malware-CNC	Rules for known malicious command and control activity for identified botnet traffic. These include call home, downloading of dropped files, and exfiltration of data.
SQL Injection	Rules that are designed to detect SQL injection attempts.

The network operator can also configure a signature whitelist, which provides the opportunity to define a list of signature IDs in the format of GeneratorID:Signature:ID. Any application flow that matches a signature ID defined in the list is ignored and passed through the IDS/IPS engine without action. This is useful for suppressing false indications of an attack with legitimate network traffic.

The Snort engine can operate in either Detection mode, where threats are only detected and logged, or Protection mode, where the engine detects and drops the threat while also providing a log of the event. vManage also provides a multitude of configurable IDS/IPS alert log levels to fit the security requirements of the organization.

Before an IDS/IPS policy can be configured, the network operator must upload a security virtual image to vManage under the software repository section (as discussed previously, this is the LxC container that will host Snort). The security virtual image can be downloaded from the Cisco software portal and is packaged in TAR format. In addition, the network operator's Cisco CCO username and password must be configured under the vManage Settings, IPS Signature Update section for automatic signature updates to succeed. Figure 10-17 shows the process of uploading a security virtual image to vManage.

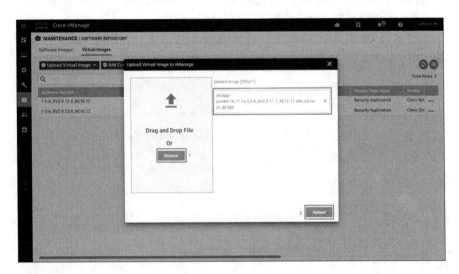

Figure 10-17 *Security Virtual Image Upload*

In addition to uploading the security virtual image, the policy will need to be configured as illustrated in Figure 10-18.

Figure 10-18 *IDS/IPS Policy Configuration*

Once the IDS/IPS policy options are configured, a target VPN or VPNs must be defined in order for the engine to know which segments on the branch WAN Edge router need application flows redirected through the Snort engine for processing.

In addition to the syslog server configuration, the policy summary section of the workflow allows for the network operator to configure the failure mode of the Snort engine. The **Fail-close** option drops all IPS/IDS traffic when there is an engine failure or engine reboot. The **Fail-open** option allows all IPS/IDS traffic when there is an engine failure or engine reboot. The default option is **Fail-open**.

Figure 10-19 provides a high-level depiction of how application flows are passed through the Snort engine in an ISR.

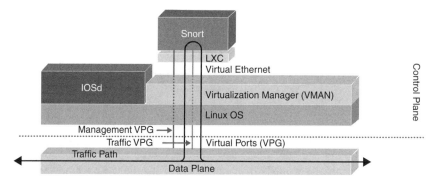

Figure 10-19 *Snort Traffic Engine*

Note If an application service-based security feature has never been enabled on a particular ISR before, a container installation task will automatically begin after the security policy is attached to the branch template. Once this installation is complete, the security policy will be enabled. This task can be monitored for successful completion by navigating to the active task pane at the top right of the Cisco vManage dashboard.

The last step to enable IDS/IPS on a branch WAN Edge router is to attach the IDS/IPS policy to a branch device template.

Note As a best practice, configure a Security App Hosting template to be referenced under the Container Profile section. The template can retain the default settings.

Monitoring of IDS/IPS statistics can be accessed through the main security dashboard shown in Figure 10-20. For more complete details, you can also monitor IDS/IPS statistics through the Intrusion Prevention section of the device dashboard. The security dashboard screen can show historical top signature hits by count or by severity and even display which remote site is contributing to these hits the most. In addition, this view can provide details around which source and destination IPs and VPNs are involved with the signature hits.

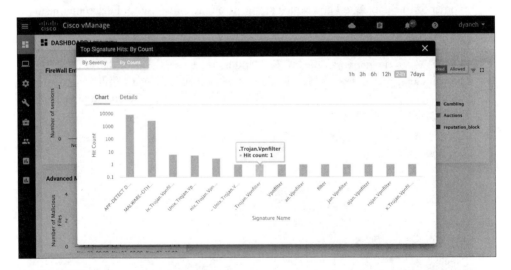

Figure 10-20 *IDS/IPS Security Dashboard View*

The Intrusion Prevention device dashboard screen also provides a view of signature hits by severity or count, but with more granularity and historical resolution, as shown in Figure 10-21. In addition, this view of the feature can provide the IPS version, when the signatures were last updated, and descriptions of the signatures being hit. From this screen, the network operator can access a hyperlink to learn more about the specific signature being hit in the environment.

Figure 10-21 *IDS/IPS Device Dashboard View*

Only ISR and CSR platforms that support IOS-XE SD-WAN code are capable of running the IDS/IPS functionality.

Please refer to the Cisco SD-WAN Security Configuration Guide published on the Cisco documentation site for additional deployment details.

Note   More detailed IPS/IDS statistics can be gathered through the Real Time section of the device dashboard or via CLI **show** command sets.

URL Filtering

URL Filtering is another Cisco SD-WAN security function that leverages the Snort engine for inspection of HTTP and HTTPS payloads, in order to provide comprehensive web security at the branch. The URL Filtering engine enforces acceptable use controls to block or allow websites. An administrator can choose to permit or deny websites based on 82 different categories, the site's web reputation score, and a dynamically updated URL database. Custom black and white lists can also be created with customized end-user notifications, in order to bypass the URL Filtering engine for websites that are internal or trusted.

When an end user requests access to a particular website through their web browser, the URL Filtering engine inspects the web traffic and first queries any custom URL lists. If the URL matches an entry in the whitelist, access is granted with no further inspection or processing. If the URL matches an entry in the blacklist, access is denied with no further inspection. When access is denied, the user can be redirected to a block page with a customizable message or can also be redirected to a custom URL (if an internal block page already exists and is desired to be leveraged). If the URL is not on either list, it is subject to inspection and will then be compared against the blocked or allowed categories policy. If allowed through the category inspection, the web reputation will then be considered and, based on the strictness of the policy, the page will either be allowed or blocked. As a final step, the URL Filtering database is consulted. This process can either utilize a cloud-hosted database or locally hosted one. If cloud based, the lookup result is cached in memory so that the next identical lookup match can happen more efficiently. Figure 10-22 illustrates the URL Filtering process and how risky domain requests are handled.

Note   To support URL Filtering functionality, an ISR must be configured with a minimum of 8GB of DRAM and 8GB of system flash if doing cloud lookup. A minimum of 16GB of DRAM and 16GB of system flash is required if doing on-box database lookup.

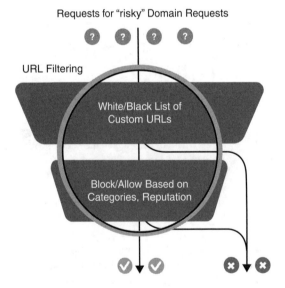

Figure 10-22   *URL Filtering Process*

Before a URL Filtering policy can be configured, the network operator must upload a security virtual image to vManage under the software repository section (as discussed in the "Intrusion Detection and Prevention" section of this chapter). The security virtual image can be downloaded from the Cisco software portal and is packaged in TAR format.

If a security virtual image was previously uploaded for another Cisco SD-WAN security functionality, no additional image is required.

Like all other security features available in Cisco SD-WAN, the first place to start is by navigating to the security section and either building a new security policy (following the simple workflow to build a URL Filtering policy) or directly navigating to the URL Filtering policy subsection under Custom Options. Figure 10-23 highlights the process. No matter how the URL Filtering policy is configured, it must eventually be tied to an overall security policy, which is then attached to the branch WAN Edge router template.

The following is a summary of steps required to configure a URL Filtering policy in Cisco SD-WAN:

Step 1.   **Create a new URL Filtering policy.** Name the policy.

Step 2.   **Configure web categories.** Specify the blocked or allowed web category list.

Step 3.   **Configure the web reputation.** Specify the web reputation for allowed websites.

Step 4.   **Configure whitelist URL list (optional).** Specify the URLs that should always be allowed.

Step 5.   **Configure blacklist URL list (optional).** Specify the URLs that should always be blocked.

Step 6.   **Configure block page (optional).** Specify the block page content.

Step 7.   **Configure the alerts and logs (optional).** Specify which alerts should be generated.

Step 8.   **Configure target VPNs.** Specify the VPNs to be inspected.

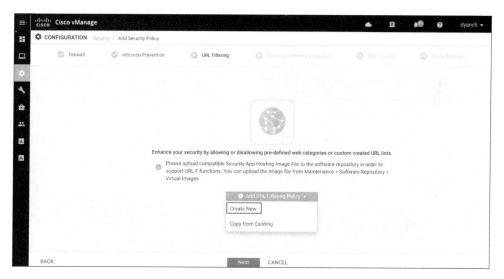

Figure 10-23   *URL Filtering Policy Workflow*

The URL Filtering engine allows for the network operator to select from a list of five reputation levels. The website's reputation will be considered if it does not match any custom lists and was allowed through the configured web categories. The URL Filtering web reputation engine will allow sites based on a numerical value (between –10 and 10) assigned to the site by Cisco Talos. Sites that either meet the configured reputation level or are of a lower risk level will be allowed. Administrators can approve websites using preconfigured reputation levels (that is, Trustworthy or High Risk). A whitelist and black-list can also be specified that can leverage regular expression entries for more flexibility. Figure 10-24 depicts the policy behavior as well as the configuration options available.

Figure 10-24   *URL Filtering Configuration*

For blocked websites, the network operator can select between a built-in block page (with customizable content) and a redirect URL. URL Filtering alerts are user definable and can provide insight into blacklist, whitelist, and reputation/category hits.

Once the URL Filtering policy options are configured, a target VPN or VPNs must be defined in order for the engine to know which segments on the branch WAN Edge router need to be inspected by the URL Filtering engine.

Lastly, the security policy containing the URL Filtering policy must be attached to a branch template for deployment.

Note   As a best practice, configure a Security App Hosting template to be referenced under the Container Profile section. The template can retain default settings. If the WAN Edge router is equipped with 16GB flash and 16GB memory, and on-box URL Filtering database is required, select "high" for the Resource Profile option in the template.

Note If an application service-based security feature has never been enabled on a particular ISR before, a container installation task will automatically begin after the security policy is attached to the branch template. Once this installation is complete, the security policy will be enabled. This task can be monitored for successful completion by navigating to the active task pane at the top right of the Cisco vManage dashboard.

Monitoring of the URL Filtering statistics can be accessed through the main security dashboard or, for more complete details, through the URL Filtering section of the device dashboard. The security dashboard screen can show the top hitting blocked and allowed URL categories by percentage as well as the amount of times the category was hit, as illustrated in Figure 10-25. In addition, this view can provide details around which WAN Edge router on the Cisco SD-WAN is contributing to the category hits.

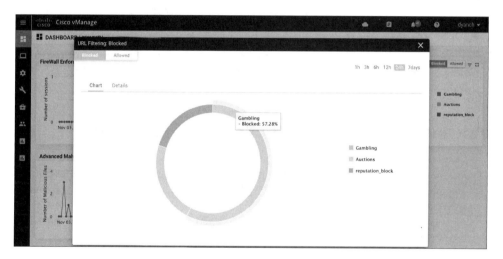

Figure 10-25 *URL Filtering Security Dashboard View*

The device dashboard URL Filtering screen, shown in Figure 10-26, presents the same data in a bar graph format with more historical resolution and includes reputation block counts.

Only ISR and CSR platforms that support IOS-XE SD-WAN code are capable of running the URL Filtering functionality.

Please refer to the Cisco SD-WAN Security Configuration Guide published on the Cisco documentation site for additional deployment details.

Figure 10-26 *URL Filtering Device Dashboard View*

Note   More detailed URL Filtering statistics can be gathered through the Real Time section of the device dashboard or via CLI **show** command sets.

Advanced Malware Protection and Threat Grid

Advanced Malware Protection (AMP) and Threat Grid are the newest additions to Cisco SD-WAN security. As with URL Filtering, both AMP and Threat Grid leverage the Snort engine and Talos for inspection of file downloads and detection of malware in real time. AMP can block malware trying to enter your network using antivirus detection engines, one-to-one signature matching, machine learning, and fuzzy fingerprinting. Figure 10-27 shows this process at a high level.

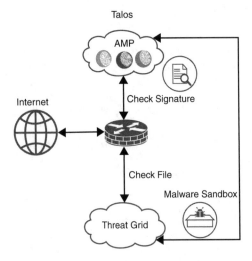

Figure 10-27 *Advanced Malware Protection Process*

Cisco Talos experts analyze millions of malware samples and terabytes of data per day and push that intelligence to AMP. AMP then correlates files, telemetry data, and file behavior against this context-rich knowledge base to proactively defend against known and engaging threats. If the AMP cloud is unable to determine if the file being inspected is good or bad, advanced sandboxing through Threat Grid can be leveraged and retrospective analysis can be performed. Threat Grid combines advanced sandboxing with threat intelligence into one unified solution to protect organizations from malware. With a robust, context-rich malware knowledge base, the network operator can understand what malware is doing (or attempting to do), how large a threat it poses, and how to defend against it.

When a file is downloaded, the Snort file preprocessor on the WAN Edge router identifies the file download, computes the SHA256 hash for the file, and looks it up in the local cache to learn if it is a known good or bad hash. If no match is found in the local database, the hash is sent to the AMP cloud for identification. The AMP cloud can then respond with one of three responses:

- **Clean:** If clean, the file download is allowed to complete.

- **Malicious:** If malicious, the file download is interrupted and stopped.

- **Unknown:** If unknown (provided that Threat Grid is enabled) and active content is found, the WAN Edge router sends the file to Threat Grid for sandboxing. The WAN Edge router queries Threat Grid for a period of time and then queries AMP for retrospection. Threat Grid then updates the new status of the hash in the AMP cloud once it is known.

> **Note** As of the publication of this book, the current SD-WAN code supports a maximum exportable file size of 10MB.

The following is a summary of steps required to configure an Advanced Malware Protection and Threat Grid policy in Cisco SD-WAN:

Step 1. **Create a new AMP policy.** Name the policy.

Step 2. **Configure AMP cloud region.** Specify the region to use for AMP cloud: North America (NAM), Europe (EU), or Asia Pacific (APJC).

Step 3. **Configure the AMP alerts log level.** Specify which alerts level should be considered.

Step 4. **Enable Threat Grid file analysis (optional).** Enable Threat Grid file analysis, if applicable.

Step 5. **Configure Threat Grid API key.** Specify the Threat Grid API key.

Step 6. **Configure file types.** Specify, from a list, the file types to be inspected.

Step 7.   **Configure the Threat Grid alerts log level.** Specify which alerts level should be considered.

Step 8.   **Configure target VPNs.** Specify the VPNs to be inspected.

> **Note**   To support AMP functionality, an ISR must be configured with a minimum of 8GB of DRAM and 8GB of system flash.

Before an AMP policy can be configured, the network operator must upload a security virtual image to vManage under the software repository section, as depicted in the "Intrusion Detection and Prevention" section of this chapter. The security virtual image can be downloaded from the Cisco software portal and is packaged in TAR format.

Like all other security features available in Cisco SD-WAN, the first place to start is by navigating to the security section and either building a new security policy (following the simple workflow to build an AMP policy) or directly navigating to the AMP policy subsection under Custom Options, as shown in Figure 10-28. No matter how the AMP policy is configured, it must eventually be tied to an overall security policy, which is then attached to the branch WAN Edge router template.

Figure 10-28   *AMP Policy Workflow*

The AMP engine allows for the network operator to configure the AMP cloud region in order to have the most optimal experience, based on the location of the branch site. Cisco supports AMP clouds in North America, Europe, and Asia. Three levels of alerts logging can also be configured: Info, Warning, and Critical. If the SD-WAN license acquired provides entitlement to Thread Grid, the API key must be configured before it can be used. Once file analysis is enabled, the Threat Grid cloud region must also be selected.

Figure 10-29 depicts the workflow in vManage. Once the AMP and Threat Grid policy options are configured, a target VPN or VPNs must be defined in order for the engine to know which segments on the branch WAN Edge router need to be inspected by the AMP engine.

Lastly, the security policy containing the AMP policy must be attached to a branch template for deployment.

> **Note**   As a best practice, configure a Security App Hosting template to be referenced under the Container Profile section. The template can retain the default settings. If the WAN Edge router is equipped with 16GB flash and 16GB memory and Threat Grid is being leveraged in the policy, select "high" for the Resource Profile option in the template.

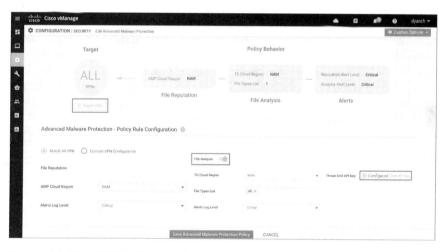

Figure 10-29   *AMP Policy Configuration*

> **Note**   If an application service-based security feature has never been enabled on a particular ISR before, a container installation task will automatically begin after the security policy is attached to the branch template. Once this installation is complete, the security policy will be enabled. This task can be monitored for successful completion by navigating to the active task pane at the top right of the Cisco vManage dashboard.

Monitoring of the AMP statistics can be accessed through the main security dashboard or, for more complete details, through the AMP section of the device dashboard. The security dashboard screen, shown in Figure 10-30, can show historical information on the number of malicious files being detected via AMP and the number of files being exported to Threat Grid for analysis. This view can also provide details around which WAN Edge router is contributing to the most AMP cloud reputation hits.

Figure 10-30 *AMP Security Dashboard View*

The AMP device dashboard provides a historical view of the number of file hashes the AMP cloud has registered as well as the AMP cloud response of those file hashes. In addition, this view details the filename, the hash value, the file type, the disposition, the timestamp, the VPN, and the action the WAN Edge router took for the file. Figure 10-31 portrays the AMP device dashboard.

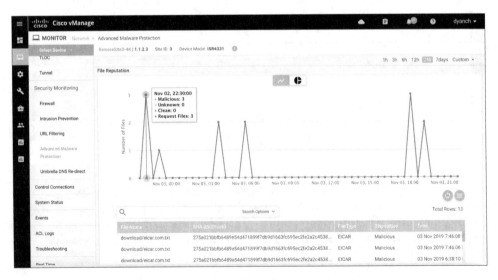

Figure 10-31 *AMP Filtering Device Dashboard View*

Only ISR and CSR platforms that support IOS-XE SD-WAN code are capable of running the Advanced Malware Protection and Threat Grid functionality.

Please refer to the Cisco SD-WAN Security Configuration Guide, published on the Cisco documentation site, for additional deployment details.

Note   More detailed AMP statistics can be gathered through the Real Time section of the device dashboard or via CLI **show** command sets.

DNS Web Layer Security

Cisco SD-WAN security leverages the Cisco Umbrella cloud in order to bring a comprehensive, VPN-aware, suite of web security tools and enhanced cloud application visibility to the branch. DNS Web Layer security integration prevents enterprise branch users and guests from accessing inappropriate content or malicious sites that might contain malware, phishing attacks, and other security risks. Once registered with Umbrella cloud, the WAN Edge router intercepts DNS requests from the LAN and redirects them to Umbrella resolvers. If the requested page is a known malicious site or is not allowed (based on the policies configured in Umbrella portal), the DNS response will contain the IP address for an Umbrella-hosted block page. The DNS response will contain the IP address of the destination website if the site is considered to have good reputation, is not malicious, and is allowed by the policy configured on the Umbrella portal. If Umbrella is not completely certain that the page being requested is safe, Intelligent Proxy can be enabled so that the Umbrella cloud acts as a man-in-the-middle. In this way, Umbrella can inspect the page data as it loads to avoid compromising the security of the end user.

DNS Web Layer security supports DNSCrypt, EDNS, and TLS decryption as well. In the same way that SSL turns HTTP web traffic into HTTPS encrypted web traffic, DNSCrypt turns regular DNS traffic into encrypted DNS traffic that is secure from eavesdropping and man-in-the-middle attacks. It does not require any changes to domain names or how they work; it simply provides a method for securely encrypting communication between the end user and the DNS servers in Umbrella cloud. Extension mechanisms for DNS (EDNS) is a specification for expanding the size of several parameters of the DNS protocol, so as to carry metadata (such as VPN ID) for additional context that can be leveraged in an Umbrella cloud policy.

In some scenarios, it may be important not to intercept DNS requests for internal resources and pass them on to an internal or alternate DNS resolver. To meet this requirement, the WAN Edge router can leverage local domain bypass functionality, where a list of internal domains is defined and referenced during the DNS request interception process. Any domain defined in the list is ignored, and no interception or redirection occurs. Figure 10-32 highlights the DNS Web Layer security process from a high level.

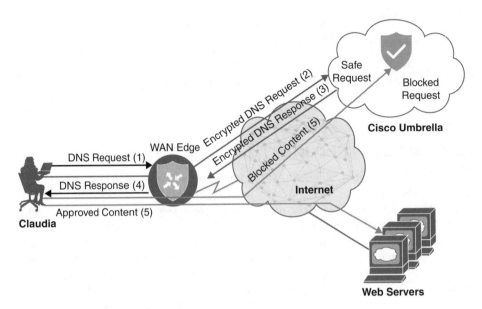

Figure 10-32 *DNS Web Layer Security Process*

The following is a summary of steps required to configure DNS Web Layer security with Cisco Umbrella:

Step 1. **Create a new DNS Security policy.** Name the policy.

Step 2. **Generate and register Umbrella API token.** In the Umbrella cloud portal, generate an API token and configure vManage with the token so as to register with Umbrella cloud.

Step 3. **Configure local domain bypass list (optional).** Define the list of local domains that should bypass inspection.

Step 4. **Configure DNS server IP.** Specify the DNS server to use for redirection: Umbrella default or a custom DNS.

Step 5. **Configure DNSCrypt.** Enable or disable DNSCrypt.

Step 6. **Configure target VPNs.** Specify the VPNs to be inspected.

Note DNS Web Layer security enforcement through Umbrella cloud requires a specific SD-WAN license tier. Cloud application visibility through Umbrella cloud portal is available in all SD-WAN license tiers.

Before a DNS security policy can be configured, the network operator must register vManage with the Umbrella cloud portal through the generation and application of an Umbrella API token. This token facilitates the automatic registration of the WAN Edge router with Umbrella cloud so that interception and redirection of DNS requests are authorized and successful. Refer to the Umbrella cloud portal documentation in order to learn how to generate an Umbrella API token. Configure the API token in vManage under the Custom Options, Umbrella API Token menu of the security policy.

Like all other security features available in Cisco SD-WAN, the first place to start is by navigating to the security section and either building a new security policy (following the simple workflow to build a DNS security policy) or directly navigating to the DNS security policy subsection, under Custom Options, as shown in Figure 10-33. No matter how the DNS security policy is configured, it must eventually be tied to an overall security policy, which is then attached to the branch WAN Edge router template.

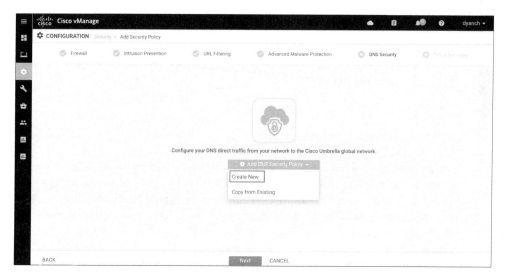

Figure 10-33   *DNS Security Policy Workflow*

The DNS security policy allows for the network operator to verify that the Umbrella registration status is configured. If the registration status is not configured, tooltips are provided to direct the network operator on how to configure vManage with the API token. A local domain bypass list can also be configured and can support "*" for wildcard matching, but an entry cannot be more than 240 characters in length. The default DNS server IP of Umbrella can be used in the policy or, alternatively, a custom DNS server IP can be set. DNSCrypt can be enabled or disabled in the DNS security policy as well. Figure 10-34 illustrates these available options and settings.

Once the DNS security policy options are configured, a target VPN or VPNs must be defined in order for the engine to know which segments on the branch WAN Edge router are candidates for DNS interception and redirection.

Lastly, the security policy containing the DNS security policy must be attached to a device template for deployment.

Figure 10-34   *DNS Security Configuration*

vManage provides only basic monitoring of DNS security interception and redirection, as shown in Figure 10-35. Detailed monitoring around policy enforcement, cloud app visibility, and other Umbrella cloud–specific information should be consumed through the Umbrella cloud portal itself. The Umbrella DNS Re-direct section of the vManage device dashboard provides a historical overview of DNS requests that were redirected to Umbrella, DNS requests that were bypassed using Local Domain Bypass, timestamps, a count of Umbrella registered VPNs, and the status of DNSCrypt.

Figure 10-35   *DNS Security Device Dashboard View*

Note As of the publication of this book, only IOS-XE SD-WAN supports DNS Web Layer security with Umbrella configuration through security policy. Viptela OS supports interception and redirection, but only through the use of a data policy, which is beyond the scope of this chapter.

All ISR, ASR, and CSR platforms that support IOS-XE SD-WAN code are capable of running the DNS Web Layer security functionality.

Please refer to the Cisco SD-WAN Security Configuration Guide published on the Cisco documentation site for additional deployment details.

Cloud Security

While this chapter focuses mainly on Cisco SD-WAN integrated security, it is important to note that other security models, such as cloud-delivered firewalls, do exist and are valid architectures to bring security to the branch in a Cisco SD-WAN environment. While integrated security provides a convenient and efficient way to consume and manage security at the branch, it can also place a compute burden on the WAN Edge router—effectively lowering its forwarding performance. However, as long as the proper WAN Edge router is selected, based on the required bandwidth for the branch, this is usually not a problem.

Cloud-delivered firewalls provide a means to offload this compute burden onto the provider's cloud environment, freeing up resources on the WAN Edge router to forward traffic unencumbered. Cloud-delivered firewalls, connected via IPsec or GRE tunnels, are terminated either directly on a WAN Edge router's DIA circuit or at a hub site where Internet traffic is backhauled to. Figure 10-36 illustrates some of the common cloud security connectivity options.

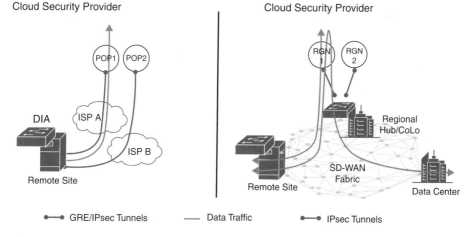

Figure 10-36 *Cloud Security Connectivity*

Because Cisco SD-WAN supports the configuration and connectivity of standards-based IPsec and GRE tunnels, virtually any cloud-delivered firewall solution can be seamlessly integrated into a WAN Edge router. Simply create a standards-based IPsec or GRE tunnel feature template, fill out the necessary parameters to establish the tunnel, and attach it to a device template. Figure 10-37 shows this configuration pane.

Note   As of the publication of this book, IOS-XE SD-WAN only supports standards-based IPsec configuration on a service-side VPN. Viptela OS supports both standards-based IPsec and GRE configurations on either the service- or transport-side VPN.

Figure 10-37   *Standards-Based IPsec Tunnel Configuration*

Historical monitoring of the IPsec or GRE tunnel's utilization, errors, drops, and so on can be found in the device dashboard under the interface section. Figure 10-38 rebreak: show-cases this monitoring as well as the received and transmitted data rates for both IPv4 and IPv6.

More detailed information about the IPsec or GRE tunnel can be gleaned through the Real Time section of the device dashboard, as shown in Figure 10-39. There are multiple device options available to choose from, such as IPsec IKE Inbound Connections and IPsec Outbound Connections.

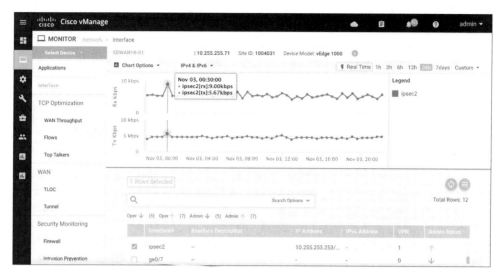

Figure 10-38   *IPsec Tunnel Monitoring*

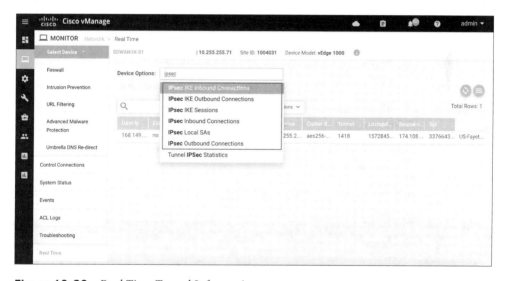

Figure 10-39   *Real-Time Tunnel Information*

Please refer to the Cisco SD-WAN configuration guides, published on the Cisco documentation site, for additional deployment details.

Note   More detailed standards-based IPsec and GRE statistics can be gathered through the Real Time section of the device dashboard or via CLI **show** command sets.

vManage Authentication and Authorization

The final component of Cisco SD-WAN security is the hardening of the SD-WAN network management system called vManage. vManage plays a critical role in the overall security of the enterprise. For this reason, it supports a multitude of authentication and authorization methods and functionalities.

Local Authentication with Role-Based Access Control (RBAC)

Users can be authenticated into vManage through a built-in local database that can be found in the Administration section. These users can then be tied to a user group, providing customized access to the solution. There are three predefined user groups: netadmin, operator, and basic. The netadmin user group provides unfettered read and write access to the entirety of vManage. The operator user group provides read-only access to vManage. The basic user group provides read-only access to the interface and system sections of vManage. Custom user groups can also be created, and a combination of read and write access to all components of vManage can be configured.

The following is a summary of steps required to configure a new local database user:

Step 1. **Add user.** Within the Administration Manage Users section, click **Add User** under the Users tab.

Step 2. **Configure full name.** Specify the user's full name.

Step 3. **Configure username.** Specify the user's desired username.

Step 4. **Configure password.** Specify and confirm the user's password, which can later be changed at first login, if necessary.

Step 5. **Select user group.** Select from one of the three predefined user groups or a custom user group.

Figure 10-40 illustrates the process for adding users and groups.

Figure 10-40 *Add Users*

The following is a summary of steps required to configure a custom user group:

Step 1.   **Add user group.** Within the Administration Manage Users section, click **Add User Group** under the User Groups tab.

Step 2.   **Configure user group name.** Specify the user group name.

Step 3.   **Select read and write access.** Select the desired read and write access levels.

When you're creating a user group, read and write options are available for various features. Figure 10-41 showcases the user group configuration pane in vManage.

Figure 10-41   *Add User Groups*

RBAC can also be made to be VPN aware. That is to say, a user can be tied to a specific user group that is assigned to an RBAC group that only provides visibility into a single VPN or a subset of VPNs.

The following is a summary of steps required to configure RBAC by VPN:

Step 1.   **Configure VPN segments.** Within the Administration VPN Segments section, enter a segment name and VPN number. Figure 10-42 illustrates the process to add a VPN number to a VPN segment. This is a way for vManage to tie a VPN number to a name so that it can be referenced later on in a VPN group.

Step 2.   **Configure a VPN group.** Within the Administration VPN Group section, enter a VPN group name and description, create the RBAC user group, and assign a segment or multiple segments to the VPN group.

A VPN group is a way for vManage to tie a single or multiple segments to a group that can then be attached to a custom RBAC user group. This RBAC user group will appear in the user group section of vManage and can then be tied to the user itself. Figure 10-43 illustrates the process to create a VPN group.

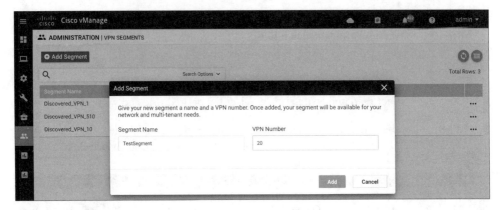

Figure 10-42 *Add VPN Segment*

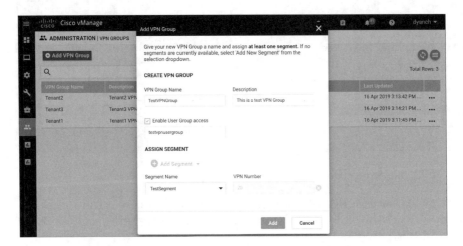

Figure 10-43 *Add VPN Group*

Step 3.   **Assign the user to the user group.** Select the newly created RBAC user group.

Configure the user to be in the newly created RBAC user group so that, when the user logs in, only the visibility information from the VPNs assigned to the VPN group is consumable. Figure 10-44 shows how to assign a user to a user group.

When a user who is assigned to a user group that is attached to a VPN group logs in, only relevant information to the VPNs allocated in the VPN group will be visible. This includes Device Health, Site Health, WAN Edge Health, and Top Applications. This can be seen in Figure 10-45, as it showcases what can be seen in the **TestVPNGroup.**

Figure 10-44   *Assign RBAC User Group*

Figure 10-45   *RBAC by VPN Visibility*

Remote Authentication with Role-Based Access Control (RBAC)

vManage also supports remote authentication with role-based access control through the use of a RADIUS/TACACS or Single Sign-On (SSO) authentication server. Figure 10-46 depicts the RADIUS and TACACS configuration pane within vManage. To authenticate via RADIUS/TACACS, simply configure a AAA vManage feature template or manually configure the RADIUS/TACACS server information via vManage CLI. User groups can still be leveraged with remote authentication as long as the authentication server can pass the group name as a parameter to vManage.

Figure 10-46 *RADIUS/TACACS Configuration*

To authenticate via SSO, upload a SAML 2.0–compliant metadata file to vManage by navigating to Identity Provider Settings under the vManage settings section. Figure 10-47 highlights how to enable the Identity Provider.

Figure 10-47 *SSO Configuration*

Please refer to Cisco SD-WAN configuration guides, published on the Cisco documentation site, for additional deployment details.

Summary

This chapter covered all aspects of Cisco SD-WAN security, including integrated functionality, such as Application-Aware Enterprise Firewall, IDS/IPS, URL Filtering, AMP, DNS Web layer security, cloud-delivered firewall connectivity, and vManage authentication and authorization. Cisco's goal with SD-WAN security is to ensure that no matter what your requirements may be at the branch, a viable option exists to ensure that the appropriate security posture can be attained, managed efficiently, and accessed securely.

Review All Key Topics

Review the most important topics in the chapter, noted with the Key Topic icon in the outer margin of the page. Table 10-3 lists these key topics and the page numbers on which each is found.

Table 10-3   *Key Topics*

Key Topic Element	Description	Page
Section	Application-Aware Enterprise Firewall	352
Figure 10-11	Security Policy Application	358
Section	Intrusion Detection and Prevention	360
Section	URL Filtering	367
Section	Advanced Malware Protection and Threat Grid	372
Section	DNS Web Layer Security	377

Define Key Terms

Define the following key terms from this chapter and check your answers in the glossary:

Direct Internet Access (DIA), zone, IDS/IPS, RBAC

Chapter Review Questions

1. Cisco SD-WAN Application-Aware Enterprise Firewall is not VPN aware.
   a. True
   b. False

2. What are the three actions that can be set in a firewall policy?

   a. Pass

   b. Inspect

   c. Redirect

   d. Export

   e. Drop

3. Logging is not available for Application-Aware Enterprise Firewall policies.

   a. True

   b. False

4. What signature sets are available for selection in an IDS/IPS policy? (Choose three.)

   a. Strict

   b. Balanced

   c. Relaxed

   d. Connectivity

   e. Security

5. Which two Snort engine modes are supported during an engine failure or engine reboot?

   a. Fail-block

   b. Fail-close

   c. Fail-pass

   d. Fail-wide

   e. Fail-open

6. Before an IDS/IPS policy can be configured, the network operator must upload a security virtual image to vManage under the software repository section.

   a. True

   b. False

7. URL Filtering requires a minimum of 4GB DRAM and 4GB flash to be deployed.

   a. True

   b. False

8. What URL Filtering feature can be leveraged to explicitly block certain websites?

   a. Categories

   b. Reputation

   c. URL blacklist

   d. URL whitelist

9. URL Filtering visibility includes which of the following information? (Choose two.)

   a. URLs accessed

   b. Session count

   c. Website reputation

   d. Blocked and allowed categories by percentage

10. The maximum exportable file size for file analysis is 1000 MB.

    a. True

    b. False

11. To configure file analysis for Advanced Malware Protection, which tasks are valid? (Choose three.)

    a. Configure Threat Grid API key.

    b. Configure file types list.

    c. Enable file analysis.

    d. Enable HTTPS inbound to the WAN Edge router.

    e. Configure a security rule for Threat Grid.

12. AMP visibility has the ability to display the malware filename.

    a. True

    b. False

13. How is the Cisco Umbrella API token generated?

    a. Automatically during vManage bootup

    b. Manually in vManage Umbrella settings

    c. By the Cisco SE and provided to the customer by email

    d. In the Cisco Umbrella portal

14. If a customer wants the DNS Web layer security redirection process to ignore a specific set of domains, what feature can be leveraged?

    a. Corporate domain bypass

    b. Domain filtering

    c. Local domain bypass

    d. Domain rules

15. Which two privilege types can be assigned to a user group in vManage?

    a. Read

    b. Erase

    c. Reboot

    d. Administer

    e. Write

16. RBAC by VPN allows some users to configure some VPN features but not others.

    a. True

    b. False

17. Which three remote authentication types are supported by vManage?

    a. Single Sign-On (SSO)

    b. RADIUS

    c. Local

    d. TACACS

Chapter 11

Cisco SD-WAN Cloud onRamp

This chapter covers the following topics:

- **Cisco SD-WAN Cloud onRamp:** This section covers what Cisco SD-WAN Cloud onRamp is and why it is relevant to your organization.

- **Cloud onRamp for SaaS:** This section of the chapter covers the concepts and configuration of Cloud onRamp for SaaS.

- **Cloud onRamp for IaaS:** This section of the chapter covers the concepts and configuration of Cloud onRamp for IaaS.

- **Cloud onRamp for Colocation:** This section of the chapter covers the concepts and configuration of Cloud onRamp for colocation.

Cisco SD-WAN Cloud onRamp

In recent years, not only has the industry seen applications migrating to the cloud on a massive scale, but "born in the cloud" is becoming the de facto standard for application development and delivery. At the same time, the rapid adoption of business-critical cloud services by nearly all organizations across every vertical is fueling all things cloud and unveiling new challenges for network architects. These challenges include the following:

- **Providing reliable, flexible, and secure cloud connectivity models:** There are a multitude of ways to reach public or private cloud workloads and applications these days. Network architects are now tasked to provide reliable and secure connectivity from the branch, hub, or data center to these workloads and applications.

- **Ensuring optimal cloud application performance and visibility:** Since most networks have multiple egress points to the Internet, it is important to ensure the best path is utilized on a per-application basis and that performance of the path is collected and available for reporting.

■ **Designing scalable, multi-cloud architectures:** Organizations are starting to realize the benefits of a multi-cloud environment when it comes to private and public cloud workload placement. Ensuring that these architectures are scalable, easy to spin up and spin down, and stay cost-effective is key.

Cisco SD-WAN Cloud onRamp provides simple, yet highly effective workflows in vManage to optimize connectivity to Software as a Service (SaaS) applications by choosing the best-performing path in the network. Path selection is based on performance measurements obtained from all available paths. In the case where a specific path experiences degradation, the traffic is dynamically moved to a more optimal path. Cloud onRamp also automates scalable, multi-cloud connectivity to Infrastructure as a Service (IaaS) workloads by instantiating virtual SD-WAN Edge routers in a transit model and then connecting the transit network to both the SD-WAN overlay and the backend workloads. Finally, Cloud onRamp for colocation enables secure, efficient, and highly flexible service-chaining architectures to reach applications hosted in colocation facilities. Figure 11-1 shows the different types of cloud onRamp offered by Cisco SD-WAN.

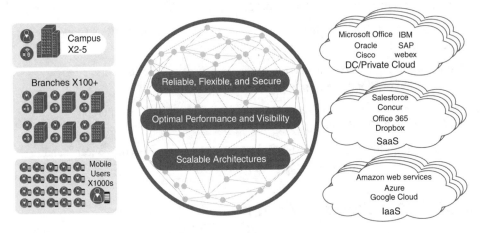

Figure 11-1 *Cisco Cloud onRamp Options*

Cloud onRamp for SaaS

As more applications move to the cloud, the traditional approach of backhauling traffic over expensive or low-performance WAN transports to the data center or hub for centralized Internet egress is quickly proving not to be the most optimal method for cloud application consumption. Current WAN infrastructures were never designed with cloud applications in mind: They can introduce latency and degrade the end-user experience, while the aggregation of traffic at a data center or hub often poses bottlenecks and capacity ceilings.

Network architects are tasked with reevaluating the design of their WANs to support a cloud transition, reduce network costs, and increase the visibility and manageability of their cloud traffic while ensuring an excellent user experience. Network architects are turning to inexpensive broadband Internet services to find ways to intelligently route trusted SaaS cloud-bound traffic directly from remote branches.

With Cloud onRamp for SaaS, the SD-WAN fabric continuously measures the performance of a designated SaaS application, such as Microsoft Office 365, through all available paths from a branch, including designated backhaul paths. For each path, the fabric computes a quality-of-experience score ranging from 0 to 10, with 10 being the best performance. This score gives network administrators visibility into application performance that has never before been available. Most importantly, the fabric automatically makes real-time decisions to choose the best-performing path between the end users at a remote branch and the cloud SaaS application. Enterprises have the flexibility to deploy this capability in several ways, according to their business needs and security requirements.

The benefits of Cloud onRamp for SaaS include the following:

- Improved branch-office user experience for SaaS applications by using the best-performing network path

- Increased SaaS application resiliency with multiple network path selections and active monitoring

- Visibility into SaaS application performance by using probes that measure real-time data

- Operational simplicity and consistency through centralized control and management of SaaS application policies

Figure 11-2 shows an overview of the Cloud onRamp for SaaS components.

One common use case is direct cloud access from a remote site. Direct cloud access allows a remote site to access SaaS applications directly from the Internet. Cloud onRamp for SaaS permits only the designated application traffic to use the directly connected Internet transport securely, while all other Internet-bound traffic takes the usual path, which could be through a regional hub, a data center, or a carrier-neutral facility. This feature allows the remote site to bypass the latency of tunneling Internet-bound traffic to a central site, subsequently improving the connectivity to the prioritized SaaS application. This feature is commonly referred to as Direct Internet Access (DIA). The Cisco SD-WAN Edge router chooses the most optimal Internet path for access to these SaaS applications. Different applications could traverse different paths because the path selection is calculated on a per-application basis.

If any SaaS application path becomes unreachable or its performance score falls below an unacceptable level, the path is removed as a candidate path option. If all paths cannot be path candidates because of reachability or performance, then traffic to the SaaS application follows the normal, routed path.

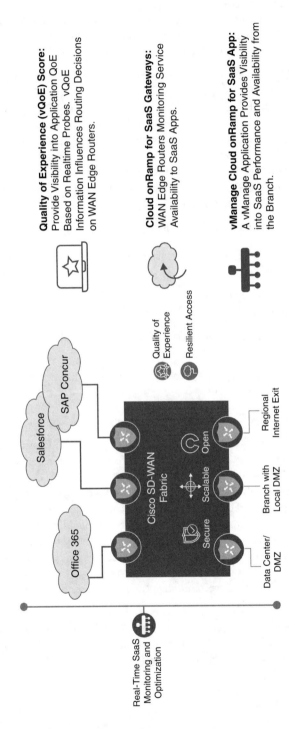

Figure 11-2 *Cloud onRamp for SaaS*

Quality of Experience (vQoE) Score: Provide Visibility into Application QoE Based on Realtime Probes. vQoE Information Influences Routing Decisions on WAN Edge Routers.

Cloud onRamp for SaaS Gateways: WAN Edge Routers Monitoring Service Availability to SaaS Apps.

vManage Cloud onRamp for SaaS App: A vManage Application Provides Visibility into SaaS Performance and Availability from the Branch.

Figure 11-3 illustrates a remote site using DIA to access SaaS applications.

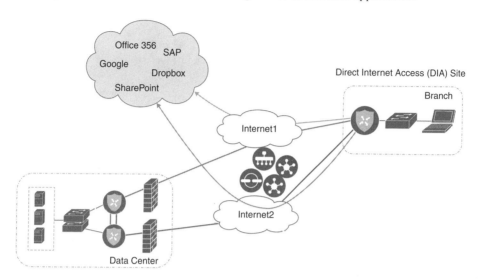

Figure 11-3   *Direct Cloud Access/Direct Internet Access*

Another common use case is cloud access through a gateway. Many enterprises do not use DIA at the branch office because either their sites are connected by only private transports or centralized policy or security requirements don't permit it. They may use data centers, regional hubs, or even carrier-neutral facilities to enable Internet connectivity. In this case, SaaS traffic is tunneled to the best-performing gateway site, where it is subsequently routed to the Internet to reach the requested SaaS application service. Note that different remote sites and different applications may use different gateway sites and paths, depending on the application and measured application performance. Remote sites that use gateway sites for Internet access are referred to as client sites.

Figure 11-4 illustrates cloud access through a gateway.

Finally, a third deployment model, the hybrid approach, makes it possible to have a combination of DIA sites and client/gateway sites. When you define both DIA sites and gateway sites, SaaS applications can use either the DIA exits of the remote site or the gateway sites for any given application, depending on which path provides the best performance. DIA sites are technically a special case of a client site, but the Internet exits are local instead of remote.

Note   At the time of this writing, the following SaaS applications are supported: Intuit, Concur, Oracle, Amazon AWS, Salesforce, Zendesk, Dropbox, Sugar CRM, Office 365, Zoho CRM, Google Apps, Box, and GoTo Meeting.

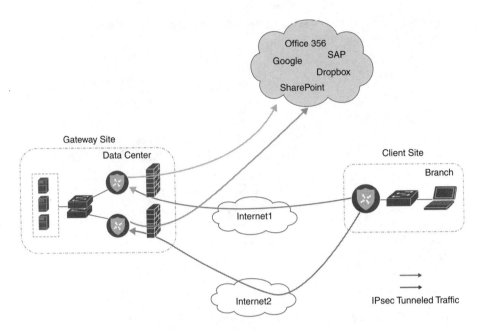

Figure 11-4 *Cloud Access Through a Gateway*

The Cloud onRamp for SaaS feature actively monitors SaaS application performance from each site over multiple paths. The WAN Edge router views performance statistics differently, depending on whether it is part of a DIA, gateway, or client site. A DIA or gateway site calculates performance statistics of the SaaS application directly, but a client site does not. SaaS performance from a client site depends on the SaaS application performance from a gateway site, plus the performance of the path from the client site to that gateway site.

In the case of a DIA or gateway site, the WAN Edge router issues numerous HTTP requests to each SaaS application over every available path to the application. Over a 2-minute sliding window, it calculates the average loss and latency for each application and path pair.

Using this data, the WAN Edge router calculates a quality of experience (vQoE) score. To get this score, the WAN Edge router accounts for average loss and latency. vManage then collects this data and keeps a record of expected average loss and latency values for all of the SaaS applications. If the actual measured loss and latency are less than the expected loss and latency, then a vQoE score of 10 is given. If actual loss and latency are more than the expected loss and latency, then a vQoE score that reflects a percentage of the baseline performance on a 10-point scale is assigned.

vManage assigns a color and vQoE status to each application and path. A vQoE score of 8 to 10 is green or good, a score of 5 to 8 is yellow or average, and a score of 0 to 5 is red or bad. For any application, the WAN Edge router takes a moving average over several 2-minute time periods and then picks the path with the higher vQoE score.

Figure 11-5 and Figure 11-6 detail how vQoE is calculated.

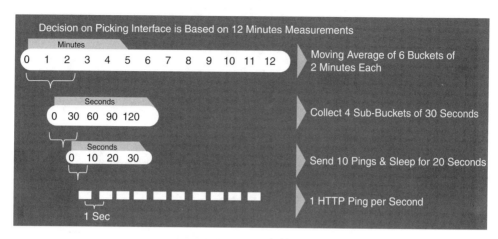

Figure 11-5 *vQoE Measurements*

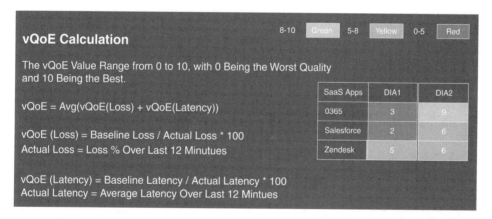

Figure 11-6 *vQoE Score Calculation*

As covered in the previous section, the gateway site issues HTTP requests directly to the SaaS application and calculates loss and latency of the application, along each of its Internet exit paths. It relays this information back to the client sites via the Overlay Management Protocol (OMP), which runs between the WAN Edge routers and establishes and maintains the control plane in the overlay network. The client site uses Bidirectional Forward Detection (BFD), which runs between WAN Edge routers over the IPsec tunnels to detect loss, latency, and jitter on the path to the gateway site. Figure 11-7 illustrates this process.

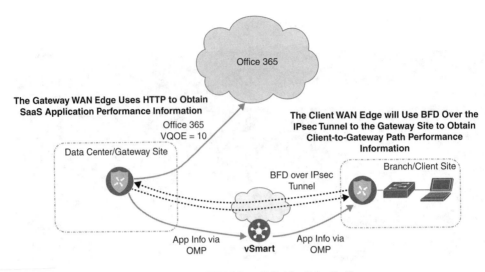

Figure 11-7   *Obtaining Performance Metrics for Client/Gateway Sites*

DIA sites execute the same probing process for their locally connected Internet circuits in addition to leveraging probe information to and from gateway sites. Figure 11-8 illustrates this process.

Cisco SD-WAN Deep Packet Inspection (DPI) identifies SaaS applications. When a flow starts for the first time, the traffic takes the path indicated by the routing table. After a couple of packets, DPI identifies the application and stores its identity in a cache so that any subsequent flows going to that destination are sent out the optimal exit determined by the vQoE score, instead of the normal routed path. DPI does not redirect the initial application flow because the redirection would cause network address translation (NAT) changes that would break TCP. Figure 11-9 shows how Cloud onRamp for SaaS handles the application flow.

> **Note**   For dual WAN Edge sites: Because DPI is used to classify flows on a WAN Edge device, it is important for traffic to be symmetric; that is, DPI should be able to see both request and response traffic. If traffic from a branch office takes a routed path to the Internet out of one WAN Edge routers but the return traffic comes back through a different WAN Edge router, DPI may not be able to classify the traffic correctly so that a local exit or gateway can be chosen for it. It will continue to be routed normally. Care should be taken with routing metrics to ensure symmetry for normally routed traffic.

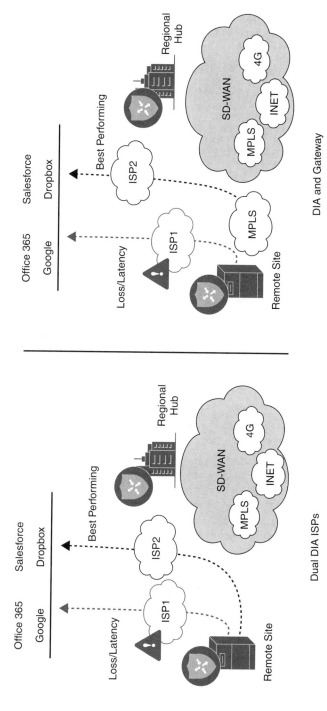

Figure 11-8 *Obtaining Performance Metrics for DIA sites*

In order to reach the SaaS applications to calculate performance statistics in the case of gateway and DIA sites, the WAN Edge router needs to first resolve the names of the Cloud onRamp SaaS applications into IP addresses. It performs this task by using the Domain Name System (DNS) server addresses defined in VPN 0. The router initiates a separate DNS query to the same application on each of its local Internet exits. When a host at a site issues a DNS query, the DPI engine intercepts it. If the local DIA Internet exit is the best path and if the query is for a Cloud onRamp SaaS application, the WAN Edge router acts as a proxy and overrides the user DNS settings by forwarding the query to the DNS server defined under VPN 0 over the best-performing DIA Internet exit. If the best path is through a gateway WAN Edge router, then the DNS query is forwarded to the gateway, which intercepts it and forwards it to the DNS server under VPN 0 over its best-performing Internet exit. The DPI engine forwards any DNS queries for non-Cloud onRamp applications normally according to the routing table.

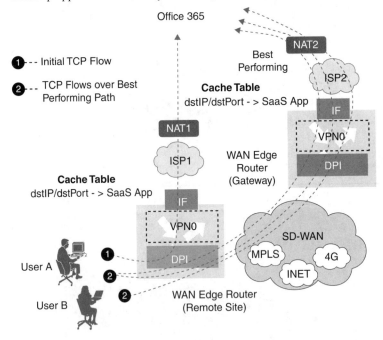

Figure 11-9 *Cloud onRamp for SaaS and NAT*

Figure 11-10 illustrates this point.

Because of the built-in workflows integrated into vManage, configuring Cloud onRamp for SaaS is very simple. However, before configuration can begin, several prerequisites must first be met. The lists that follow describe these prerequisites.

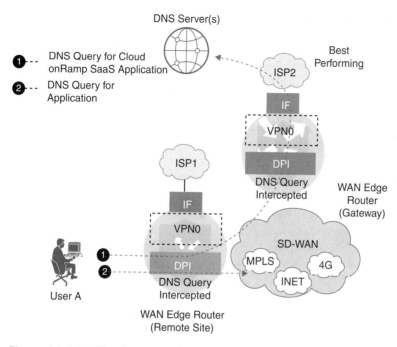

Figure 11-10 *Cloud onRamp for SaaS DNS Interception*

Note The information presented in this section of the book has been adapted from the Cloud onRamp for SaaS Validated Design Guide. For detailed step-by-step instructions and more technical tips, refer to the Validated Design Guide found on Cisco.com.

Prerequisites for all site types (DIA, client, or gateway):

■ WAN Edge routers need to be in vManage mode as opposed to CLI mode. Simply attach a template to the WAN Edge router and it will be in vManage mode.

■ The minimum Viptela OS WAN Edge router software version is 16.3.0 to configure DIA sites and 17.1.0 to configure gateway sites, but you should use the latest recommended maintenance release. The minimum IOS-XE WAN Edge router software version is 17.2.1, but you should use the latest recommended maintenance release.

■ A default route that directs traffic out to the Internet (perhaps through a data center, regional hub, carrier-neutral facility, or even locally) and can reach the SaaS applications must be present in the service VPNs before you configure the Cloud onRamp for SaaS feature. The first couple of packets need to take the traditional routing path before the Cisco SD-WAN DPI engine can identify the application and cache it so that subsequent flows can be directed to the Internet by a DIA path or a gateway site path, whichever is more optimal at that time. The initial flow continues to take the routed path until completion.

Prerequisites for DIA or gateway sites only:

- Network address translation (NAT) configuration: In order for SaaS traffic to be able to exit the site locally (for both DIA and gateway sites), NAT configuration is required under each VPN 0 physical interface attached to the Internet or Internet path. This requirement is necessary for the interface to be a candidate for local exit, regardless of any other NAT configured for the site. Enabling NAT, by default, causes translation of the source IP address of a site user to the outside IP address of the WAN Edge router when it uses the interface as a local exit to the SaaS applications.

- Default route for local exit: You must have at least one default route defined under VPN 0 to allow the tunnel to connect to the remote sites and data centers through one or more of the physical interfaces. You can either statically define the configuration of this default route or obtain it via Dynamic Host Configuration Protocol (DHCP). For DIA and gateway sites, this default route gives the next-hop information for the direct Internet exits when the Cloud onRamp for SaaS feature is configured.

- DNS server defined in VPN 0.

The following is a summary of steps required to configure Cloud onRamp for SaaS in Cisco vManage:

Step 1.   **Enable Cloud onRamp for SaaS globally.** In the vManage Settings page, enable Cloud onRamp for SaaS.

Step 2.   **Define the SaaS applications.** Define a list of SaaS applications to be monitored.

Step 3.   **Configure DIA sites (optional).** Select the sites that will be configured as DIA sites.

Step 4.   **Configure gateway sites (optional).** Select the sites that will be configured as gateway sites.

Step 5.   **Configure client sites (optional).** Select the sites that will be configured as client sites.

First, start by enabling Cloud onRamp for SaaS globally by navigating to the Settings section of vManage, as shown in Figure 11-11.

Enable Cloud onRamp for SaaS and save the changes, as shown in Figure 11-12.

To define the SaaS applications, first select the cloud icon at the top of the vManage GUI window and then select **Cloud onRamp for SaaS**, as shown in Figure 11-13. Alternatively, you can go to **Configuration > Cloud onRamp for SaaS** from the menu on the left side of the GUI.

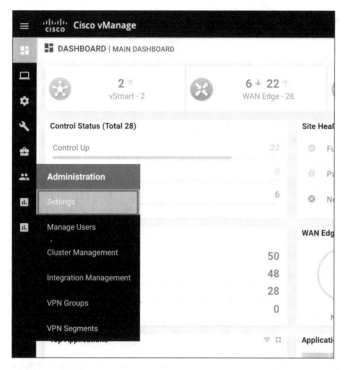

Figure 11-11 *vManage Settings Page*

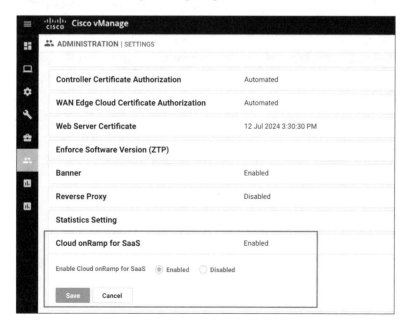

Figure 11-12 *Enabling Cloud onRamp for SaaS Globally*

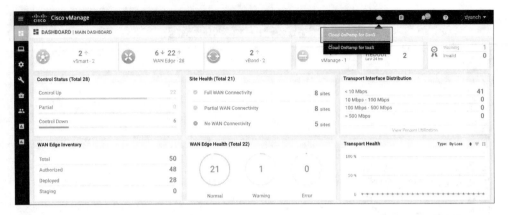

Figure 11-13   *Accessing Cloud onRamp for SaaS*

A screen pops up that welcomes you to Cloud onRamp for SaaS, states that Cloud onRamp for SaaS has been enabled, and instructs you to add applications and VPNs, client sites, gateways, and DIA sites; it invites you to start using Cloud onRamp for SaaS through the dashboard. Click the **Manage Cloud onRamp for SaaS** drop-down menu and select **Applications** to enable the desired SaaS applications, as shown in Figure 11-14.

Figure 11-14   *Defining Applications*

If the goal is to configure Direct Internet Access (DIA) sites, navigate to the DIA sites section under the Manage Cloud onRamp for SaaS screen, as shown in Figure 11-15.

Attach the sites that are deemed to be DIA sites so that vManage and vSmart can push the appropriate configuration and policy to the devices, as shown in Figure 11-16.

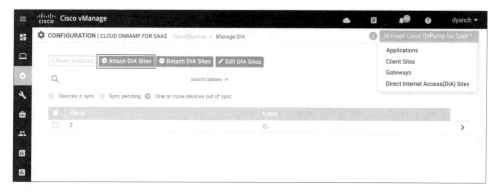

Figure 11-15 *DIA Site Configuration*

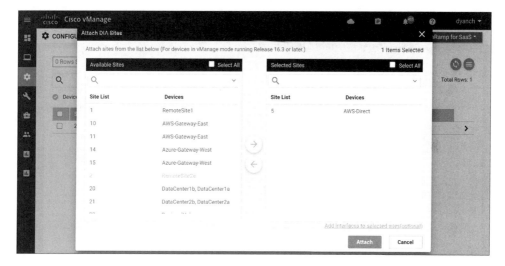

Figure 11-16 *Attaching DIA Sites*

Optionally, to configure specific interfaces for DIA, select **Add Interfaces** to selected sites at the bottom of the pop-up screen. Select the WAN Edge router interfaces in the textbox drop-down menu that you will use as direct exits for the SaaS applications, as shown in Figure 11-17. Select **Save Changes**.

Using the Task View section of vManage, verify that all configurations and policies have been pushed out successfully, as shown in Figure 11-18. This process can take 30 seconds or longer.

Figure 11-17 *Adding Optional DIA Interfaces*

Figure 11-18 *Cloud onRamp for SaaS Configuration Push*

If you're configuring gateway sites, follow the preceding instructions after navigating to the **Gateways** section and clicking **Attach Gateways,** as shown in Figure 11-19.

Figure 11-19 *Gateway Site Configuration*

If you're configuring client sites, follow the preceding instructions after navigating to the **Client Sites** section and clicking **Attach Sites**, as shown in Figure 11-20. Selecting interfaces will not be available when configuring a client site since client sites do not break out locally.

Figure 11-20   *Client Site Configuration*

vManage provides built-in monitoring for Cloud onRamp for SaaS. When you monitor Cloud onRamp for SaaS, you can view vQoE performance scores, view the network path selected for each application and site, and view the detailed loss and latency data for each application and path as well.

The main Cloud onRamp for SaaS page displays each configured SaaS application as a widget. Each widget lists the number of active sites, WAN Edge devices that use that application, and the number of WAN Edge devices that show vQoE scores in the good, average, and bad ranges, as shown in Figure 11-21. Note that these vQoE scores are shown only for the best-performing path according to each WAN Edge device.

Figure 11-21   *Cloud onRamp for SaaS Monitoring*

From this page, select an application widget to get additional details about the vQoE scores and optimal paths selected. The resulting page will show the list of sites, the WAN

Edge name, the vQoE status (a symbol indicating good, average, or bad), the vQoE number score, and the optimal path in use (local exit or gateway, selected local interface or system IP of the gateway, and an indication of the IPsec tunnel transports used to reach the remote gateway), as shown in Figure 11-22.

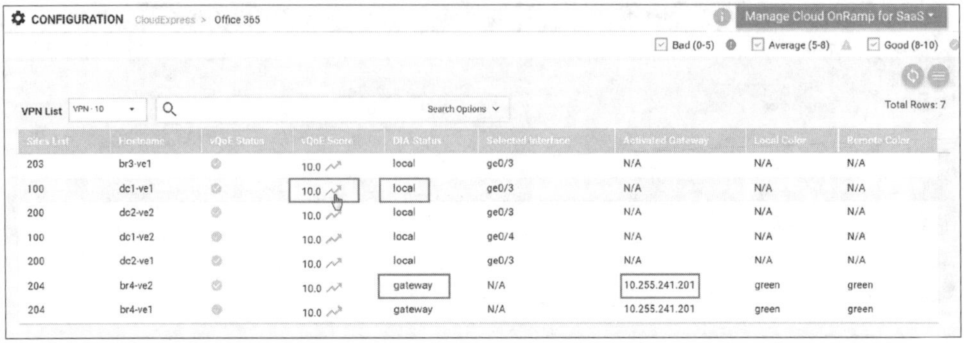

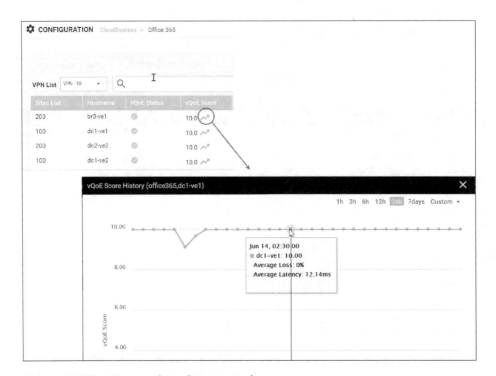

Figure 11-22 *Application-Specific Performance by Site*

If you select an arrow under the vQoE score column, a window will pop up to show the vQoE score history on a graph. You can see a 1-, 3-, 6-, 12-, or 24-hour view, a 7-day view, or a custom view of this data, as shown in Figure 11-23.

Figure 11-23 *Historical Application Performance*

You can make vManage display detailed loss and latency data on a per-SaaS-application basis by navigating to the device dashboard and selecting the Real Time option. The CloudExpress Applications output shows each application, the optimal path that has been chosen, and the mean latency and loss associated with the application for each optimal path, as shown in Figure 11-24.

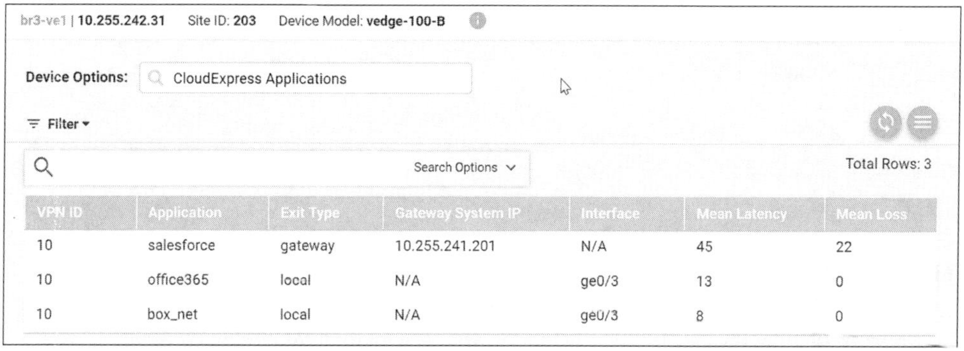

br3-ve1 | **10.255.242.31**   Site ID: **203**   Device Model: **vedge-100-B**

Device Options: CloudExpress Applications

Filter ▾

Search Options ∨   Total Rows: 3

VPN ID	Application	Exit Type	Gateway System IP	Interface	Mean Latency	Mean Loss
10	salesforce	gateway	10.255.241.201	N/A	45	22
10	office365	local	N/A	ge0/3	13	0
10	box_net	local	N/A	ge0/3	8	0

Figure 11-24   *Real-Time CloudExpress Applications*

The CloudExpress Gateway Exits output shows each application, what the gateway exits are, and the mean latency and loss associated with the application for each gateway path available, as shown in Figure 11-25. It also indicates the tunnel transport that is taken to reach the gateway site (Local Color/Remote Color columns).

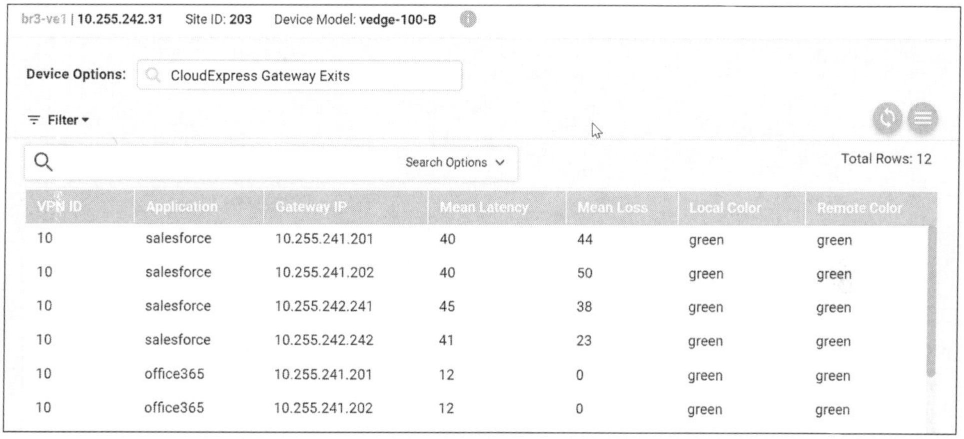

br3-ve1 | **10.255.242.31**   Site ID: **203**   Device Model: **vedge-100-B**

Device Options: CloudExpress Gateway Exits

Filter ▾

Search Options ∨   Total Rows: 12

VPN ID	Application	Gateway IP	Mean Latency	Mean Loss	Local Color	Remote Color
10	salesforce	10.255.241.201	40	44	green	green
10	salesforce	10.255.241.202	40	50	green	green
10	salesforce	10.255.242.241	45	38	green	green
10	salesforce	10.255.242.242	41	23	green	green
10	office365	10.255.241.201	12	0	green	green
10	office365	10.255.241.202	12	0	green	green

Figure 11-25   *Real-Time CloudExpress Gateway Exits*

The **CloudExpress Local Exits** output shows each application and the mean latency and loss associated with each of its local Internet exits, as shown in Figure 11-26.

VPN ID	Application	Interface	Mean Latency	Mean Loss	Last Updated
10	salesforce	ge0/3	45	56	14 Jun 2018 1:30:48 P
10	salesforce	ge0/4	45	44	14 Jun 2018 1:30:48 P
10	office365	ge0/3	13	0	14 Jun 2018 1:30:48 P
10	office365	ge0/4	13	0	14 Jun 2018 1:30:48 P
10	box_net	ge0/3	10	0	14 Jun 2018 1:30:48 P
10	box_net	ge0/4	8	0	14 Jun 2018 1:30:48 P

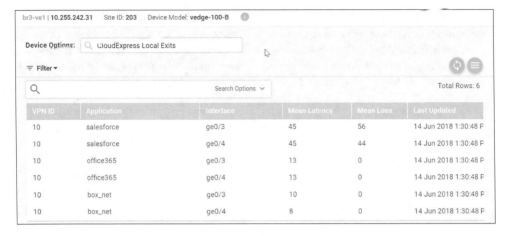

Figure 11-26 *Real-Time CloudExpress Local Exits*

Finally, the OMP CloudExpress Routes output shows the OMP routes received from the various gateways and the mean latency and loss associated with the applications and paths originating from them, as shown in Figure 11-27.

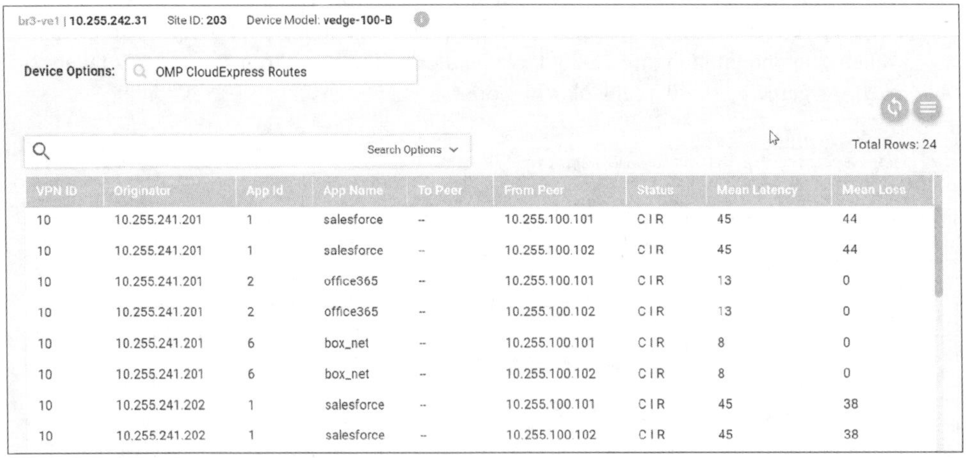

VPN ID	Originator	App Id	App Name	To Peer	From Peer	Status	Mean Latency	Mean Loss
10	10.255.241.201	1	salesforce	--	10.255.100.101	C I R	45	44
10	10.255.241.201	1	salesforce	--	10.255.100.102	C I R	45	44
10	10.255.241.201	2	office365	--	10.255.100.101	C I R	13	0
10	10.255.241.201	2	office365	--	10.255.100.102	C I R	13	0
10	10.255.241.201	6	box_net	--	10.255.100.101	C I R	8	0
10	10.255.241.201	6	box_net	--	10.255.100.102	C I R	8	0
10	10.255.241.202	1	salesforce	--	10.255.100.101	C I R	45	38
10	10.255.241.202	1	salesforce	--	10.255.100.102	C I R	45	38

Figure 11-27 *Real-Time CloudExpress Routes*

Cloud onRamp for IaaS

In a multi-cloud world, organizations are quickly realizing the benefits of cloud computing services by leveraging Infrastructure as a Service (IaaS). IaaS providers, such as Amazon Web Services (AWS) and Microsoft Azure, allow organizations to more rapidly and cost-effectively develop and deliver new applications. Instead of procuring, installing, and managing hardware, which could take months to accomplish, you can easily use the on-demand and scalable compute services in an IaaS environment. This allows you to focus your resources on applications rather than on managing the data center and physical infrastructure. With the use of IaaS, expenses shift from fixed costs for hardware, software, and data center infrastructure to variable costs based on the usage of compute resources and the amount of data transferred between the private data center, campus, branch locations, and the IaaS cloud provider. Because of this new consumption model, you must be able to monitor the usage of such resources for cost tracking and/or internal billing purposes.

A virtual private cloud (VPC) is an on-demand virtual network, logically isolated from other virtual networks within a public cloud. Most public IaaS cloud providers, such as AWS, allow traffic to flow between different virtual private clouds within a single region and recently between regions through VPC peering connections. However, AWS does not allow traffic to transit through a VPC, meaning traffic must either originate or terminate within a VPC, not simply pass through it. This means that as the number of VPCs increases, the amount of peering between the VPCs increases dramatically, if full-mesh connectivity between VPCs is a requirement.

Cloud onRamp for IaaS extends the fabric of the Cisco SD-WAN overlay network into public cloud instances, allowing branches with WAN Edge routers to connect directly to public cloud application providers. By eliminating the need for a physical data center, Cloud onRamp for IaaS improves the performance of applications hosted in the cloud.

Note At the time of this writing, both Amazon Web Services (AWS) and Microsoft Azure IaaS environments are supported by Cloud onRamp for IaaS. Other IaaS providers will be supported in later releases. This section of the chapter will focus on demonstrating how Cloud onRamp for IaaS is deployed for an AWS environment only, but the process is virtually the same for Microsoft Azure.

Cloud onRamp for IaaS is designed to alleviate design and scale issues by provisioning a transit VPC within the IaaS public cloud provider. A transit VPC is a VPC that has the single purpose of transporting traffic between other VPCs as well as campus and branch locations.

Figure 11-28 illustrates this design.

Within the Cisco Cloud onRamp workflow, one or more cloud instances can be created. Each cloud instance corresponds to an AWS account and region in which one or more transit VPCs can be created and to which one or more host VPCs can then be mapped. Multiple AWS accounts can be added to Cisco Cloud onRamp by adding either AWS Identity and Management (IAM) roles or access keys. These are used by Cisco Cloud onRamp to make the necessary application programming interface (API) calls to create the transit VPC and map host VPCs to the transit VPC.

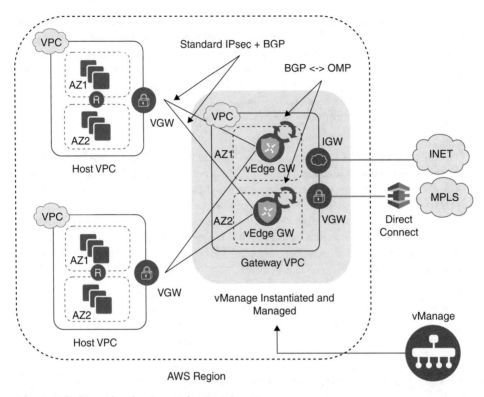

Figure 11-28 *Cloud onRamp for IaaS Design*

Within the Cisco Cloud onRamp workflow, you specify an IPv4 Classless Inter-Domain Routing (CIDR) block range when creating the transit VPC. The IPv4 CIDR range you configure is automatically divided up to create the necessary subnets within the transit VPC. Cisco Cloud onRamp uses AWS APIs to create the AWS logical components, including the transit VPC, subnets, network interfaces, Internet gateway (IGW), and elastic IP addresses (public routable IP addresses).

A pair of redundant Cisco WAN Edge Cloud routers is implemented within a VPC dedicated to function as a transit point for traffic between host VPCs. The Cisco WAN Edge Cloud routers are each deployed within a different availability region within the transit VPC for greater resilience in case of failure. Each Cisco WAN Edge Cloud router is automatically provisioned with the following:

■ A management VPN (VPN 512), available via an AWS elastic IP address (public IP address)

■ A transport VPN (VPN 0), also available via an AWS elastic IP address

■ One or more service VPNs (VPNs 1, 2, and so on)

The transit VPC also provides the entry point from AWS into the Cisco SD-WAN Secure Extensible Network (SEN). The AWS VPN gateway at each host VPC establishes redundant site-to-site VPN connections to each Cisco WAN Edge Cloud router within the transit VPC, through the service VPN side of the Cisco WAN Edge Cloud routers.

When you map a host VPC to the transit VPC, Cisco Cloud onRamp uses AWS APIs to automatically create a redundant pair of AWS site-to-site VPN connections at the host VPC. Each AWS IPsec VPN connection is mapped to one of the two Cisco WAN Edge Cloud routers within the transit VPC. Each Cisco WAN Edge Cloud router within the transit VPC functions as a customer gateway from an AWS perspective. Each AWS site-to-site VPN connection consists of a pair of IPsec tunnels established to the same customer gateway. Therefore, a total of two IPsec tunnels is established from each host VPC to the transit VPC.

Figure 11-29 illustrates this point.

Multiple host VPCs can be mapped to the same service VPN at the transit VPC. This provides connectivity between the host VPCs. Alternatively, individual host VPCs can be mapped to separate service VPNs at the transit VPC—if network segmentation is required.

Figure 11-30 illustrates this point.

Because of the built-in workflows integrated into vManage, configuring Cloud onRamp for IaaS is very simple. However, before configuration can begin, several prerequisites must first be met:

- Verify you have available tokens/licenses for two additional Cisco WAN Edge Cloud routers in vManage.

- Configure a device template for the Cisco WAN Edge Cloud routers that will be used within the transit VPC.

- Deploy the device template to the Cisco WAN Edge Cloud routers that will be used within the transit VPC. You cannot complete the Cloud onRamp for IaaS workflow unless the virtual WAN Edges being deployed have templates with a basic configuration attached to them. A sample base template can be found in the Cloud onRamp for IaaS Deployment Guide accessible on Cisco.com.

- **Verify** you meet the AWS prerequisites such as elastic IP limits, VPC limits, and so on.

Note The information presented in this section of the book has been adapted from the Cloud onRamp for IaaS Deployment Guide. For detailed step-by-step instructions and more technical tips, refer to the Deployment Guide found on Cisco.com.

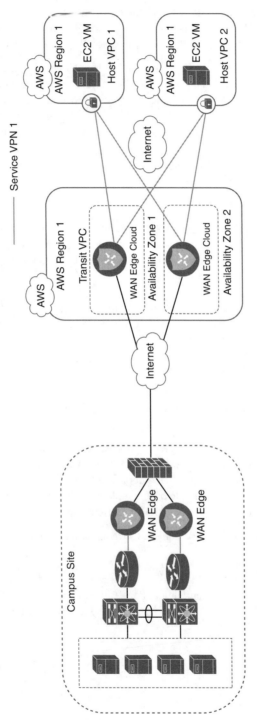

Figure 11-29 *Cloud onRamp for IaaS Single Segment*

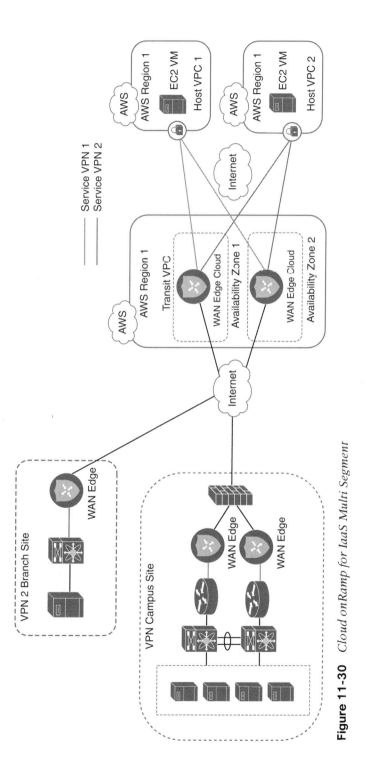

Figure 11-30   *Cloud onRamp for IaaS Multi Segment*

The following is a summary of steps required to configure Cloud onRamp for IaaS:

Step 1.   **Add a new cloud instance.** Navigate to the Cloud onRamp for IaaS workflow and begin the workflow.

Step 2.   **Select the cloud provider and configure access credentials.** Select either AWS or Azure and provide the API key.

Step 3.   **Add a transit VPC.** Select a region and create transit VPCs.

Step 4.   **Discover and map host VPCs to the transit VPC.** Map the discovered host VPCs to the desired transit VPC.

Begin by navigating to the Cloud onRamp for IaaS section of vManage and selecting **Add New Cloud Instance** to start the workflow. Cloud onRamp for IaaS can be found either under the **Configuration** tab of vManage, as shown in Figure 11-31, or by clicking the cloud icon at the top right of the screen and selecting **Cloud Onramp** for IaaS.

Figure 11-31   *Cloud onRamp for IaaS Navigation*

Select the cloud provider from the screen in Figure 11-32. For the purposes of this example, Cloud onRamp for IaaS using Amazon Web Services will be selected and deployed.

Cisco Cloud onRamp uses API calls to create the AWS transit VPC with two Cisco WAN Edge Cloud router instances as well as to map existing AWS spoke VPCs to the transit VPC. Either an AWS Identity and Management (IAM) role or an access key can be used to make the necessary API calls. In the example in Figure 11-33, an access key for AWS credentials will be used. The Cloud onRamp for IaaS Deployment Guide discusses how to generate the access key if you do not already have one.

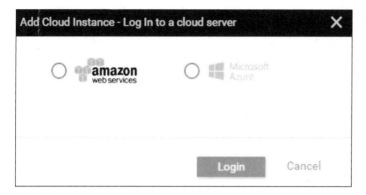

Figure 11-32   *Add Cloud Instance*

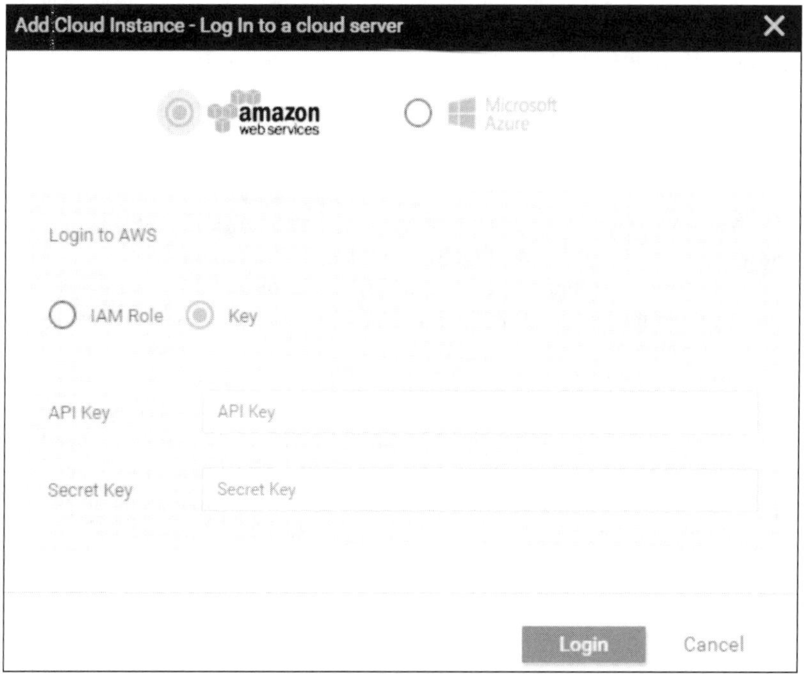

Add Cloud Instance - Log In to a cloud server   ✕

amazon
web services   Microsoft
Azure

Login to AWS

◯ IAM Role   ◉ Key

API Key   API Key

Secret Key   Secret Key

Login   Cancel

Figure 11-33   *Log in to a Cloud*

Enter the AWS access key ID in the API Key field, and enter the AWS secret access key in the Secret Key field shown in Figure 11-33. Click the **Login** button when you have entered the AWS credentials.

Upon entering your AWS credentials, you will be taken to the next step in the workflow: adding a transit VPC.

From the drop-down menu next to Choose a Region, select the AWS region in which you want to create a transit VPC, as shown in Figure 11-34. The following information must be provided to continue the deployment:

- **Transit VPC Name:** This is the name of the transit VPC created by Cisco Cloud onRamp within AWS.

- **WAN Edge Version:** This is the version of software that will run on the redundant pair of Cisco WAN Edge Cloud routers. Once the Cisco WAN Edge Cloud routers are running within the transit VPC, if necessary, you can upgrade the code version they are running to a higher release through vManage.

- **Size of Transit vEdge:** This is the type of AWS compute resource allocated to the WAN Edge cloud routers. The larger the C4 instance, the more vCPUs, memory, and network performance but at a higher per-hour rate.

- **Device 1 and Device 2:** These are the unused and licensed WAN Edge Cloud routers previously deployed with a basic template. The UUID of these routers should populate the drop-down.

- **Transit VPC CIDR (optional):** The default CIDR for the transit VPC is 10.0.0.0/16. There must be sufficient address space to create six subnets within the CIDR block. Only IPv4 addressing is supported.

- **SSH PEM Key:** By default, AWS EC2 instances are accessed using an SSH keypair. This is different from the AWS credentials discussed earlier. You must have an SSH keypair already configured under the same user ID used for the AWS access key discussed earlier. Refer to the Cloud onRamp for IaaS Deployment Guide for detailed instructions on how to generate an SSH keypair in AWS.

Once you have filled in the fields, you can choose to create just the transit VPC at this time by clicking the **Save and Finish** button. Alternatively, you can choose to proceed to the discovery and mapping of spoke VPCs to the transit VPC by selecting the **Proceed to Discovery and Mapping** button. In this example, the host VPCs are mapped to the transit VPC in a separate procedure.

After a few minutes, the Task View screen should appear, confirming that the transit VPC with a redundant pair of Cisco WAN Edge Cloud routers has been created within AWS, as shown in Figure 11-35.

Note   Note that the configuration deployed on the Cisco WAN Edge Cloud routers within the transit VPC can be modified at any time by making the appropriate changes to the template within vManage and deploying the changes to the devices.

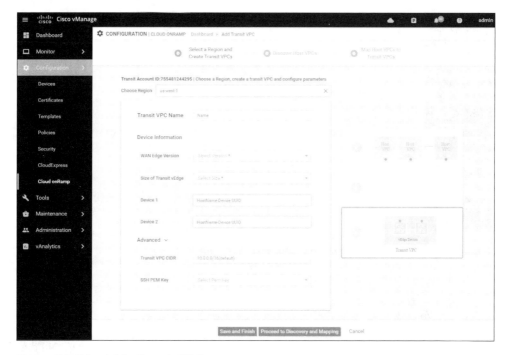

Figure 11-34 *Add a Transit VPC*

Figure 11-35 *Successful Creation of a Transit VPC*

Before host VPCs can be mapped to the transit VPC, they must first be discovered within Cisco Cloud onRamp. In the navigation panel on the left side of the screen, select **Configuration** and then select **Cloud onRamp**. This will bring you to the initial Cisco Cloud onRamp screen, as shown in Figure 11-36.

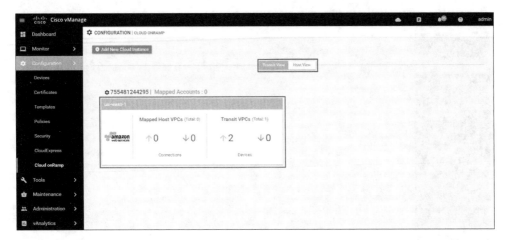

Figure 11-36 *Cloud onRamp for IaaS Existing Cloud Instance*

The IaaS cloud instance created in the previous procedure will appear when the **Transit View** tab is selected. As you can see in Figure 11-36, a single AWS cloud instance now exists. You can verify which AWS region the cloud instance resides in by clicking the **Mapped Accounts** link shown in Figure 11-36. Within this cloud instance, a single transit VPC with two Cisco WAN Edge Cloud routers has been created. Both Cisco WAN Edge Cloud routers are up, as indicated by the green arrow.

At this point, there are no host VPCs mapped to the transit VPC within the cloud instance. Host VPCs connect to the transit VPC through AWS site-to-site VPN connections that use elastic IP addresses (publicly routable IP addresses) at the transit VPC. Host VPCs must first be discovered and then mapped to the transit VPC.

Click the AWS cloud instance widget to which you wish to map host VPCs within the Cisco Cloud onRamp screen. This will bring up additional details regarding the cloud instance. Figure 11-37 shows an example.

Figure 11-37 *Mapped Host VPCs*

The details screen has two tabs: Host VPCs and Transit VPCs. In Figure 11-37, the Host VPCs tab is selected. The Host VPCs tab has two subtabs: Mapped Host VPCs and Unmapped Host VPCs. By default, the Mapped Host VPCs subtab is selected. As can be seen in Figure 11-37, no host VPCs are currently mapped to the transit VPC within the cloud instance.

Multiple transit VPCs can be configured within a single cloud instance (AWS account within a region). When multiple transit VPCs exist within a cloud instance, host VPCs can be mapped to any one of the transit VPCs.

Select the **Un-Mapped Host VPCs** tab. The screen will change to look as shown in Figure 11-38.

Figure 11-38   *Un-Mapped Host VPCs Tab*

Host VPCs must first be discovered by Cisco Cloud onRamp before they can be mapped to a transit VPC. The discovery process uses AWS API calls to discover the VPCs within the AWS account you select.

From the drop-down menu next to **Select one account**, select the account from which you wish to discover host VPCs.

When you entered the AWS credentials within this deployment guide, they were associated with an AWS account. The AWS account number associated with this account should appear within the drop-down menu. You can also enter new accounts by clicking in the **New Account** button at the bottom of the drop-down menu. A pop-up screen asking for the account credentials will appear, as shown in Figure 11-39.

For this example, the host VPCs were created under the same account as the transit VPC.

Click the **Discover Host VPCs** button. The screen should update to show the VPCs available to be mapped to a transit VPC. Figure 11-40 shows an example.

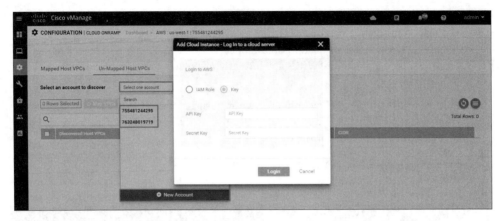

Figure 11-39   *Add a New Account*

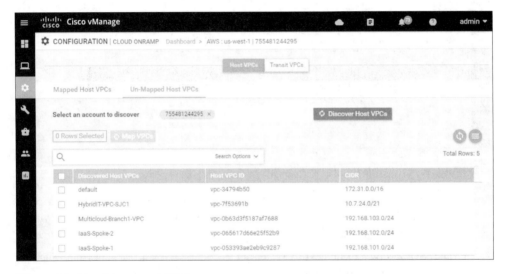

Figure 11-40   *Discovered VPCs*

> **Note**   Only VPCs within the AWS account selected and within the same AWS region as the transit VPC will appear. VPCs must also have a name tag associated with them within AWS for them to appear within Cisco Cloud onRamp. The default VPC automatically created by AWS for each region typically does not have a name tag associated with it. If you want the default VPC for the AWS region to appear within the list of VPCs to map to the transit VPC, you must assign a name tag to it within AWS before it can be discovered.

Select the host VPCs that you want to map and click the **Map VPCs** button, as shown in Figure 11-41.

Figure 11-41 *Map VPCs*

For this example, both host VPCs IaaS-Spoke-1 and IaaS-Spoke-2 were selected from the preceding picture. The pop-up screen in Figure 11-42 will then appear.

Map Host VPCs

> ⚠ OnRamping multiple VPCs with overlapping subnets will cause network routing issues.

Transit VPC	Cloud_onRamp_Transit_VPC1 ✕
VPN	1 ✕
Route Propagation ⓘ	⬤ Disabled

Map VPCs   Cancel

Figure 11-42 *Transit VPC Mapping Details*

If there is only one transit VPC configured within the cloud instance, the Transit VPC field will be filled in for you. If there are multiple transit VPCs within the cloud instance, then from the drop-down menu select the transit VPC to which you wish to map the host VPC.

You have the choice of mapping the host VPC to any of the service VPNs you have defined within the device template attached to the Cisco WAN Edge Cloud router instance. Each host VPC can be mapped to a single service VPN. Mapping host VPCs to the same service VPN allows communication between the host VPCs. Mapping host VPCs to different service VPNs provides network isolation of the host VPCs from each other and allows only branch and campus sites with the same service VPN to access the host VPC.

Enabling **Route Propagation** will propagate the BGP routes to both host VPCs. By default, **Route Propagation** is disabled.

Click the **Map VPCs** button. After a few minutes, the Task View screen should appear, confirming that the host VPC has been mapped to the transit VPC, as shown in Figure 11-43.

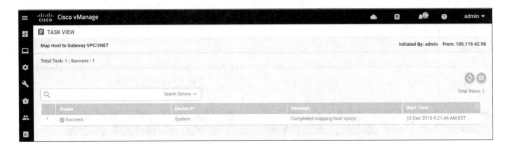

Figure 11-43 *Successful Mapping of Both Host VPCs to the Transit VPC*

When you monitor Cisco Cloud onRamp, you can view the following:

- The connectivity state of each host VPC
- The state of the transit VPC
- Detailed traffic statistics for the IPsec VPN connections between the transit VPC and each host VPC

To view the connectivity state of each host VPC, select the cloud icon at the top of the vManage GUI and then click **Cloud onRamp for IaaS.** You will come to a page displaying each configured cloud instance as a widget. Each widget will list how many host VPCs are mapped to any of the transit VPCs within the cloud instance as well as how many transit VPCs are defined for the cloud instance. Figure 11-44 shows an example.

The aggregate number of host VPCs that are reachable is indicated with a green "up" arrow under **Mapped Host VPCs.** Likewise, the aggregate number of host VPCs that are unreachable is indicated with a red "down" arrow. The color-coded up and down arrows indicate whether the IPsec VPN tunnels connecting the host VPC with the transit VPC are up or down.

Figure 11-44 *Cloud Instance Widget*

The aggregate number of Cisco WAN Edge Cloud routers that are reachable is indicated with a green up arrow under **Transit VPCs**. Likewise, the aggregate number of Cisco WAN Edge Cloud routers that are unreachable is indicated with a red down arrow. In the case of transit VPCs, the color-coded up and down arrows indicate whether the logical Cisco WAN Edge Cloud router is reachable or not. Generally, reachability indicates whether the Cisco WAN Edge Cloud router is running or not. Since there are two Cisco WAN Edge Cloud routers per transit VPC, the number of devices shown here should be twice the number of transit VPCs.

Although the widget can be used to quickly display whether any of the Cisco WAN Edge Cloud routers is down/unreachable or whether any of the host VPCs is unreachable, it does not tell you which specific Cisco WAN Edge Cloud router is down/unreachable or which host VPC is unreachable. For this information you must look further within the cloud instance.

Click the IaaS cloud instance deployed. You can see specific details regarding whether individual host VPCs are up or down as well as their associated transit VPC. You can also see which service VPN the host VPC is mapped to at the transit VPC. Figure 11-45 shows an example.

Figure 11-45 *Per-Host State Details*

When you click the **Transit VPCs** tab, you will be taken to a screen that displays the state of each transit VPC within the cloud instance. Figure 11-46 shows an example.

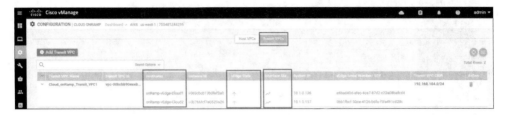

Figure 11-46   *Transit VPC State*

Although the more detailed information discussed in the previous procedure is useful in determining if a given Cisco WAN Edge Cloud router is up or down, it doesn't provide any information regarding the traffic between the transit VPC and each host VPC.

Click the graph icon for one of the Cisco WAN Edge Cloud routers under the **Interface Stats** column shown in Figure 11-46.

A pop-up screen displaying statistics for the IPsec VPN connections between the Cisco Cloud onRamp router and the host VPC(s) is displayed. Figure 11-47 shows an example.

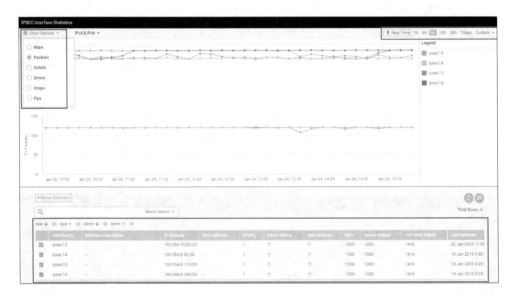

Figure 11-47   *Host VPC VPN Statistics*

Statistics are displayed in both the transmit and receive directions—from the perspective of the Cisco WAN Edge Cloud router logical IPsec interfaces configured within the transit VPN. By default, statistics are displayed for all IPsec interfaces. You can remove an interface from the graph by unselecting it in the panel below the graph.

Cloud onRamp for Colocation

The traditional architectural method of delivering traffic optimization (such as load balancing, security policy, WAN optimization, and so on) relied on centralized provisioning of elements, such as firewalls, intrusion detection/prevention sensors, data leak prevention systems, URL filtering, proxies, and other such devices at aggregation points within the network (most commonly the organization's data centers). For SaaS applications and Internet access, this approach resulted in backhauling user traffic from remote sites into the main data centers, which increased application latency and negatively impacted overall user experience. For applications hosted in the data center, this approach resulted in the potential waste of data center bandwidth resources. Additionally, this architectural method also proved to be challenging to effectively mitigate security incidents, such as virus outbreaks, malware exploits, and internally sourced denial of service attacks.

Today, as we move into the era of SD-WAN, this problem is exacerbated by the architectural shift into a distributed access model. Branches and users are now free to access SaaS applications and Internet resources directly—bypassing the aggregation points highlighted earlier. While this provides a much more efficient method of moving data from point A to point B, it poses a challenge to IT teams looking to maintain their traditional optimization and security policies.

Figure 11-48 shows how Cloud onRamp for Colocation provides a solution to this problem by creating a hybrid model.

In addition to the challenges previously listed, the following items also create pain points for many customers wishing to optimize cloud access:

- It is becoming increasingly difficult to apply optimization policies uniformly across private and public applications.

- Some IaaS and SaaS vendors simply do not provide the necessary optimization and security policy sought by many IT teams.

- Those IaaS and SaaS providers that do offer optimization and security policies typically do so in a way that is not consistent with your enterprise policy.

- Ultimately, there exists an inconsistency in the application of policies across users, devices, applications, and cloud resources.

Cisco SD-WAN offers support for both centralized and distributed architectural models. By leveraging service insertion policies and/or intelligent routing, Cisco SD-WAN can steer traffic of interest wherever necessary to satisfy policy. It is this core function that gave birth to the concept of regionalized service chaining. Coupled with Cisco Cloud onRamp for Colocation, Cisco SD-WAN can establish strategic demarcation points between users/devices and the resources they access. By positioning optimization/security network elements in strategic points across the network, regional service chaining strikes the right balance between operation, cost, application quality of experience, and the ability to effectively mitigate security incidents.

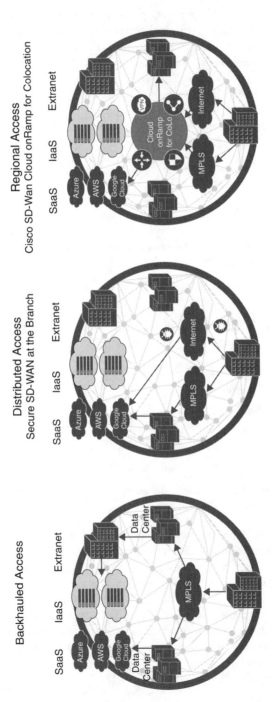

Figure 11-48   *The WAN of Yesterday, Today, and Tomorrow*

Choosing to move to a regionalized model with service chaining comes with many benefits, such as the following:

- **Security:** Distributed policy enforcement offers simple and secure access, deployment, and control.

- **Scalable architecture:** The flexible architecture of Cloud onRamp for Colocation allows you to scale out as required. Cisco Cloud Services Platform (CSP) negates the need to order, cable, rack, and stack dedicated appliances when capacity needs increase or changes need to be made.

- **Performance agility:** The ability to spin up new network elements on demand offers improved performance agility. Optimize application performance by strategically placing Cloud onRamp for Colocation in colocation centers that are closest to your SaaS and IaaS cloud providers.

- **Flexibility:** The solution supports both Cisco virtual network functions (VNFs) and third-party VNFs.

- **Cost savings:** By having various strategic locations to connect to various clouds (including private clouds), enterprises can optimize the costs of circuits to connect their users to applications. Circuit costs for a colocation facility are significantly lower than in a private data center.

Figure 11-49 shows how traffic shifts from a data center model to a center of data model. Users, devices, and things exist on the left, and the resources they access (centers of data) are shown on the right. Cloud onRamp for Colocation sits on the demarcation between these groups. Any traffic moving from left to right within the drawing must pass through Cloud onRamp to satisfy business policy.

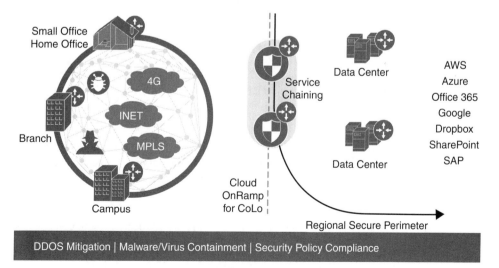

Figure 11-49 *Regionalized Service Chaining*

Why Colocation?

Colocation centers allow you to rent equipment, bandwidth, or space in a secure public data center. These facilities provide flexibility to directly connect with a variety of telecommunications, network, and cloud service providers at a fraction of what it would cost to run direct connections to a private data center. One of the greatest benefits to utilizing a colocation center, however, is its geographical coverage. A colocation facility not only provides high-speed access into public and private cloud resources, but also its geographical presence ensures that you can strategically select a facility (or multiple facilities) in close proximity to your users. Hence, with Cisco SD-WAN and Cisco Cloud onRamp for Colocation, you can ensure your users' traffic need only travel a short distance to the nearest colocation—where that traffic will be optimized, further secured, and transmitted to its intended destination over a high-speed backbone.

How It Works

Establishing regional service chaining is a useful approach in maintaining the organization's optimization and security policies that were once used in a centralized architecture. In this case, policy enforcement can happen on demand by modifying SD-WAN policies to steer application traffic of interest to the nearest colocation facility without the need to re-engineer the network at either remote sites or data centers. Traffic steering can be as granular as a single application or as coarse as the entire remote site's traffic. Once this traffic reaches the colocation facility, it will be shuttled through the appropriate service chain (hosted by Cisco Cloud onRamp for Colocation) as dictated by SD-WAN policy. It's important to note that Cisco SD-WAN is not a requirement for Cloud onRamp for Colocation. Cisco SD-WAN greatly simplifies traffic steering, however, and will be the focus of the example for this section.

Initial traffic steering is performed by Cisco SD-WAN Edge routers (running either IOS-XE or Viptela OS). Through intelligent routing, Deep Packet Inspection, and/or service insertion policy, the ingress router will identify the traffic, analyze its destination, and steer the traffic through the nearest colocation facility (when necessary). It is also important to note that this traffic steering is not limited to IaaS, SaaS, or Internet destinations. In fact, organizations seeking to provide inter-site security and optimization can also utilize Cisco Cloud onRamp for Colocation with service chaining, such as when WAN optimization is necessary.

As mentioned, network functions (such as load balancers, IDS/IPS, firewalls, proxies, and so on) are typically virtualized or hosted within Cisco Cloud onRamp for Colocation and are installed in a colocation facility within geographic proximity to the users it will service.

Figure 11-50 shows the high-level architecture of the solution.

These virtual or physical network services are then directly connected to the Cisco WAN Edge router via the LAN interface. This router then, in essence, announces the presence of these network functions through BGP or OMP service routes (or even via a default route). For traffic that must adhere to a particular optimization or security policy, ingress

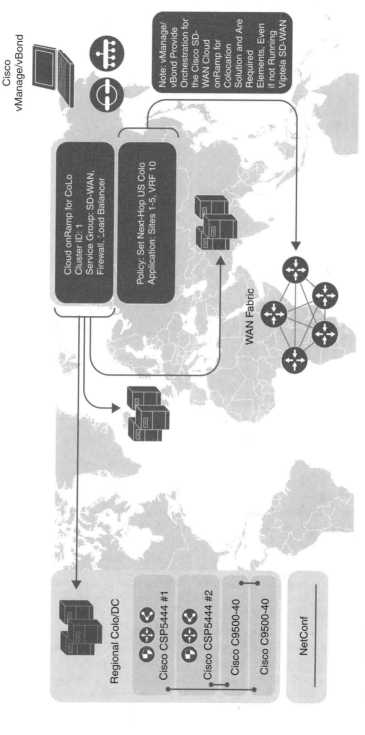

Figure 11-50 *High-Level Architectural View*

routers will select the nearest colocation router announcing the presence of these net-work services and forward their traffic appropriately. Again, strategically placed Cloud onRamp for Colocation clusters allow administrators to minimize the latency penalty for inter-site, Internet, SaaS, and IaaS traffic—thus providing a high quality of experience (QoE) without having to sacrifice security or optimization.

By utilizing this approach, coupled with the templating capabilities of Cisco SD-WAN, administrators can quickly and easily onboard new colocations and/or service chains into the WAN fabric without the need to adjust policy.

Figure 11-51 shows the physical components that make up the solution.

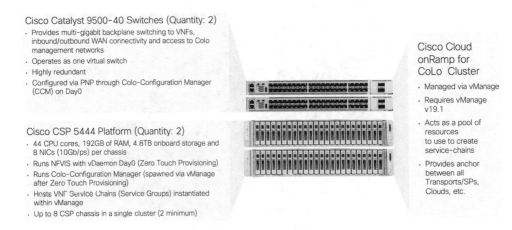

Cisco Catalyst 9500-40 Switches (Quantity: 2)
- Provides multi-gigabit backplane switching to VNFs, inbound/outbound WAN connectivity and access to Colo management networks
- Operates as one virtual switch
- Highly redundant
- Configured via PNP through Colo-Configuration Manager (CCM) on Day0

Cisco CSP 5444 Platform (Quantity: 2)
- 44 CPU cores, 192GB of RAM, 4.8TB onboard storage and 8 NICs (10Gb/ps) per chassis
- Runs NFVIS with vDaemon Day0 (Zero Touch Provisioning)
- Runs Colo-Configuration Manager (spawned via vManage after Zero Touch Provisioning)
- Hosts VNF Service Chains (Service Groups) instantiated within vManage
- Up to 8 CSP chassis in a single cluster (2 minimum)

Cisco Cloud onRamp for CoLo Cluster
- Managed via vManage
- Requires vManage v19.1
- Acts as a pool of resources to use to create service-chains
- Provides anchor between all Transports/SPs, Clouds, etc.

Figure 11-51   *Cloud onRamp for Colocation Cluster*

Service Chaining for a Single Service Node

In the case of a service chain with a single service node, application traffic of interest is steered from the source WAN Edge router across the SD-WAN fabric to the Colocation Edge router announcing the service. Once the traffic passes through the network service (a firewall, for instance), either it is forwarded back to the Colocation Edge router (which then forwards it to the original destination router across the SD-WAN fabric) or it is for-warded out of the network service chain toward the public cloud/Internet.

Both control and data policies can be used for this type of service chaining. The main difference between them is that data policies are sent from vSmart controllers to the SD-WAN routers, while control policies stay only on the vSmart controllers (that is, similar to how a BGP route reflector would modify routes prior to announcing them to neighbors). Knowing this, it is important to note that with control policies, since vSmart controllers do not "see" actual data packets, matching policy rules can only be on control plane identifiers (such as site IDs, OMP routes, and so on). Data policies do not have this limitation, as these policies are enforced directly on the SD-WAN router.

Figure 11-52 depicts how a single service chain node is inserted into the fabric by lever-aging SD-WAN policy.

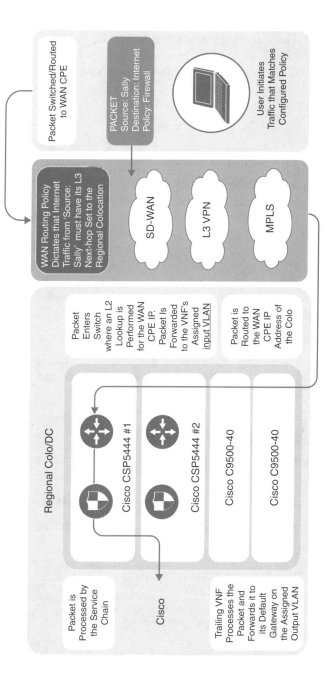

Figure 11-52 *Simplified Packet Walkthrough*

In all cases, the network service is advertised into the SD-WAN fabric via OMP. Service advertisement is done in the VPN context, which gives service insertion even further flexibility with regard to managed service providers and multitenancy. Not only can service insertion be regionalized, but also different VPNs can potentially utilize different services in the same region. This level of flexibility may not be required for common deployment scenarios.

In the case of a firewall service, Cisco SD-WAN fabric also supports provisioning trusted and untrusted side interfaces. In such a case, policies can be orchestrated in such a way that site-to-site traffic is forwarded across the untrusted zone and trusted zone interfaces appropriately, with regard to traffic direction. OMP, in fact, advertises two services—one for the trusted interface and one for untrusted interfaces. As such, traffic symmetry can be maintained.

 ## Service Chaining for Multiple Service Nodes

In the case of multiple service nodes (such as a firewall, followed by a proxy or load balancer), application traffic of interest is steered from the source WAN router to the Colocation Edge router hosting the network service. Traffic is then handed off to the first element of the service chain. Once processed by the network service element, traffic then follows that device's routing table to the next element. If allowed by the second network service element, it is then forwarded to the third element (and so on). When traffic has progressed through the entire service chain, it is then forwarded either out to the public cloud/Internet or back to the Colocation Edge router (which, in turn, would send the traffic to the original destination).

Figure 11-53 depicts the life of a packet as it travels from end user to cloud destination.

Just as in the case of the single service node, both control and data policies can be used for the service insertion. The same differences between data and control policies are true for a multinode service chain.

Service Chaining and the Public Cloud

The positioning of Cisco Cloud onRamp for Colocation clusters within colocations is mainly influenced by the following factors:

- Amount of available bandwidth to accommodate inbound traffic

- Geographic proximity to the source of transmission to minimize backhaul latency

- Availability of cross-connects with public cloud providers

- Availability of power, cooling, space, and so on

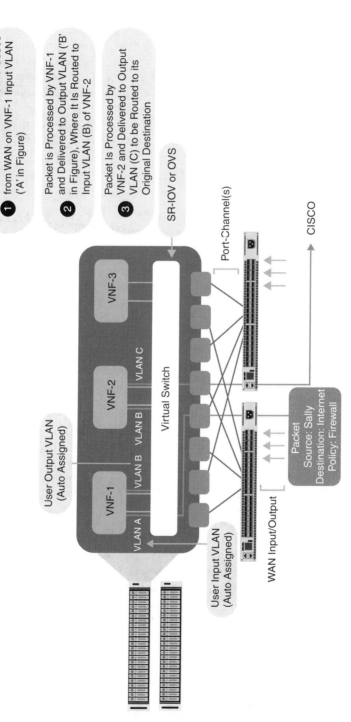

1 Packet/Frame Delivered to C9500 from WAN on VNF-1 Input VLAN ('A' in Figure)

2 Packet is Processed by VNF-1 and Delivered to Output VLAN ('B' in Figure), Where It Is Routed to Input VLAN (B) of VNF-2

3 Packet Is Processed by VNF-2 and Delivered to Output VLAN (C) to be Routed to its Original Destination

SR-IOV or OVS

Port-Channel(s)

CISCO

VNF-3

VNF-2

VNF-1

Virtual Switch

VLAN A   VLAN B   VLAN B   VLAN C

User Output VLAN (Auto Assigned)

User Input VLAN (Auto Assigned)

WAN Input/Output

Packet
Source: Sally
Destination: Internet
Policy: Firewall

Figure 11-53 *Detailed Packet Walkthrough*

Infrastructure as a Service

Considering the factors in the preceding list, it is feasible to provision Cisco Cloud onRamp for Colocation within the transit path of traffic destined to IaaS resources. There are two options to consider when utilizing this type of deployment, though both yield the same result. The first is via direct connection to the cloud provider. Amazon AWS refers to this service as DirectConnect, while Microsoft Azure refers to the service as ExpressRoute. In either case, a physical connection is made between your Cisco Cloud onRamp for Colocation cluster and your resources within the cloud service provider. The second option is via legacy VPN. With this option, a VPN is built between your Cisco Cloud onRamp for Colocation cluster and the cloud service provider. In both instances, the cloud provider will use BGP to peer with Cloud onRamp for Colocation VNF elements to advertise appropriate prefixes. These prefixes are then propagated throughout the WAN or SD-WAN fabric.

Figure 11-54 shows how Cloud onRamp for Colocation can be integrated with other features, such as Cloud onRamp for IaaS (discussed previously). Here, Cloud onRamp for IaaS is used to build automated connectivity into the IaaS cloud while Cloud onRamp for Colocation is used to optimally connect end users to this integration point.

Service chaining for IaaS resources happens in much the same way as with any other service chainable resources. Traffic of interest will be directed to the nearest colocation facility, where it will be processed by Cloud onRamp for Colocation service chains and forwarded to the IaaS provider. If you will recall, Cisco SD-WAN has the capability of extending the SD-WAN fabric to the AWS/Azure cloud (a feature known as Cloud onRamp for IaaS). Though logically this solution seems ideal, the advantage that Cisco Cloud onRamp for Colocation brings to the table is one of reduced latency and optimization. With Cloud onRamp for Colocation, remote sites do not need to transit the Internet (and be subjected to potential latency issues). Instead, IaaS-bound traffic will move to the nearest colocation facility, where it will be processed by a service chain and forwarded on a high-speed backbone link to the IaaS provider, thus minimizing latency and guaranteeing a high-quality experience for the end user.

Software as a Service

SaaS resources, by nature, present a unique challenge to network architecture since the only way to reach these resources is via the Internet. Distributed Internet access (as with SD-WAN) has solved this problem by allowing direct access to these resources from the branch location. However, again, we are confronted with the issue of how to optimize and secure this traffic, without sacrificing the distributed architecture that provides a high-quality experience. Cisco SD-WAN, coupled with Cloud onRamp for Colocation, provides a two-pronged solution to this dilemma.

Ideally, Cloud onRamp for Colocation clusters will be placed in a colocation (or colocations) that has direct connectivity to the SaaS provider's resources. Given this advantage, we know that the object of the game will be to get our user traffic to the nearest colocation as quickly and efficiently as possible to capitalize on the colocation's high-speed transport into the SaaS provider's cloud. To accomplish this, Cisco SD-WAN offers the Cloud onRamp for SaaS feature. This feature utilizes HTTP probing to identify which circuits within the organization offer the least amount of loss and latency to reach a given SaaS application. When this feature is enabled, remote sites will begin to probe SaaS applications via their locally attached Internet circuit. In addition, probes can also be sent through colocations. In theory, Cloud onRamp for Colocation–enabled locations will have the best loss and latency into the provider's cloud and, hence, be chosen as the primary path for reaching the application. In the event of loss or latency within the colocation, one of two outcomes is possible: the traffic will be diverted to the "next best" performing colocation or it will utilize the locally attached Internet circuit, as shown in Figure 11-55.

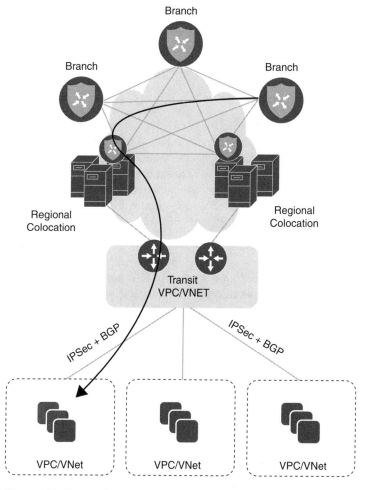

Figure 11-54 *Infrastructure as a Service via Colocation*

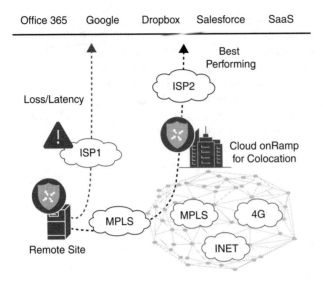

Figure 11-55 *Infrastructure as a Service via Colocation*

Redundancy and High Availability

High availability and redundancy for service chains are achieved both by provisioning two identical service chains (on separate CSPs within the same colocation) and through the use of multiple colocation facilities hosting the same set of services. In such a case, chassis redundancy is provided through the use of two or more CSPs in the Cisco Cloud onRamp for Colocation cluster. Service chain redundancy is provided either through identical service chains spread across multiple chassis or multiple colocations.

The Cisco Cloud onRamp for Colocation solution monitors each service chain element for uptime and throughput. Upon failure, the device will be rebooted automatically. It is assumed, however, that individual service chain elements also maintain either Active/Active or Active/Standby failover session state. In essence, the automatic reboot should trigger the element to "fail over" to its identical device residing on the second chassis.

Service Chain Design Best Practices

An enterprise would typically go through the following stages while designing its service chains for Cloud onRamp for Colocation:

- Identify virtual network functions (VNFs).

- Design service chains.

- Design the Cloud onRamp for Colocation clusters(s).

As an example, the connection patterns emerge from an analysis of a typical customer network, as shown in Figure 11-56.

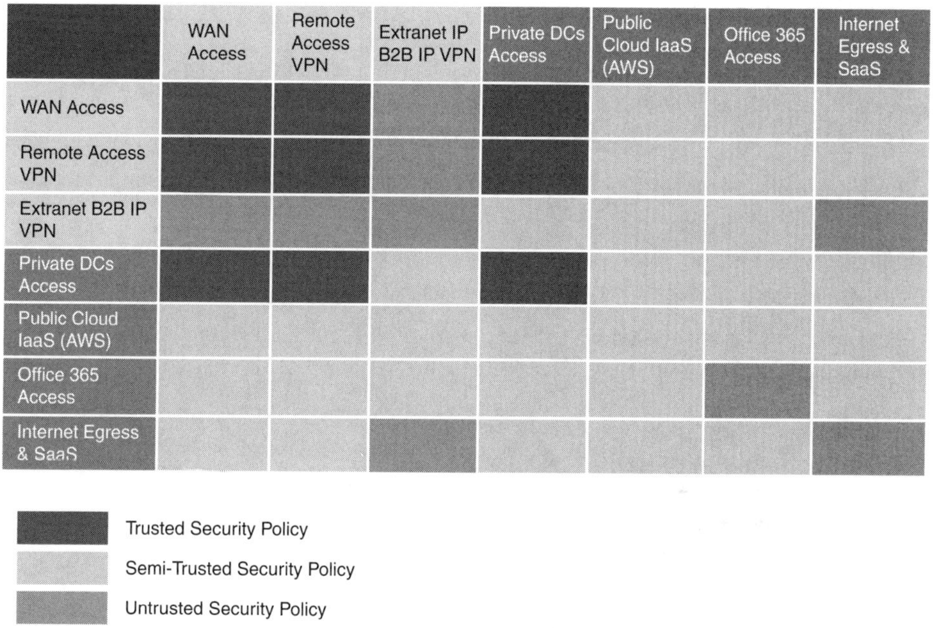

	WAN Access	Remote Access VPN	Extranet IP B2B IP VPN	Private DCs Access	Public Cloud IaaS (AWS)	Office 365 Access	Internet Egress & SaaS
WAN Access	Trusted	Trusted	Semi-Trusted	Trusted	Semi-Trusted	Semi-Trusted	Semi-Trusted
Remote Access VPN	Trusted	Trusted	Semi-Trusted	Trusted	Semi-Trusted	Semi-Trusted	Semi-Trusted
Extranet B2B IP VPN	Semi-Trusted	Semi-Trusted	Semi-Trusted	Semi-Trusted	Semi-Trusted	Semi-Trusted	Untrusted
Private DCs Access	Trusted	Trusted	Semi-Trusted	Trusted	Semi-Trusted	Semi-Trusted	Semi-Trusted
Public Cloud IaaS (AWS)	Semi-Trusted	Semi-Trusted	Semi-Trusted	Semi-Trusted	Semi-Trusted	Semi-Trusted	Semi-Trusted
Office 365 Access	Semi-Trusted	Semi-Trusted	Semi-Trusted	Semi-Trusted	Semi-Trusted	Trusted	Semi-Trusted
Internet Egress & SaaS	Semi-Trusted	Semi-Trusted	Untrusted	Semi-Trusted	Semi-Trusted	Semi-Trusted	Untrusted

- Trusted Security Policy
- Semi-Trusted Security Policy
- Untrusted Security Policy

Figure 11-56 *Source and Destination Matrix*

Based on this information, service-chaining policies can be derived. The table in the figure shows which groups cannot interact with each other (medium blue), which groups can interact but with certain controls (light blue), and which groups can interact without additional services (dark blue). Knowing this information will help determine the type of VNFs needed. For example, when creating a service chain for traffic coming from your employees, you may require fewer firewalls, as the source of such traffic is considered to be trusted.

Cisco Cloud onRamp for Colocation supports both Cisco VNFs and third-party VNFs. Based on your traffic patterns and volume, select the VNF that suits your need best.

Consider the following when selecting VNFs and their placement for your service chains:

- SR-IOV versus DPDK: Your service chain design depends on the VNFs you have identified and their support of each of these traffic forwarding modes.

- High availability (HA).

- Port channeling.

Next, evaluate your compute needs. By default, a cluster must include two CSP 5444 appliances along with two Catalyst 9500 series 40-port switches. This combination provides high-throughput and ample compute capability for most applications (44 CPU cores, 192GB RAM, 5TB hard disk space). Each individual cluster is capable of expanding to eight CSP 5444 appliances, however. Bear in mind that additional CSPs will reduce the number of switch ports available for integrating physical network appliances within your service chains.

Configuration and Management

The entire Cisco Cloud onRamp for Colocation architecture utilizes the same dashboard as the Cisco SD-WAN solution. Hence, all provisioning, troubleshooting, monitoring, and configuration are done within the workflows of vManage.

In this section, we will briefly show how to create a cluster, followed by a simple data policy, to set up a typical service chain.

Cluster Creation

First, verify vManage version via the **Help > About** screen, as shown in Figure 11-57. At a minimum, Cloud onRamp for Colocation requires version 19.1 of vManage.

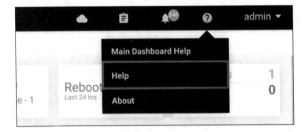

Figure 11-57   *vManage Help*

Ensure that CSP and C9K device licenses exist within the **Configuration > Devices** screen on vManage. If not, ensure that valid licenses exist within the appropriate Smart Account for this cluster. These device licenses can then be manually downloaded and imported into vManage or automatically downloaded from the Smart Account (via the **Configuration > Devices** screen).

From the **Configuration** menu within vManage, choose **Cloud onRamp for Colocation**, as shown in Figure 11-58.

Before proceeding, ensure that the cluster is correctly cabled. Cloud onRamp for Colocation is designed to be turnkey and prescriptive. Hence, the cluster must be cabled in a prescriptive manner. A cabling guide can be found in the Cloud onRamp for Colocation solution guide on the Cisco documentation website.

Once the cluster is physically cabled and powered on, click the **Configure and Provision Cluster** button. Enter a name, site ID, location, and description for your cluster, as shown in Figure 11-59. With the exception of Site ID, other values are recommended to be unique.

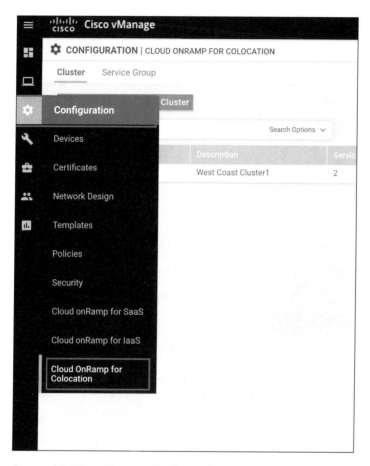

Figure 11-58 *vManage Configuration*

Figure 11-59 *Configure and Provision Cluster*

Identify the appropriate switches and CSPs for this cluster by clicking the Switch and CSP icons in the middle of the screen. Provide a name, select a serial number, and click the **Save** button, as shown in Figure 11-60.

Figure 11-60 *CSP and Switch Allocation*

Set credentials for this cluster by clicking the **Credentials** button. By default, CSPs and C9Ks will ship with well-known passwords. It is best practice to set a new, complex password for these devices within this workflow. At a minimum, you should reset the Admin account password, as shown in Figure 11-61, though you may optionally create a new user.

Note Cluster credentials provide command-line access to the CSP and C9K devices. In most circumstances, CLI access to these devices is not required for cluster provisioning and management.

When finished, click the **Save** button.

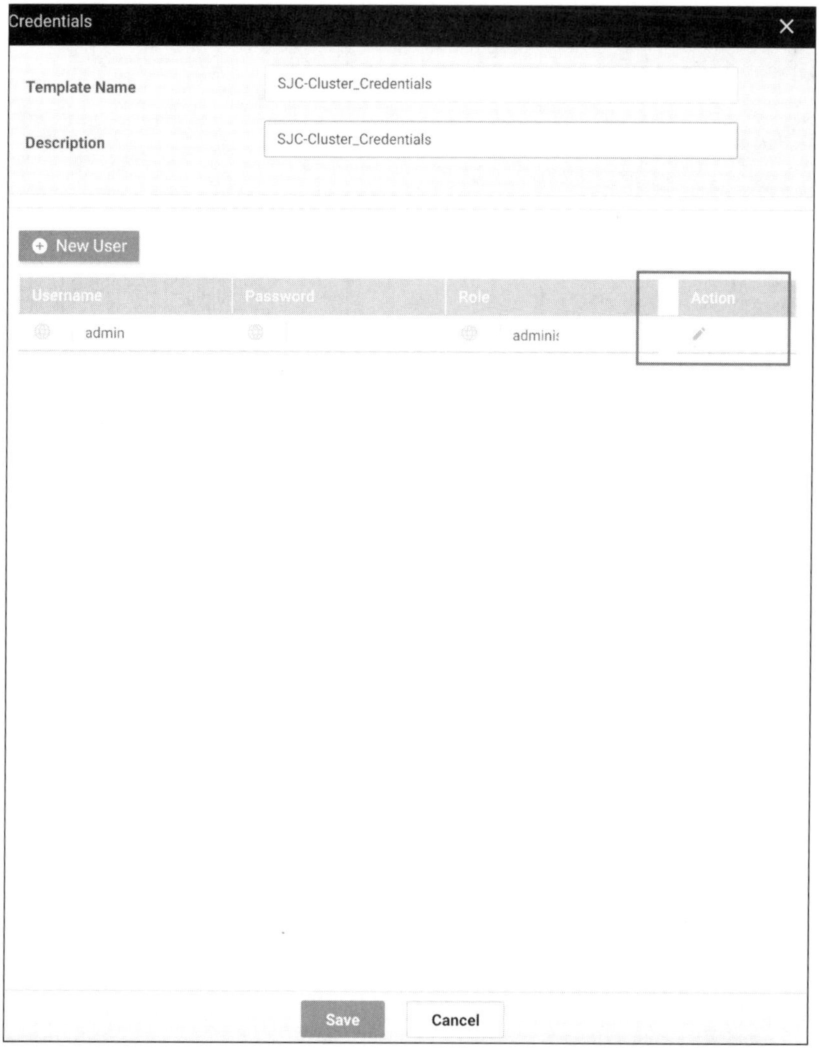

Figure 11-61 *Cluster Credentials*

Next, specify resource pool settings by clicking the **Resource Pool** button. These settings allow vManage to stitch together service chain elements as well as allow those service chain elements to boot up with basic configuration parameters for bootstrap purposes (for example, these settings would allow a Firepower Threat Defense virtual firewall to automatically contact Firepower Management Center as soon as it is booted and without user intervention), as shown in Figure 11-62. These values will be unique to your environment, and some are oftentimes provided by the colocation provider. Click the **Save** button when finished.

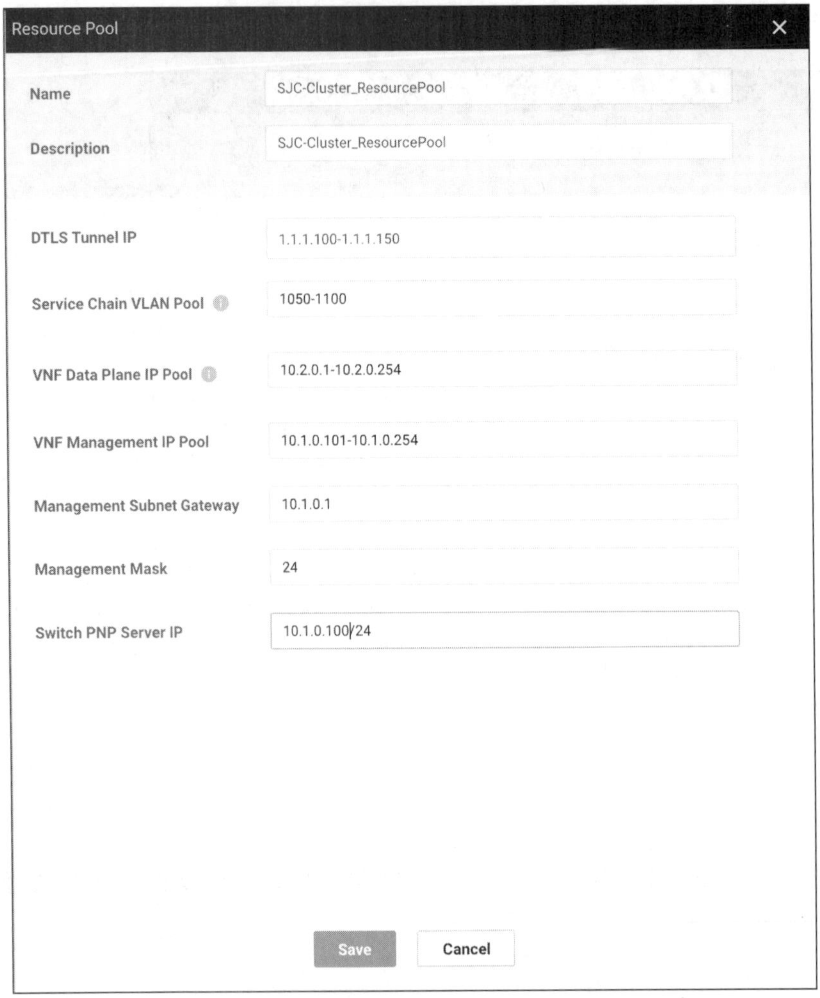

Figure 11-62   *Cluster Resources*

■ **DTLS Tunnel IP:** Analogous to System IP in Cisco SD-WAN nomenclature and only used when a VNF joins the SD-WAN fabric.

■ **Service-chain VLAN Pool:** Pool of VLANs that vManage will use to stitch VNFs together from a Layer 2 perspective.

■ **VNF Data Plane IP Pool:** Pool of IP addresses that vManage will use to stitch VNFs together from a Layer 3 perspective.

■ **VNF Management IP Pool:** Pool of IP addresses that vManage will use to automatically assign management addresses to the management interface of a booting VNF (where applicable).

- **Management Gateway Prefix:** Default gateway for management subnet.

- **Management Mask:** Subnet mask for management subnet.

- **Switch PNP Server IP:** Auto-populated from Management IP Pool but can be manually specified, if desired. This setting identifies the IP address that Colo Configuration Manager will use to communicate directly with the switches. You must configure the address shown in this field as the DHCP Option 43 parameter in your management subnet DHCP server.

> **Note** Because switches do not join the SD-WAN fabric, they have no way of directly communicating with vManage for provisioning updates. Colo Configuration Manager, or CCM, is a component that automatically spawns with cluster creation and is used to proxy-switch configuration from vManage. It does not require intervention from the administrator for provisioning, managing, or monitoring purposes and should only be accessed under Cisco TAC supervision.

The cluster is now ready to be provisioned. As a final (optional) step, consider adding an NTP and syslog server to this cluster by clicking the **Cluster Settings** button. Because Cisco SD-WAN relies heavily on certificate authentication, accurate timekeeping is paramount. Hence, an NTP server is strongly recommended. When finished, click the **Save** button.

Activate the new cluster by clicking the ellipsis (far right side of screen) and choosing **Activate**. The following screen should appear. To preview the configuration that will be provisioned, click on each of the CSPs in the left pane. When ready, click the **Configure Devices** button, as shown in Figure 11-63.

Figure 11-63 *Cluster Activation*

Note Although four devices are being provisioned (at a minimum), this task will prompt the user to confirm configuration on only three devices (two CSPs and one Colo Configuration Manager).

Cluster activation can take up to 45 minutes. You can review the status of activation via the workflow screen that appears after clicking the Configure Devices button in the previous step. Alternatively, you can revisit this screen via the Task menu in the upper-right corner of vManage.

As previously discussed, switches do not directly attach to the SD-WAN fabric and, hence, require a local resource for proxy configuration from vManage. In the preceding steps, an IP address was defined for Colo Configuration Manager. The Catalyst 9500 switches, upon bootup, will automatically begin searching for this local resource as part of their bootstrap (PNP) process. In the case shown in Figure 11-64, the switches will learn of CCM via DHCP Option 43. You must configure the Management subnet DHCP server with the appropriate Option 43 information. In Cisco IOS-XE, review the following example. The CCM IP address defined in Figure 11-63 and in Figure 11-64 is 10.1.0.100. Input your values where appropriate.

```
ip dhcp pool Management-DHCP-Server
 network 10.1.0.0 255.255.255.0
 default-router 10.1.0.1
 dns-server 10.1.0.1
 option 43 ascii "5A;B2;K4;I10.1.0.100;J9191"
```

Figure 11-64 *DHCP Server Configuration*

Note The ASCII information specified in the Option 43 statement specifies that the switches are to utilize HTTP/S as a transport protocol on port 9191. It is recommended not to alter these values, however. Simply replacing the preceding example's IP address (10.1.0.100) with your cluster CCM address is all that is required.

Approximately 10 minutes after cluster activation, you might notice that the task output has stopped. This is likely due to the Catalyst switches not contacting the newly created CCM. In such a case, simply reboot the switches to force them to obtain new IP addressing information with DHCP Option 43. Your cluster should then move to ACTIVE state after a few additional minutes.

Note It is entirely normal for the Catalyst switches to reboot periodically during the provisioning process as the virtual switching system is initialized and inter-chassis port channels are created.

Image Repository

Once the cluster is up and operational, you must upload applicable virtual machine images to the vManage Software Repository via **Maintenance > Software Repository**. Cloud onRamp for Colocation uses a KVM-based hypervisor. As such, QCOW2 images are the only supported disk image files. To upload a premade package for use within service chains, click the **Virtual Images** tab, followed by the **Upload Virtual Image** button.

Where necessary, a custom package can also be created to provide complete flexibility in which devices can be utilized within service chains. Click the **Add Custom VNF Package** button. Here, you can specify many package parameters (most notably, the Day0 configuration that the device should boot up with) along with uploading your QCOW2 image, as shown in Figure 11-65. When finished, click the **Save** button.

Figure 11-65 *Custom VNF Package*

Service Chain Creation

The next step in Cloud onRamp for Colocation administration is to define a new data policy. This step instructs remote routers to utilize the service chain that will be built in the proceeding steps. From the **Configuration > Policies** menu, click the button **Add Policy** (or, alternatively, you may edit an existing policy). Identify the Match criteria in the first screen (in this case, a Protected-Applications list was created). Click the **Next** button to navigate to the **Configure Traffic Rules** section, as shown in Figure 11-66. Click the button to add a new traffic data policy.

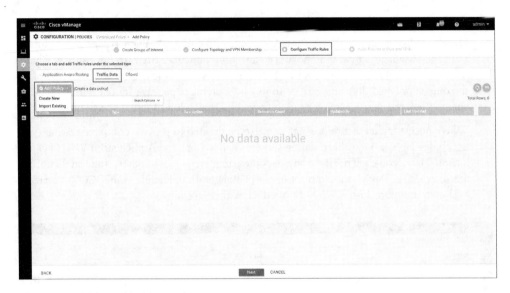

Figure 11-66   *Traffic Data Policy*

Click the **Sequence Type** button and select **Service-Chaining**. Click the **Sequence Rule** button to construct the policy. In the example shown in Figure 11-67, traffic matching the Protected-Applications list will be subjected to service chaining using the device advertising the Firewall service located at TLOC IP address 1.2.1.1.

Figure 11-67   *Source and Destination Matrix*

Save the policy sequence and proceed to the **Apply Policies to Sites and VPNs** section. Apply the new policy to the SD-WAN routers at the remote sites (this may require you to construct VPN and site lists). In addition, choose which VPN this policy is going to be applied to, as shown in Figure 11-68.

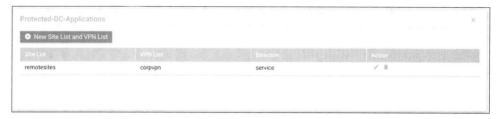

Figure 11-68 *Policy Application*

Next, a VPN configuration feature template for the colocation router (where the firewall is connected) needs to be created. This template will specify the service node IP address that corresponds to the Firewall label used in the data policy, as shown in Figure 11-69.

CONFIGURATION | TEMPLATES

Device   Feature

Feature Template > VPN

| DNS | OMP | IPv4 Route | IPv6 Route | Service | GRE Route |

Service Type		IP Addresses (Maximum: 4) or Interfaces	
⊕ ▾ FW ▾	⦿ IP Address ◯ Interface	⊕ ▾	10.10.10.1

Figure 11-69 *OMP Service Advertisement*

Next, provision the service chain on the Cloud onRamp for Colocation cluster from within the **Cloud onRamp for Colocation > Service Group** page. This step assumes that the cluster also hosts the Colocation Edge router that will be advertising the service configured in the preceding step (though this could also be a separate physical box or a traditional IOS-XE CSR, if desired). Hence, you might need to complete this step and revisit the previous steps in order to ensure that the Colocation Edge router is properly advertising the Firewall service.

From the **Configuration > Cloud onRamp for Colocation** menu, click the **Service Groups** tab. In Figure 11-70, as part of the Add Service Group workflow, you are prompted to enter ingress and egress VLANs (10 and 20, respectively).

After clicking **Add**, you will be prompted to build the service chain. From the screen in Figure 11-71, click and drag each service chain element from the left pane to the right pane (assuming the Custom chain option was selected in the previous workflow screen).

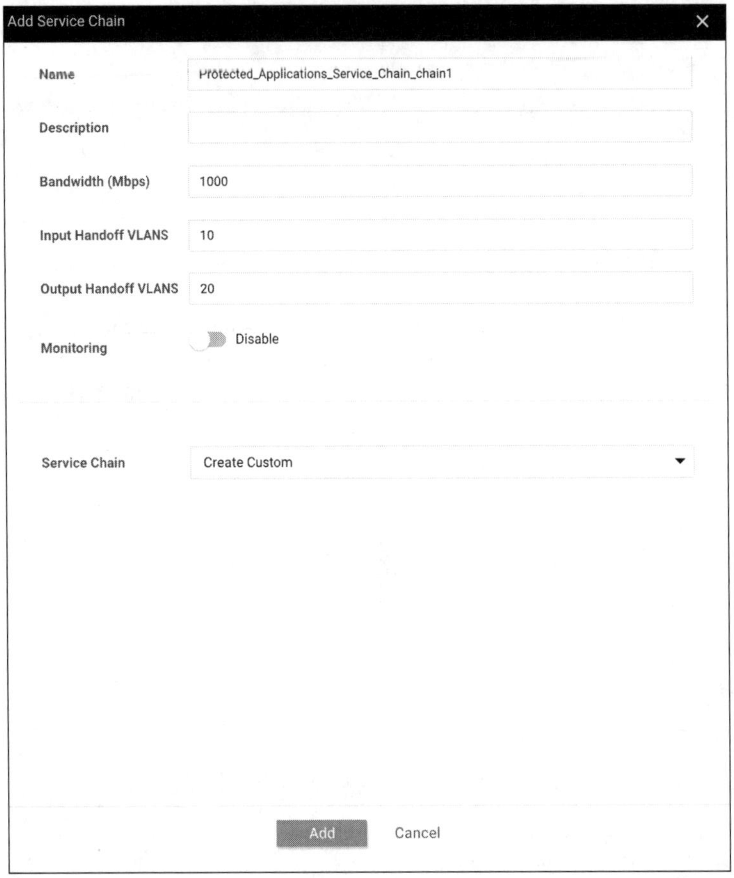

Add Service Chain   ✕

Name	Protected_Applications_Service_Chain_chain1
Description	
Bandwidth (Mbps)	1000
Input Handoff VLANS	10
Output Handoff VLANS	20
Monitoring	⬤▷ Disable
Service Chain	Create Custom ▾

Add   Cancel

Figure 11-70 *Add Service Chain*

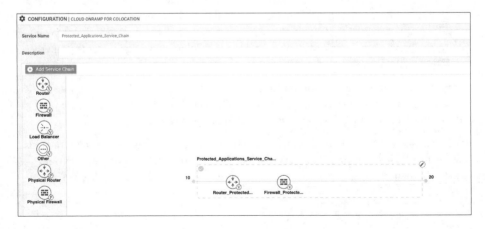

Figure 11-71 *Service Chain Creation*

Click each of the service chain elements to configure their parameters as appropriate. As discussed previously, some variables within this screen (see Figure 11-72) will be provided by the customer, and others will be pulled from the Cluster Resources configuration pools created in the cluster creation section.

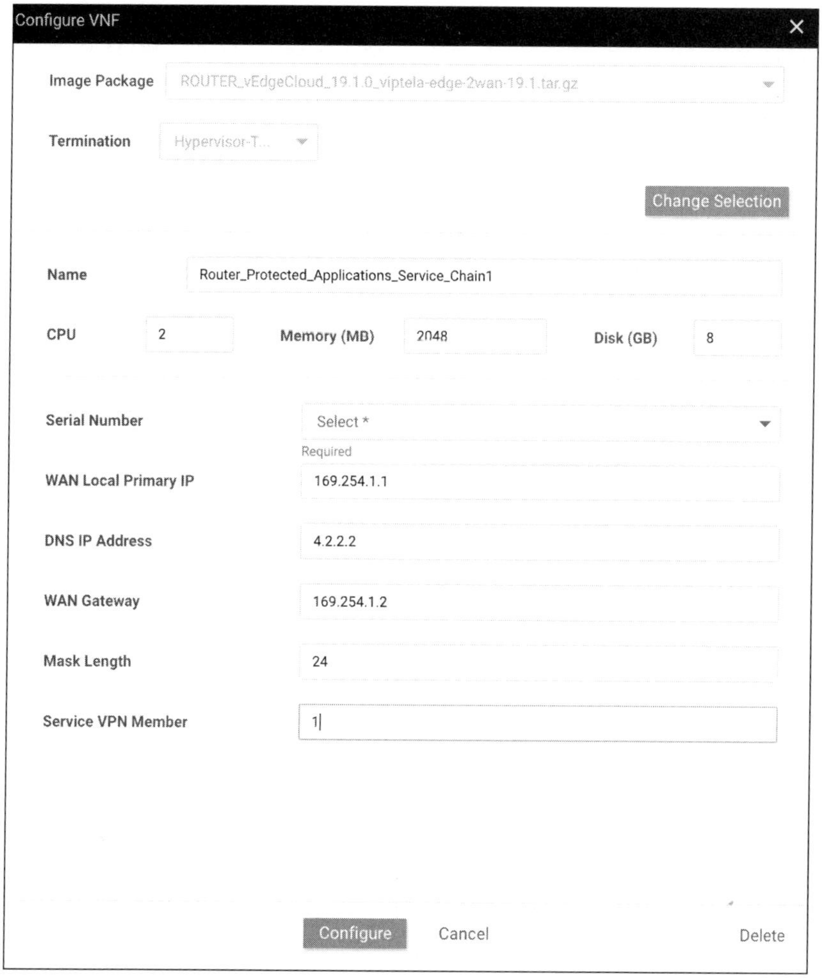

Figure 11-72 *VNF Definition*

Once complete, click the ellipsis to the right of the new service chain and choose the **Attach Cluster** option. The configuration established from Figure 11-72 now accomplishes the following:

- Establishes a Colocation Edge router to join the colocation to the SD-WAN fabric
- Provisions a firewall as the second element of the service chain

- Configures the Colocation Edge router to advertise the existence of the firewall through OMP service route announcements

- Configures a data policy to force remote site routers to seek out a colocation offering firewall services with which to forward traffic in the "Protected Applications" list

Monitoring

Service chain and cluster status can be viewed via the Colocation Clusters tab of the **Monitoring > Network** menu, as shown in Figure 11-73. Click the cluster name to view health and performance statistics.

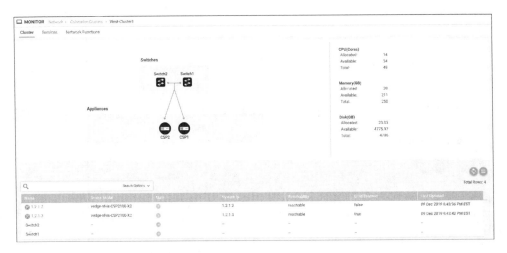

Figure 11-73 *Colocation Cluster*

From the screen in Figure 11-73, you can view CSP health by clicking the CSP in the lower pane. Service chain health and status can be viewed by clicking the **Services** tab. You can view the Services screen as a list or graphical representation using the **Table | Diagram** option, as shown in Figure 11-74. In the Diagram view, hovering over the service chain element presents the user with information specific to the VNF, as shown in Figure 11-75.

Figure 11-74 *Service Chain Status*

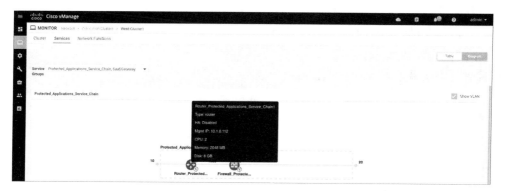

Figure 11-75   *Service Chain Status (Diagram View)*

You can review individual VNF health via the **Network Functions** tab in the upper-left corner of this screen. You can view metrics such as CPU, Hard Disk, and Network I/O by clicking the respective tabs in the left pane, as shown in Figure 11-76.

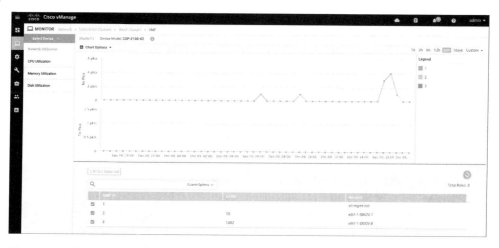

Figure 11-76   *VNF Health*

Summary

This chapter covered all aspects of Cisco SD-WAN Cloud onRamp, including onRamp for SaaS, IaaS, and Colocation. With onRamp for SaaS, on one hand, the Cisco SD-WAN fabric improves branch-office user experience by using the best-performing network path, increasing application resiliency, and providing path and performance visibility. OnRamp for IaaS, on the other hand, extends the SD-WAN fabric into public cloud instances and provides all the benefits of Cisco SD-WAN directly to the front doorsteps of cloud workloads. Finally, Cloud onRamp for Colocation allows for distributed security enforcement, a scalable architecture through the use of CSP and VNFs, and performance agility by strategic placement of colocation access points.

Review All Key Topics

Review the most important topics in the chapter, noted with the Key Topic icon in the outer margin of the page. Table 11-1 lists these key topics and the page numbers on which each is found.

Table 11-1 *Key Topics*

Key Topic Element	Description	Page
Paragraph	Direct cloud access use case	395
Paragraph	Cloud onRamp for IaaS concept	413
Paragraph	Cloud onRamp for Colocation concept	429
Section	Service Chaining for Single Service Node	434
Section	Service Chaining for Multiple Service Nodes	436

Define Key Terms

Define the following key terms from this chapter and check your answers in the glossary:

Direct Cloud Access, colocation, transit VPC

Chapter Review Questions

1. Cisco Cloud onRamp for SaaS requires a Cisco SD-WAN Edge router to be placed in the SaaS cloud.

   a. True
   b. False

2. What are the three Cloud onRamp for SaaS site types?

   a. Gateway site
   b. DIA site
   c. Local site
   d. Client site
   e. Hub site

3. Cloud onRamp for SaaS supports dual Internet and MPLS transport sites.

   a. True

   b. False

4. Cloud onRamp for SaaS DPI does not redirect the initial application flow after detection.

   a. True

   b. False

5. Which two real-time outputs provide information about Cloud onRamp for SaaS?

   a. CloudExpress Applications

   b. CloudExpress Paths

   c. CloudExpress Gateway Exits

   d. CloudExpress Local Paths

   e. CloudExpress Statistics

6. Which three things is a WAN Edge Cloud router provisioned with automatically?

   a. Management VPN

   b. Transport VPN

   c. BGP AS

   d. SNMP ID

   e. Service VPN

7. How many Cisco SD-WAN WAN Edge Cloud routers are provisioned in a single transit VPC or VNET during the Cloud onRamp for IaaS process?

   a. It depends on the scale of the network.

   b. Two

   c. Four

   d. Eight

8. When logging in to an AWS cloud instance during the Cloud onRamp for IaaS process, both IAM role and API key methods are supported.

   a. True

   b. False

9. When you monitor Cisco Cloud onRamp for IaaS, which of the following can you view? (Select three.)

   a. The connectivity state of each host VPC

   b. The concurrent sessions going through the transit VPC

   c. The state of the transit VPC

   d. Detailed traffic statistics for the IPsec VPN connections between the transit VPC and each host VPC

10. Cloud onRamp for Colocation includes which of the following components? (Select all that apply.)

    a. Cisco CSP

    b. Cisco Catalyst 9K

    c. Cisco WAN Edge Cloud router

    d. Cisco Identity Services Engine

11. Cisco Cloud onRamp for Colocation supports which two types of service insertion?

    a. Control policy

    b. Local policy

    c. Data policy

    d. CLI policy

    e. OMP policy

Chapter 12

Cisco SD-WAN Design and Migration

This chapter covers the following topics:

- **Cisco SD-WAN Design Methodology:** This section covers the methodology behind SD-WAN design across the enterprise.

- **Cisco SD-WAN Migration Preparation:** This section of the chapter covers the recommended steps to prepare for migrating an enterprise to Cisco SD-WAN.

- **Cisco SD-WAN Data Center Design:** This section of the chapter goes into detailed data center design options and migration techniques.

- **Cisco SD-WAN Branch Design:** This section of the chapter goes into detailed branch design options and migration techniques.

- **Cisco SD-WAN Overlay and Underlay Integration:** This section of the chapter discusses optimal connectivity methods between migrated and non-migrated sites.

Cisco SD-WAN Design Methodology

For most organizations, migrating to Cisco SD-WAN is done in a brownfield environment and is a rare opportunity to re-architect the entire wide area network—an opportunity that might only present itself every decade or so. The WAN is such a critical and sensitive component of a typical organization's business that approvals for lengthy outages necessitated by pervasive design changes are a rarity. This means that it is common to see many years of incremental changes done by a multitude of individuals (with different skillsets and design methodologies) along with temporary fixes or adjustments that were never re-evaluated. Coupled with inconsistent configurations and connectivity models, this all results in complexities that, oftentimes, not a single person on staff may fully comprehend.

Designing your next-generation WAN is a golden opportunity to really dig deep into your WAN. You can learn how it operates, understand all the complexities and caveats that lie within, and propose a scalable, high-performing, easy-to-manage next-generation solution. It is crucial that the individuals leading the Cisco SD-WAN design and deployment dissect the existing WAN architecture in order to have a solid understanding of routing, topology, high availability, failover, and traffic flow patterns. This is in an effort to discover all the potential problems that may arise during migration. With this information on hand, you can utilize the incredibly comprehensive toolsets that are native to Cisco SD-WAN to effectively solve these problems intelligently and efficiently. During this process, the ultimate goal should be to remove unnecessary complexity, either through the evaluation of why that complexity existed initially and if it is still required or through replacing it with the intelligent application-aware and flexible fabric that Cisco SD-WAN offers.

The goal of this section is to present design recommendations garnered through years of Cisco SD-WAN implementation experience that will allow an organization to gracefully migrate to this new architecture while ensuring that the existing WAN is not disrupted. Ideally, the legacy WAN and the Cisco SD-WAN should be able to operate like ships in the night. An example of such a recommendation might be to selectively place Cisco SD-WAN hubs across your enterprise in order to act as transit points between migrated and non-migrated sites. Another such recommendation might be to provide high availability at branch sites through the use of Virtual Router Redundancy Protocol (VRRP) between an existing non-Cisco SD-WAN router and the new SD-WAN router.

Truthfully, there are many ways to migrate to Cisco SD-WAN—some better than others. In the end, however, everything always comes back to the fundamental routing and traffic engineering concepts we know and love today. Rest assured that Cisco SD-WAN is unparalleled in its support for comprehensive routing and traffic engineering toolsets, including best path manipulation options, advanced routing protocol features, filtering and tagging, and an overlay management protocol that provides traffic engineering flexibility like never before seen in the industry.

Cisco SD-WAN Migration Preparation

Preparing for Cisco SD-WAN migration can be thought of as one of the most important steps in the journey to Cisco SD-WAN enablement. Solid preparation will set an organization up for success during all stages of migration, including data center deployment, branch deployment, and policy configuration. Here are some of the most important preparations to make prior to beginning the migration:

■ **Data center and branch site physical and logical diagramming:** To have a good understanding of the existing architecture at data centers and branch sites, it is important to collect up-to-date physical and logical diagrams. This comes in handy to ensure there is sufficient power, cooling, rack space, and port density and to visualize how the Cisco SD-WAN routers will be connected to the existing network.

- **Collection of existing device configurations:** Collecting and reviewing the existing device configurations ensures that all considerations have been made around Cisco SD-WAN feature support and enablement. You don't want to realize, in the middle of a site turnup, that a specific feature you were using prior to the Cisco SD-WAN migration is not yet supported or that you have not made provisions to ensure that the feature would still function as designed after the migration.

- **Analysis of existing topology, routing, and traffic engineering:** Having a good understanding of existing routing and traffic engineering in the network will allow you insert Cisco SD-WAN into the network with ease. It will allow you to determine if anything needs to be changed during the migration or if a specific consideration needs to be made to ensure that the same network behaviors exist post-migration. This might include topology design, data center affinity configuration, equal-cost multipath routing, high availability configuration, and failover behavior.

- **Bandwidth capacity planning:** In many designs, the data center can become a hub either temporarily or permanently. For this reason, it is important to plan ahead to ensure that WAN bandwidth is sufficient pre- and post-migration.

- **Allocation of new physical and logical network resources:** In most cases, there will be new Cisco SD-WAN routers added to the data centers in the environment. 1Gbps or 10Gbps connectivity will need to be provided for the LAN and WAN. New subnets and IP addresses will need to be cut for transit and management networking. Planning this out ahead of time will allow you to scale consistently and contiguously.

- **Configuration of new or existing network entities:** Pre-stage the configuration required on new or existing network devices for a smooth deployment. This could include the configuration of a new VPN, VLANs, transit links, routing processes, prefix lists, route filters, autonomous systems, and so on.

- **Documentation of Cisco SD-WAN-specific configuration values:** As mentioned in previous chapters, the Cisco SD-WAN fabric has many unique values that must be configured in order to build the secure extensible network. This includes values such as the system IP, site ID, encapsulation type, and transport color. It may also include other parameters such as TLOC priority, TLOC weight, upstream and downstream transport bandwidth, GPS coordinates, hostnames, DNS, management loopbacks, and more. Deployment is much smoother when all of these variables are predefined and well documented.

- **Cisco SD-WAN policy design and configuration:** Cisco SD-WAN policy dictates the groups of interest (prefix-lists, site-lists, and so on), network topology, traffic engineering, overlay routing, Application-Aware Routing, security posture, quality of service classification, application visibility, and much more. Prior to migration, the Cisco SD-WAN policy should be fully thought out, predefined, configured, and activated so that sites rolling onto the fabric inherit the policy and adhere to it immediately. A well-constructed and executed policy will ensure that the migration is smooth and that post-migration performance is high.

■ **Cisco SD-WAN device template configuration and attachment:** One of the most powerful features of Cisco SD-WAN is templating. Device and feature templates allow for a modular and flexible configuration model that can be fully preconfigured and attached to Cisco SD-WAN routers before they even join the overlay. This allows you to pre-stage hundreds of remote sites with vManage, waiting and ready to push configuration as soon as the Zero Touch Provisioning process is initiated. Spend time prior to the deployment figuring out how these templates should be designed based on site structure and functionality, what configurations should be made as variables, and what those variable entries actually are.

Cisco SD-WAN Data Center Design

In nearly all cases, the data center is the first site to be migrated to Cisco SD-WAN. While there are many ways to design SD-WAN into the data center, the most commonly deployed and strongly recommended approach is to insert and run the solution in parallel with the existing WAN. This is accomplished by standing up Cisco SD-WAN routers alongside the current WAN Edge infrastructure (behind the Multiprotocol Label Switching [MPLS] CE/PE or Internet Edge routers) and providing the routers connectivity to WAN transports indirectly. This is especially true when an organization doesn't have the luxury of providing the Cisco SD-WAN router dedicated circuits or handoffs for all the transports already in service. It is common to see new SD-WAN routers leveraging private connectivity through an existing MPLS CE/PE router and public connectivity through an existing secure Internet Edge firewall. Figure 12-1 depicts this architecture.

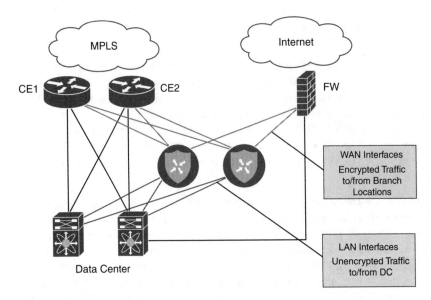

Figure 12-1 *Data Center Dedicated Pod*

This design allows the data center to act as a transit site for traffic between non-Cisco SD-WAN and Cisco SD-WAN sites and allows for a gradual migration of remote sites to Cisco SD-WAN without affecting the legacy network. This type of design also decouples and removes fate sharing between non-migrated and migrated sites, as they are landing on separate WAN Edges in the data center with distinct domains for routing and control. This same design can be used when migrating from legacy overlay technologies, such as Dynamic Multipoint VPN (DMVPN) and Group Encrypted Transport VPN (GETVPN), to Cisco SD-WAN.

In some environments, transiting the hub and the potential for added latency may be a concern. Designating multiple regional hubs as transit points for dedicated geographies and configuring the overlay routing to leverage these hubs intelligently is a common solution to this problem. For example, you may want to designate a US West hub, a US East hub, an APAC hub, and an EMEA hub. Each of these hubs handles the transit traffic between its respective regions.

An alternative, albeit much more complex and operationally expensive, method of solving the same latency problem is to mix overlay and underlay networking to provide a direct path between non-migrated and migrated sites. The section "Cisco SD-WAN Overlay and Underlay Integration" addresses this approach later in the chapter.

Transport-Side Connectivity

As detailed in the previous chapters, Cisco SD-WAN routers have a transport-side VPN and a service-side VPN that need to be integrated into the existing network. The most common way to integrate transport-side connections on the SD-WAN router into the network is by dedicating a single interface in VPN 0 per carrier/transport. Routing can be as simple as a default route to the next-hop carrier edge equipment or gateway. The only requirement is that the Cisco SD-WAN router transport interface IP address must be reachable on that particular underlay. For example, one way to leverage an existing MPLS transport as a part of the Cisco SD-WAN overlay could be by connecting a VPN 0 interface directly to the MPLS CE over a /30 transit network. A static default route toward that MPLS CE is configured, and the MPLS CE must advertise that transit network into the underlay. Leveraging an Internet transport is nearly an identical process, with the exception that the VPN 0 interface can connect to an existing DMZ or Internet Edge. It can be provided either a public or private IP address on a larger subnet, and it might or might not be behind network address translation (NAT). Figure 12-2 details this type of connectivity.

Note Cisco highly recommends that you ensure that all Cisco SD-WAN routers have connectivity into all transports being leveraged as a part of the overlay in order for high availability and for Application-Aware Routing to work optimally. Typically, this is achieved by providing direct connectivity from each Cisco SD-WAN router into every WAN or Internet Edge router or through the use of Transport Locator (TLOC) extensions.

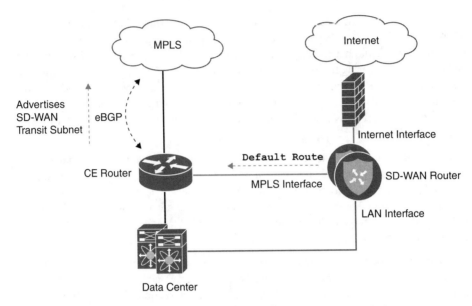

Figure 12-2 *Data Center Direct Transport Side*

> **Note** If NAT is required in order to provide connectivity to the Internet for the Cisco SD-WAN router, it is recommended to configure a static 1:1 NAT whenever possible to avoid tunnel bring-up issues that might occur in some uncommon scenarios.

Indirect connectivity to the Transport Edge is also supported and can be accomplished through the use of VLANs and dedicated interfaces or sub-interfaces. In this example, three VLANs are provisioned: VLAN 10 for the LAN service-side connection, VLAN 20 for the MPLS transport-side connection, and VLAN 30 for the transit between the data center core and the CE router. Routing to the WAN Edge remains the same as in the directly connected design. Figure 12-3 details this type of connectivity.

While this approach is simple and effective, utilizing a routing protocol on a VPN 0 transport interface may be required in some scenarios where direct connectivity to the edge of the WAN is not feasible, or some type of path manipulation or underlay traffic engineering is required. In this scenario, a routing protocol such as BGP or OSPF can be configured in order for the router to learn more specific prefixes, and traditional route policies can be applied inbound and outbound.

> **Note** When utilizing a routing protocol on VPN 0 to gain access to the underlay, it is important to ensure that the correct and optimal path to peer tunnel endpoints for that particular transport is followed through the local network. This is not a concern when connecting directly to the edge of the WAN since it always guarantees that the next hop will carry the tunnel traffic directly onto the desired transport.

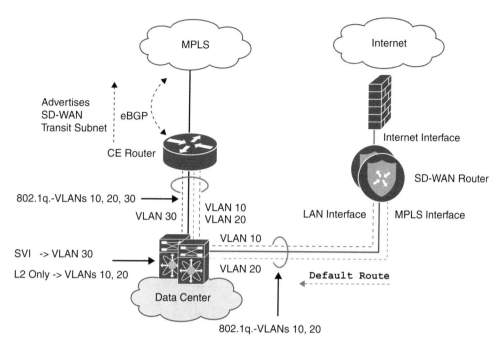

Figure 12-3 *Data Center Indirect Transport Side*

In some advanced topologies, an organization may want to leverage multiple CE routers and circuits to the same service provider for overlay connectivity and may also want to retain granular path selection and control via Cisco SD-WAN policy. Because a single transport color cannot be used twice by the same Cisco SD-WAN router, two alternative TLOC designs exist to meet these requirements.

Loopback TLOC Design

With this design, a loopback interface is configured as a conventional TLOC and is advertised towards both CE routers via two connections (one to each CE). This way, both CEs can reach the Cisco SD-WAN tunnel endpoint configured on the loopback, and the Cisco SD-WAN router can reach the underlay via both CEs. The drawback to this solution is that it requires additional routing complexity. In addition, because there is only a single color configured, path selection granularity via Cisco SD-WAN policy is also limited. It should be noted that two modes exist for this loopback—bind mode and the standard mode. In bind mode, the loopback is bound to a physical interface and traffic destined to the loopback will be carried to and from the mapped physical interface. This can be used when you have connected subnets on the transport side and want to use a loopback to form control connections and data tunnels. Figure 12-4 showcases the bind mode option.

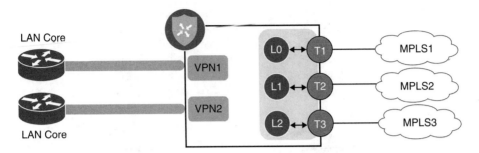

Figure 12-4 *Loopback TLOC Bind Mode*

In the standard mode, the loopback interface is not bound to any physical interface.
Traffic destined to the loopback can go through any physical interface based on a hash
lookup. Figure 12-5 illustrates this.

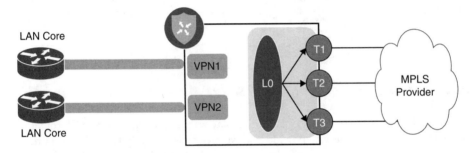

Figure 12-5 *Loopback TLOC Standard Mode*

Note It is important to note that in the normal mode, information collected via
Bidirectional Forwarding Detection (BFD) can be on any of the interfaces. Because of this,
the liveliness info can be seen as different for each remote site, even though the remote
sites are on the same local color at this location.

Service-Side Connectivity

Service-side connectivity is commonly achieved by provisioning one or two interfaces
in a service VPN and connecting them into the data center core. The data center core is
typically a point in the network where aggregation of legacy routes and Cisco SD-WAN
routes occurs and allows for natural transitive connectivity. Usually, a routing protocol
(such as BGP) is run between the Cisco SD-WAN router and the data center core so that
the Cisco SD-WAN router can learn both data center and legacy WAN routes as well as
advertise migrated site routes back toward the data center. External BGP (eBGP) is typically the protocol of choice, as it provides built-in loop prevention mechanisms (AS Path

and Site of Origin) and has a very flexible and comprehensive path selection algorithm. This algorithm can be manipulated in both directions via route policy. For instance, a route policy could match a set of routes from the overlay and set a local preference in order to influence the data center core. BGP Multi-Exit Discriminator (MED) can also be leveraged for path selection and is actually carried within Overlay Management Protocol (OMP) for vSmart path selection in the overlay. Lastly, BGP also provides granular tagging and filtering mechanisms through the use of route maps, prefix lists, and communities. Figure 12-6 details this type of connectivity.

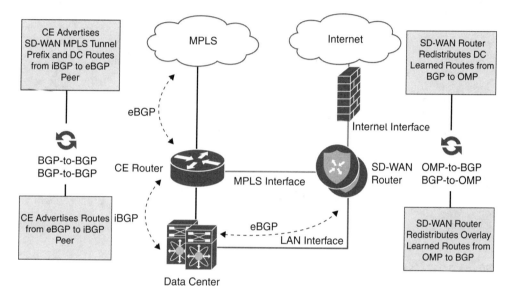

Figure 12-6 *Service-Side BGP*

While eBGP is usually the recommended service-side routing protocol, depending on the platform, Cisco SD-WAN supports iBGP, OSPF, EIGRP, Static Routing, and configuration of the first-hop redundancy protocol VRRP as well. Selecting an appropriate service-side routing protocol for an organization depends completely on the existing network configuration, required features and functionality, as well as operator comfort level.

In some instances, using a service-side routing protocol that is different from the existing routing protocol deployed in the data center core can add complexity—especially when it comes to route redistribution between the two protocols. To avoid this complexity, it may be worth considering the same routing protocol on the Cisco SD-WAN router that is found on the data center core. An alternative approach is to connect and peer the service side of the SD-WAN router directly with an existing WAN Edge router (that is, the MPLS CE) already running BGP. This way no additional redistribution needs to occur on the data center core since the WAN Edge router is already providing this functionality. Routes from the Cisco SD-WAN overlay would be learned by the WAN Edge router, and as long as the routing policy permits, they will be redistributed into the protocol running on the data center core. Conversely, the routes learned on the WAN Edge router from the data center core would be redistributed into BGP and learned by both the Cisco SD-WAN router and the service provider. The diagram in Figure 12-7 details this type of connectivity.

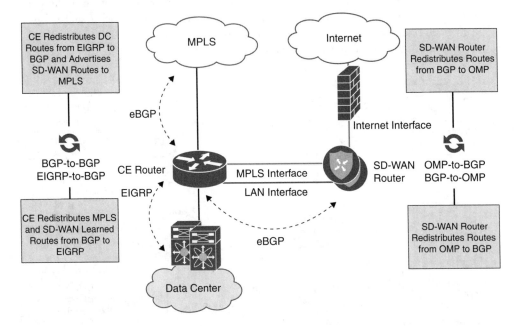

Figure 12-7   *Service-Side CE Integration*

Note   As with any other routing integration exercise, it is important to ensure that path selection occurs as desired, loops are avoided, failover performs as expected, and routing is not suboptimal. The aforementioned route manipulation, filtering, and tagging tools supported on Cisco SD-WAN should be leveraged to achieve this.

Keep in mind that while the aforementioned Cisco SD-WAN data center designs are the most recommended and widely deployed, many other methods of providing transport and service-side connectivity do exist and can be investigated for their value, specific to the organization's needs. For instance, sub-interfaces can be leveraged for both LAN and WAN connectivity if port density is a concern or if the requirement to transit through a switch of transparent firewall is applicable. In the end, we are dealing with traditional routing and switching, and many basic design concepts still hold true.

Finally, once all remote sites have been migrated to Cisco SD-WAN, it is possible (but not mandatory) to decommission the legacy WAN Edge routers terminating the transport circuits. The transport circuits will need to be re-terminated on the Cisco SD-WAN routers directly, which could potentially change the connectivity design and configuration.

In short, control plane connectivity will need to be provided to VPN 0 in some manner. While decommissioning the legacy WAN Edge routers might seem like the right thing to do, many organizations opt to keep them in service so as to retain compartmentalization and minimize complexity. Figure 12-8 illustrates this potential post-migration design where the WAN Edge router is removed.

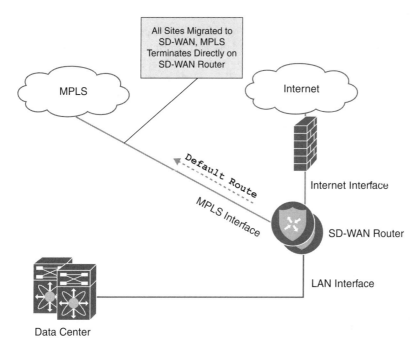

Figure 12-8 *Direct Transport Termination*

Note Refer to Cisco's published migration guides and Cisco Validated Design guides for detailed step-by-step instructions on migration and sample configurations.

Cisco SD-WAN Branch Design

Once the data centers have been migrated to Cisco SD-WAN, the branches can then follow suit. Cisco SD-WAN branch design can be a bit tricky when compared to the data center. Most organizations have branches that come in all shapes and sizes with different topologies, WAN connectivity models, high availability, and additional services (such as voice and security) that need to be taken into consideration. This migration to Cisco SD-WAN could be your opportunity to enforce standardized branch designs and make use of the power of device and feature templates. Because it would not be feasible to detail how to migrate every single branch design, the following portion of this chapter will focus on those designs that are most common.

Complete CE Replacement—Single Cisco SD-WAN Edge

The replacement (or upgrade) of a single WAN Edge to a Cisco SD-WAN Edge requires downtime, as there is no other router to forward traffic during the migration. This design is very straightforward and simply requires you to physically or logically terminate the circuits on the transport side of the Cisco SD-WAN Edge router as well as connect the service side to a LAN core. No routing protocol is required on the transport side, as a default route(s) is used to direct traffic to the respective carrier's next-hop IP address. Both Layer 2 and Layer 3 service-side connectivity is supported. The Cisco SD-WAN Edge can connect to the LAN via 802.1Q sub-interfaces and act as the Layer 3 gateway for all of the service-side VLANs. Alternatively, depending on the platform, the Cisco SD-WAN Edge can peer with a Layer 3 LAN core via BGP, OSPF, or EIGRP. In the Layer 2 design, the connected subnets are automatically redistributed into OMP and end-to-end reachability is achieved. Figure 12-9 depicts this type of L2 design.

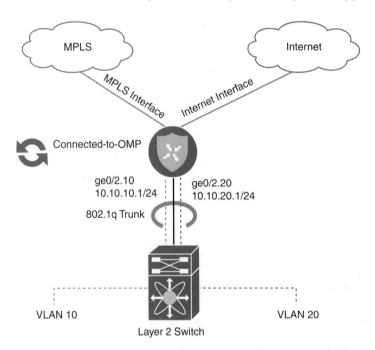

Figure 12-9   *Complete CE Replacement—Single Router L2 Branch*

In the Layer 3 design, the routing protocol used on the service side must be redistributed into OMP, and OMP must be redistributed into the service-side routing protocol explicitly. Figure 12-10 depicts these designs.

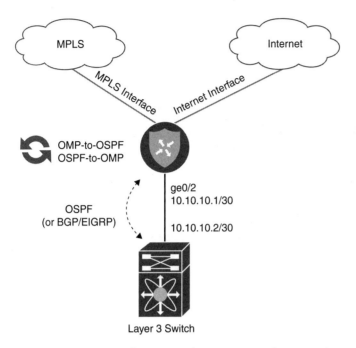

Figure 12-10   *Complete CE Replacement—Dual Router L3 Branch*

Complete CE Replacement—Dual Cisco SD-WAN Edge

Branches that require high availability might have two WAN Edge routers that need to be replaced. In this scenario, it is possible to provide a near hitless cutover since one router can be replaced or upgraded at a time while the other router continues forwarding traffic. Using routing protocol path manipulation and/or VRRP priority adjustment, it would be necessary to first ensure that all the inbound and outbound traffic is shifted to flow over the router not being initially upgraded. Once one of the routers is replaced or converted to Cisco SD-WAN, traffic can then be shifted over to the newly brought up Cisco SD-WAN overlay network while the other router is also replaced or upgraded.

In this design, depicted in Figure 12-11, both Cisco SD-WAN routers have access to all transports directly—either through multiple handoffs or by utilizing multiple IP addresses and WAN Edge switching infrastructure.

In addition, users have the choice of leveraging a routing protocol or VRRP and static routing for service-side integration, as illustrated in Figure 12-12.

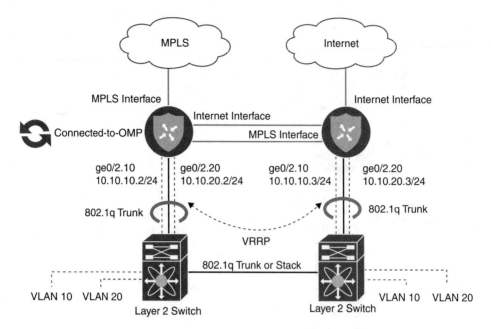

Figure 12-11   *Complete CE Replacement—Dual Router L2 Branch*

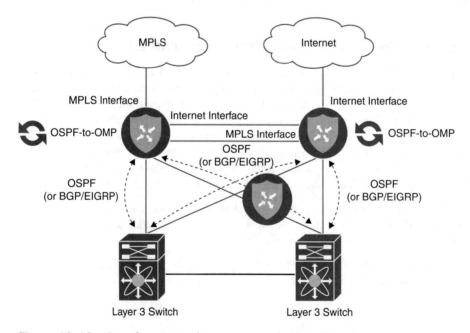

Figure 12-12   *Complete CE Replacement—Dual Router L3 Branch*

It is a very common scenario where only a single physical handoff and IP address is available on a given transport and yet that transport must be terminated into two Cisco SD-WAN routers. It is highly recommended that both routers have direct or indirect connectivity into all transports being leveraged for the Cisco SD-WAN overlay so that high availability and Application-Aware Routing performs optimally. In this scenario, a public color and private color TLOC extension can be used to meet the requirement. A TLOC extension is a direct or indirect connection between two Cisco SD-WAN routers that extends a locally terminated TLOC to a peer Cisco SD-WAN router. This allows a Cisco SD-WAN router to leverage a non-locally connected transport as a part of the Cisco SD-WAN overlay. TLOC extensions can be bidirectional (if both transports need to be extended) or unidirectional (if only a single transport is to be extended). Figure 12-13 showcases bidirectionally configured TLOC extensions.

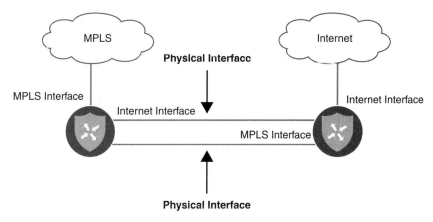

Figure 12-13 *TLOC Extension Dedicated Interfaces*

In some scenarios, it might be necessary to use sub-interfaces to configure TLOC extensions directly between two routers or through a LAN core, as there may not be sufficient physical interfaces free. Figure 12-14 depicts this option.

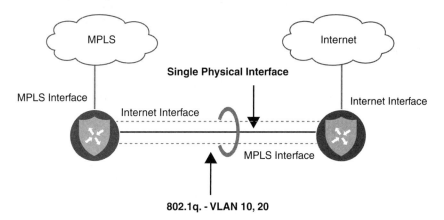

Figure 12-14 *TLOC Extension Sub-Interfaces*

In addition, IOS-XE-based Cisco SD-WAN routers support Layer 3 TLOC extension via GRE. This removes the requirement for the routers to have direct Layer 2 adjacency to one another. Hence, they can be geographically separated (as might be the case in a campus environment with multiple data centers).

When extending a private color via TLOC extension, you need to allocate a new enterprise routable transit network for the connection between Cisco SD-WAN routers. On the router extending the locally connected private transport, a dynamic routing protocol should be configured in VPN 0 and peered with the service provider in order to advertise reachability of the new transit network. A route policy can be configured in order to filter inbound and outbound routes so that only the transit network is advertised out and no other networks are learned. Remember, in most cases a default route toward the service provider is all that is needed for tunnel building and control plane connectivity. The Cisco SD-WAN router receiving the extension is not aware of anything different and configures its end of the extension as a standard private TLOC with a default route pointing toward the adjacent next-hop IP on the newly created transit network. Figure 12-15 highlights the private TLOC extension.

Note   Ensure that the Cisco SD-WAN router receiving the extension is able to build control connections through the peer by allowing the transit network to be learned by the data center (where the control components might reside) or allowed through the Internet Edge firewall, where it can egress to reach the cloud controller complex.

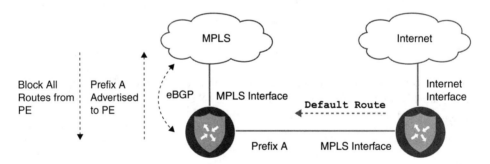

Figure 12-15   *TLOC Extension Private*

Extending a public color via TLOC extension is configured a bit differently than private TLOC extensions. With a public TLOC extension, any locally significant private transit network can be allocated between Cisco SD-WAN routers to build the connectivity. On the router extending the public transport, enable NAT on the egress interface toward the transport so that a unique private-to-public mapping can occur for both of the Cisco SD-WAN routers communicating with other remote sites and the controller complex. Like with a private TLOC extension, the Cisco SD-WAN router receiving the extension is not aware of anything different and configures its end of the extension as a standard public TLOC with a default route pointing toward the adjacent peer's next-hop IP on the newly created transit network. Figure 12-16 shows an example of a public TLOC extension.

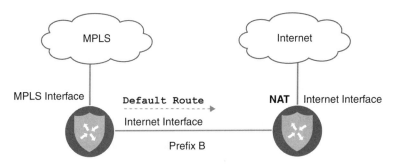

Figure 12-16 *Public TLOC Extension*

Integration with Existing CE Router

Sometimes a branch design calls for the integration of the Cisco SD-WAN router with an existing CE router. For example, some MPLS carriers provide and manage the CE router and, as a part of the contract, the router cannot be removed from the branch site. In other cases, the existing CE router may be providing other services for the branch that must stay intact post-migration (such as voice gateway functionality). In order for the Cisco SD-WAN router to have connectivity into the MPLS underlay, the design must be made such that the Cisco SD-WAN router can tunnel through the existing MPLS CE. This can easily be accomplished by connecting a physical or logical transport-side interface, configured as a private TLOC in a /30 transit network, to an available interface or sub-interface on the existing CE router. The Cisco SD-WAN router would then be configured with a default route pointing to the next-hop IP address of the MPLS CE. In addition, to provide connectivity to the tunnel endpoint IP address, the MPLS CE router will need to advertise this transit network into the underlay network via a routing protocol such as BGP. The diagram in Figure 12-17 depicts this scenario.

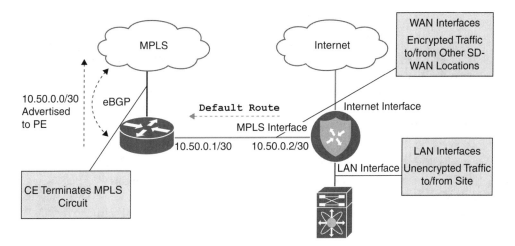

Figure 12-17 *Branch CE Integration*

Integration with a Branch Firewall

It isn't uncommon for a branch site to have a firewall terminating Internet connectivity and providing services such as Direct Internet Access (DIA), secure access control, zone-based segmentation, URL filtering, NAT, and IDS/IPS. Because of the routing DNA embedded in Cisco SD-WAN, there are all sorts of methods to integrate with a branch firewall, depending on the desired traffic flow and traffic visibility requirements.

Firewalls can be inserted at the WAN Edge north of the SD-WAN router, in parallel with the Cisco SD-WAN router or even behind the Cisco SD-WAN router in either a Layer 3 routed or Layer 2 transparent mode. Choosing the appropriate integration model depends on several factors, such as physical connectivity, logical traffic flow, traffic visibility requirements, segmentation architecture, NAT requirements, and so on. The only requirement for the Cisco SD-WAN router is that it is provided transport-side Internet connectivity for control and data plane tunnels as well as service-side LAN connectivity to receive and forward user traffic in and out of the overlay.

If all Internet-bound traffic is backhauled to a data center or hub egress point, firewall integration is very straightforward. In this design, the firewall terminates the Internet connection directly and provides access to the WAN Edge through either an allocated public IP address in a DMZ or through NAT (1:1 or PAT).

Note   While Cisco SD-WAN supports tunneling through several types of NAT, symmetric and port-restricted NAT can cause tunnel establishment failures (especially if this type of NAT is on both sides of the tunnel). Refer to the Cisco SD-WAN Validated Design guides for details on supported NAT configurations.

Secure DIA is one of the key benefits of migrating to Cisco SD-WAN, and the following design options are focused on providing this functionality.

In some networks, it is beneficial for the firewall to provide DIA functionality to clients since it may be running advanced security services such as URL filtering. With this design, Internet-bound traffic ingresses the service side of the Cisco SD-WAN router and, instead of performing NAT and local egress itself, the Cisco SD-WAN router forwards the traffic over another service-side link to the adjacent firewall. The firewall can then perform inspection, access control, and NAT prior to forwarding the traffic to the Internet. Traffic to private network destinations follows the Cisco SD-WAN overlay. This is most optimal when the Internet handoff has more than one physical port. Figure 12-18 details this design.

If a dedicated handoff to the Internet is not available, an alternative design would be to connect the transport side of the SD-WAN router to the firewall. In this way, the Cisco SD-WAN router has access to the Internet for control and data plane tunnels while also keeping a separate service-side connection to forward Internet-bound traffic to the firewall for processing and local egress. Figure 12-19 details this design.

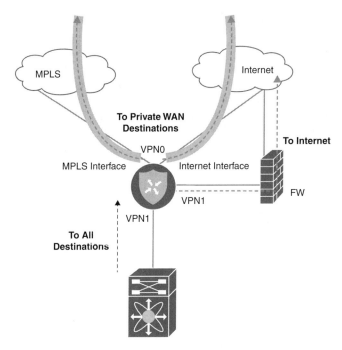

Figure 12-18 *DIA Through Firewall*

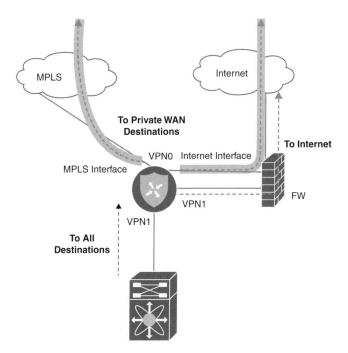

Figure 12-19 *Transport and DIA Through Firewall*

Lastly, if you wish for all traffic to flow through the Cisco SD-WAN router and only a single connection exists between the router and the firewall, consider the following design. With this design, only a single Cisco SD-WAN transport-side connection is required and is utilized for both tunneling and Direct Internet Access. NAT is configured on the Cisco SD-WAN transport-side interface connected to the firewall, and SD-WAN policy can selectively break out Internet-bound traffic to the underlay. The firewall receives this Internet-bound traffic and may perform a second NAT, as it sends the traffic to the Internet. It is important to note that because the Cisco SD-WAN router is performing NAT (which is a requirement for Cisco SD-WAN routers to break out traffic locally), the firewall loses visibility into the original client source IP addresses. Figure 12-20 showcases this design.

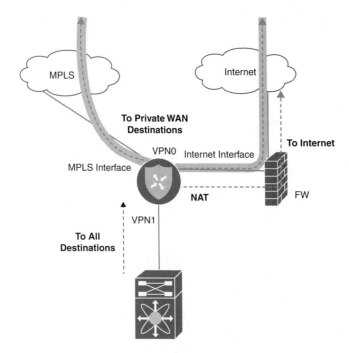

Figure 12-20   *Transport and DIA Through Firewall Single Link*

Integration with Voice Services

Some branch sites may have voice services, such as SRST, deployed that need to stay functional post-migration. As of version 19.2, there is no voice service integration on routers running Cisco SD-WAN code. Therefore, a dedicated voice gateway must be implemented. A dedicated voice gateway can be an existing CE not running Cisco SD-WAN code but providing SRST and PSTN services. Or it can be a completely separate router configured solely for voice. One such way to integrate a dedicated voice services gateway would be to connect it to the LAN as if it was a host on the network. Either a routing protocol can be configured to advertise the loopback IP address terminating the voice services or VRRP can be implemented to take over voice services should the Cisco SD-WAN overlay incur an outage. Figure 12-21 illustrates the L2 voice service integration design.

As mentioned earlier, voice services can also leverage L3 in this design. Figure 12-22 illustrates the L3 voice service integration design.

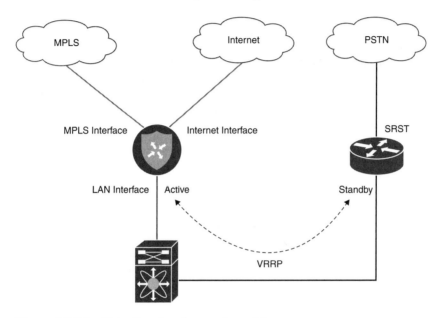

Figure 12-21   *Voice Services Integration—L2*

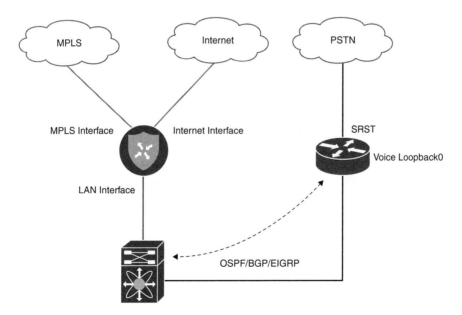

Figure 12-22   *Voice Services Integration—L3*

Cisco SD-WAN Overlay and Underlay Integration

This section details how integration between the underlay and overlay networks can be achieved through several design options.

Overlay Only

To minimize complexity and the potential for routing loops, it is recommended to adhere to the aforementioned designs for data center and branch migration. These designs have been proven time and time again to provide a graceful migration solution for organizations of all sizes, complexities, and applications types. Overlay-only-based migrations provide a clear and deterministic traffic flow and are easy to control, scale, and troubleshoot. Figure 12-23 showcases a Cisco SD-WAN site to a non-Cisco SD-WAN site design.

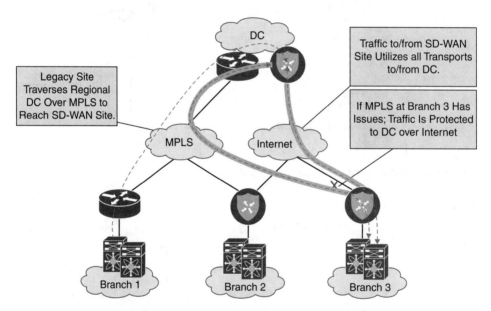

Figure 12-23 *SD-WAN to Non-SD-WAN Site Overlay-Only Traffic Flow*

Understanding the traffic flow from an SD-WAN site to another SD-WAN site is also critical. Figure 12-24 highlights the traffic flow patterns experienced when employing an overlay-only design.

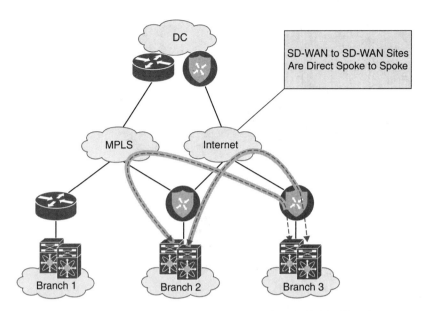

Figure 12-24   *SD-WAN to SD-WAN Site Overlay-Only Traffic Flow*

Overlay with Underlay Backup

If a branch site leveraging MPLS and Internet for the Cisco SD-WAN overlay has only a single Cisco SD-WAN router employed alongside the MPLS CE, another design opportunity exists that can allow for a backup path to become active if the Cisco SD-WAN router were to fail. For this design to work properly, routing needs to be manipulated in such a way that the site prefixes advertised by the MPLS CE into the underlay are less preferred in the network than those being advertised by the Cisco SD-WAN router into the overlay. Conversely, from the perspective of the LAN, the Cisco SD-WAN router should be the preferred path to reach remote networks. Figure 12-25 illustrates this.

This manipulation of path preference ensures that the traffic flow stays symmetric over the Cisco SD-WAN fabric and only utilizes the underlay if the Cisco SD-WAN router were to fail. One way to manipulate path preference for the underlay is to only advertise local site prefixes from the MPLS CE to the service provider using BGP AS path prepending. Figure 12-26 depicts this type of scenario. Naturally, the data center will advertise the remote site prefixes learned from the data center Cisco SD-WAN router into the underlay with a shorter AS path, ensuring a more preferred, symmetric flow.

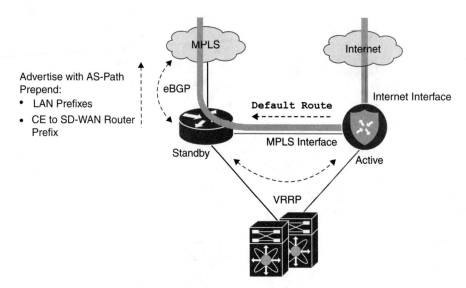

Figure 12-25 *Overlay with Underlay Backup—L2 Design*

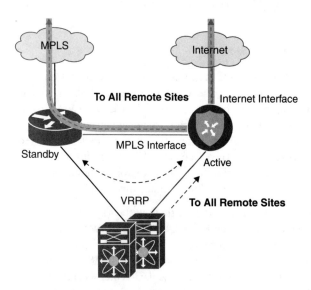

Figure 12-26 *Overlay with Underlay Backup—L2 Design Traffic Flow*

It should be noted that LAN-side routing also needs to be manipulated in order to prefer the Cisco SD-WAN router (for normal operation) and fail over to the MPLS CE during an impaired state. This can be accomplished in a Layer 2 branch by running VRRP between the Cisco SD-WAN router and the MPLS CE (with the Cisco SD-WAN router having the higher priority). Figure 12-27 depicts this design option.

In a Layer 3 branch design, advertising remote prefixes to the LAN with a more attractive metric from the Cisco SD-WAN router is also an option. Figure 12-28 illustrates.

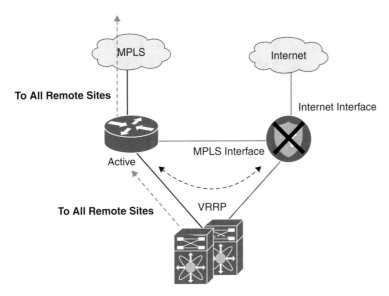

Figure 12-27   *Overlay with Underlay Backup—L2 Design Traffic Flow During Failover*

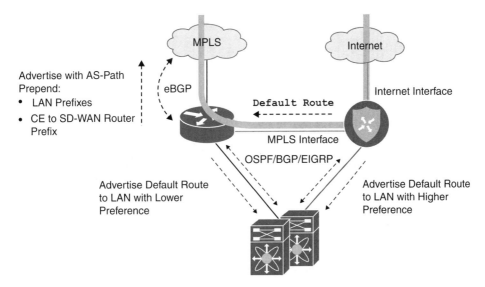

Figure 12-28   *Overlay with Underlay Backup—L3 Design*

Finally, for the underlay backup architecture to work correctly, it is important to do some filtering at the data center. To ensure that remote branch routes are learned and preferred through the overlay (and asymmetry or route looping is avoided), create a filter outbound toward the Cisco SD-WAN router to limit the learned routes to those originating from the data center. Make sure to also advertise a default or summary into the overlay. Figure 12-29 depicts this design consideration.

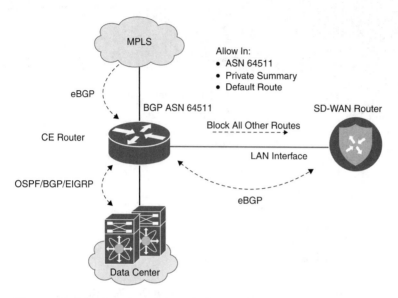

Figure 12-29   *Overlay with Underlay Backup—Data Center Considerations*

Figure 12-30 reviews the traffic flow patterns experienced when employing an overlay with an underlay backup design.

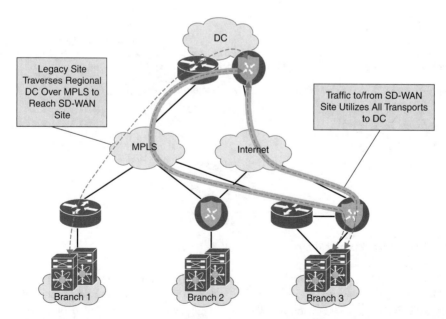

Figure 12-30   *Overlay with Underlay Backup Traffic Flow*

It is also important to see the traffic flow during a failover condition. This helps visualize the path the traffic will take during a failure scenario. Figure 12-31 highlights the backup traffic flow during a failover event.

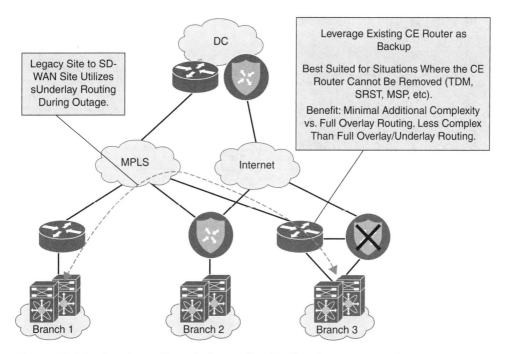

Figure 12-31 *Overlay with Underlay Backup Traffic Flow During Failover*

Full Overlay and Underlay Integration

For some organizations, due to strict application latency requirements, select branches migrated to Cisco SD-WAN may need to communicate directly to non-migrated branches through a lower latency underlay path. For example, CIFS traffic can be relatively sensitive to latency and may suffer by going through an additional hop at the data center for transit to another site. To meet this latency requirement, it is possible to architect the solution in such a way that the overlay path is used to communicate with migrated sites and the underlay path is used to communicate with non-migrated sites. In contrast to the aforementioned design options, this section showcases the traffic patterns experienced when employing a full overlay and underlay integration design. Figure 12-32 shows routing from a non-Cisco SD-WAN site to a Cisco SD-WAN site.

It is also critical to see the traffic flow of a Cisco SD-WAN site to another Cisco SD-WAN site while leveraging a full overlay and underlay integration design. Figure 12-33 illustrates this concept.

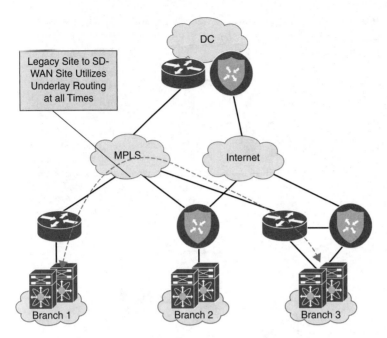

Figure 12-32   *Full Overlay with Underlay Routing Legacy Site to SD-WAN Site Traffic Flow*

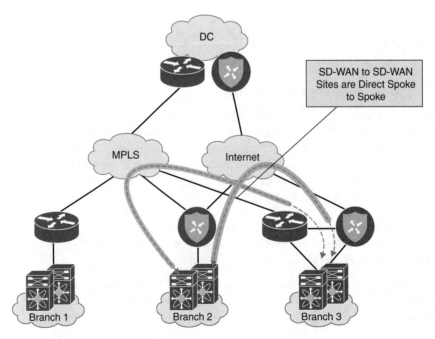

Figure 12-33   *Full Overlay with Underlay Routing Cisco SD-WAN Site to Cisco SD-WAN Site Traffic Flow*

Note   In most cases, configuring full overlay and underlay integration at every site will add a significant amount of routing complexity to the network and, in some environments, can be a challenge to scale and control. Typically, voice applications can handle 300ms of round-trip latency and therefore this design might not even be required.

One way to implement full overlay and underlay integration at a branch is through the use of an existing MPLS CE router. This design is similar to the MPLS CE integration solution discussed previously, save for the exception that the CE continues to advertise the site prefixes into the MPLS underlay at the same time that the Cisco SD-WAN router advertises the site prefixes into the overlay. Both the MPLS CE router and Cisco SD-WAN router advertise prefixes from the WAN into the LAN. However, Cisco SD-WAN migrated site prefixes (including data center prefixes learned via the MPLS CE) should be advertised with a more attractive metric so as to retain traffic symmetry and to force Cisco SD-WAN sites to talk to each other via the overlay. While any routing protocol can be used to achieve this design, iBGP is recommended for its native anti-transit logic. If any other routing protocol is used, tagging and filtering mechanisms should be employed so as to avoid making the branch into a transit site. Figure 12-34 shows this design option.

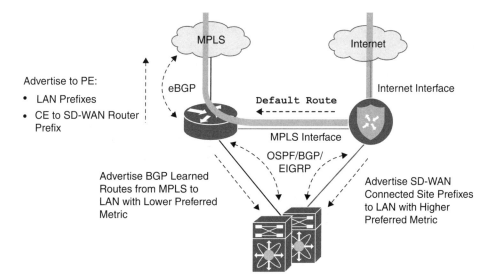

Figure 12-34   *Full Overlay with Underlay Routing CE Integration*

Figure 12-35 shows the traffic flow for a branch with two transports. Traffic can flow directly through an Internet interface as well as an interface that is connected to an existing MPLS CE router.

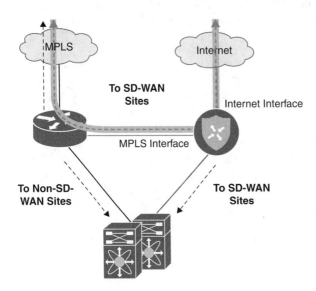

Figure 12-35 *Full Overlay with Underlay Routing CE Integration Traffic Flow*

Full overlay and underlay integration can also be achieved when no dedicated MPLS CE is present and only a Cisco SD-WAN router exits at the branch. The same principles apply as if there was a separate CE terminating the MPLS connection; however, TLOC termination on the SD-WAN router is a bit different. Instead of configuring the TLOC on the physical interface connected to the MPLS carrier like normal, a loopback interface is created in VPN 0 and configured as the TLOC. The physical WAN interface is bound to the loopback by using the aforementioned "bind" command. A routing protocol is configured between the Cisco SD-WAN router and the carrier in order to advertise the tunnel interface IP address for control and data plane tunnel termination. A VPN 0 interface is then configured and connected to a downstream (LAN-side) Layer 3 switch or looped back into a service VPN interface on the Cisco SD-WAN router. Finally, a routing protocol can be configured on this transit link to learn and advertise routes between the overlay. This configuration, in effect, creates a route leak between VPNs. Figure 12-36 shows this design option.

Figure 12-37 illustrates the traffic flow for a site location with no integration with a CE device.

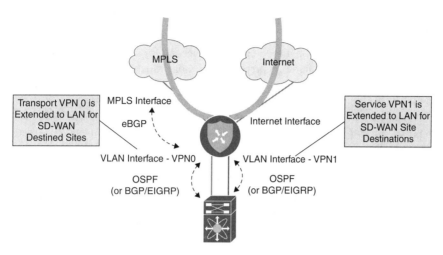

Figure 12-36 *Full Overlay with Underlay Routing Without CE Integration*

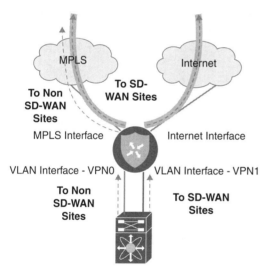

Figure 12-37 *Full Overlay with Underlay Routing Without CE Integration Traffic Flow*

Note Additional tagging, filtering, and best path manipulation may be required at both the data center and the remote sites participating in full overlay/underlay connectivity, depending on how routing between the overlay and underlay is accomplished. From a routing perspective, there are many valid ways to achieve full overlay and underlay integration. Each of these options deserves special attention to detail so as not to cause route looping and suboptimal routing. Every environment will come with its own set of complexities and caveats, and it therefore behooves you to think through all of the different possible scenarios specific to your organization's network that could affect the flow of traffic during and after migration.

Summary

This chapter covered the design methodology recommended for a migration to Cisco SD-WAN. The importance of migration preparation, validated data center and branch designs, as well as overlay and underlay integration techniques was discussed. Migrating to Cisco SD-WAN requires a solid discovery and design period where ample time is spent understanding the existing network thoroughly while also thinking about its future state. Preparation, prior to deploying the Cisco SD-WAN network, is key in ensuring that data center and branch cutovers are executed flawlessly. Understanding the benefits and caveats of all the supported data center and branch designs allows the network architect to select one that meets the requirements of the business and provides additional Cisco SD-WAN functionalities, while maintaining resiliency and performance. All networks have a degree of complexity, and the goal is to migrate to Cisco SD-WAN gracefully without increasing this complexity.

Review All Key Topics

Review the most important topics in the chapter, noted with the Key Topic icon in the outer margin of the page. Table 12-1 lists these key topics and the page numbers on which each is found.

Table 12-1 *Key Topics*

Key Topic Element	Description	Page
Section	Loopback TLOC Design	465
Paragraph	TLOC Extension Concept	473
Section	Cisco SD-WAN Overlay and Underlay Integration	480

Chapter Review Questions

1. Most SD-WAN deployments are done in a greenfield environment.
   a. True
   b. False

2. What are some reasons for a migration to Cisco SD-WAN? (Choose three.)
   a. Application-Aware Routing
   b. Centralized policy
   c. Fast convergence
   d. Scalability
   e. Improved performance

3. Migration to SD-WAN is a hard cut, where all data centers and remote sites are migrated simultaneously.
   a. True
   b. False

4. What are some of the most important preparations that should be made prior to migration? (Choose three.)

   a. Reloading all routers

   b. SD-WAN device template configuration and attachment

   c. Ensuring all routers have a maintenance contract

   d. Analysis of existing topology, routing, and traffic engineering

   e. SD-WAN policy design and configuration

5. What are some classification criteria that can be configured in a list in preparation for policy deployment? (Choose three.)

   a. SNMP OID lists

   b. Prefix-lists

   c. Site-lists

   d. Interface lists

   e. VPN ID lists

6. What type of SD-WAN-specific configuration values should be defined prior to migration? (Choose three.)

   a. Site-IDs

   b. VPN IDs

   c. OSPF hello and dead timers

   d. BGP med values

   e. TLOC colors

7. Standing up SD-WAN routers alongside the current WAN Edge infrastructure is the preferred method for data center SD-WAN router integration.

   a. True

   b. False

8. From a design perspective, how can you improve latency when migrating to SD-WAN while transiting hubs?

   a. Enable TCP optimization

   b. Move the sites closer to each other

   c. Designate multiple regional hubs as transit points

   d. Use dedicated Layer 2 circuits

9. The most common way to integrate transport-side connections on the SD-WAN router into the network is by sharing a single interface in VPN 0 for all carriers/transports.

   a. True

   b. False

10. What is the difference between bind and unbind mode when configuring a loopback TLOC?

   a. Bind mode forms control connections, and unbind mode does not.

   b. Unbind mode takes less router CPU than bind mode.

    c. Unbind mode allows for public and private color connectivity, whereas bind mode does not.

    d. Blnd mode ensures traffic destined to the loopback will be carried to and from the mapped physical interface. Unbind mode does not have this behavior.

11. What are three different Cisco SD-WAN branch design options?

    a. Complete CE replacement with a single SD-WAN router

    b. SD-WAN router running inline bridge mode

    c. Integration with existing CE router

    d. Complete CE replacement with dual SD-WAN routers

12. A TLOC extension can only be configured for private colors.

    a. True

    b. False

13. SD-WAN integration with existing firewalls and voice services is not supported.

    a. True

    b. False

14. Which routing protocols are supported for service-side integration with the LAN? (Choose three.)

    a. OMP

    b. OSPF

    c. ISIS

    d. EIGRP

    e. ODR

    f. eBGP

15. What important consideration needs to be made at the data center if implementing overlay and underlay integration designs?

    a. Only OSPF should be used.

    b. ECMP should be configured.

    c. SD-WAN routers should be running the latest code.

    d. Filtering toward the SD-WAN router should be configured.

Chapter 13

Provisioning Cisco SD-WAN Controllers in a Private Cloud

This chapter covers the following topics:

- **SD-WAN Controller Functionality Recap:** This section is a recap of the SD-WAN controllers' functionality.

- **Certificates:** This section covers the various options for certificate management in the SD-WAN solution.

- **vManage Controller Deployment:** This section covers the deployment of the vManage controller. vManage is utilized for day-to-day management and monitoring of the Cisco SD-WAN fabric.

- **vBond Controller Deployment:** This section covers installation and setup of the vBond controller. vBond is the component that authenticates and brings all the components in the SD-WAN fabric together.

- **vSmart Controller Deployment:** This section covers deployment options for vSmart in a private cloud, on-premises lab environment. vSmart is the control plane of the SD-WAN fabric.

SD-WAN Controller Functionality Recap

This section is meant to provide a recap of the SD-WAN controllers' functionality. There are three distinct controllers in the SD-WAN fabric:

- **Management plane:** The management plane is provided by vManage. vManage is the single pane of glass for onboarding, provisioning, monitoring, and troubleshooting. Once the SD-WAN components are deployed, this is where most day-to-day operations will be performed.

- **Orchestration plane:** The orchestration plane functionality is provided by the vBond controller. vBond authenticates and authorizes all of the SD-WAN components. The vBond controller also provides connectivity information about the vSmart and vManage controllers. For environments that utilize NAT, vBond also provides NAT traversal capabilities.

- **Control plane:** The control plane component is referred to as vSmart. The vSmart controller provides all routing and data plane policies to the routers in the environment.

This chapter covers certificate deployment options as well as the installation procedure for each of the SD-WAN controllers. The information in this chapter will be applicable for IT teams looking to deploy the solution within the following environments:

- On-premises

- Private cloud

- Lab

Before the SD-WAN controllers can be deployed, a brief discussion of Certificate Authorities (CAs) is warranted. Certificates issued by trusted CAs are an important component of control plane authentication between controller and WAN Edge routers. Each controller and WAN Edge router is equipped with a certificate (signed by a mutually trusted CA) that it can use to identify itself to other solution elements. Should you choose to manage this functionality yourself, there are plenty of enterprise CA options available. Some common choices are Microsoft Certificate Services, OpenSSL, and even Cisco Identity Services Engine. Choosing which enterprise CA to use is not in scope for this book. However, automatic and manual enrollment with the Cisco Managed CA, Symantec/DigiCert CA, and an enterprise CA will be discussed in this section.

Keep in mind that the process outlined in this chapter is only relevant should you choose not to have Cisco manage this functionality. In most circumstances, when the decision is made to move forward with cloud-managed controllers, Cisco deploys and manages the controller infrastructure (including certificates) for the organization. With an on-premises, private cloud, or lab deployment model, the IT team will be responsible for managing the infrastructure. This includes controller redundancy, software upgrades, and backups. Cisco SD-WAN controllers are delivered as virtual appliances. Supported hypervisors for this deployment method are VMware ESXi and KVM. Once the virtual appliances are deployed, the process is the same for ESXi and KVM. All three controller virtual appliances (OVAs) can be downloaded from Cisco.com. Going forward, the three deployment methods discussed (on-premises, lab, and private cloud) will simply be referred to as *on-premises*. Screenshots might be slightly different, depending on the version that is being implemented. In this section, we'll be installing the latest version, 19.2. Figure 13-1 illustrates the differences between cloud and on-premises.

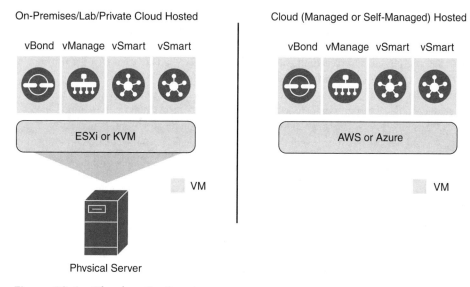

On-Premises/Lab/Private Cloud Hosted

vBond vManage vSmart vSmart

ESXi or KVM

VM

Physical Server

Cloud (Managed or Self-Managed) Hosted

vBond vManage vSmart vSmart

AWS or Azure

VM

Figure 13-1 *Cloud vs. On-Premises*

The installation process has a specific order that needs to be followed. Details around this will be discussed in each individual section. The high-level order of operations is as follows:

Step 1. Deploy virtual machines for vManage, vBond, and vSmart.

Step 2. Bootstrap and configure the vManage controller.

Step 3. Bootstrap and configure the vBond controller.

Step 4. Bootstrap and configure the vSmart controller.

Step 5. Install licensing file or sync with Cisco Smart Account.

> **Note** Retrieving licensing is beyond the scope of this book. Your Cisco Account Team or Partner can answer any questions about licensing.

The Cisco SD-WAN solution strives to achieve the highest level of security, and no component is allowed on the fabric unless it has been authenticated and authorized. There is a detailed process that each of these components goes through when coming online. This is discussed, in detail, in Chapter 3, "Control Plane and Data Plane Operations." At a high level, each component will authenticate the others using their certificates. Once this process is complete, the control, management, and orchestration planes are established. Full configuration will then be pushed to the vSmart and vBond controllers from vManage.

When controllers are deployed on-premises, special considerations need to be made. If requirements call for deployment of the controllers in a data center, then routing must be in place to reach the vManage, vBond, and vSmart from the WAN Edges. This means that all WAN Edges and controllers must be able to reach the VPN 0 transport interfaces of other solution elements via their own VPN 0 transport interfaces. There are a couple of ways that this can be achieved. Namely, controller VPN 0 prefixes can be leaked into the underlay routing table, or a default route can be installed to influence controller traffic to the data center. By leaking these VPN 0 routes, the controllers will have connectivity between the elements. Alternatively, for deployments where the controllers need to be reachable via the Internet, you can utilize NAT. In such a case, vBond will require a static 1:1 NAT while other controllers can be behind PAT. If you recall, vBond facilitates NAT traversal and detects when other solution elements are behind NAT. Hence, vBond must be directly reachable from the Internet to perform this function. Another option for deployment is to place the controllers in a DMZ, wherein publicly routable addressing is applied directly to the controller VPN 0 interfaces. The same rules apply for routing with this design, however. Specifically, solution elements should have accessibility to these addresses via their VPN 0 transport interface. For transports that don't need to facilitate control connectivity to the controllers (such as with MPLS, wherein the controllers are only reachable via the Internet), you must restrict control connections via the **max-control-connections 0** command. This command is applied to the transport tunnel interface.

Certificates

As discussed in Chapter 4, "Onboarding and Provisioning," certificates are critical to the secure integrity of the Cisco SD-WAN solution. Not only does the solution use a whitelist model to authenticate the solution components, but each controller also provides its identity via a certificate. Each controller (vManage, vBond, and vSmart) will mutually authenticate each other via these certificates and build their control plane connections. This process is shown in Figure 13-2 but will be discussed in more detail later in this chapter. Likewise, WAN Edges will also validate these certificates to ensure that these controllers are authenticated and authorized.

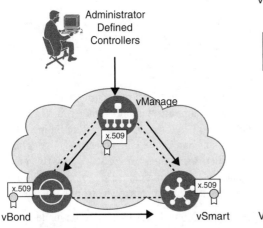
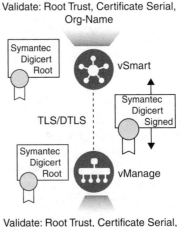

Figure 13-2 *Controller-Based Connectivity*

Controllers are administratively defined, and each controller is manually configured to connect to the vBond. It is from this connection that the solution components learn about each other. Two whitelist files are generated and distributed by vManage. The first whitelist is a controller list that is created by manually adding the controllers to the vManage GUI. This list gets distributed to vBond, where it is pushed to the vSmart controllers during the authentication process. The controller list contains the certificate serial numbers for each of the controllers. These serial numbers are used as part of the authentication process. The second whitelist identifies the approved WAN Edges in the environment. This list can be downloaded from the PnP portal at https://software.cisco.com or can be retrieved via the Sync Smart Account mechanism within vManage. Once retrieved, the list is distributed to the other controllers by vManage. Figure 13-3 depicts these two processes.

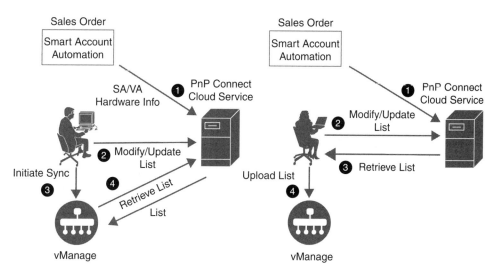

Figure 13-3 *Upload WAN Edge List Processes*

Before any whitelists can be exchanged, however, controllers must authenticate each other. The following process elaborates on the authentication that occurs. Once authentication is complete, secure control plane connectivity can be achieved and whitelist information can be distributed to controller elements.

1. First, the controller to be authenticated presents its certificate. Certificate trust will be validated by checking to make sure the certificate presented is signed by a mutually trusted root CA. Note that the root CA certificate chain must be installed on all devices before this can occur. By default, root certificates are already installed for the Symantec, DigiCert, and Cisco CAs. Hence, manually installing the root CA chain is only required when using your own CA. This is a two-way authentication, and each controller authenticates the other one in parallel. See Figure 13-4 for an example between the vBond and vSmart controllers.

2. Inside the sending controller's certificate is the organization name. This value is checked against the locally configured one. This organization name needs to match enterprise-wide.

3. The receiving controller verifies the peer's certificate serial number against the authorized whitelist received from vManage. Note that when the vBond is being authenticated, this serial number is not used.

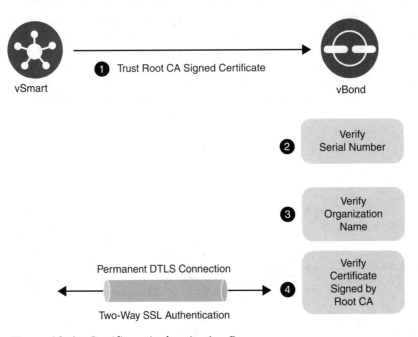

Figure 13-4 *Certificate Authentication Process*

Obviously, before a controller can authenticate itself with a certificate, it must first obtain one. The first step in obtaining a certificate is to generate a certificate signing request (CSR) from each controller. This process can be done when the controller is added to vManage or the network administrator can perform this operation manually via the controller's CLI. Once the certificate is signed, it can either be installed manually or automatically on the controller. When onboarding virtual components such as vEdge Cloud devices, things are a little different. vManage will act as a sub-CA to the root CA and sign the certificates for these devices. Figure 13-5 illustrates the automatic enrollment process, though there are multiple ways to perform the certificate signing process:

■ **Automated certificate signing request with Symantec/DigiCert CA:** For this option, a CSR is generated via the vManage GUI for each controller and automatically sent to the Symantec/DigiCert CA. Once this is complete, a Cisco CSOne case needs to be opened and the signing request will be authorized. After the signing request is authorized, the Symantec/DigiCert CA will generate certificates. vManage will automatically retrieve the certificate(s) and install them on the corresponding controllers. The root chain for the Symantec and DigiCert CA is preloaded with the controller and does not require any additional attention.

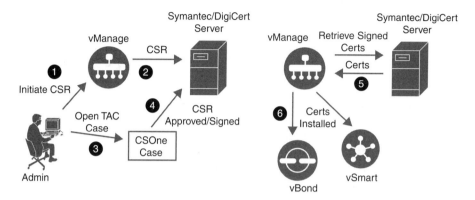

Figure 13-5 *Automatic Enrollment for Symantec/DigiCert Certificates*

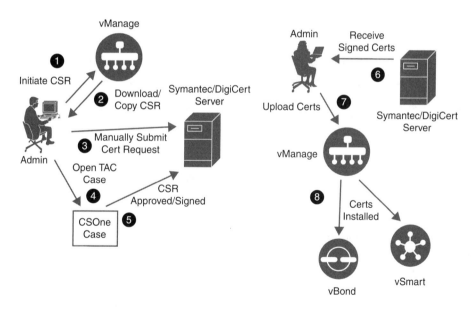

Figure 13-6 *Manual Enrollment for Symantec/DigiCert Certificates*

- **Manual certificate signing request with Symantec/DigiCert CA:** With the manual option, shown in Figure 13-6, the administrator will generate a CSR for each controller and manually upload the file to the Symantec/DigiCert portal. A CSOne case will then need to be opened and, once the CSR is authorized, the administrator will receive the certificate via email or via download link. The administrator will then need to manually install this certificate via the vManage GUI. vManage will then push the certificate to the relevant controller. This type of deployment would be utilized if the controllers have no Internet connectivity or a firewall is blocking HTTP/HTTPS connectivity to the Symantec/DigiCert portal. As mentioned previously, the root chain for the Symantec and DigiCert CA is preloaded on the controllers and no additional attention is needed.

- **Automatic certificate signing request with Cisco PKI CA:** This option requires the controllers to be running version 19.1 or later. This option is similar to the automatic Symantec/DigiCert method. The only difference, however, is that once the request is submitted to the Cisco PKI, a CSOne case does not need to be opened. The request will be signed automatically. Likewise, vManage will retrieve and install the certificate for each of the controllers. Figure 13-7 depicts this process. This is the recommended method, as no intervention is needed. As with the Symantec/DigiCert methods, the root chain for the Cisco PKI CA is preloaded with the controller and no additional attention is necessary.

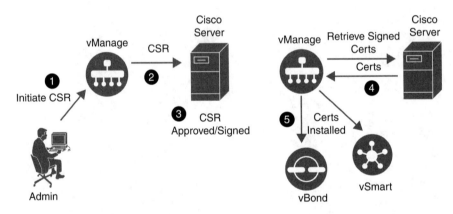

Figure 13-7 *Automatic Enrollment for Cisco PKI Certificates*

- **Manual certificate signing request with Cisco PKI CA:** This option requires the controllers to be running version 19.1 or later. This option is identical to the automated Cisco PKI method; however, in the absence of Internet connectivity, an administrator will need to manually generate and upload the CSR to the PnP portal at https://software.cisco.com. Once the CSR is authorized, the administrator will need to manually retrieve the certificate(s) from the PnP portal and upload it to vManage, where it will be distributed to the other controllers. Figure 13-8 highlights this process. As with all other options, the root chain for the Cisco PKI CA is preloaded on the controllers and no additional attention is required.

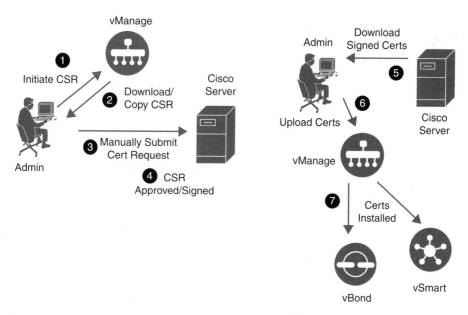

Figure 13-8 *Manual Enrollment for Cisco PKI Certificates*

- **Certificate signing request with Enterprise CA:** If the deployment will be utilizing an enterprise CA for certificates, the process is similar to the manual steps listed previously with some slight differences. Specifically, the administrator will need to install the root chain from the enterprise CA on each controller. Once this is completed, a certificate signing request can be generated for the corresponding controllers via the vManage GUI. The administrator would then download the CSR and submit the request for signing to the enterprise CA. Once the CSR is authorized and a certificate is generated, the same process noted previously can be used to upload the signed certificate to the vManage GUI for the appropriate controller. Figure 13-9 illustrates this process.

Note For the following sections, OpenSSL will be utilized as an enterprise CA.

 vManage Controller Deployment

Before the vManage controller can be deployed, the virtual environment must be prepped. The network administrator should plan to have IP address information for the VPN 0 (control plane) interface and the VPN 512 (out-of-band management) interface.

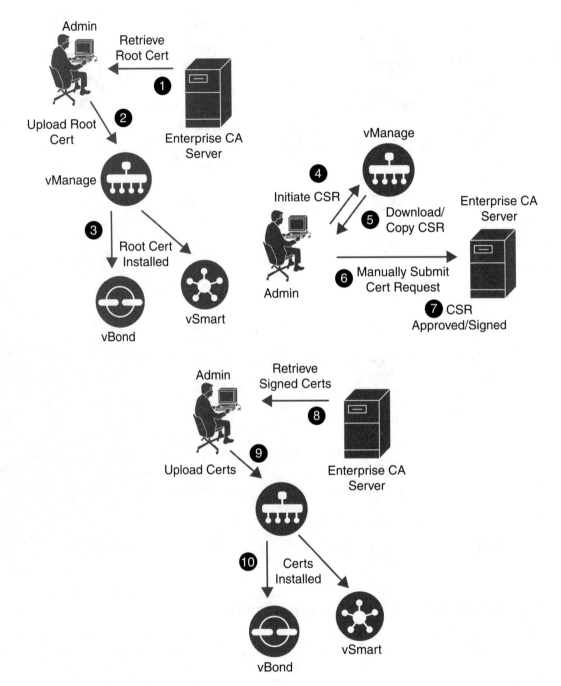

Figure 13-9 *Manual Enrollment for Enterprise CA*

VPN 512 addressing is not a requirement but, depending on the design, it may be necessary (especially if the controllers are in an isolated network, such as a DMZ).

For the remainder of this section, we'll use the subnets noted in Table 13-1.

Table 13-1   *Controller Subnets*

VPN	Network	Subnet Mask
VPN 0	209.165.200.224	255.255.255.224
VPN 512	192.168.1.0	255.255.255.0

In this example, the version being deployed is 19.2; however, the process is the same for earlier versions as well. Consider reviewing the certificate sections discussed previously as well, as there are many options to consider prior to building out the control infrastructure. For our examples, we'll be using an enterprise CA.

The remainder of this section will cover deployment of the vManage controller on VMware ESXi. Here are the steps being performed:

Step 1.   Deploy virtual machine for vManage.

Step 2.   Bootstrap and configure vManage controller.

Step 3.   Set the organization name and vBond address in vManage.

Step 4.   Install the root CA certificate.

Step 5.   Generate, sign, and install the certificate onto the vManage controller.

The process to install the vManage virtual machine is similar to deploying any other kind of virtual machine. The Open Virtual Appliances (OVAs) for the controllers can be downloaded from https://www.cisco.com. Once the OVA is deployed, an additional hard disk will need to be added for the database. This drive needs to be at least 100 GB.

Note   At the time of publishing, the OVA location is https://software.cisco.com/download/home/286320995/.

Step 1: Deploy vManage Virtual Appliance on VMware ESXi or KVM

After installing the OVA, right-click on the virtual machine and select **Edit Settings** (see Figure 13-10).

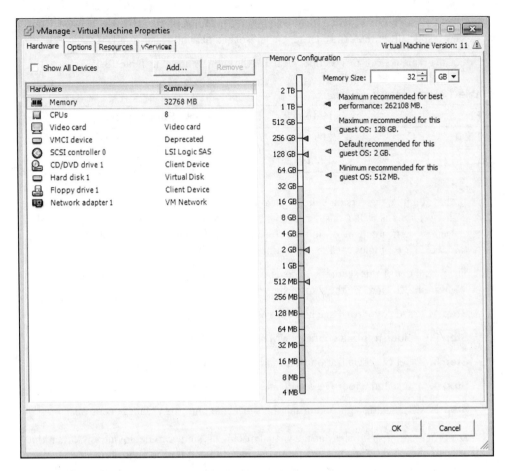

Figure 13-10 *VMware Settings Window*

Click the **Add** button, select **Hard Disk**, and click **Next** (see Figure 13-11).

Select **Create a new virtual disk**, click **Next**, and set the size to at least 100 GB. Click **Next** until you are back to the **Virtual Machine Properties** window. Click **OK** to save the settings (see Figure 13-12).

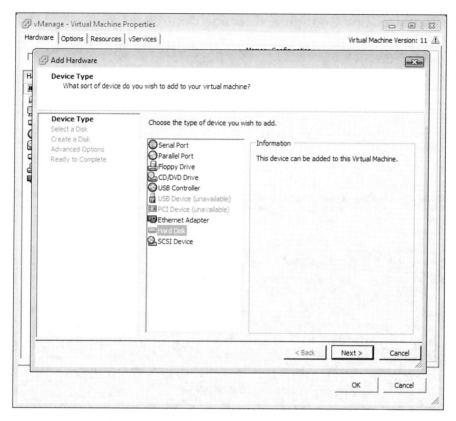

Figure 13-11   *Add Hardware Wizard*

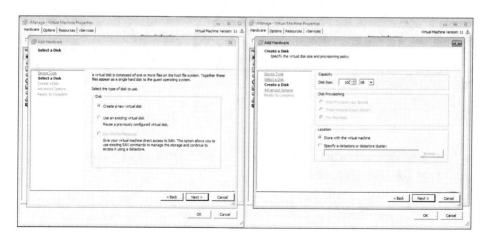

Figure 13-12   *Create New Virtual Disk*

Once you are finished, power up the virtual machine.

Step 2: Bootstrap and Configure vManage Controller

Now that the vManage virtual machine is properly configured and powered up, the network administrator can begin to configure basic settings.

Open the VMware console for this virtual machine and (once the system prompts you for a login) enter the default username and password of **admin**. Upon initial login, you will be prompted to format the virtual disk that was just added. Select the disk and type **yes** to format it. Depending on the size of this virtual disk, it could take some time. Once this process completes, the system will reboot automatically. Figure 13-13 illustrates the initial bootup process.

Figure 13-13   *Initial Bootup*

Step 3/4: Set Organization Name and vBond Address in vManage; Install Root CA Certificate

Now that the virtual disk is formatted, you can begin to apply the initial bootstrap configuration. The initial configuration must contain the following information:

- Organization name

- System IP

- Address of the vBond controller

- Site ID

- IP address for VPN 0

- (Optional) an address for VPN 512

- (Optional) NTP server

There are two methods by which to accomplish these tasks. First, you could apply an IP address to the VPN 512 interface and use the vManage GUI to create feature templates that define these parameters. Alternatively, the administrator can input this information via CLI. For our example, we'll be focusing on the CLI example because it's generally considered the easiest method. vManage runs Viptela OS, so in some ways the syntax is similar to Cisco IOS.

The system context is where items such as organization name, system IP, site ID, and the address of the vBond controller will be set; optionally, you will want to set an NTP server as well. This will ensure that all your controllers are using the same time. When time isn't the same across all controllers, you can experience authentication issues between them. To access configuration mode, you will type **config terminal** or **conf t**. Once in configuration mode, you will need to navigate to the system context by executing the **system** command. Example 13-1 provides a sample configuration.

Example 13-1 *vManage Initial System Configuration*

```
vmanage# config terminal
Entering configuration mode terminal
vmanage(config)# system
vmanage(config-system)# system
vmanage(config-system)# site-id 100
vmanage(config-system)# system-ip 10.10.10.10
vmanage(config-system)# organization-name "Cisco Press"
vmanage(config-system)# vbond 209.165.200.226
vmanage(config-system)# ntp server 209.165.200.254
vmanage(config-server-209.165.200.254)# vpn 0
```

Now that the system information has been set, IP address information can be applied. This setup will contain configuration in VPN 0 and VPN 512. As a reminder, VPN 0 is required and will be where control plane connections with other controllers and WAN Edges will be terminated, and VPN 512 will be for out-of-band access. If out-of-band access isn't required, then VPN 512 configuration is optional. To access these configuration contexts, you simply type the **vpn** command, followed by the VPN you want to configure. Example 13-2 provides a sample configuration. Note the addition of the **tunnel-interface** command. This command instructs vManage to use this interface as a transport (control plane) interface.

Example 13-2 *vManage VPN 0 and VPN 512 Configuration*

```
vmanage(config-system)# vpn 0
vmanage(config-vpn-0)# interface eth0
vmanage(config-interface-eth0)# ip address 209.165.200.225/27
vmanage(config-interface-eth0)# tunnel-interface
vmanage(config-tunnel-interface)# no shutdown
vmanage(config-tunnel-interface)# ip route 0.0.0.0/0 209.165.200.254
vmanage(config-vpn-0)#
vmanage(config-vpn-0)# vpn 512
vmanage(config-vpn-512)# interface eth1
vmanage(config-interface-eth1)# ip address 192.168.1.10/24
vmanage(config-interface-eth1)# no shutdown
vmanage(config-interface-eth1)# ip route 0.0.0.0/0 192.168.1.254
vmanage(config-vpn-512)#
```

One difference Viptela OS has with Cisco IOS is that any configuration changes are not actually applied until you commit them. Cisco IOS XR has this feature as well. Inside Viptela OS, you can check your candidate config by running the **show config** command. There are many benefits to this, such as allowing for building out configuration and checking for syntax issues prior to activation. With classical Cisco IOS, all changes made in configuration mode are instantly applied, which could potentially cause an outage. Example 13-3 provides a sample configuration.

Example 13-3 *Commit Configuration Changes*

```
vmanage(config-vpn-512)# commit [and-quit]
Commit complete
vmanage#
```

Now that the initial bootstrap configuration has been applied, we can connect to the vManage GUI and finalize the bootstrap process. As discussed, we will use the enterprise CA method of certificate enrollment in this example. Refer to the previous section for information about other methods.

1. Connect to the VPN 512 IP address via a web browser and log in with the username of **admin** and a password of **admin**. Once you're logged in, the system presents you with a dashboard. This dashboard provides a quick overview on the state of the SD-WAN deployment, as depicted in Figure 13-14.

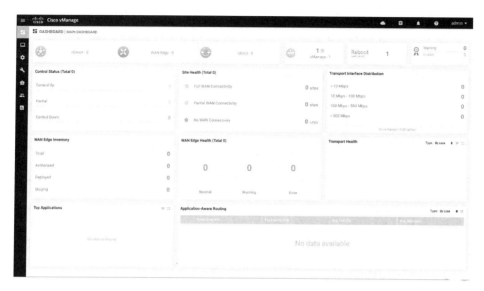

Figure 13-14 *vManage Dashboard*

2. From the menu bar on the left of the screen, click the **Administration** icon and select **Settings** (see Figure 13-15).

Figure 13-15 *vManage Menu Bar*

3. On the page that follows, navigate to the **Organization Name, vBond address,** and the **Controller Certificate Authorization** fields. Click on each of these items and select **Edit.** Here are the values that will be used:

- **Organization Name:** Cisco Press

- **vBond:** 209.165.200.226

- **Controller Certificate Authorization:** Enterprise CA

Figure 13-16 highlights how to edit these settings in vManage.

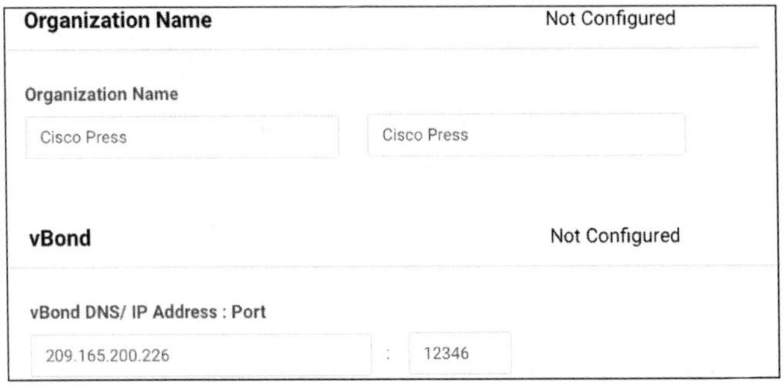

Organization Name	Not Configured
Organization Name	
Cisco Press	Cisco Press
vBond	Not Configured
vBond DNS/ IP Address : Port	
209.165.200.226	: 12346

Figure 13-16 *vManage Settings*

4. The last step that needs to be done is to change the **Controller Certificate Authorization** mode. Click **Edit** and select enterprise CA. In the box that appears, you can either upload or paste in the root CA certificate file. You might need to obtain this file from your enterprise PKI administrator. See Figure 13-17 for this process. Note that you also have the option to set the CSR properties for all CSR requests by selecting **Set CSR Properties.**

Controller Certificate Authorization   Enterprise

Certificate Signing by: ○ Cisco Automated (Recommended)   ○ Symantec Automated   ○ Manual   ● Enterprise Root Certificate

Certificate

----BEGIN CERTIFICATE----
MIIDODCCAiACCQDHUwD+eulb/jANBgkqhkiG9w0BAQaFADBeMQswCQYDVQQGEwJV
UzELMAkGA1UECAwCTkMxDDAKBgNVBAcMA1JUUDETMBEGA1UECgwKY2IzY29wcmVz
czEfMB0GA1UEAwwWdm1ibmFnZS5jaXNjb3ByZXNzLmNvbTAeFw0xOTEwMzExMjAx
MDIaFw0yMjA4MjAxMjAxMDIaMF4xCzAJBgNVBAYTAlVTMQswCQYDVQQIDAJOQzEM
MAoGA1UEBwwDUlRQMRMwEQYDVQQKDApjaXNjb3ByZXNzMR8wHQYDVQQDDBZ2bWFu
YWdlLmNpc2NvcHJlc3MuY29tMIIBIjANBgkqhkiG9w0BAQEFAAOCAQ8AMIIBCgKC
AQEA1z3FMA2TJQ24p6nlN+QyVqC5JOPexfos25axu7iYz8tFu547gOdLYDm2xp17
yGxvaytgh218QQzlI/aajmfazR15mtilHlO5ZplGuZTDjL4zsaH7tBC+yTe0sx+n
2R/zW9zZl6ts+4HdebdS7J/BFAoLkXO35zpLaxcOg8ICiGTu9TEfcRhTxUrwt1vP
UNfA5xo1diCc54keyBGCgVgPO1YUOcRKM8jAPdQxJl9gtXdVi4TuuJYmgBPWzfve
HmiZqVF0yq6R2j7A1B7Y6mGZHEOAsp+KsGEeBMg6QYxCvMWW18GEJi6YyODH3W71
EfLIPFTLyZMVrMs0T8C94FPfFwlDAQABMA0GCSqGSIb3DQEBCwUAA4IBAQCDEHS/
PZ1S82ECtSVoj4YJlA2IKRWrNuST7fndaPCGWThPtLKuVAEA7OXbwlAreBtyde1X
HPgwbPlRyoY/DTDd4bgyQy0P/+3shsG8UXaeq5bFa6KnulFpaZeaAkypN2tmeGsg
LcdZXr9NAvx3mXOj0ji6ZV0mOef5MLysvr2+Ym9olbFUr9lMaX4x9sCn2YOd3ELb
xVeYcj2VzuMCmb4GipGLzbiTNMN0mEcTRHANNO+cHDAzUOazxIBAcfwbnzzeKNZd

☐ Set CSR Properties

Import & Save   **Cancel**

Figure 13-17 *vManage Settings*

Note Once devices have been added to vManage, the organization name cannot be changed.

Step 5: Generate, Sign, and Install Certificate onto vManage Controller

The final step is to generate the certificates that will be used for vManage controller authentication.

1. Browse to the Devices Configuration section. From here, select **Certificates**. Select the **Controllers** tab at the top. Figure 13-18 shows these steps in vManage.

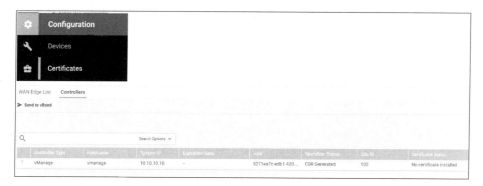

Figure 13-18 *vManage Certificate Settings*

2. From here, you can see additional information about the vManage controller. Note the **Certificate Status** column. From this screen we can also regenerate a CSR and install a certificate. Since the CSR is automatically generated by vManage, we'll download and have the enterprise CA sign it. From there, we'll install the signed certificate into the controller. To download the CSR, click the ellipsis to the far right for the respective controller. Figure 13-19 highlights the necessary pane within vManage.

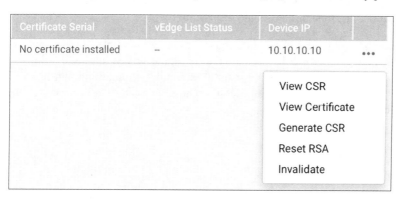

Figure 13-19 *Download CSR*

3. Select **View CSR**. From here, the CSR is displayed and you have the option to copy or download the text. Copy or download this file and submit to your Enterprise PKI administrator. Once this CSR has been submitted and signed by the enterprise CA, we can continue with installation. Figure 13-20 shows the CSR properties window within vManage.

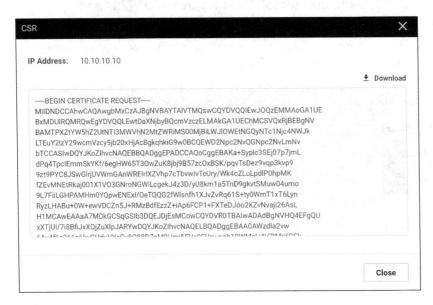

Figure 13-20 *View CSR Properties Window*

4. Once the certificate has been generated and signed by the root CA, you can install the certificate into the controller. In the right-hand corner of the main screen, locate the button that says **Install Certificate**. From here, you are prompted to either paste the contents of or upload the certificate. Click **Install**, as shown in Figure 13-21.

5. At this point, a status window appears allowing you to track the progress of certificate installation. The final output should display **Success**.

In this section, initial deployment of the vManage controller was completed. The controller was manually bootstrapped via the CLI, and the configuration was finished via the vManage GUI. This included using an enterprise CA to handle certificate enrollment. Now that the vManage controller is deployed, the administrator can move on to deploying the rest of the control plane.

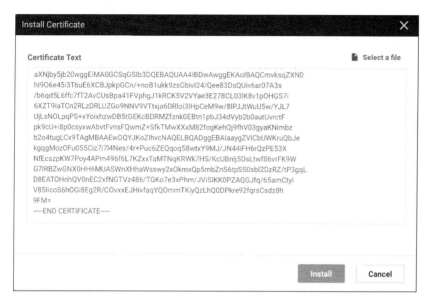

Figure 13-21 *Install Certificate Window*

vBond Controller Deployment

Now that the vManage controller has been deployed, we can begin with the vBond controller. Remember that the vBond performs a critical function in the SD-WAN deployment, as it orchestrates or glues all other components together. vBond is how WAN Edges find out about the various vManage and vSmart controllers and acts as the first line of authentication and authorization into the fabric. WAN Edges do not sustain a permanent connection to the vBond. Rather, the connection to vBond is transient. WAN Edges must be able to reach the vBond controller on all VPN 0 transports by default.

For environments that utilize the Internet as a transport, it is strongly recommended to place the vBond in a DMZ with a public IP address. Provided that vBond has a public IP address, the vSmart, vManage, and WAN Edge routers can remain behind a secured gateway performing NAT. The vBond then performs NAT detection and traversal for these devices. Refer to the NAT section in Chapter 3 for further information on this. Again, if the vBond must be behind NAT, it must be a static 1:1 NAT.

For the remainder of this section, we'll use the subnets noted in Table 13-2.

Table 13-2 *Controller Subnets*

VPN	Network	Subnet Mask
VPN 0	209.165.200.224	255.255.255.224
VPN 512	192.168.1.0	255.255.255.0

This section will cover deployment of the vBond controller. Here are steps to be performed:

Step 1. Deploy the virtual machine for vBond.

Step 2. Bootstrap and configure the vBond controller.

Step 3. Manually install the root CA certificate on vBond.

Step 4. Add the vBond controller to vManage.

Step 5. Generate, sign, and install the certificate onto the vBond controller.

The examples in this section cover deployment with version 19.2. Note that there is no specific vBond OVA because it uses the same OVA as vEdge Cloud. Hence, when the vEdge Cloud OVA is deployed, the persona is changed to be a vBond. For this deployment, the VPN 0 and VPN 512 IP addresses need to be assigned.

Note   At the time of publishing, the OVA location is https://software.cisco.com/download/home/286320995/.

Step 1/2/3: Deploy vBond Virtual Machine on VMware ESXi; Bootstrap and Configure vBond Controller; Manually Install Root CA Certificate on vBond

Once the vBond virtual machine is deployed, power up the virtual machine.

1. Similar to the vManage controller, you need to apply a bootstrap configuration via the CLI. In this step you'll set the organization name, site ID, system IP, VPN 0, and VPN 512 information. As with vManage, the first thing you'll do on vBond is set the system information. To access this configuration mode, type **config terminal** or **conf t**. Once in configuration mode, to access the system context, execute the command **system**. Pay special attention to the **vbond 209.165.200.226 local** command. Remember that we're using the vEdge Cloud image for the vBond. By specifying the **local** command, the vBond persona is enabled. Example 13-4 lists the initial system configuration.

Example 13-4   *vBond Initial System Configuration*

```
vedge# config terminal
Entering configuration mode terminal
vedge(config)# system
vedge(config-system)# system
vedge(config-system)# host-name vbond
vedge (config-system)# site-id 100
vedge(config-system)# system-ip 10.10.10.11
vedge(config-system)# organization-name "Cisco Press"
vedge(config-system)# vbond 209.165.200.226 local
vedge(config-system)# ntp server 209.165.200.254
vedge(config-server-209.165.200.254)# vpn 0
```

2. Just like with the vManage controller, you need to provide some initial settings to the VPN 0 and VPN 512 interfaces. One difference from the vManage controller is that you need to remove the tunnel **tunnel-interface** command. This process is shown in Example 13-5.

Example 13-5 *vBond VPN 0 and VPN 512 Configuration*

```
vedge(config-system)# vpn 0
vedge (config-vpn-0)# interface ge0/0
vedge(config-interface-ge0/0)# ip address 209.165.200.226/27
vedge(config-interface-ge0/0)# no tunnel-interface
vedge(config-interface-ge0/0)# no shutdown
vedge(config-interface-ge0/0)# ip route 0.0.0.0/0 209.165.200.254
vedge(config-vpn-0)#
vedge(config-vpn-0)# vpn 512
vedge(config-vpn-512)# interface eth0
vedge(config-interface-eth0)# ip address 192.168.1.11/24
vedge(config-interface-eth0)# no shutdown
vedge(config-interface-eth0)# ip route 0.0.0.0/0 192.168.1.254
vedge(config-vpn-512)#
```

3. As discussed previously, you need to save your configuration. This is completed by committing the configuration using the **commit** command, as depicted in Example 13-6.

Example 13-6 *Commit Configuration Changes*

```
vedge(config-vpn-512)# commit [and-quit]
Commit complete
vbond#
```

4. The last step to initially bootstrap the vBond controller is to install the root CA certificate. To complete this, you need to copy the root CA certificate to the vBond controller. This can be most easily accomplished with SCP (such as with Putty SCP or WinSCP). Simply use the SCP program of your choice to connect to the VPN 512 interface of vBond and copy the root certificate over. By default, the file is copied to the **/home/admin** directory on the vBond. Once copied, however, the certificate needs to be installed. This is accomplished via the **request root-cert-chain install directory** command, as demonstrated in Example 13-7.

Example 13-7 *Root Certification Chain Install*

```
vbond# request root-cert-chain install /home/admin/rootca.pem
Uploading root-ca-cert-chain via VPN 0
Copying ... /home/admin/rootca.pem via VPN 0
Updating the root certificate chain..
Successfully installed the root certificate chain
vbond#
```

Step 4/5: Add vBond Controller to vManage; Generate, Sign, and Install Certificate onto vBond Controller

The remainder of vBond bootstrapping can be done via the vManage GUI. In these steps, the network administrator will be adding the vBond controller to the SD-WAN overlay (that is, updating the whitelist discussed previously). Most notably, this will consist of generating a CSR, signing the CSR, and installing the certificate.

1. Adding the vBond to the controller whitelist is done via the vManage GUI. Once you're logged in to the vManage GUI, browse to **Configuration > Devices > Controllers** (tab). From here, select **Add Controller** and select **vBond**, as illustrated in Figure 13-22.

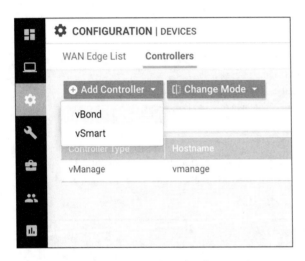

Figure 13-22 *Add vBond Controller to vManage*

2. A dialog box will be displayed. From this screen, input the management IP (VPN 512) as well as the username and password. For this example, the default values are **192.168.1.11** and **admin/admin**. Click **Add** when finished. By leaving **Generate CSR** checked, a CSR will automatically be created. Figure 13-23 showcases the necessary steps to accomplish this.

You should now see the vBond controller added to the vManage GUI. Figure 13-24 shows the successful addition of the vBond.

3. The final step is to generate the certificates that will be used for vBond controller authentication. Browse to the **Devices > Certificates > Controllers** screen in the GUI.

Just like we did with vManage, we need to download and sign the CSR. To download the CSR, click the ellipsis to the far right for the respective controller and select **View CSR**. A dialog box will appear. From here, you can download the CSR and have the enterprise CA sign the request.

Once this is complete, you can install the certificate. The process is exactly the same as with the vManage controller described previously. If everything was successful, you should see a screen similar to the one depicted in Figure 13-25.

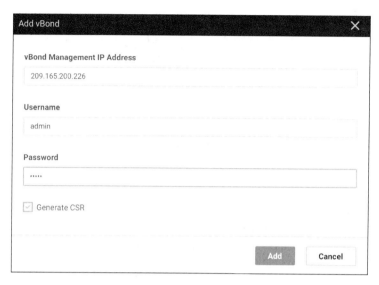

Figure 13-23 *Add vBond Controller to vManage Controller*

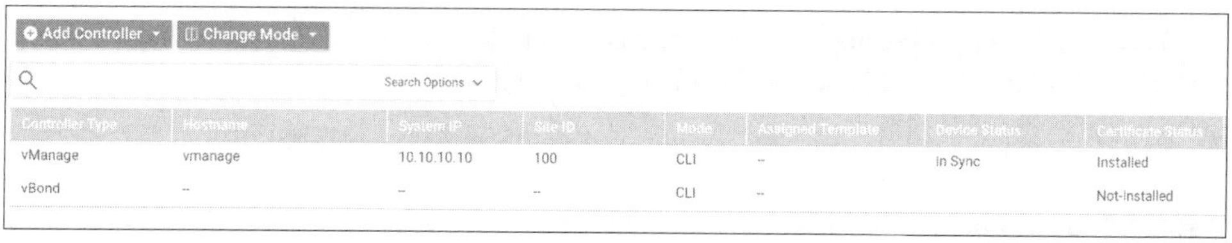

Figure 13-24 *Add vBond Controller to vManage Controller*

Figure 13-25 *Install Certificate on vBond Controller*

4. From the **Configuration > Devices > Certificates > Controllers** screen that is shown in Figure 13-26, we can now see that the vBond is in sync and vManage has learned additional values from the device (such as site ID and system IP).

Controller Type	Hostname	System IP	Expiration Date	uuid	Operation Status	Site ID
vBond	vbond	10.10.10.11	16 Mar 2021 10:41:39 PM EDT	abd5e9d7-9dee-4d0...	Installed	100
vManage	vmanage	10.10.10.10	14 Mar 2021 8:28:32 AM EDT	5271ea7c-edb1-420...	vBond Updated	100

Figure 13-26 *Controller Certificate Screen*

In this section, the vBond controller was deployed, bootstrapped, and configured and certificates were installed. The next section will cover deployment of the vSmart controller. The process for the vSmart controller is very similar to the vBond controller.

vSmart Controller Deployment

Now we have deployed the vManage and vBond controllers, the final controller to deploy is vSmart. The process is very similar to the vBond controller. After deploying the OVA, we need to provide basic bootstrap configuration, install the root CA certificate, add the controller to vManage, and facilitate certificate installation. When we add the controller, vManage will use Netconf to connect. Hence, when we add the tunnel-interface command, we'll have to apply one additional line of configuration to allow Netconf access. The process is the same if we are deploying one vSmart controller or multiple vSmart controllers. For this example, we'll be focusing on version 19.2 of the vSmart controller. The OVA for vSmart can be downloaded from https://www.cisco.com.

For the remainder of this section, we'll use the subnets noted in Table 13-3.

Table 13-3 *Controller Subnets*

VPN	Network	Subnet Mask
VPN 0	209.165.200.224	255.255.255.224
VPN 512	192.168.1.0	255.255.255.0

The remainder of this section will cover deployment of the vSmart controller, using the following steps:

Step 1.   Deploy the vSmart virtual machine from the downloaded OVA.

Step 2.   Bootstrap and configure the vSmart controller.

Step 3.   Manually install the root CA certificate on vSmart.

Step 4.   Add the vSmart controller to vManage.

Step 5.   Generate, sign, and install the certificate onto the vSmart controller.

Step 1/2/3: Deploy vSmart Virtual Machine from Downloaded OVA; Bootstrap and Configure vSmart Controller; Manually Install Root CA Certificate on vSmart

1. Install the vSmart OVA onto VMware ESXi or KVM and power up the VM. The default username and password are **admin.**

2. Now that the OVA is installed and powered up, let's apply the initial bootstrap configuration. Just like with the vBond controller, you first need to configure system options (such as site ID, system IP, organization name, and vBond address). Additionally, in Example 13-8, we'll apply the VPN 0 and VPN 512 interface information.

Example 13-8 *vSmart Initial System Configuration*

```
vsmart# config terminal
Entering configuration mode terminal
vsmart(config)# system
vsmart(config-system)# system
vsmart(config-system)# site-id 100
vsmart(config-system)# system-ip 10.10.10.12
vsmart(config-system)# organization-name "Cisco Press"
vsmart(config-system)# vbond 209.165.200.226
vsmart(config-system)# ntp server 209.165.200.254
vsmart(config-server-209.165.200.254)# vpn 0
```

3. Next on the list is to configure the VPN 0 context. This configuration is slightly different from vBond configuration, however. When the **tunnel-interface** command is applied, a firewall is enabled (since it is assumed that this interface will be connected to untrusted networks). By default, Netconf is blocked. Since vManage uses Netconf to initially connect as well as push configuration, we need to allow this. Unblocking Netconf is accomplished with the command **allow-service netconf** under the **tunnel-interface.** Example 13-9 lists these steps.

Example 13-9 *vSmart VPN 0 and VPN 512 Configuration*

```
vsmart(config-system)# vpn 0
vsmart(config-vpn-0)# interface eth0
vsmart(config-interface-eth0)# ip address 209.165.200.227/27
vsmart(config-interface-eth0)# tunnel-interface
vsmart(config-tunnel-interface)# no shutdown
vsmart(config-tunnel-interface)# ip route 0.0.0.0/0 209.165.200.254
vsmart(config-tunnel-interface)# allow-service netconf
vsmart(config-vpn-0)#
vsmart(config-vpn-0)# vpn 512
vsmart(config-vpn-512)# interface eth1
```

```
vsmart(config-interface-eth1)# ip address 192.168.1.12/24
vsmart(config-interface-eth1)# no shutdown
vsmart(config-interface-eth1)# ip route 0.0.0.0/0 192.168.1.254
vsmart(config-vpn-512)#
```

4. As we did with the vManage and vBond controllers, we need to save our commands. The **commit** command is used to accomplish this and is highlighted in Example 13-10.

Example 13-10 *Commit Configuration Changes*

```
vsmart(config-vpn-512)# commit [and-quit]
Commit complete
vsmart#
```

5. Next, the network administrator needs to manually install the root CA certificate. This is most easily achieved by copying the file to the vSmart controller using your favorite SCP program. By default, the file is copied to the **/home/admin** directory on the vSmart controller. Once this file is copied, the certificate needs to be installed. This is accomplished via the **request root-cert-chain install <directory>** command, as shown in Example 13-11.

Example 13-11 *Root Certification Chain Install*

```
vsmart# request root-cert-chain install /home/admin/rootca.pem
Uploading root-ca-cert-chain via VPN 0
Copying ... /home/admin/rootca.pem via VPN 0
Updating the root certificate chain..
Successfully installed the root certificate chain
vsmart#
```

Step 4/5: Add vSmart Controller to vManage; Generate, Sign, and Install Certificate onto vSmart Controller

The remaining bootstrap steps will be performed from the vManage GUI. The process is identical to the vBond controller to add the vSmart controller.

1. First, browse to **Configuration > Devices > Controllers** from the vManage GUI. From here, select **Add Controller** and select **vSmart**. Figure 13-27 illustrates the process.

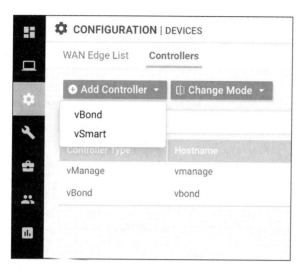

Figure 13-27   *Add vSmart Controller to vManage*

2. A dialog box will appear asking for vSmart's IP address, username, and password. You also have the option to use either DTLS or TLS. By default, we use DTLS. Leave the **Generate CSR** box checked. Figure 13-28 demonstrates the correct fields to configure within the vManage.

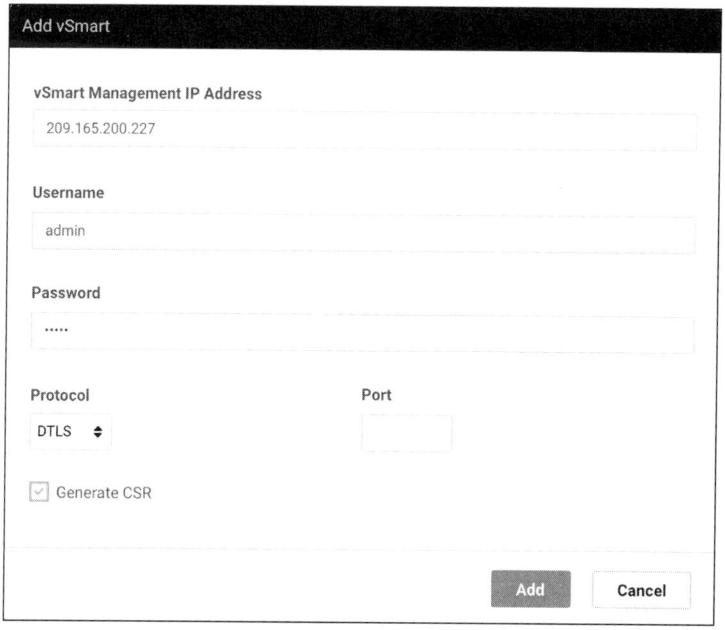

Add vSmart

vSmart Management IP Address

209.165.200.227

Username

admin

Password

•••••

Protocol   Port

DTLS ⬍

☑ Generate CSR

Add   Cancel

Figure 13-28   *Add vSmart Controller to vManage Controller*

If completed successfully, you should see the vSmart controller added with a certificate status of **Not-Installed**, as shown in Figure 13-29.

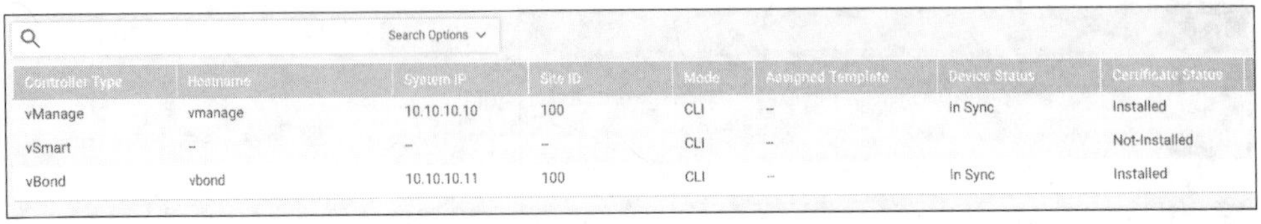

Controller Type	Hostname	System IP	Site ID	Mode	Assigned Template	Device Status	Certificate Status
vManage	vmanage	10.10.10.10	100	CLI	--	In Sync	Installed
vSmart	--	--	--	CLI	--		Not-Installed
vBond	vbond	10.10.10.11	100	CLI	--	In Sync	Installed

Figure 13-29 *Add vSmart Controller to vManage Controller*

3. The next step is to download the CSR, have it signed, and install the corresponding certificate. Figure 13-30 displays the process in the vManage controller. To access this screen, browse to **Configuration > Certificates > Controllers**. Once on this screen, click the ellipsis to the right of the vSmart controller and select **View CSR**. Copy the CSR to a text file or download the CSR.

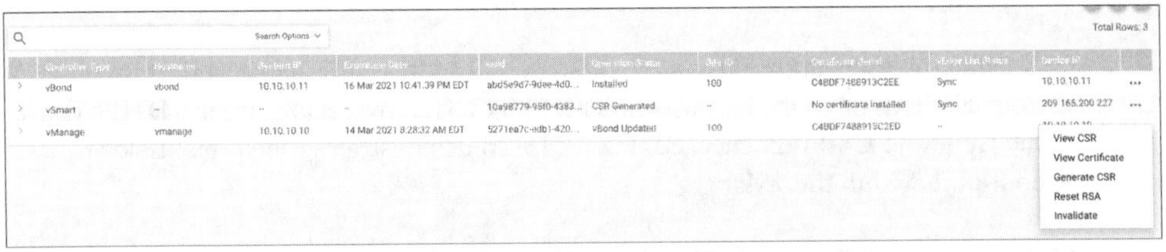

Controller Type	Hostname	System IP	Expiration Date	UUID	Operation Status	Site ID	Certificate Serial	vEdge List Status	Device IP	
vBond	vbond	10.10.10.11	16 Mar 2021 10:41:39 PM EDT	abd5e9d7-9dee-4d0...	Installed	100	C48DF748E913C2EE	Sync	10.10.10.11	...
vSmart	--	--	--	10a98779-98f0-4383...	CSR Generated	--	No certificate installed	Sync	209.165.200.227	...
vManage	vmanage	10.10.10.10	14 Mar 2021 8:28:32 AM EDT	5271ea7c-adb1-420...	vBond Updated	100	C48DF748B913C2ED	--		

View CSR
View Certificate
Generate CSR
Reset RSA
Invalidate

Figure 13-30 *Download CSR for vSmart Controller*

4. The final step is to install the signed certificate. As we did with the vBond and vManage controllers, select **Install Certificate** in the upper right-hand corner. A dialog box will appear. Either paste the contents of the certificate into the window or select the certificate file using the **Select a file** button. Once it is uploaded, click **Install**. Figure 13-31 highlights the step in vManage to install the vSmart controller certificate.

If successful, you should see a status screen stating that the certificate was installed. Navigating to **Configuration > Devices > Controllers**, as shown in Figure 13-32, you can see that some additional information has been learned about the vSmart controller.

Now that the vSmart controller is deployed, we have a fully functional SD-WAN overlay. The process to add additional vSmart controllers is exactly the same, should you need to revisit these steps in the future. At this point, you can begin building templates and policies and start onboarding WAN Edges.

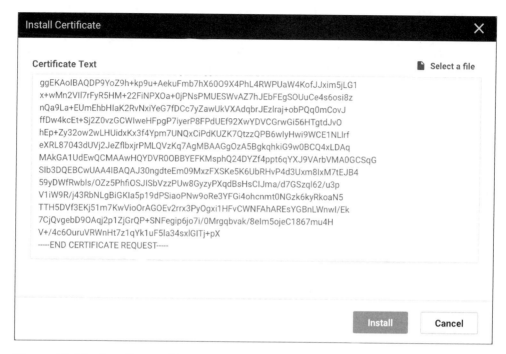

Figure 13-31 *Install Signed Certificate for vSmart Controller*

Figure 13-32 *Install Signed Certificate for vSmart Controller*

Summary

This chapter discussed how certificates are utilized in an SD-WAN fabric and also how to deploy the SD-WAN control plane, management plane, and the orchestration plane. From this information, an engineer can deploy the solution in a private cloud, on-premises, or lab deployment.

The first section covered the importance of certificates and the critical function they play with authentication and authorization. When controllers are brought online, they mutually authenticate each other and check the attributes of exchanged certificates. Only if these attributes match will the controllers be able to build connections to each other. Certificates can be managed via multiple methods, such as automatic enrollment with

Symantec/DigiCert, manual enrollment with Symantec/DigiCert, automatic enrollment with Cisco PKI, manual enrollment with Cisco PKI, and finally utilizing an enterprise CA. Starting with version 19.1 of the SD-WAN software, using automatic enrollment with Cisco PKI is the preferred mechanism because the management and support are seamless.

The final sections covered deployment of the SD-WAN controllers in a virtualized environment. Starting with the management plane, vManage was deployed and configured. Second, the orchestration plane was deployed with vBond. Finally, the control plane was deployed with the vSmart controller. This process consisted of deploying the virtual machines, initial bootstrap configuration, and adding the controllers to vManage.

Review All Key Topics

Review the most important topics in the chapter, noted with the Key Topic icon in the outer margin of the page. Table 13-4 lists these key topics and the page numbers on which each is found.

Table 13-4   *Key Topics*

Key Topic Element	Description	Page
Section	Certificates	496
Section	vManage Controller Deployment	501
Section	vBond Controller Deployment	513
Section	vSmart Controller Deployment	518

Define Key Terms

Define the following key terms from this chapter and check your answers in the glossary:

Data plane (WAN Edge), management plane (vManage), control plane (vSmart), orchestration plane (vBond), Overlay Management Protocol (OMP), Certificate Authority (CA)

Chapter Review Questions

1. What are the three controllers that make up the Cisco SD-WAN solution?

   a. vSmart

   b. vBond

   c. WAN Edge

   d. vManage

   e. vController

2. What are the three main certificate deployment options?

   a. Automatic enrollment with Symantec/DigiCert/Cisco PKI

   b. Manual enrollment with Symantec/DigiCert/Cisco PKI

   c. Self-signed certificates

   d. SSH private/public keys

   e. Enterprise CA

3. Which controller is deployed first?

   a. vManage

   b. vSmart

   c. vBond

   d. WAN Edge

   e. vCompute

4. If the vBond controller is behind a NAT, it must have a 1:1 static NAT.

   a. True

   b. False

5. Which three attributes are verified when authenticating the certificate?

   a. Organization name

   b. Trust of certificate

   c. Common name

   d. City

   e. Certificate serial number

6. Which command is a valid command to enable the vBond persona?

   a. **vbond 209.200.165.227 local**

   b. **vbond 209.200.165.227 enable**

   c. **feature vbond**

7. What protocol does vManage use to push configuration to vSmart?

   a. Netconf

   b. SSH

   c. Telnet

   d. Feature Templates

8. Which command is used to save configuration changes?

   a. **commit**

   b. **copy running-config startup-config**

   c. **save**

   d. **write memory**

   e. **BGP**

9. What is the order in which the controllers are installed?

   a. vManage > vBond > vSmart

   b. vBond > vManage > vSmart

   c. vSmart > vBond > vManage

   d. WAN Edge > vBond > vSmart > vManage

10. Which command is used to allow Netconf through the inherent firewall on the vSmart controller?

   a. **allow-service netconf**

   b. **permit netconf any any**

   c. **enable-service netconf**

   d. **feature netconf**

References

"Cisco SD-WAN CVD–Certificate Deployment," https://www.cisco.com/c/dam/en/us/td/docs/solutions/CVD/SDWAN/cisco-sd-wan-certificates-deploy-2019sep.pdf, September 2019

"Cisco SD-WAN Bring Up Sequence of Events," https://sdwan-docs.cisco.com/Product_Documentation/Getting_Started/Viptela_Overlay_Network_Bringup/01Bringup_Sequence_of_Events

Answers to Chapter Review Questions

Chapter 1

1. A, B, D. The influx of IoT, guest, and BYOD devices as well as the shift to cloud-based applications are causing a strain on the WAN. High-bandwidth applications are impeding performance in the WAN for traffic destined to branch locations.

2. A, B, E. Businesses are looking to lower operational complexity, increase usable bandwidth by using dormant backup links or commodity Internet links, and improve the overall user experience, all with a topology-independent environment.

3. A, B, E. Administrative distance, traffic engineering, and preferred path selection all come into play when having multiple links in the branch routers.

4. B. False—A software-centric approach is needed for intent-based network (IBN) adoption.

5. A, E. Software driven, automated, programmable, predictive, and business intent are the components of digital transformation.

6. A, B. SD-WAN is designed to give the business control of all routing and service level agreements (SLAs).

7. A, B, C, F. IoT devices and increased cloud consumption are IT trends, not benefits of SD-WAN.

8. A, B, E. Cisco SD-WAN can support dual MPLS, hybrid WAN, and dual Internet as options for transport.

9. B. DIA is used to offload cloud applications directly to the Internet for more efficient access to the cloud providers.

10. A. Multidomain is designed to simplify operations across multiple administrative domains, such as campus, WAN, and data center, providing a seamless end-to-end policy across all of those domains.

Chapter 2

1. A, B, D. The three controllers that make up the Cisco SD-WAN solution are vSmart, vBond, and vManage. These components make up the control, management, and orchestration planes in the environment.

2. A, B, E. The Cisco SD-WAN solution is a distributed architecture. By splitting out the components in the solution, vManage can provide a single pane of glass for all management and troubleshooting. By also moving the control plane to a central location, we can achieve greater scale while reducing complexity.

3. A, B, E. vManage provides a single viewpoint for all troubleshooting, configuration, and monitoring functions.

4. A. IPsec is used to secure and authenticate data plane connectivity. IPsec tunnels are only formed between WAN Edges.

5. A. The vSmart operates similarly to a route reflector in the sense that routing updates are only advertised to and from the vSmart. The vSmart has the capability to apply policy inbound or outbound to the prefixes it services.

6. A, B. The vBond provides authentication of all devices in the environment. The vBond is the initial point of contact and, from there, it distributes connectivity information for all other controller elements. STUN is also utilized with the vBond to detect when a component is behind a NAT.

7. A. The Cisco SD-WAN solution supports three types of multi-tenancy: Dedicated, VPN, and Enterprise.

8. A, B, E. EIGRP, OSPF, and BGP are supported on the service side (LAN) of the WAN Edge. These three protocols can be redistributed to and from OMP.

9. A, B, C. BFD is utilized to measure delay, loss, and jitter. With this information, intelligent decisions can be made to switch traffic to different transports that may perform better.

10. A. MPLS labels (RFC 4023) are used to provide different levels of segmentation for various compliance reasons. With segmentation, different types of topologies can be created per VPN. Some examples of this are hub-and-spoke, full mesh, and point-to-point.

Chapter 3

1. A. The three controllers that make up the Cisco SD-WAN solution are the vSmart, vBond, and vManage. These components make up the control, management, and orchestration planes in the environment, respectively. The vSmart controller is the brains behind the control plane and distributes routing information along with encryption information.

2. A, B, E. OMP has three types of routing advertisements. They are OMP route, TLOC route, and service route.

3. B. When two devices are behind symmetric NAT, the data plane cannot be built. This is due to the fact that symmetric NAT utilizes ports that will change depending on which device the data plane tunnel is being established with.

4. A. When using private-to-private colors, it is assumed that there is no NAT between the two, so private (pre-NAT) information is used. When communicating with a public color, NAT may be involved, so the public (post-NAT) attributes are used.

5. A. Since key exchange is handled via the vSmart controller, there is no need for the IKE session management protocol.

6. A. UDP port 12346 is used to communicate with all control elements in the SD-WAN fabric.

Chapter 4

1. A, B. Device templates can either use feature templates or CLI templates, but not a mixture of both. When a CLI template is used, it must be the full configuration of the device.

2. A, B, E. Feature templates have three different types of values that can be set. When global is used, the value of that field will be the same wherever that template is applied. The default value will use whatever the default value is for the field. Variables allow the network administrator the flexibility to set a parameter on a per-device basis, without the need for an additional template.

3. B. Device templates are specific to certain device types. Separate device templates will need to be used for different product versions.

4. A. CLI templates do not provide the same flexibility as feature templates. A CLI template must contain the full CLI configuration.

5. A. The Plug and Play process uses HTTPS for communication to the PnP server.

6. A, B, C. For automatic provisioning to be successful, a device must receive an IP address and DNS server via DHCP. Once the device has this information, it needs to be able to resolve **ztp.viptela.com** or **devicehelper.cisco.com** and have connectivity to them.

Chapter 5

1. B, C, D. URL Filtering, Application-Aware Routing, and centralized data are all types of Cisco SD-WAN policies. There is no such thing as a traffic engineering policy; traffic engineering would be achieved with a control policy or a centralized data policy.

2. B. Cisco SD-WAN policies, much like traditional Cisco ACLs and route maps, are evaluated ordinally and use first-match logic.

3. A, B, C, D, E, F. All of these are different types of lists that are used in Cisco SD-WAN.

4. B. Unlike traditional IOS, SD-WAN has explicit list types for matching in the control plane (prefix-list) versus the data plane (data-prefix-list).

5. B. The only way to filter routes from routing neighbors outside of the SD-WAN fabric is with a route map in a local policy.

6. A, B. VPN membership policies and topology policies are applied to and enforced on the vSmart controllers. Zone-Based Firewall policies are part of security policies, which are applied directly to the WAN Edge and enforced there. Cflowd policies are part of centralized data policies; they are applied to the vSmarts, but enforced on the WAN Edge.

7. C, D. Security policies and localized data policies are applied to and enforced on the WAN Edge routers. Application-Aware Routing policies are applied to the vSmarts and enforced on the WAN Edge routers. VPN membership and topology policies are applied to and enforced on the vSmarts.

8. A. Application-Aware Routing policies are applied to the vSmarts and enforced on the WAN Edge routers. Security policies and localized data policies are applied to and enforced on the WAN Edge routers. VPN membership and topology policies are applied to and enforced on the vSmarts.

9. D. All policy configuration is done on vManage. vManage is the single administration point for both the vSmarts and the WAN Edge routers.

10. B. If there is a conflict in the forwarding decisions made by an Application-Aware Routing policy and a centralized data policy, the centralized data policy will override the Application-Aware Routing policy.

Chapter 6

1. C. The only two answers that apply to centralized control policies are Accept and Reject. "Deny" is an action in a centralized data policy. The default setting of the default action in a centralized control policy is Reject.

2. B, C, D, E, F. System IP, Color, and Encapsulation are the three elements that uniquely define a TLOC. Additionally, a TLOC list will also allow the configuration of Weight and Preference. The other attributes cannot be defined as part of a TLOC list.

3. D. The TLOC attribute Weight is not part of the OMP best-path selection process. After the winners of the best paths have been determined, the Weight attribute is examined to determine how the flows should be divided proportionally among the best paths.

4. B. TLOC Preference values, not OMP Route Preference values, can be configured via feature and device templates.

5. A. A route that has a valid TLOC as a next hop will have a status code of R for "resolved." If the resolved route is also the winner of the OMP best-path selection process, then the route will have a status of "C R," where C means "chosen." If the route is installed in the local routing table, it will have a status of "C I R," where I is "installed."

6. C. Both TLOCs and OMP routes have support for an attribute called "Preference."

7. D. A VPN Membership policy specifies which VPNs the vSmart will accept updates from, and forward updates to, on a specific WAN Edge. Without the VPN being permitted by the VPN policy, the VPN can still be configured on the WAN Edge, but it will be isolated from the rest of the fabric.

8. B. Control policies that are used to leak routes must always be applied in the inbound direction.

9. B. A centralized control policy can be used to leak routes between different service-side VPNs. A centralized control policy cannot be used to leak into or out of VPN 0 or VPN 512.

10. C. Centralized control policies configured with the **export-to** action are used to leak routes between service-side VPNs.

Chapter 7

1. B. In a centralized data policy, the easiest way to match all traffic is to not configure any matching criteria. There is no concept of a "match-all" criteria in SD-WAN, and the default action will only allow certain actions to be undertaken.

2. A. The **nat use-vpn** configuration syntax always NATs traffic to VPN 0.

3. B. The **nat fallback** configuration provides a backup forwarding path across the fabric in the event that all of the local interfaces configured for NAT are down. If all of the WAN interfaces go down, **nat fallback** will not work, as there will be no way to backhaul the traffic to a different site.

4. C. In the vSmart configuration, there is only a single data policy that is configured per site ID per direction. That single policy will include sub-policies per VPN, but there are only two policies that are applied per site ID.

5. B. The **local-tloc** command sets the preference for the outbound interface to be used when forwarding traffic. In the event that the TLOC specified in the LOCAL-TLOC policy is unavailable, traffic will fall back to the routing table.

6. D. A single FEC block consists of four data packets and a parity packet that is calculated from those four data packets. In the event of the loss of any one of the data packets, the original packet can be reconstructed from the remaining three data packets and the parity packet.

7. C. FEC-adaptive begins to operate when the packet losses on a tunnel exceed 2%. Currently, this is not a user-configurable policy.

8. D. When packet duplication is configured, the duplicate packets are automatically sent down the tunnel that is currently experiencing the least amount of packet loss.

9. C. The PKTDUP RX THIS field shows the total number of unique packets that have been received at the WAN Edge, including the values received over the original path (PKTDUP RX) and the backup path (PKTDUP RX OTHER). The last two values are TX values and have nothing do with the number of packets received.

10. F. While both Viptela OS platforms and XE-SD-WAN platforms support Forward Error Correction, packet duplication, and TCP optimization, the implementations of these features are different between Viptela OS and XE-SD-WAN. As such, the features are not able to interoperate.

Chapter 8

1. D. Application-Aware Routing policies are applied on a per-site, per-VPN basis. Unlike other data policies, directionality does not play a role with AAR policies. The direction is always "from-service."

2. B. App-Route policies are a special type of centralized data policy. These policies are centrally applied on the vSmart controllers and enforced on the WAN Edge routers.

3. A, D, G. The BFD Hello Interval specifies how frequently BFD packets are sent and statistics are gathered. The App-Route Poll Interval defines the period of time to evaluate the BFD statistics and produce an average. This forms a single "bucket." The App-Route Multiplier specifies how many App-Route Poll Intervals to consider (how many "buckets" to consider) when calculating tunnel performance. The number of tunnels, colors, and SLA classes has no impact on the statistic calculation process. The BFD Hello Multiplier is used for liveliness detection and is not part of the App-Route process.

4. C. The maximum (and default) number of App-Route Poll Intervals that can be used for tunnel performance calculations is six. This value is configured using the App-Route Poll Interval Multiplier.

5. D. Tunnels are reevaluated for compliance with SLA classes after each App-Route Poll Interval. The Hello Interval controls how often BFD packets are transmitted by the router and, thus, how often they are received by the router. The Hello Multiplier is used for Path Liveliness detection, not for Application-Aware Routing.

6. B. As of version 19.2, a single WAN Edge router can only have four different SLA classes configured.

7. C. As of version 19.2, a router and, thus, single WAN Edge router can only have four different SLA classes configured.

8. C. The Backup SLA Preferred Color option applies when no colors, not just the options configured under Preferred Colors, are able to meet the required SLA.

9. B. When configured, the Strict option will drop traffic when *all* available colors fail to meet the requirements of the SLA class, not only the colors specified in the Preferred Colors field.

10. A. An AAR policy will only make path selection decisions between multiple equal-cost routes. If one route is more preferred, that route will always be chosen by the forwarding engine regardless of the AAR policy or the performance of the tunnels.

Chapter 9

1. C. Localized policies are configured and enforced on the local WAN Edge routers. vBond and vSmart are completely independent of localized policies. vPolicy does not exist.

2. B. False. As centralized policies are applied to the vSmart, and localized policies are applied to the WAN Edge routers, the configurations are completely independent and will use different lists.

3. A. Localized policies are scoped to a specific device. While uncommon, it would be possible for every device to have a different localized policy.

4. A, B. Localized control policies support the Accept and Reject actions. The Drop action is only available in a localized data policy. The Inspect and Pass actions are specific to Zone-Based Firewalls.

5. B. False. As all of the traffic is traversing in tunnels, all of the necessary firewall and NAT states will have already been established. Ensuring symmetric flows through a single WAN Edge router is important for the fidelity of the deep packet inspection and application recognition data.

6. A, C. Localized data policies support the Accept and Drop actions. The Reject action is only available in a localized control policy. The Inspect and Pass actions are specific to Zone-Based Firewalls.

7. D. Current code supports eight queues per interface on WAN Edge routers.

8. A. LLQ and priority queuing functionalities are only supported in queue 0.

9. A. Control plane traffic is automatically mapped to queue 0.

10. A, B, D. While shapers are part of QoS, they are configured under the interface configuration and are not part of the localized policy configuration. Class-maps are used to map the forwarding classes to hardware queues. qos-schedulers are used to configure the forwarding parameters of each traffic class. qos-maps are used to tie all of the schedulers together into a single policy.

Chapter 10

1. B. On the contrary, the Application-Aware Enterprise Firewall is completely VPN aware. Firewall policies are applied on a per-VPN basis.

2. A, B, E. Three main actions can be set, per sequence entry, in a firewall policy: Inspect, Drop, and Pass.

3. B. High-Speed Logging is an available logging option for a firewall policy.

4. B, D, E. Only three options for signature sets exist today for IDS/IPS: Balanced, Connectivity, and Security.

5. B, E. The Fail-close option drops all the IPS/IDS traffic when there is an engine failure. The Fail-open option allows all the IPS/IDS traffic when there is an engine failure. The default option is Fail-open.

6. A. An IDS/IPS policy cannot be configured unless a security virtual image is first uploaded to the software repository in vManage.

7. B. To support URL Filtering functionality, an ISR must be configured with a minimum of 8GB of DRAM and 8GB of system flash if doing cloud lookup, and 16GB of DRAM and 16GB of system flash if doing on-box database lookup.

8. C. A URL blacklist can be configured to explicitly block certain websites in the URL policy configuration.

9. B, D. Between the security dashboard and device dashboard, vManage can provide the blocked and allowed categories by percentage, as well as the URL session count.

10. B. As of the writing of this book, the current SD-WAN code supports a maximum exportable file size of 10 MB.

11. A, B, C. At a minimum, file analysis must be enabled, a file types list must be specified, and the Threat Grid API key must be configured.

12. A. The filename of the malware detected is displayed in the device dashboard section of vManage.

13. D. To generate the API token, the user must log in to the Cisco Umbrella portal and navigate to the API token generation page.

14. C. The WAN Edge router can leverage local domain bypass functionality, where a list of internal domains is defined and referenced during the DNS request interception process. Any domain defined in the list is ignored and no interception or redirection occurs.

15. A, E. When configuring a user group, Read and Write privileges can be assigned on a per-feature basis.

16. B. RBAC by VPN is for visibility only, not configuration.

17. A, B, D. In addition to local database authentication, vManage supports SSO, RADIUS, and TACACS for remote authentication.

Chapter 11

1. B. Cloud onRamp for SaaS is not a book-ended solution. Cloud onRamp for SaaS uses a unique HTTPS probe to monitor the performance of the path to the SaaS application.

2. A, B, D. The three types of Cloud onRamp for SaaS sites are gateway, DIA, and client sites.

3. A. A site configured for Cloud onRamp for SaaS can have Internet or MPLS transports to reach SaaS applications.

4. A. DPI does not redirect the initial application flow because the redirection would cause network address translation (NAT) changes that would break the TCP flow.

5. A, C. The CloudExpress Applications output shows each application, the optimal path that has been chosen, and the mean latency and loss associated with the application for each optimal path. The CloudExpress Gateway Exits output shows each application, what the gateway exits are, and the mean latency and loss associated with the application for each gateway path available.

6. A, B, E. Each Cisco WAN Edge Cloud router is automatically provisioned with a management VPN, a transport VPN, and a service VPN.

7. B. Only two cloud routers are provisioned per transit VPC.

8. A. Cloud onRamp for IaaS supports both IAM role and API key login methods for connecting to a cloud instance.

9. A, C, D. Cisco vManage provides the connectivity state of each host VPC, the state of the transit VPC, as well as the detailed traffic statistics for the IPsec VPN connections between the transit VPC and each host VPC.

10. A, B, C. Cloud onRamp for Colocation is a bundle and includes the Cisco CSP, the Cisco Catalyst 9K, and Cisco WAN Edge Cloud routers.

11. A, C. Service insertion with Cloud onRamp for Colocation can be achieved via either a control policy or a data policy.

Chapter 12

1. B. On the contrary, most SD-WAN deployments are done in a brownfield environment with existing complexity.

2. A, B, E. Cisco SD-WAN provides Application-Aware Routing and visibility as well as improved performance through leveraging multiple active paths. These features are enabled through centralized policy.

3. B. Migration to Cisco SD-WAN is a graceful procedure, as long as preparation is performed and appropriate designs are implemented.

4. B, D, E. Among many other things, device templates and policy can be designed and deployed prior to SD-WAN migration. In addition, analysis of the existing topology, routing, and traffic engineering can be done ahead of time.

5. B, C, E. Groups of interest can be defined in SD-WAN policy ahead of SD-WAN migration. This includes prefix-lists, site-lists, VPN IDs, and application lists.

6. A, B, E. Site-IDs, VPN IDs, system IPs, and TLOC colors are all SD-WAN-specific values that can be predefined and planned for ahead of migration to SD-WAN.

7. A. This design allows the data center to act as a transit site for traffic between non-SD-WAN and SD-WAN sites and allows for a graceful and gradual migration of remote sites to SD-WAN without ever affecting the legacy network.

8. C. Designating multiple regional hubs as transit points for dedicated geographies and configuring overlay routing to leverage these hubs intelligently can minimize site-to-site latency during migration.

9. B. The most common way to integrate transport-side connections on the SD-WAN router into the network is by dedicating a single interface in VPN 0 per carrier/transport and designating a unique color, public or private (depending on the type of transport), for each.

10. D. In bind mode, each loopback is bound to a physical interface, and traffic destined to the loopback will be carried to and from the mapped physical interface. In unbind mode, the loopback interface is not bound to any physical interface. Traffic destined to the loopback can go through any physical interface based on a hash lookup.

11. A, C, D. Many valid branch designs exist, but a complete replacement of the CE router, either with a single SD-WAN router or dual SD-WAN routers, is supported. Integration with an existing CE router is also supported.

12. B. TLOC extensions can be configured for either public or private colors.

13. B. Cisco SD-WAN can integrate with existing firewalls in many ways. As of IOS-XE, SD-WAN 19.2 code integration with existing voice services, such as SRST, can be accomplished as long as it is not attempted on the SD-WAN router.

14. B, D, F. Cisco SD-WAN supports a wide range of routing protocol for both LAN- and WAN-side integration, including OSPF, eBGP, iBGP, and EIGRP.

15. D. To ensure that remote branch routes are learned and preferred through the overlay (and asymmetry and route looping are avoided), you can create a filter outbound toward the SD-WAN router in order to limit the learned routes to those originating from the data center. Make sure to also advertise a default or summary into the overlay.

Chapter 13

1. A, B, D. The three controllers that make up the Cisco SD-WAN solution are vSmart, vBond, and vManage. These components make up the control, management, and orchestration planes in the environment.

2. A, B, E. The Cisco SD-WAN solution supports three main certificate deployment models. These include automatic enrollment with either Symantec, DigiCert, or Cisco PKI; manual enrollment with either Symantec, DigiCert, or Cisco PKI; and Enterprise CA.

3. A. vManage is instantiated first. Once vManage is deployed, you can begin to deploy the vBond and vSmart controllers.

4. A. The vBond controller must have a public IP address, whether configured directly on VPN 0 or behind a NAT gateway, in which case it must be a 1:1 NAT. This allows vBond to facilitate NAT traversal in the data plane between WAN Edges.

5. A, B, E. When the controllers mutually authenticate each other, they verify three things: the certificate organization name must match the organization name that the controller has configured, the certificate must be generated by a mutually trusted root CA, and the certificate serial number must be in the controller whitelist.

6. A. To enable the vBond persona on the vEdge Cloud component, the **local** keyword is added to the **vbond** command.

7. A. vManage uses Netconf to push templates and policies to the vSmart controller.

8. A. The **commit** command is used to save and apply configuration changes. This differs from IOS, where any config changes are applied instantly upon entering them.

9. A. vManage is instantiated first; then vBond and vSmart are installed and configured.

10. A. By default, Netconf is blocked when enabling the **tunnel-interface** command. To allow connectivity via Netconf, the command **allow-service netconf** needs to be applied.

Example 7-17

This example shows the full and complete policy for all of the configuration that was performed in Chapters 6 and 7.

```
policy
 control-policy DC_Inbound_Control_Policy
    sequence 1
     match tloc
      originator 10.0.10.1
     !
     action accept
      set
       preference 500
      !
     !
    !
    sequence 11
     match tloc
      originator 10.0.10.2
     !
     action accept
      set
       preference 400
      !
     !
    !
    sequence 21
     match tloc
      originator 10.0.20.1
     !
     action accept
```

```
       set
        preference 500
        !
       !
      !
     sequence 31
      match tloc
       originator 10.0.20.2
       !
      action accept
       set
        preference 400
        !
       !
      !
     sequence 41
      match route
       vpn-list SERVICE_VPN
       prefix-list _AnyIpv4PrefixList
       !
      action accept
       export-to vpn-list CLIENT_VPNS
       set
        omp-tag 100
        !
       !
      !
   default-action accept
  !
 control-policy North_America_Reg_Mesh_with_FW
     sequence 1
      match tloc
       site-list DCs
       !
      action accept
       !
      !
     sequence 11
      match tloc
       site-list North_America_Branches
       !
      action accept
       !
      !
```

Example 7-17   541

```
       sequence 21
        match route
         prefix-list Default_Route
         site-list North_America_DC
         !
        action accept
         set
          preference 100
          !
         !
        !
       sequence 31
        match route
         site-list DCs
         prefix-list _AnyIpv4PrefixList
         !
        action accept
         !
        !
       sequence 41
        match route
         site-list North_America_Branches
         prefix-list _AnyIpv4PrefixList
         !
        action accept
         !
        !
       sequence 51
        match route
         site-list Europe_Branches
         prefix-list _AnyIpv4PrefixList
         !
        action accept
         set
          service  FW
          !
         !
        !
     default-action reject
    !
   vpn-membership vpnMembership_373293275
       sequence 10
        match
         vpn-list CLIENT_VPNS
         !
```

```
        action accept
         !
        !
       sequence 20
        match
         vpn-list CorporateVPN
         !
        action accept
         !
        !
       sequence 30
        match
         vpn-list SERVICE_VPN
         !
        action accept
         !
        !
       sequence 40
        match
         vpn-list PCI_VPN
         !
        action accept
         !
        !
      default-action reject
      !
     control-policy Euro_Reg_Mesh_with_FW_MultiTopo
        sequence 1
         match tloc
          site-list DCs
          !
         action accept
          !
         !
        sequence 11
         match tloc
          site-list Europe_Branches
          !
         action accept
          !
         !
        sequence 21
         match route
          prefix-list Default_Route
          site-list Europe_DC
```

Example 7-17   543

```
 !
 action accept
  set
   preference 100
   !
  !
 !
sequence 31
 match route
  site-list DCs
  prefix-list _AnyIpv4PrefixList
  !
 action accept
  !
 !
sequence 41
 match route
  site-list Europe_Branches
  vpn-list CorporateVPN
  prefix-list _AnyIpv4PrefixList
  !
 action accept
  !
 !
sequence 51
 match route
  site-list Europe_Branches
  vpn-list PCI_VPN
  prefix-list _AnyIpv4PrefixList
  !
 action accept
  set
   tloc-list Europe_DC_TLOCs
   !
  !
 !
sequence 61
 match route
  site-list North_America_Branches
  prefix-list _AnyIpv4PrefixList
  !
 action accept
  set
   service  FW
   !
```

```
       !
     !
  default-action reject
 !
 control-policy Branch_Extranet_Route_Leaking
    sequence 1
     match route
      vpn 101
      prefix-list _AnyIpv4PrefixList
      !
     action accept
      export-to vpn-list SERVICE_VPN
      set
       omp-tag 101
       !
      !
     !
    sequence 11
     match route
      vpn 102
      prefix-list _AnyIpv4PrefixList
      !
     action accept
      set
       omp-tag 102
       !
      export-to vpn-list SERVICE_VPN
      !
     !
  default-action accept
 !
 data-policy _CorporateVPN_Branch_-1923459860
  vpn-list CorporateVPN
    sequence 1
     match
      app-list AUDIO_VIDEO_APPS
      source-ip 0.0.0.0/0
      !
     action accept
      count CORP_AUDIO_VIDEO_199743323
      loss-protect fec-adaptive
      loss-protection forward-error-correction adaptive
      set
       local-tloc-list
        color mpls
```

Example 7-17   545

```
  !
  !
 !
sequence 11
 match
  destination-data-prefix-list INTERNAL_ADDRESSES
  !
 action accept
  count INTERNAL_PCKTS_199743323
  !
 !
sequence 21
 match
  app-list TRUSTED_APPS
  source-ip 0.0.0.0/0
  !
 action accept
  nat use-vpn 0
  nat fallback
  count CORP_DCA_199743323
  !
 !
sequence 31
 match
  app-list YouTube
  source-ip 0.0.0.0/0
  !
 action accept
  count CORP_YOUTUBE_199743323
  set
   local-tloc-list
    color biz-internet
    encap ipsec
  !
  !
 !
sequence 41
 match
  app-list Facebook
  source-ip 0.0.0.0/0
  !
 action accept
  count CORP_FACEBOOK_199743323
  set
   vpn 1
```

```
         tloc-list Europe_DC_INET_TLOCS
        !
       !
      !
     sequence 51
      match
       app-list Google_Apps
       source-ip 0.0.0.0/0
      !
      action accept
       count UMBRELLA_PCKTS_199743323
       set
        service  IDP local
       !
      !
     !
  default-action accept
  !
  vpn-list PCI_VPN
     sequence 1
      match
       source-data-prefix-list PAYMENT_SERVERS
      !
      action accept
       count PCI_PCKTS_-1949123913
       set
        local-tloc-list
         color mpls
       !
       loss-protect pkt-dup
       loss-protection packet-duplication
      !
     !
     sequence 11
      match
       destination-data-prefix-list PAYMENT_SERVERS
      !
      action accept
       count PCI_PCKTS_-1949123913
       set
        local-tloc-list
         color mpls
       !
       loss-protect pkt-dup
       loss-protection packet-duplication
```

Example 7-17   547

```
    !
    !
  default-action accept
!
  vpn-list GUEST_ACCESS_VPN
    sequence 1
     match
      destination-data-prefix-list BOGON_ADDR
      !
     action drop
      count GUEST_DROPPED_PKTS_-939522740
      !
    !
    sequence 11
     match
      source-ip 0.0.0.0/0
      !
     action accept
      nat use-vpn 0
      count GUEST_DIA_PKTS_-939522740
      !
    !
  default-action drop
!
data-policy _CorporateVPN_DC_Corp_1741652260
  vpn-list CorporateVPN
    sequence 1
     match
      app-list AUDIO_VIDEO_APPS
      source-ip 0.0.0.0/0
      !
     action accept
      count CORP_AUDIO_VIDEO_-430111853
      loss-protect fec-adaptive
      loss-protection forward-error-correction adaptive
      set
       local-tloc-list
        color mpls
       !
      !
    !
  default-action accept
!
  vpn-list PCI_VPN
    sequence 1
```

```
        match
         source-data-prefix-list PAYMENT_SERVERS
         !
        action accept
         count PCI_PCKTS_1715988207
         set
          local-tloc-list
           color mpls
          !
         loss-protect pkt-dup
         loss-protection packet-duplication
         !
        !
      sequence 11
       match
        destination-data-prefix-list PAYMENT_SERVERS
        !
       action accept
        count PCI_PCKTS_1715988207
        set
         local-tloc-list
          color mpls
         !
        loss-protect pkt-dup
        loss-protection packet-duplication
        !
       !
  default-action accept
  !
 lists
  app-list AUDIO_VIDEO_APPS
   app-family audio-video
   app-family audio_video
   !
  app-list Facebook
   app facebook
   app facebook_messenger
   app fbcdn
   app facebook_mail
   app facebook_live
   !
  app-list Google_Apps
   app android-updates
   app blogger
   app chrome_update
```

Example 7-17   549

```
app gcs
app gmail
app gmail_mobile
app gmail_basic
app gmail_basic
app gmail_chat
app gmail_drive
app gmail_mobile
app google_picasa
app google_desktop
app google_cache
app google_play_music
app google
app google_translate
app google_groups
app google_localguides
app google_gen
app gmail_drive
app google_calendar
app google_classroom
app google_skymap
app google_tags
app google_maps
app gcs
app google_code
app google_toolbar
app gstatic
app google_spaces
app google_accounts
app google_sprayscape
app google-services
app google-services-audio
app google-services-media
app google-services-video
app google_accounts
app google_ads
app google_analytics
app google_appengine
app google_cache
app google_calendar
app google_code
app google_desktop
app google_docs
app google_photos
app google-docs
```

```
            app google-downloads
            app google_earth
            app google_earth
            app google-earth
            app google_groups
            app google_maps
            app google_photos
            app google_picasa
            app picasa
            app google_play
            app google-play
            app google_plus
            app google-plus
            app google_plus
            app google_safebrowsing
            app google_skymap
            app google_spaces
            app google_tags
            app google_toolbar
            app google_translate
            app google_trusted_store
            app google_weblight
            app googlebot
            app gstatic
            app gtalk
            app gtalk-chat
            app gmail_chat
            app gtalk-ft
            app gtalk-video
            app gtalk-voip
            app hangouts
            app hangouts-audio
            app hangouts-chat
            app hangouts-file-transfer
            app hangouts-media
            app hangouts-video
            app youtube
            app youtube_hd
            app youtube_hd
           !
        app-list TRUSTED_APPS
          app webex-meeting
          app webex_weboffice
          app webex
          !
```

Example 7-17   551

```
app-list YouTube
 app youtube
 app youtube_hd
!
data-prefix-list BOGON_ADDR
 ip-prefix 10.0.0.0/8
 ip-prefix 100.64.0.0/10
 ip-prefix 127.0.0.0/8
 ip-prefix 172.16.0.0/12
 ip-prefix 192.168.0.0/16
!
data-prefix-list INTERNAL_ADDRESSES
 ip-prefix 10.0.0.0/8
!
data-prefix-list PAYMENT_SERVERS
 ip-prefix 10.2.10.0/24
!
prefix-list Default_Route
 ip-prefix 0.0.0.0/0
!
site-list BranchOffices
 site-id 100-199
!
site-list DCs
 site-id 10-50
!
site-list Europe_Branches
 site-id 102-103
!
site-list Europe_DC
 site-id 20
!
site-list North_America_Branches
 site-id 101
!
site-list North_America_DC
 site-id 10
!
tloc-list Europe_DC_INET_TLOCS
 tloc 10.0.20.1 color biz-internet encap ipsec preference 500
 tloc 10.0.20.2 color biz-internet encap ipsec preference 400
!
tloc-list Europe_DC_TLOCs
 tloc 10.0.20.1 color mpls encap ipsec
 tloc 10.0.20.1 color biz-internet encap ipsec
```

```
      tloc 10.0.20.2 color mpls encap ipsec
      tloc 10.0.20.2 color biz-internet encap ipsec
     !
     vpn-list CLIENT_VPNS
      vpn 101
      vpn 102
     !
     vpn-list CorporateVPN
      vpn 1
     !
     vpn-list GUEST_ACCESS_VPN
      vpn 3
     !
     vpn-list PCI_VPN
      vpn 2
     !
     vpn-list SERVICE_VPN
      vpn 100
     !
     prefix-list _AnyIpv4PrefixList
      ip-prefix 0.0.0.0/0 le 32
     !
    !
   !
  apply-policy
   site-list Europe_Branches
    control-policy Euro_Reg_Mesh_with_FW_MultiTopo out
   !
   site-list BranchOffices
    data-policy _CorporateVPN_Branch_-1923459860 from-service
    control-policy Branch_Extranet_Route_Leaking in
    vpn-membership vpnMembership_373293275
   !
   site-list DCs
    data-policy _CorporateVPN_DC_Corp_1741652260 from-service
    control-policy DC_Inbound_Control_Policy in
   !
   site-list North_America_Branches
    control-policy North_America_Reg_Mesh_with_FW out
   !
  !
```

Glossary of Key Terms

A

App-Route Multiplier Determines how many App-Route poll intervals should be considered when making the determination about the SLA compliance of the tunnels. The default value is 6, and the maximum is 6. This value is configured per router.

App-Route Poll Interval Defines the period of time to collect Bidirectional Forwarding Detection (BFD) probes for analyzing the statistical performance of the SD-WAN tunnels and making a determination about SLA compliance. This value is configured per router.

Application Programming Interface (API) A flexible interface beyond the traditional user interface that can be used programmatically to manage and monitor an application, device, or operating system.

Artificial Intelligence (AI) The use of compute power to make human-like and informed decisions based on real-time data in the environment.

B

backup-sla-preferred-color An optional configuration argument that allows

for the specification of a selected color or colors to use when forwarding a class of traffic in the event that no tunnels meet the required SLAs.

BFD Hello Interval Specifies how often a WAN Edge router will send a BFD probe on a tunnel. This value is configured per router, per color.

BFD Multiplier Specifies how many consecutive BFD probes can be sent without a response before the tunnel is declared to be down. This value is configured per router, per color.

Bring Your Own Device (BYOD) A common enterprise administrative policy that allows for employees to connect to enterprise networks or the Internet with personal devices such as phones and tablets.

C

Centralized Policy A centralized policy can affect the entire Cisco SD-WAN fabric and is activated on the vSmart controllers.

Certificate Authority (CA) An entity that is responsible for signing certificate requests and issuing SSL certificates. Since SD-WAN components are configured to trust the organization's root CA, any certificate generated or signed by the root CA is also trusted. Hence, SD-WAN components will inherently trust the identity of one another since they share the same mutual trust of the signing root CA.

Cisco Application Centric Infrastructure (Cisco ACI)   A software controller–based solution by Cisco that uses SDN to deploy, monitor, and manage enterprise data centers and clouds.

Cisco Software-Defined WAN (Cisco SD-WAN)   A software controller–based solution by Cisco that uses SDN to deploy, monitor, and manage wide area networks.

Cloud   Shared compute and application resources that exist in a domain away from the physical enterprise network, such as the Internet or a shared data center. Examples include Amazon Web Services (AWS) and Microsoft Azure.

Colocation   A colocation (colo) is a data center facility in which a business can rent space for servers and other computing hardware. Typically, a colo provides the building, cooling, power, bandwidth, and physical security while the customer provides servers and storage.

Color   An attribute that allows the solution to identify specific transports with a color and influence how the data plane is built.

Command Line Interface (CLI)   Method of configuring network devices individually by inputting configuration commands.

Control Plane (vSmart)   This element is where all control and centralized policy will be enforced. Calculation of the routing table and distribution of encryption keys are handled by the vSmart.

Control Policy   A control policy manipulates routing information and can be used to affect how traffic is forwarded through a WAN Edge.

D

Data Plane (WAN Edge)   The component where data traffic is terminated and encapsulated across the SD-WAN fabric. The data plane is only built between WAN Edges.

Data Policy   A data policy directly impacts the forwarding of traffic flows through the WAN Edge router.

Direct Cloud Access   Forwards SaaS traffic (such as Office 365, Salesforce, Box, Google, and so on) from the branch directly to the Internet or the backhaul path to the data center (DC) based on candidate path performance. It ensures the best SaaS application experience and also reduces the IT WAN cost.

Direct Internet Access (DIA)   Accessing the Internet through local egress at the remote site rather than backhauling through a data center.

E–I

Extranet   An extranet is a restricted communications network, typically used to allow business partners in different organizations to have a private and secure communication channel.

Forward Error Correction   The process of including additional information, called parity, into a message so that if part of the message is lost or corrupted, the whole message can still be recovered.

IDS/IPS   Intrusion detection systems (IDSs) analyze network traffic for signatures that match known cyberattacks. Intrusion prevention systems (IPSs) also analyze packets, but they can also stop the packets from being delivered based on what kind of attack is detected, thus helping stop the attack.

Inbound Control Policy   A control policy that is applied to OMP updates sent from the WAN Edge to the vSmart and applied before the vSmart performs the best-path selection algorithm.

Infrastructure as a Service (IaaS)

Virtualized hardware that is outsourced to providers and that typically runs in the cloud.

Internet of Things (IoT) A collection of nontraditional network-connected devices that are typically unmanned, such as manufacturing equipment, lighting, security cameras, and door locks.

L–M

Localized Policy A localized policy will only affect a single WAN Edge router and is configured in the device template.

Machine Learning A subset of artificial intelligence (AI) used to gather data and information from the network environment to constantly learn, adapt, and improve the accuracy of the AI.

Management Plane (vManage) The element where day-to-day administration of the SD-WAN fabric will be achieved. vManage is the single pane of glass where configuration, troubleshooting, software upgrades, and monitoring will be achieved.

Multidomain An end-to-end network architecture that comprises different types of solutions to fit the requirements of each individual environment, such as campus, WAN, data center, and cloud.

Multi-topology A network design where different VPN segments have different logical topologies. Some VPNs may be able to establish direct communication with each other, while other VPN segments may have to communicate indirectly via a third site, and other VPN segments may not be able to communicate at all.

N–O

NAT Fallback The process of forwarding traffic that would have been NAT'ed through a local egress interface across the SD-WAN fabric instead when no local interfaces are configured for NAT in an operational state.

OMP Route The route advertisement responsible for carrying information about data prefixes. These routes are usually LAN subnets.

Orchestration Plane (vBond) vBond is the glue that brings all the other components together. The orchestration plane distributes vManage and vSmart information to the WAN Edges and also authenticates all the Cisco SD-WAN components.

Originator A matching criterion that is used to select the WAN Edge that did the initial advertisement of a route or TLOC.

Outbound Control Policy A control policy that is applied to OMP updates that are sent from the vSmart to the WAN Edge and applied after the vSmart performs the best-path selection algorithm.

Overlay Management Protocol (OMP) The routing protocol of the fabric. OMP is utilized to distribute all routing information, encryption keys, and other policy information. OMP runs inside of a DTLS/TLS tunnel between the vSmart and WAN Edges.

P–R

Packet Duplication The process of forwarding a redundant copy of a traffic flow down a duplicate path in order to protect against packet loss.

Preferred Color An optional configuration argument that allows for the specification of a selected color or colors to use when forwarding a class of traffic, as long as these classes are compliant with the SLA Class.

Quality of Services (QoS) The categorization and prioritization of traffic in a network typically based on application type and requirements.

Role-Based Access Control (RBAC) A policy-neutral, access-control mechanism defined around roles and privileges. The components of RBAC such as role-permissions, user-role, and role-role relationships make it simple to perform user assignments.

S

Service Insertion The process of redirecting a network flow to an additional device for the purposes of performing a function on the traffic. Common network services include firewalls, load balancers, and caching engines.

Service Level Agreement (SLA) A commitment made by a service or application provider to customers for a minimum level of service or uptime.

Service Route A route that advertises a service, such as a firewall or intrusion prevention system, to the rest of the network. Policy can be deployed that forces traffic through these services.

SLA Class List A type of list that allows the administrator to specify the maximum loss, latency, and/or jitter on an SD-WAN tunnel that a specific class of traffic is forwarded across.

Software as a Service (SaaS) Software applications that are outsourced to providers and that typically run in the cloud.

Software-Defined Networking (SDN) A process by which network flows, rules, and operations are defined and deployed from a centralized controller rather than on each individual network device.

Strict An optional configuration argument that specifies that the class of traffic should be dropped rather than forwarded in the event that no classes meet the required SLA.

T

TLOC A route that distributes next-hop information and also connects the fabric to the physical underlay. Data plane deployment can be influenced by manipulating Transport Locator (TLOC) information.

tloc-list A list element that can contain references to one or more TLOCs described by their system IP, color, and encapsulation. It may also include the optional arguments of Weight and Preference.

Transit VPC Using a transit VPC is a common strategy for connecting multiple, geographically disperse virtual private clouds (VPCs) and remote networks in order to create a global network transit center. A transit VPC simplifies network management and minimizes the number of connections required to connect multiple VPCs and remote networks.

V–Z

Virtualization Applications and software that are abstracted from the underlying physical hardware resources and run as virtual instances.

vSmart vSmart is the control plane of the fabric. The vSmart acts as a Border Gateway Protocol (BGP) route reflector but is responsible for distributing encryption keys as well.

Zone A zone is a grouping of one or more VPNs.

Index

N

O

P

packet duplication, 274–280

packet forwarding, App-Route policies, 304

    SLA class action, 306–315

    traditional lookup in the routing table, 305–306

packet loss, protecting applications from, 269–270

    FEC (Forward Error Correction), 270–274

    packet duplication, 274–280

pairwise encryption keys, 86–87

parity packets, 271, 274

path quality monitoring, App-Route policies, 298

path selection, OMP, 56–58

PnP (Plug and Play), 101–102

policers, 119

policies. *See also* App-Route policies; centralized policies; control policies; data policies; localized policies

    centralized, 110–112, 117, 134–136

        activation, 125–127

        application-aware routing, 112

        cflowd, 112

        construction, 118, 122–125

        control, 111

        isolating remote branches from each other, 136–149

        monitoring, 147

        multi-topology, 206–210

        VPN membership, 111

    construction, 115–118

    definition, 119–122

    domains, 113–114

    firewall, 354

    lists, 118–119

    localized, 112–113

    matching criteria, 120–121

    packet forwarding order of operations, 127–128

    saving, 147

port restricted cone NAT, 77–80

PoS (point of sales) systems, 5–6

preferred-color command, 312

prefix lists, 118–119

on-premises deployment, 494

    Cisco SD-WAN (Software-Defined WAN), 38

    installation process, 495

previewing, localized data policies, 335–336

private cloud deployment, Cisco SD-WAN (Software-Defined WAN), 38

Q

QoS (quality of service), 2–3, 5–6, 8, 112, 319–320, 339

    policies, configuration

        assign traffic to forwarding class, 339–341

        configure scheduling parameters for each queue, 341–342

        configure the transport interface with the QoS map, 343–346

        map forwarding classes to hardware queues, 341

        map schedulers into a single QoS map, 342–343

W

Z

Connect, Engage, Collaborate

The Award Winning Cisco Support Community

Attend and Participate in Events

Ask the Experts
Live Webcasts

Knowledge Sharing

Documents
Blogs
Videos

Top Contributor Programs

Cisco Designated VIP
Hall of Fame
Spotlight Awards

Multi-Language Support

https://supportforums.cisco.com

REGISTER YOUR PRODUCT at CiscoPress.com/register
Access Additional Benefits and SAVE 35% on Your Next Purchase

- Download available product updates.
- Access bonus material when applicable.
- Receive exclusive offers on new editions and related products.
  (Just check the box to hear from us when setting up your account.)
- Get a coupon for 35% for your next purchase, valid for 30 days.
  Your code will be available in your Cisco Press cart. (You will also find
  it in the Manage Codes section of your account page.)

Registration benefits vary by product. Benefits will be listed on your account page under Registered Products.

CiscoPress.com – Learning Solutions for Self-Paced Study, Enterprise, and the Classroom
Cisco Press is the Cisco Systems authorized book publisher of Cisco networking technology, Cisco certification self-study, and Cisco Networking Academy Program materials.

At **CiscoPress.com** you can
- Shop our books, eBooks, software, and video training.
- Take advantage of our special offers and promotions (ciscopress.com/promotions).
- Sign up for special offers and content newsletters (ciscopress.com/newsletters).
- Read free articles, exam profiles, and blogs by information technology experts.
- Access thousands of free chapters and video lessons.

Connect with Cisco Press – Visit CiscoPress.com/community
Learn about Cisco Press community events and programs.

Cisco Press

ALWAYS LEARNING   PEARSON